MOTOCOURSE™

THE WORLD'S LEADING GRAND PRIX & SUPERBIKE ANNUAL

CMG PUBLISHING

CONTENTS

MOTOCOURSE 2005–2006

is published by
Crash Media Group Ltd
Number One
The Innovation Centre
Silverstone Circuit
Silverstone
Northants NN12 8GX
United Kingdom
Tel: +44 (0)870 3505044
Fax: +44 (0)870 3505088
Email: info@crash.net
Website:www.crashmediagroup.com

Printed in England by
Butler and Tanner Ltd,
Frome, Somerset

ISBN: 1 905334 05 2

DISTRIBUTORS

Vine House
Waldenbury
Chailey
East Sussex BN8 4DR
Tel: +44 (0)1825 723398
Email: sales@vinehouseuk.co.uk

Menoshire Ltd
Unit 13
21 Wadsworth Road
Perivale
Middlesex UB6 7LQ
Tel: +44 (0)20 8566 7344
Fax: +44 (0)20 8991 2439

NORTH AMERICA
Motorbooks International
PO Box 1
729 Prospect Avenue
Osecola
Wisconsin 54020, USA
Tel: (1) 715 294 3345
Fax: (1) 715 294 4448

**Left: Valentino Rossi after his win
in the 2005 French Grand Prix at
Le Mans.**

**Dust-jacket: Valentino Rossi scored
a second successive MotoGP title
aboard the Yamaha M1 and a fifth
consecutive premier class
championship.**

**Title page: 2005 World Superbike
champion Troy Corser on his
Corona Alstare Suzuki.
Photographs: Gold & Goose**

Editor's Acknowledgements

The Editor and staff of MOTOCOURSE wish to thank the following for their assistance in compiling the
2005/6 edition: Marc Petrier (FIM), Paul Butler and Mike Trimby (IRTA), Eva Jirsenska (Dorna),
Chuck Aksland, Katie Baines, Jerry Burgess, Peter Clifford, Gavin Emmett, Ali Forth, Isabelle Lariviere,l
Iain Mackay, Roberta Vallorosi, Debbie van Zon, Ian Wheeler and Rupert Williamson, as well as numerous
colleagues and friends.

Photographs published in AUTOCOURSE 2005–2006 have been contributed by:
Chief photographers: Gold & Goose; *Contributing photographers:* Clive Challinor, Dave Collister;
Tom Htnatiw/Flick of The Wrist Photography; Martin Heath; John McKenzie; Dave Purves; Neil Spalding;
Andrew Wheeler; Yamaha

editor
MICHAEL SCOTT

publisher
BRYN WILLIAMS

text editor
JENNIFER SCOTT

results and statistics
KAY EDGE

sales promotion
STUART DENT

art editor
STEVE SMALL

design and production
ROSANNE DAVIS
MIKE WESTON

office manager
WENDY SALISBURY

chief photographers
GOLD & GOOSE
Peter J. Fox
David Goldman
Mirco Lazzari
Patrik Lundin
Telephone +44 (0)20 8444 2448

MotoGP bike illustrations
ADRIAN DEAN
f1artwork@blueyonder.co.uk

FOREWORD by WAYNE RAINEY

Yamaha's previous World Champion – 1990, 1991, 1992

VALENTINO ROSSI's MotoGP title is the perfect way for Yamaha to start their next 50 years.

What can I say about Rossi that hasn't already been said? It seems everything he touches turns to gold – he seems to have the whole package.

He has the might of the whole Yamaha corporation behind him – they are putting a lot into MotoGP, and it definitely shows with their motorcycle. The M1 is a beautiful machine.

We did see some of the other riders stepping up this season. It's taken longer than I would have thought. Their target is Rossi. They've seen him do his magic, so they know where they need to work on their programmes. But there's still a gap from Rossi to the next group.

I was very fortunate to race in an era when the top guys were real close. All of them could be World Champion, and all of the were – Eddie Lawson, Mick Doohan, Wayne Gardner and especially Kevin Schwantz. Racing against them automatically elevated me, and I elevated them. It would be nice to see the current group continue to use Rossi to raise their game. It would make racing even more interesting than it is… for Rossi as well as the fans. Maybe that would make him hang around another year or two. That's what needs to happen.

There's no doubt that the four-stroke MotoGP bikes have made racing safer. They're very fast in a straight line, but more predictable for the rider at their limits. The power band is much wider, and riders use one gear for much longer. With the 500, you'd get more than 100 horsepower all in an instant. That explosive nature made the 500 a very difficult beast to tame. The electronics and tyres have also added to

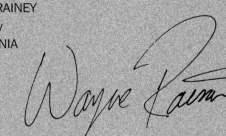

safety, and these things are understood better now than in my day. Nowadays riders can hope for longer careers.

TV statistics and crowd figures show that many more people are watching MotoGP now than ever before. The US GP close to my house was a sell-out, which was important to me. There's more involvement now from the industry as a whole, with everyone focused on the four-stroke. Factories can now develop special projects at the highest level of racing, and that trickles down to production bikes. MotoGP is good for the industry. And from what I see, Dorna is doing a good job.

It's a pleasure to write the foreword for MOTOCOURSE. I've always looked forward to the great pictures and all the different features. As a rider, you would find out things you didn't know about during the year, and see a different perspective. Nowadays I find myself going back to my MOTOCOURSE collection, to compare lap times, check up on races. Once in a while I'll pull one out at random and just open a page, and see where it brings me. When you retire, you need to look back and go right to that moment. That's what MOTOCOURSE provides for me.

We can look forward from this 30th edition to the next 30 years. Then we'll be able to look back 60 years. That'll be something.

WAYNE RAINEY
Monterey
CALIFORNIA

Wayne Rainey

SPECIAL PLACES

"Il Laureato" – Rossi wrote the script, in smooth black lines of rubber.
Photograph: Gold & Goose

There are some special places in MotoGP.

One is the rise at the end of the main straight at Mugello. The fastest bikes are doing well over 200 mph, and the front wheels lift over the brow. As they land, they must brake hard, to shed 100 mph and four gears in a real hurry, then get it all collected for a sweeping uphill loop.

Another is the set of left-handers leading onto Phillip Island's straight. The many kinks at Assen... Brno's exacting downhillers... Donington's Craner Curves... Istanbul's flat-in-fifth Turn 11, the new fastest corner in the world. Even the silly twiddly tracks like Valencia and Sachsenring have their special places, where (if you have the right accreditation) you can hang over the barrier, and marvel at a 250-horsepower 990cc racing motorcycle bellowing and skittering at absolute full stretch.

You get the picture. MotoGP in 2005 was memorable. Five years into the new Millennium and four into the reign of the terror four-strokes – soon to be banned because they're just too fast – we are in momentous times for motorbike racing.

This year, and this book, repeatedly celebrates the same theme: Rossi the genius, Rossi the giant, Rossi the history man. His talents seemed endless; his enjoyment of them endlessly infectious.

Millions are under his spell. And in MotoGP, they're all under his thumb.

Valentino's serial success has more or less done for the last generation. Most of them are beaten before they've engaged second gear.

This past year made amends. Marco Melandri and Nicky Hayden both defeated Rossi, the former twice. Both are at relatively early stages of their careers, and will get stronger.

At the same time, a tide of youthful talent is sweeping up through from the smaller classes. Next year Dani Pedrosa, tsar of 250s, will be the most significant of several youthful recruits.

Rossi's dominance, far from being stifling, has actually created a vibrancy that is having a revitalising effect.

The machines took a step forward in electronic refinement and performance – lap records and race times kept on dropping; a burgeoning tyre war between Michelin and Bridgestone added another element . Honda's second defeat in a row by Yamaha and Rossi turned the pressure up still further.

Next year will be the last of the big 990s, due for replacement by new-generation 800s in 2007. If it is half as good as it promises to be, we will one day look back on the five 990cc years as a golden age.

MotoGP continued to grow steadily in 2005. The return of the USA to the calendar was hugely popular and highly significant – though problematical as ever, because of track safety issues. China had none of those, putting Laguna Seca to shame. But Shanghai also had no spectators. Nor did the third addition, Turkey – another fine venue. But the TV was good in all cases, and that is what matters most.

The strangeness of the year was a disturbing emigration of sponsors. This needs to be reversed. Perhaps the new 800s will do that in 2007.

In the meantime, there is one more year of 990s. When they're gone, those special places may not be so special ever again.

MICHAEL SCOTT
Wimbledon, London, 2005

FIM WORLD CHAMPIONSHIP 2005

TOP TEN RIDERS

The Editor's Choice

Photography by
Gold & Goose

IF you were to make a top ten of all time, who of the current crop would be on it? No question. Rossi would be at or very near the top. This year he eclipsed Mike Hailwood in the number of GPs won. Never mind the history. He also eclipsed every one of his 2005 rivals, repeatedly and sometimes humiliatingly. Valentino hardly put a foot wrong all year. And when he did, as usual, he came out smiling anyway.

Thus when he rammed the back end of Melandri at Motegi, and crashed at more than 100 mph at Valencia, in both cases, he walked away. He was very lucky.

More to the point, and in spite of it being a foregone conclusion, Rossi illuminated the season with a number of superb races. The competition was closer this year than last, when only Gibernau challenged. Rossi thrived on it.

His summary dismissal of Gibernau at the last corner of the first-race set the tone: he would brook no nonsense from that quarter. As the year wore on, he found both Melandri and Hayden pressing harder. When it mattered, he had little trouble dealing with them.

By rights, Rossi's domination and the highly predictable title outcome should have detracted from the excitement. His nature precludes that – a combination of showmanship, charm, exuberance and shining talent. Even when you know he's going to win, he's a pleasure to watch.

This is a remarkable era of racing. Rossi's Era. We are lucky to be able to experience it at first hand. People will look back in awe.

VALENTINO ROSSI

Gauloises Yamaha Team

2005 World Championship – 1st (MotoGP)

Race wins – 11

Pole positions – 5

Career GP wins – 79 (40 MotoGP, 13 500cc, 14 250cc, 12 125cc)

World Championships – 7 (4 MotoGP, 1 500cc, 1 250cc, 1 125cc)

Born 16 February, 1979, Urbino, Italy

MARCO MELANDRI

Team MoviStar Honda

2004 World Championship – 2nd (MotoGP)

Race wins – 2

Career GP wins – 19 (2 MotoGP, 13 10 250cc, 7 125cc)

World Championships – 1 (250cc)

Born 7 August, 1982, Ravenna, Italy

WHAT a change for the former boy-wonder, once following more closely in Rossi's footsteps. In his time, Melandri has been the youngest-ever 125 race winner, and champion in the 250 class. He moved straight to MotoGP... and fell on hard times. Yamaha's M1 was for him an invitation to crash every time he pushed hard – 14 times in 2004 – and by the second year his relationship with the second-string Yamaha team had soured considerably.

His confidence was as bruised by the experience as his body. When Fausto Gresini picked him to join Gibernau in his satellite Honda team, he was taking a bit of a chance. Or perhaps not...

The maturing rider rapidly showed that the team principal's faith was well justified, finishing on the rostrum in the first race. He was challenging Rossi by Assen-time, and won the last two races of the year. A slump in between those points wasn't helped by a nasty injury at Rossi's hands at Motegi. The way Melandri fought back showed real strength and commitment.

The vehicle for this was Honda's RC211V, and the bike suited his style so well that it might have been tailor-made. It massaged his talent in the same way that the Yamaha had punished it.

Compared with Melandri's obvious target, this is a weakness. Rossi has proved he can win on any bike; Melandri needed a Honda.

At the same time, his progress from bruised battler to double race winner was very assured. If he can continue to get better at the same rate, he will soon be very hard for anybody to beat.

3 LORIS CAPIROSSI

Ducati Marlboro Team

2005 World Championship – 6th (MotoGP)

Career GP wins – 25 (3 MotoGP, 2 500cc, 12 250cc, 8 125cc)

World Championships – 3 (1 250cc, 2 125cc)

Born 4 April, 1973, Bologna, Italy

Small but hard, Loris Capirossi made his name with three smaller-class world titles with a particular style of riding. This combined conspicuous daring with an assertiveness with the machine, bending it to his will sometimes in spite of itself. The image of Loris hanging on to the handlebars, throttle pinned wide open, while his bike bucks and weaves beneath him, is strong.

That approach has not yielded consistently good results in the big class, either with two-strokes or four-strokes. There was never any doubt about his potential or his competitive urge – Capirossi could often produce brilliance. Just not all the time.

Racing is all about having the right package; the rider just a part of it. And at the end of 2005, the ingredients all came together... the powerful Ducati was responding better than ever to rider input, and more importantly the Bridgestone tyres were as good as anything anyone could get.

In this way, Capirossi hit the rostrum at Brno, and decisively won the next two races. His form meant that he would be a serious threat at Phillip Island as well. Instead, a heavy practice crash left him injured, returning only for a below-par run in the final round.

The exciting thing about Loris's wins was the way he achieved them – just by being his old self. Well into his thirties, with 231 GP starts behind him, at Motegi especially he looked like a teenager. He was wringing the Desmosedici's neck, and every time it fought back he would wring it even harder. Attaboy!

NICKY HAYDEN

Repsol Honda Team

2005 World Championship – 3rd (MotoGP)

Race wins – 1

Pole positions – 3

Career GP wins – 1 (MotoGP)

Born 30 July, 1981, Owensboro, USA

Honda won Hayden from Yamaha in a tug-of-love after he had won the AMA Superbike title in 2002, but his first two years on a full factory Honda were never more than promising. All eyes were on the American for his third season – it was time to deliver. It was easy to forget he was still just 23 at the start of the year, with just 30 GP starts, compared with (say) Rossi on 140, Biaggi on 197, or Barros on 241.

All the same, people had expected more from the AMA champion, and sooner.

Under this sort of pressure, there is no doubt that the affable, modest and thoroughly likeable Kentucky Kid (once known as "Mr Dirt") produced a very impressive season. Working with a new crew chief, Kiwi Pete Benson, he put together a package that was fast from the start.

Being fast for more than a few laps, especially at the end of the race, was Nicky's stated goal; and again that took longer than he might have hoped.

Victory at home was a massive boost to his confidence, however. That US win can be put down to intimate local knowledge of a highly technical circuit; but there was a different Hayden to be seen in subsequent races, and a string of four rostrums, including two seconds, in the final races was the proof of it.

In fact, while other riders may be jealous of Hayden's privileged position with HRC, his progress hasn't actually been that slow, and he will start 2006 at a higher level again.

DANI PEDROSA

5

Telefónica MoviStar Honda

2005 World Championship – 1st (250cc)

Race wins – 8

Pole positions – 5

Career GP wins – 24 (16 250cc, 8 125cc)

World Championships – 3 (2 250cc, 1 125cc)

Born 29 September, 1985, Sabadell, Spain

It is hard, when you know only the public face of Dani Pedrosa to realise he was still a teenager when he won his third World Championship. He has the mien of an altogether older, harder man – stern and unsmiling, utterly focused.

There is another Dani, a teenager with an impish sense of humour. Few people outside his circle see it, for it is well hidden behind the race face he wears for most of the weekend. The nickname "Laughing Boy" is deeply ironic.

Pedrosa is not just a remarkably talented rider. He has also developed his race-craft and tactics to a high degree. This is another reason why he appears so mature while still so young.

The protégé of former 500 GP winner Alberto Puig,

Dani found himself with some tougher opposition for his second 250 title, and he dealt with it in his familiar masterly fashion, making full use of whatever machine advantage he might have had.

He showed something else in 2005 – real courage. He fractured his shoulder in one of his three crashes at Motegi, but told nobody, until after he'd come back to win the title in Australia.

Next year, Dani is in the big class, and will surely need some time to learn – though he was dazzlingly fast in early tests. The 800s of the year after that might suit his small stature even better (though nobody told Capirossi that). The question is whether Rossi will still be around when Dani reaches full strength… for that would be an interesting battle.

SETE GIBERNAU

Team MoviStar Honda

2005 World Championship – 7th (MotoGP)

Race wins – 0

Pole positions – 5

Career GP wins – 9 (8 MotoGP, 1 500cc)

Born 15 December, 1972, Barcelona, Spain

Sete told us all himself. He'd had a superb season. There had been just one missing ingredient ... race results. Apart from that, a proud year of achievement for the glamorously turned out Spanish racer that Rossi nicknamed "Hollywood".

And this was truly so. Sete rode better than he ever had before, and better than any other Honda rider. Not only fastest qualifier of the year on aggregate, he equalled Rossi's five pole positions, and exceeded his victor's number of laps in the lead, by 113 to 109.

It was just that last lap. And though four times second was better than anyone else, the rest was a sorry litany of serial disaster and lost opportunity. Sete made mistakes under pressure, running wide three times while leading – even falling off. He was

also prey to the sort of rotten luck that might have been scripted: rain victim at Estoril, tyre mystery in China, out of gas at Brno, engine blow-up at Valencia. If he didn't mess it up himself, something else would intervene.

Sete excelled in almost every department, but forgot something crucial... how to race. It is only respectful to his obvious riding talent to accept that this lapse might be temporary. Although with his age (32) and experience (160 starts), it's bound to be a worry.

Now on a Ducati, Sete has the chance to regain his rightful place... close to, but somewhere behind Valentino Rossi.

He certainly captured the attention in 2005, and deserved a lot more sympathy than he got.

7 SHINYA NAKANO

Kawasaki Racing Team

2005 World Championship – 10th (MotoGP)

Career GP wins – 6 (250cc)

Born 10 October, 1977, Chiba, Japan

The Japanese rider's career might have been different had Yamaha kept faith with him. Instead, they let him go at the end of 2003 – and their loss was Kawasaki's gain.

Highly rated by rivals and fans alike, the cheery Nakano brought plenty with him when he joined the green team... not only his consistent riding and analytical skills, but also a measure of self-respect. It worked both ways. A team that had been languishing in its first season came back much stronger – moving past their closest rivals Suzuki. And the rider regained momentum, with a full factory team where his status was assured.

Nakano actually achieved better individual race results last year, but produced a stronger overall performance in 2005. He frequently qualified well, and was always to be taken into account in the race, even if he wasn't on the fastest or most manageable machine.

In this way, he was only out of the top ten twice, while none of his three non-finishes were his own fault. A blow-up at Motegi cost him dear, then Gibernau knocked him off while with the front runners at Sepang a week later. Either of these Bridgestone-friendly races might have given him a best finish of the year.

It would be interesting to see what Nakano would be doing on a fully competitive machine. It remains to be seen whether Kawasaki can take another technical step forward for next year, when they have a new engine. If they do, they can be sure that Nakano will make the most of it.

TONI ELIAS

Fortuna Yamaha Team

2005 World Championship – 12th (MotoGP)

Career GP wins – 9 (7 250cc, 2 125cc)

Born 12 March, 1983, Manresa, Spain

THE best way to qualify for this listing is to bring excitement when you ride. Elias has always done that in his career in 125 and 250, where he was often dazzling. In 2003, he won five races to 250 champion Poggiali's four.

Stocky, tough-looking, with a disarming toothy grin, Elias moved to the big class this year, and adapted quickly to the M1 Yamaha, a motorcycle that doesn't suit everybody. He started out pushing, and quickly outclassed his more four-stroke experienced team-mate Xaus. When he was fit, his progress on the M1 was consistently impressive. In Turkey, the penultimate round, he double-bluffed and out-charged no less a rider than Colin Edwards for sixth.

The problem was a big gap in the middle of the season. Testing the day after only the fourth round at

Le Mans, Elias did fall victim to the M1's hard-to-handle nature, and among a number of injuries, a wrist fracture would cost him dear for many weeks to come. He missed three races, and was not at full strength for the next four either.

He finished with a flourish, however – favourite of sponsors Fortuna, and going with them to replace Gibernau in the front-running Gresini Honda team. The same move served Melandri well

Elias has been overshadowed by Pedrosa through much of his career – a position he fostered when he decided to break free from the same Alberto Puig-led Telefónica stable to build an independent career. Without the same patronage, it hasn't always been easy, but Elias has his own influential supporters, and is earmarked for a big future all the same.

9 CARLOS CHECA

2005 World Championship – 9th (MotoGP)

Career GP Wins: 2 (500cc)

Born 15 October, 1972 – Sant Fruitos, Spain

Carlos Checa's six years with Yamaha seemed to have taken him firmly over the hill ... and when the Spanish rider was selected for the second Ducati seat in place of Troy Bayliss, there was much muttering about how the influence of sponsors was having a bad effect on the choice of riders. After all, it had been way back in 1998, back in the old 500cc days, that Carlos had won a race.

Like Melandri, however, Carlos turned the corner on a different motorcycle. It took time to get to grips with the Desmosedici's special ways, but when the Bridgestone tyres got good after Brno, Carlos was ready to make the most of it.

In the last six races, he was twice on the rostrum, and only once lower than fifth. If only he could find better qualifying speed, he might have done better still.

Checa's form wasn't good enough for him to keep his ride at Ducati – sponsor favour or no. But it was close enough to a second flowering for him to be snapped up for the Pons Honda team, where he will ride the V5 Honda for the first time.

As second chances go, it's the latest in a string of them for the personable Carlos, who has developed a fine line in dry humour in the intervening years. If he can ride for 2006 like he did the latter part of 2005, he will have deserved it.

10

COLIN EDWARDS

Gauloises Yamaha Team

2005 World Championship – 4th (MotoGP)

World Championships – 2 (World Superbike)

Born 27 February, 1974, Houston, USA

It is a cross that Colin Edwards must bear that everyone expects more of him. When he delivers – as this year at Le Mans, Laguna Seca and Assen in particular – it seems that this should be normal. When he finds himself struggling, as he did rather too often during 2005, he is castigated as a major disappointment.

For a double World Superbike champion, this may be fair. On the other hand, it doesn't take into account that, for a racing hero, MotoGP MotoGP has been a rather rocky road. His first year was on the Aprilia, a major handful in anybody's language; his second was on a Honda, that for some reason gave him chatter problems that worried the other V5 riders much less.

For his third year, he was team-mate to one of the greatest racers of all time. He was in the back seat even before he started.

Colin did have more trouble than he should have during the season, and his results were erratic. But he was adapting once again to a motorcycle he hadn't ridden before – his third completely different motorcycle in three years. At this level, that it a hard task.

He did well enough, on his good days, to earn a suspended sentence from his critics. But anything less than regular top results in his second year on the factory Yamaha would be likely to seal his fate, to the accompaniment of a reinforced chorus of his dreaded nay-sayers and armchair world champions.

MONEY TALKS LOUDEST

By MICHAEL SCOTT

Above: Behind closed doors... the paddock village at Catalunya.

Photograph: Gold & Goose

MOTOGP four-strokes have changed grand prix racing more in four years than anything before in its history of more than 50. And it's not just the technicalities... the acquisition of poppet valves. Everything but the actual substance has changed – the profile, the way of working, the surrounding paddock, the manner of motorcycle racing, all radically altered. Only Sunday afternoon remains the same.

Motorcycles have personalities of their own – highly individual. It is clear in retrospect that the nature of the 990s compared with the 500s has played a part in those changes.

The 500cc two-strokes improved upon the purity of tradition, taking racing to an esoteric ivory tower of exclusivity and excellence. Technically irrelevant, they existed only to race against one another. This coloured the whole fabric. Motorcycle GP racing took place because of itself and on its own behalf. The participants were there also purely in their own interests, and for their own interest.

Going four-stroke aligned racing with the real world of business, with all its functions and functionaries. And the real world has invaded.

It is of no relevance whether this is good or bad. It's unstoppable, a sign of success. Commercialisation of sport is the inevitable goal, when it is commercially owned and managed for the profit of the investors. And almost all of the commercial signs were good... increasing TV audiences, a growing calendar, and a star like Rossi to put a rocket under the global recognition factor. There remained, at the end of 2005, a major conundrum. In a business that showed every possible sign of booming, why were the sponsors running away?

There were three, possibly four, major sponsorship losses... Telefónica MoviStar, Gauloises, BMW, and possibly Camel. In fact, each departure came about for a different reason, so to suggest a trend may be trying too hard. As one frustrated money-seeker pointed out, much of the big-spend from sponsors is entirely whimsical... in that the basic decision is almost always at the whim of one powerful man. If he happens to like motorbike racing, then the budget can be enormous. But he might at any moment decide he prefers soccer, or clay-pigeon shooting. All the same, the losses were too severe to be shrugged off with quite the same whimsy, amounting to an annual spend of at least $50-million. And that was not all.

As well as outside backing, MotoGP also lost support from within: Aprilia left the class after three somewhat fruitless years. The troubled Italian company's new owners, Piaggio, continued whole-hearted support of the smaller classes, but after equivocating for a while, firmly shelved the costly Cosworth-developed three-cylinder MotoGP machine. Then, halfway through the year, another manufacturer pulled the plug... KTM. The Austrian firm, also making big inroads in 125 and starting in 250, had embarked rather half-heartedly on a project developing and supplying their hitherto still-born V4 engine to Team Roberts for MotoGP. During the summer break they abruptly pulled out, leaving the England-based team bereft.

This left a thriving race series facing thin grids, down to 18-strong at Australia. This may get worse next year, with Teams Pons and Roberts searching for sponsorship, and the Blata WCM squad in a very uncertain position. The inevitably vaulting costs of four-stroke racing have hit smaller teams very hard. Dorna already in 2005 put financial and other backing towards propping up some which have fallen on hard times. Like Team Roberts, and the d'Antin squad, both of whom expect to be running next year. Team Roberts also have back-door backing from none other than the Honda Racing Corporation, well aware of the need to forestall any further loss of people to beat, with an agreement to supply engines for the England-built chassis for 2006.

It will be, after all, an interim year, a sort of no-man's land. The 990cc MotoGP machines will, at the end of it, be headed for the museum.

Some think that the new generation of 800s offer salvation, a fresh impetus. There were reports of at least one and maybe two all-new engines in preparation for the big change of 2007 – the first by Mario Illien, one of the founders of F1 engine firm Ilmor, recently sold to Mercedes Benz.

There were other encouraging signs that, if outside backing may be faltering at present, GP racing's original support system – from within itself – has regained considerable vitality. A stream of talent rising up the ladder, 125 to 250 to MotoGP, had by the end of 2005 swelled to become a river. And there is plenty more to come.

It is easy to lean towards tales of woe and to the signs of

financial disaster, but the positive side is very strong, and the reverse flow of sponsorship cash simply a bizarre quirk. It is also easy to believe that fairly soon a balance will be achieved, and the obvious commercial value of MotoGP will attract the outside backing it currently so sorely lacks… and perhaps sooner rather than later. In fact, it had better be sooner, because quite what will happen when Rossi goes is another story…

The final and potentially one of the most significant developments came late in the year, when the ultimate owners of MotoGP rights, venture capitalists CVC, made a new purchase… taking over from Bernie Ecclestone as majority shareholders of F1.

Quite what this will mean to MotoGP is not clear, but it does now form part of a portfolio including the world's most commercially successful motorsport. Will MotoGP step up onto the rostrum, or will it remain as a very junior partner?

THE MONEY DRAIN AND THE POWER GAME

Gauloises pulled out of MotoGP sponsorship at the end of 2005 because they felt they had been dealt a bad hand by Yamaha. They had a contract in place to sponsor the factory team… then it transpired that Yamaha's top rider, Rossi, wouldn't be riding for that team. Some $20-million gone west.

Telefónica MoviStar did the same thing for much the same reason, except in this case it was Honda. The factory team poached the rider they had nurtured from his earliest racing days, Dani Pedrosa. That's another $15-million or so.

Nobody upset BMW, as far as we can tell. They simply decided to go elsewhere with the backing that included the support-series BMW Cup, as well as a fleet of safety and support vehicles.

But it was Honda who faced up to Camel at the last race of the year, rejecting their estimated $12- to $15-million and triggering a row not yet resolved at the time of writing. This put HRC 2:1 up on Yamaha in the field of sponsor-bashing.

The argument centred on Max Biaggi, and here was proof of the whimsical nature of sponsorship. Biaggi is a personal favourite of a senior executive at Camel brand owners JTI. During the course of 2005, however, he became persona non grata to HRC. They decided he would never again ride a Honda. So when Camel proposed putting the fallen hero, dumped from the factory squad, into their satellite team, HRC bluntly refused.

To teams hungry for sponsorship, this sort of attitude is incomprehensible. Sponsors who get to pay enough also get to choose the riders. This is a fact of life. BMW apart, the above cases show that this same attitude does not prevail in the upper echelons. And this is a significant shift in the balance of power. To some, a sinister shift…

It is hard to know to what extent Yamaha were wrong-footed by Rossi in their contretemps with Gauloises, or whether they went into it with their eyes wide open. After all, the value of keeping him on to win titles for them and enhance their brand worldwide is even higher than the Gauloises cash. It is in any case tobacco money, tainted money, already in a fearsome squeeze of (as yet largely untested) new European and other legislation. Nobody knows for how much longer this long-standing and generous source of funding will be available, but it's not to be relied upon forever.

The same applies to Camel, over in the Honda camp – but this was surely not a consideration. HRC's factory team had been through a second bad season, although in 2005 they had managed to win a race, which was one better than 2004. But it was junior rider Nicky Hayden whose home-race triumph took the chequered flag; clear number one rider Biaggi had been a serious disappointment, mixing occasional strong races with a series of year-end stumbles, and grumbling almost non-stop. A strong challenge for second overall fell to pieces in the closing stages, and after another outburst in Turkey, where Max had finished a year's-worst 12th, Honda had had enough. After Rossi had proved once again that riders ultimately outrank engineers, they were smarting. Somebody had to be punished, and Max had virtually volunteered for the role.

This leads to a larger issue. In questions of rank, Honda's perception is clear enough: they are at the top. Both Telefónica MoviStar and Camel gave them the opportunity to

assert themselves.

On the surface, they were regaining the important element of control over rider choice. More than that, they were demonstrating their power and status. As they privately admitted at Valencia, even the biggest-spending sponsors are nowadays a relatively small part of the vastly increased overall costs of racing the new four-stroke MotoGP bikes. The factories are spending so much more while sponsorship levels have remained

relatively static; the importance of the sponsors has declined proportionally.

This is undoubtedly true for Honda, who decline to reveal MotoGP budget or costs, but who certainly spend a great deal more than anybody else, Yamaha included. Honda can afford to do so. And they can afford to lay down the law to their sponsors. Yamaha obviously feel the same, whether voluntarily or not is open to question.

Other manufacturer teams are in sharp contrast. Kawasaki and Suzuki, for example, are reduced to scratching for income, even selling VIP paddock hospitality packages; Team Roberts is hunting hard to replace the lost Proton; WCM is also bereft of big-bucks backing. Only circumstances would prevent any of these from doing almost anything a sponsor asked. In fact, Suzuki turned the Camel/Biaggi package away for want of

Cartoonist Sprockett's exclusive view on the Italian GP (top), and Gibernau's smashing performance in Germany.

Below: A new flag to racing. For 2005, race stoppages were themselves stopped in favour of flag-to-flag . The white flag with a red cross meant riders were permitted to pit to change bikes. First deployed when it rained mid-race in Portugal, it worked against the luckless Gibernau (below).
Photograph: Gold & Goose

Bottom: US GP winner Nicky Hayden gate-crashed Yamaha's party.

capacity, having just signed up two riders and a sponsor deal with Rizla for 2006. Kawasaki accepted, planning to run a third bike for Biaggi... only to be told that Bridgestone would not be able to supply enough tyres.

The overall meaning is simple.

Honda are flexing their muscles, and calling the shots. If this drives sponsors away, so be it. If the other factories can then not afford to compete fully, or even at all, so be it.

At least everybody will know just who is the boss.

800CC – MORE LIKE REAL RACING BIKES?
The choice of 990cc for the new MotoGP class of 2002 was not quite arbitrary. Certain functions had to be fulfilled.

The new bikes must be seen as specialised prototypes, which ruled out round numbers – like 750cc or 1000cc. Being 990cc made them special.

They also had to be fast enough to outclass the prevailing 500cc two-strokes, instantly. There was not the luxury of a couple of years of development; they had to be faster out of the box.

The death of Daijiro Kato at the start of the second season put the spotlight on safety, and started a movement to cut power and speeds, already reliably beyond 200mph and getting faster all the time. MotoGP's peculiar structure means that

technical rules are written by the manufacturers themselves, and their MSMA association started to confer.

One can only imagine how difficult these discussions must have been with such disparate parties as Aprilia and Kawasaki, Ducati and Honda. Eventually a compromise was announced at the first race of 2003: from 2007 the capacity would be cut to 900cc.

This seemed like a small difference. It would set back overall performance only slightly, but would at the same time offer more-or-less continuous development: losing ten percent capacity off a 990cc engine is a simple enough matter of adjusting bore and stroke.

Decisions have to be unanimous, but Honda made it known at once they were not in agreement, arguing the case for a much more radical reduction, with 700 or 750cc seen as ideal for the next generation. But the decision was made, and the die cast. Or so it seemed. That view did not take into account HRC's determination to have their way, or their power in persuading the others to step into line.

Thus 2005 started with news that the MSMA – now under presidency of HRC president Suguru Kanazawa (on a rotational basis, he pointed out) – were "reconsidering". The outcome was made known at the Italian GP in June, with barely 18 months to go before the new machines will appear. No longer would they be 900cc clones of the current generation. The new 2007 plan was for a much more savage cut – to 800cc.

This had several effects – the most trenchant that the change was big enough to require fresh engine design and thinking. An 800cc engine would be significantly smaller and higher-revving. Nobody could adapt a 990, nor would the same ground-rules apply. Where current development work concentrates on taming an excess of power, smaller engines would be trying to maximise it.

New thinking is in itself no bad thing. Indeed, development of relevant engine technology is one very good reason for a factory to justify money spent on racing. The drawback is only in costs, already spiralling since the four-strokes arrived. Starting from scratch again would heavily favour Honda, the richest of the protagonists.

Again, the MSMA's decision was unanimous; again there were dissenting voices immediately afterwards. None louder than Ducati's, who had lost the argument to ban pneumatic valve springs. The need for high revs will become acute with the smaller engines, and the advantage of their desmodromic system much more valuable than at present. (HRC later nobly revealed they had no plans to use pneumatics, but they may have had their fingers crossed.)

It remains to be seen just what the 800s will bring with them, but the machines will demand higher levels of technology than the galumphing 990s. They will be more exotic, especially in detail. They will be more like racing bikes.

They will also be more difficult to ride than the current bikes... peakier, twitchier, revvier. More like the old two-strokes in fact, although HRC's Kanazawa points out that electronic over-rides – the most rapid field of technical development – will counteract this tendency.

Rossi is not convinced by the "more-like-two-strokes" argument, although he has already changed his mind... once insisting that he found the 500s, more exacting, exciting and enjoyable to ride than the 990s. "I think the MotoGP bikes as they are now are better – very nice, very fast," he said. "For sure, with 800cc we will lose some of the taste. I think these one-litre bikes will pass into history." He and his peers were lucky, he said, to have ridden them.

But he was reserving final judgement, expecting to start testing a 2007 prototype Yamaha mid-season in 2006. "I will wait and see."

So must we all. All major participants were already working on the next generation of MotoGP prototype, with tantalising rumours suggesting that Honda already have a V3 motor up and running, plus confirmation of a V4 from former Ilmor designer Mario Illien, and rumours of another German-designed in-line triple.

Can the others afford to compete? Can they afford not to?

Stand by for a new generation of the most specialised and

advanced racing prototypes ever seen, bristling with electronics, special materials and new techniques. Stand by for the future. It will be exciting.

And when, after a year or so (as Kanazawa predicts) the new machines reach and exceed the speeds and performances of the current 990s, try and remember that the change was originally proposed in the interest of cutting speeds and improving safety.

THE RIDERS' LADDER

The racing 500s were consigned to history because of irrelevance. The 250s now occupy the same position. They exist because they existed already. Their days must obviously be numbered.

It is far from clear, however, what to do about it. A junior class is required, and since the Flammini Group has the contract on road-based motorcycles, help cannot be sought from the showrooms.

One suggestion is simply for smaller-size prototype four-strokes... reduced-capacity MotoGP bikes, in other words. The difficulty is obvious: it costs just as much to build a 400cc prototype as an 800cc or 990cc prototype. The cost does not lie in the quantity of metal used.

Another is for a 400cc single-cylinder class – following the lead set by motocross. Objections are raised because of the nature of the beast. They would sound old-fashioned, for one thing. Nor would they necessarily be especially cheap. Would they be fast enough?

During 2005, the difficulties of resolving the question led to a stay of execution. Everybody knows the 250s are living on borrowed time, but the MSMA and Dorna have lent them some more... until 2012.

The status quo confers many advantages. The two-stroke 250 twins are relatively simple, and relatively inexpensive to buy and to run. A hands-off policy by the Japanese factories has meant an end to full factory teams from that quarter, although from Europe Aprilia's factory squad has been joined this year by Fantic and KTM.

Another aspect was of crucial importance in the successful fight-back of the 250s. This season has firmly re-established the 250 class as the rider's ladder.

This is more important than on first sight, because it finally overturns an expectation that the new four-strokes would favour recruits from elsewhere... in particular, World Superbikes. It was thought that four-stroke experience would be of paramount importance.

Well, it's obviously no drawback, but so far not one of the ex-World or other Superbike classes has actually dazzled, though some have flickered from time to time – like Colin Edwards and latterly Nicky Hayden, at last becoming a serious championship threat. Troy Bayliss seemed ultimately out of his depth; fellow ex-SBK champion Neil Hodgson was never taken seriously, while his former SBK team-mate Ruben Xaus started in spirited fashion, but spent 2005 falling off the back of the bus.

This year's fastest-rising MotoGP star was Marco Melandri, who had trod the boards traditionally, Rossi-style, moving up through the classes from bottom to top. Toni Elias, in his first year, was also highly impressive, injury permitting. Another class-by-class rookie.

Even more significant were the newcomers who enlivened the 250 class – a trio of teenage talent which had dominated 125s the year before: Andrea Dovizioso, Jorge Lorenzo and Hector Barbera. At the same time, new age limits engendered further movement. The reduced maximum (to 27) meant that several senior riders moved up or retired, opening the way for 16 rookies at the start of the year – almost half the entry, with more joining during the season.

Next year, this tidal flow continues – the top two in the 250 championship, Dani Pedrosa and Casey Stoner, moving up to MotoGP. They will be joined by another ex-SBK candidate Chris Vermeulen, the trio significantly reducing the average age of the class.

Vermeulen is another with the chance to prove that World Superbikes can produce MotoGP winners, after an impressive pair of substitute rides in 2005 on a Honda... though his

choice of the Suzuki will not make it easy.

In the end, a good rider is a good rider, and his actual training and background not that important. Following the 125/250/MotoGP path does gives a rider some tangible advantages over a Superbike rival, such as familiarity with the circuits and the lifestyle, and important experience in setting up true racing bikes, with adjustable suspension and gearing. A talented rider can quickly learn these things.

Much more important is the system. More businesslike in this way as well as others, racing (read "Dorna") has worked at establishing a clear career path for a teenage would-be world champion. Start at the bottom, but in GP racing, and you are on this path, and in a position where you will be known to team managers and talent spotters from the earliest opportunity. That is why Vermeulen is lucky to find a slot. A year later, with Lorenzo & Co. pushing on through, and more coming behind, it would have been harder.

It's mainly Dorna's doing – with significant help from Alberto Puig and the Telefónica MoviStar initiative – a fruitful programme based around the Spanish 125 championship, which has launched Pedrosa and Elias, among others. This is reflected in the national bias of the 125 class. Last year, most riders were Italian: 13 to eight Spaniards. This year, the rookie-friendly entry list shifted the ratio heavily the other way, 14 Spaniards to just six Italians.

From Spain comes some salvation for British riders, after a long barren spell. It is thanks to Dorna's MotoGP Academy – the current evolution of Puig's evolving training scheme. Two teenagers were picked for this training course. Danny Webb found his way to the rostrum in Spain; Bradley Smith did even better, coming within one point of the Spanish title by winning the last two rounds.

It was an encouraging start, but there is a long way yet to travel. Like any ladder, it goes one step at a time.

Top: Pedrosa will still need the riders' ladder in 2006.

Above: Jorge Lorenzo leads team-mate Hector Barbera... two major talents on the way up.
Photograph: Gold & Goose

23

TECHNICAL REVIEW
WORLD CHAMPIONSHIP TO ORDER

by NEIL SPALDING

Above: Gauloises Yamaha, up close.

Photograph: Gold & Goose

IN 2005 Yamaha's racing department had a lot to deliver. The year before, they had scooped the championship, with Valentino Rossi demonstrating his phenomenal riding skills to tame an admittedly under-par machine sufficiently to make it a winner at his first attempt. Now they were under orders to do it again.

Yamaha's 2004 M1 was a hybrid, mostly 2003 parts with selected items modified by Masao Furusawa's motorcycle engineering division and fine-tuned by Jerry Burgess and his crew. The engine had the most changes, including a new four-valve head and a different crankshaft.

The company's directive for 2005 was to defend the championship to coincide with Yamaha's 50th anniversary. No small task. It's difficult enough to win MotoGP in any year without somebody telling you when you have to do it. To help deliver Yamaha's birthday present Furusawa and his engineers put together possibly the ultimate across-the-frame, four-cylinder racing motorcycle.

In the opposite corner Honda were still coming to terms with the loss of direction suffered with the departure of both their top rider and his race engineer. They were not happy with the way their 2004 chassis worked on corner entry, and after a lot of testing they opted to use a selection of parts from both 2004 and 2003 on their 2005 works bikes. To get as much information as possible they hired riders with radically different riding styles, but still they found it difficult to construct a bike to beat the Yamaha/Rossi combination.

The supporting cast were also having their ups and downs. Ducati had finished 2004 apparently severely chastened following their power delivery and weight distribution difficulties at the start of the year. Kawasaki had proven their new chassis, lighter but still suffering quite ridiculous levels of wheelspin and a lack of grip. Suzuki had a chassis that handled delightfully, but then again, MotoGP chassis technology with a low-power engine should handle pretty well. The rest of the Europeans were having problems. Aprilia's new owners put a quick halt to any delusions of MotoGP grandeur, Kenny Roberts's England-based GP Motorsports facility had discovered that developing four stroke engines wasn't as easy as it looked, and WCM dug out their old four-cylinders and crossed their fingers that Czech minibike company Blata would indeed turn up with the promised 990cc V6.

In the tyre world Bridgestone, Michelin and Dunlop continued their all-out battle. The Japanese contenders had upped the stakes, introducing test teams with Suzuki, Kawasaki and most especially Ducati, circumventing rules forbidding pre-testing at GP tracks.

On the Ducati, Bridgestone's tyres showed form during early winter testing, but we had to wait until mid-season at Brno before they finally got a rear carcase and compound mix that really suited their chassis. Bridgestone had more luck with Kawasaki and Suzuki early in the year, especially in the wet, but it was only when they got Michelin away from the security of Europe that they really delivered. Bridgestone showed new form from Brno onwards. Motegi's pole and win with Ducati were not overly surprising considering the number of laps their test teams had done there; but the continuance of that form to Malaysia and beyond was quite unexpected and showed serious intent.

Dunlop too started to find compounds and constructions that made sense once they had some track time on the d'Antin Ducati. Dunlop's improvement was most easily measured at WCM, where Ellison was able to knock two-and-a-half seconds off 2004 Brno times. Some of that was Ellison, some of that was the WCM, but a substantial chunk was Dunlop.

Electronic throttles went from being flighty and temperamental to must-have equipment. The need to maintain performance with a reduced fuel capacity, from 24 to 22 litres, brought a significant change from previous attempts at traction control, where excess power was bled off by dropping sparks. The 2005 version made sure the excess power wasn't developed in the first place. This not only improved rider feel, but as a direct result less fuel was used.

The new norm, with a four-cylinder engine, was to give the rider direct control of only two cylinders. The other two, along with the ignition timing map and the overall fuel maps, were under the control of a computer. This first compared front and rear wheel speeds, and the rate of acceleration of both wheels and the crankshaft. This left some bikes sounding slightly curious as teams juggled ignition maps and independently operated throttles to achieve the best possible combination of accurate throttle response, grip and wheelspin.

Magneti Marelli became the majority choice in pit lane, supplying software and know-how, but with most teams developing their own tailor-made packages.

YAMAHA – BALANCE IS ALL

Yamaha started testing very early indeed. Rossi's first ride on his 2005 bike was immediately after the end of the 2004 season. Absolutely determined to win, Yamaha made sure the bike was delivered to Rossi a full six months before the first race. Whether it was qualifying tyres, supreme determination or a very good motorcycle, Rossi promptly went faster on the new bike than he had in the race three days before.

Yamaha's 2005 bike was still called an M1. A logical extension of the 2004 machine, it was nonetheless almost completely new, only clutch and wheels seemingly unchanged. The engine was narrower across the cylinder block, although not across the crankshaft, and shorter as well. The in-line four's downside is width, and Yamaha's 2005 engine may be the smallest one-litre four ever made.

Motorcycle design is all about packaging. You must put the weight in the right place, but you must also fit a 990cc engine, 22 litres of fuel, 12 to 15 litres of airbox, an exhaust system, a frame and electronics as well as the rider behind the smallest possible fairing. The packaging is further complicated by the need to get cooling air both in and out, and to get the output shaft in the right place for the swing-arm and chain.

The engine was shrunk across the barrels by moving the cam drive from a chain on the right of the block to a series of gears running up the back on the bike's centre line. This allowed the barrel assembly to only be as wide as the four cylinders and their water jacket. The balance shaft that in 2004 ran full width behind the crankshaft now appeared to be just long enough to drive the cam gears, perform its balancing function, and trans-

mit power to the clutch. The alternator that previously lived on the end of this shaft was driven off the top of the clutch-basket primary gear. Everything that rotates was as close to the centre line as possible. The crank still turned backwards, aiding low-speed chassis agility by counteracting some of the gyroscopic forces generated by the wheels.

The engine retained the four-valves-per-cylinder layout introduced at the start of 2004 but developed significantly more power. Furusawa, now Executive Officer of Yamaha's engineering operations department, confirmed that last year's chain-drive cam was a limitation to increasing revs. Gear drive made high revs far more reliable, which let Yamaha tune the motor for power at higher rpm.

The rear of the engine was also redesigned, with Yamaha using a vertically stacked gearbox very similar to those on its sporting street bikes. This moved the clutch up the back of the cylinder block and allowed Yamaha to bring the second shaft of the gearbox almost vertically underneath the first. Yamaha had needed to lower the gearbox output shaft slightly to maintain the centre of gravity that Rossi had preferred while regaining a closer to ideal relationship between output shaft, swing-arm pivot and rear axle.

The revised engine architecture allowed Yamaha to build a chassis narrower around the front engine mounts. One of the improvements seen in 2004 was these front mounts, which appeared to allow additional deflection at the steering head. When added to the old engine and chassis, they used up much of the space previously occupied by radiator exhaust ducts. This had a knock-on effect both in terms of cooling and drag. The 2005 motor allowed much bigger exhaust ducts, enabling greater flow

Below left: Spy shot between the forks shows Yamaha's neatened wiring arrangements at the headstock substation.

Bottom left: Ruben Xaus's Yamaha shows short version of tailpipe.
Photographs: Neil Spalding

Below: Compact packaging and revised chassis design improved Yamaha's airflow.
Photograph: Gold & Goose

Below: Below: Honda had seven variations on the RC211V theme on track in 2005. This one is Troy Bayliss's machine.
Photograph: Gold & Goose

through the radiator, improving cooling and reducing drag. The new gearbox allowed the chassis to be shorter and the swing-arm longer, and thus less prone to strong reaction to the forces that are created when 240-plus horsepower are transmitted to the rear wheel by the chain.

The repackaging of the motor and the chassis changes were all designed to maximize handling efficiency. The Yamaha is claimed to roll in faster, turn faster, pitch less, and to be more stable on corner entry. These were areas that Honda admitted were weak spots before the year had even started. Yamaha seldom had the highest top speed, but it got to that speed very quickly out of corners, and was devilishly effective going into them. A salutary lesson to those who think that all that matters are power and top speed.

In addition to the mechanical tour-de-force, Yamaha perfected their electronic throttle system. Still called the Idle Control System (ICS), this is nothing less than a full new-style ride-by-wire package. Two throttle butterflies respond directly to the rider's commands and two are driven by a computer, to constantly deliver the right amount of torque for the occasion. The riders freely admit that the engine would be unrideable without the smoothing effects of the Magneti Marelli based system. It allowed Yamaha to develop an ever more peaky motor while still giving riders the illusion of a broad accessible power band. And it reduced fuel consumption by eight percent. While they were at it, Yamaha also cleaned up their previously very untidy wiring loom, leaving a system that looked elegantly simple.

Yamaha also made sure that their subsidiaries played their part in the defence of their first MotoGP title. Öhlins suspension is used by the majority of teams within MotoGP, but is a subsidiary of Yamaha Motor. They certainly delivered, with new front forks on the M1 from its first test onwards, and a revised rear shock arriving for testing at Le Mans. This took several GPs

to perfect, but by Assen was standard equipment on both works bikes. There followed several races where both Rossi and Edwards were on the podium. At those races, the Yamaha was the better motorcycle, whereas before it had required the genius of Rossi to complete the package.

HONDA – INTO THE WILDERNESS

In all its fields of operation, Honda seems to have the genius of being able to design a completely new vehicle that somehow looks just like the previous version, only sleeker. It is no different with the RC211V. The bike campaigned from the start of the year by the works team was a combination of a more powerful motor in a chassis that looked identical to the 2003 version. The customer bikes appeared to be copies of the works 2004 machines, and for most the year stayed unchanged. However the works bikes of Gibernau, Biaggi and Hayden enjoyed several upgrades.

From the start Honda fitted the three works bikes with adjustable steering heads, which not only allowed some movement of the head forwards and backwards, but also allowed the rider to change the angle.

The works riders' complaints that the bike was difficult to turn compared to the Yamaha did get a response, with a new chassis available to Biaggi and Gibernau from Sachsenring on. This moved the headstock forward something like 10 mm, about what you'd expect for a one-degree change in steering-head angle, while keeping the wheelbase the same. Just one GP later, at Brno, Honda brought a new RC211V. Available for testing only after an unexplained 30-hour delay, this bike was completely new – the engine some eight mm shorter thanks to a slightly stacked gearbox, allowing a longer swing-arm. The chassis and bodywork were also completely new, with some additional aerodynamic benefits.

Above: MoviStar Honda clearly shows non-adjustability of swing-arm pivot position.
Photograph: Gold & Goose

Left: Searching for length, high-level exhaust for rear cylinders does a full loop within the seat hump.
Photograph: Neil Spalding

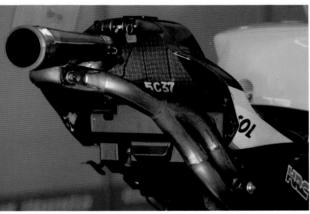

If we include satellite teams, Honda had seven different basic chassis on track at various times of the year. First the customer bikes, then the three works HRC bikes with their adjustable headstocks and 2003-design swing-arms. A second version of these three works bikes had repositioned swing-arm pivots. By Assen, all three top riders had at least one chassis with this modification available. Then there was the "long-head-stock" version available to Biaggi and Gibernau from Sachsenring, the new prototype bike, and another version using the normal HRC chassis with a swing-arm very similar to that on the prototype. Following tests of a works chassis after Brno, Marco Melandri had a hybrid works/customer chassis from Motegi.

In engine terms, the customer bikes were substantially more powerful than last year but remained unchanged. The works bikes, which appeared to have had an upgrade mid year, were more powerful than the customer bikes in any event, with the prototype pulling another ten horsepower on top. Rossi may well have won the championship but it's not as if Honda weren't trying.

Honda give very few details of engine changes, but one of the classic ways to judge an engine's peak rev range is to look at the length of the exhaust primary pipes. The 2005 bike may have had a very similar exhaust system to that used in late 2003 and early 2004, but the primary pipes join together somewhat earlier. The shorter primary length, approximately 50 mm, is the sort of figure you would expect if the engine were peaking about a thousand rpm higher, Honda later confirmed a 16,500-rpm limit. Following engine problems at Motegi, HRC confirmed that they had instructed all their teams to reduce limits by 500 rpm. We believe that the RC211V has a shorter stroke engine now than originally, but more serious work may now be needed to remain competitive in the 990cc formula's swansong year.

As the engine gets more powerful, and we assume peakier, more time is needed for setup. The tools for that are becoming increasingly sophisticated. Last year Honda gave details of a differential throttle system that gave the rider far more control in the lower gears. At the time, they said it operated in the first three only. Project leader Kyoichi Yoshii admitted this year that it had for most of the time been available in all six. At the same time he confirmed that Honda now had a base setting that seemed to fit most riders, and adjustments to this were only necessary for special circumstances.

Further details of Honda's system came out at Brno where Gibernau's bike mysteriously expired on the last lap while trading places for the lead with Rossi. The bike had run out of fuel. With the team vehemently denying having started the race with a less than full tank, HRC eventually revealed they had a system on each bike that monitors fuel usage during the race. This measures the duration of each fuel pulse, leaning out less critical areas of the fuel map if fuel needs to be rationed. It was this system that appeared to have failed. It was a matter of some sensitivity for Honda.

This also highlights the fact that a five-cylinder 990cc engine running to 16,500 rpm peak during a MotoGP race is getting remarkably close to its new 22-litre fuel limit. While the sport may be thought to suffer, and we don't want to see many races settled with one or other of the top bikes running out of fuel, it does give racing a more environmentally sound image if we learn to moderate fuel usage while maintaining high power outputs.

DUCATI – DESMO DAWN

Top: Ducati's unconventional steel-tube chassis is proudly displayed.
Photograph: Gold & Goose

Above: Some switchgear remained unused as electronic variations were discarded.
Photograph: Neil Spalding

Ducati arrived in 2005 with a significantly better-sorted machine, then they dropped the ball just before the first race at Jerez. The 22-litre rule was always going to hit the high-revving bikes harder, and Ducati has the hardest-revving of them all. While the factory claims 16,500 rpm, there is no doubt that the bike is capable of more than that, and on occasion it is fuelled to take into account 18,000 rpm, although that is unlikely to be under acceleration. The fuel question focused minds very hard indeed back in Bologna.

Ducati's waste-saving strategy seemed to be to shut down the engine when not really needed. "Conventional" 2005 MotoGP technology used a slipper clutch and some sort of active fast tick-over system to ensure a smooth run into the corner, and that the rider can come back onto the power with no jerks or lurches. Ducati reasoned that if they could disengage the engine smoothly, allow the rider to do his down shifts, and then re-engage the motor equally smoothly as soon as the rider reapplied the throttle, then they could cut out 70 metres of fuel use every corner. A small saving, but probably enough to maintain full power for the rest of the lap.

A standard clutch was used, with "some magic", according to Ducati Corse chief Claudio Domenicali, this being the addition of a computer-operated automatic extra control, with a small hydraulic pump and a special slave cylinder.

The same technology could help a bike launch off the line, with the computer looking after maximum power and traction. The system sounded quite surreal at Jerez, with a large red motorcycle apparently cutting its engine completely as it passed the end of the garages. The rider could be heard changing down, and the second the throttle was reapplied near the corner apex the motor would burst into life and the bike roar off again.

Unfortunately Ducati simply ran out of time to set the system up correctly. It was run all the way through practice at Jerez, and it wasn't until Capirossi hurt his ankle in a crash in final qualifying that they gave up. When the bikes came out for race-

day warm-up suddenly slipper clutches were back in operation. The system didn't reappear for the rest of the year, but the operating switchgear remained stubbornly on top of the triple clamp, defiantly ignoring the fact that it had nothing to control.

If Ducati were panicking about fuel consumption and a major fuel saving strategy was binned just before the first race, how come they never ran out of fuel? The answer is that they did – or rather the 2004 d'Antin bike of Rolfo did at Laguna following excessive wheelspin.

An intriguing feature of all the Ducatis was how, before the start of each race, a set of surgeons pliers clamped off the tank breather once the bike had been filled for the race. Ducati have a close technical partnership with Shell, who said that until this year all requests had been for more power. Shell won't confirm any such action, but they're capable of making a fuel and oil package angled more towards low friction and fuel economy than pure power and this, along with a well-developed ride-by-wire system seems to have been enough to get the bikes to the finishing line.

While the bike went through several different setups during the course of the year – different offsets, fork positions and (just before Loris's winning streak) a change of swing-arm pivot position – the only significant change appeared to be the use by Capirossi of carbon-fibre outer fork tubes. While these are lighter, the real reason for the choice is that they are 30-percent stiffer. This allows Capirossi more extreme setups on the front, with the stronger fork tubes better able to resist bending back than the aluminum units – the risk being that the tyre will make contact with the cylinder head. Part-way through the year, in response to ever more extreme chassis settings, and the proximity of the front tyre under braking, the bodywork surrounding the front cylinder head disappeared, making a bit of a mockery of their own wind tunnel work.

Without a doubt their Bridgestone tyres limited Ducati's race performances in the early part of the year. But when Bridgestone got it right and delivered tyres that not only stuck but also remained stable through to the end of the race, the Ducati not only ran at the front. It won outright.

KAWASAKI – PROMISE UNFULFILLED

In 2004, Kawasaki replaced their ponderous first MotoGP design with some superb new lightweight chassis, built in conjunction with SRT (Suter Racing Technology) in Switzerland. One of the best-designed and packaged motorcycles in the pit lane, it suffered badly from lack of traction and drive, due to the "screamer" nature of its in-line-four engine. In 2005 all that changed. Kawasaki hired Ichiro Yoda from Yamaha, main development engineer on the M1 project since its inception. He was fully aware of Yamaha's R&D programme, and in fairly quick order the Kawasaki became capable of top-six finishes.

It is not quite clear what happened first, but by Jerez Kawasaki were testing a very strange-sounding motor, a true big-bang engine. Using the original crankshaft, two pistons fired together, and 180 degrees of crank rotation later the other two pistons would fire. Then there would be one-and-a-half revs before the next power pulse.

The effect was dramatic. Suddenly Nakano had drive, and the tyres gripped not only coming out of the corners but going in as well. This first version became christened the B2. At the same time Kawasaki tried a second version, B3. This had two pistons firing together, the other two firing as normal.

Big bang theory is to provide enough time between pulses for the tyre to regain grip. You would think that the delivery of 495cc worth of power in a single pulse would be more likely to break traction, but it seems that the downsides of big power pulses are greatly outweighed by the upsides, and that breaking up the flow of power really does improve grip. The bigger bangs had some cost though, with the primary gears changed after every day's use.

For the first part of the year, the team concentrated on the B2 version, but following the success of their ride-by-wire system they tried again with the B3.

This system was the second major development, arriving for Shanghai. Initially put on Jacque's bike for a test, he found it so easy to use that both bikes were immediately fitted with it. This helped Jacque to a sensational second place in the pouring rain in Shanghai. The same system stopped Nakano in the same race, but that failure seems to have been quite rare.

Similar in concept to the Yamaha system and also Magneti Marelli, this puts three cylinders under the rider's direct control, and uses a computer to open the remaining throttle butterfly, as well as varying ignition timing and even dropping the occasional spark. This gave maximum traction combined with maximum rider feel.

Highly adjustable, the system let crew chief and rider choose the most appropriate from the various parameters under its control. As such, tuning this system was a learning experience, the setup at the start of each GP reflecting the lessons learnt at the previous races. While Kawasaki wouldn't admit it, some of their competitors are quite sure that the combination of their big-bang engine and sophisticated ride-by-wire allowed them to use softer-compound Bridgestones at quite a few of the circuits, to their advantage.

Kawasaki's basic engine package still looks very similar to the original "super-Superbike" debuted three years ago. Yoda's influence appears to have allowed Kawasaki to try again at increasing power but, at Motegi at least, with the same embarrassing smoky results.

Kawasaki were well on the way with a new "built-in-Japan" 990cc package when the rules for 2007 were changed. We can expect to see the new version on track immediately after the end of the season.

Below: Kawasaki's Big Bang was a step in the right direction.
Photograph: Neil Spalding

Bottom: Crucial chassis area behind engine shows room to move for swing-arm pivot.
Photograph: Gold & Goose

SUZUKI – AWAITING SALVATION

Suzuki had their hopes dashed yet again. They have one of the best-handling bikes in pit lane, but the factory insists on using its own in-house engine management system. While this means their street bikes can have the benefit of knowledge gained, it is currently holding back the MotoGP team quite badly.

Suzuki have a ride-by-wire system seemingly quite similar to the Magneti Marelli, in so far as two butterflies are under the control of the rider and two appear to be operated automatically. The difference lies in the operating parameters. Suzuki's basic data for traction control is gained from monitoring crankshaft acceleration. What we now consider "normal" traction control not only does this, but also compares front and rear wheel speeds, and allows technicians to modify throttle position, ignition timing and cylinder firing to get the best feel at any given circuit. With a system based purely on the rate of crankshaft acceleration, Suzuki could find the engine being tricked into producing less power merely by a fast transition from upright to full lean, where the reduced gearing of the smaller tyre diameter could fool the system into activating.

The year started well, with a new motor tune releasing another 20 hp and 1,000 rpm. In addition the valve springs that needed so much maintenance in 2004 were meant to stop breaking. While an additional 20 hp certainly helped, Suzuki did not gain the massive jump in mid-range acceleration enjoyed by Honda and Yamaha. In addition to trying different exhaust pipes and experimenting with intake lengths, the team spent a lot of time trying different airbox volumes and intake systems. All of these variables can make big differences to the quantity and rev range of maximum torque, but in the end you need an engine that is basically good before you can hope to get the right result from these relatively small adjustments.

Suzuki's shortage of real power certainly helped them as soon as it got wet. Roberts led at Shanghai, until a big-end went (an unheard-of failure until then), and did well again at Donington in the pouring rain to finish second.

All through the year the combination of a second-grade ride-by-wire system and a lack of serious grunt left Suzuki relying on rider ambition for a good result. Hopkins used Bridgestone's excellent qualifying tyres to their maximum effect on several occasions.

There was an increasing number of visits from senior Suzuki personnel as the year went on leaving the team confident of a substantial investment in the current 990cc engine before the new 800 formula starts in 2007.

Proton KR powered by KTM – WRONG TURN

Proton KR's own ill-starred V5 engine project came to an end in 2004. It had proved, if anybody needed it proving, that building a MotoGP engine was not easy, and certainly wasn't going to be done within the limited budgets of a non-factory team – especially when they had to compete with customer Honda teams for quality sponsors.

At the same time, KTM had a seemingly competitive four-cylinder pneumatic-valve-spring 75-degree 990cc V4 engine sitting in their museum, a stillborn project shelved when the enormity of the costs of MotoGP became apparent. On the other side of Europe, Proton KR had a really nice chassis, and no engine; while MotoGP promoter and ringmasters Dorna needed to put a British rider on the grid to keep the BBC happy. Out of all this came what seemed to be a dream deal; KTM could use their engine, KR Proton their chassis, and Shane Byrne could ride, while Dorna made sure the team had the Michelin tyres they craved. In theory, everybody would live happily ever after.

Unfortunately, the deal suffered from the start, as somewhere in the mix the chassis didn't work with the engine or the

engine didn't work with the chassis. It was just a question of who was telling the story.

After the first two races KTM invested in a run of ten engines, which suffered teething troubles. When they started down the path of revised exhausts and up-rated engine specifications, everything was quickly spiralling into the high-cost vortex from which they had previously shied away. Sometime around the middle of June, the US company Polaris committed to buying 24 percent of KTM's stock; within a month of that deal the designer of the engine left KTM to rejoin BMW, and shortly after that KTM withdrew from the project. The resulting legally complex spat was disappointing. As this was written KR Proton were looking for alternative engine suppliers. Honda was a likely choice but it won't be a cheap option.

The Proton KR powered by KTM was an interesting machine. To see it being warmed up in its garage was to see Formula 1 technology in its most basic form. Rather than the noisy but spectacular warming-up process indulged in by all the other teams they simply connected their engine's water supply to a combined water pump and kettle and brought it up to temperature nice and gently. Once the bike was on track things were not so simple.

The first chassis lasted only two races before a drastically different version was brought out, the engine almost 40 mm further forward and the swing-arm also 40mm longer to suit. This was an attempt to allow Byrne to spin up the rear tyre and steer the bike out of corners on the power; it didn't seem to work. The chassis' arrival coincided with the ten production engines, and a run of embarrassing bottom-end failures during the first few races.

Airbox size was increased dramatically and different exhausts were built by Akrapovic, all to little avail. The bike stayed stubbornly at the back of the field, with KTM looking for additional power and the Proton KR team trying to find a chassis setup that would at least let them exit corners at a reasonable speed.

WCM – WAITING FOR ELE*
* Extinction Level Event

WCM benefited from a dramatic increase in grip from their Dunlop tyres during the course of the year. By far the simplest and oldest bike in pit lane, the only real change to the WCM this year was a much longer swing-arm, and a rider who was prepared to give it everything.

The bike is a basic across-the-frame four, using a combination of GSX-R 1000 race parts and early Yamaha R1 internal parts. In accordance with the first year's MotoGP rulebook these are encased in Prototype WCM castings.

WCM's riders had Blata all over their leathers for most of the year. This reflected a deal by which the team should have taken delivery after the first few races of V6 990cc motorcycles built by the ambitious Czech minibike firm Blata. Just when they were expected to show up, an announcement was made that they would be ready by Brno. This was another false promise. The sonorous six may yet arrive, but you have to ask what sense it makes to build a MotoGP bike when the basic design will only be good for one year's competition.

In the absence of the V6 WCM have got to find some way to extend the life of their now time-expired in-line fours for next year. They may find solace in the new technical rulebook, which no longer prohibits parts from serial production. Indeed with the permission of the manufacturer any engine can be used.

With the advent of another generation of much-improved Superbike engines WCM could do worse than to apply to use one of those, with a very mild change to the bore. In a perfect world, they might be able to persuade KTM to let them borrow the engines gathering dust at Mattighofen. How they will approach 2007 and the 800cc formula is another matter entirely.

Opposite: Suzuki reveals carbon-fibre sub-frame and deep-section swing-arm. Handling was its strong suit.
Photograph: Gold & Goose

Below: WCM had simplest electronics of all.
Photograph: Neil Spalding

Above: WCM's electronic dashboard is blank in the pits.
Photograph: Gold & Goose

Opposite: KTM-powered Proton is warmed up in silence, F1-style.
Photograph: Neil Spalding

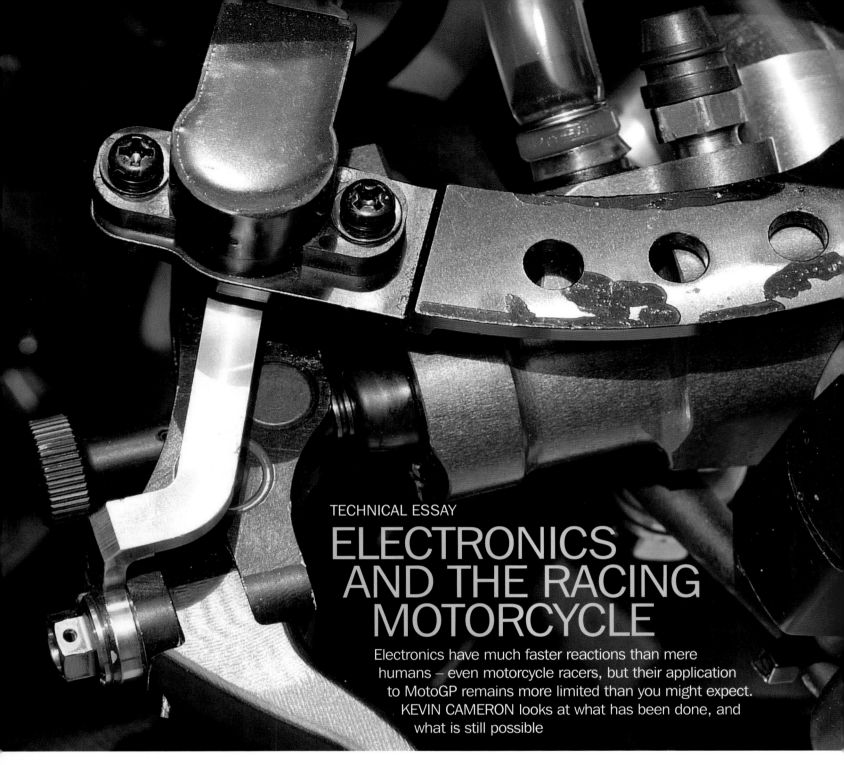

TECHNICAL ESSAY

ELECTRONICS AND THE RACING MOTORCYCLE

Electronics have much faster reactions than mere humans – even motorcycle racers, but their application to MotoGP remains more limited than you might expect. KEVIN CAMERON looks at what has been done, and what is still possible

Left: Simple switch, complex consequences. Honda handlebar offers rider various options.
Photograph: Gold & Goose

WHEN MotoGP came into being, it was assumed by many even within the sport that the new class would become "Formula One on two wheels". That meant exotic, ultra-high-revving engines teetering on the leading edge of technology – and it meant space-age electronic controls.

In reality, the use of electronics in MotoGP splits into two camps. The first (successful) camp employs electronic controls topically - only for specific jobs for which its function is unambiguous. Honda initially and now Yamaha do this well. Limited use of electronics includes the obvious – engine control by means of stored maps for ignition and fuel injection, plus the shifter switch and the use of data acquisition from multiple sensors to aid in machine set-up. Less obvious but still of limited scope are rev limiters, variable intake and exhaust devices, engine braking control by means of fast-acting throttle positioners (using engine power during deceleration to cancel any desired fraction of engine friction), Honda's clever differential throttle, and electronically modifiable suspension damping.

The second camp takes its brief from aviation and F1, and seeks by integrating several related functions into a "global" control system to reach a higher level of performance than could be reached by an unaided human.

In high performance aircraft, two situations have stimulated such development.

Firstly, when operating at high angles of attack and low airspeed, control functions couple and overlap each other in confusing ways. It is then attractive to separate the pilot from the control surfaces (normally connected to the pilot's stick and rudder pedals by steel control cables) and to insert a computer between. The computer unscrambles the confusion and executes the pilot's will rather than his specific control movements. Its instructions come from software writers interpreting data from a vehicle dynamic model, from full-scale testing, and from specialized tunnel and rig tests.

Secondly, as vehicles are made more responsive, they become less stable. As with motorcycles, the relaxation of stability to achieve faster control response makes airplanes subject to oscillations which can cause complete control loss and structural failure. The solution was to develop computer-driven artificial stability, which by superhuman response speed and fast control actuators keep the aircraft headed correctly, oscillation-free. Aircraft thus designed can be compared with an arrow flying backward; at the slightest deviation from straight, the arrow instantly flips around the other way – and human reflex is too slow to keep the arrow straight.

It was easier to implement these functions as a global control system than to contemplate how to seamlessly superimpose the computer's corrections upon a conventional cable

Why not automate clutch, throttle and gearchange in a drive-by-wire system to eliminate all this? With a back-torque-limiting clutch and engine-braking cancellation, such a system might assure stable braking and corner entry, and would optimize the application of power during acceleration to prevent slide-outs and high-sides. Big advantages.

Who could resist? After all, such automation is now routine on many heavy highway trucks and high-end sports cars. Piece of cake! Let's do it!

Remember that aircraft fly-by-wire developers worked with reliable dynamic models. No universally respected motorcycle dynamic model exists, and developing one is difficult because firstly the behavior of tyres is so complex, and secondly MotoGP constructors cannot match the R & D budgets of major air forces. Despite this, drive-by-wire seemed to be a way to solve several problems at one stroke.

Honda, after reportedly at least one ambitious control experiment that failed, decided to rely upon what its engineers knew best – development of a very refined but conventional motorcycle, assisted in small respects by electronic systems of modest scope. Honda had resources appropriate to this kind of development. Yamaha, Aprilia, and Suzuki gambled on more ambitious controls – and lost in such a big way that Honda's early dominance made the first MotoGP seasons more exhibition than racing. At the time, the press eagerly attributed this success to F1-style electronics but we now know that the RC211 V was mainly a very good, easy-to-ride motorcycle. The grip-destroying spikes and dips that naturally appear in an engine's torque curve as it is developed to higher and higher horsepower were carefully neutralized, using the same techniques that have given us today's extremely powerful but civilized sportbikes.

A hidden cost of deploying global control systems prematurely was that their chronic failure badly spooked several talented riders. Think of trying to race, knowing the computer will deal you numerous uncommanded full throttles per lap. Don't worry, it was just a computer glitch. We've got it fixed now. Give us some hot laps.

Only when the Rossi/Burgess team moved to Yamaha did that company focus completely on development of a refined motorcycle with only "topical" electronic controls. Then they too became successful.

In 2003 Ducati surprised everyone by achieving some podiums and a win. Their philosophy was to develop maximum power with all its spikes and dips, then smooth the delivery electronically by engine mapping. Their experience in MotoGP has been a battle between the need to deliver smooth power in lower gears, and the company's evident faith that raw power can win races. Results, while showing occasional promise, have

Below: **Plugged in and downloading –**
Kawasaki technician gathers data.
Photograph: Neil Spalding

control system (a wrestling match was not the desired outcome). Problems always seem to pop up at the interfaces, so eliminating cable-to-computer transitions via a global control system was just common sense. Military aviation had the funding to do this job thoroughly, and the result – as seen on aircraft such as the Dassault Mirage 2000 and GD F-16 – is called "fly-by-wire".

In MotoGP, the novel and pressing problem was not steering stability but the effect of braking upon it. Two-stroke 500s had not faced this problem because their engine friction upon throttle closure is moderate. With MotoGP's doubled four-stroke displacement, engine friction increased enough to drag the back tyre, provoking hop when upright or making the tyre slide out without warning as the machine rolled over into turns. With nearly 100% weight transfer onto the front wheel during braking, too little rear tyre footprint remained to damp the weave instability mode (lateral swinging of the rear of the machine at two to three cycles per second). The combination of increased disturbance and reduced damping provoked chassis weave oscillations that could build up in one or two seconds sufficient to cause a corner entry crash. Downshifting added another disturbance – torque spikes that could cause hop, either provoking weave or shaking the chassis enough to start front-end chatter.

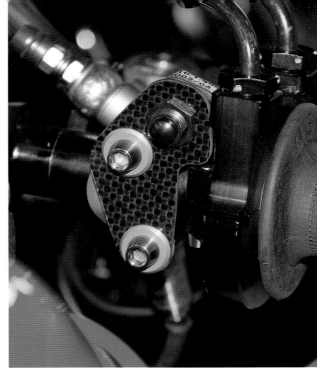

Above: Like all the factory riders, Alex Hofmann can relying on a bit of electronic help as he unleashes excess horsepower for his circumstances.

Top right: Ducati throttle... but rider had direct control of only some of its functions.
Photographs: Gold & Goose

Right and above right: Yamaha shows details of its partial fly-by-wire system.
Photographs: Neil Spalding

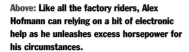

not confirmed this strategy.

Are anti-spin and yaw-control systems – now common in upper-end autos – about to take the life and flair out of MotoGP? If they are, why don't they work? Look at any race – the top men spin and slide the least, but behind them comes a parade of lurid sliders, men riding desperately over their heads in a madcap attempt to keep position - and their contracts. Electronic control would help all riders equally, but there are huge differences between the best and worst Hondas and Yamahas. Just switch on those systems, boys, and see you on the podium!

This is not to say that such systems won't be developed – such things are surely under study. In the meantime, some very fine conventional motorcycles have been developed, with rideability all motorcyclists can applaud. This is useful progress.

What else? Variable ride height is often discussed. Dragsters are built very low so they can accelerate harder without lifting their front wheels. Road racers need ground clearance to keep their engine crankcases off the ground in corners. Variable ride height offers us both by lowering the machine 50 to 75mm when upright, then restoring full height as the bike leans over into a turn. Such a system would allow fuller use of engine power during low-speed acceleration, and might cut one or even two seconds from laptime. We don't have it now because its failure modes are frightening. Aircraft fly-by-wire systems employ triplexed or quadruplexed electronics, backed by a separate, single-channel system. It can be done – it just hasn't happened yet.

Electronic damping control will come soon, and we've already seen Ohlins CES, which substituted software commands for the flexing washer stacks now used. Need an altered damping curve? A few taps on the laptop and it's installed – no removal, depressurization, oil dump, and restacking of washers. Suspension/chassis engineers today would like to damp only specific, troublesome frequencies such as the front chatter frequency, the heave mode, pitch mode, and chassis twist frequencies. Otherwise, they'd prefer to let the suspension move unimpeded. An electronic system of sufficiently fast response could do this, detecting the onset of the unwanted oscillation and then nipping up in phase with its velocity peaks.

Beyond that is full active suspension, in which wheel motions are driven, not by the bumps in the road, but by on-board actuators. As a suspension deflection begins, it would be detected by an accelerometer, and a fast acting "suspension jack" would move the affected wheel to zero out the chassis acceleration. Such a system could come much closer to smooth, steady tyre loading than the present passive system. It could easily implement variable ride-height. It would also likely be banned at once as "destabilizing" (you can't chew gum in class unless you bring enough for everyone).

The holy grail of automatic systems is variable valve timing (VVT), which can make engines deliver both strong, smooth bottom power and extreme top power. Without VVT, the closest approach to this is to employ short, fixed valve timing (smooth at lower speeds) with large lift or valve area (supplying the engine's airflow needs even at high rpm). Pneumatic springs beckon because their higher valve accelerations can better combine high valve lift and short timing even at high rpm. Many VVT mechanisms exist in production vehicles, but in racing it is expensive enough just to achieve stability and reliability in a fixed-timing valve system.

The automation of throttle, clutch, and gear-change faces formidable problems. An experienced rider can integrate their functions in a versatile way, responding to a wide variety of situations. Can a computer-driven system do as well? Can it do it without coming into conflict with the rider's style? Before you answer yes, tell me why a motorcycle still has two separate brake systems. Surely it would be child's play to integrate them by some automatic device into a system that always does the right thing? Care to take a shot at writing the software?

Speaking of braking, why is there no ABS in MotoGP? This is because ABS was developed for the much simpler automotive application. On production ABS bikes its use is advised only when the machine is upright, but in road racing braking continues into the roll-over when entering turns. The idea of ABS is inviting. The application is difficult.

Everyone is excited at the prospects of using GPS information to tell the motorcycle where it is on the circuit. With it, the system can say, "Here, we're approaching the pull-out at the bottom of the Corkscrew at Laguna Seca – increase low-speed compression damping to prevent bottoming". Reportedly, tests with such a system initially failed because riders cannot always use exactly the same line in a given corner. Ducati used GPS data to allow its experimental engine-braking system to declutch the engine completely on approach to particular corners, then smoothly re-engage it for the drive out of the corner. Initial results were encouraging but problems prevented its continued use. GPS data will definitely be a partner in future control systems because it has the potential to break some traditional compromises.

Honda's differential throttle attacks the long-standing problem of throttle sensitivity. For quick response, racing motorcycles have one-eighth-turn throttles, but quick throttles lack the sensitivity to control wheelspin in lower gears. On some 500 two-strokes the ancient clock-maker's fusee, or snail pulley was revived. This winds cable slowly at small throttle, then faster and faster as the throttle is opened. Honda's new-last-year system employed a differential gear. By analogy to a car's differential, the rider's throttle is one axle shaft, a stepper motor is connected to the other axle, and the driveshaft is the output that operates the throttles. If the stepper motor remains stationary, the relation between rider throttle and butterflies is fixed. To slow the throttle, you send a message to the computer to rotate the stepper motor backward at 20%, 50%, or any desired fraction of the rotation of the rider throttle (which has a throttle position sensor on it already). Changing the throttle sensitivity in any gear is a matter of taps on the laptop keyboard.

When any rider shows outstanding skill there is an immediate outcry that his team must be using an anti-spin system. People point to wheel-speed sensors, saying, "I told you so". In fact, tachometer data is all that's needed to implement spin detection. A simple differentiator and some arithmetic extract from tacho data the rate of increase of rear wheel speed. Rates of increase are compared with norms for the circuit. If they are exceeded by some percentage, the engine control is instructed to retard the ignition to reduce engine torque (a much faster means of torque control than winching throttles open and closed). Such a system would be complicated by the fact that maximum possible rates of longitudinal acceleration vary with track, position on the track, track condition, weather, tyre type and condition, and most of all, by analogy with ABS, the angle of lean. Gosh, folks, this is starting to sound pretty complicated.

Okay, we'll use wheel-speed sensors instead – we'll measure spin by comparing front and rear wheel speeds. That works – until there is a wheelie.

Then let's implement anti-spin as yaw control, as is done in some expensive autos. We'll use a yaw rate detector to sense the back end letting go. But this prevents the use of intentional throttle-steering. Who decides what yaw rate is too much, and in which corner? If the system prevents throttle-steering, the bike runs wide. It's the old man-vs-system wrestling match again. Can we get our trick system up and working without spooking our highly-paid riders so badly they permanently lose the confidence to give their best? This is a serious question.

Uh, well, we'll keep on adding more gizmos, like triplex inertial platforms, GPS, and lots of sensors, and we'll write a million lines of control code, and... but wait. We already have a system on board very much like that - the rider. The rider's inner ear is an inertial platform with its "gyros" and accelerometers. The rider has angle sensors, actuators, visual, auditory, and positional pattern recognition and the rest of it. While not as fast as a computer, the rider learns and is versatile and resourceful. Will it always remain true – as is the case at present - that the best investment in MotoGP is to give that rider a very refined conventional motorcycle whose responses are predictable and controllable? Or will the day come when the motorcycle's on-board computer becomes the rider, with the human astride reduced to the role of hostage?

It remains to be seen.

FIFTY YEARS OF YAMAHA

Yamaha celebrated their 50th anniversary this year, with a second consecutive MotoGP title. For a company that has always had racing at the heart of its development and philosophy, there could be few better ways.

Motorcycle racing historian COLIN McKELLAR picks out five landmark bikes, one per decade, thatbest express Yamaha's ethic of success through simplicity, eschewing engineering vanity in favour of balanced and logical design

Top: Happy Birthday... to me! Yamaha's year-end celebrations.
Photograph: Gold & Goose

Above and above centre: Phil Read's RD56. At top, he is at record speed at the 1964 TT, its first title year, breaking Honda's three-year grip.
Photographs: Henk Keulemans

Right: Rossi goes retro at Valencia.
Photograph: Gold & Goose

1955 to 1965
Phil Read and the RD56

Within ten years of the birth of the company, Yamaha had become the world leader in two-stroke motorcycle racing technology. This is remarkable for several reasons.

Firstly, Yamaha was created to build motorcycles as an off-shoot of the Nippon Gakki Company, which had been established by Tarakusu Yamaha in 1888 to build musical instruments. Other than the years under military control during World War Two, when they had been commandeered to produce aircraft propellers and fuel tanks, the company had no experience in complex mechanical engineering.

Secondly, the first Yamaha motorcycle produced in 1955 was a replica of a German DKW two-stroke with a design dating from 1935. Minimal original design or development went into the 125cc YA1, doing little to provide Yamaha engineers with a greater understanding of the two-stroke combustion process.

Finally, Yamaha were late in coming to Europe to enter truly competitive racing, arriving in 1961, two years later than bitter rivals Honda. Their first season in GP racing did not match the success they had achieved in Japan, which had commenced in 1955, when the YA1 had won both the Mount Fuji and Mount Asama races.

Yet by 1963, Yamaha had produced a 250 two-stroke twin that was to bring them their first world championship and set them up to become the dominant manufacturer of two-stroke racing machinery for almost 30 years. How was this possible?

The RD56, as it was classified by the company, was a two-stroke rotary-valve twin housed in a frame that was modelled on the Norton "Featherbed" frame, renowned for its excellent handling during the 1950s. It was a perfect package of contemporary technology, with a fine balance of reliable power and handling. This was something that came to be Yamaha's trademark, the creation of a race bike whose handling would make the bike competitive, despite lower engine power than rival machinery.

The RD56 was a landmark race bike. Four-stroke technology that had dominated post-war racing was under threat. The potential of the two-stroke had been clear for some years as the small MZ factory, working out of East Germany, had shown towards the end of the 1950s. Patient and exhaustive work by MZ engineer Walter Kaaden had established greater understanding of the two-stroke engineering principles.

Yamaha had combined this knowledge with advances in metallurgy that had enabled them to develop reliable large-capacity two-stroke engines. The RD56 used alloy cylinders with chrome bores, along with pistons with narrow cast-iron rings. The dimensions of the ports in the wall of the cylinders and the dimensions of the exhaust pipes showed a new understanding of the dynamics of the two-stroke combustion process. Reliable delivery of higher power levels, driving a chassis that handled well by the standards of the day, was the recipe for the challenge that was to topple Honda from their world championship position.

Initially trusted to the star of the Yamaha team of riders, Fumio Ito, he demonstrated its potential in its sole race of 1962, at the Japanese GP, coming home second behind Honda's 250 world champion Jim Redman on the four-cylinder Honda. A limited-budget three-race season in 1963 resulted in a legendary battle between the two of them at the Isle of Man TT, with victory again going to Redman by just 27 seconds in a race lasting over 2 hours. The result was repeated at the Dutch TT, but a week later, Yamaha won their first GP at the lightening-fast Spa circuit in Belgium. There was no looking back.

Ito was Yamaha's man. He'd been their chief rider since their first foray into international competition at the Island of Catalina in 1958. He had led their team in the abortive 1961 GP season in Europe. Now with a competitive machine, it was expected that he would be the Yamaha star of 1964, fighting hard for Honda's defeat. Sadly this was not to be. Injuries sustained at the non-championship Singapore GP of 1964 ended his racing career, and the burden passed to the shoulders of the new European rider signed by Yamaha, Phil Read. After a frustrating

SIMPLICITY ABANDONED – YAMAHA'S WILDER SHORES

When people talk about the Golden Age of Japanese GP racing in the 1960s, reference is often made to the collection of multi-cylinder engineering masterpieces that Honda built. Their design drive was to lower reciprocating weight in order to increase engine speeds and raise power levels. This was Honda's credo.

Two-stroke rivals Yamaha and Suzuki were tempted into following suit, the latter's 50cc three-cylinder that was designed, built and tested, but never raced, represented the ultimate miniature racing two-stroke engine.

Yamaha's knee-jerk reaction to the appearance of the six-cylinder 250 Honda at the 1964 Italian GP was to lay down their own plans for a multi-cylinder 250, hoping that it would be completed in time to salvage something of the 1965 season. In fact the simple RD56 performed wonderfully well and retained Yamaha's title that year without any help from the new bike.

All the same, Yamaha persisted and their answer to Honda's six debuted at the 1965 Italian GP.

The bike that appeared at the track was a water-cooled V-4 250, with rotary valve induction, producing a claimed 65 bhp at 13,500 rpm. The front pair of cylinders was almost horizontal, set at a 70-degree angle to the rear cylinders. Contra-rotating crankshafts drove the eight-speed gearbox via a separate jackshaft which was also used to drive the water pump. An air-cooled version had been built and rejected due to difficulties cooling both pairs of cylinders. The penalty that water-cooling brought was another 24kg to an already heavy bike. It was to get heavier as attempts were made to cure its handling problems by clamping lead weights to the lower rails of the frame.

Rather naively, Yamaha had assumed that the impeccable frame used on the RD56 would be able to cope with the new engine. Rather than develop a new frame, Yamaha focused on weight reduction, and magnesium was used throughout the engine, including the carburettors. By the 1967 season, the lower weight, greater power, improved handling and above all reliability was almost enough to defeat Hailwood on Honda six. Almost, but not quite, and Yamaha were only able to regain the title in 1968, after Hailwood's and Honda's withdrawal from GP racing.

The V4-250 was joined at the end of 1966 by a 125cc clone, the RA31, using the same rolling chassis as its big brother. The result was altogether a better bike, thanks primarily to its lower weight and a better match between power output and chassis strength. It was enough for the title in 1967, defeating two-stroke rival Suzuki, but the bike remained unproven against Honda, who had dropped out of the class after 1966.

For 1968 Yamaha were left to divvy up the 250 and 125 class between themselves as Honda and Suzuki watched from the sidelines. New regulations had been announced for 1969, limiting machines in both classes to just two cylinders and six-speed gearboxes, Technical innovation would have to take a different path in the search for a better race bike. Team rivalry provided the spice that kept the interest in the racing, with the legendary battles developing between Bill Ivy and Phil Read. Phil defied team orders to take both titles, much to Yamaha's chagrin. He was never forgiven and reciprocated by spending the rest of his career doing his best to defeat the official Yamaha riders.

The RD05 and the RA31 were typical of the exotica produced by Japanese factories in the 60s. Dominated by their engines, they were the product of a philosophy that equated success with the power available at the rear wheel. It would take many years before the design of race bikes looked at the whole package to create winning machinery. Yamaha achieved this insight during the development of the YZR500. It became their trademark. Undoubtedly the lessons gained during the 1960s on the 250 and 125 V4s contributed to the speed of Yamaha's enlightenment two decades later.

Above: Two legends... Giacomo Agostini and the Yamaha TZ750 at Daytona in 1974. It was his first ride for the factory, and the machine's debut. He won. Like Rossi, the 15-times World Champion had switched to Yamaha from the dominant factory team, MV Agusta. Ago gave Yamaha their first 500-class title in 1975, the first also for a two-stroke, changing the sound and face of racing until the MotoGP era.

Top left: Simple genius: Jarno Saarinen on the TZ250 in 1927.
Photographs: Henk Keulemans

Top right: Masao Furusawa, current racing boss, shares a laugh with Agostini.
Photograph: Gold & Goose

1963 season riding antique Gileras in the 500 class, Read was ready to light a fire under the Redman/Honda combination.

The 1963 run in Europe had revealed weaknesses in the RD56 carburetion, frequently resulting in oiled plugs. In addition it was felt that a lowered engine position in the frame would improve the handling. Yamaha's meagre R&D resources meant that the new bike was not ready at the start of the 1964 season. So the distinctive orange tank RD56 was wheeled out for Read for the early races, with the new version of the bike appearing mid-season, complete in the red and white livery that was to be used by Yamaha for many years to come. After a couple of races to shake down the new bike, Read got into his stride to take four GP wins on the trot, forcing Honda to reveal their new six-cylinder machine prematurely in a desperate attempt to hang on to the world championship. It was in vain, and Yamaha and Phil Read took their first 250 world championship title.

Surprisingly, Read and the RD56 resisted the Honda onslaught for another season, demonstrating that a well-balanced package could be more effective than the powerful but heavy, technical masterpiece that was the six-cylinder RC 165. But as the season progressed the struggle became tougher, and it was time for a replacement for the 56. Yamaha turned to their own engineering prowess to produce the 250 V4 RD05, and embarked on their own evolutionary road to turn the complex machine into a championship winner.

The 56 was pensioned off to selected riders in national championships around Europe, finally disappearing from the

circuits in 1967 as spares dried up. It was a brilliantly simple machine, which had enabled Yamaha to realise their world championship ambitions and establish the company as the leader of the two-stroke revolution taking place in the sport of motorcycle racing.

1965 to 1975
Jarno Saarinen and the TD-TZ

No race bike ever built has meant more to the sport than the Yamaha production racer, the TZ. For a period of about 20 years, between 1970 and 1990, literally thousands of the TZs, and its air-cooled predecessor, the TD, packed race grids, victory podiums and race reports, forming the mainstay for national and international racing. Factory TDs and TZs running in the GPs were responsible for over 100 GP wins during this period. Over 90 percent of the bikes that competed in the 350cc GP class until its demise in 1982 were Yamaha production racers. Several generations of riders developed and honed their racing skills from the seat of a TZ, before moving on to greater things. You'd be hard pressed to find a post-1970 500cc world champion who had not, at some time in his career, been found scratching around a track on a TZ. It is one of the greatest success stories of the sport.

The TZ can trace its heritage back to the second All Japan Clubmans Race that was held in August 1959. Open to all bikes of which at least 40 units had been sold, the new Yamaha sports twin, the YDS1, was used as the base model with a kit available for competition racing. First time out, it came home in third place behind two Honda CR71s, but a month later at the subsequent race, Osamu Mashiko brought the Yamaha production racer its first victory.

It was immediately decided to promote this close relationship between street bike and racing bike internationally, and a number of the race kits found their way to the American and Australian market where the YDS1 was sold. Known as the Asama racer or YDS1R, the bike was underpowered, handled poorly, was unreliable and ugly to boot. It had nothing going for it, except it was an affordable way to start racing on a shoe-string.

After the exposure to competitive racing in Europe in 1961, Yamaha decided to take the full step towards offering a factory production racer for sale. From the 1962 introduction of the YDS2, the race kit was fitted at source, and the resulting racer brought to market as the TD1. It was still unreliable and scarcely competitive, but by 1964, with the arrival of the TD1B, a real race bike was beginning to develop. The Daytona race of that year saw the B take the first two places, and it began winning races regularly in the USA.

Although becoming more commonplace in Europe, it was the arrival of the TD1C in 1967, that heralded the flood that was to take place. With the C, the major flaw of the TD1 was at last

corrected; the clutch was moved from the end of the crankshaft to the primary transmission shaft. With the clutch no longer running at engine speeds, snapped crankshafts and exploding clutch baskets were a thing of the past.

The TD1 and its spares were cheap and it was discovered that they responded well to experimental engine development work by mechanics and riders looking for an edge over the competition. A whole industry developed modifying cylinders, pistons and exhausts to change the power characteristics of the engine. The most effective changes were often incorporated as standard in the subsequent model. By the end of the 1960s, Yamaha acknowledged the importance of this work by publishing regular bulletins outlining the changes being made in the paddock. From 1969, the TD domination of 250 racing was complete, from club races through to GPs, almost without exception, riders were running TDs. TR versions were available for the flourishing 350 class, many riders competing in both races.

One of these riders was Finn Jarno Saarinen. In 1970, he bought himself a TD2 and went GP racing, joining the band of racing junkies known as the Continental Circus, and finishing fourth in his first season. His aggressive riding style, unassuming character and ability to do so well when lack of money forced him to scavenge the paddock for discarded drive chains and tyres, endeared him to the public and his fellow riders. Sponsorship in 1971 from the Finnish Yamaha importer brought him his first GP win and third place in the world championship. For 1972, Yamaha produced a water-cooled version of the over-the-counter TD3 production racer and allocated them to their most-favoured GP riders. Mid-season one of them went to Saarinen and he won the next four races on the trot, bringing home the world championship as a result. From 1973, the TZ250 and TZ350 were available to anyone with a racing habit and a modestly healthy bank account.

Perhaps the pinnacle of achievement of the Yamaha production racers were the 1972 and 1973 Daytona 200-Mile races. Open to all machines with a displacement up to 750 cc, Kawasaki and Suzuki entered their three-cylinder two-stroke 750s, joining four-strokes entered by Triumph, BSA and Harley. As the other Japanese two-strokes failed and the years finally caught up with the uncompetitive British and American four-strokes, it was Don Emde on an air-cooled TR2B who sensationally took the 1972 win. It was said by some that good fortune had smiled on Yamaha that day, but when Jarno Saarinen led home two other TZ350 riders in the 1973 Daytona 200, becoming the first foreign rider ever to win the event, the legend of the giant-killing Yamaha production racer was complete.

The TZ250 continues to be produced to this day. As the interest in 250 racing outside of GPs has waned, so too has the importance of the TZ. But looking back into history, it is impossible to over-state the impact and influence that the bike has had on the sport.

1975 to 1985
Everyman's Racer – the TZ750

The first incarnation of a "Superbike" racing class, the FIM Formula 750, was a two-stroke party, and the TZ750 turned it into a Yamaha party. Desperate to retain some illusions that the 750 Triumphs, BSAs and Nortons were high-performance sports bikes, the British racing body, the ACU, convinced the FIM to invent a new world championship to prove this. Modelled on the AMA regulations from the USA, the class was introduced in 1973, but the collapse of the British industry was so rapid that it was all but dead by then.

Instead, the championship became the playground of the Japanese two-strokes, with active interest from Kawasaki and Suzuki, using their road going 750s as a basis for the race bikes, as had been intended when the class was introduced. The street bike heritage of the racers was thought to be safeguarded by the regulation requiring that a bike would only be homologated for the class if at least 200 units of the basic model had been built and sold. When Yamaha decided to gatecrash the party in 1974, they turned the rule on its head, simply building 200 race machines and selling them with ease in Europe, the USA and Australia.

The first TZ750 was essentially a doubled up TZ350, with four cylinders and a capacity of 694cc, although it did feature the reed valves that Yamaha were beginning to introduce on their two-strokes. Out of the crate, it had much more power than any contemporary riders had ever experienced, but was actually not that difficult to ride, with a big fat power band of 3,000 rpm to play with. Handling was good, once a slight wobble that developed on fast straights had been dialled out with suspension adjustments. Reports of 180 mph top speeds had riders drooling with anticipation.

The TZ750's debut at the 1974 Daytona 200 saw Giacomo Agostini take the win, his first race for Yamaha and his first race on a two-stroke. The Yamaha was all set to make a clean sweep of the F750 world championship, then the FIM decided they would ban the machine, as it broke the spirit of the class and its intended street bike heritage.

Once this had been sorted out for 1975, there was no holding the TZ back, and it totally dominated the class for the next five years. So complete was its superiority that the FIM felt there was little interest in a one-make championship, and suspended the series in 1979.

The big TZ became a remarkably multi-functional bike. The engines were snapped up by sidecar drivers for their open-class races that were still very popular in Europe. The infamous TZ Miler dirt track machines were developed and raced in the USA a couple of times by Kenny Roberts and Steve Baker, with Roberts taking his legendary win at the Indianapolis Mile in 1975 ahead of the all-conquering XR750 Harleys. Occasional

Above and top: Kenny Roberts in 1978. The Californian was key to Yamaha's resurgence in the late 1970s, and became King in the process. Advance guard of an army of talent from the USA, Kenny arrived in 1978, and in a classic duel defeated the reigning Barry Sheene and the Suzuki at his first attempt. Kenny won the title for three years straight, and later founded the team that took Wayne Rainey to triple victory.

Photographs: Yamaha

Above: Serial champion of a golden age –
Wayne Rainey in 1991.
Photograph: Gold & Goose

Top: Rainey in action on the YZR in 1990,
his first championship year
Photograph: Yamaha

TZ750s were entered in endurance races, usually with pre-dictable early retirement. A major upset almost occurred at the 1979 Bol D'Or when it finished runner-up in the 24 hour race, deprived of victory by a late crash. There were even a couple of Californian loons who managed to convince the US licensing authorities to declare their TZ750 street-legal and issue licence plates. Love will find a way.

The TZ750 was not exposed to a wildly radical development program. It wasn't needed, it won almost every race it was entered for. In 1975, the full 750cc capacity was provided, and factory bikes started appearing housed in the mono-shock chassis that had by now become Yamaha's trademark, with the OW31 moniker. A couple of years later the over-the-counter TZ750D appeared as a replica of the OW31, but with less magnesium and titanium alloy than the factory bikes.

Although two more models were to follow with slight detail changes, the 1977 TZ750 was essentially the end of the line. In total almost 600 TZ750s were built and sold, for ten years ruling open class racing with a level of performance that was closer to the 500cc pinnacle of road racing than anyone really could reasonably expect. A Superbike by anyone's standard.

1985 to 1995
Wayne Rainey and the YZR500

Competition between Honda and Yamaha has always been fierce since their first clashes in the early days of racing in Japan, but never been as intense as the bitter rivalry in the 500cc class of Grand Prix racing during the 1980s and 1990s. Yamaha's weapon in this war was the YZR, that of Honda the NSR. The two companies invested millions to demonstrate the superiority of their products on the racetrack, resulting in open, unpredictable racing.

Race wins were evenly divided between the two until Kevin Schwantz started to spoil the fun with his Suzuki towards the end of the 1980s. Greatest winners were the fans, treated to a decade of excitement and spectacle that secured the sport's pop-

ularity as it continued its commercial evolution towards MotoGP.

The YZR traced its heritage to a decade of two-stroke experimentation that had its origins in the Yamaha decision to wrest the 500cc crown from MV Agusta, the defenders of the four-stroke faith. Other than a brief and unsuccessful challenge from Honda (the 1966 constructors championship notwithstanding), MV had for 15 years been the undisputed King of the Blue Riband class, until Yamaha and Jarno Saarinen entered the arena in 1973.

The first factory machine, the OW19, was an in-line four-cylinder piston-ported two-stroke, with reed valve induction. With Saarinen in the saddle, it crushed the MVs of Agostini and Read at the opening two races, with a broken drive chain preventing a third consecutive win. Saarinen's death at the next race in Italy prompted Yamaha's withdrawal from the 1973 championship, with MV again winning by default. It had been a close call for the Italians, prompting them to execute a crash development program that improved the bikes enough for them to defend the challenge that now came from lost son Agostini, who had jumped ship for Yamaha. It was just a delay of execution, and in 1975 Yamaha took their first 500cc title, and Agostini his last. It was the end of an era and the end of MV. The two-stroke had completed its conquest of motorcycle racing.

Yamaha were committed to the piston-ported race engine design for all their multi-cylinder racers, and continued to develop their OW 500cc racers along these lines. Their greatest two-stroke rival, Suzuki, decided that the rotary-valve engine offered the better induction principle and brought the RG500 square-four to the class. Initially the Barry Sheene/RG combination proved unbeatable, until Yamaha teamed Kenny Roberts with the OW and three World Championships were the result. But by the end of 1980, the piston-ported 500 development was considered to be exhausted. The last innovations that had been introduced to ward off defeat included power valves controlling exhaust port height, and reversed outer cylinders to enable better exhaust pipe design. It was scarcely enough, but now there was nowhere left to go.

Desperate to maintain their position in 500 class racing Yamaha swallowed their pride and built an RG500 replica, the 1981 OW54. It went to the GPs under-developed, and this cost Roberts and Yamaha the championship. With the experience of a year's racing the 1982 OW60 was a much better machine and could have won the title in 1982 had Roberts been riding it. Instead it was left to a small group of semi-factory riders, including Barry Sheene, to campaign the bike, while Roberts wrestled with Yamaha's new two-stroke flagship, the V4 OW61, with rotary valves. This was the very first V4 two-stroke 500 and was to define the engine format for the class for the remaining 20 years of 500cc GP racing.

The OW61 was innovative, but flawed. Designing a rotary-valve V4 with the valves and carburettors located within the V proved difficult, and compromised the effectiveness of the design in many ways. In addition, Yamaha decided to experiment with a totally new chassis, using a horizontally mounted rear-shock which theoretically could have helped the handling, but in practice made the bike almost unrideable. Roberts struggled all year, and again the title went to an RG500. Interestingly Honda's own first V4 the 1984 NSR, was equally quirky, with exhausts passing over the engine and the fuel tank slung under the bike.

But the V-4 concept was sound and the 1983 OW70 demonstrated its potential with Roberts as close as was possible to the championship, denied by Spencer and the agile three-cylinder reed-valve NS500 from Honda. By the end of the 1983 season, the OW70 was clearly the most powerful machine in the paddock, so Honda built themselves the V4 NSR.

Yamaha regained faith in piston-ported engines with reed valves, following the NS500 successes of the previous two years. The final step in OW chassis evolution brought forth the first of the modern "Deltabox" frames employing aluminium twin spars and bell-crank suspension with a vertically mounted shock absorber. The YZR was born and Eddie Lawson took the 1984 title for Yamaha.

For the years to come there were detail changes to the bike, but the essential basic design was fixed. Contra-rotating crankshafts were introduced from 1985 with the OW81, with the claim that the neutralisation of the gyroscopic effects of the rotating cranks improved handling. The last of the true OWs, the 1988 OW98, had the angle of the V widened from 60 to 70 degrees, to create more room for the carburettors and reed valves. Following Honda's lead, Yamaha introduced the "Big Bang" YZR in 1992, with a 90-degree firing interval. Experimentation with different materials resulted in a stiffer chassis, that was actually found to make the bike more difficult to ride. Wayne Rainey more than any rider suffered from these pragmatic experiments to improve the effectiveness of the YZR, causing him frequently to ignore the latest factory product in favour of older but proven technology.

The link-up with Rainey marked the high-water mark for the YZR at the start of the 1990s. With almost stagnant evolution of the 500cc bikes, the winning margin started to become increasingly reliant on rider and team. From 1990, Team Roberts, Yamaha and Wayne Rainey were the trinity that dominated the class, and three world titles were their reward. After Wayne's tragic accident in 1993 (leading on points again), success was to turn to Repsol, Doohan and Honda. Further changes to the YZR including the introduction of 54x54 square bore-and-stroke, and revised porting in 1996 and 1997, were in vain. Despite this, the YZR was never far from the competition, gaining the constructors title in 2000, but not the riders championship.

Although living in the shadow of the NSR as the era of the 500cc two-stroke drew to a close, the technology that was developed for the YZR found its way to many race and street machines, especially in the area of frame design. In addition it built the foundation for the success that was to come to Yamaha in the MotoGP class as they accepted the challenge of four-stroke racing at the highest level.

Below: Sustained evolution: Rainey's title-winning YZR of 1991.
Photograph: Henk Keulemans

1995 to 2005
Valentino Rossi and the M1

The turn of fortune that Yamaha has undergone over the last decade of GP racing has been spectacular and dramatic. Living in Honda's shadow during the Doohan years was frustrating in the extreme, with the maturity of two-stroke technology as well as GP regulations limiting fresh approaches to the creation of a winning package. The transition to a four-stroke base for top class GP racing created the space manufacturers needed for the implementation of innovative ideas for motorcycle racing technology. Yamaha grasped the opportunity with both hands.

On the eve of introduction of the new regulations, the general belief was that Honda's decades of support for the racing four-stroke coupled with the deep pockets of their racing division, would make them almost unassailable. This was not to be.

In fact, the introduction of the new MotoGP regulations enabled Yamaha to do what they do best: choose the simplest design to get the job done, rejecting ostentatious exotica born from engineering vanity; then embark on a painstaking, assiduous, tireless and relentless path of development, to create the best racing motorcycle in the world. Driven by this philosophy, the Yamaha M1 MotoGP bike was born.

Simplicity for Yamaha meant that the M1 adopted the almost-universal engine configuration for large capacity sports bikes: the in-line four-cylinder.

Although this may seem to have been the easy choice, it was based on a thorough analysis of the consequences in chassis design for different engine configurations. The shorter engine of the in-line four, would in turn permit a shorter wheelbase and allow the engine to be placed well forward. This was felt to be essential, the key to a good-handling, agile bike. Simplicity also meant using carburettors on the 2002 M1, despite fuel injection adventures in the past on the Superbike R7. Five-valve engines have been Yamaha's four-stroke trademark, and the first M1 kept the tradition going. There's always been a big debate on the effect of the rotating crankshaft on chassis behaviour and Yamaha chose to have the crank rotate backwards, necessitating a countershaft to drive the transmission. Perhaps driven by the speculation that the anticipated power levels of the MotoGP bikes would destroy race tyres, the 2002 M1 appeared at the first races with a displacement well under the permitted 990 cc at about 930cc. By mid-season a full-capacity engine had appeared. Rounding off the package was a chassis that closely resembled that of the two-stroke YZR500 that had been

ridden by M1 riders Checa and Biaggi for the previous two years. Yamaha aimed to reduce the variables to a minimum. Keep it simple.

Perhaps it was too simple. During the first few races, the bikes were clearly down on top speed and struggling. In particular engine braking had been a real problem – the rear wheel locking up as the riders stamped down the gearbox. But the intensity of the development program was soon apparent. The factory worked hard to enhance the slipper clutch using electronics to blip the throttle as the riders changed down (this was widely misreported as a clutch booster system). By the fourth race, the bikes were faster and the engine braking problem solved. Throughout the rest of the year, there were new components at almost every race, with experimental traction control tried in practice, but not raced. Fuel injection was also being developed as the use of electronics to control fuel delivery would add even greater flexibility. Although a step behind Honda, especially the Honda ridden by Valentino Rossi, the M1 took 12 podium places, including two victories by Biaggi.

Then Biaggi was fired. True to character he had been quite outspoken in his comments on the bike's weaknesses, and tensions in the team lead to the split. The M1 development had been a joint affair, with Max focusing on the engine and Checa on the handling. For 2003, all development work would be in Carlos Checa's hands with some support from other M1 riders such as Abe, Barros and new MotoGP rider Marco Melandri.

The year was a disaster for Yamaha, with injury-plagued Barros unable to mount an effective challenge and Checa unable to play the role of both developer and top GP racer. Although development continued, the focus on increasing chassis rigidity saw the team moving in the wrong direction, the bike becoming especially twitchy mid-corner as the throttle was cracked open. Despite engine improvements giving it good top speed, the package was not working.

The factory decided to take drastic action, and it was announced in May 2003 that Masao Furusawa would be taking over the racing team. Actually Furusawa was Yamaha's Mr. Fix-it, heading a tiger team to observe, analyse and recommend changes to projects within Yamaha that were not delivering the goods. His assignment raised the profile of the project within the company, opening doors to financial and other resources that may otherwise have been out of reach. The results were dramatic.

In essence the second generation of the M1 was sketched out. It was decided to replace the five-valve cylinder heads with four-valve versions that offered better combustion efficiency at the 16,000 rpm engine speeds used. A technique was resurrected that had been employed so successfully on the two-stroke bikes of the 1990s, the "big bang" engine. As before, this seemed to produce a more effective power delivery, emulating the torquey output of a V-engine, from the small compact in-line four-cylinder engine. An ideal combination. The chassis also underwent a major change, with the rear suspension top mounting point at the rear of the engine, and a swing arm with heavy under-bracing. Carlos Checa took it out after the last GP of 2003 and immediately improved on his best race lap time of the day before.

But the final piece of the package that Furusawa managed to assemble was the best rider in the world, Valentino Rossi. Exploiting his dissatisfaction with Honda's cavalier attitude towards its riders, Rossi was persuaded to make the move, taking most of his team with him. Typically Honda swore to create a new engine to crush the Rossi/Yamaha combination, underlining the attitude that had caused Rossi to leave.

For the first tests of the season in January 2004, Yamaha lined up all versions of the bikes they had available – four- and five-valve heads, regular/irregular firing order, different chassis. Rossi's choice fell immediately on the configuration Yamaha themselves had wanted to pursue, four-valve big-bang engine in

the chassis Checa had found to be so effective.

Rossi and team chief Jerry Burgess also convinced Yamaha to position the engine slightly higher in the frame to get better braking performance, also lengthening the wheelbase a little to maintain stability. With this package, the team were ready, and embarked on one of the most sensational GP seasons in the history of the sport.

Victory at the opening round in South Africa astounded everyone, including Rossi himself, but gave the team the one vital ingredient that was missing, self-confidence. With changes in the electronics to improve driveability, traction control and engine braking, coupled with small adjustments to the chassis, by mid-season Rossi and the M1 had become dominant, and the championship was theirs.

Despite the success, a gruelling winter test program was instigated, Yamaha not wishing to slow the development momentum. It was exhausting for the team, but did result in a bike that, for the first time, was possibly better than the Honda, once front and rear suspension settings were dialled in. The experience of the team, combined with the strong analytical skills of Rossi, led to race-winning set-ups at all but six of the 17 rounds in 2005. The dominant 2005 MotoGP championship was a fine way to celebrate 50 years of Yamaha racing.

Left: M1 expressed Yamaha's philosophy of relative simplicity.
Photograph: Gold & Goose

TEAM-BY-TEAM
MOTOGP
REVIEW

2005 Teams and Riders
MICHAEL SCOTT
STEPHEN MARKS

MotoGP Bike Illustrations
ADRIAN DEAN

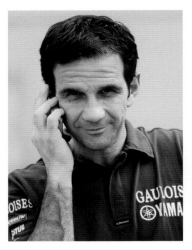

Photographs: Gold & Goose

DAVIDE BRIVIO
Team Director

VALENTINO ROSSI

Born: **February 16, 1979** – Urbino, Italy

GP Starts: **157** (97 MotoGP/500cc, 30 250cc, 30 125cc)

GP Wins: **79** (53 MotoGP/500, 14 250cc, 12 125cc)

World Championships: **7** (5 MotoGP/500cc, 1 250cc, 1 125cc)

COLIN EDWARDS

Born: **February 27, 1974** – Houston, Texas

GP Starts: **49** (MotoGP)

GAULOISES YAMAHA M1

ENGINE

Type: **990cc in-line four, close firing intervals, DOHC, four valves per cylinder**

Power: **Around 220 PS**

Ancillaries: **Magneti Marelli electronics, NGK sparking plugs, EFI, two chokes ride-by-wire**

Lubrication: **Motul**

Transmission: **Gear primary drive with direction-reversing balance shaft, multiplate dry slipper clutch, six-speed constant mesh cassette-type gearbox, DID chain**

CHASSIS

Fabricated aluminium twin-beam

Weight: **148kg**

Dimensions: **length, wheelbase, height, width n/a**

Fuel: **22 litres, Motul**

Suspension: **Front: Öhlins TT25 42mm forks; Rear: Öhlins TT440 gas shock with linkage**

Wheels: **16.5-inch Marchesini**

Tyres: **Michelin**

Brakes: **Brembo carbon 380mm front, Yamaha steel rear**

Sponsors
Gauloises
Michelin
Motul
Magneti Marelli
Alpinestars
Beta
Termignoni

Technical Suppliers
Brembo
NGK
DID
Öhlins

IN 2002, Yamaha shifted the factory team from their long-standing base in the Netherlands to Italy, at the headquarters of Yamaha Motor Europe near Monza, from where the Belgarda Yamaha factory Superbike team had been operated. Until the end of last year, however, the team was still run out of Holland, where Yamaha Motor Racing managing director Lin Jarvis was based.

At the start of 2005, however, Jarvis and staff moved to the Italian base, further consolidating the enterprise. The links with the Belgarda Yamaha team were now indivisible, flagged by team director Davide Brivio, who had managed the Superbike team before moving to MotoGP.

The team operated closely with the Yamaha factory staff, headed by project leader Masahiko Nakajima, though technical director Ichiro Yoda had gone to Kawasaki.

The factory team had revised sponsorship arrangements compared with 2004, when Checa ran in Fortuna colours and Rossi in Gauloises. This year, the Fortuna backing was passed to the Tech 3 satellite team, and both the official machines ran in identical Gauloises blue, except for two GPs. In the US round at Laguna Seca both bikes ran in the famous yellow/black bumblebee livery of the US racing team of the 1970s; and in Valencia in the white/red colours of Yamaha Europe's racing bikes of the same era. Both were in celebration of the company's 50th birthday.

VALENTINO ROSSI PIT CREW
Jeremy BURGESS: Chief Mechanic (above)

Mechanics
Bernard ANSIAU Alex BRIGGS
Brent STEPHENS

Gary COLEMAN (assistant/logistics)
Hiroya ATSUMI: Yamaha Engineer
Matteo FLAGMINI: Telemetry

COLIN EDWARDS PIT CREW
Daniele ROMAGNOLI: Chief Mechanic (above)

Mechanics
Walter CRIPPA Antonio SPADA
Javier ULLATE

Roberto BRIVIO (assistant/logistics)
Yoichi NAKAYAMA: Yamaha Engineer
Andrea ZUGNA: Telemetry

TEAM STAFF
Lin JARVIS: Managing Director
Masahiko NAKAJIMA: Project leader
Davide BRIVIO: Team Director
Marc CANELA: Team Co-ordinator
Rupert WILLIAMSON (Sponsorship)

Brivio had been instrumental in the critical enticement of Rossi from Honda, and remained in charge of a team broadly unaltered from 2004.

Rossi (26) remained the centre of attention. Winner of the title for the past four years straight, thrice with Honda and once with Yamaha, there was no doubting who was the jewel in the crown, and the team revolved around him accordingly. To devastating effect. Rossi's determined domination began at the first race.

His pit crew was unchanged, headed by experienced Australian Jerry Burgess, with compatriot Alex Briggs prominent by his side. Burgess was going for his tenth title in the class, his portfolio running via Mick Doohan to Wayne Gardner almost 20 years ago. His creed – a direct and simple approach to the task of making the most of what you have – meshed perfectly with Yamaha, the M1 and the rider, and he was key to their success both last year and this.

There was a new team-mate on the other side of the garage... former double Superbike World Champion Colin Edwards (31). The Texan Tornado was in his third team in three years of MotoGP – Aprilia, Honda and now Yamaha. This put the amiable rider back with the marque that gave him his first international experience in Superbikes. His crew chief, Daniele Romagnoli, was new to the post, promoted from within the squad.

It was to be a difficult season for Edwards, completely overshadowed by his team-mate, and he found himself with more to learn than he expected. He was still making adjustments to his riding style at the final races. Edwards finished with a couple of good results, three times on the rostrum and a fine second in the USA, and his optimism unquenched.

The season ended in controversy concerning sponsorship. Midway through the year Rossi had signed up for 2007, on condition that he could bring his own sponsors for a so-called satellite team. This grossly offended Gauloises, who believed that by contracting to sponsor the factory team, they would automatically also get the factory's top rider. Gauloises seemed certain to quit racing; their stablemates Fortuna departed to replace MoviStar at the Gresini Honda team, taking promising young rider Toni Elias with them.

It was not known what sponsor's colours Rossi or indeed Edwards would run next year. The future of their satellite team was also in doubt, although there was the possibility of a Dunlop-backed rescue, running Roberto Rolfo and another as-yet unnamed rider.

For 2006, Yamaha might find themselves free to race in corporate colours even more often than in 2005. *MS*

MAKOTO TANAKA
Team Manager

3

MAX BIAGGI

Born: June 26, 1971, Rome, Italy
GP Starts: 214 (127 MotoGP/500cc, 87 250cc)
GP Wins: 42 (13 MotoGP/500cc, 29 250cc)
World Championships: 4 (250cc)

69

NICKY HAYDEN

Born: July 30, 1981, Owensboro, USA
GP Starts: 47 (MotoGP)
GP wins: 1 (MotoGP)

Photographs: Gold & Goose

REPSOL HONDA RC211v

ENGINE

Type: 990cc 75.5-degree V5, close firing intervals, DOHC, four valves per cylinder

Power: more than 240 PS

Ancillaries: HRC electronics, NGK sparking plugs, all-active ride-by-wire EFI

Lubrication: Repsol

Transmission: gear primary drive, multiplate dry slipper clutch, six-speed constant mesh cassette-type gearbox, RK chain

CHASSIS

Fabricated aluminium twin-beam

Weight: 148kg +

Dimensions: 2,050mm length, 1,440mm wheelbase, 1,140mm height, 645mm width

Fuel: 22 litres, Repsol

Suspension: Front: Showa 47mm forks; Rear: Showa gas shock with linkage

Wheels: 16.5-inch Enkei

Tyres: Michelin

Brakes: Brembo carbon 314mm front, HRC steel 218mm rear (Hayden 255 mm rear)

+44 (0)121 603 1554   © 2005 ADRIAN DEAN

REPSOL renewed their faith in Honda for 2005, after 11 years of sponsoring the factory team, in spite of what they called "the hiccup" of not a single race win last year.

The factory squad, operated out of Belgium, but overseen directly from HRC's headquarters in Japan, instituted a number of changes to avoid a repetition of these circumstances.

Rider-wise, Alex Barros was out, having failed for various reasons to provide the development impetus they had lost with the departure of Rossi and crew chief Burgess. He was replaced as senior rider by Max Biaggi (33).

To some, this was a surprising choice. Max had left Honda amid angry accusations at the end of 1998 for Yamaha. He'd been dropped by them at the end of 2002, and returned to Honda, if only with a satellite team on a "production" bike, the Camel Pons squad. At the time, he had said he hoped to regain favour with HRC, so that he could get a top factory bike. "If I am a good boy, then I will get some cake," he said. The top Repsol ride is as good as it gets.

Biaggi is an experienced race winner and former serial 250 champion, and HRC hoped he would provide the clear leadership required to regain lost ground.

The other major change was the return of long-time Honda racing legend Erv Kanemoto, after an interim year at Suzuki, to offset the loss of Burgess. The Japanese-American engineer's racing success goes back to Freddie Spencer in the 1980s. His title of Technical Director was in line with the original intention for his role – overseeing both riders. In fact, it worked out differently, even during pre-season testing. Erv and Max worked closely together, somewhat leaving Hayden's side of the garage free to find its own way.

This might have been the cake Max had been dreaming about. As it turned out, for whatever reason, the mix was not successful and the icing did not set. Max finished second in Italy and Japan, and at that stage still seemed a possible title runner-up. But he frequently had trouble qualifying, and again complained about the machine, and everybody's inability to make it steer to his liking. A string of bad races at the end of the year pushed HRC too far, and in the end they responded by dispensing with his services. "We are very disappointed with his results," said HRC managing director Satoru Horiike.

Erv, hard-pressed to find elusive technical answers to Biaggi's questions was always available for advice to the other side of the pit, but the structure meant that Nicky Hayden (23) was relatively independent. He made the most of it.

In his third year on the factory bike, he worked from the start at forging a relationship with newly promoted chief mechanic Pete Benson. The American and the Kiwi formed a partnership that gained strength through the year, boosted by victory in the USA.

They added some solid end-of-year rostrums. This bodes well for their future together.

HRC top brass were frequently present at the track, with president Suguru Kanazawa attending a number of races, and likewise affable MS Mr Horiike. In the same way there were always a number of factory engineers present, some for the long-haul, others only now and then. The general manager was Tsutomu Ishii.

Honda worked with their familiar technical partners – Michelin tyres, Showa suspensions, and their own in-house electronics. *MS*

Top: Power posse – the factory Repsol Honda squad.

Above left and left: Biaggi with Erv Kanemoto (left) **in his pit, and on his motorcycle.**

Above: Managing director Satoru Horiike.

Far left: Nicky Hayden, with crew chief Pete Benson, scored the team's only win.
Photographs: Gold & Goose

FAUSTO GRESINI
Team Owner and Manger

SETE GIBERNAU

Born: December 15, 1972 – Barcelona, Spain	
GP Starts: 160 (141 MotoGP/500cc, 19 250cc)	
GP Wins: 9 (MotoGP/500cc)	

MARCO MELANDRI

Born: August 7, 1982 – Ravenna, Italy	
GP Starts: 121 (45 MotoGP, 47 250cc, 29 125cc)	
GP Wins: 19 (2 MotoGP, 10 250cc, 7 125cc)	
World Championships: 1 (250cc)	

Photographs: Gold & Goose

MOVISTAR HONDA RC211V

ENGINE

Type: 990cc 75.5-degree V5, close firing intervals, DOHC, four valves per cylinder

Power: more than 240 PS

Ancillaries: HRC electronics, NGK sparking plugs, all-active ride-by-wire EFI

Lubrication: Castrol

Transmission: gear primary drive, multiplate dry slipper clutch, six-speed constant mesh cassette-type gearbox, RK chain

CHASSIS

Fabricated aluminium twin-beam

Weight: 148kg +

Dimensions: 2,050mm length, 1,440mm wheelbase,1,140mm height, 645mm width

Fuel: 22 litres, Elf

Suspension: Front: Showa 47mm forks; Rear: Showa gas shock with linkage

Wheels: 16.5-inch Enkei

Tyres: Michelin

Brakes: Brembo carbon 314mm front, HRC steel 218mm rear

+44 (0)121 603 1554

© 2005 ADRIAN DEAN

Sponsors
Movistar
Castrol
Devil
Domino
Michelin
Piolanti
AEG
Berner
Black Prince
Polini
Seven

Technical Sponsors
Alcantara
Atlas Copco
Beta
Bike Lift
Blue Box
Mokador
Ghigi
Roland
San Benedetto
Zanussi Professional

THE senior of Honda's three satellite teams was acknowledged as such by HRC, with Sete Gibernau on a factory machine from the outset. When Sete ran into the longest period of disastrous misfortune in racing memory, his junior team-mate Marco Melandri reached maturity seemingly overnight after joining the team only for this year, and by the end of the season he too had a hybrid factory machine.

The year reinforced this status, with Melandri's second overall making them not just the best satellite team, but the best of any of the Honda teams.

Fausto Gresini's tight-knit organisation has an impressive reputation in the paddock, as a "tidy" outfit. This has been built up over almost ten years of steady growth, with a string of impressive results for the Rimini-based Italian-accented squad.

Gresini was a formidable 125 rider, with two World Championships – he still holds the class record with 11 consecutives wins. Retired in 1994, in 1997 he founded the team that has grown to the stature it enjoys today. With technical director Fabrizio Cecchini, Gresini entered the 500cc class, fielding Alex Barros on a factory-linked V-twin Honda.

By 2000, Team Gresini had proved itself, and the next turning point was to be entrusted by Honda with their factory machine and favourite rider, Daijiro Kato. With Telefónica MoviStar backing and the riding genius of the taciturn Japanese star, Team Gresini became the dominant force in 250s, and in

2002 moved back to the top class, with Kato Rookie of the Year, on a two-stroke 500.

Kato's tragic death at the first round of 2003 was another turning point, with the stricken team contemplating quitting. The success of new second rider Sete Gibernau, who claimed four race wins, each dedicated to his fallen team-mate, renewed their spirit. In 2004, Gibernau was second to Rossi, with four more wins. Team Gresini started 2005 as serious title contenders.

Typically, the team stepped up to the plate. Nobody could have anticipated the way it happened.

Prize fighter Sete Gibernau won the pre-season tests at Catalunya, and was leading as they approached the final hairpin of the opening GP. Until Rossi clattered underneath him, sending him ricocheting into the gravel trap. The senior rider was fast at almost every other track, but a variety of problems would intervene before the chequered flag. At Brno he even ran out of fuel. More often, the non-finishes were through some or other mistake by a rider who seemed unable to regain race-winning confidence.

Was it only good luck that new team member Marco Melandri turned out to be the revelation of the year? The 2002 250 champion was straight off two injury-strewn and downbeat years on Yamaha's M1. He clicked with the Honda from the earliest tests (when the team blanked off the on-board

SETE GIBERNAU PIT CREW

Juan MARTINEZ: Chief Mechanic (above)

Mechanics
Pedro CALVET Simone ALESSANDRINI
Fabio ROVELLI
Luigi TRABATTONI (assistant)
Naoki TOMISAWA: Engines
Francesco FAVA: Telemetry

MARCO MELANDRI PIT CREW

Fabrizio CECCHINI: Chief Mechanic (above)

Mechanics
Ivan BRANDI Alverto PRESUTTI
Andrea BONASSOLI
Ryoichi MORI: Engines
Diego GUBELLINI: Telemetry

TEAM STAFF
Fausto GRESINI:
Chairman and Managing Director

Carlo MERLINI: Commercial
and Marketing Director

Fabrizio CECCHINI: Technical Director

lap-timer, so he could concentrate only on the machine); finished the first race on the rostrum, and in spite of a mid-season slump and a Motegi injury, resumed progress to claim his first win at the penultimate round, following it up straight away with another. His final second place overall meant that in terms of individual results, this was not only the best of the satellite teams, but the best Honda team per se, though the factory Repsol squad did outpoint them in the Team standings.

In the pits, Sete continued with fellow-Spaniard Juan Martinez as his chief mechanic, the earnest-looking bespectacled technician giving him a machine capable of pole position five times in 17 races. Melandri had the benefit of the experience of team fellow-founder Fabrizio Cecchini taking care of his machine.

Castrol were among the important sponsors, running an oil development programme tailored directly to the Honda RC211V.

Team Gresini was an innocent victim of the departure from motorcycle racing of Telefónica MoviStar at the end of the year – major sponsors for five years. The team's status was underlined by the willingness of another significant Spanish sponsor to step into the breech. Fortuna brought promising ex-Yamaha rookie Toni Elias with them – for Gibernau had found pastures new, with Ducati, taking Martinez with him. *MS*

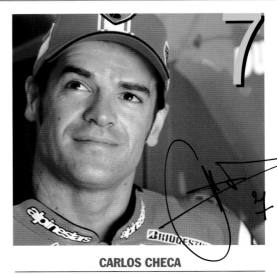

LIVIO SUPPO
Project Manager

LORIS CAPIROSSI

Born: April 4, 1973 – Bologna, Italy
GP Starts: 231 (120 MotoGP/500cc, 84 250cc, 27 125cc)
GP Wins: 25 (5 MotoGP/500cc, 12 250cc, 8 125cc)
World Championships: 3 (1 250cc, 2 125cc)

CARLOS CHECA

Born: October 15, 1972 – Sant Fruitos, Spain
GP Starts: 185 (157 MotoGP/500cc, 27 250cc, 1 125cc)
GP Wins: 2 (500cc)

Photographs: Gold & Goose

MARLBORO DUCATI DESMOSEDICI GP5

ENGINE

Type: 989cc 90-degree V4, close firing intervals, DOHC, four valves per cylinder, desmodromic valve gear

Power: 230-plus PS at 16,500rpm

Ancillaries: Magneti Marelli electronics, NGK sparking plugs, EFI with automatic fast tickover

Lubrication: Shell Advance Ultra 4

Transmission: gear primary drive, multiplate dry slipper clutch, six-speed constant mesh cassette-type gearbox, Regina chain

CHASSIS

Multi-tube adjustable steel trellis, aluminium swing-arm

Weight: 148kg

Dimensions: 2,100mm length, n/a wheelbase, 1,180mm height, 750mm width

Fuel: 22 litres, Shell Racing V-Power

Suspension: Front: Öhlins TT25 42mm forks; Rear: Öhlins ST45 gas shock with linkage

Wheels: 16.5-inch Marchesini

Tyres: Bridgestone

Brakes: Brembo carbon 320mm front, steel 200mm rear

+44 (0)121 603 1554   © 2005 ADRIAN DEAN

Sponsors
Marlboro
Alice
Shell Advance
Breil
Bridgestone

Technical Suppliers
AMD
Brembo
CHT
Gnutti
Lampo
Magneti Marelli
Regina
SKF
Termignoni
USAG
Öhlins

THE Bologna-based factory faced 2005 with renewed spirit, after a bruising 2004. Joining MotoGP one year after it had started, Ducati won a race in their first season. In their second, they had lost much of the impetus achieved.

For 2005, there were two major changes in an otherwise fundamentally little-altered team. The first was the replacement of Troy Bayliss with Carlos Checa, the former a Ducati stalwart, the latter after six more or less lacklustre years with Yamaha.

The second was a surprise shift from Michelins to Bridgestones.

The abandonment of the class-leading tyres was something of an adventure. The reason, MotoGP project manager Livio Suppo explained when the news broke, was as much to break out of the Michelin loop as anything. Firstly, they would benefit from more clearly tailored tyre development. Secondly, there would be some tracks that would suit the Japanese tyres, and others that wouldn't. But at the good tracks, they would be in a much smaller field of potential winners than was the case with Michelin. Events would fully justify the philosophy, but Ducati would have to wait.

A true factory team, with Ducati Corse chief Claudio Domenicali a frequent pit presence, along with such as designer Felippo Prezzioso and aerodynamicist Alan Jenkins; it operated under the supervision of technical director Corrado

Cecchinelli, who has held the position since the first arrival of the Desmosedici in 2003. Suppo was another in a team of stalwarts; sponsors Marlboro had also been there from the very start.

So too had Loris Capirossi (32), with two full years on the bike, and winner of their one GP so far. The former 125 and 250 champion would visit the rostrum only once in the first ten races, with third at home in Italy.

At the 11th round, the new-generation Bridgestones came good, and Loris started a run that showed how twilight was a shade that seemed to suit this veteran's career. Capirossi was again riding with the abandonment that characterised his younger years. Second at Brno was followed by a pair of back-to-back wins at Motegi and Malaysia. There might have been more, but two races later Loris fell heavily in practice at Phillip Island, and only returned, still hurt, for the final round.

New team-mate Carlos Checa (32) was another old hand, after ending his Yamaha years as distant team-mate to Rossi. He was not the only one hoping he'd be able to revive a flagging career on a bike more suited to his beefy riding style than the flighty M1. As the whole combination gathered strength in the late races, he went a long way towards justifying these hopes. Although he didn't retain the contract, his eventual form earned him a slot on a Pons Honda for 2005, sponsorship willing.

SHINICHI ITO

Born: December 7, 1966 – Miyagi, Japan

GP Starts: 65 (MotoGP/500cc)

Left: Capirossi's machine gets fettled.

Below left: Capirossi dominated for Ducati and Bridgestone in Japan and Malaysia.

Below: The watchful eyes of Claudio Domenicali.
Photographs: Gold & Goose

LORIS CAPIROSSI PIT CREW

Massimo BRACCONI: Chief Mechanic

Mechanics

Davide MANFREDI Massimo MIRANO

Mark ELDER Luciano BERTAGNA

Roberto BONAZZI: Track Engineer (above)

Marco FRIGERIO: Telemetry

CARLOS CHECA PIT CREW

Bruno LEONI: Chief Mechanic

Mechanics

Roberto CLERICI Paul HALLETT

Giorgio CASTURA Lorenzo GAGNI

Christhian PUPULIN: Track Engineer (above)

Davide MARELLI: Telemetry

TEAM STAFF

Claudio DOMENICALI: Managing Director

Livio SUPPO: Project Manager

Corrado CECCHINELLI: Technical Director

Dario RAIMONDI: Team Manager

Capirossi's crew was basically unchanged from last year, under control of Roberto Bonazzi. On Checa's side of the pit, a new track engineer, Cristhian Pupulin, took over.

Ducati also worked closely with Shell on fuel and oil, making valuable progress. But the biggest significance was their partnership with Bridgestone. The pair ran a test team on a number of circuits, with former GP rider Shinichi Ito in the saddle, and felt the benefits of this tailored tyre development at the end of the year. Ito's sole GP outing, as a Turkey GP substitute for Capirossi, ended in an ignominious black flag. *MS*

Left: Checa gained strength in his one Ducati season.

Far left: Technical director Corrado Cecchinelli (grey hair) exults after Capirossi's win in Japan.
Photographs: Gold & Goose

SITO PONS
Team Director

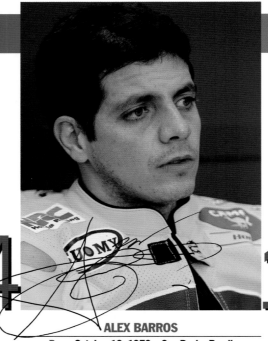

4

ALEX BARROS
Born: October 18, 1970 – Sao Paulo, Brazil
GP Starts: 258 (227 MotoGP/500cc, 14 250cc, 17 80cc)
GP Wins: 7 (MotoGP/500cc)

12

TROY BAYLISS
Born: March 30, 1969 – Taree, Australia
GP Starts: 44 (43 MotoGP, 1 250cc)

CAMEL HONDA RC211V

ENGINE

Type: 990cc 75.5-degree V5, close firing intervals, DOHC, four valves per cylinder

Power: more than 240 PS

Ancillaries: HRC electronics, NGK sparking plugs, all-active ride-by-wire EFI

Lubrication: Elf

Transmission: gear primary drive, multiplate dry slipper clutch, six-speed constant mesh cassette-type gearbox, RK chain

CHASSIS

Fabricated aluminium twin-beam

Weight: 148kg +

Dimensions: 2,050mm length, 1,440mm wheelbase, 1,140mm height, 645mm width

Fuel: 22 litres, Elf

Suspension: Front: Showa 47mm forks; Rear: Showa gas shock with linkage

Wheels: 16.5-inch Enkei

Tyres: Michelin

Brakes: Brembo carbon 314mm front, HRC steel 218mm rear

+44 (0)121 603 1554 © 2005 ADRIAN DEAN

Sponsors

JT International
Correos
Leo Vince
Tenuta Dada Di
Casalenza

Technical Suppliers

Michelin
Sparco
Sanyo
Brembo
Renault Trucks
Stahlwille
Showa
NGK
Ferve
A³

TEAM STAFF

Sito PONS: Team Principal
Félix RODRIGUEZ: Team Co-ordinator
Malcolm SAYER: Marketing and Commercial Director
Michele MORISETTI: Press and PR

I N 2005 double 250cc World Champion Sito Pons recovered his role as the owner of a two-man team, with the experienced duo of Alex Barros (34) and Troy Bayliss (36) aboard satellite Honda RC211Vs. The team had spent 2004 with a huge dividing wall running down the centre of the garage, with Max Biaggi and Makoto Tamada running bikes with different tyre suppliers, Michelin and Bridgestone respectively. Effectively there were two one-man teams under the Camel umbrella.

Sito's team is generally regarded as being one of the most professional outfits in MotoGP. Administering from his Barcelona headquarters, Pons is a hard task-master, and the team is immaculately presented, from the bikes and the pit garage to the leather sofas in his hi-tech hospitality suite.

Towards the end of 2004, it seemed as though Pons was once again struggling for support from Honda, an apparently annual loggerhead which has stretched the fraught relationship between the Spaniard and the Japanese factory to the limit. 2005 saw him recover one of the stars from the team's heyday years in the early part of the millennium, Barros, who had twice beaten Rossi on board the RC211V in 2002. The Brazilian veteran would spearhead the team's chances in more familiar surroundings than those he endured in a disappointing year with the factory squad.

The early season signs were promising, fourth and sixth in

the first round at Jerez, seemingly confirming the team's faith in their veteran pairing. The capture of Ducati stalwart Bayliss had been a big gamble, and pre-season tests seemed to show that his aggression, and unfamiliarity with the subtle use of the clutch in downshifting, would not marry well with the Honda.

Barros's win at race two in Estoril, his adopted home-race after the cancellation of the Rio GP, added further to the team's stock. Fastest in all three sessions, qualified on pole, he rode a gutsy last 12 laps, skating across puddles, after early leader Gibernau fell foul of the changing conditions.

Then came a sharp downturn in fortunes. On occasion Camel Honda prepared a machine to tackle the best of the factory-run bikes, but there were times when consistency became an issue. Barros only featured once more on the podium, at the waterlogged Donington Park, his 250th Grand Prix. The final part of his season was hit by front-end problems, a killer blow for the latest of the late-brakers.

In turn, Bayliss would only equal his Jerez sixth at Laguna Seca, where he had the advantage of track knowledge. Far too many crashes and a real lack of confidence belied the usually fiery and upbeat nature of the Aussie. Then, training at home before the Japanese GP, Bayliss' MotoGP career would come to an abrupt end after a motocross accident shattered his wrist. He will now return to the World Superbike paddock, back with

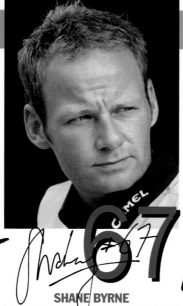

72   67   17   54

TOHRU UKAWA
Born: May 18, 1973 – Chiba, Japan
GP Starts: 127 (50 MotoGP, 77 250cc)
GP Wins: 5 (1 MotoGP, 4 250cc)
* NB: Also rode for Moriwaki Racing

SHANE BYRNE
Born: December 10, 1976 – Lambeth, Great Britain
GP Starts: 19 (MotoGP)
* NB: Also rode for Team Roberts

CHRIS VERMEULEN
Born: June 19, 1982 – Brisbane, Australia
GP Starts: 2 (MotoGP)

RYUICHI KIYONARI
Born: September 23, 1982 – Kawagoe, Japan
GP Starts: 14 (MotoGP)

ALEX BARROS PIT CREW
Ramon FORCADA: Chief Mechanic (above)
Mechanics
Joan CASAS, Xavi CASANOVAS,
Paco LOPEZ, Tomas FONCEA

TROY BAYLISS PIT CREW
Santi MULERO: Chief Mechanic (above)
Mechanics
Carlos BARTOLOME, Carles FABREGAT
Jose Manuel ESCAMEZ, Alejandro TEJEDO
Ramon AURIN: Telemetry
Hitoshi TAGAWA: Engines

the Ducati factory team.

Former Camel Honda rider Tohru Ukawa took his place at Motegi, Shane Byrne in Malaysia and Qatar, performing decently on his first ride on the RCV at two new tracks. Chris Vermeulen took over for two races, fresh from second overall in WSBK, admirably finishing ahead of Biaggi in Turkey, earning himself a Suzuki contract for 2006.

Byrne was enlisted for the final round at Valencia, but replaced at the last minute by Ryuichi Kyonari, BSB runner up.

There had been threats that Camel would leave Pons at the end of the year, but at the last round at Valencia the team had seemed settled on another two-rider set-up, with two more veterans, Max Biaggi and Carlos Checa. Until a late-night change of heart on race Sunday. In the media centre, the team's press officer announced in full voice that Camel would no longer support the team, because Honda refused to give Biaggi a bike. Just where he and his tobacco money will end up remains a mystery, but talented 250cc runner-up Casey Stoner has taken advantage, and seems likely to join Checa on the team next year, adding a fresh element to an experienced team in need of a boost.

As an important member of Spain's racing establishment, Sito Pons has led something of a charmed life in MotoGP over the years, able to rely on help and support to solve sponsorship crises in the past. All expected him to come up smiling. *SM*

Above top left and top centre: Veteran Barros was the team's driving force, with a win at Estoril.

Above centre left: Chris Vermeulen was in and out of the team like a blur.

Left: Troy Bayliss had a hard year that ended early.
Photographs: Gold & Goose

Photographs: Gold & Goose

HARALD ECKL
General Manager

SHINYA NAKANO

Born: October 10, 1977 – Chiba, Japan	
GP Starts: 114 (80 MotoGP/500, 34 250cc)	
GP Wins: 6 (250cc)	

ALEX HOFMANN

Born: May 25, 1980 – Mindelheim, Germany	
GP Starts: 77 (35 MotoGP, 41 250cc, 1 125cc)	

KAWASAKI NINJA ZX-RR

ENGINE

Type: 990cc in-line four, close firing intervals, DOHC, four valves per cylinder

Power: More than 230 PS at 15,000 rpm

Ancillaries: Magneti Marelli electronics, NGK sparking plugs,

EFI with one choke ride-by-wire

Lubrication: Fuchs Silkolene Titan GT1

Transmission: Gear primary drive, multiplate dry slipper clutch, six-speed constant mesh cassette-type gearbox, EK chain

CHASSIS

Fabricated aluminium twin-beam

Weight – 148kg

Dimensions: length, height and width n/a, 1,420mm wheelbase (adjustable)

Fuel: 22 litres, Elf

Suspension: Front: Öhlins TT25 42mm forks; **Rear:** Öhlins TT44 gas shock with linkage

Wheels: 16.5-inch JB Magtan

Tyres: Bridgestone

Brakes: Brembo carbon 305mm front, steel 220mm rear

+44 (0)121 603 1554

© 2005 ADRIAN DEAN

Sponsors
Fuchs Petrolub
Arlen Ness
Erdinger Weissbrau
JP Interactive
MAN

Technical Suppliers
Akrapovic
Bridgestone
AFAM
MRA
NGK

TEAM STAFF

Harald ECKL: General Manager

Ichiro YODA: Technical Director

Michael BARTHOLEMY: Team Co-ordinator

Naoya KANEKO: Technical Co-ordinator

Danilo CASONATO: Chief Data and Electronics Engineer

Andrea DOSOLI: Fuel Injection Technician

Tomy OMATA: Suspension

Ian WHEELER: Marketing and Communications

RUN by former racer Harald Eckl since back in World Superbike days, the factory Kawasaki GP team was entering its third year of MotoGP, after a process of steady change and development. After a downbeat first season, results had been steadily getting better.

Most of this was driven from within the team, based in Germany, with Eckl's influence and experience in European racing. New chassis were sourced from former rider Eskil Suter in Switzerland, electronics and engine tuning also from Europe, bringing significant improvements in the second year, which continued into the third, most especially with their own version of a simple big bang.

For the third year, the team added a new level of expertise and experience, recruiting two key people direct from Yamaha.

One was the vastly experienced mechanic and crew chief Fiorenzo Fanali, whose spannering experience goes back to MV Agusta days with Agostini, with a host of other famous names including Kenny Roberts Snr. and Eddie Lawson. He took over as crew chief to Shinya Nakano.

The other was even more significant... Yamaha's previous technical director Ichiro Yoda, whose intimate knowledge of the successful M1 engine, like the Kawasaki an in-line four, would prove an important guide to future developments, including an all-new 990cc motor for 2006.

Last year, Kawasaki had also changed tyres, from Dunlop to Bridgestone. The Japanese tyre manufacturers had wanted to work with full factory teams (Suzuki being the other), and the move suited the team, as Nakano scored their first MotoGP rostrum with third at Motegi.

They kept the same pair of riders. Nakano (27) was in his second year with the team, after being unexpectedly dropped by Yamaha at the end of the previous season. The Japanese rider started 2005 as one of the most respected riders in the paddock. Although his best race finish of the year would be fifth, his consistent strength would bring further credit to his reputation. He signed to stay with the team at the end of it.

Alex Hofmann (24) would have a very different season. The German's hopes were ruined by injury... the first in a demo run before the Portuguese GP. He battled through the middle part of the year, then crashed again at Motegi, breaking more bones. Luck seemed against Hofmann at every turn, and his contract was not renewed. Instead Eckl signed up ex-250 rider Randy de Puniet alongside Nakano.

The rider who brought the green machines their best result ever in top-class racing was former 250 World Champion Olivier Jacque (31), currently without a ride for a second season. At his first attempt, in near flood conditions in China, "OJ" took second place.

Fanali headed Nakano's crew; Hofmann's side was headed by the experienced Christophe Bourguignon.

OLIVIER JACQUE

Born: **August 29, 1973** – Villerupt, France

GP Starts: **131** (51 MotoGP/500cc, 80 250cc)

GP Wins: **7** (250cc) World Championships: **1** (250cc)

ICHIRO YODA   NAOYA KANEKO

Left: **Shinya Nakano prepares for some Ninja action.**
Photograph: Gold & Goose

SHINYA NAKANO PIT CREW

Fiorenzo FANALI: Chief Mechanic (above)

Mechanics

Benoit LEFEBVRE   Florian FERRACCI
Jason CORNEY   Josef BUCHNER

Gerold BUCHER: Telemetry

ALEX HOFMANN PIT CREW

Christophe BOURGUIGNON: Chief Mechanic

Mechanics

Timothy PALMER   Stewart MILLER
Emanuel BUCHNER   Daniel PETAK

Emmanuel ROLIN: Telemetry

Kawasaki had a good season, all told, but Eckl was worried by the end of it that they would not be able to continue with their semi-independent development. The factory planned to be more directly involved with forthcoming machines, starting with the all-new 990 (more Yamaha-like, with a balance shaft) for just one year.

Nakano liked the new motor in post-season tests, and increased commitment and investment from the factory, applied constructively, could power another step forward.   *MS*

Above: **Nakano's fairing shows primitive rider-cooling technology.**

Above left: **Three-strong in Germany, with bikes for (from left) Hofmann, Jacque and Nakano.**

Centre far left. **And then Jacque and Hofmann crashed into each other in the first corner.**

Above centre: **Beneath the green.**

Left: **Jacque leads Biaggi at Istanbul.**
Photographs: Gold & Goose

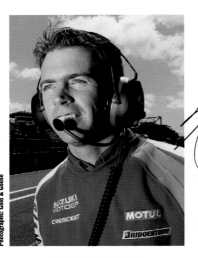

PAUL DENNING
Team Manager

KENNY ROBERTS Jr.

Born: July 25, 1973 – Mountain View, USA	
GP Starts: 143 (125 MotoGP/500cc, 18 250cc)	
GP Wins: 8 (500cc)	
World Championships: 1 (500cc)	

JOHN HOPKINS

Born: May 22, 1983 – Ramona, USA	
GP Starts: 61 (MotoGP/500cc)	

SUZUKI GSV-R – XR-E3

ENGINE

Type: 990cc 65-degree V4, close firing intervals, DOHC, four valves per cylinder

Power: 240 + PS at 15,500rpm

Ancillaries: Mitsubishi electronics, NGK sparking plugs, EFI with two chokes ride-by-wire

Lubrication: Motul

Transmission: Gear primary drive, multiplate dry slipper clutch, six-speed constant mesh cassette-type gearbox, RK chain

CHASSIS

Fabricated aluminium twin-beam

Weight: 148kg

Dimensions: 2,600mm length, 1,450mm wheelbase, 1,150mm height, 660mm width

Fuel: 22 litres, Elf

Suspension: Front: Öhlins TT25 42mm forks; Rear: Öhlins TT44 gas shock with linkage

Wheels: 16.5-inch JB Magtan

Tyres: Bridgestone

Brakes: Brembo carbon 305 or 314mm front, steel 200mm rear

+44 (0)121 603 1554   © 2005 ADRIAN DEAN

Sponsors
Motul
NGK
Bridgestone
Toyo Radiator
RK
DID
AFAM
Yoshimura
Kokusan
Denki
Mitsubishi
DAF
Mac Tools
Dread
Autocom

Technical Suppliers
Öhlins
Brembo
JB
Magtan

THE all-American line-up of John Hopkins and Kenny Roberts Jr. remained the same as in 2003 and 2004, but Team Suzuki MotoGP came into the 2005 season with a major change at the top – long-standing manager Garry Taylor was replaced at the helm.

The team had been unable to reproduce the kind of form that took them to the world title in 2000, and after over thirty years service to the factory, Taylor was replaced by the boss of the successful BSB championship winners Crescent Suzuki, Paul Denning. It was felt that the time was right for youthful dynamism to boost the team's fortunes.

It represented a major step for the Hamamatsu firm. More significantly, they were unable to make enough forward progress with the GSV-R in order to match the improvements of top bikes, and as such any personnel changes were merely superficial.

With Yamaha having shown how it was viable for the smaller Japanese factories to put one over the mighty Honda, confidence of a Suzuki revival was high at the start of the year. Crucially though, Yamaha's change of fortunes had come along with the arrival of Rossi and Co., allied to a determined effort on the factory's part to invest the necessary resources to support the riders' wishes. Unfortunately Suzuki seem to have been unable to match Yamaha in this area.

True, it was the team's most successful year since the MotoGP machines were introduced in 2002 (when Kawasaki were in their fledgling year and Ducati still hadn't arrived), although the single podium finish in the wet at Donington for Roberts was still only a slight improvement on the single third place he achieved in Brazil in 2002.

At the same time, the existing test team was given more importance, with Bridgestone's backing, as with Kawasaki and Ducati. Former factory Suzuki rider Nobu Aoki was given the job of test rider, as well as a handful of wild card rides.

The team structure continued much the same as in previous seasons: Stuart Shenton as crew chief for Hopkins's side of the

9

NOBUATSU AOKI
Born: August 31, 1971 – Sumaga, Japan
GP Starts: 166 (109 MotoGP/500cc, 57 250cc)

Above: The end of a long dry season... in more ways than one. Roberts on the podium at Donington.

Above left: Roberts leads Rossi and Barros in the race.

Left: Hopkins kept trying all year.

Below left: Headgear bonding: Suzuki's MotoGP squad.

Photographs: Gold & Goose

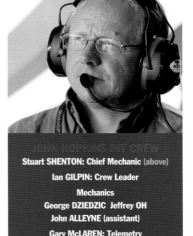

Photographs: Gold & Goose

KENNY ROBERTS PIT CREW
Tom O'KANE: Chief Mechanic (above)
Simon WESTWOOD: Crew Leader
Mechanics
Tsutomo MATSUGANO Ray HUGHES
Mark FLEMING (assistant)
Renato PENNACHIO: Telemetry

JOHN HOPKINS PIT CREW
Stuart SHENTON: Chief Mechanic (above)
Ian GILPIN: Crew Leader
Mechanics
George DZIEDZIC Jeffrey OH
John ALLEYNE (assistant)
Gary McLAREN: Telemetry

TEAM STAFF
Paul DENNING: Team Manager
Masahito IMADA: Group Leader
Howard PLUMPTON: Operations Manager
Shinichi SAHARA: Technical Manager
Keiichiro FUKUZAWA: Engine Development
Hiroshi JINMON: Chassis Development

garage, whilst respected engineer Tom O'Kane was drafted in for Roberts, from his father's Proton team.

Clearly progress had been made though, with lap times having significantly improved compared to previous seasons, especially in qualifying, and with the more consistent performance of the Bridgestones. However with Ducati and Kawasaki now both on the tyre brand, the pecking order for top material remained unclear, and the old racing adage, that as you make steps forward the rest make bigger ones, will be ringing true around the ears of Suzuki top brass.

Even Denning acknowledged this, with echoes of past end-of-season comments from Taylor, "Whilst we can be positive about having made moves forward from 2004, the team, the riders, Suzuki and myself personally are far from satisfied with this level of performance. and the winter months will be a true test of all of us to make sure that we fulfil a better potential in 2006."

The potential is certainly there, John Hopkins has signed for another two years, after being courted by both Honda and Ducati, and the Anglo-American continued to demonstrate the raw talent which has seen him consistently impress during his four years in MotoGP. Hopkins was once again the youngest rider in the class, and a career-best fifth in Japan, where tyres were at optimum performance, showed that when things are right for the 22 year-old, he will challenge at

the front.

The same could also be said about Kenny Roberts Jr.(31), who has openly admitted that he will not push beyond the limit if the risk is not worth taking. Leading in the rain-soaked races in both China and Britain, where the water played its habitual role as the great leveller, seemed to back up his own theory. Despite having had an indifferent year, the veteran did clinch the team's only podium finish at Donington, and though he was forced to retire with engine problems in Shanghai, Roberts might have been considered to have done enough to keep his ride for next season.

It was thought that Denning had been keen to end the team's relationship with Roberts at the beginning of the year, yet ironically it was whilst uncharacteristically pushing beyond the limit at the super-fast Doohan corner at Phillip Island that the former World Champion's season was ended with a broken wrist. His tenure as lead Suzuki rider also came to an abrupt end.

Roberts will be replaced by the talented young Australian Chris Vermeulen, who makes the move over from Superbikes after having turned his nose up at Honda's offer to wait another year before coming to MotoGP. It could just be the coup that forces Suzuki forward. Under the guidance of Denning, a young-looking squad just needs the factory's backing to make that giant leap up to regularly finishing on the podium. *SM*

HERVÉ PONCHARAL
Team Director

TONI ELIAS
Born: March 16, 1983 – Manresa, Spain
GP Starts: 97 (14 MotoGP, 48 250cc, 35 125cc)
GP Wins: 9 (7 250cc, 2 125cc)

RUBEN XAUS
Born: February 18, 1978 – Barcelona, Spain
GP Starts: 38 (33 MotoGP, 5 250cc)

Photographs: Gold & Goose

FORTUNA YAMAHA M1

ENGINE

Type: 990cc in-line four, close firing intervals, DOHC, four valves per cylinder

Power: Around 220 PS

Ancillaries: Magneti Marelli electronics, NGK sparking plugs, EFI, two chokes ride-by-wire

Lubrication: Motul

Transmission: Gear primary drive with direction-reversing balance shaft, multiplate dry slipper clutch, six-speed constant mesh cassette-type gearbox, DID chain

CHASSIS

Fabricated aluminium twin-beam

Weight: 148kg

Dimensions: Length, wheelbase, height, width n/a

Fuel: 22 litres, Motul

Suspension: Front: Öhlins TT25 42mm forks; Rear: Öhlins TT440 gas shock with linkage

Wheels: 16.5-inch Marchesini

Tyres: Michelin

Brakes: Brembo carbon 380mm front, Yamaha steel rear

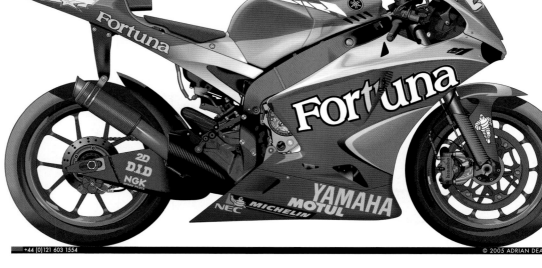

+44 (0)121 603 1554   © 2005 ADRIAN DEAN

Sponsors
Fortuna
Yamaha
Motul

Technical Sponsors
Michelin
NEC
Alpinestars
Flex
Brembo
2D
AFAM
NGK
DID
Öhlins

TEAM STAFF

Hervé PONCHARAL: Team Manager
Gérard VALLE: Team Co-ordinator

SINCE winning the 250cc World Championship in 2000, the French Tech 3 team owned by Hervé Poncharal has seen its stock gradually slide, with major decisions seemingly taken out of the team's hands one by one as factory and sponsors staked their claim. The team moved into MotoGP directly after winning the 250 title with Olivier Jacque, and it was his pairing with Shinya Nakano which brought the best out of them. Nakano's fifth place in the 2001 championship, the team's debut year, promised much for the future, but like so many of the privately owned teams, they were soon to fall foul of the extra costs of the four-stroke machines.

Whereas previously the team could be seen as possible title challengers, the structure of Yamaha meant they became very much the "second string" outfit, and Poncharal even remarked at the beginning of 2005 that his team were not out to win championships, but to "develop young talent for the factory's benefit."

Even that secondary role may have been palatable for former racer Poncharal, whose passion for the sport is still infectious even after nearly 20 years as a team owner. However, when his signing of French 250 rider Randy de Puniet was vetoed by team sponsors Fortuna in favour of the all-Spanish rider line-up of Toni Elias (22) and Ruben Xaus (27), he readily admitted that he was no longer in charge of his own team and feared for its future.

With this subtext it would be easy to suggest that there were no positives to be drawn from the season, but that would be wrong. True, it became clear very quickly that Xaus was never going to adapt to the M1, nor repeat the performance on the Ducati that silenced the nay-sayers, such as the podium finish of Qatar in 2004.

His aggressive style, roughly hewn from the Ducati Superbike school, represents the antithesis of Rossi's smooth and harmonious piloting of a MotoGP machine, and with the new M1 having been moulded around the World Champion, Xaus was just not able to haul himself up to the level required. The huge blisters on his posterior after the first lengthy test session just added injury to the insult.

As if to back up the team's position at the mercy of sponsors, at one point it looked as though Xaus wouldn't even travel to the flyaway races. Luckily for all concerned the sponsors were talked out of such drastic action.

Amidst all the doom and gloom there was a bright spot, however, and it came in the form of the gifted class rookie Elias. It was soon obvious he was to be the team's hope of salvation, and when he took an impressive ninth at Le Mans the smile had returned to Poncharal's face. However in a cruel twist of fate, the following day at tests Elias broke his wrist, condemning him to the sidelines for three races and seriously interrupting his forward progress. It was therefore some relief for

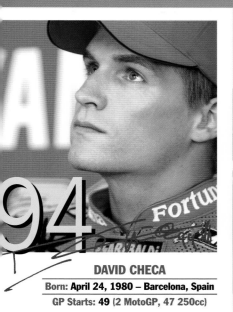

94

DAVID CHECA

Born: April 24, 1980 – Barcelona, Spain
GP Starts: 49 (2 MotoGP, 47 250cc)

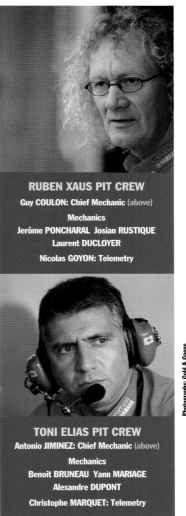

RUBEN XAUS PIT CREW

Guy COULON: Chief Mechanic (above)

Mechanics
Jerôme PONCHARAL Josian RUSTIQUE
Laurent DUCLOYER

Nicolas GOYON: Telemetry

TONI ELIAS PIT CREW

Antonio JIMINEZ: Chief Mechanic (above)

Mechanics
Benoit BRUNEAU Yann MARIAGE
Alexandre DUPONT

Christophe MARQUET: Telemetry

Photographs: Gold & Goose

the team when Elias bounced back into the limelight. Performances such as that at Turkey stood out. He had made his way up to fourth, only to run off the track, drop to ninth and then claw his way back up the field to pass Edwards on the run in to the line for an inspiring sixth.

Later in the season it became apparent that he was effectively tied to the sponsors and their money, and he became a hot property, courted by a number of teams. Unfortunately for Tech 3 they didn't have the pulling power of the Gresini Honda team and he was quickly snaffled away, much

to the disgust of Poncharal.

As such, next season Tech 3 is once again at the mercy of sponsors and Yamaha, and with the flight of Gauloises and Fortuna sponsorship, things have reached a critical point. Poncharal seemed likely to have only one rider next year, Britain's James Ellison, and no major sponsor for the time being. With the team also switching from Gallic partners Michelin to Dunlop, things could be about to get even more difficult... unless Ellison is capable of lifting the team as Elias did in 2005. *SM*

JIR KONICA MINOLTA HONDA

LUCA MONTIRON
Team Manager

MAKOTO TAMADA

Born: November 4, 1978 – Ehime, Japan
GP Starts: 47 (46 MotoGP, 1 250cc)
GP Wins: 2 (MotoGP)

JURGEN VAN DEN GOORBERGH

Born: December 29, 1969 – Breda, Holland
GP Starts: 165 (94 MotoGP/500cc, 71 250cc)

JIR KONICA MINOLTA HONDA RC211V

ENGINE

Type: 990cc 75.5-degree V5, close firing intervals, DOHC, four valves per cylinder

Power: more than 240 PS

Ancillaries: HRC electronics, NGK sparking plugs, all-active ride-by-wire EFI

Lubrication: Elf

Transmission: gear primary drive, multiplate dry slipper clutch, six-speed constant mesh cassette-type gearbox, DID chain

CHASSIS

Fabricated aluminium twin-beam

Weight: 148kg +

Dimensions: 2,050mm length, 1,440mm wheelbase, 1,140mm height, 645mm width

Fuel: 22 litres, Elf

Suspension: Front: Showa 47mm forks; Rear: Showa gas shock with linkage

Wheels: 16.5-inch Enkei

Tyres: Michelin

Brakes: Brembo carbon 314mm front, HRC steel 218mm rear

+44 (0)121 603 1554   © 2005 ADRIAN DEAN

Sponsors:
Konica-Minolta
Honda
HRC
Classeditori
Ecodem
Diadora
Flex Berik (Arlen Ness)

Technical Suppliers:
Vuemme
Michelin
GPR
Sinter
Eurodiesel
Beta
DID

GIANLUCA Montiron set up Japan Italy Racing (JiR) along with Tetsuo Iida, the former president of Honda Europe, at the beginning of 2005, after a season as one half of the Camel Honda garage. A very good season... Makoto Tamada was undoubtedly one of the riders of 2004, after guiding his Honda to two victories – in Brazil and more importantly in Japan.

In 2003, the team had run Tamada as a lone rider under Pramac sponsorship. With the Japanese ace continuing in 2005, the team was looked upon favourably by Honda when allotting their machines, and with the arrival of Konica Minolta, an excitingly different sponsor from the Japanese electronics sector, the team was set for great things in 2005.

It seems however that the most decisive factor in the team's success did not lie with the machinery or the backing of a multinational. It was the decision of Japanese tyre manufacturer Bridgestone to end their association with the Honda-backed outfit.

For several years the Honda factory had made no secret of its desire to take the MotoGP crown with a Japanese rider on Bridgestones. Hence the multi-million dollar development programme, which began away from the actual races in 2001, led by legendary tuner Erv Kanemoto, with Shinichi Ito and Nobuatsu Aoki as riders. This led to their first race wins with Tamada in 2004.

Unfortunately for Konica Minolta Honda, Bridgestone's decision to team up with Ducati in the off-season meant that their hand was forced as far as tyres were concerned. The Japanese tyre manufacturer could not produce a sufficient number of tyres to keep supplying Tamada. This meant they moved to Michelin, which in the team's official view meant that Tamada should be able to challenge at every round. For a team whose success was bred out of finding an apparent advantage in extreme conditions, it was a concern.

Tamada struggled to adapt to the French rubber, and the team was no longer as high up the pecking order for tyres as they had been with Bridgestone. The newly developed Michelins with an improved edge grip to match the Bridgestones took time to filter down to Tamada, whose unique style (shoulder brushing the kerb) they should have suited.

A fractured scaphoid for Tamada before the Portuguese GP, just the second on the calendar, compounded his problems, and he would not fully recover until his home round later in the year.

In the meantime his replacement Jurgen van den Goorbergh would take a creditable sixth in the wet in China, and 14th in France, with Tamada eventually returning at the Italian GP. Sixth remained the team's best until Tamada rode into a fine third in his home GP, showing glimpses of the kind of rider Honda had expected would provide more opposition to the dominant Rossi.

The season tailed off with a couple more top ten finishes, and 11th overall for the rider. Tamada did just enough to hang on to his seat for another year, but question marks over which brand of tyres the team will use next year will not help him to fulfil Honda's hopes.

Team boss Luca Montiron kept the faith. "With a bit more luck, next year Makoto will be able to keep in good physical shape, which will allow him to fight always with the fastest riders, because he was born to win." *SM*

MAKOTO TAMADA PIT CREW
Hirano YUTAKA: Chief Mechanic
Mechanics
Andreini GUGLIELMO Marco BONESSO
Maroco ROSA GASTALDO
Alessandro LA BARBA: Telemetry

TEAM STAFF
Iida TETSUO: Chairman

Gianluca MONTIRON: Managing Director/Team Manager

Giulio BERNARDELLE: Technical Director (below)

Jacopo ZODO: Commercial and Marketing Director

LUIS d'ANTIN
Team Director

44

ROBERTO ROLFO

Born: **March 23, 1980 – Turin, Italy**	
GP Starts: **119 (17 MotoGP, 102 250cc)**	
GP Wins: **3 (250cc)**	

PIT CREW: ROBERTO ROLFO

Andre LAUGIER: Chief Mechanic (above)
Mechanics
Martín ZABALA, Marco BALEIRON
Giuseppe OGNO

Photographs: Gold & Goose

D'ANTIN DUCATI DESMOSEDICI

ENGINE

Type: **989cc 90-degree V4, close firing intervals, DOHC, four valves per cylinder desmodromic valve gear**

Power: **more than 220 PS at 16,000 rpm**

Ancillaries: **Magneti Marelli electronics, NGK sparking plugs, EFI with automatic fast tickover**

Transmission: **gear primary drive, multiplate dry slipper clutch, six-speed constant mesh cassette-type gearbox, Regina chain**

CHASSIS

Multi-tube adjustable steel trellis, aluminium swing-arm

Weight: **148kg**

Fuel: **22 litres**

Suspension: Front: **Öhlins TT25 50mm forks;** Rear: **Öhlins ST45 gas shock with linkage**

Wheels: **16.5-inch Marchesini**

Tyres: **Dunlop**

Brakes: **Nissin carbon 305 or 320mm front, steel 220mm rear**

+44 (0)121 603 1554   © 2005 ADRIAN DEAN

Sponsors
Regione Piemonte
Pramac Group
Technical Suppliers:
Dunlop
AFAM
Regina
Öhlins
Beta
Speed Fiber
Arlen Ness
Brembo

TEAM STAFF

Luis D'ANTIN: Chairman and Managing Director

Andre LAUGIER: Technical Director

AT the end of last season, the D'Antin MotoGP team parted company with former World Superbike stars Neil Hodgson and Ruben Xaus, and the break-up was less than amicable. Money issues hung menacingly over the team's head, and Xaus even claimed that he remained unpaid for his efforts. With this in mind, the team may not quite have the appeal of others for some riders, but it still represents a good chance for them to get a first shot at MotoGP. As it proved for Roberto Rolfo in 2005.

The Spanish outfit has been a regular in MotoGP class for several years, having moved up from 250s once team owner Luis d'Antin had retired himself from racing, mainly running Yamaha machines. In fact, the team is extremely successful at national level in Spain, with the R1 and R6. So it was once upon a time in MotoGP, when Norick Abe spent four years riding for the team, and took two victories on board the YZR500.

With the arrival of the four-strokes, however, and the subsequent rise in costs of leasing engines from factories, coupled with the loss of long-term sponsor Antena 3 television, D'Antin has spent the last three seasons in desperate need of financial support. Before the ill-fated year of Hodgson and Xaus, the team ran a single Yamaha with Shinya Nakano on board, until like Abe before him, he realised he was surplus to factory requirements and signed for Kawasaki.

D'Antin took the split as an opportunity to make a switch in machine supplier, leasing the previous season's Ducati Desmosedicis. Xaus even managed to guide it onto the podium at Qatar. Ever opportune, the team also managed to snare the Pramac sponsorship money, once the engineering firm's deal with Honda came to an abrupt end. This meant they could stay afloat and field a single Ducati in 2005.

D'Antin recruited 25-year-old Italian Roberto Rolfo, with extra sponsorship coming from his regional government, and from Dunlop tyres. Rolfo's relationship with the Midlands tyre manufacturers was strong, after having done considerable development work in the 250 class, and they chose him to spearhead their project as they attempt to work their way up through the echelons of MotoGP once again.

As expected, given his means, Rolfo never stood out, but he had a season which epitomised his consistency as a rider, and the former 250cc championship runner-up impressed many with his tenacity and ever-positive attitude. Rolfo is a rare crasher, and if nothing else will have saved the team pots of money in terms of spare parts when compared to Xaus. A best of tenth came in the wet at Donington, and in total he collected eight other point-scoring rides, impressing particularly in dusty conditions in Qatar, where he took a notable 12th ahead of Byrne on the Honda and Xaus on the Yamaha.

D'Antin's aim was for a two-rider team next year on improved Ducatis, but there was no confirmation as to riders. *SM*

FRANCO BATTAINI

Born: July 22, 1972 – Brescia, Italy

GP Starts:139 (17 MotoGP, 122 250cc)

JAMES ELLISON

Born: September 19, 1980 – Kendal, Great Britain

GP Starts: 22 (MotoGP)

PETER CLIFFORD
Director of Racing

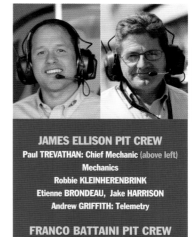

Photographs: Gold & Goose

JAMES ELLISON PIT CREW
Paul TREVATHAN: Chief Mechanic (above left)
Mechanics
Robbie KLEINHERENBRINK
Etienne BRONDEAU, Jake HARRISON
Andrew GRIFFITH: Telemetry

FRANCO BATTAINI PIT CREW
Gerard ROUSSEL: Chief Mechanic (above right)
Mechanics
Michael LARSSON, Jez WILSON
Jan LUYTEN: Telemetry

BLATA HARRIS-WCM

ENGINE

Type: 990cc in-line four, DOHC, four valves per cylinder

Power: 200 + PS

Ancillaries: Life Racing electronics, NGK sparking plugs, EFI

Lubrication: Motul

Transmission: gear primary drive, multiplate dry slipper clutch, six-speed constant mesh cassette-type gearbox

CHASSIS

Fabricated aluminium twin-beam

Weight: 155kg

Dimensions: 2,100mm length, 1,475mm wheelbase, 1,100mm height, 720mm width

Fuel: 22 litres, Elf

Suspension: Front: Öhlins 42mm forks; Rear: Öhlins TT44 gas shock with linkage

Wheels: 16.5-inch PVM

Tyres: Dunlop

Brakes: Brembo carbon 320mm front, PVM steel 210mm rear

+44 (0)121 603 1554   © 2005 ADRIAN DEAN

Sponsors
Blata
Harris Performance

Technical Suppliers
Dunlop
Sebimoto
Wiseco
MRA
BST Wheels

TEAM STAFF

Bob MacLEAN: Principal

Peter CLIFFORD: Managing Director

Francois CHARLOT: Technical Director

Jori NEVALAINEN: Research and Development

THE smallest team in racing had fallen on hard times after losing the Red Bull sponsorship and the satellite-team Yamahas at the end of 2002, but had refused to succumb to circumstances. Even when their self-built Yamaha R1-based MotoGP machine suffered serial disqualification in 2003, they soldiered on with development of their own engine parts, to return for a full 2004 season, albeit technically outclassed.

For 2005 they forged a new alliance with Czech Republic minibike factory Blata. Team manager Peter Clifford moved the team from Austria to a new base not far from Brno, and long before the end of last season Blata announced ambitious plans to build a V6 MotoGP machine, as well as a road scooter and a future full-size motorcycle. At first they hoped to have the V6 ready in time for pre-season testing. The next target was the early part of the season, the third was after the summer break for Brno.

Nothing more than drawings and promises ever materialised, however. One reason was that Blata was waiting for government funding; another was that they were now very fully occupied with legal actions, in an attempt to stop Chinese manufacturers flooding the market with cheap copies of their staple production models (themselves, said some, already cheap copies).

This left the team hamstrung for development, consigned to racing their already outclassed machines for yet another year. Their Dunlop tyres showed a significant improvement, but with horsepower levels and acceleration simply not in the same class as even the slowest of the other motorcycles, they were never going to be doing more than picking up scraps and hoping for bad weather. Often, the riders only had one bike each at their disposal.

The WCM team was still a slick outfit, belying their slender resources to achieve consistency and reliability. Francois Charlot was technical director, with crew chiefs Paul Trevathan and Gerard Roussel serving Ellison and Battaini respectively.

James Ellison (24) had joined the team as a substitute last year for six races, and was full time for 2005. The Kendall rider had come to prominence in British Superbikes, and although the machine was not competitive, it was a good opportunity for him to show his abilities on the world stage. He made the most of it, scoring one point in the second round, and finishing 13th in the rain in China. He scored again in Qatar and Australia, but his best result was eclipsed by team-mate Franco Battaini's 11th (albeit last) at the depleted Motegi race.

Battaini (32) was having a first season in MotoGP after racking up more than 120 starts in the 250 class.

WCM ended the season in a state of uncertainty. "Anything is possible, though further backing from Blata is dependent on government funding," said Clifford. Another distant possibility was use of the KTM engines. Given the experience of Proton with the Austrian firm, this might be regarded as clutching at straws.

MS

TEAM ROBERTS

KENNY ROBERTS
Team Principal

Photographs: Gold & Goose

67

SHANE BYRNE
Born: December 10, 1976 – Lambeth, Great Britain
GP Starts: 19 (MotoGP)
* NB: Also rode for Camel Honda

99

JEREMY McWILLIAMS
Born: April 4, 1964 – Carmoney, N.I.
GP Starts: 175 (117 MotoGP/500cc, 58 250cc)
GP Wins: 1 (250cc)

80

KURTIS ROBERTS
Born: November 17, 1978 – Turlock, USA
GP Starts: 21 (10 MotoGP, 11 250cc)

KR Powered by KTM/V5

KTM GP1 Engine

Type: 990cc, 75-degree V4, even firing intervals, DOHC, four valves per cylinder, pneumatic valve springs

Power: more than 240 PS, maximum engine speed – 17,000rpm

Ancillaries: EFI electronics, two injectors per cylinder, Champion sparking plugs

Lubrication: Agip, dry sump

KR V5 Engine

Type: 990cc 60 degree V5, close firing intervals, DOHC, four valves per cylinder

Power: Approx. 200 PS

Ancillaries: EFI electronics Lubrication: Mobil 1

Transmission: gear primary drive, multiplate dry slipper clutch, six-speed constant mesh cassette-type gearbox, Regina chain

Chassis: Machined and fabricated aluminium twin-beam

Weight: 148kg +

Fuel: 22 litres

Suspension: Front: Ohlins; Rear: Ohlins

Wheels: Marchesini **Tyres:** Michelin

Brakes: Nissin carbon front, Nissin steel rear

+44 (0)121 603 1554   © 2005 ADRIAN DEAN

KURTIS ROBERTS PIT CREW

Tom JOJIC: Chief Mechanic
Mechanics
Howard GREGORY   Craig CUMMINGS
Dave CRABTREE   Phil TRAVES
Brian HARDEN Telemetry
Nick DAVIS: Spares
Dave ELLIS: Transport
Colin MORRIS: Transport

Partners
Dunlop/Michelin
2D Telemetry
Regina
Vaz
Magical Racing
WRP Racing Products

TEAM STAFF

Kenny ROBERTS: Team Principal
Chuck AKSLAND: Team Manager
Charlie MOODY: Operations Manager
www.teamkr.com

Proton Team KR suffered a blow at the end of 2004, with the loss of the bulk of their sponsorship from Proton Cars, which brought the development programme of their England-made V5 engine to a close. In truth, this had always lagged behind the major factories, largely through a lack of comparable finance. Based in the heart of the F1 belt in England at Banbury, they had an advanced chassis, and no engine.

In fact, signs of salvation had come before the end of the season, when they had adapted their carved-from-solid chassis (designed by F1 guru John Barnard) to fit the V4 KTM MotoGP motor, which had been shelved when the Austrian company cancelled their own project midway through the previous year. Early tests showed the motor to be powerful and promising, and over the winter a complex deal was put in place, with the assistance of Dorna. Proton Team KR would be "Powered by KTM" for the forthcoming season.

The arrangement married several interests. The BBC wanted a British rider to add interest to their live race broadcasts. The team would have preferred old hand Jeremy McWilliams (41), but the BBC preferred the younger Shane "Shakey" Byrne (28) who had racked up nine starts in 2004 in a troubled season on the Aprilia. Dorna brokered this deal to the team, with the considerable sweetener of Michelin tyres. KTM would provide engines, which would

be developed during the year, and would finance certain elements of the project.

The constituents were there, but the balance was wrong, and in retrospect it showed from early in the season, with a string of poor results as the team struggled with an engine with quite the wrong power characteristics. They were also short on quantity, missing the Shanghai race altogether because they had run out of engines. The first and only engine upgrade came for the next race, the French GP, bringing with it reliability problems.

Byrne was having trouble adjusting to the bike and finishing races, with crashes and minor injuries conspiring with unreliability, as well as a lack of bottom-end and mid-range horsepower and throttle response, to make his life difficult.

He scored the team's only point of the year at the US GP, but already relations between Proton and KTM were souring. The bomb dropped before the Czech Republic GP – KTM announced they would no longer supply engines. Because of contract problems with Byrne (signed to KTM rather than the team), McWilliams had a single outing on the old V5 at the Brno race. They came back for one last race at Valencia, Kurtis Roberts (26) riding the V5 again.

The team was still seeking sponsorship for next year, but had secured an agreement with HRC to supply engines for one rider.

MS

MORIWAKI RACING

MAMORU MORIWAKI
Team Director

TOHRU UKAWA
Born: May 18, 1973 – Chiba, Japan
GP Starts: 127 (50 MotoGP, 77 250cc)
GP Wins: 5 (1 MotoGP, 4 250cc)
* NB: Also rode for Camel Honda

NAOKI MATSUDO
Born: July 25, 1973 – Chiba, Japan
GP Starts: 86 (1 MotoGP, 85 250cc)

MORIWAKI

+44 (0)121 603 1554   © 2005 ADRIAN DEAN

	TEAM	POINTS
1	GAULOISES YAMAHA TEAM	546
2	REPSOL HONDA TEAM	379
3	MOVISTAR HONDA MOTOGP	370
4	DUCATI MARLBORO TEAM	295
5	CAMEL HONDA	220
6	KAWASAKI RACING TEAM	150
7	FORTUNA YAMAHA TEAM	130
8	TEAM SUZUKI MOTOGP	126
9	KONICA MINOLTA HONDA	103
10	TEAM D'ANTIN - PRAMAC	25
11	BLATA WCM	14
12=	MORIWAKI	1
12=	TEAM ROBERTS	1

2005
MOTOGP CONSTRUCTORS' CHAMPIONSHIP

	CONSTRUCTOR	POINTS
1	YAMAHA	381
2	HONDA	341
3	DUCATI	202
4	KAWASAKI	126
5	SUZUKI	100
6	BLATA	13
7=	PROTON KR	1
7=	MORIWAKI	1

Moriwaki occupy a unique position in modern racing... an independent constructor using Honda engines, supplied by HRC. As the personal hobby horse of Mamoru Moriwaki, founder of the legendary Japanese tuning and racing firm bearing his name, the project relies on a long-standing national old-boy network.

The MotoGP bike is the latest in a spasmodic series of Moriwaki 250 and 500 machines over the years, used to test his sometimes unorthodox engineering ideas in design and construction. The four-stroke machine has appeared from time to time as a wild card entry since 2002, with little success achieved by riders including Olivier Jacque and Andrew Pitt.

The biggest change for this year was a switch from Dunlop to Michelin tyres. In other respects, the mainly conventional machine - aside from the tubular frame - remained as before.

Two riders exercised the machine in 2005, with Tohru Ukawa (31) claiming its first finish in the points when he was 15th in the streaming rain in China, in a break from testing duties in Japan for HRC.

Fellow-Japanese rider Naoki Matsudo (31) had less luck at Motegi, crashing out on the first lap.

This was the final year for the project, but it has set a new trend. HRC intended to continue the practice of supplying engines to independent chassis constructors, replacing Moriwaki next year with Team Roberts, and their British-built machine. In this way, the dream of following the F1 model, of independent constructors using manufacturers' engines, is being kept alive.   *MS*

casey stoner

dani pedrosa

jorge lorenzo

hector barbera

sebastian porto

hiroshi aoyama

250cc: TALENT RISES TO THE TOP

WHAT is the point of the 250 class? With MotoGP going four-stroke, and dwindling support from the major factories, it seemed to be heading for an outside window, to leave a suicide note.

Several things happened in 2005 to stem this movement, with a renewed commitment (until 2012) from manufacturers to keep providing the increasingly irrelevant machines, and a massive blood transfusion of riding talent and vitality. At the same time, the class's role as a training ground for MotoGP, once thought to have been ceded to the four-stroke Superbikes, was substantially reinforced.

The new blood came firstly thanks to the new maximum age limit in the 125 class, forcing a number of seasoned veterans to move up (and in some cases return) to the class. At the same time, a corps of talented 125 teenagers from the opposite end of the age scale stormed into 250 racing, on a fast track towards MotoGP.

The numbers tell the story. Of a permanent entry of 30, no less than 12 were class rookies, only a handful of whom did not have previous 125 experience, and some of whom (like 125 champion Dovizioso and several close 2004 rivals) were very serious contenders. Two more class newcomers – rising Australian Casey Stoner and former 125 Champion Roberto Locatelli – were returning to 250s after dropping back down to the smallest class.

There had also been some notable losses from last year's line up. Race winners Toni Elias and Fonsi Nieto had both gone, the former to MotoGP, the latter to a

dire attempt at World Superbikes. One-time challenger Franco Battaini was also up to MotoGP; former champion Manuel Poggiali down to 125s, along with lesser lights Hector Faubel and Alex Baldolini. Johan Stigefelt had also gone.

There was a certain amount of factory backing from Aprilia and to a lesser extent Honda, but it remained a class of haves and have-nots. But the front group was boosted; while the privateer battle for the lower points-scoring positions remained a secondary highlight.

The 30-strong entry list was dominated again by Aprilia, their seasoned V-twin in all its many variations providing motive power for fully half the riders. Honda had a ten-strong portfolio, while Yamaha's presence had dwindled to an extremely low-key two.

There were two new marques on the list, however. Fantic arrived, with their own new V-twin in its shakedown season with a two-strong team; while KTM were entered... though in fact their motorcycle would not be ready until almost halfway through the year.

APRILIA

As ever, the difference in quality between the best and the worst of the 15 Aprilia V-twins was very large; as ever, the exact specifications of a wide range of mix-and-match machines also varied considerably. The factory continued the policy of favouring some teams with hand-me-down parts throughout the season, whether by contract or to help a promising effort; and this engendered some horse-trading throughout the field.

What was certain was that the official factory team,

MS Aprilia Corse, fielded the state-of-the-art motorcycle, and the best always went to new top rider Alex de Angelis (21 at the first race, from San Marino), up from his position as apprentice last year, filling the gap left by the disappointing Poggiali. In turn, Simone Corsi (18), another class rookie up from 125s, took that role, in the same team livery.

There were several other high-level Aprilia teams, the most notable by results being the Carrera Sunglasses squad run out of Italy by former racer Lucio Cecchinello. The rider line-up was strong – the veteran former 125 champion Roberto Locatelli (30), back for another try at 250s; and the rising Australian Casey Stoner (19), a protégé of Cecchinello.

Hardly less senior was the Spanish Aprilia Aspar squad, in authoritative Repsol colours, and run by former 80cc and 125cc multiple champion Jorge "Aspar" Lorenzo. Two seasoned riders joined forces. Argentinean Sebastian Porto (26) was the most experienced 250 rider on the grid, with 140 starts in the class by the end of the season. Frenchman Randy de Puniet (24) had switched teams but not machines. It was a strong pairing.

It was hard to grade the quality of machinery for the rest, although again one team traditionally was especially favoured... the experienced Italian Campetella squad, in their virulent pink-and-yellow livery. Rider-wise, they were not so strong, fielding the two bottom scorers from last year, Taro Sekiguchi (29, former Japanese and European champion) and 20-year-old Italian Alex Baldolini, in his third season. Sekiguchi ran into trouble at pre-season tests, crashing heavily, and was replaced in

alex de angelis

randy de puniet

chaz davies

yuki takahashi

anthony west

andrea dovisioso

mid-season by Hugo Marchand (23, from France).

British hope Chaz Davies (18) missed out on a Campetella ride because of a want of sponsorship, and stayed with the Aprilia Germany team for another season. As team-mate he had Colombian newcomer Martin Cardenas (23), in his first GP season after winning the Spanish 600cc championship last year.

The last two-rider team was French – the SCRAB squad, fielding Sylvain Guintoli (22) and rookie Gregory Leblanc (19), the former set for a strong season at privateer level; the latter for replacement for the final races by compatriot Erwan Nigon (21), and for the last race by Mathieu Gines (16).

Three Italian one-rider teams ran with class rookies who had left 125 racing because of the age limit. All had been strong runners in that class. The Italian Team Nocable.It ran German Steve Jenkner (28). The Abruzzo Racing Team fielding Andrea Ballerini (31) and Matteoni Racing running fellow-Italian Mirko Giansanti (28).

HONDA

Honda's RS250R machine comes in two guises: the production version, and the HRC-development model, which carries a "W" (for "Works") suffix, and is a very different motorcycle. Of course, there is room to move within those categories, and it was obviously the case that Pedrosa's title-winning motorcycle was quite a bit more "W" than the RS250R-W run by (for example) class rookie Barbera.

The top team was again the Spain-based Telefónica MoviStar Honda outfit managed by Alberto Puig, with seasoned crew chiefs Mike Leitner and Gilles Bigot (formerly with Alex Crivillé) in the pits.

Leitner worked with defending champion Dani Pedrosa (19, in his second 250 year, from Spain), unquestioned peak of the pit pyramid. Favoured in every possible way, Pedrosa would repay that privilege in full. His team-mate was again Japanese Hiroshi Aoyama (23) who, although considered an HRC favourite for a future MotoGP career, quit at year's end to move to KTM instead for 2006.

Two other teams ran with R-W models.

The Spanish Fortuna Honda team was established in the class, fielding Elias and Rolfo last year. They too had a couple of class rookies, who were on the same railway line as Dovizioso. Spaniards Hector Barbera (18) and Jorge Lorenzo (17), with four and three 2004 125 race wins respectively. Barbera was second overall; the younger Lorenzo fourth, and both were being groomed for the big time.

Team Scot, from Italy, had come up from the 125 class along with their title winner Andrea Dovizioso. Still only 19, the Italian was on a career express train. His companion was a series rookie, Japan's Yuki Takahashi (20), fifth in Japan last year.

Production machines were chosen by three privateer teams, all of whom had HRC development parts. Spain-based Wurth Honda ran the experienced Alex Debon (29, from Spain), and 26-year-old Czech Republic rider Radomil Raus. The German Kiefer-Bos-Castrol squad fielded one rider, their countryman Dirk Heidolf (28). Holland's Arie Molenaar Racing ran the Czech Republic's Jakub Smrz.

YAMAHA

Yamaha had no direct involvement, but the long-standing Germany-based UGT Kurz team continued to run with the marque, at a very low level, and with a number of riders, all but one rookies. They started out with Hungarian Gabor Rizmayer (23) and Franz Aschenbrenner (18, from Germany), for the first race only. He was replaced by 28-year-old Swede Frederic Watz, for three races. Then came another two Swedes, Nicklas Cajbac (19) and Andreas Martensson (21), as well as Bulgarian Alexander Todorov (20), who also had a short tenure. France's Erwan Nigon also ran for the team, finishing the season with Cajbac on the other machine.

FANTICS/KTM

The new bikes in the pits were V-twin Fantics, in their first season, with former 125 champion Arnaud Vincent (30) and Gabriele Ferro (16, from Italy). In a year of inevitable teething troubles, neither finished in the points.

This was not so for the other new marque, KTM. Rider Anthony West (23) had been kept waiting until Donington Park before the bike was ready, but finished second in the wet. Meltdown was approaching, however, and the new bike's lack of reliability and propensity for seizing meant rider and team parted company at Qatar, in between practice and the race.

thomas luthi

mika kallio

marco simoncelli

gabor talmacsi

mattia pasini

julian simon

125cc: VARIETY APLENTY

Aprilia dominated the smallest class also in terms of numbers, with 15 out of the 36-strong grid on the Italian motorcycles. Another 12 chose Hondas, again with a wide range of machine levels in all cases.

Some teams for both marques had factory help – but they were private teams at heart. The remainder of the entry list was made up of something closer to full factory teams – very much so in the case of the three-rider KTM squad, slightly less for the four-strong Derbi-Gilera stable, and likewise for the pair of Malagutis.

The introduction this year of a maximum age limit of 27 forced out a number of old hands, and opened the doors to a flood of no less than 16 rookies, almost half the field. The oldest rider at the start of the year was 26-year-old Fabrizio Lai; there were six 15-year-old recruits entered for the first race of the year, with more to come during the year.

The class was thriving.

APRILIA

There were three teams sharing the top of the Aprilia tree.

The most successful was to be the Italy-based Noca-ble.It squad, fielding 18-year-old Marco Simoncelli in his

third season, and ready to hit the big time. His team-mate was Joan Olive (20, from Spain).

Jorge Martinez had a two-rider Master Aspar team, with riders Sergio Gadea (20) and Hector Faubel (21), both from Spain, the latter down from 250s as a class rookie. Martinez also ran a junior team, with two more Spanish youngsters, Jordi Carchano (20) and Julian Miralles (16), a rookie whose father made a name in the smallest classes in the Eighties.

The other top team was Italian, with the alliterative title of Totti Top Sport, and Mattia Pasini as lead rider. The 19-year-old Italian was in his second season, and would make a strong showing. His rookie team-mate, Manuel Hernandez (20), was from Spain.

The experienced Semprucci team from Italy, back from a year running Malaguti, ran German Dario Giuseppetti (20), and Czech rookie Karel Abraham (15).

The final two-rider squad was Team Hungary, with Hungarian rider Imre Toth (19) joined by Swiss rookie Vincent Braillard (19).

Aprilia numbers were completed by three more rookies in one-rider teams – Italians Lorenzo Zanetti (17, Fontana Sport), Andrea Iannone (15, Abruzzo Racing Team) and Raffael de Rosa (18, Matteoni Racing).

fabrizio lai

moyoshi yama

hector faubel

sergio gadea

juan olive

alvaro bautista

manuel poggiali

mike di meglio

pablo nieto

HONDA

The top team, with HRC support, was the Racing World team, where ex-rider Gino Borsoi, foul of the age limit, had slipped into the role of team chief. He replaced himself with ex-Gilera rider Fabrizio Lai (26), and retained French rider Mike di Meglio (17). They were a strong pair.

Kit parts went to four riders – the most notable turning out to be Thomas Luthi (18), the Swiss farm boy in this third full season, after missing much of last year injured.

The Italian Angaia Racing team had a pair of rookies, Japan's Toshihisa Kuzuhara (24) and Italian Federico Sandi (15), also with kit parts; as was Dutch rider Raymond Schouten (20).

The Seedorf RC3 team, hobbyhorse of Dutch footballer Clarence Seedorf, was back, with Spaniard Alvaro Bautista (20) joined by countryman Aleix Espargaro (15), in his first season.

Angel Rodriguez (19) was in a one-rider Galicia team; Ajo Motosport ran a pair of rookies, Alexis Masbou (17) and Tomoyoshi Koyama (22). German newcomer Sandro Cortese (15) rode in the Kiefer-Bos-Castrol Honda

KTM

A full factory team in a swathe of orange, KTM's squad was headed by redoubtable Austrian veteran tuner and entrant Harald Bartol, joined in the pit by former 500-class and MotoGP guru Warren Willing.

Their rider line-up was three-strong.

Mika Kallio (22) had joined KTM mid-season in 2003, and though still awaiting his first race win, was poised for a strong season.

His team-mate (and erstwhile title challenger) was Hungarian Gabor Talmacsi (23), in his fifth 125 season and off a Malaguti last year, headed for a chequered season.

The third KTM rider was also new to the machine, rising Spaniard Julian Simon (18), in his third season

MALAGUTI

The two-rider team run by former racer Olivier Liegeois took a step backwards this year in terms of riders after scoring points last year with Talmacsi. They started the year with two rookies, Italian Michele Pirro (18) and German Sascha Hommel (15), but neither lasted the year,

and by the end they had the more experienced Gioele Pellino (21, Italy) and rookie Jules Cluzel (16, France) on their machines.

DERBI/GILERA

Differently named but technically identical, the Derbi and Gilera teams also shared senior team management, in the urbane Italian Giampiero Sacchi. Derbi had a Spanish sponsor and address; Gilera likewise, but Italian.

Each had one experienced rider, and one less seasoned. For Derbi, the senior of their Spanish pairing was Pablo Nieto (24), returning to the team with which his father Angel won the first of his 13 titles in the early 1970s. His team-mate was rookie Nicolas Terol (16).

Gilera regained the services of Manuel Poggiali (22), who had won them the title in 2001. In the interim the San Marino rider had won the 250 title on an Aprilia, followed last year by a dismal season in defence. Now he was back where he started, and among friends.

His team-mate Lukas Pesek (19, from the Czech Republic) joined Gilera from Honda for his second full season.

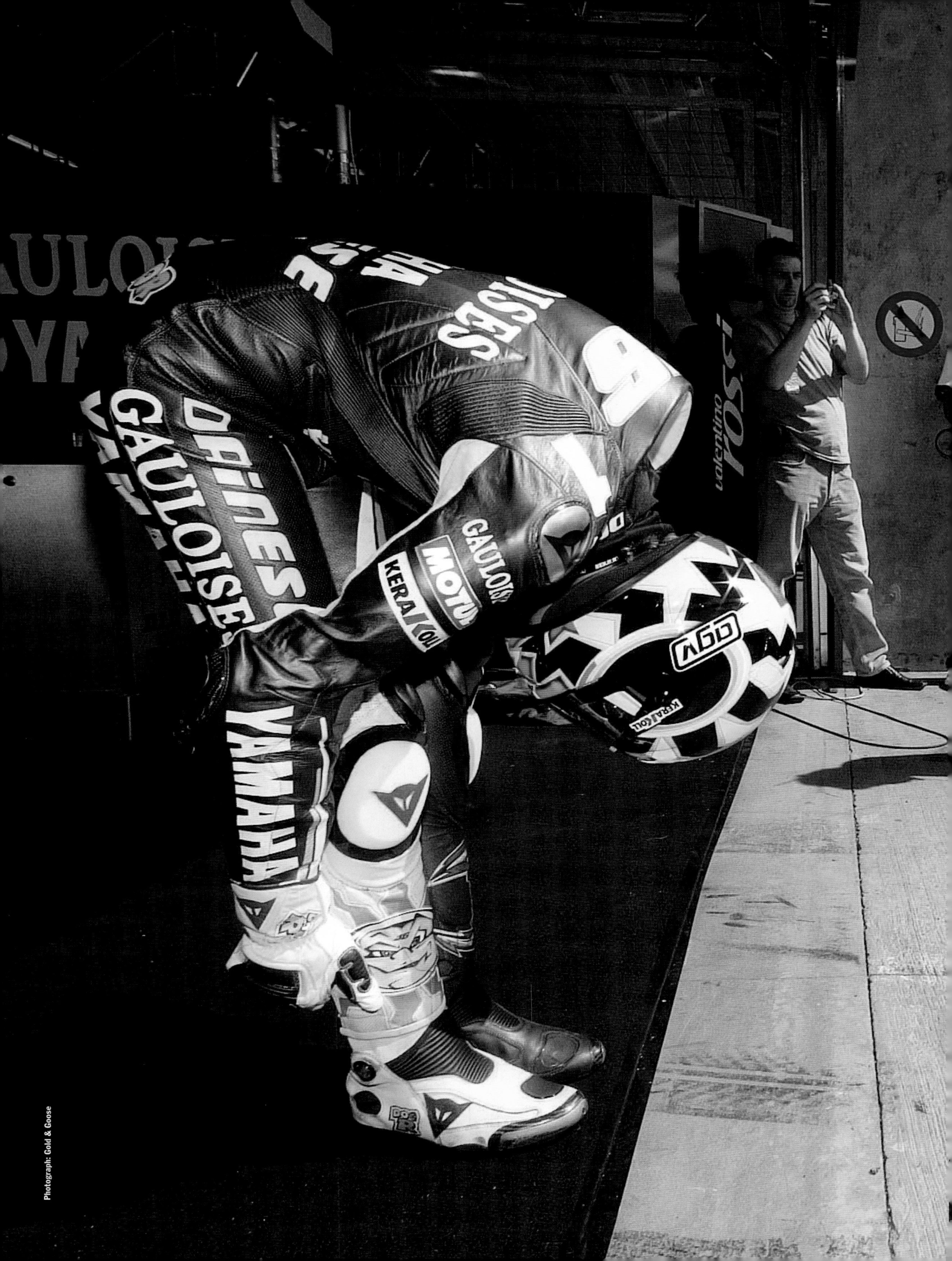

Photograph: Gold & Goose

GRANDS PRIX
2005

FIM WORLD CHAMPIONSHIP • ROUND 1

SPANISH GP
JEREZ

**Wounded shoulder or wounded pride?
Gibernau was winged in more ways than
one.**
Photograph: Gold & Goose

Above: Point of contact in last corner drama. Sequence shows the collision of trajectories; Inset above shows where Gibernau ended up.

Right: Rossi unrepentant. "It was a race of motorcycles."
Photographs: Gold & Goose

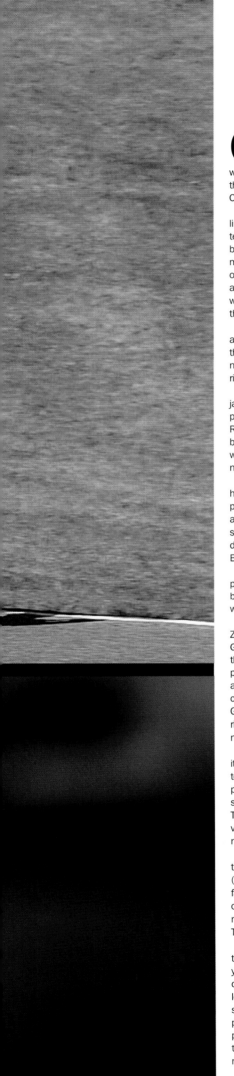

ONE undesired consequence of the extended winter testing ban was pre-season fatigue. All the factory teams had followed and several had exceeded a rigorous round-the-world schedule. It started on January 23 at Sepang, returning there, then Phillip Island and Qatar before the Spanish climax at Catalunya and Jerez, with the first race two weeks later.

Another was few surprises. By the time the MotoGP field lined up for the first single Saturday one-hour qualifying session, test-wearied riders eager to get racing, the order had already been established. From the bottom: Proton's last-minute agreement meant they had tested only perfunctorily; WCM were still on the old in-line fours, the promised V6 delayed again; Suzuki and Kawasaki had both shown clear improvement (the latter with a still very new Big Bang engine); while Ducati had shown a threat to return to form.

The main contenders were still Yamaha and Honda, the former as much by the grace of Rossi as by technical prowess: although the latest M1 had major detail developments, they were not yet necessarily improvements. And Honda, humiliated by a superior rider on an inferior machine in 2004, had come back flying.

Testing had also warned of narrower horizons. Already at the jamboree Catalunyan test – the one with all the TV and trumpets and a BMW M1 as the first prize of the year– Gibernau and Rossi had emerged as the cream, Biaggi's first falter there had been followed by an inexplicable further slump at Jerez tests a week later. He would be complaining about hypersensitive corner entry for the year to come.

Gibernau had won the televised 40-minute dash-for-the-hatchback; accomplished actor Rossi engaged in a new form of pantomime on his thwarted slow-down lap – punching the air in a gesture of frustration. The grand master really was having something of a struggle getting the new M1 balanced and handling right. This would persist for two or three races to come. But it wouldn't stop Valentino.

Nor would Gibernau, trying to close the entry to the final hairpin bend on the crucial final corner of the last lap – only to be barged firmly into the gravel, in a move that set the tone for the whole season to come. He had led all but three of the 27 laps.

Nor yet would a personal letter from FIM President Francesco Zerbi, in the following week. Addressed privately to Rossi and Gibernau, couched in the Italian lawyer's preferred baroque style, this rather vaguely enjoined the pair of them to keep their competitive instincts in check – so far and no further – without actually accusing anyone of doing anything wrong. "In the same circumstances, I would do it again," was Rossi's response; that of Gibernau's team less jaunty. Fausto Gresini was angry that both riders were dealt with equally, when clearly Gibernau had been innocent; Zerbi irate that a private letter had been made public.

It was not so easy to attach blame, but Race Direction viewed it from several angles, including closed-circuit TV, and, according to chief Paul Butler: "We all decided it was a racing incident." No protests were lodged, nor was any reprimand considered necessary. This was sharply at variance with the disqualification of Tamada at Motegi in 2003, in a similar incident with the same victim, and would have echoes at Motegi this year too. These matters, insisted Butler, are decided "case by case".

The crowd were clear whose side they were on, however. On the slowdown lap they chanted at Valentino: "Hijo de puta" (Son of a whore). "I probably lost 40 percent of my Spanish fans today," he grinned later. But, as he added: "It was a race of motorcycles." And the final truth was clear: Rossi had outmanoeuvred, out-fought, out-barged and out-raced the home hero. This set the bar for the whole year to come.

One important question, as the field assembled for the first time minus Aprilia, concerned the future of MotoGP. Here one year before, the MSMA had announced that from 2007, engine capacity would be cut from 990cc to 900cc. Now, with less less than two years to go, the MSMA were reconsidering, with something closer to 750 of 800cc more realistic. New MSMA president, HRC boss Suguru Kanazawa ("It was my turn to be president") explained HRC's point of view. "We want no limit to the machines. MotoGP is an experimental field, and displacement and weight should be the only limits." In any case, he

continued, it would only take a year or two for power output to rise again, current MotoGP engines being relatively soft compared with F1. Higher tuning would make the bikes harder to ride, but increasingly sophisticated electronics would ameliorate this, he predicted. Taken to the logical conclusion, this means any reduction in engine size, far from a safety measure, is a charter for high technology.

The riders already had a foretaste of more mettlesome engines thanks to the new fuel tank regulations, down by two litres to 22. This meant leaner injection settings, leading in turn to snappier throttle response. The Honda riders barely noticed it – most of the problems had been tuned out immediately after the first test, according to Hayden; though Gibernau allowed that the MotoGP bikes were becoming more like the old 500 two-strokes, "which personally I like". Rossi and his fellow Yamaha riders obviously had more of a problem, particularly coming onto the throttle mid-corner. "There is a little delay – it is more aggressive on the throttle. They want to limit speeds and performance for safety, but maybe this is more unsafe," he said.

A similar sensation, for different reasons, prevailed at Ducati. At Catalunya their new engine-braking system had appeared for the first time – replacing the slipper clutch with what sounded like a freewheel device. Designer Filippo Prezioso said it used "a standard clutch ... with some magic", but details were closely guarded. This system also saved fuel, bypassing the throttle-blipping phase completely. Corner entries sounded as if the riders were doing plug chops; the key was how seamlessly the clutch could re-engaged when the throttle was re-opened. Not smoothly enough for Checa, who crashed at the tests and was still nursing a dislocated shoulder. Ducati insisted they both use it all the same ... and then Capirossi fell heavily in Saturday morning practice. Clever the system might be, friendly to the riders it was not. It was dropped on race morning, on the rather flimsy grounds that it caused chain stretch on starting ... and that was the last that was heard of it this year.

MOTOGP RACE – 27 laps

Gibernau and Rossi were still avoiding eye contact at the post-practice conference, where the latter had seized pole in the dying minutes. Rossi credited Michelin's latest qualifying tyres, saying: "My bike works very well when the grip is high," and adding: "Tyre choice will be very critical;" to which Gibernau responded testily: "When is tyre choice not critical?" He had led all three "free practice" sessions, and remained on top until Rossi's sudden and emphatic access to the front. This lent weight to the theory that Rossi had been sandbagging.

Melandri was on the front row in his first outing on a Honda – a quick adaptation; the second saw Nakano in the middle, again exceeding expectations of the Kawasaki, and top Bridgestone runner. Hayden was faster, Capirossi slower – heroic after his heavy crash and cracked ankle bones, and more proof of the merits of Bridgestone's qualifiers and Costa's painkillers. Tamada, Barros and Bayliss were on row three; then Hopkins behind Hofmann's Kawasaki, a disappointing start for Suzuki. Roberts was down in 14th; Edwards way off form, 15th fastest and 1.75 seconds down on his new team-mate's pole time.

Race morning warm-up brought a frisson as Rossi slid off, blaming a mechanical or electronic malfunction, but he was unhurt and ready to go again for the race.

After mixed and mainly windy weather in practice, race day was sunny but gusty and dusty. Gibernau was first off the line, Rossi pushed past into the first corner but was wide at the exit, then lost another place to Hayden further round the lap. Melandri a close fourth was heading Nakano, Bayliss, Capirossi and the gang; Xaus crashed exiting the last corner, rejoining, pitting for running repairs, then again for a ride-through penalty (he'd broken the speed limit first time through). No home GP joy.

Melandri hung with the first three only for a while, as Rossi regained second at Dry Sack hairpin on lap five. Now Gibernau put the hammer down, gaining an advantage of almost a second in three laps, but Rossi closed up remorselessly, faster round the more technical sections. Hayden was losing ground,

Top: Shane Byrne made a shaky two-lap debut on the Proton KTM.

Top right: Elias, getting to grips in his first 990 race.

Above: Edwards leads Biaggi, Checa and Nakano in qualifying.

Right: A problem shared, a problem halved? Independent team owners Kenny Roberts and Bob MacLean (Blata WCM) confer.
Photographs: Gold & Goose

up to almost two seconds adrift, but he was closing again when he fell under braking for the hairpin on lap 20. He was unrepentant. "I won't apologize for trying hard and wanting to learn. If every time the pace gets hot I just back off and cruise home in third I'm never going to make that next step," he said a week later in Portugal.

As the race drew on, the front end had a familiar appearance, Rossi hounding Gibernau, waiting his chance. It came at the last hairpin at the end of lap 24; Gibernau said later he had let him through, so as to position himself for a last-lap attack. The stop-watch made this plausible, for the Honda started the last lap only three tenths behind the Yamaha.

Rossi was right on the limit. And then over it, as his bike jinked under braking for Dry Sack hairpin, and he ran wide past the apex. This had not been Gibernau's planned passing point, but he didn't have much choice, and the pair banged fairings at least twice as Sete made sure he retained the lead through the next corners. Rossi was breathing down his neck through the Nieto double-rights.

Then followed a masterpiece of tactics, carried through with sheer aggression. Anybody who thought Rossi was any sort of angel was now emphatically disabused.

There remained two sweeping 90-degree right-handers, taken in one smooth line, before a short dash to the acute final left-hand hairpin. Rossi ran inside and slightly ahead of Gibernau into the first of the rights, but there was room enough for Gibernau to sneak back inside of him and ahead again on the exit. The consequence was to put Gibernau too far to the right, however, and tight on the entry for the second part. As a result, his exit was slightly compromised. For Rossi, the opposite was true. His slower first corner gave him a better run through the second. He emerged going faster than Gibernau… by enough to squeeze inside and alongside under braking. He wasn't ahead, but there was little choice for Gibernau. He could have stayed wide, and possibly cut inside on the exit. Possibly. Instead he tried to hold his line only to get hit from behind, and

carried out all the way onto the grass and thence the gravel. He stayed wheels down, and crossed the line in a distant, pained and disgruntled second place.

An epic start to the season.

And a humbling experience for many of the others... big names condemned to a side-show scrap for the places.

Melandri was a lone third, promoted by Hayden's headlong dive. Behind him Nakano held on valiantly as Checa closed steadily from eighth on lap one, accompanied by Tamada. They'd both taken fast-starter Bayliss by lap seven, and were closing on the Kawasaki, at this stage two seconds ahead. Barros was also moving through rapidly from a slow getaway, past Bayliss by half distance, leaving the Australian now awaiting the arrival of Edwards.

There was some shuffling among this lot, a collision between Tamada and Checa losing the latter several places, as it jolted his shoulder injury. Barros led them as they caught Nakano on lap 15, Tamada up close, Bayliss hanging on, then Edwards heading Checa, Biaggi and Hofmann. Only Barros got ahead of Nakano's precisely ridden Kawasaki at the finish, then Bayliss came back, a second adrift.

Biaggi had managed to make some improvement over the weekend, after qualifying 16th and finishing the first lap one place lower. Still complaining of corner entry problems, he gained a place as Tamada faded in the closing laps. Seventh was better than it might have been for Honda's troubled new top dog.

Tamada was busy with Edwards at the end, two more disappointing performances; Checa was off the back of the pair, well ahead of Hofmann.

Elias could be pleased with 12th first time out on a 990; injured Capirossi soldiered on to 13th; Hopkins's softer tyre choice left him losing ground at the end; Rolfo took the last point in his class debut, ahead of the WCMs and two-stopper Xaus. Roberts retired from 14th before half-distance with a throttle software glitch. Byrne's Proton KTM lasted two laps before the return of a misfire sent him pitwards.

250 cc RACE – 26 laps

The smaller classes used the old system, free practice in the mornings, timed on both Friday and Saturday afternoons. Pedrosa and Porto disputed it throughout, the champion holding the upper hand, class returnee Stoner close in third, and de Puniet completing three Aprilias on the front row. Barbera was on row two; fellow ex-125 rookies Lorenzo and Dovizioso led row three.

The 250s faced a gusty start; Pedrosa blew strong and steady throughout, leading into the first corner and all the way to the flag. If there was to be an end to processional 250 racing, this would not be it.

Porto stayed close and pushed for as long as he could, but after four laps the gap started to stretch steadily, to be more than a second after nine laps and two seconds by half distance. Pedrosa was coping with the hazardous crosswinds; Porto had another consideration, a "strange noise from my engine", and from then on he settled for second, and Pedrosa was in control of a gap that remained constant to the finish.

Main picture: Barros, Tamada and Bayliss close on Nakano – but only the Brazilian would get past.

Inset below: Racing's craziest fans enjoy a panoramic view.
Photographs: Gold & Goose

Aoyama and Barbera had started well, heading de Angelis on lap one. The younger rider was soon losing places; Aoyama hung on a bit longer, but succumbed to a forceful de Angelis on lap five. By then, de Puniet was ahead of both, in a brief blaze of glory. Seventh at the end of lap one, he set fastest lap fifth time round and was soon hounding Porto. He never did get past, and fell victim to the dusty track on lap 12, slithering off in somewhat familiar style.

Stoner had been carving through hardly less impressively. Eleventh after lap one, he was past de Angelis on lap eight. Now he inherited third, five seconds behind Porto. That lasted only two laps, and he too crashed out on the clearly treacherous surface, another rostrum possibility lost. "I don't know why it happened," he said later.

De Angelis was now coming under mild pressure from a re-formed pack led by Aoyama, until he and Barbera had a collision at Turn One starting lap nine. He fell, Barbera rejoined in tenth. De Angelis watched Stoner fall ahead of him at half distance, inheriting a now unthreatened rostrum spot.

Behind him, 125 champion Dovizioso's yellow Honda was heading Lorenzo's similar bike; another older 125 refugee Locatelli behind, Debon losing ground behind. Barbera was coming back, however, past his erstwhile rivals and finally taking fifth from team-mate Lorenzo on the last corner, Dovizioso less than a second ahead.

Locatelli was a lone seventh from Debon. Two more ex-125 men, Corsi and Giansanti, were ninth and tenth. Ten seconds behind, Chaz Davies emerged the victor of a three-strong privateer battle, with Hungarian rookie Rous behind, after Smrz crashed out on the last lap.

125 cc RACE – 23 laps

The first race of the day started in high winds, with dust billowing over the track. Marco Simoncelli was on pole, from Pasini, Luthi and Lai, in the new reduced-age "125 Lite" class.

Talmacsi's orange KTM led for the first half-lap. Pasini took over by the end of it, then Luthi after two more, for a spell. This was over the line… elsewhere on the track they were back and forth and blown all over the place. When Kallio took the lead over the line for the first time on lap seven, there was a pack of seven riders pulling clear.

By half distance, Nieto and Lai also took turns at heading the gang, with paint being freely swapped all around the track. This was a good time for Luthi and Simoncelli to start drawing away slowly but steadily, ahead of the perils of the pack.

They had gained more than 2.5 seconds when Luthi suddenly slowed and pulled to the side, his race run. From then on Simoncelli was alone, and still 1.4 seconds clear at the flag.

Pasini and Talmacsi had lost touch with the battle, leaving Nieto, Lai and Kallio hard at it, until Nieto slithered off at the last hairpin with three laps to go, climbing back quickly to save 12th place.

Lai was in second… until a few yards from the end. Kallio dived under him into the last hairpin to claim the place by a tenth of a second.

Pasini held fourth from a pressing Talmacsi; five seconds back former champion Poggiali (Gilera) eventually prevailed over Faubel.

Top left: De Angelis served notice, with third.

Top right: Pedrosa made his presence felt from the start – pulling away from Porto and de Puniet.

Above left: First-time winner Simoncelli (58) looks for a way past Lai.

Above: The 125 race started in a haze of dust.

Opposite: Melandri was overjoyed with a podium in his first Honda race.
Photographs: Gold & Goose

CIRCUITO DE JEREZ

PELUQUI
EXPO 92
FERRARI
ANGEL NIETO
MICHELIN
CURVA
DRY SACK
DUCADOS
SITO PONS

CIRCUIT LENGTH: 2.745 miles/4.423 km

GRAN PREMIO MARLBORO DE ESPAÑA

10 APRIL 2005 • FIM WORLD CHAMPIONSHIP ROUND 1

MotoGP

27 laps, 74.196 miles/119.421 km

Pos.	Rider (Nat.)	No.	Machine	Laps	Time & speed
1	Valentino Rossi (I)	46	Yamaha	27	45m 43.156s 97.383 mph/ 156.722 km/h
2	Sete Gibernau (E)	15	Honda	27	45m 51.787s
3	Marco Melandri (I)	33	Honda	27	46m 01.616s
4	Alex Barros (BR)	4	Honda	27	46m 10.094s
5	Shinya Nakano (J)	56	Kawasaki	27	46m 10.815s
6	Troy Bayliss (AUS)	12	Honda	27	46m 11.665s
7	Max Biaggi (I)	3	Honda	27	46m 13.774s
8	Makoto Tamada (J)	6	Honda	27	46m 20.043s
9	Colin Edwards (USA)	5	Yamaha	27	46m 20.764s
10	Carlos Checa (E)	7	Ducati	27	46m 22.834s
11	Alex Hofmann (D)	66	Kawasaki	27	46m 25.439s
12	Toni Elias (E)	24	Yamaha	27	46m 38.613s
13	Loris Capirossi (I)	65	Ducati	27	46m 45.528s
14	John Hopkins (USA)	21	Suzuki	27	47m 02.502s
15	Roberto Rolfo (I)	44	Ducati	27	47m 16.763s
16	James Ellison (GB)	77	Blata	26	46m22.019s
17	Franco Battaini (I)	27	Blata	26	46m 42.560s
18	Ruben Xaus (E)	11	Yamaha	24	46m 04.511s
	Nicky Hayden (USA)	69	Honda	20	DNF
	Kenny Roberts (USA)	10	Suzuki	11	DNF
	Shane Byrne (GB)	67	Proton KR	2	DNF

Fastest lap: Rossi, 1m 40.596s, 98.353 mph/158.284 km/h (record).

Previous record: Valentino Rossi, I (Honda), 1m 42.788s, 96.256 mph/154.909 km/h (2003).

Event best maximum speed: Melandri, 181.4 mph/291.9 km/h (qualifying practice).

Qualifying: 1 Rossi, 1m 39.419s; 2 Gibernau, 1m 39.915s; 3 Melandri, 1m 40.179s; 4 Hayden, 1m 40.465s; 5 Nakano, 1m 40.542s; 6 Capirossi, 1m 40.648s; 7 Tamada, 1m 40.707s; 8 Barros, 1m 40.720s; 9 Bayliss, 1m 40.774s; 10 Hofmann, 1m 40.812s; 11 Hopkins, 1m 40.825s; 12 Checa, 1m 40.948s; 13 Elias, 1m 41.029s; 14 Roberts, 1m 41.058s; 15 Edwards, 1m 41.176s; 16 Biaggi, 1m 41.233s; 17 Xaus, 1m 42.286s; 18 Rolfo, 1m 43.523s; 19 Battaini, 1m 44.576s; 20 Byrne, 1m 44.728s; 21 Ellison, 1m 44.833s.

Fastest race laps: 1 Rossi, 1m 40.596s; 2 Hayden, 1m 40.892s; 3 Gibernau, 1m 40.897s; 4 Melandri, 1m 41.043s; 5 Nakano, 1m 41.467s; 6 Biaggi, 1m 41.525s; 7 Edwards, 1m 41.596s; 8 Barros, 1m 41.603s; 9 Tamada, 1m 41.723s; 10 Bayliss, 1m 41.828s; 11 Checa, 1m 41.851s; 12 Capirossi, 1m 42.189s; 13 Elias, 1m 42.246s; 14 Hofmann, 1m 42.275s; 15 Roberts, 1m 42.458s; 16 Hopkins, 1m 42.606s; 17 Rolfo, 1m 44.011s; 18 Ellison, 1m 45.575s; 19 Xaus, 1m 45.691s; 20 Byrne, 1m 46.018s; 21 Battaini, 1m 46.243s.

World Championship: 1 Rossi, 25; 2 Gibernau, 20; 3 Melandri, 16; 4 Barros, 13; 5 Nakano, 11; 6 Bayliss, 10; 7 Biaggi, 9; 8 Tamada, 8; 9 Edwards, 7; 10 Checa, 6; 11 Hofmann, 5; 12 Elias, 4; 13 Capirossi, 3; 14 Hopkins, 2; 15 Rolfo, 1.

---

250 cc

26 laps, 71.448 miles/114.998 km

Pos.	Rider (Nat.)	No.	Machine	Laps	Time & speed
1	Daniel Pedrosa (E)	1	Honda	26	45m 36.679s 93.998 mph/ 151.275 km/h
2	Sebastian Porto (ARG)	19	Aprilia	26	45m 38.815s
3	Alex de Angelis (RSM)	5	Aprilia	26	46m 06.361s
4	Andrea Dovizioso (I)	34	Honda	26	46m 13.218s
5	Hector Barbera (E)	80	Honda	26	46m 14.178s
6	Jorge Lorenzo (E)	48	Honda	26	46m 14.407s
7	Roberto Locatelli (I)	15	Aprilia	26	46m 21.717s
8	Alex Debon (E)	6	Honda	26	46m 33.018s
9	Simone Corsi (I)	24	Aprilia	26	46m 39.523s
10	Mirko Giansanti (I)	32	Aprilia	26	46m 47.387s
11	Chaz Davies (GB)	57	Aprilia	26	46m 57.469s
12	Radomil Rous (CZ)	64	Honda	26	46m 57.629s
13	Alex Baldolini (I)	25	Aprilia	25	45m 39.345s
14	Andrea Ballerini (I)	8	Aprilia	25	45m 53.365s
15	Gregory Leblanc (F)	38	Aprilia	25	46m 23.618s
16	Gabor Rizmayer (H)	12	Yamaha	25	46m 34.357s
	Jakub Smrz (CZ)	96	Honda	25	DNF
	Alvaro Molina (E)	41	Aprilia	25	DNF
	Hugo Marchand (F)	9	Aprilia	19	DNF
	Steve Jenkner (D)	17	Aprilia	14	DNF
	Casey Stoner (AUS)	27	Aprilia	13	DNF
	Randy de Puniet (F)	7	Aprilia	11	DNF
	Yuki Takahashi (J)	55	Honda	10	DNF
	Hiroshi Aoyama (J)	73	Honda	8	DNF
	Arnaud Vincent (F)	21	Fantic	8	DNF
	Dirk Heidolf (D)	28	Honda	5	DNF
	Sylvain Guintoli (F)	50	Aprilia	2	DNF
	Martin Cardenas (COL)	36	Aprilia	1	DNF
	Franz Aschenbrenner (D)	16	Yamaha		DNQ
	Yves Polzer (A)	42	Aprilia		DNQ
	Gabriel Ferro (I)	20	Fantic		DNQ

Fastest lap: de Puniet, 1m 44.459s, 94.716 mph/152.431 km/h.

Previous record: Daijiro Kato, J (Honda), 1m 44.444s, 94.729 mph/152.452 km/h (2001).

Event best maximum speed: de Puniet, 155.8 mph/250.8 km/h (race).

Qualifying: 1 Pedrosa, 1m 42.868s; 2 Porto, 1m 43.195s; 3 Stoner, 1m 43.212s; 4 de Puniet, 1m 43.444s; 5 de Angelis, 1m 43.744s; 6 Aoyama, 1m 43.813s; 7 Barbera, 1m 44.038s; 8 Locatelli, 1m 44.330s; 9 Lorenzo, 1m 44.345s; 10 Dovizioso, 1m 44.426s; 11 Takahashi, 1m 44.462s; 12 Corsi, 1m 44.706s; 13 Jenkner, 1m 44.764s; 14 Debon, 1m 45.267s; 15 Smrz, 1m 45.364s; 16 Guintoli, 1m 45.374s; 17 Molina, 1m 45.648s; 18 Baldolini, 1m 45.734s; 19 Davies, 1m 45.988s; 20 Rous, 1m 46.007s; 21 Giansanti, 1m 46.090s; 22 Heidolf, 1m 46.256s; 23 Ballerini, 1m 46.881s; 24 Cardenas, 1m 47.103s; 25 Leblanc, 1m 47.183s; 26 Marchand, 1m 47.515s; 27 Rizmayer, 1m 48.003s; 28 Vincent, 1m 48.262s; 29 Aschenbrenner, 1m 50.409s; 30 Polzer, 1m 50.609s; 31 Ferro, 1m 58.033s.

Fastest race laps: 1 de Puniet, 1m 44.459s; 2 Pedrosa, 1m 44.548s; 3 Porto, 1m 44.571s; 4 Stoner, 1m 44.779s; 5 de Angelis, 1m 45.002s; 6 Barbera, 1m 45.207s; 7 Locatelli, 1m 45.263s; 8 Dovizioso, 1m 45.382s; 9 Aoyama, 1m 45.473s; 10 Lorenzo, 1m 45.510s; 11 Debon, 1m 45.779s; 12 Takahashi, 1m 45.807s; 13 Corsi, 1m 46.198s; 14 Jenkner, 1m 46.220s; 15 Giansanti, 1m 46.430s; 16 Baldolini, 1m 46.916s; 17 Smrz, 1m 46.993s; 18 Rous, 1m 47.041s; 19 Davies, 1m 47.297s; 20 Molina, 1m 47.331s; 21 Heidolf, 1m 47.869s; 22 Guintoli, 1m 48.084s; 23 Ballerini, 1m 48.650s; 24 Leblanc, 1m 49.251s; 25 Marchand, 1m 49.337s; 26 Rizmayer, 1m 49.502s; 27 Vincent, 1m 52.783s; 28 Cardenas, 1m 58.361s.

World Championship: : 1 Pedrosa, 25; 2 Porto, 20; 3 de Angelis, 16; 4 Dovizioso, 13; 5 Barbera, 11; 6 Lorenzo, 10; 7 Locatelli, 9; 8 Debon, 8; 9 Corsi, 7; 10 Giansanti, 6; 11 Davies, 5; 12 Rous, 4; 13 Baldolini, 3; 14 Ballerini, 2; 15 Leblanc, 1.

---

125 cc

23 laps, 63.204 miles/101.729 km

Pos.	Rider (Nat.)	No.	Machine	Laps	Time & speed
1	Marco Simoncelli (I)	58	Aprilia	23	42m 27.960s 89.311 mph/ 143.732 km/h
2	Mika Kallio (SF)	36	KTM	23	42m 29.378s
3	Fabrizio Lai (I)	32	Honda	23	42m 29.470s
4	Mattia Pasini (I)	75	Aprilia	23	42m 36.242s
5	Gabor Talmacsi (H)	14	KTM	23	42m 36.890s
6	Manuel Poggiali (RSM)	54	Gilera	23	42m 41.611s
7	Hector Faubel (E)	55	Apilia	23	42m 42.550s
8	Joan Olive (E)	6	Aprilia	23	42m 45.124s
9	Julian Simon (E)	60	KTM	23	42m 45.222s
10	Manuel Hernandez (E)	43	Aprilia	23	42m 59.107s
11	Mike di Meglio (F)	63	Honda	23	43m 02.697s
12	Pablo Nieto (E)	22	Derbi	23	43m 02.761s
13	Jordi Carchano (E)	28	Aprilia	23	43m 05.106s
14	Aleix Espargaro (E)	41	Honda	23	43m 17.551s
15	Nicolas Terol (E)	18	Derbi	23	43m 19.589s
16	Imre Toth (H)	45	Aprilia	23	43m 22.568s
17	Mateo Tunez (E)	86	Aprilia	23	43m 22.707s
18	Federico Sandi (I)	10	Honda	23	43m 22.920s
19	Julian Miralles (E)	84	Aprilia	23	43m 23.487s
20	Sandro Cortese (D)	11	Honda	23	43m 38.824s
21	Andrea Iannone (I)	29	Aprilia	23	43m 50.657s
22	Karel Abraham (CZ)	44	Aprilia	23	43m 54.486s
23	Raymond Schouten (NL)	16	Honda	23	44m 06.063s
24	Sascha Hommel (D)	31	Malaguti	23	44m 15.421s
25	Vincent Braillard (CH)	26	Aprilia	22	43m 37.185s
	Tomoyoshi Koyama (J)	71	Honda	21	DNF
	Alexis Masbou (F)	7	Honda	20	DNF
	Daniel Saez (E)	49	Aprilia	19	DNF
	Dario Giuseppetti (D)	25	Aprilia	16	DNF
	Thomas Luthi (CH)	12	Honda	15	DNF
	Toshihisa Kuzuhara (J)	9	Honda	15	DNF
	Sergio Gadea (E)	33	Aprilia	10	DNF
	Lukas Pesek (CZ)	52	Derbi	9	DNF
	Angel Rodriguez (E)	47	Honda	6	DNF
	Raffael de Rosa (I)	35	Aprilia	3	DNF
	Michele Pirro (I)	15	Malaguti	0	DNF
	Alvaro Bautista (E)	19	Honda	0	DNF
	David Bonache (E)	48	Honda	0	DNF
	Lorenzo Zanetti (I)	8	Aprilia	0	DNF
	Patrik Vostarek (CZ)	87	Honda		DNQ

Fastest lap: Nieto, 1m 49.176s, 90.624 mph/145.845 km/h.

Previous record: Stefano Perugini, I (Aprilia), 1m 47.766s, 91.809 mph/147.753 km/h (2003).

Event best maximum speed: Pasini, 136.1 mph/219.0 km/h (race).

Qualifying: 1 Simoncelli, 1m 46.996s; 2 Pasini, 1m 47.397s; 3 Luthi, 1m 47.747s; 4 Lai, 1m 47.873s; 5 Kallio, 1m 47.934s; 6 Talmacsi, 1m 48.286s; 7 Faubel, 1m 48.611s; 8 de Rosa, 1m 48.632s; 9 Zanetti, 1m 48.764s; 10 Koyama, 1m 48.810s; 11 Poggiali, 1m 48.898s; 12 Pesek, 1m 49.088s; 13 Nieto, 1m 49.155s; 14 Simon, 1m 49.174s; 15 Hernandez, 1m 49.386s; 16 di Meglio, 1m 49.473s; 17 Carchano, 1m 49.592s; 18 Gadea, 1m 49.666s; 19 Toth, 1m 49.719s; 20 Bautista, 1m 49.767s; 21 Cortese, 1m 49.991s; 22 Espargaro, 1m 50.039s; 23 Kuzuhara, 1m 50.219s; 24 Olive, 1m 50.255s; 25 Sandi, 1m 50.443s; 26 Terol, 1m 50.452s; 27 Braillard, 1m 50.524s; 28 Masbou, 1m 50.586s; 29 Iannone, 1m 50.619s; 30 Miralles, 1m 50.660s; 31 Giuseppetti, 1m 50.676s; 32 Tunez, 1m 50.945s; 33 Rodriguez, 1m 51.212s; 34 Pirro, 1m 51.283s; 35 Schouten, 1m 51.970s; 36 Abraham, 1m 52.284s; 38 Saez, 1m 52.456s; 39 Bonache,

Fastest race laps: 1 Nieto, 1m 49.176s; 2 Simoncelli, 1m 49.195s; 3 Lai, 1m 49.216s; 4 Pasini, 1m 49.295s; 5 Luthi, 1m 49.297s; 6 Kallio, 1m 49.298s; 7 Talmacsi, 1m 49.516s; 8 Poggiali, 1m 49.951s; 9 Simon, 1m 49.974s; 10 Carchano, 1m 50.178s; 11 Olive, 1m 50.205s; 12 Koyama, 1m 50.251s; 13 Faubel, 1m 50.301s; 14 Pesek, 1m 50.325s; 15 Espargaro, 1m 50.336s; 16 Gadea, 1m 50.348s; 17 Masbou, 1m 50.439s; 18 Hernandez, 1m 50.691s; 19 di Meglio, 1m 50.718s; 20 Terol, 1m 50.931s; 21 de Rosa, 1m 51.085s; 22 Braillard, 1m 51.201s; 23 Tunez, 1m 51.412s; 24 Toth, 1m 51.450s; 25 Sandi, 1m 51.609s; 26 Miralles, 1m 51.617s; 27 Cortese, 1m 51.820s; 28 Rodriguez, 1m 51.980s; 29 Giuseppetti, 1m 52.221s; 30 Iannone, 1m 52.354s; 31 Abraham, 1m 52.607s; 32 Saez, 1m 52.781s; 33 Kuzuhara, 1m 52.844s; 34 Schouten, 1m 53.140s; 35 Hommel, 1m 53.365s.

World Championship: 1 Simoncelli, 25; 2 Kallio, 20; 3 Lai, 16; 4 Pasini, 13; 5 Talmacsi, 11; 6 Poggiali, 10; 7 Faubel, 9; 8 Olive, 8; 9 Simon, 7; 10 Hernandez, 6; 11 di Meglio, 5; 12 Nieto, 4; 13 Carchano, 3; 14 Espargaro, 2; 15 Terol, 1.

81

Main picture: First lap, and with Gibernau already two seconds clear, Barros heads Biaggi, Rossi and Melandri.

Right: A second misfortune in two races as Gibernau crashes out of the lead.

Far right: The umbrella girls really needed their umbrellas.

Photographs: Gold & Goose

ESTORIL
PORTUGUESEGP

FIM WORLD CHAMPIONSHIP • ROUND 2

F LAG-TO-FLAG regulations for rain-hit races have the benefit of putting the tyre-change decision into the hands of the rider, but still had many detractors. For one, the new system meant riders would be racing in pit lane, albeit under revised rules – the speed limit now 60km/h (37.3 mph) rather than 80, and no overtaking. With mechanics, team managers and hangers-on milling about, the possibilities of collision still seemed high. As it turned out, the first application of the rule brought out quite another aspect... the risk taken by the race leader, when obliged by circumstances to keep racing on slicks in deteriorating conditions.

The visit to Estoril had been brought forward by fully six months, from the original October 23 date, to take the place of the Rio race, cancelled just weeks before the season began. At least the two events shared a common language. In consequence, the already reliably severe and unpredictable weather of the Atlantic seaboard was even worse – and on race day it was bad enough that for the first time the new white flag was shown in anger. This meant riders could pit to change bikes if they wanted, as long as they were on different tyres, but that the race would go on regardless. The decision was taken on lap eight of 28, but disobligingly, the weather did neither one thing nor the other, with minor spotting of rain now and then at various points on the track, but nothing serious. Until finally a heavier shower (the first of several more) fell on the sharp right-hander at the end of the long straight.

The location was crucial, because the first of the riders to arrive at a fully wet corner was the long-time leader, Gibernau, starting his 17th lap. He paid the price, and in so doing warned all but one of those following of the sudden deterioration in grip. The exception was Hopkins, headlong out of eighth.

It was dry for the start, with everyone using slicks, but the weather was clearly imminently changeable, after rain in morning warm-up. Gusty winds brought in squalls of dampness as the race progressed, a display-case of meteorological variations that weren't quite rain and weren't quite not rain either. Barros set fastest lap, 1.2 seconds off his pole time, on lap seven; from then on times dropped off by a second or so, but stayed fairly consistent, even after the white flag was shown.

The weather itself took little notice of the flag. Conditions remained tricky, lap times consistent. None of the riders entertained any thoughts of pitting for a bike on better tyres. This lasted until the 17th lap, which new leader Barros took almost five seconds longer to complete than the previous.

Now there were 11 laps left, but with parts of the track still dry, even on slicks it wasn't worth risking what Rossi estimated would be "40 or 50 seconds" to swap bikes. Everybody soldiered on, on tip-toes, with lap times varying wildly as conditions changed. It was a draining exercise in survival – another meaning perhaps of flag-to-flag – but still a stern test of riding skills.

The activities in the pits kept the crewmen warm, with two or even three changes of tyres. Rossi's chief Burgess explained the process. "For the start, you have the spare bike on the same dry tyres, in case there's a problem on the warm-up lap. Straight away we changed that to wet tyres. Then as the race wears on, with say ten laps to go, you fit a softer-compound wet."

Still, although Edwards and Bayliss also fell, nobody was hurt. There'd been enough of that already. With cold winds blowing dust across the surface and nine of the 13 corners running to the right, letting the left of the tyre cool down, a number had tasted tarmac in practice, including Gibernau, Elias, Xaus, Hayden, Melandri and Hopkins. The hardest to fall was Bayliss, looping over the bars on Friday afternoon. Tough as you like, Bayliss at first seemed concussed, but was back out later in the same session.

Least fortunate was Makoto Tamada, who fell on his fifth lap of the qualifying session. Hopes of racing on Sunday were thwarted by severe pain. Several days later in Japan doctors diagnosed what had been missed at the track and even at his first hospital visit – a cracked scaphoid (wrist) bone that required surgery. Much had been expected of Makoto on Michelins. Now he was to miss three races.

Kawasaki rider Alex Hofmann suffered a physically similar and race-wise equally costly injury even before the meeting began, in ignominious circumstances. It was all too embarrassing. A photocall and public promo had been arranged in the streets round the Estoril casino, with a handful of MotoGP bikes parading. The Camel Honda team had remembered to take tyre-warmers; the Kawasaki team had not. And so Alex's parade was altogether more spectacular than planned, with a low-speed low-side crash that fractured his wrist. There is nothing new in big-name riders spoiling their GP seasons with crashes and injuries sustained at other events. The big risks used to be the big-money races, until Honda banned factory riders from participating after Freddie Spencer was injured in the Transatlantic series of 1984. There is irony to be observed in the modern version, of a rider suffering injury not while earning extra money to fund his GP habit, but by poodle-faking and sponsor-pleasing to justify the money he nowadays can cream off the side of it.

The publicity stunt was to little effect, with the bad spring weather possibly further depressing the appeal to the crowd. Barely 26,000 turned up for the race, some 100,000 less than at not-too-distant Jerez the previous weekend, and there were murmurings that this might be the last of the series. If so, that would still leave three races on the Iberian peninsula.

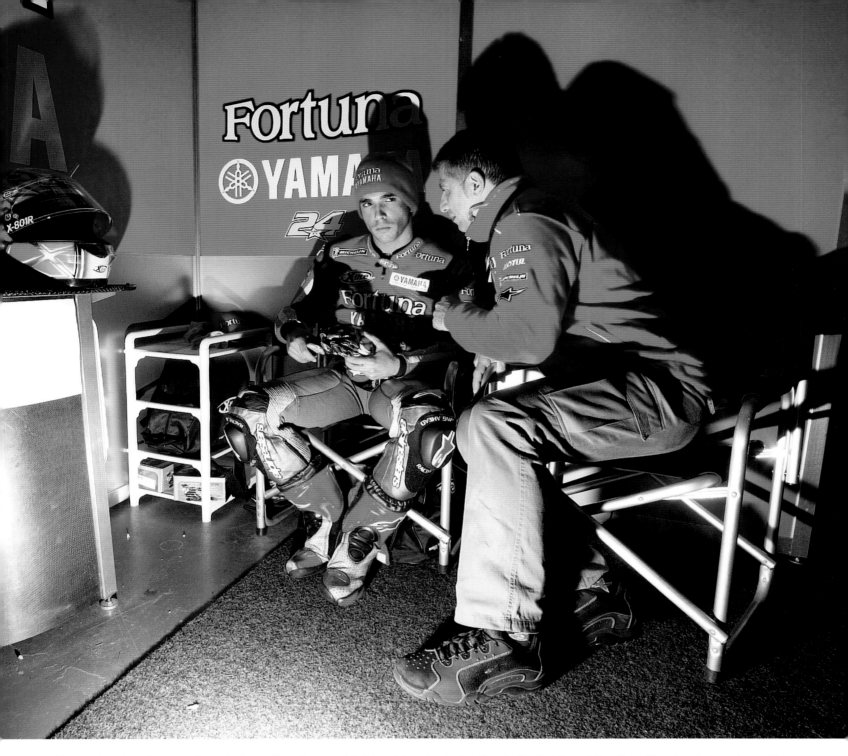

More amateur dramatics among the main players, the acting this time coming from Sete. There'd been quite a song and dance the preceding week about the shoulder injury sustained in the Jerez collision, but after physiotherapy, injections and ultrasound treatment he was officially cleared fit to race. Things were not easy, he insisted, saving his gravest claims for Saturday evening, after slipping off in the morning session, requiring more painkilling injections prior to qualifying. He could run three or four laps okay, he said, but after five control was difficult. His credibility on this matter, already undermined by the jibes of a disbelieving Rossi, was further reduced by his commanding performance in the next day's race.

The man in charge at the end, as he had been throughout practice, was Alex Barros, who at 34 became the oldest rider to win a premier-class GP since Jack Findlay won the Austrian GP in 1977. Riding a Suzuki, he was 42. It was Barros's first victory in more than two years. More than that: "I've never been fastest in every session then won the race before." Ironically enough, this was after being demoted by Honda from factory to satellite team. The man he swapped with, Biaggi, again suffered by comparison, qualifying eighth, though redeeming himself somewhat with a steadfast pursuit of Rossi in the race. His 33rd podium finish lifted him one clear of Mamola, with whom he shares the distinction of the most successful rider never to have won the title, with 13 wins apiece.

Estoril is mainly a slow track, with a devilish first-gear uphill chicane ... but average speeds and reputation are regained by the final fast corner, a long right-hander of ever-increasing radius, and the subsequent long downhill straight, where a Ducati again narrowly won the top speed battle, Checa running 206.3 mph/332.0 km/h, a pack of Hondas barely slower.

MOTOGP RACE – 28 laps

Barros quite dominated practice and qualifying, run in mainly cool and windy conditions, to take only the fifth pole in his long career. He had the grimacing Gibernau alongside, then Checa's Ducati, nudging Rossi to head row two. The Jerez winner was still in trouble, however, complaining that his bike felt "nervous" all weekend. This problem would be solved by suspension changes and raising the ride height in tests the day after the race, though continuing bad weather meant it would take a race or two before they could be sure of the benefit.

Gibernau was fastest in the dash down to the tight funnel into the first corner, and had a lead of almost two seconds by the end of a blistering first lap, over Biaggi and Barros, Rossi and Melandri close, Edwards and Hopkins behind.

By lap two Barros had taken up the pursuit, and never let Gibernau out of his sight. By the same token, Gibernau never let him get closer than just under a second (on lap ten – Barros

Above: Biaggi was happy to settle for a podium.

Opposite: Body language – for once, Rossi didn't mind getting beaten. Barros had led every practice session as well.

Below: The beautiful art in the connoisseur's class: first-time 250 winner Stoner leads de Puniet and Dovizioso, Pedrosa fades behind.

Photographs: Gold & Goose

had earlier set fastest lap). It was still 1.2 seconds as Sete started his 17th and final lap. "I know what I'll do next time I see the white flags. I'll make sure I'm not leading," he would say later; at the time he was fuming at a lack of warning that the first corner was suddenly a whole lot wetter than it had been the lap before. "I wasn't touching the brakes or hardly touching my knee. But when you're on slick tyres and it's f***ing pouring with rain and nobody tells you, it's impossible not to crash."

The rain and the loss of the leader of course changed the complexion of the race, but made little difference to Barros. He had ten seconds in hand over Rossi and Biaggi, and the luxury of that cushion to ease his role of pioneer in the changing conditions. His lap times varied widely as he tested the waters, but he had plenty in hand to remain comfortable in spite of Rossi's fast final lap. The veteran did everything right all weekend, but also needed a dose of luck (actually Gibernau's bad luck) to pull off the victory.

Rossi had taken third off Biaggi on lap four, now a second behind Barros. But unusually instead of hauling in the older rider, he continued to lose ground. And Biaggi stayed in close and faithful company, seldom more than half a second adrift, even after the weather changed and the lap times stretched out. Never close enough to attack, he only slackened his pursuit with one lap to go. Discretion yielded a rostrum, a welcome relief given his continuing difficulties adapting to the factory Honda.

Melandri had lost pace behind the leaders from the early laps, soon to be engaged with Edwards, who went ahead on lap four, but only for three laps. They remained hard at it. Close behind, Hopkins was working hard, only losing touch with this battle after half distance. Meanwhile, Checa had managed to get away from an off-form Hayden, and on lap 15, the Ducati powered past the Suzuki down the straight. Checa had gained a little gap when Hopkins crashed out on the wet first corner two laps later.

Ahead of him, Edwards adapted better to the changed conditions and finally got ahead of Melandri once and for all. He had opened up a gap of better than three seconds when he also slipped off at the same first corner. "It was like ice," he commented. Edwards hurriedly remounted, losing only two places as Melandri and the now-close Checa came skittering past through the spray. The Ducati rider was on a charge, and managed to get ahead of Melandri on the final lap, only to run wide

immediately, dropping behind again.

Edwards was a long way back, likewise Hayden, still well clear of Nakano's Kawasaki. The American had been troubled by an attack from Bayliss after the rain began, the Australian charging past, only to fall victim to the conditions. He also remounted to save a handful of points, behind Capirossi and Xaus. Capirossi had again been riding in pain, with his fresh ankle injury.

There'd been a desultory sort of battle at the back in the closing stages; Bayliss remained half-a-second ahead of Roberts's rather unexpected flying last lap – the former World Champion ignited by belated ambition. Only Rossi was faster. This avoided the factory Suzuki from getting beaten by class rookies Rolfo and Elias. Ellison's WCM took the final point, two laps down. Aside from Gibernau and Hopkins, Battaini was the only non-finisher, pitting in the early stages.

Byrne had a downbeat second KTM race, starting from pit lane after throttle problems on the warm-up lap, and finishing behind Ellison.

250 cc RACE – 26 laps

TThe 250s opened the day, under lowering skies. The track had mostly dried, however, with a distinct racing line threading between dark patches. De Puniet took pole narrowly from Porto, with three Hondas next: Pedrosa, Dovizioso and Barbera, leading row two. Stoner was 12th.

Porto seized the lead, and galloped into the distance, fully two seconds clear after the first lap, doubled one lap later. He was in a race of his own … but it would not last. After four laps, he later explained, his rear tyre seemed to start disintegrating. He was soon losing pace.

Pedrosa had passed de Angelis, de Puniet and Dovizioso to take second at the end of lap two, and stayed there, Stoner well placed behind, the gap to Porto gradually shrinking. By lap ten the defending champion was taking chunks out of it; on lap 12 both he and Dovizioso were ahead of the Argentine, with Stoner, de Angelis and de Puniet close behind, the first six covered by less than 1.5 seconds.

As half-distance passed, they had split into two groups: Pedrosa led Dovizioso and Stoner; then a growing gap to the next trio, where Porto was soon behind de Puniet and de Angelis, and would drop out of contention. Now it seemed like a familiar scenario: Pedrosa in control, ready to move decisively ahead in the

Right: Aprilia factory cadet Corsi takes shelter before his second 250-class start.

Far right: All chuckles for ex-racer and now team owner Cecchinello after protégé Stoner's maiden class win.

Photographs: Gold & Goose

Above: Two-faced. Bamboozled on the last lap, de Puniet had reason to look glum.

Below: KTMs lead the 125 brawl, first-time winner Kallio ahead. Talmacsi (14) will soon crash, Simoncelli (58) will lose ground, but Faubel (55) will escape from the mid-pack for a photo finish.

Far right: The sun did appear... when it was all over.

Photograph: Gold & Goose

closing laps, the remainder left to a vain and straggling pursuit. But this race proved how the influx of new blood had rewritten the rules in the 250 class.

Pedrosa later said he had gone too hard too early. Unable to shake off his pursuers, by lap 18 he was instead under the most severe pressure, with the top five all closed up again. Pedrosa still led over the line, from de Puniet, Dovizioso, Stoner and de Angelis, but they were almost five abreast, and he was about to be swamped. Next time round he was fourth. Troubled by a sliding rear, "I thought it would be the same for the other riders, but when I dropped to the back of the group I realised I had more problems than them," he said later. He kept tactfully quiet about another problem ... a fogging visor on his new Nolan helmet. This problem would affect him and other similarly-clad riders in races to come, at some further cost.

De Puniet's Aprilia made the running for the next four laps, Dovizioso tucked in behind, but Stoner was heading steadily forwards, and he surged into the lead at the end of a dramatic 23rd lap. His earlier attack on de Puniet had run both wide, letting Dovizioso to the front, working hard in the turns to make up for his Honda's lack of speed. Stoner waved an apology to the Frenchman, and set about the Italian, ahead as they crossed the line.

Stoner held on until they started the final lap De Puniet snatched the lead into the first turn, only to make a slip a little further round. This brought him within range of Dovizioso, and their skirmish through the slow uphill twists gave Stoner the gap he needed to guarantee victory, by less than half a second.

Dovizioso clung on to a fine second in only his second GP; Pedrosa managed to recapture fourth from de Angelis on the final lap, the pair now a couple of seconds adrift.

Fifteen seconds away, Aoyama finally won a long Honda battle with compatriot Takahashi. Guintoli was next, the last to pass the ailing Porto.

Lorenzo was tenth, after charging through from near the back

after a lap two contretemps, finally catching the scrapping Barbera and Smrz and outpacing both.

De Angelis had the consolation of fastest lap, but the poor conditions meant he was two seconds shy of the record; Davis ended a weekend of problems with his disappointing new bits-and-pieces Aprilia with a race crash.

125 cc RACE – 23 laps

Unusually last of the day, the smallest class laid on a race with much more drama and tension than the few changes of lead would suggest.

The maturing strength of KTM was obvious in qualifying, when Kallio claimed his and the marque's first pole, heading a close front row from Luthi, Simoncelli and Faubel. It would be the last-named's Aprilia that would give him the most trouble.

For a short while there were two KTMs, with Talmacsi taking up second place behind fast-away Kallio on the second lap. The Hungarian crashed out, however, on the third.

By now Faubel had tagged on, and the pair started to escape as Pasini, Lai and a gaggle of others scrapped close behind. The gap was more than 2.5 seconds after ten laps, at which stage Luthi was in third, from Lai and Pasini, a little spread out, with di Meglio and Simon scrapping behind.

Kallio barely had time to draw breath, and on lap 18 Faubel stormed past, leading for four laps, the orange bike shadowing his every move until the penultimate lap when Kallio struck back. He was 0.023 seconds ahead over the line, and leading by less next time round as he claimed his first win of the season by an amazing eight thousandths!

Luthi seemed safe in third, until a last-lap lunge from Lai closed a gap of almost a second to less than a tenth over the line, the young Swiss rider just holding his rostrum place. Pasini fell back from this group towards the finish, with not only recovering slow starter Poggiali but also the battling Koyama and Bautista ahead by the finish.

ESTORIL CIRCUIT

CURVA 2 LAMY GANCHO

ORELHA ESSES

PARABOLICA
INTERIOR
PARABOLICA
AYRTON
SENNA

CURVA 1

CIRCUIT LENGTH: 2.598 miles/4.182 km

betandwin.com
GRANDE PREMIO
DE PORTUGAL

17 APRIL 2005 • FIM WORLD CHAMPIONSHIP ROUND 2

MotoGP

28 laps, 72.772 miles/117.096 km

Pos.	Rider (Nat.)	No.	Machine	Laps	Time & speed
1	Alex Barros (BR)	4	Honda	28	47m 14.053s 92.425 mph/ 148.743 km/h
2	Valentino Rossi (I)	46	Yamaha	28	47m 16.824s
3	Max Biaggi (I)	3	Honda	28	47m 20.124s
4	Marco Melandri (I)	33	Honda	28	47m 43.599s
5	Carlos Checa (E)	7	Ducati	28	47m 43.827s
6	Colin Edwards (USA)	5	Yamaha	28	47m 58.269s
7	Nicky Hayden (USA)	69	Honda	28	48m 11.174s
8	Shinya Nakano (J)	56	Kawasaki	28	48m 13.900s
9	Loris Capirossi (I)	65	Ducati	28	48m 21.771s
10	Ruben Xaus (E)	11	Yamaha	28	48m 36.484s
11	Troy Bayliss (AUS)	12	Honda	28	48m 47.582s
12	Kenny Roberts (USA)	10	Suzuki	28	48m 48.104s
13	Roberto Rolfo (I)	44	Ducati	28	48m 50.009s
14	Toni Elias (E)	24	Yamaha	28	48m 50.545s
15	James Ellison (GB)	77	Blata	26	47m 19.474s
16	Shane Byrne (GB)	67	Proton KR	24	47m 53.289s
	Sete Gibernau (E)	15	Honda	16	DNF
	John Hopkins (USA)	21	Suzuki	16	DNF
	Franco Battaini (I)	27	Blata	8	DNF
	Makoto Tamada (J)	6	Honda		DNS

Fastest lap: Barros, 1m 38.480s, 94.992 mph/152.875 km/h.

Previous record: Valentino Rossi, I (Yamaha), 1m 38.423s, 95.047 mph/152.964 km/h (2004).

Event best maximum speed: Checa, 206.3 mph/332.0 km/h (qualifying practice).

Qualifying: 1 Barros, 1m 37.202s; 2 Gibernau, 1m 37.329s; 3 Checa, 1m 37.456s; 4 Rossi, 1m 37.643s; 5 Melandri, 1m 37.835s; 6 Capirossi, 1m 38.000s; 7 Edwards, 1m 38.003s; 8 Biaggi, 1m 38.009s; 9 Hayden, 1m 38.123s; 10 Nakano, 1m 38.283s; 11 Hopkins, 1m 38.412s; 12 Xaus, 1m 38.949s; 13 Bayliss, 1m 39.033s; 14 Roberts, 1m 39.628s; 15 Elias, 1m 39.836s; 16 Rolfo, 1m 41.327s; 17 Ellison, 1m 41.699s; 18 Byrne, 1m 41.705s; 19 Battaini, 1m 41.728s; 20 Tamada, 1m 41.930s.

Fastest race laps: 1 Barros, 1m 38.480s; 2 Gibernau, 1m 38.513s; 3 Biaggi, 1m 38.848s; 4 Melandri, 1m 39.102s; 5 Rossi, 1m 39.142s; 6 Hopkins, 1m 39.413s; 7 Hayden, 1m 39.492s; 8 Bayliss, 1m 39.535s; 9 Nakano, 1m 39.545s; 10 Checa, 1m 39.556s; 11 Edwards, 1m 39.584s; 12 Capirossi, 1m 40.103s; 13 Elias, 1m 41.228s; 14 Roberts, 1m 41.328s; 15 Xaus, 1m 41.397s; 16 Rolfo, 1m 42.058s; 17 Ellison, 1m 43.229; 18 Byrne, 1m 44.061s; 19 Battaini, 1m 44.315s.

World Championship: 1 Rossi, 45; 2 Barros, 38; 3 Melandri, 29; 4 Biaggi, 25; 5 Gibernau, 20; 6 Nakano, 19; 7 Checa and Edwards, 15; 8 Bayliss, 15; 10 Capirossi, 10; 11 Hayden, 9; 12 Tamada, 8; 13 Elias and Xaus, 6; 15 Hofmann, 5; 16 Roberts and Rolfo, 4; 18 Hopkins, 2; 19 Ellison, 1.

---

250 cc

26 laps, 67.574 miles/108.732 km

Pos.	Rider (Nat.)	No.	Machine	Laps	Time & speed
1	Casey Stoner (AUS)	27	Aprilia	26	45m 36.009s 88.898 mph/ 143.067 km/h
2	Andrea Dovizioso (I)	34	Honda	26	45m 36.413s
3	Randy de Puniet (F)	7	Aprilia	26	45m 36.440s
4	Daniel Pedrosa (E)	1	Honda	26	45m 38.018s
5	Alex de Angelis (RSM)	5	Aprilia	26	45m 38.213s
6	Hiroshi Aoyama (J)	73	Honda	26	45m 53.864s
7	Yuki Takahashi (J)	55	Honda	26	45m 53.923s
8	Sylvain Guintoli (F)	50	Aprilia	26	45m 59.819s
9	Sebastian Porto (ARG)	19	Aprilia	26	46m 02.416s
10	Jorge Lorenzo (E)	48	Honda	26	46m 21.930s
11	Hector Barbera (E)	80	Honda	26	46m 27.542s
12	Jakub Smrz (CZ)	96	Honda	26	46m 32.929s
13	Alex Debon (E)	6	Honda	26	46m 40.112s
14	Mirko Giansanti (I)	32	Aprilia	26	46m 45.521s
15	Martin Cardenas (COL)	36	Aprilia	26	46m 54.517s
16	Dirk Heidolf (D)	28	Honda	26	46m 59.949s
17	Simone Corsi (I)	24	Aprilia	26	47m 02.959s
18	Andrea Ballerini (I)	8	Aprilia	26	47m 03.188s
19	Radomil Rous (CZ)	64	Honda	26	47m 03.341s
20	Gabor Rizmayer (H)	12	Yamaha	25	47m 25.537s
21	Yves Polzer (A)	42	Aprilia	24	46m 19.845s
	Chaz Davies (GB)	57	Aprilia	19	DNF
	Gregory Leblanc (F)	38	Aprilia	10	DNF
	Alex Baldolini (I)	25	Aprilia	9	DNF
	Roberto Locatelli (I)	15	Aprilia	8	DNF
	Alvaro Molina (E)	41	Aprilia	7	DNF
	Arnaud Vincent (F)	21	Fantic	4	DNF
	Hugo Marchand (F)	9	Aprilia	0	DNF
	Franz Aschenbrenner (D)	16	Yamaha		DNQ
	Gabriele Ferro (I)	20	Fantic		DNQ

Fastest lap: de Angelis, 1m 43.484s, 90.399 mph/145.483 km/h.

Previous record: Toni Elias, E (Honda), 1m 41.595s, 92.080 mph/148.188 km/h (2004).

Event best maximum speed: Corsi, 171.7 mph/276.4 km/h (qualifying practice no. 2).

Qualifying: 1 de Puniet, 1m 41.104s; 2 Porto, 1m 41.152s; 3 Pedrosa, 1m 41.285s; 4 Dovizioso, 1m 41.462s; 5 Barbera, 1m 41.597s; 6 de Angelis, 1m 41.700s; 7 Aoyama, 1m 41.790s; 8 Lorenzo, 1m 42.049s; 9 Locatelli, 1m 42.116s; 10 Corsi, 1m 42.206s; 11 Takahashi, 1m 42.250s; 12 Stoner, 1m 42.269s; 13 Guintoli, 1m 42.395s; 14 Smrz, 1m 42.815s; 15 Davies, 1m 43.151s; 16 Debon, 1m 43.232s; 17 Giansanti, 1m 43.254s; 18 Baldolini, 1m 43.472s; 19 Rous, 1m 43.768s; 20 Molina, 1m 43.895s; 21 Heidolf, 1m 43.916s; 22 Marchand, 1m 43.946s; 23 Leblanc, 1m 44.205s; 24 Ballerini, 1m 44.639s; 25 Rizmayer, 1m 45.049s; 26 Cardenas, 1m 45.505s; 27 Polzer, 1m 48.109s; 28 Vincent, 1m 48.129s; 29 Aschenbrenner, 1m 52.029s; 30 Ferro, 2m 38.980s.

Fastest race laps: de Angelis, 1m 43.484s; 2 de Puniet, 1m 43.504s; 3 Stoner, 1m 43.563s; 4 Dovizioso, 1m 43.739s; 5 Pedrosa, 1m 43.825s; 6 Lorenzo, 1m 44.177s; 7 Aoyama, 1m 44.305s; 8 Takahashi, 1m 44.335s; 9 Guintoli, 1m 44.532s; 10 Locatelli, 1m 44.613s; 11 Porto, 1m 44.626s; 12 Barbera, 1m 45.046s; 13 Smrz, 1m 45.559s; 14 Davies, 1m 45.569s; 15 Giansanti, 1m 45.753s; 16 Heidolf, 1m 45.890s; 17 Cardenas, 1m 45.960s; 18 Debon, 1m 46.166s; 19 Corsi, 1m 46.699s; 20 Rous, 1m 46.713s; 21 Ballerini, 1m 46.766s; 22 Leblanc, 1m 48.093s; 23 Baldolini, 1m 49.512s; 24 Molina, 1m 50.224s; 25 Rizmayer, 1m 50.263s; 26 Polzer, 1m 52.954s; 27 Vincent, 1m 58.390s.

World Championship: : 1 Pedrosa, 38; 2 Dovizioso, 33; 3 de Angelis and Porto, 27; 5 Stoner, 25; 6 Barbera, de Puniet and Lorenzo, 16; 9 Debon, 11; 10 Aoyama, 10; 11 Locatelli and Takahashi, 9; 13 Giansanti and Guintoli, 8; 15 Corsi, 7; 16 Davies, 5; 17 Rous and Smrz, 4; 19 Baldolini, 3; 20 Ballerini, 2; 21 Cardenas and Leblanc, 1.

---

125 cc

23 laps, 59.777 miles/96.186 km

Pos.	Rider (Nat.)	No.	Machine	Laps	Time & speed
1	Mika Kallio (SF)	36	KTM	23	41m 19.431s 86.778 mph/ 139.656 km/h
2	Hector Faubel (E)	55	Aprilia	23	41m 19.439s
3	Thomas Luthi (CH)	12	Honda	23	41m 22.329s
4	Fabrizio Lai (I)	32	Honda	23	41m 22.371s
5	Manuel Poggiali (RSM)	54	Gilera	23	41m 30.707s
6	Tomoyoshi Koyama (J)	71	Honda	23	41m 32.974s
7	Alvaro Bautista (E)	19	Honda	23	41m 32.978s
8	Mattia Pasini (I)	75	Aprilia	23	41m 33.924s
9	Julian Simon (E)	60	KTM	23	41m 34.141s
10	Marco Simoncelli (I)	58	Aprilia	23	41m 34.625s
11	Mike di Meglio (F)	63	Honda	23	41m 34.639s
12	Pablo Nieto (E)	22	Derbi	23	41m 55.949s
13	Alexis Masbou (F)	7	Honda	23	41m 56.289s
14	Toshihisa Kuzuhara (J)	9	Honda	23	41m 56.348s
15	Manuel Hernandez (E)	43	Aprilia	23	41m 56.456s
16	Aleix Espargaro (E)	41	Honda	23	41m 56.504s
17	Jordi Carchano (E)	28	Aprilia	23	42m 14.340s
18	Joan Olive (E)	6	Aprilia	23	42m 16.247s
19	Michele Pirro (I)	15	Malaguti	23	42m 19.192s
20	Sergio Gadea (E)	33	Aprilia	23	42m 20.677s
21	Angel Rodriguez (E)	47	Honda	23	42m 20.775s
22	Imre Toth (H)	45	Aprilia	23	42m 24.207s
23	Nicolas Terol (E)	18	Derbi	23	42m 29.846s
24	Raffaele de Rosa (I)	35	Aprilia	23	42m 29.946s
25	Sandro Cortese (D)	11	Honda	23	42m 30.108s
26	Andrea Iannone (I)	29	Aprilia	23	42m 30.740s
27	Federico Sandi (I)	10	Honda	23	42m 30.793s
28	Julian Miralles (E)	84	Aprilia	23	42m 32.634s
29	Dario Giuseppetti (D)	25	Aprilia	23	42m 34.399s
30	Raymond Schouten (NL)	16	Honda	23	42m 37.688s
31	Vincent Braillard (CH)	26	Aprilia	23	42m 38.310s
32	Patrik Vostarek (CZ)	87	Honda	22	42m 05.454s
	Karel Abraham (CZ)	44	Aprilia	12	DNF
	Gabor Talmacsi (H)	14	KTM	2	DNF
	Lukas Pesek (CZ)	52	Derbi	2	DNF
	Sascha Hommel (D)	31	Malaguti		DNQ
	Carlos Ferreira (P)	50	Honda		DNQ

Fastest lap: Faubel, 1m 46.654s, 87.712 mph/141.159 km/h.

Previous record: Hector Barbera, E (Aprilia), 1m 45.573s, 88.610 mph/142.604 km/h (2004).

Event best maximum speed: Olive, 146.2 mph/235.3 km/h (qualifying practice no. 1).

Qualifying: 1 Kallio, 1m 45.279s; 2 Luthi, 1m 45.393s; 3 Simoncelli, 1m 45.622s; 4 Faubel, 1m 46.059s; 5 Pesek, 1m 46.060s; 6 Talmacsi, 1m 46.205s; 7 Pasini, 1m 46.369s; 8 Lai, 1m 46.440s; 9 Simon, 1m 46.503s; 10 Poggiali, 1m 46.517s; 11 Bautista, 1m 46.566s; 12 di Meglio, 1m 46.752s; 13 Hernandez, 1m 47.132s; 14 Nieto, 1m 47.252s; 15 Kuzuhara, 1m 47.428s; 16 Koyama, 1m 47.442s; 17 Espargaro, 1m 47.583s; 18 Olive, 1m 47.597s; 19 Cortese, 1m 47.639s; 20 Masbou, 1m 47.705s; 21 Toth, 1m 47.749s; 22 Pirro, 1m 48.127s; 23 Gadea, 1m 48.157s; 24 Carchano, 1m 48.364s; 25 Terol, 1m 48.437s; 26 Sandi, 1m 48.493s; 27 Miralles, 1m 48.535s; 28 Iannone, 1m 48.583s; 29 de Rosa, 1m 48.584s; 30 Braillard, 1m 48.680s; 31 Giuseppetti, 1m 48.896s; 32 Schouten, 1m 48.986s; 33 Rodriguez, 1m 49.196s; 34 Abraham, 1m 50.349s; 35 Vostarek, 1m 51.138s; 36 Hommel, 1m 52.785s; 37 Ferreira, 1m 55.286s.

Fastest race laps: : 1 Faubel, 1m 46.654s; 2 Kallio, 1m 46.660s; 3 Luthi, 1m 46.732s; 4 Lai, 1m 46.914s; 5 Bautista, 1m 46.999s; 6 Pasini, 1m 47.074s; 7 Poggiali, 1m 47.078s; 8 di Meglio, 1m 47.116s; 9 Koyama, 1m 47.201s; 10 Simon, 1m 47.260s; 11 Simoncelli, 1m 47.423s; 12 Talmacsi, 1m 47.872s; 13 Hernandez, 1m 47.904s; 14 Espargaro, 1m 47.955s; 15 Nieto, 1m 47.980s; 16 Kuzuhara, 1m 47.997s; 17 Masbou, 1m 48.130s; 18 Rodriguez, 1m 48.342s; 19 Gadea, 1m 48.440s; 20 Carchano, 1m 48.867s; 21 Olive, 1m 49.020s; 22 Pirro, 1m 49.172s; 23 Sandi, 1m 49.197s; 24 Iannone, 1m 49.212s; 25 Toth, 1m 49.267s; 26 de Rosa, 1m 49.268s; 27 Cortese, 1m 49.277s; 28 Terol, 1m 49.350s; 29 Miralles, 1m 49.440s; 30 Giuseppetti, 1m 49.447s; 31 Braillard, 1m 49.855s; 32 Schouten, 1m 49.924s; 33 Abraham, 1m 51.572s; 34 Vostarek, 1m 52.553s; 35 Pesek, 1m 56.604s.

World Championship: : 1 Kallio, 45; 2 Simoncelli, 31; 3 Faubel and Lai, 29; 5 Pasini and Poggiali, 21; 7 Luthi, 16; 8 Simon, 14; 9 Talmacsi, 11; 10 di Meglio and Koyama, 8; 13 Nieto and Olive, 8; 15 Hernandez, 7; 16 Carchano and Masbou, 3; 18 Espargaro and Kuzuhara, 2; 20 Terol, 1.

FIM WORLD CHAMPIONSHIP • ROUND 3

GP
SHANGHAI

Above: Gibernau is powerless to resist a good old-fashioned Jacque attack.

Right: Rossi's scooter recce left him dizzy. Racing was worse.

Far right: Pictogram track had some fancy swirls.

Below: Jurgen van den Goorbergh was a second last-minute substitute, and a creditable sixth.

Photographs: Gold & Goose

QUITE what the Chinese thought of their first motorcycle GP may be divined from the contrast between the almost-empty grandstands (official crowd was 25,000, though it was hard to see them) and the shoulder-to-shoulder throngs in Shanghai the next day, massed in vast numbers to celebrate the second of the two day Labour break. It seemed to have passed most of them by completely.

For the foreign visitors, the first-ever motorcycle grand prix in China, less than one year after F1's Shanghai debut, was approached with some trepidation. Faced pre-race with red tape rivalled only by the other addition to this year's calendar, the US GP, nobody was quite sure what to expect upon arrival at this most foreign of foreign races.

When they left, it was with tales of awe – about the circuit and facilities, about Shanghai, and about the tireless and good-natured welcome from the new hosts, who did just about everything right. Give or take a medical helicopter snafu that delayed the first MotoGP practice by two-and-a-half hours. And that the flown-in BMW "Safety Car" aquaplaned and spun on standing water just before the big race, spreading mud across the track… though that was with Dorna's regular driver Carlos Pratola rather than any local influence.

They left also with a new hero or two. None greater than Olivier Jacque, recruited at short notice for Hofmann's Kawasaki. The Frenchman won the 250 title in 2000, but his career in the big class petered out soon after the arrival of the four-strokes, and he was now in a second season without a ride. Why not? he thought, when Harald Eckl rang him out of the blue. "I feel like the hair in the soup, as we say in France," he said, at the pre-race conference, sitting next to the likes of Rossi. Three days later, after a quite extraordinary display of prowess in the streaming wet took him from 15th on the grid to second in the race, he added: "Today I felt like a fish in water." He surely meant "frog", but in the excitement the lapse could be forgiven. Many were left wondering, on the long flight home, how such a talented rider could have been overlooked for the past two years, while others apparently less deserving were left to soldier on and on. It was of course only a coincidence that Max Biaggi racked up a landmark 200 starts at Shanghai, and Kenny Roberts Jr. 150, and in any case the latter put on a reputation-redeeming show, if only briefly.

Another last-minute replacement did the same thing, only less so. Jurgen van den Goorbergh, fresh from a painful break-up with his Ducati Supersport team, got the late call from Konika Minolta's Luca Montiron, and took Tamada's Honda from 19th on the grid to a fine sixth. It had taken the Dutchman a long time to secure a top Honda seat, if only for a race or two, and he made the most of it.

Equally unexpected and admirable, though somewhat short-lived, was another comeback, and further proof how the dire weather changed the footing. Kenny Roberts Jr. hadn't actually gone away since winning the title in 2000, but mostly might as well have done. Never one to take risks in a hopeless task, as the Suzukis (both 500 and 990) fell further behind the opposition so too did his willingness to race. Now the wet conditions and virgin track served up a perfect scenario for an ex-champion to prove his worth. Kenny leapt into the lead, and was steadily if slowly extending it, inching away from Rossi. Then the

Suzuki suddenly broke. It was a big-end, an unprecedented failure on an engine whose more usual weakness is top-end entanglements. Kenny went home with the point only half proved: nobody would ever know how it would have panned out in the end. He would get another chance at Donington Park.

The conditions also yielded an interesting statistic... this was the first time since MotoGP began in 2002 that a Honda had finished lower than second.

The circuit was extraordinary, from the twin-tower grand-stands linked by bridges containing (among other things) extensive press facilities to the contorted overall layout, said to resemble the Chinese character "Shang" (meaning Lofty, or Above). In many ways, from the perspective of MotoGP, it seemed a strange way to spend US $400-million, to end up with a tortuous track more Mickey Mouse than Confucius. The average speeds told the story.

At 5.281 km, only Assen and Brno have a longer lap, and the 1.2km straight exceeded those of Mugello and Catalunya, both in distance and speed... Checa's Ducati clocked 213.0 mph/342.9 km/h, Capirossi and a gaggle of Hondas not much slower. Rossi was down at 205.5 mph/330.8 km/h, the Kawasakis and Suzukis both hitting 202.5 mph/326 km/h at the new fastest straight of the season. But average speeds were way down the list, slower even than the Sachsenring, faster only than Jerez, Estoril and Valencia. Because, unlike the long straights on those other tracks, this one ended in a slow hairpin, one of two first-gear corners on a highly contorted lay-out which set new standards of loopiness.

Whether it was slavish adherence to F1's preference for lots of slow corners or simply the demands of the pictogram, designers had taken the concept of the hairpin further than ever, by bending the U over another 90 degrees. In this way a 180-degree turn became one of 270 degrees, followed by a 90-degree bend in the opposite direction. "For MotoGP, we need more open corners... like Sepang. The first corner especially goes on forever. It's very difficult to find the line," said Rossi.

Below: Roberts would inch away from Rossi... but after four laps engine failure took him from hero to heartbreak.
Photograph: Gold & Goose

MORIWAKI

TIGER
SAHARA

NISIN

MICHELIN

NGK
SPARK PLUG

D.I.D.

DESIGN FACTO

AFA

Gibernau said it was fun, like sliding a motorbike round a car-park, but hardly an arena for Grand Prix-level speeds or skills. Same for everybody, of course, and unusually equally new to everybody. There was no possibility for prior experience, nor even a Playstation simulation, a favourite way for track novices to get basic familiarity. At least the surface was sweet, as Nicky Hayden would have it.

The run-off was not so peachy, the most serious example so far of the growing conflict in safety requirements of bikes and cars. The latter prefer hard standing, so that they can brake and regain control after running off, rather than being marooned in the loose stuff. Bikes need gravel traps to slow both machine and rider. The compromise here was gravel on top of asphalt, but it quickly became clear that there was not enough of it, as one rider after another ran off the track only to go scooting across the traps, unable to brake and barely to steer, but also not losing much speed. It was a first attempt, said the FIM's Claude Danis; next year the gravel would be deeper.

The biggest problem was the weather – race day rain was so heavy that the first race, the 125s, was delayed by half-an-hour because of serious flooding. Rain is rain, and racing carries on... but there was a significant side effect, which had first surfaced at Estoril. There Pedrosa had been the most significant victim of visor fogging on his Nolan helmet. He was not the only one afflicted, and this weekend the fogging problems were a great deal worse. Melandri is another Nolan user, but he showed some racing spirit and saved his bacon by borrowing a Shoei helmet from his pal Dovizioso. Pedrosa tried his team-mate Aoyama's Shoei on the sighting lap, but it was too big, and he had to revert to his Nolan, and the same fogging problem spoiled another race. The GP helmets are prototypes, and this triggered an emergency redesign back at the factory.

The question remained among the pristine empty grand-stands... for whose benefit had this race been run? If not for the people, then it must be for the larger good of China, and certainly of Dorna and the MotoGP series. Biggest beneficiaries, probably, will be the cigarette sponsors, free from the European, American and Australian curbs on advertising and branding, although in this regard much remains to be seen.

For a first attempt, the Chinese GP was a landmark, and a welcome surprise to the first-time visitors. There was nothing to be done about the weather. If only they could do something about that pictogram track.

MOTOGP RACE – 22 laps

Rain on Friday afternoon and iffy conditions on Saturday further cut down set-up time at a track where not even gearing was known in advance, for a field missing Byrne and the Proton KR, which had run out of KTM motors.

Melandri came out of it all best, until team-mate Gibernau snitched away his first pole by more than a tenth. Capirossi's Ducati claimed a rare front row; Rossi was down in sixth, still chasing front-end grip and 1.1 seconds off pole. Hopkins hurtled round with huge daring and angles of lean for a close fourth. The Suzuki is well balanced, and often shows strongly in the early stages, before the other bikes have been dialled in.

All the set-up fears came to naught, with heavy and persistent rain on race day. The map had been redrawn, including large puddles and rain still falling steadily as the grid formed.

Gibernau headed a ball of spray off the line, but ran wide at the first corner. It was proof of what he already knew from the sighting lap. He had landed on the wrong side of a tyre conundrum.

Michelin, fearing the combination of a drying track with the fastest straight of the year would destroy a softer treaded wet tyre, had recommended all their riders to fit a harder-compound rear wet. Gibernau had not tried it in practice, other riders had. But on the sighting lap, he didn't like the feel of it.

On the grid, he asked his team to fit the softer rear he'd chosen previously. Team boss Gresini decided to follow Michelin's cautious advice, and declined. Ironically enough, it stayed wet enough for the softer rear, and it might easily have been a race-winning combination for rain specialist Sete. Instead he never

did get the measure of the tyre, then in the final three laps something did go seriously wrong – vibrating and losing grip, he dropped back to a disgruntled fourth, parking directly against the pit wall. "I wasn't sure I could even finish the last lap," he said later, in a long and sombre press briefing. His title hopes had suffered another bitter blow.

Hopkins took over briefly, but by the end of a frantic first lap Roberts headed Rossi, Elias, Hopkins, Gibernau, Biaggi and Melandri.

The leading pair pulled away rapidly, and Roberts was looking convincing as he crossed the line a second ahead to start lap five. A couple of corners later he slowed suddenly. That was that.

Conditions were dire. Bayliss crashed out on the same lap, then Checa also under braking for the last corner, sliding miles on his back down pit lane.

Gibernau was grimly holding on to second, five seconds behind the lone Rossi, from Biaggi, Elias, Hopkins and Jacque, going like a train from 11th on lap one. "I realised from the start I could go faster than everybody," he would explain. An equally happy rainmaster van den Goorbergh was next, then Barros and Melandri, the Brazilian soon into the pits for a ride-through penalty for a jumped start. Elias was in the same boat, a fine chance cruelly spoiled when he rejoined at the back. He hadn't left early, but taken the wrong position, for a four-bike 250/125 grid rather than the three-by-three MotoGP grid.

This promoted Hopkins to fourth, but he showed how hard he was riding, missing his braking point and doing a gravel gallop to rejoin 11th.

Biaggi was engaged now and then with Gibernau, Jacque closing rapidly. The Italian was losing ground again when the Frenchman pounced, and then he did so even faster.

Now, approaching half distance, the flying part-time super-hero set about Gibernau, taking slices out of him under braking and in the corners but visibly slower on the straight. On lap 15 he was by and moving ahead rapidly. With seven laps left, could he close a 6.1-second gap to the leader?

He took three tenths on the next lap, eight tenths on the next, and so on. On lap 18 Rossi set fastest lap so far in his bid to stay ahead, and Jacque immediately posted a faster one... but as they started the final lap he was still 2.5 seconds away, 1.7 at the flag. He'd waited a long time for this result, he said later, and had decided by then that second was good enough. Good enough also for Kawasaki's best ever finish in the premier class, the marque's first rostrum since Ballington was third in Finland in 1981.

Gibernau held third, his pace still close to the leaders', Biaggi a little slower and some eight seconds behind. But a new thread of action was forming behind him. Mid-race, van den Goorbergh had been four seconds from the factory Honda; at the same time Melandri was picking up speed. He passed the Dutchman on lap 16, quickly closed on Biaggi to take fourth one lap later. He was seven-odd seconds from Gibernau, and lapping faster, though not by enough.

Gibernau's lap times show how the tyre vibration struck on the third from last – suddenly he was three seconds slower, and easy meat for Melandri, who swept past on the final lap for his second rostrum in three races.

Another lap and Biaggi would also have passed Gibernau – he missed by just a second, van den Goorbergh close behind, then Hopkins, who had worked his way forwards again. Edwards had passed Hayden in spite of vision problems; then came Xaus. Barros was 11th, setting fastest lap of the race on the second-last lap, and cursing the luck that had turned so severely since Estoril. "I am sure I could have been on the podium," he said.

Capirossi was down in 12th, blaming a bad rear tyre choice... Jacque had proved that Bridgestone certainly did have good tyres available; Ellison was a steadfast 13th. Elias was 14th and angry after his spoiled chance, ahead of wild card Tohru Ukawa, with first points for the Moriwaki Honda, now on Michelins. Rolfo was another six seconds back; Battaini crashed out with six laps to go; Nakano had quit the race early after an electronically triggered misfire on the first lap.

Right: Stoner takes Dovizioso. He was able to withstand constant attack for a second straight win.

Below: Second season, first win... and by inches. 125 victor Pasini celebrates.

Bottom: Delayed by flooding, the 125s set off for their first lap – Lai heading Kallio, Luthi, Talmacsi and the pack.

Bottom right: Max Biaggi celebrated his 200th GP.

Photographs: Gold & Goose

250 cc RACE – 21 laps

Stoner bounced back from a morning crash for his first 250 pole, first by an Australian since Greg Hansford in 1979. He'd displaced Pedrosa by less than two hundredths, class rookies Dovizioso and Lorenzo making three Hondas on the front row.

The rain was falling again as Pedrosa led out from Dovizioso, Stoner lying fifth into the first tight loops. Dovizioso took the lead onto the long back straight, Pedrosa already suffering vision problems; Stoner outbraked the Italian at the end of that straight, and the pair were immediately pulling away at better than a second a lap. With two laps left, they were more than 20 seconds clear.

Dovizioso had looked consistently threatening, but Stoner was ready for the last-lap attack, making sure he had a margin of safety at the crucial overtaking points – the end-of-straight hairpin and the following left-hander onto the pit straight. It was two in a row for the Australian Aprilia rider.

Pedrosa was in trouble. He lost third to de Puniet on lap four, de Angelis following past almost at once, then Barbera, Porto and Aoyama. The group were still sorting out positions; by the halfway mark de Puniet and de Angelis had a small lead over Porto and Aoyama. Pedrosa was hanging on grimly; Barbera now dropping away.

Aoyama had the most in hand, however. He passed Porto and de Angelis in one lap, de Puniet on the next, and pulled away for a safe rostrum, seven seconds clear of de Angelis as the bedraggled pack splashed over the line. Porto was two seconds down, a gloomy Pedrosa unable to stay in touch.

De Puniet had left the party with four laps left, gesticulating angrily as his Aprilia went onto one cylinder, but spluttering on to finish 18th.

Barbera was safe but lonely in seventh, Corsi was well down,

just two-and-a-half seconds clear of Lorenzo, who had been moving forward steadily after a bad start, finishing lap one 15th. His last victims had been Takahashi, with Debon, Guintoli, Baldolini, Smrz and Heidolf filling the points. Ballerini was the only rider to crash; all other non-finishers pitted.

125 cc RACE – 19 laps

A second successive pole for Kallio suggested perhaps at last the long run without a back-to-back 125 winner might be broken. Simoncelli was close, however, with Talmacsi's KTM and hot Swiss teenager Luthi completing the front row.

Flooding delayed the start by 30 minutes, and though conditions were drying, the track remained mainly wet. Emerging from the spray for a thrilling finale were long-time leader Lai and persistent rival Pasini, almost alongside through the last corner. Several collisions later, the latter was inches ahead over the line.

The pair had exchanged the lead a couple of times over the first eight laps, pulling away from all but Talmacsi... Kallio had already dropped out of the leading pack, leaving Koyama, Luthi and Simoncelli to squabble over fourth.

The whole of the last lap was thrilling on a track with plenty of grip in the wet, Pasini and Lai changing places twice earlier in the lap. Talmacsi had lost touch in the closing stages, finishing four seconds adrift.

Luthi prevailed over rookie Koyama, Simoncelli was held at bay in sixth. Behind another rookie Espargaro managed to fend off Nieto – the Derbi rider had picked his way through from 16th on lap one.

In spite of the conditions, only two riders fell – local wild card Chow and Sandro Cortese.

SHANGHAI
INTERNATIONAL
CIRCUIT

CIRCUIT LENGTH:
3.300 miles/5.281 km

TAOBAO.com
GRAND PRIX OF CHINA

1 MAY 2005 • FIM WORLD CHAMPIONSHIP ROUND 3

MotoGP

22 laps, 72.182 miles/116.182 km

Pos.	Rider (Nat.)	No.	Machine	Laps	Time & speed
1	Valentino Rossi (I)	46	Yamaha	22	50m 02.463s 86.560 mph/ 139.304 km/h
2	Olivier Jacque (F)	19	Kawasaki	22	50m 04.163s
3	Marco Melandri (I)	33	Honda	22	50m 19.037s
4	Sete Gibernau (E)	15	Honda	22	50m 21.369s
5	Max Biaggi (I)	3	Honda	22	50m 22.014s
6	Jurgen vd Goorbergh (NL)	16	Honda	22	50m 24.085s
7	John Hopkins (USA)	21	Suzuki	22	50m 28.346s
8	Colin Edwards (USA)	5	Yamaha	22	50m 33.496s
9	Nicky Hayden (USA)	69	Honda	22	50m 41.762s
10	Ruben Xaus (E)	11	Yamaha	22	50m 43.454s
11	Alex Barros (BR)	4	Honda	22	50m 46.477s
12	Loris Capirossi (I)	65	Ducati	22	50m 46.864s
13	James Ellison (GB)	77	Blata	22	50m 55.912s
14	Toni Elias (E)	24	Yamaha	22	51m 08.316s
15	Tohru Ukawa (J)	72	Moriwaki	22	51m 11.943s
16	Roberto Rolfo (I)	44	Ducati	22	51m 17.756s
	Franco Battaini (I)	27	Blata	16	DNF
	Kenny Roberts (USA)	10	Suzuki	5	DNF
	Troy Bayliss (AUS)	12	Honda	4	DNF
	Carlos Checa (E)	7	Ducati	4	DNF
	Shinya Nakano (J)	56	Kawasaki	2	DNF

Fastest lap: Barros, 2m 13.716s, 88.345 mph/142.178 km/h (record).

Previous record: New Circuit.

Event best maximum speed: Checa, 213.1 mph/342.9 km/h (qualifying practice).

Qualifying: 1 Gibernau, 1m 59.710s; 2 Melandri, 1m 59.873s; 3 Capirossi, 2m 00.480s; 4 Hopkins, 2m 00.666s; 5 Hayden, 2m 00.747s; 6 Rossi, 2m 00.821s; 7 Checa, 2m 00.902s; 8 Elias, 2m 01.081s; 9 Roberts, 2m 01.085s; 10 Nakano, 2m 01.098s; 11 Barros, 2m 01.117s; 12 Bayliss, 2m 01.328s; 13 Edwards, 2m 01.401s; 14 Biaggi, 2m 01.502s; 15 Jacque, 2m 02.072s; 16 Xaus, 2m 02.869s; 17 Rolfo, 2m 03.886s; 18 Ukawa, 2m 04.223s; 19 van den Goorbergh, 2m 04.594s; 20 Battaini, 2m 05.468s; 21 Ellison, 2m 06.496s.

Fastest race laps: 1 Barros, 2m 13.716s; 2 Jacque, 2m 14.133s; 3 Rossi, 2m 14.225s; 4 Hopkins, 2m 14.607s; 5 Melandri, 2m 14.717s; 6 Gibernau, 2m 15.120s; 7 Edwards, 2m 15.175s; 8 Hayden, 2m 15.282s; 9 Ellison, 2m 15.400s; 10 van den Goorbergh, 2m 15.524s; 11 Biaggi, 2m 15.626s; 12 Capirossi, 2m 15.755s; 13 Xaus, 2m 16.249s; 14 Elias, 2m 16.520s; 15 Ukawa, 2m 16.560s; 16 Roberts, 2m 16.591s; 17 Rolfo, 2m 16.853s; 18 Battaini, 2m 17.391s; 19 Checa, 2m 17.949s; 20 Bayliss, 2m 18.905s; 21 Nakano, 2m 30.849s.

World Championship: 1 Rossi, 70; 2 Melandri, 45; 3 Barros, 43; 4 Biaggi, 36; 5 Gibernau, 33; 6 Edwards, 27; 7 Jacque, 20; 8 Nakano, 19; 9 Checa, 17; 10 Hayden, 16; 11 Bayliss, 15; 12 Capirossi, 14; 13 Xaus, 12; 14 Hopkins, 11; 15 van den Goorbergh, 10; 16 Elias and Tamada, 8; 18 Hofmann, 5; 19 Ellison, Roberts and Rolfo, 4; 22 Ukawa, 1.

250 cc

21 laps, 68.901 miles/110.901 km

Pos.	Rider (Nat.)	No.	Machine	Laps	Time & speed
1	Casey Stoner (AUS)	27	Aprilia	21	48m 07.205s 85.923 mph/ 138.280 km/h
2	Andrea Dovizioso (I)	34	Honda	21	48m 07.454s
3	Hiroshi Aoyama (J)	73	Honda	21	48m 28.639s
4	Alex de Angelis (RSM)	5	Aprilia	21	48m 35.794s
5	Sebastian Porto (ARG)	19	Aprilia	21	48m 39.084s
6	Daniel Pedrosa (E)	1	Honda	21	48m 47.725s
7	Hector Barbera (E)	80	Honda	21	48m 53.537s
8	Simone Corsi (I)	24	Aprilia	21	49m 08.820s
9	Jorge Lorenzo (E)	48	Honda	21	49m 11.466s
10	Yuki Takahashi (J)	55	Honda	21	49m 13.028s
11	Alex Debon (E)	6	Honda	21	49m 15.350s
12	Sylvain Guintoli (F)	50	Aprilia	21	49m 16.858s
13	Alex Baldolini (I)	25	Aprilia	21	50m 08.321s
14	Jakub Smrz (CZ)	96	Honda	21	50m 08.572s
15	Dirk Heidolf (D)	28	Honda	21	50m 09.098s
16	Roberto Locatelli (I)	15	Aprilia	21	50m 12.502s
17	Frederik Watz (S)	18	Yamaha	21	50m 14.566s
18	Randy de Puniet (F)	7	Aprilia	21	50m 20.660s
19	Gabor Rizmayer (H)	12	Yamaha	21	50m 33.404s
20	Zi Xian He (CHN)	62	Yamaha	20	48m 40.297s
21	Shi Zhao Huang (CHN)	58	Yamaha	20	48m 40.728s
	Mirko Giansanti (I)	32	Aprilia	18	DNF
	Andrea Ballerini (I)	8	Aprilia	17	DNF
	Radomil Rous (CZ)	64	Honda	17	DNF
	Gregory Leblanc (F)	38	Aprilia	14	DNF
	Steve Jenkner (D)	17	Aprilia	2	DNF
	Chaz Davies (GB)	57	Aprilia	2	DNF
	Zhu Wang (CHN)	60	Aprilia		DNQ
	Hugo Marchand (F)	9	Aprilia		DNQ
	Zheng Peng Li (CHN)	61	Aprilia		DNQ
	Zhi Yu Huang (CHN)	59	Honda		DNQ

Fastest lap: Dovizioso, 2m 15.608s, 87.113 mph/140.195 km/h (record).

Previous record: New circuit.

Event best maximum speed: Stoner, 170.1 mph/273.8 km/h (qualifying practice no. 1).

Qualifying: 1 Stoner, 2m 06.196s; 2 Pedrosa, 2m 06.214s; 3 Dovizioso, 2m 06.473s; 4 Lorenzo, 2m 06.544s; 5 Aoyama, 2m 06.615s; 6 Barbera, 2m 07.437s; 7 de Puniet, 2m 07.653s; 8 Porto, 2m 07.665s; 9 Corsi, 2m 07.709s; 10 Takahashi, 2m 07.889s; 11 de Angelis, 2m 08.018s; 12 Locatelli, 2m 08.567s; 13 Davies, 2m 08.840s; 14 Debon, 2m 08.886s; 15 Guintoli, 2m 09.016s; 16 Baldolini, 2m 09.057s; 17 Ballerini, 2m 09.166s; 18 Heidolf, 2m 09.212s; 19 Smrz, 2m 09.420s; 20 Rous, 2m 09.579s; 21 Giansanti, 2m 09.673s; 22 Rizmayer, 2m 11.900s; 23 Leblanc, 2m 12.237s; 24 Jenkner, 2m 12.743s; 25 Watz, 2m 13.260s; 26 Zhao Huang, 2m 13.307s; 27 He, 2m 14.434s; 28 Wang, 2m 18.458s; 29 Marchand, 2m 19.113s; 30 Li, 2m 19.312s; 31 Yu Huang, 2m 24.652s.

Fastest race laps: 1 Dovizioso, 2m 15.608s; 2 Stoner, 2m 15.701s; 3 de Angelis, 2m 15.995s; 4 Aoyama, 2m 16.045s; 5 de Puniet, 2m 16.374s; 6 Porto, 2m 16.446s; 7 Pedrosa, 2m 16.566s; 8 Lorenzo, 2m 16.905s; 9 Barbera, 2m 17.612s; 10 Corsi, 2m 17.639s; 11 Takahashi, 2m 17.889s; 12 Debon, 2m 17.985s; 13 Guintoli, 2m 18.325s; 14 Ballerini, 2m 18.400s; 15 Watz, 2m 19.760s; 16 Smrz, 2m 19.929s; 17 Baldolini, 2m 20.008s; 18 Rous, 2m 20.091s; 19 Smrz, 2m 20.122s; 20 Rizmayer, 2m 21.260s; 21 Locatelli, 2m 21.357s; 22 Giansanti, 2m 21.361s; 23 Zhao Huang, 2m 23.053s; 24 He, 2m 23.486s; 25 Leblanc, 2m 23.867s; 26 Davies, 2m 30.142s; 27 Jenkner, 2m 43.626s.

World Championship: 1 Dovizioso, 53; 2 Stoner, 50; 3 Pedrosa, 48; 4 de Angelis, 40; 5 Porto, 38; 6 Aoyama, 27; 7 Barbera, 23; 9 Debon and de Puniet, 16; 11 Corsi and Takahashi, 15; 13 Guintoli, 12; 14 Locatelli, 9; 15 Giansanti, 8; 16 Baldolini and Smrz, 6; 18 Davies, 5; 19 Rous, 4; 20 Ballerini, 2; 21 Cardenas, Heidolf and Leblanc, 1.

125 cc

19 laps, 62.339 miles/100.339 km

Pos.	Rider (Nat.)	No.	Machine	Laps	Time & speed
1	Mattia Pasini (I)	75	Aprilia	19	46m 30.273s 80.441 mph/ 129.457 km/h
2	Fabrizio Lai (I)	32	Honda	19	46m 30.338s
3	Gabor Talmacsi (H)	14	KTM	19	46m 35.226s
4	Thomas Luthi (CH)	12	Honda	19	46m 39.058s
5	Tomoyoshi Koyama (J)	71	Honda	19	46m 40.980s
6	Marco Simoncelli (I)	58	Aprilia	19	46m 42.232s
7	Aleix Espargaro (E)	41	Honda	19	46m 56.224s
8	Pablo Nieto (E)	22	Derbi	19	46m 57.425s
9	Lukas Pesek (CZ)	52	Derbi	19	46m 58.427s
10	Julian Simon (E)	60	KTM	19	46m 58.980s
11	Mika Kallio (SF)	36	KTM	19	47m 02.761s
12	Manuel Poggiali (RSM)	54	Gilera	19	47m 14.590s
13	Michele Pirro (I)	15	Malaguti	19	47m 28.891s
14	Joan Olive (E)	6	Aprilia	19	47m 29.649s
15	Hector Faubel (E)	55	Aprilia	19	47m 30.152s
16	Toshihisa Kuzuhara (J)	9	Honda	19	47m 31.109s
17	Alvaro Bautista (E)	19	Honda	19	47m 35.749s
18	Andrea Iannone (I)	29	Aprilia	19	47m 36.627s
19	Raymond Schouten (NL)	16	Honda	19	47m 43.472s
20	Mike di Meglio (F)	63	Honda	19	47m 44.969s
21	Alexis Masbou (F)	7	Honda	19	48m 12.566s
22	Jordi Carchano (E)	28	Aprilia	19	48m 16.500s
23	Julian Miralles (E)	84	Aprilia	19	48m 18.996s
24	Wai On Cheung (CHN)	38	Honda	19	48m 23.185s
25	Federico Sandi (I)	10	Honda	19	48m 37.064s
26	Nicolas Terol (E)	18	Derbi	19	48m 51.692s
27	Karel Abraham (CZ)	44	Aprilia	19	48m 51.864s
28	Raffaele de Rosa (I)	35	Aprilia	19	48m 54.714s
29	Sergio Gadea (E)	33	Aprilia	18	47m 10.684s
30	Imre Toth (H)	45	Aprilia	17	47m 08.450s
31	Ho Wan Chow (CHN)	39	Honda	15	47m 48.516s
	Dario Giuseppetti (D)	25	Aprilia	17	DNF
	Sandro Cortese (D)	11	Honda	11	DNF
	Angel Rodriguez (E)	47	Honda	6	DNF
	Manuel Hernandez (E)	43	Aprilia	3	DNF
	Vincent Braillard (CH)	26	Aprilia	0	DNF
	Sascha Hommel (D)	31	Malaguti	0	DNF
	You Rhao Zhou (CHN)	85	Honda	0	DNF

Fastest lap: Lai, 2m 23.967s, 82.055 mph/132.055 km/h (record).

Previous record: New circuit.

Event best maximum speed: Kallio, 144.6 mph/232.7 km/h (warm-up).

Qualifying: 1 Kallio, 2m 13.535s; 2 Simoncelli, 2m 13.631s; 3 Talmacsi, 2m 14.293s; 4 Luthi, 2m 14.341s; 5 Simon, 2m 14.530s; 6 Lai, 2m 14.773s; 7 Pesek, 2m 14.954s; 8 Koyama, 2m 15.085s; 9 Kuzuhara, 2m 15.130s; 10 Faubel, 2m 15.489s; 11 Pirro, 2m 15.607s; 12 di Meglio, 2m 15.627s; 13 Bautista, 2m 15.995s; 14 Nieto, 2m 16.179s; 15 Pasini, 2m 16.259s; 16 Espargaro, 2m 16.316s; 17 Poggiali, 2m 16.376s; 18 Cortese, 2m 16.408s; 19 Masbou, 2m 16.433s; 20 Hernandez, 2m 16.450s; 21 Iannone, 2m 16.734s; 22 Gadea, 2m 17.079s; 23 Miralles, 2m 17.357s; 24 Rodriguez, 2m 17.424s; 25 Toth, 2m 17.575s; 26 de Rosa, 2m 17.650s; 27 Olive, 2m 17.654s; 28 Giuseppetti, 2m 18.000s; 29 Abraham, 2m 18.165s; 30 Terol, 2m 18.260s; 31 Braillard, 2m 18.337s; 32 Schouten, 2m 18.356s; 33 Carchano, 2m 18.767s; 34 Sandi, 2m 18.826s; 35 Hommel, 2m 18.851s; 36 Cheung, 2m 21.609s; 37 Chow, 2m 22.649s; 38 Zhou, 2m 46.312s.

Fastest race laps: 1 Lai, 2m 23.967s; 2 Pasini, 2m 24.162s; 3 Koyama, 2m 24.528s; 4 Luthi, 2m 24.779s; 5 Espargaro, 2m 24.812s; 6 Pesek, 2m 24.865s; 7 Nieto, 2m 24.882s; 8 Olive, 2m 25.030s; 9 Simoncelli, 2m 25.109s; 10 Talmacsi, 2m 25.137s; 11 Faubel, 2m 25.460s; 12 Kallio, 2m 25.939s; 13 Simon, 2m 25.977s; 14 Miralles, 2m 26.202s; 15 Poggiali, 2m 26.470s; 16 Pirro, 2m 26.802s; 17 Schouten, 2m 26.910s; 18 Bautista, 2m 26.946s; 19 Kuzuhara, 2m 27.046s; 20 Iannone, 2m 27.068s; 21 Masbou, 2m 27.349s; 22 Carchano, 2m 27.457s; 23 Cortese, 2m 27.475s; 24 Gadea, 2m 27.573s; 25 di Meglio, 2m 28.435s; 26 Terol, 2m 28.680s; 27 Abraham, 2m 29.005s; 28 de Rosa, 2m 29.094s; 29 Sandi, 2m 29.122s; 30 Giuseppetti, 2m 29.934s; 31 Cheung, 2m 30.668s; 32 Rodriguez, 2m 31.280s; 33 Chow, 2m 33.126s; 34 Toth, 2m 35.205s; 35 Hernandez, 2m 36.947s.

World Championship: 1 Kallio, 50; 2 Lai, 49; 3 Pasini, 46; 4 Simoncelli, 41; 5 Faubel, 30; 6 Luthi, 29; 7 Talmacsi, 27; 8 Poggiali, 25; 9 Koyama, 21; 10 Simon, 20; 11 Nieto, 16; 12 Espargaro, 11; 13 di Meglio and Olive, 10; 15 Bautista, 9; 16 Hernandez and Pesek, 7; 18 Carchano, Masbou and Pirro, 3; 21 Kuzuhara, 2; 22 Terol, 1.

FIM WORLD CHAMPIONSHIP • ROUND 4

FRENCHGP
LE MANS

A handshake after Rossi beat Gibernau once more, but no eye contact. The victor prefers to keep his eyes on the road.
Photograph: Gold & Goose

Right: Rostrum-bound, Edwards silenced the nay-sayers. For a while.

Below: Rossi and Jeremy Burgess had plenty to smile about.
Photographs: Gold & Goose

THE return to the home continent and familiar ground – to bike racing's version of normality – was marked by more bad weather, though somewhat less disruptive than in China. Proper monsoon conditions on Friday afternoon and again on Saturday morning gave riders a first chance to wet-test the all-new surface of the looping u-turns and short straights of the Bugatti circuit, and both grip and consistency won praise, after recent years where just the opposite was the case.

Sunday's weather was threatening enough for the "Wet Race" board to be displayed before the MotoGP off, but in fact it stayed dry – perhaps to the relief of Olivier Jacque, back for a second Kawasaki outing. After China, much was expected, and it was going to be hard to deliver. "I set the standard too high," smiled the still rather bemused Frenchman ruefully before the start of the weekend. "Since then my telephone hasn't stopped ringing – I hope I find time to race." He did, and 11th was much more in line with the Kawasaki's true potential.

Fellow China charger van den Goorbergh was also back, but only waiting at first, as the prematurely returned Tamada bravely essayed the first free practice, only to pull out in pain. Rain in two of three remaining sessions left Jurgen painfully short of dry time on the Honda. "I'm still learning things the others learned in pre-season testing. The bike is my boss at the moment," he said, after finishing 14th in what would turn out to be his final outing.

It was time for another personality to flower – not for the first time – Colin Edwards. The Tornado had been feeling the criticism of those who expected more of his third MotoGP year, and now was getting it from supposed friends on his own web-site. As often on a new surface, he was running smooth and fast, and after qualifying second he invited his critics, those "armchair world champions", to kiss his ass. The invitation was renewed after a rostrum finish. Edwards had again been behind

his team-mate Rossi, but this time only narrowly, after leading for much of the race.

The Rossi talk was all about contracts – from the fanciful to the extreme. It was definitely true that he and Yamaha were soon to open negotiations, possibly for a two-year deal. Nobody really knew into which category the big rumour fitted, that he was heading for a berth in F1 sooner rather than later, and that Ferrari virtually had the tyre warmers on already. This was backed by somewhat implausible "insider" whispers that in fact Ferrari had played down his single F1 test last year, and that he had in fact been close to lap record pace from the off.

Yamaha's team manager Davide Brivio was implicated in leaking the news, after some comments were splashed in the Italian press that Rossi would be in F1 in 2007. Brivio protested his innocence: Rossi himself found a witty way of laying the question to one side. "For me, the media is becoming a big problem," he told a pre-race press briefing. "I see nothing new. Everybody is managing my words.

"So now I say – I will finish my career in MotoGP. I will never stop. I will be here for another ten years."

A daunting prospect for all the other riders. Or perhaps stimulating. The expected rivals were still variously struggling... Biaggi remaining at odds with his factory machine – consistency in complaints was however matched by some consistency in mainly top-five race results; Gibernau was running faster than ever, but increasingly flummoxed by a rival who could go faster still, and his Portugal crash had cost him dear; Hayden was struggling to make the step between fast sometimes and fast all race long; Barros was inconsistent; Capirossi hampered by early injury and in making the switch to Bridgestone tyres on the still fast but wayward Ducati; Tamada was out hurt.

Melandri was the only one actually exceeding expectations, and he spoke to MOTOCOURSE at Le Mans about how his

former close friendship with Rossi had already changed as a result. "Before, was good. Now it is so-so. I saw the same thing with Sete. He and Valentino were friendly, but when Sete started to go fast, Valentino made some distance. I think with me it started at Jerez last year, where I passed him in the wet. Afterwards, Valentino said in the Italian press that if it had been dry, I would never have passed him.

"I am sorry, because we were friends for a long time. If you are slower than him, then you can be friends. Valentino has a lot of power. A lot of riders think that they cannot beat him. It's not the same for me. I raced against Valentino on pocket bikes and mini-cross. For me, Valentino is just another rider." Not this weekend, he wasn't; not for the first or last time Rossi demonstrated how much he was holding in reserve by setting a new record on the final lap, on spent tyres.

Proton were back, and team manager Chuck Aksland was anxious to quell dire rumours that were spreading after the team, already absent from China, had cancelled planned tests of the second-generation KTM V4 motor. There were rumours of KTM refusing requests from Roberts for more financial support. Not true, said Aksland. There had been "some details" between themselves and KTM that had seen the tests cancelled, but the team's commitment to developing the machine and completing the season remained. KTM told a different story, about a new arrangement to share costs. It was the start of a breakdown that would have dire consequences by the end of the summer break.

Anyway, the new engine was at hand for a troublesome debut, Byrne seldom managing more than a lap or two without some sort of problem, ranging from oil control to a puzzling reluctance to perform. That turned out the result of overtight bearing tolerances, rather than the electronics they had suspected. The oil problem? Earlier in the programme, there'd been a spell of piston failures during bench-testing. An oil radiator used then, and contaminated with swarf, had found its way onto a motorcycle, and this was damaging the new motors. A string of blow-ups meant Byrne was obliged to fall back on the single surviving Mk1 motor, both for qualifying and for a short-lived race – a heavy first-lap high-side rendering questions of engine endurance redundant. At least he had good news about handling... chassis revisions had improved the British rider's front-end feel.

In the smallest class, KTM were denied another race win, but Kallio remained at the head of the table. The debut of the new 250 KTM remained in abeyance for the moment, but rider Anthony West was back. Replacement for injured Columbian rookie Martin Cardenas in the Aprilia Germany team, this was his chance to blow out the cobwebs after injury at Phillip Island ended his season last year. And back with a bang... West was fastest out of 18 riders who did go out by a massive 3.4 seconds. In the race, however, he finished well out of the points.

MOTOGP RACE – 28 laps

Practice was dry Friday morning and for Saturday afternoon's qualifying hour, streaming wet for the other two hours. Everyone was short of dry set-up time. Most riders found this vexing. It was a measure of the balance Rossi had by now found with his 2005 machine that he put it differently, after taking his second pole of the season. He described it as "useful", giving a chance to perfect both wet and dry settings.

Edwards and Melandri made the front row; Gibernau led the second from Hayden and the amazing Nakano; times were very close, with a dozen riders within eight tenths of pole.

Hayden led away towards the evocative Dunlop bridge; in the middle of the chicane that nowadays precedes it Biaggi pushed Checa wide, and the latter's subsequent route towards a crash in the gravel took Rolfo with him, though he remained upright. Byrne crashed out alone slightly further round the lap. Hopkins was involved in a private drama way behind – the servo motor for the GSV-R's throttle system failed on the warm-up lap, and he couldn't even keep up with the safety car. As the others took off he sputtered into the pits to jump onto his spare, luckily still fitted with dry tyres for just such an eventuality, and started from pit lane just in time before the leaders finished lap one.

By the end of the first time round the 180-degree loops and short straights, Edwards was in front of his compatriot's Honda, Capirossi third, and a gap opening on Melandri, who was waiting for his tyres to stick better. Nakano had started well, and headed slow-off-the-line Rossi and Gibernau.

On lap three the champion started to impose, passing Nakano and Melandri in successive corners. Adrift of the leaders by 1.7 seconds, he took just two laps to catch up, flying straight past Capirossi, who would never regain contact, blaming a too-soft rear tyre choice.

Hayden was in familiar all-action mode, Rossi tucked in behind until he saw his chance, running inside at the wide Museum loop. Again, Hayden immediately lost touch, as Rossi settled down behind Edwards, comfortably awaiting developments.

Gibernau had been following through, past Barros, then catching Melandri and the still-fast Nakano. He despatched the latter on lap seven, but took a couple more before he could finally make a pass stick over his determined young team-mate.

He was five seconds behind now, but his harder tyre choice was already paying dividends and by lap 14 had closed down and passed Capirossi, and was gaining on the leaders. Hayden was a relatively easy target as Gibernau set one fastest lap after another, taking third on lap 16, just two seconds adrift of the leading Yamahas.

He kept on charging, and was on the pair on lap 18.

Now Rossi made a rare slip. Failing to outbrake Edwards at the end of the back straight, he took to the kerbs at the subsequent fast chicane. He rejoined in third, but was ahead of Gibernau again one lap later.

Now came his second chance. At the corner before the back straight he slipped inside Edwards. The American stayed wide, hoping to regain the lead on the exit... only to shake his head in surprise as Gibernau promptly dived through the gap as well.

Now it was between the two of them. Gibernau maintained his furious pace, but it turned out Rossi had an answer to everything. His last lap was the fastest of the race, a new record.

Behind Melandri and Nakano, Barros had been pulling Biaggi and rookie Elias along, the youngster losing touch after six laps. By then Biaggi was in front and both about to engage with Nakano. Max then closed on Melandri for a fight to the flag. Barros took longer to pass Nakano, and had hardly done so when he crashed out.

The pair ahead were closing on Capirossi as they battled, and ahead on lap 16. Hayden was next, and four laps later they both passed him as well. Now Melandri led Biaggi most times over the line, and managed to do so again, by half a second, after the final last-lap joust.

Capirossi was next, then Nakano, with Elias only two seconds adrift of the now misfiring Kawasaki. Some way back, Jacque was battling with Bayliss, who had got ahead with seven laps left, and narrowly stayed there. Another big gap, then Xaus managed to fend off Roberts. Van den Goorbergh was a long way back, Rolfo regained the track on lap one to take the final point, ahead of Hopkins and Battaini, whose WCM team-mate Ellison crashed out on lap three.

250 cc RACE – 26 laps

Pedrosa was on pole by almost half a second from Stoner, then Lorenzo and Porto. Home hero de Puniet was more than a second down, with a lack of dry time leading in this case to a wide spread of times.

It didn't lead to a widely spread race – anything but, with the influx of young blood reinforcing the revival of tooth-and-nail 250 racing, hardly known since Kato came in 2000 to string the field out.

Rookie Dovizioso led out, pursued by Pedrosa, Stoner, de Puniet, Porto and Barbera, the last named losing touch at the same time as Lorenzo moved steadily forward from eighth on lap one. By the eighth he was with the group, Pedrosa now at the back. Dovizioso was resisting Stoner, with de Puniet finally and clearly taking third off team-mate Porto.

Lorenzo was torrid, picking off Pedrosa on lap nine as Dovizioso

Top: Yamaha team director Davide Brivio on the podium with his two charges.

Above centre: Pensive Hayden, yet to find speed for the full race, had plenty to think about.

Above: Tamada was happy to be back, but pulled out after one practice session.

Left: Max Biaggi, and the fearsome concentration in his eyes – bad weather brought out clear visors.

Photographs: Gold & Goose

Above: Pedrosa heads Dovizioso, Stoner, de Puniet and the 250 gang, Aoyama (73) prominent on the outside.

Right: De Puniet did everything but win his home GP.

Below: Gadea, heading for second, leads Kallio. He would stay there to the end.

Opposite: Gibernau's expression says it all.

Photographs: Gold & Goose

dropped to third a little way ahead. Next time round, Lorenzo had passed Porto and Dovizioso to take that place.

Stoner's lead had lasted three laps, then the crowd cheered as de Puniet pushed inside with a daring inside line at the fast first corner. Lorenzo moved straight into second, and on lap 16 his charge was finally rewarded with his first time leading a 250 GP. But there were old hands close to him, this was vintage 250 racing, and de Puniet was at home. He moved straight to the front for another two laps.

Now there were eight to go, and time for Pedrosa to put on the pressure, passing Lorenzo and Stoner in one lap. A new record on lap 19 saw him take the lead, and he kept going at furious speed. Only de Puniet and Dovizioso could go with him, Stoner and Lorenzo outpaced.

On the last lap but one, de Puniet kicked once more, with a tough move at the chicane. He held on as they started the final lap... and all the way to the penultimate corner. He ran a little wide, and Pedrosa was ready and waiting to take advantage, to win by a quarter of a second. Dovizioso was just over a second behind, then Stoner and Lorenzo breathless behind them.

Aoyama came through to push Barbera seventh, with Debon and Guintoli closing to the finish, Takahashi dropping away.

125 cc RACE – 24 laps

Half a second covered a close front row, with Luthi snatching his first pole from Kallio in the closing minutes. Faubel was alongside, then Talmacsi on the second KTM.

The Swiss rider was unbeatable. Luthi led every lap but the second, when Lai nosed ahead briefly. After that he pulled away steadily from a typical brawl for second, gaining half-a-second or more on some laps. It was a lonely race, and an unstoppable first win.

Lai played a slowly fading role in the next gang, losing touch before half distance and ultimately retiring. Faubel had already pulled into the pits by then, leaving two KTMs – Kallio and Talmacsi – engaged with Frenchman di Meglio's Honda. Then on lap 13 Simoncelli had caught up, and he made his way to the front of the group with a series of brave passes, including one under a yellow flag.

He was lying second when IRTA showed him the board ordering him back to fifth place.

Gadea also caught up the group, and he also made an illegal pass, but Race Direction judged that he had immediately given way again to reverse the order. By the finish he had his hands full fighting off Kallio, with di Meglio, Simoncelli and Talmacsi close behind.

Nieto was a distant seventh, then Simon, Toth and Poggiali tenth, his season failing to gain any momentum.

LE MANS – BUGATTI CIRCUIT

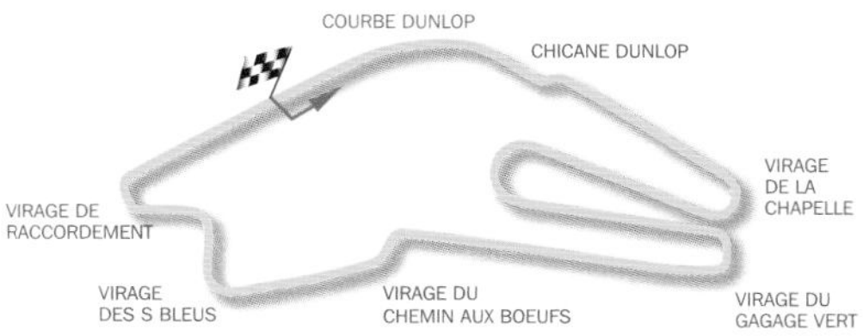
COURBE DUNLOP
CHICANE DUNLOP
VIRAGE DE LA CHAPELLE
VIRAGE DE RACCORDEMENT
VIRAGE DES S BLEUS
VIRAGE DU CHEMIN AUX BOEUFS
VIRAGE DU GAGAGE VERT

CIRCUIT LENGTH: 2.597 miles/4.180 km

GRAND PRIX ALICE DE FRANCE

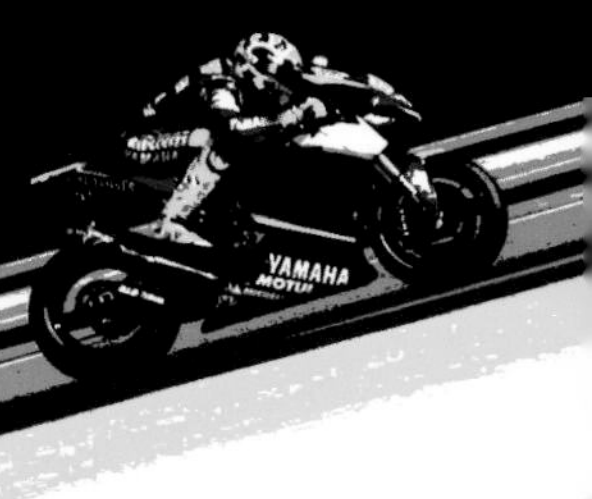

15 MAY 2005 • FIM WORLD CHAMPIONSHIP ROUND 4

MotoGP

28 laps, 72.716 miles/117.040 km

Pos.	Rider (Nat.)	No.	Machine	Laps	Time & speed
1	Valentino Rossi (I)	46	Yamaha	28	44m 12.223s 98.714 mph/ 158.864 km/h
2	Sete Gibernau (E)	15	Honda	28	44m 12.605s
3	Colin Edwards (USA)	5	Yamaha	28	44m 17.934s
4	Marco Melandri (I)	33	Honda	28	44m 19.499s
5	Max Biaggi (I)	3	Honda	28	44m 19.926s
6	Nicky Hayden (USA)	69	Honda	28	44m 33.993s
7	Loris Capirossi (I)	65	Ducati	28	44m 36.887s
8	Shinya Nakano (J)	56	Kawasaki	28	44m 48.163s
9	Toni Elias (E)	24	Yamaha	28	44m 50.285s
10	Troy Bayliss (AUS)	12	Honda	28	45m 04.830s
11	Olivier Jacque (F)	19	Kawasaki	28	45m 05.525s
12	Ruben Xaus (E)	11	Yamaha	28	45m 12.565s
13	Kenny Roberts (USA)	10	Suzuki	28	45m 12.737s
14	Jurgen vd Goorbergh (NL)	16	Honda	28	45m 30.216s
15	Roberto Rolfo (I)	44	Ducati	28	45m 44.456s
16	John Hopkins (USA)	21	Suzuki	27	44m 50.726s
17	Franco Battaini (I)	27	Blata	27	45m 22.642s
	Alex Barros (BR)	4	Honda	12	DNF
	James Ellison (GB)	77	Blata	2	DNF
	Shane Byrne (GB)	67	Proton KR	0	DNF
	Carlos Checa (E)	7	Ducati	0	DNF

Fastest lap: Rossi, 1m 33.678s, 99.814 mph/160.635 km/h (record).

Previous record: Max Biaggi, I (Honda), 1m 34.088s, 99.379 mph/159.935 km/h (2004).

Event best maximum speed: Biaggi, 188.7 mph/303.7 km/h (race).

Qualifying: 1 Rossi, 1m 33.226s; 2 Edwards, 1m 33.449s; 3 Melandri, 1m 33.465s; 4 Gibernau, 1m 33.467s; 5 Hayden, 1m 33.514s; 6 Nakano, 1m 33.536s; 7 Hopkins, 1m 33.594s; 8 Biaggi, 1m 33.699s; 9 Checa, 1m 33.727s; 10 Capirossi, 1m 33.773s; 11 Barros, 1m 33.876s; 12 Elias, 1m 33.991s; 13 Jacque, 1m 34.403s; 14 Roberts, 1m 35.068s; 15 Bayliss, 1m 35.231s; 16 Xaus, 1m 35.772s; 17 Byrne, 1m 36.249s; 18 Rolfo, 1m 36.319s; 19 van den Goorbergh, 1m 36.595s; 20 Ellison, 1m 37.265s; 21 Battaini, 1m 37.341s.

Fastest race laps: 1 Rossi, 1m 33.678s; 2 Gibernau, 1m 33.906s; 3 Melandri, 1m 33.965s; 4 Biaggi, 1m 34.206s; 5 Hayden, 1m 34.355s; 6 Edwards, 1m 34.366s; 7 Capirossi, 1m 34.658s; 8 Barros, 1m 34.740s; 9 Nakano, 1m 34.856s; 10 Elias, 1m 35.191s; 11 Hopkins, 1m 35.406s; 12 Jacque, 1m 35.720s; 13 Roberts, 1m 35.763s; 14 Bayliss, 1m 35.786s; 15 Xaus, 1m 35.991s; 16 Rolfo, 1m 36.258s; 17 van den Goorbergh, 1m 36.706s; 18 Ellison, 1m 38.996s; 19 Battaini, 1m 39.642s.

World Championship: 1 Rossi, 95; 2 Melandri, 58; 3 Gibernau, 53; 4 Biaggi, 47; 5 Barros, 43; 6 Edwards, 41; 7 Nakano, 27; 8 Hayden, 26; 9 Jacque, 25; 10 Capirossi, 23; 11 Bayliss, 21; 12 Checa, 17; 13 Xaus, 16; 14 Elias, 15; 15 van den Goorbergh, 12; 16 Hopkins, 11; 17 Tamada, 8; 18 Roberts, 7; 19 Hofmann and Rolfo, 5; 21 Ellison, 4; 22 Ukawa, 1.

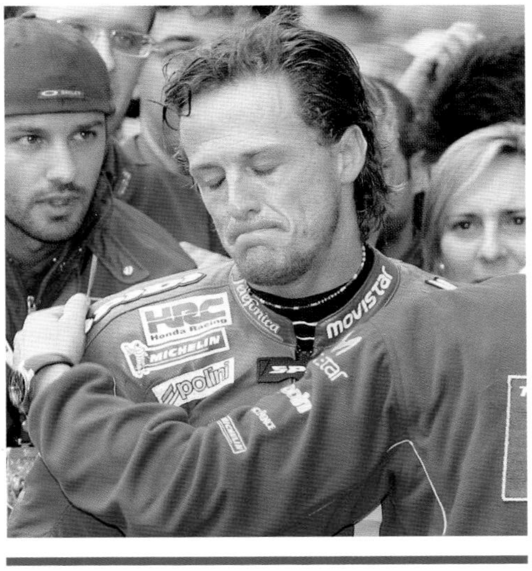

250 cc

26 laps, 67.522 miles/108.680 km

Pos.	Rider (Nat.)	No.	Machine	Laps	Time & speed
1	Daniel Pedrosa (E)	1	Honda	26	42m 55.152s 94.406 mph/ 151.932 km/h
2	Randy de Puniet (F)	7	Aprilia	26	42m 55.403s
3	Andrea Dovizioso (I)	34	Honda	26	42m 56.706s
4	Casey Stoner (AUS)	27	Aprilia	26	42m 59.382s
5	Jorge Lorenzo (E)	48	Honda	26	43m 01.179s
6	Hiroshi Aoyama (J)	73	Honda	26	43m 19.121s
7	Hector Barbera (E)	80	Honda	26	43m 25.819s
8	Alex Debon (E)	6	Honda	26	43m 27.191s
9	Sylvain Guintoli (F)	50	Aprilia	26	43m 27.604s
10	Yuki Takahashi (J)	55	Honda	26	43m 32.924s
11	Simone Corsi (I)	24	Aprilia	26	43m44.437s
12	Chaz Davies (GB)	57	Aprilia	26	43m 44.661s
13	Alex Baldolini (I)	25	Aprilia	26	43m 44.682s
14	Roberto Locatelli (I)	15	Aprilia	26	43m 44.923s
15	Andrea Ballerini (I)	8	Aprilia	26	43m 45.047s
16	Jakub Smrz (CZ)	96	Honda	26	43m 57.274s
17	Mirko Giansanti (I)	32	Aprilia	26	43m 57.764s
18	Anthony West (AUS)	14	Aprilia	26	44m 12.510s
19	Gregory Leblanc (F)	38	Aprilia	26	44m 12.654s
20	Erwan Nigon (F)	63	Aprilia	26	44m 13.534s
21	Radomil Rous (CZ)	64	Honda	26	44m 17.850s
22	Gabor Rizmayer (H)	12	Yamaha	25	43m 24.437s
	Sebastian Porto (ARG)	19	Aprilia	13	DNF
	Alex de Angelis (RSM)	5	Aprilia	7	DNF
	Frederik Watz (S)	18	Yamaha	6	DNF
	Steve Jenkner (D)	17	Aprilia	0	DNF
	Dirk Heidolf (D)	28	Honda	0	DNF
	Hugo Marchand (F)	9	Aprilia		DNS
	Arnaud Vincent (F)	21	Fantic		DNQ
	Samuel Aubry (F)	65	Honda		DNQ
	Gabriele Ferro (I)	20	Fantic		DNQ
	Marc Antoine Scaccia (F)	47	Yamaha		DNQ
	Zheng Peng Li (CHN)	61	Aprilia		DNQ

Fastest lap: de Puniet, 1m 37.594s, 95.809 mph/154.189 km/h (record).

Previous record: Daniel Pedrosa, E (Honda), 1m 38.202s, 95.216 mph/153.235 km/h (2004).

Event best maximum speed: Dovizioso, 156.0 mph/251.0 km/h (race).

Qualifying: 1 Pedrosa, 1m 37.391s; 2 Stoner, 1m 37.880s; 3 Lorenzo, 1m 37.882s; 4 Porto, 1m 38.123s; 5 Dovizioso, 1m 38.448s; 6 de Puniet, 1m 38.554s; 7 de Angelis, 1m 38.588s; 8 Guintoli, 1m 38.641s; 9 Barbera, 1m 38.707s; 10 Aoyama, 1m 38.729s; 11 Davies, 1m 39.447s; 12 Smrz, 1m 39.516s; 13 Takahashi, 1m 39.528s; 14 Ballerini, 1m 39.540s; 15 Debon, 1m 39.599s; 16 Locatelli, 1m 39.737s; 17 Corsi, 1m 39.855s; 18 Giansanti, 1m 40.239s; 19 Baldolini, 1m 40.355s; 20 Jenkner, 1m 40.495s; 21 Nigon, 1m 40.857s; 22 Leblanc, 1m 41.420s; 23 Heidolf, 1m 41.444s; 24 Rous, 1m 41.464s; 25 West, 1m 42.339s; 26 Rizmayer, 1m 42.540s; 27 Marchand, 1m 42.700s; 28 Watz, 1m 43.061s; 29 Vincent, 1m 44.587s; 30 Aubry, 1m 46.103s; 31 Ferro, 1m 46.430s; 32 Scaccia, 1m 47.251s; 33 Li, 21m 31.231s.

Fastest race laps: 1 de Puniet, 1m 37.594s; 2 Pedrosa, 1m 37.665s; 3 Dovizioso, 1m 37.797s; 4 Stoner, 1m 37.980s; 5 Lorenzo, 1m 38.297s; 6 Porto, 1m 38.726s; 7 de Angelis, 1m 38.880s; 8 Aoyama, 1m 39.189s; 9 Barbera, 1m 39.228s; 10 Debon, 1m 39.329s; 11 Takahashi, 1m 39.365s; 12 Guintoli, 1m 39.433s; 13 Baldolini, 1m 39.852s; 14 Davies, 1m 39.908s; 15 Ballerini, 1m 40.048s; 16 Giansanti, 1m 40.180s; 17 Smrz, 1m 40.181s; 18 Locatelli, 1m 40.206s; 19 Corsi, 1m 40.231s; 20 Leblanc, 1m 40.333s; 21 West, 1m 40.386s; 22 Nigon, 1m 40.630s; 23 Rous, 1m 40.932s; 24 Rizmayer, 1m 42.842s; 25 Watz, 1m 43.276s.

World Championship: 1 Pedrosa, 73; 2 Dovizioso, 69; 3 Stoner, 63; 4 de Angelis, 40; 5 Porto, 38; 6 Aoyama and de Puniet, 36; 8 Barbera and Lorenzo, 34; 10 Debon, 24; 11 Takahashi, 21; 12 Corsi, 20; 13 Guintoli, 19; 14 Locatelli, 11; 15 Baldolini and Davies, 9; 17 Giansanti, 8; 18 Smrz, 6; 19 Rous, 4; 20 Ballerini, 3; 21 Cardenas, Heidolf and Leblanc, 1.

125 cc

24 laps, 62.328 miles/100.320 km

Pos.	Rider (Nat.)	No.	Machine	Laps	Time & speed
1	Thomas Luthi (CH)	12	Honda	24	41m 52.772s 89.307 mph/ 143.726 km/h
2	Sergio Gadea (E)	33	Aprilia	24	41m 55.852s
3	Mika Kallio (SF)	36	KTM	24	41m 56.035s
4	Mike di Meglio (F)	63	Honda	24	41m 57.009s
5	Marco Simoncelli (I)	58	Aprilia	24	41m 57.083s
6	Gabor Talmacsi (H)	14	KTM	24	41m 57.654s
7	Pablo Nieto (E)	22	Derbi	24	42m 18.595s
8	Julian Simon (E)	60	KTM	24	42m 19.121s
9	Imre Toth (H)	45	Aprilia	24	42m 24.383s
10	Manuel Poggiali (RSM)	54	Gilera	24	42m 25.624s
11	Lorenzo Zanetti (I)	8	Aprilia	24	42m 26.042s
12	Aleix Espargaro (E)	41	Honda	24	42m 33.392s
13	Dario Giuseppetti (D)	25	Aprilia	24	42m 36.249s
14	Manuel Hernandez (E)	43	Aprilia	24	42m 38.162s
15	Sandro Cortese (D)	11	Honda	24	42m 46.696s
16	Julian Miralles (E)	84	Aprilia	24	42m 49.712s
17	Gioele Pellino (I)	42	Malaguti	24	42m 54.160s
18	Mathieu Lussiana (F)	88	Honda	24	43m 00.327s
19	Federico Sandi (I)	10	Honda	24	43m 00.522s
20	Raffaele de Rosa (I)	35	Aprilia	24	43m 00.931s
21	Karel Abraham (CZ)	44	Aprilia	24	43m 02.679s
22	Nicolas Terol (E)	18	Derbi	24	43m 03.933s
23	Andrea Iannone (I)	29	Aprilia	24	43m 09.669s
24	Raymond Schouten (NL)	16	Honda	24	43m10.414s
	Fabrizio Lai (I)	32	Honda	18	DNF
	Alexis Masbou (F)	7	Honda	16	DNF
	Mathieu Gines (F)	74	Honda	16	DNF
	Tomoyoshi Koyama (J)	71	Honda	15	DNF
	Jules Cluzel (F)	89	Honda	15	DNF
	Jordi Carchano (E)	28	Aprilia	11	DNF
	Michele Pirro (I)	15	Malaguti	11	DNF
	Vincent Braillard (CH)	26	Aprilia	11	DNF
	Alexis Michel (F)	90	Honda	10	DNF
	Alvaro Bautista (E)	19	Honda	9	DNF
	Hector Faubel (E)	55	Aprilia	7	DNF
	Lukas Pesek (CZ)	52	Derbi	6	DNF
	Joan Olive (E)	6	Aprilia	6	DNF
	Angel Rodriguez (E)	47	Honda	4	DNF
	Toshihisa Kuzuhara (J)	9	Honda		DNS
	Yannick Deschamps (F)	73	Honda		DNS

Fastest lap: Kallio, 1m 43.373s, 90.452 mph/145.569 km/h.

Previous record: Andrea Dovizioso, I (Honda), 1m 42.651s, 91.089 mph/146.593 km/h (2004).

Event best maximum speed: Kuzuhara, 133.1 mph/214.2 km/h (qualifying practice no. 1).

Qualifying: 1 Luthi, 1m 43.405s; 2 Kallio, 1m 43.688s; 3 Faubel, 1m 43.939s; 4 Talmacsi, 1m 43.940s; 5 Simoncelli, 1m 44.005s; 6 Pesek, 1m 44.088s; 7 Lai, 1m 44.201s; 8 Simon, 1m 44.325s; 9 di Meglio, 1m 44.468s; 10 Gadea, 1m 44.610s; 11 Masbou, 1m 44.694s; 12 Nieto, 1m 44.770s; 13 Olive, 1m 44.791s; 14 Koyama, 1m 44.820s; 15 Poggiali, 1m 45.000s; 16 Hernandez, 1m 45.014s; 17 Bautista, 1m 45.019s; 18 Toth, 1m 45.120s; 19 Cortese, 1m 45.147s; 20 Rodriguez, 1m 45.157s; 21 Zanetti, 1m 45.521s; 22 Kuzuhara, 1m 45.625s; 23 Miralles, 1m 45.629s; 24 Espargaro, 1m 45.651s; 25 Cluzel, 1m 45.838s; 26 Giuseppetti, 1m 45.906s; 27 Braillard, 1m 45.916s; 28 Carchano, 1m 46.068s; 29 Sandi, 1m 46.084s; 30 de Rosa, 1m 46.215s; 31 Gines, 1m 46.291s; 32 Lussiana, 1m 46.415s; 33 Terol, 1m 46.460s; 34 Iannone, 1m 46.470s; 35 Pirro, 1m 46.616s; 36 Schouten, 1m 46.649s; 37 Abraham, 1m 47.154s; 38 Deschamps, 1m 47.358s; 39 Pellino, 1m 47.781s; 40 Michel, 1m 48.485s.

Fastest race laps: 1 Kallio, 1m 43.373s; 2 Luthi, 1m 43.585s; 3 Simoncelli, 1m 43.690s; 4 Gadea, 1m 43.771s; 5 di Meglio, 1m 43.848s; 6 Faubel, 1m 43.913s; 7 Talmacsi, 1m 43.950s; 8 Masbou, 1m 44.212s; 9 Poggiali, 1m 44.387s; 10 Bautista, 1m 44.451s; 11 Simon, 1m 44.451s; 12 Nieto, 1m 44.468s; 13 Lai, 1m 44.475s; 14 Koyama, 1m 44.541s; 15 Zanetti, 1m 44.579s; 16 Olive, 1m 44.828s; 17 Pesek, 1m 44.915s; 18 Toth, 1m 45.059s; 19 Hernandez, 1m 45.132s; 20 Espargaro, 1m 45.219s; 21 Giuseppetti, 1m 45.241s; 22 Cortese, 1m 45.319s; 23 Miralles, 1m 45.505s; 24 Carchano, 1m 45.544s; 25 Braillard, 1m 45.675s; 26 Abraham, 1m 45.720s; 27 Lussiana, 1m 46.050s; 28 Gines, 1m 46.129s; 29 Pellino, 1m 46.159s; 30 Sandi, 1m 46.215s; 31 Schouten, 1m 46.219s; 32 Pirro, 1m 46.224s; 33 de Rosa, 1m 46.282s; 34 Iannone, 1m 46.321s; 35 Terol, 1m 46.538s; 36 Cluzel, 1m 46.653s; 37 Rodriguez, 1m 47.188s; 38 Michel, 1m 50.491s.

World Championship: 1 Kallio, 66; 2 Luthi, 54; 3 Simoncelli, 52; 4 Lai, 49; 5 Pasini, 46; 6 Talmacsi, 37; 7 Poggiali, 31; 8 Faubel, 30; 9 Simon, 28; 10 Nieto, 25; 11 di Meglio, 23; 12 Koyama, 21; 13 Gadea, 20; 14 Espargaro, 15; 15 Olive, 10; 16 Bautista and Hernandez, 9; 18 Pesek and Toth, 7; 20 Zanetti, 5; 21 Carchano, Giuseppetti, Masbou and Pirro, 3; 25 Kuzuhara, 2; 26 Cortese and Terol, 1.

ITALIANGP
MUGELLO

Rossi view of the fans - he gave them what they came for.
Photograph: Martin Heath

ROSSI mania is an international phenomenon, but nobody can grasp the full scale of it until they see it at Mugello. Especially when he wins... as he has done five times in nine visits in all three classes, and for the past three years straight. His stature can be gauged from his latest honour – academic decoration from the University of Urbino (his birthplace)... a "Doctorate ad Honorem" in Communication and Publicity. The ceremony, where he was presented with a scroll, a gown and a mortarboard was attended by more than 1,500 people. It justified the legend on his special helmet – "The Real Doctor", as well as "Il Laureato" (The Graduate) on the back. And explains why the delighted Rossi, sweating profusely, donned the same mortarboard on the rostrum.

Anything that fervent is also inevitably somewhat sinister, particularly in the narrowing confines of the steep-sided valley athwart which the magnificent circuit plunges and swoops. Especially when it is echoing to cheers for Rossi and boos to Gibernau. And especially in a country where melodrama and mayhem often go hand in hand. Big changes have been forced on the Ferrari-owned circuit and its operators after problems with track invasions and traffic gridlock in the past, and moves to limit crowd numbers, manage their movement, and control traffic were largely successful. Even so, there were still armed guards posted at the back of Rossi's pit, just in case.

It was a very Italian race, too, with Rossi, Biaggi, Capirossi and Melandri making all the running up front. The grandeur of the track layout is matched by a propensity for very close racing at very, very high speeds. In fact, the numbers weren't quite as high as in China, nor even quite as fast as last year, but Checa's Duke still ran 211.6 mph/340.5 km/h. This at the point where tucked-in riders cross a brow, wheels in the air, landing to brake hard for the first corner. The high-speed artistry and courage are a match for Assen and Phillip Island.

So, once again, are the MotoGP bikes just too fast? This question had already been answered in the affirmative some time before; by how much had been in dispute ever since, even after the MSMA had announced at last year's Spanish GP that they planned to cut capacity from 990cc to 900 for 2007. Honda's discontent had been made clear more or less at once, by Jerez this year the MSMA were letting it be known they were reconsidering. At Mugello, the decision came... a Honda-pleasing extra 100cc lopped off: from 2007 the machines will be 800cc. Yamaha signified broad agreement (or at least acceptance), likewise Suzuki and Kawasaki. Others were less pleased. Ducati were still arguing after the fact that pneumatic valve springs should be banned... this to preserve any advantage of their desmodromic system. Kenny Roberts looked resigned, and said: "It'll be the end for this KTM engine." And at the far end Blata saw the relevance of their still-awaited V6 curtailed still further. "We always thought it would only be a two-year engine," said team boss Peter Clifford. "Now it will be one-year."

Rossi had a typically memorable comment. "For sure, it will not have the same taste as 1000cc. We are lucky – maybe these bikes we are riding now will go into legend. But these bikes are starting to go too fast." Biaggi was also in favour of cutting overall power. "Maybe they will be a little bit slower, but already we cannot use the horsepower in the first three gears."

Another new rule for 2007, also aimed at curbing power increases, was a further reduction in fuel tank sized, from 22 to 21 litres; a reminder that so far this year fears that riders might be running out of gas at the end of races had not so far come to pass.

And with immediate effect, "ship-to-shore" radios were also banned. This made little practical difference; in spite of a number of attempts nobody had been able to make the system work properly. One problem was simply making the intercoms audible; another that riders tend to stop listening when they're riding with total concentration. The obvious application for communication would be a wet race, to call a rider in for a tyre change, or (as Gibernau needed in Portugal) to warn him of a sudden change in conditions. Now it will never be used.

The injury profile had shuffled its victims – Tamada and Hofmann were both back, consigning Jacque to a hanging-around role; the absentee this time was the unlucky Toni Elias, who had sustained fractures in his left ankle, arm and wrist, crashing while testing at Le Mans the day after the GP. The wrist injury, the dreaded broken scaphoid, was the most troublesome and serious, and though he tried to return a week later, he would be out of action for three races, spoiling a so-far promising class debut. His place was taken by some-time 250 rider David Checa, younger brother of Carlos, fresh from victory at the Le Mans 24-Hour race.

Racing was close also in the smaller classes. In the 250s, rookie Lorenzo had another charging ride, leading for a second race in succession then claiming a fine second in a close battle. And it was almost too close in the smallest class, which ended with one of those accidents that seem always to be waiting to happen when the leading pack is as close as this. On the final long and fast downhill left, with only yards left to run, leader Mika Kallio slipped and flicked over the high-side, under the wheels of Hector Faubel, in with a chance of bettering his career-best second in Portugal. He couldn't avoid running over him, and both looped at speed into the gravel. By some miracle, neither was seriously hurt.

The Graduate...

Main picture: Rossi treats the fans to some Michelin smoke.

Far left: As always, they want more.

Far left, inserts: Tavullia lies over the Apennines, with a café for fan club HQ. Rossi has made the little town famous.

Below: Full marks. The Real Doctor had given another master class.
Photographs: Gold & Goose

Above: At lap-record speed, Biaggi flew past Melandri.

Right: Tamada was back again, this time fit to race.

Centre right: Alex Hoffman, back in the saddle and in the points.

Photographs: Gold & Goose

MOTOGP RACE – 23 laps

There were a dozen within a second of pole, positions something of a lottery. But with the same winner – a demonstration of perfect pit work saw Rossi once again reel off an unbeatable lap on soft qualifiers in the dying seconds of practice. It was possible also to get it wrong: the pit crews of Biaggi, Melandri and Hayden all underestimated the time taken by the out lap, and their riders crossed the line after the chequered flag, wasting their second set of qualifiers.

Capirossi led into the first corner, after one of the big Duke's trade-mark drag-strip starts, Gibernau and the rest lining up behind him, Rossi sixth or so. His first lap was a stormer, however, and he gained two places into that first corner, was up into third on the tricky Casanova-Savelli swoop off the hill. By now Gibernau was in front. Rossi despatched Capirossi also on the last long right-hander, and dived past Gibernau at the next fast chicane. Rossi leads!

Melandri was fast behind him, seizing second on lap two, but the way Rossi drew away was demoralising, two seconds clear and still stretching after six laps. Gibernau was falling back, blaming a lack of front-end bite; he ceded third to Biaggi on lap four, and he was under pressure from Capirossi one lap later when down he went – a second race crash of the year. "I was over-riding the bike. It was my fault," he said later. "I was strug-

gling to do the lap times from the start. It's all about risking, and it's all about racing. I wanted to win or nothing."

Biaggi brought the race back to life. He flew past Melandri with a new record on lap five, and rapidly closed the two-second gap on Rossi, on his tail by lap nine. Melandri had followed along, and now the real racing began, with both Honda riders having a clear speed advantage on the long straight.

Melandri was the first to attack, leading the tenth lap; directly afterwards Rossi and Biaggi put him third, and pulled away slowly over the next five laps. At the same time, Capirossi was closing again from behind, and when Biaggi attacked successfully (also at Casanova-Savelli) on lap 17 to lead for four laps, both Melandri and Capirossi closed up to make four up front. But the latter pair were far too busy with one another to challenge for the lead, Capirossi powering past time and again on the straight only to run wide in one of the subsequent turns.

Rossi was in control, albeit narrowly, with Biaggi pushing every inch of the way; Capirossi had finally managed to stay in front of Melandri all the way round lap 22, and they crossed the line almost together on the 23rd, less than four seconds back. A fine and very Italian GP.

A similar distance behind, a good battle for fifth finally went to Checa. He'd succumbed to Hayden on lap seven while struggling with a full fuel load, but after half distance Checa was the fastest man on the track as he closed again, finally pushing

past on lap 19, to be chased all the way.

Hopkins had started well, hounding Hayden for a lap or two until the Hondas of Barros and Tamada both piled past, followed by Edwards. Barros, hampered by a poor grid position, was the fastest, running close to the race leaders' times as he escaped the group for a lonely chase after Checa and Hayden, still three seconds behind at the end.

Tamada and Edwards finished close together in that order, a strong ride from the returned Japanese injury victim but a disappointment for the American after his last-race rostrum. "I'm as mystified as anyone. Every refinement to the bike seems to leave us in the same position. We struggled to get it working – the race was an uphill battle," he said later.

Hopkins lost the group, managing to hold Nakano at bay for the first ten laps, finally finishing five seconds adrift. By the end he was kept busy managing a gap over the returned Hofmann's Kawasaki, the German in turn busy fending off a last-lap lunge by Bayliss, having passed the struggling Australian with eight laps left.

Xaus, another ex-Ducati rider struggling with his new Japanese machine, was another eight seconds back at the flag, with a disgruntled Roberts trailing his Suzuki in behind for the last point. He'd slowed so much in the final laps that he'd come under threat from Byrne's Proton, the new KTM engine lacking acceleration but with good top-end speed (203.9 mph/328.1 km/h, beating the Suzukis and Kawasakis handsomely) and improved handling from the new chassis to get him past Rolfo's Dunlop-shod 2004 Ducati in the closing stages.

Battaini was 18th, ahead of David Checa's Yamaha after the

Top left: Loris Capirossi at full lean for Ducati's first rostrum of the season.

Centre left: Private team owners Luis d'Antin and Luca Montiron find common ground.

Below: Three Hondas and a Yamaha – Hayden, Rossi, Biaggi and Gibernau – make a 200mph eight-wheeler at one of racing's most spectacular sections of track.
Photograph: Gold & Goose

new boy pitted on lap one with "a strange feeling from the rear", before rejoining. Ellison had retired after one lap.

250 cc RACE – 21 laps

Unstoppable rookie Lorenzo took his first class pole by the most slender of margins from Stoner, with Dovizioso and de Puniet completing the first row. Pedrosa was seventh fastest, behind de Angelis and Porto on the second row, but still less than half-a-second off pole.

The defending champion got the drop to lead off the line, but the company was close and pressing, and he was consigned to fourth on lap two, with de Puniet now leading from Stoner and Dovizioso. Next time round, Stoner was in front, and he held the lead until well after half distance, the pursuers swapping to and fro in an eventful race. De Angelis had moved to join the party early on, with Pedrosa, de Puniet and Dovizioso still going strong, Porto losing touch behind.

Lorenzo was the man to watch. Seventh after the first lap, he was soon moving forward, past Porto on lap five. At the same time, ahead of them, de Puniet crashed out again.

Dovizioso was drifting out of touch now, and Lorenzo closed quickly and pounced on lap seven, and then took two more laps to close down a second's gap on the leaders. He hadn't finished yet. On lap ten he took third from Pedrosa, and firmly resisted subsequent attempts on lap 13 to reverse the position, all the while sniffing at de Angelis close in front. Even more impressive was his aggression at the start of lap 15, when he swept from third to first in one outbraking move.

He led for three laps, but with no visor fogging or other problems Pedrosa was waiting for the close of play to give his best. He showed his class when he came out best in a reshuffle on the straight at the end of lap 19, with de Angelis second, then Stoner, Lorenzo suddenly back to fourth.

By the final lap, Pedrosa was inching away, half-a-second clear; while Lorenzo had barged past Stoner into third with an all-elbows move mid-chicane. In the last corner, the thrusting Spaniard did the same to de Angelis, who was just two thousandths ahead of Stoner over the line.

Porto was still less than five seconds behind, fending off Barbera, who had caught up from a slow start, both of them having passed the fading Dovizioso. He had more trouble in store, losing seventh to Aoyama three laps from the end, narrowly failing to regain it over the line. Aoyama had earlier been back and forth with compatriot Takahashi, until he crashed out five laps from the end.

Corsi had an up-and-down race to ninth, well clear of the next gang disputing tenth. Chaz Davies won out, after Smrz collided with Guintoli in the thick of it, splitting the group and dropping Ballerini and Giansanti off the back.

Locatelli and Vincent were among a number of fallers.

125 cc RACE – 20 laps

Top speeds of the smallest bikes were close, with Zanetti's Aprilia fastest of the weekend at 145.8 mph (234.7 km/h). Hondas, Gileras and a stable-mate Derbi were faster than the top KTM (Kallio's), which was only 13th, but a mere two mph slower. But Kallio and team-mate Talmacsi led practice, the former's third pole of the year. The Aprilias of Faubel and Pasini completed the front row.

The race was as close as the speeds. Kallio led away and was in front across the line for 15 of the 20 laps. In fact only Faubel and Simoncelli also led over the line, and of course Talmacsi on the final lap. But Luthi was the fifth in the leading pack, and they were exchanging positions at every point, and often three or four abreast, with Luthi also taking a short spell up front.

Just after the midway point, Simoncelli was flicked off through one of the fast chicanes, leaving just four in a fearsome brawl.

Kallio had opened a small but significant gap on the final lap, apparently running for the flag. But he was trying too hard, and the final long left-hander, running downhill towards the finish line, was his nemesis … and that of Faubel close behind. Kallio was instantly over the high side, and his trajectory carried him right under the Spaniard's wheels. It was a spectacular crash.

Earlier on the lap, Talmacsi had nosed past Luthi, and now found himself leading. He managed to hang on to his first victory by less than a tenth. Luthi's reward for second was the championship lead.

Pasini and Koyama had been racing it out behind the leaders for almost full distance, until Olive and Gadea closed up. Gadea sputtered to a stop on the last lap; Olive managed to lead the remaining trio over the line by inches, for his first podium in three years. Pasini was next, then Koyama.

Three seconds behind, Poggiali came through to snitch sixth from Simon by a couple of tenths; Lai, Kuzuhara and Masbou made up the top ten.

AUTODROMO INTERNAZIONALE
DEL MUGELLO

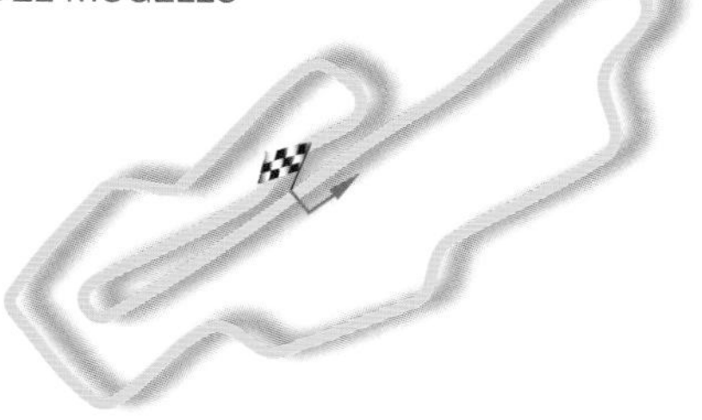

CIRCUIT LENGTH: 3.259 miles/5.245 km

GRAN PREMIO ALICE D'ITALIA

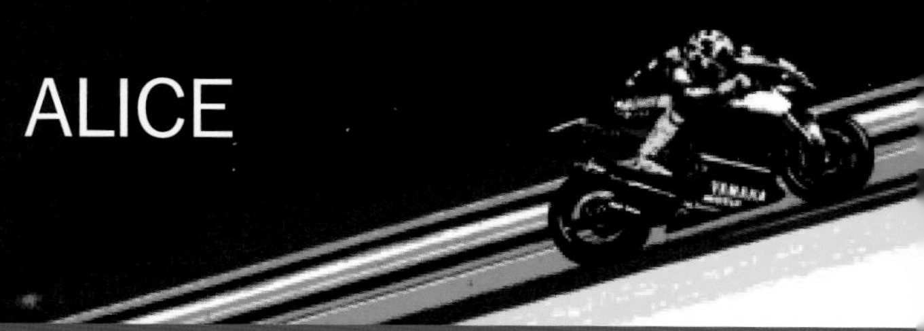

5 JUNE 2005 • FIM WORLD CHAMPIONSHIP ROUND 5

MotoGP

23 laps, 74.957 miles/120.635 km

Pos.	Rider (Nat.)	No.	Machine	Laps	Time & speed
1	Valentino Rossi (I)	46	Yamaha	23	42m 42.994s 105.288 mph/ 169.444 km/h
2	Max Biaggi (I)	3	Honda	23	42m 43.353s
3	Loris Capirossi (I)	65	Ducati	23	42m 46.868s
4	Marco Melandri (I)	33	Honda	23	42m 46.973s
5	Carlos Checa (E)	7	Ducati	23	42m 50.892s
6	Nicky Hayden (USA)	69	Honda	23	42m 51.198s
7	Alex Barros (BR)	4	Honda	23	42m 54.566s
8	Makoto Tamada (J)	6	Honda	23	43m 08.368s
9	Colin Edwards (USA)	5	Yamaha	23	43m 08.479s
10	Shinya Nakano (J)	56	Kawasaki	23	43m 19.543s
11	John Hopkins (USA)	21	Suzuki	23	43m 24.631s
12	Alex Hofmann (D)	66	Kawasaki	23	43m 26.653s
13	Troy Bayliss (AUS)	12	Honda	23	43m 26.910s
14	Ruben Xaus (E)	11	Yamaha	23	43m 34.569s
15	Kenny Roberts (USA)	10	Suzuki	23	43m 53.269s
16	Shane Byrne (GB)	67	Proton KR	23	43m 55.576s
17	Roberto Rolfo (I)	44	Ducati	23	43m 56.041s
18	Franco Battaini (I)	27	Blata	22	43m 01.858s
19	David Checa (E)	94	Yamaha	22	44m 23.120s
	Sete Gibernau (E)	15	Honda	5	DNF
	James Ellison (GB)	77	Blata	0	DNF

Fastest lap: Biaggi, 1m 50.117s, 106.548 mph/171.472 km/h (record).

Previous record: Gibernau, 1m 51.133s, 105.573 mph/169.904 km/h (2004).

Event best maximum speed: Checa, 211.6 mph/340.5 km/h (free practice no. 3).

Qualifying: 1 Rossi, 1m 49.223s; 2 Gibernau, 1m 49.361s; 3 Biaggi, 1m 49.458s; 4 Hayden, 1m 49.546s; 5 Hopkins, 1m 49.556s; 6 Capirossi, 1m 49.633s; 7 Melandri, 1m 49.805s; 8 C. Checa, 1m 49.811s; 9 Nakano, 1m 49.856s; 10 Tamada, 1m 49.951s; 11 Roberts, 1m 50.052s; 12 Edwards, 1m 50.176s; 13 Barros, 1m 50.281s; 14 Hofmann, 1m 51.056s; 15 Xaus, 1m 51.585s; 16 D. Checa, 1m 51.610s; 17 Bayliss, 1m 51.764s; 18 Byrne, 1m 52.117s; 19 Rolfo, 1m 53.010s; 20 Ellison, 1m 54.177s; 21 Battaini, 1m 54.820s.

Fastest race laps: 1 Biaggi, 1m 50.117s; 2 Rossi, 1m 50.291s; 3 Melandri, 1m 50.338s; 4 Capirossi, 1m 50.728s; 5 C. Checa, 1m 50.856s; 6 Gibernau, 1m 50.938s; 7 Barros, 1m 50.963s; 8 Hayden, 1m 50.974s; 9 Tamada, 1m 51.388s; 10 Edwards, 1m 51.504s; 11 Bayliss, 1m 52.120s; 12 Nakano, 1m 52.136s; 13 Hofmann, 1m 52.145s; 14 Hopkins, 1m 52.208s; 15 Roberts, 1m 52.531s; 16 Xaus, 1m 52.712s; 17 Rolfo, 1m 53.273s; 18 D. Checa, 1m 53.725s; 19 Byrne, 1m 53.907s; 20 Battaini, 1m 55.335s.

World Championship: 1 Rossi, 120; 2 Melandri, 71; 3 Biaggi, 67; 4 Gibernau, 53; 5 Barros, 52; 6 Edwards, 48; 7 Capirossi, 39; 8 Hayden, 36; 9 Nakano, 33; 10 C. Checa, 28; 11 Jacque, 25; 12 Bayliss, 24; 13 Xaus, 18; 14 Hopkins and Tamada, 16; 16 Elias, 15; 17 van den Goorbergh, 12; 18 Hofmann, 9; 19 Roberts, 8; 20 Rolfo, 5; 21 Ellison, 4; 22 Ukawa, 1.

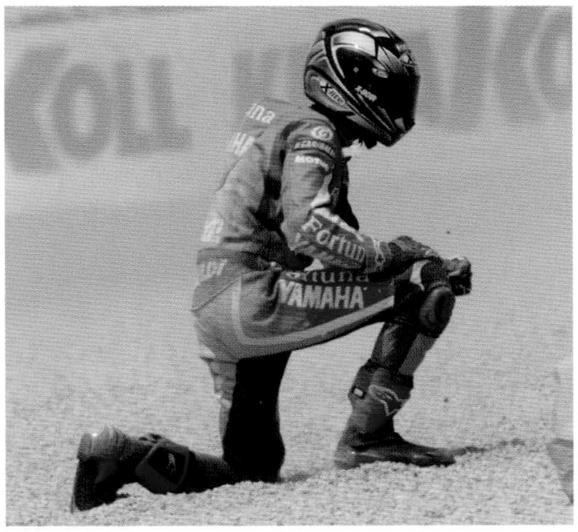

250 cc

21 laps, 68.439 miles/110.145 km

Pos.	Rider (Nat.)	No.	Machine	Laps	Time & speed
1	Daniel Pedrosa (E)	1	Honda	21	40m 31.909s 101.314 mph/ 163.049 km/h
2	Jorge Lorenzo (E)	48	Honda	21	40m 33.095s
3	Alex de Angelis (RSM)	5	Aprilia	21	40m 33.466s
4	Casey Stoner (AUS)	27	Aprilia	21	40m 33.499s
5	Sebastian Porto (ARG)	19	Aprilia	21	40m 38.015s
6	Hector Barbera (E)	80	Honda	21	40m 40.200s
7	Hiroshi Aoyama (J)	73	Honda	21	40m 43.710s
8	Andrea Dovizioso (I)	34	Honda	21	40m 43.778s
9	Simone Corsi (I)	24	Aprilia	21	40m 53.884s
10	Chaz Davies (GB)	57	Aprilia	21	41m 14.290s
11	Andrea Ballerini (I)	8	Aprilia	21	41m 14.408s
12	Mirko Giansanti (I)	32	Aprilia	21	41m 14.991s
13	Radomil Rous (CZ)	64	Honda	21	41m 38.173s
14	Gregory Leblanc (F)	38	Aprilia	21	41m 48.814s
15	Hugo Marchand (F)	9	Aprilia	21	42m 00.178s
16	Alvaro Molina (E)	41	Aprilia	21	42m 03.320s
17	Martin Cardenas (COL)	36	Aprilia	21	42m 07.561s
18	Jarno Ronzoni (I)	71	Aprilia	21	42m 11.370s
	Yuki Takahashi (J)	55	Honda	16	DNF
	Gabor Rizmayer (H)	12	Yamaha	16	DNF
	Yves Polzer (A)	42	Aprilia	13	DNF
	Sylvain Guintoli (F)	50	Aprilia	11	DNF
	Jakub Smrz (CZ)	96	Honda	11	DNF
	Frederik Watz (S)	18	Yamaha	9	DNF
	Alex Baldolini (I)	25	Aprilia	6	DNF
	Randy de Puniet (F)	7	Aprilia	5	DNF
	Alex Debon (E)	6	Honda	3	DNF
	Roberto Locatelli (I)	15	Aprilia	1	DNF
	Arnaud Vincent (F)	21	Fantic	0	DNF
	Dirk Heidolf (D)	28	Honda	0	DNF
	Gabriele Ferro (I)	20	Fantic		DNQ

Fastest lap: de Angelis, 1m 54.332s, 102.619 mph/165.150 km/h (record).

Previous record: Shinya Nakano, J (Yamaha), 1m 54.462s, 102.503 mph/164.963 km/h (2000).

Event best maximum speed: Aoyama, 170.6 mph/274.5 km/h (race).

Qualifying: 1 Lorenzo, 1m 53.494s; 2 Stoner, 1m 53.548s; 3 Dovizioso, 1m 53.674s; 4 de Puniet, 1m 53.714s; 5 de Angelis, 1m 53.841s; 6 Porto, 1m 53.889s; 7 Pedrosa, 1m 53.991s; 8 Barbera, 1m 54.000s; 9 Aoyama, 1m 54.815s; 10 Ballerini, 1m 54.971s; 11 Smrz, 1m 55.054s; 12 Corsi, 1m 55.111s; 13 Takahashi, 1m 55.205s; 14 Guintoli, 1m 55.378s; 15 Baldolini, 1m 55.676s; 16 Locatelli, 1m 55.794s; 17 Davies, 1m 55.879s; 18 Giansanti, 1m 55.885s; 19 Marchand, 1m 57.032s; 20 Leblanc, 1m 57.213s; 21 Heidolf, 1m 57.395s; 22 Ronzoni, 1m 57.668s; 23 Rous, 1m 57.794s; 24 Polzer, 1m 57.803s; 25 Vincent, 1m 57.846s; 26 Debon, 1m 58.019s; 27 Rizmayer, 1m 58.372s; 28 Molina, 1m 58.399s; 29 Watz, 1m 58.636s; 30 Cardenas, 1m 59.689s; 31 Ferro, 2m 03.009s.

Fastest race laps: 1 de Angelis, 1m 54.332s; 2 Pedrosa, 1m 54.381s; 3 Lorenzo, 1m 54.522s; 4 Stoner, 1m 54.660s; 5 de Puniet, 1m 54.779s; 6 Dovizioso, 1m 54.845s; 7 Barbera, 1m 55.136s; 8 Porto, 1m 55.200s; 9 Corsi, 1m 55.271s; 10 Aoyama, 1m 55.346s; 11 Takahashi, 1m 55.390s; 12 Baldolini, 1m 55.708s; 13 Davies, 1m 55.892s; 14 Guintoli, 1m 56.018s; 15 Giansanti, 1m 56.072s; 16 Ballerini, 1m 56.220s; 17 Smrz, 1m 56.221s; 18 Rous, 1m 57.614s; 19 Leblanc, 1m 57.851s; 20 Molina, 1m 58.350s; 21 Marchand, 1m 58.574s; 22 Watz, 1m 58.934s; 23 Cardenas, 1m 59.144s; 24 Polzer, 1m 59.206s; 25 Ronzoni, 1m 59.352s; 26 Rizmayer, 1m 59.495s; 27 Debon, 1m 59.741s; 28 Locatelli, 2m 08.189s.

World Championship: 1 Pedrosa, 98; 2 Dovizioso, 77; 3 Stoner, 76; 4 de Angelis, 56; 5 Lorenzo, 54; 6 Porto, 49; 7 Aoyama, 45; 8 Barbera, 44; 9 de Puniet, 36; 10 Corsi, 27; 11 Debon, 24; 12 Takahashi, 21; 13 Guintoli, 19; 14 Davies, 15; 15 Giansanti, 12; 16 Locatelli, 11; 17 Baldolini, 9; 18 Ballerini, 8; 19 Rous, 7; 20 Smrz, 6; 21 Leblanc, 3; 22 Cardenas, Heidolf and Marchand, 1.

125 cc

20 laps, 65.180 miles/104.900 km

Pos.	Rider (Nat.)	No.	Machine	Laps	Time & speed
1	Gabor Talmacsi (H)	14	KTM	20	40m 12.658s 97.260 mph/ 156.524 km/h
2	Thomas Luthi (CH)	12	Honda	20	40m 12.718s
3	Joan Olive (E)	6	Aprilia	20	40m 27.371s
4	Mattia Pasini (I)	75	Aprilia	20	40m 27.383s
5	Tomoyoshi Koyama (J)	71	Honda	20	40m 27.737s
6	Manuel Poggiali (RSM)	54	Gilera	20	40m 30.698s
7	Julian Simon (E)	60	KTM	20	40m 30.858s
8	Fabrizio Lai (I)	32	Honda	20	40m 31.341s
9	Toshihisa Kuzuhara (J)	9	Honda	20	40m 32.791s
10	Alexis Masbou (F)	7	Honda	20	40m 32.969s
11	Michele Conti (I)	61	Honda	20	40m 41.284s
12	Alvaro Bautista (E)	19	Honda	20	40m 44.449s
13	Manuel Hernandez (E)	43	Aprilia	20	40m 44.475s
14	Lorenzo Zanetti (I)	8	Aprilia	20	40m 47.400s
15	Raffaele de Rosa (I)	35	Aprilia	20	40m 47.420s
16	Andrea Iannone (I)	29	Aprilia	20	40m 57.961s
17	Aleix Espargaro (E)	41	Honda	20	40m 58.068s
18	Dario Giuseppetti (D)	25	Aprilia	20	41m 01.117s
19	Michele Pirro (I)	15	Malaguti	20	41m 01.268s
20	Gioele Pellino (I)	42	Malaguti	20	41m 01.273s
21	Nicolas Terol (E)	18	Derbi	20	41m 02.070s
22	Pablo Nieto (E)	22	Derbi	20	41m 02.118s
23	Jordi Carchano (E)	28	Aprilia	20	41m 05.783s
24	Lorenzo Baroni (I)	91	Aprilia	20	41m 15.545s
25	Imre Toth (H)	45	Aprilia	20	41m 17.893s
26	Raymond Schouten (NL)	16	Honda	20	41m 17.947s
27	Karel Abraham (CZ)	44	Aprilia	20	41m 17.965s
28	Vincent Braillard (CH)	26	Aprilia	20	41m 20.539s
29	Luca Verdini (I)	92	Aprilia	20	41m 50.895s
	Mika Kallio (SF)	36	KTM	19	DNF
	Hector Faubel (E)	55	Aprilia	19	DNF
	Sergio Gadea (E)	33	Aprilia	19	DNF
	Mike di Meglio (F)	63	Honda	17	DNF
	Federico Sandi (I)	10	Honda	14	DNF
	Marco Simoncelli (I)	58	Aprilia	11	DNF
	Sandro Cortese (D)	11	Honda	10	DNF
	Angel Rodriguez (E)	47	Honda	9	DNF
	Nico Vivarelli (I)	93	Honda	8	DNF
	Lukas Pesek (CZ)	52	Derbi	7	DNF
	Simone Grotzki Giorgi (I)	62	Aprilia		DNQ

Fastest lap: Luthi, 1m 59.464s, 98.211 mph/158.055 km/h.

Previous record: Gino Borsoi, I (Aprilia), 1m 58.969s, 98.620 mph/158.713 km/h (2003).

Event best maximum speed: Zanetti, 145.8 mph/234.7 km/h (race).

Qualifying: 1 Kallio, 1m 58.662s; 2 Talmacsi, 1m 59.152s; 3 Faubel, 1m 59.712s; 4 Pasini, 1m 59.776s; 5 Simoncelli, 1m 59.796s; 6 Luthi, 1m 59.947s; 7 Conti, 2m 00.037s; 8 Simon, 2m 00.152s; 9 Lai, 2m 00.178s; 10 Pesek, 2m 00.203s; 11 di Meglio, 2m 00.387s; 12 Rodriguez, 2m 00.493s; 13 Olive, 2m 00.519s; 14 Kuzuhara, 2m 00.572s; 15 Gadea, 2m 00.599s; 16 Zanetti, 2m 00.623s; 17 Poggiali, 2m 00.664s; 18 Pirro, 2m 00.716s; 19 Baroni, 2m 00.718s; 20 Koyama, 2m 00.931s; 21 de Rosa, 2m 00.964s; 22 Masbou, 2m 00.982s; 23 Espargaro, 2m 00.995s; 24 Vivarelli, 2m 01.101s; 25 Pellino, 2m 01.170s; 26 Cortese, 2m 01.275s; 27 Nieto, 2m 01.312s; 28 Hernandez, 2m 01.392s; 29 Bautista, 2m 01.397s; 30 Iannone, 2m 01.445s; 31 Schouten, 2m 01.571s; 32 Toth, 2m 01.596s; 33 Carchano, 2m 01.680s; 34 Terol, 2m 02.065s; 35 Giuseppetti, 2m 02.210s; 36 Abraham, 2m 02.422s; 37 Verdini, 2m 02.887s; 38 Sandi, 2m 03.659s; 39 Braillard, 2m 03.749s; 40 Grotzki Giorgi, 2m 04.058s.

Fastest race laps: 1 Luthi, 1m 59.464s; 2 Faubel, 1m 59.464s; 3 Kallio, 1m 59.551s; 4 Simoncelli, 1m 59.586s; 5 Talmacsi, 1m 59.648s; 6 Pesek, 1m 59.743s; 7 Lai, 1m 59.749s; 8 Koyama, 1m 59.911s; 9 Olive, 1m 59.983s; 10 Gadea, 2m 00.034s; 11 Pasini, 2m 00.174s; 12 Simon, 2m 00.191s; 13 Poggiali, 2m 00.256s; 14 Kuzuhara, 2m 00.387s; 15 Conti, 2m 00.482s; 16 Masbou, 2m 00.491s; 17 di Meglio, 2m 00.496s; 18 Hernandez, 2m 00.506s; 19 Zanetti, 2m 00.523s; 20 de Rosa, 2m 00.802s; 21 Espargaro, 2m 00.856s; 22 Pellino, 2m 00.888s; 23 Rodriguez, 2m 00.918s; 24 Iannone, 2m 00.986s; 25 Bautista, 2m 01.128s; 26 Cortese, 2m 01.184s; 27 Pirro, 2m 01.252s; 28 Terol, 2m 01.256s; 29 Vivarelli, 2m 01.359s; 30 Sandi, 2m 01.468s; 31 Nieto, 2m 01.648s; 32 Giuseppetti, 2m 01.698s; 33 Toth, 2m 01.805s; 34 Baroni, 2m 01.854s; 35 Carchano, 2m 01.873s; 36 Abraham, 2m 01.989s; 37 Braillard, 2m 01.992s; 38 Schouten, 2m 02.167s; 39 Verdini, 2m 03.890s.

World Championship: 1 Luthi, 74; 2 Kallio, 66; 3 Talmacsi, 62; 4 Pasini, 59; 5 Lai, 57; 6 Simoncelli, 52; 7 Poggiali, 41; 8 Simon, 37; 9 Koyama, 32; 10 Faubel, 30; 11 Olive, 26; 12 Nieto, 25; 13 di Meglio, 20; 14 Gadea, 20; 15 Espargaro, 15; 16 Bautista, 13; 17 Hernandez, 12; 18 Kuzuhara and Masbou, 9; 20 Pesek, Toth and Zanetti, 7; 23 Conti, 5; 24 Carchano, Giuseppetti and Pirro, 3; 27 Cortese, de Rosa and Terol, 1.

Gibernau finds some shade on the grid.
There was nowhere to hide in the race.
Photograph: Gold & Goose

BARCELONA
CATALUNYANGP
FIM WORLD CHAMPIONSHIP • ROUND 6

Above: Loris Capirossi practices his new-found throttle control.

Right: David Checa and Ruben Xaus show off their Miro-inspired leathers on the grid.

Photographs: Gold & Goose

IT was too early to be a turning point in the season... which in any case already seemed well set in the obvious direction. But this race was surely a turning point for Sete Gibernau. The only rider reckoned strong enough to challenge Rossi, he led most of the race, only to be put firmly in his place at the end of it. Just as had happened, more or less, one year ago. This single result, coming after the humiliating defeat at Jerez, was enough to change the way his home fans thought about Sete.

Spanish riders are thought to have an easy ride in MotoGP. Plentiful sponsorship has led to some unexpectedly long careers, but just one premier class title – Alex Criville, in 1999. But even unsuccessful Spaniards could always rely on the support of their countrymen, and Gibernau is hardly a lame duck racer. As in France, and everywhere really, Sete was riding brilliantly. He qualified on pole; his best lap was all but 1.5 seconds faster than his own record of last year, his race time an amazing 45.8 faster. Quite a ride.

This sort of performance from, for example, a Dutch, German or British rider, would surely elevate his national status. In the case of Gibernau, it was not good enough. From this point, the press and fans had a different view. Gibernau was a failure, ran the canon. This is the downside of when racing starts to achieve

the sort of popularity of football; the reverse of the coin whose obverse was the sponsorship and backing in the first place. This was a significant phase in the development of the belittlement of Gibernau.

Because no matter how brilliantly Sete rode from his pole position start, Rossi could always do more – stalking him without pity, then pouncing, his afternoon culminating in a searing new lap record on the 23rd of 25 laps, all but 1.5 seconds faster than Gibernau's record of last year. It was the fourth in a string of five wins in a row for Valentino, whose package for the season was quite obviously comprehensive and complete. He had everything he needed to show his riding talent and race craft, and he had plenty of both of those.

This late-race run was in spite of dire tyre warnings. A full resurface over the winter had ironed out the bumps – especially those troublesome switchbacks of tarmac distorted by the extraordinary loads of F1 braking... but it had brought other problems. This track comprises not only a very long straight (fastest this year was Capirossi at 205.02 mph (331.4 km/h), five mph slower than Barros's 339.4 on the Honda last year), but also a punishing series of very long medium to high-speed corners, where the bike is on its side for long periods of time.

The punishment to the rears is obvious and easily seen, with long tyre-smoking slides at several corners; Catalunya also exacts unusual demands on front tyres.

Michelin and Bridgestone had been forewarned in pre-season tests, which proved previous data and experience to be right out of date. "It's like coming to a new track," said Michelin's Nicolas Goubert. Bridgestone runners were struggling even more, with all suffering front-end problems.

Tyres were not the only issues for the Suzuki riders Hopkins and Roberts. New engine top-end parts might have improved mid-range throttle response some, but it was subtle at best, and the machines still lagged in mid-range grunt, making a hard task for the riders. Each tackled it in his own way, Hopkins putting in superhuman efforts to little effect, after being obliged to pit for a tyre change; Roberts plodding on within the limits of the possible, gaining one point, more than a minute and a half behind the leader.

Hopkins, his face scorched after a fiery Italian post-race misadventure involving Shakey Byrne and some waste racing fuel, had other problems, leading to a remarkable record... breaking the new 60 km/h pit-lane speed limit by a resounding 70 mph. He was timed at 172 km/h (114.235 mph) as he dashed out at the end of session to try to get in a qualifying lap (he missed it by some five seconds). Having already been hit with the full panoply of the FIM's incremental fine structure – US $100 for the first, $500 for each thereafter – for three offences at Jerez, he'd decided "I'm going to get my money's worth."

Over at Ducati, the issue of fuel consumption shed some oblique light on a rather surprising fact of Loris Capirossi's riding. Seems he had never before much considered the use of a balanced part-open throttle. All his racing life, the twistgrip had always been wound wide open or fully shut, "for 15 or 16 years," he said. It seemed barely plausible that, in his third year on the Ducati and after winning a GP on it here two years before, he was only now becoming aware of the facility for smaller throttle movements, but his team said that the data bore this out. This all came into the open with the installation of a fuel consumption gauge, reading in grams-per-lap. Both riders had it at Mugello; only Capirossi kept it, to remind him after a hot lap to take it easy for the next, both to save fuel and tyre wear. Hmmm.

Toni Elias was back in the paddock, hoping that intensive treatment to his broken scaphoid would allow him to take part in his home GP, where the Tech 3-team Yamahas were displaying new livery inspired by Catalan artist Miro, in dashing red and yellow. Alas, though he bravely ran 22 laps on Friday morning, he could manage only eight in the afternoon, succumbing to the pain and ceding his motorcycles to reserve David Checa for a second race in a row.

Team-mate Xaus reinforced his growing reputation for crashing hard and (mercifully) bouncing back with a spectacular tumble at the closing stadium section. He ended up at an unprotected stretch of wall. On Saturday; earlier on the lap, after the first downhill swoop, Dovizioso also fell in practice, lucky to escape serious injury after slamming into an unprotected stretch of tyre wall. Both areas had gained an air-fence lining by race day. Riders' safety committee member Rossi, asked about this belated measure, explained that Dovizioso's crash especially had been in an unexpected place, but had been triggered because the corner exit kerb there (and elsewhere) was too short, and he had touched the grass while still accelerating out.

For old hands, the return of another famous name – one of the five-strong 125 wild card pack was young Stefan Bradl, 15-year-old son of 1991 250cc runner-up Helmut, on a KTM. A regular German and European championship runner, Stefan hoped to run the full season in 2006, and eventually "go one better than my father". His first attempt ended in retirement.

Below: John Hopkins: conspicuous efforts to compensate.
Photograph: Gold & Goose

Above: Gibernau collides with Melandri in the early stages... both were lucky to stay on board.

Top right: A warm embrace from mentor Alberto Puig for three-in-a-row winner Pedrosa.

Centre right: Porto's hopes ended early, in the gravel.

Bottom right: Pedrosa fans got what they had come for.

Photographs: Gold & Goose

MOTOGP RACE – 25 laps

Gibernau won the battle for pole from team-mate Melandri, Rossi on the far end of row one, Biaggi leading the second. Rossi was slow off the line, and Gibernau led the pack as it funnelled into the first turn, from Melandri, Biaggi and Hayden, Rossi next and on the move. He picked off Hayden and Biaggi on consecutive corners, Max then unwittingly helping by running wide and letting Hayden and Barros through as well. Then Rossi set about the MoviStar Hondas, actually nosing into the lead in the stadium section, Melandri fighting hard. They crossed the line with Gibernau narrowly ahead of Melandri and Rossi, from Hayden, Barros and Biaggi.

A hectic first lap, with more action before the race settled down... Melandri inside Gibernau at the end of the back straight to lead for the next three laps, Rossi moving into second, then taking the lead on lap four, Barros riding very hard to get to third behind Gibernau, and Melandri fourth. Gibernau had bashed into Melandri's back tyre during all this; luckily neither went down.

Rossi led for just one lap, then Gibernau took over for almost the rest of the race, Rossi his faithful companion. The next trio – Hayden, Melandri and Barros – were in a state of almost constant flux, but losing ground. Up front, the outcome remained in doubt only if you were a prepared to ignore the past and recent history.

On the 23rd lap, Rossi unleashed the inevitable. Taking a faster exit from the downhill corner onto the long front straight, he sped by on the inside and into turn one to set his blistering record lap, maintaining a similar pace to the finish.

Gibernau had thought he might be able to fight, but the higher pace was too much for his tired rear tyre. "I couldn't flick the bike when I needed to, and Valentino used that to pass," he said. He had to accept second again, by just over a second... a cruel if inevitable fate after leading for so long.

Seven seconds behind at the flag, the next three were at it

all race long. Melandri regained third from Hayden with nine laps left, the pair back and forth from then on. But Barros was close and attentive, and on lap 23 the final order was established ... Melandri taking over the rostrum position, and Hayden consigned to fifth. Melandri credited improved corner speeds as the fuel load lightened; Hayden blamed a lack of side grip that cost him dear on the long corners, especially the left leading into the crucial last three right-handers.

A little way back, neither catching nor losing much, Biaggi held sixth from the sixth to the last lap, struggling (he explained) with continuing handling problems, different from those of Mugello, but no better overall. Braking was improved, he said, but the handling and cornering were worse, punishing the tyres. "I could never take part in the game and it makes me very sad," he said.

Seventh-placed Edwards had come through from tenth on lap one, but never did get quite close enough to Biaggi to attack, dropping away again by the finish. He'd chosen a medium rear tyre rather than the hard compound favoured by the rest, and it was a mistake. "It got to where you just couldn't hold any lean angle," he said later.

Bayliss had a race to redeem his fading fortunes. Qualifying 15th, a dire start left him 18th on lap one, but he picked his way through steadily for the rest of the afternoon, firmly taking eighth off Nakano on the second-last lap. It was to be something of a false dawn, as he struggled to adapt from years of Ducatis to the very different character of the Honda.

Nakano nearly lost ninth as well to a late charge from Xaus, whose last-corner attack failed by only 0.54 seconds. Best of the Bridgestone runners, the Japanese rider had his hands full containing the slides for the last ten laps, he said. The similarly shod Ducatis were next, Checa clear of Capirossi, both sliding badly. "It felt as though it was wet," complained the Italian.

David Checa was right on Capirossi over the line, taking three points in only his second GP. Rolfo's Dunlop-shod Duke was next, then Roberts on Bridgestones, dropping way off the pace to claim the last point.

Hofmann had pitted from 14th place after 12 laps to replace his rear Bridgestone. Back on track, he had repassed the two WCMs of Ellison and Battaini by the end, all a lap down.

There were only two non-finishers. Tamada was an early de-parture, losing the front after working his way past Biaggi to a close sixth, on the sixth lap; Hopkins had dropped to 16th before also pitting for a tyre change, only to pull in from plumb last three laps later.

250 cc RACE – 23 laps

Pedrosa and his rising new rival Lorenzo headed the front row on their Hondas, the Aprilias of Porto and de Puniet alongside. Dovizioso's heavy crash on Saturday morning meant he missed final qualifying, starting from ninth on row three.

The lights triggered a burst of power from all but pole man Pedrosa, who almost stalled. It was de Puniet up front as Dani managed to regain momentum, finishing the first lap ninth, with an all-action brawl between the two of them.

Porto was pushing hard, third behind another Spaniard in the mix, Hector Barbera, when he slipped off on lap two; De Puniet's run lasted only one more lap before he followed suit, though he was able to run straight to his bike and rejoin in last place for a sterling recovery.

Barbera took over the lead, then de Angelis for six hectic laps. Pedrosa had joined the front group after only three laps, bringing Dovizioso with him; now the defending champion settled in to bide his time while the race developed. Barbera was ahead again as they started lap 11, when came the incident that thinned the competition in favour of the ultimate winner.

Lorenzo claimed that de Angelis had run wide on the entry to Repsol corner, then cut in again across his nose; the Italian that Lorenzo had attempted a crazy inside pass when he already had the line. The outcome was both in the gravel, with Lorenzo frac-turing his collarbone; and Pedrosa seizing the lead for the first time. He gained almost two seconds over the next two laps, then continued to stretch away to a margin of better than five, his third win in a row, and the first at Catalunya in this class by a Spaniard.

Two laps later Barbera started to feel the increased pace, with Stoner taking advantage to seize second, the Spanish youngster next succumbing to Dovizioso on lap 13, and one lap later to teenager Corsi on the second factory Aprilia, in the front pack from the start. The class rookies then started a phase that would end badly for Barbera. After exchanging puzzling hand gestures, things got violent as Corsi swerved to his left at the end of the

Above right: De Puniet leads the 250s into the first turn, from Porto (19), Barbera (obscured), de Angelis (blue MS bike) and Aoyama (73), with Lorenzo on his outside. Stoner (27) is prominent ahead of Dovizioso; Davies (57) is mid-field after a good start, but winner Pedrosa is lost in the pack.

Top left: Andrea Dovizioso bounced back from a heavy fall to take a fourth podium of the year.

Above: Simoncello battles with Kallio. He prevailed for second.

Right: Pasini's runaway made him the first to win two 125 races this year.

Far right: If the caps fit, wear them. Rossi was on a roll.

front straight after yet another change of places, sideswiping Barbera's front wheel. Tyres smoking, the Spaniard was saved from a violent crash mainly by his momentum, but it cost him one place as Aoyama came past, and now his bike began to slow. He dropped steadily away to a pointless 16th.

The Japanese factory Honda rider was on his way forward after an unusual race: he'd started well, but on lap three had run off the track after getting his finger caught up in the brake! He rejoined in 15th, and now took fourth off Corsi with two laps to go, the front runners now stretched apart by Pedrosa's convincing run.

Another remarkable ride came from de Puniet, who had been 26th and last on lap three on his luckily barely damaged Aprilia. He wasted no time in slicing through the backmarkers to sixth.

His final victims had been Takahashi and Guintoli, who had been locked in battle since before half distance. The Japanese rider took seventh by a tenth; with Giansanti similarly shading Baldolini and Debon for ninth.

Smrz, Ballerini and Jenkner all crashed out in short order, the last remounting for 19th; Davies retired to the pits with three laps left.

125 cc RACE – 22 laps

Kallio took pole on a close front row; Luthi led the first lap. But the normal brawl failed to materialise, in a most unusual 125 runaway.

Pasini took the lead on the second lap, with Luthi and Kallio losing tenths each lap, until after eight laps the gap was more than a second. By now Kallio was in second, and Luthi in turn dropping back.

Pasini's progress carried on all the way to the flag, by when he was almost ten seconds ahead, becoming the first rider to win two races this season and deposing Luthi from the points lead in the process. It was very different from his win by inches in China, by just six hundredths.

Anyone seeking excitement needed only to watch Simoncelli. On the first lap a coming together with Kuzuhara dropped him to 16th. He was soon advancing impressively, moving into the top ten with a vaulting lap five when he overtook no less than four riders to take seventh. He carried on the same way, passing Simon, Talmacsi and the now-fading Luthi for fourth on lap ten. Then Faubel retired from third place. Pasini was out of reach, but Simoncelli closed up on Kallio, who complained of badly sliding tyres in the latter half of the race, and took him with seven laps to go, stretching his advantage to the flag.

There was a good fight for fourth, with Talmacsi managing to stay ahead of Koyama. They dropped off Simon and Luthi, but by the finish Poggiali had joined the two, losing fifth again to Koyama on the last lap. Luthi was two seconds back, his hands full keeping Simon behind.

CATALUNYA CIRCUIT – BARCELONA

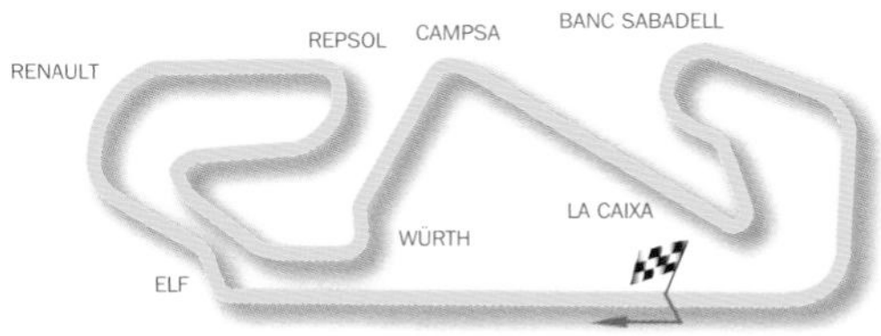
RENAULT
REPSOL
CAMPSA
BANC SABADELL
WÜRTH
LA CAIXA
ELF

CIRCUIT LENGTH: 2.937 miles/4.727 km

GRAND PREMIO GAULOISES DE CATALUNYA

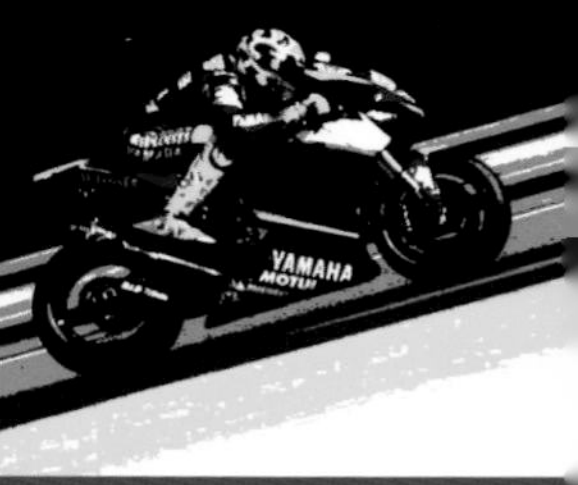

12 JUNE 2005 • FIM WORLD CHAMPIONSHIP ROUND 6

MotoGP

25 laps, 73.425 miles/118.175 km

Pos.	Rider (Nat.)	No.	Machine	Laps	Time & speed
1	Valentino Rossi (I)	46	Yamaha	25	43m 16.487s 101.810 mph/ 163.848 km/h
2	Sete Gibernau (E)	15	Honda	25	43m 17.581s
3	Marco Melandri (I)	33	Honda	25	43m 24.297s
4	Alex Barros (BR)	4	Honda	25	43m 24.691s
5	Nicky Hayden (USA)	69	Honda	25	43m 24.760s
6	Max Biaggi (I)	3	Honda	25	43m 28.538s
7	Colin Edwards (USA)	5	Yamaha	25	43m 35.249s
8	Troy Bayliss (AUS)	12	Honda	25	43m 59.118s
9	Shinya Nakano (J)	56	Kawasaki	25	44m 03.125s
10	Ruben Xaus (E)	11	Yamaha	25	44m 03.179s
11	Carlos Checa (E)	7	Ducati	25	44m 16.844s
12	Loris Capirossi (I)	65	Ducati	25	44m 20.351s
13	David Checa (E)	94	Yamaha	25	44m 20.472s
14	Roberto Rolfo (I)	44	Ducati	25	44m 26.745s
15	Kenny Roberts (USA)	10	Suzuki	25	44m 40.218s
16	Shane Byrne (GB)	67	Proton KR	25	44m 51.111s
17	Alex Hofmann (D)	66	Kawasaki	24	43m 43.269s
18	James Ellison (GB)	77	Blata	24	43m 52.521s
19	Franco Battaini (I)	27	Blata	24	43m 56.686s
	John Hopkins (USA)	21	Suzuki	16	DNF
	Makoto Tamada (J)	6	Honda	5	DNF

Fastest lap: **Rossi,** 1m 43.195s, **102.466 mph/164.903 km/h (record).**

Previous record: **Sete Gibernau, E (Honda),** 1m 44.641s, **101.050 mph/162.624 km/h (2004).**

Event best maximum speed: **Capirossi,** 205.3 mph/330.3 km/h **(race).**

Qualifying: **1 Gibernau,** 1m 42.337s; **2 Melandri,** 1m 42.390s; **3 Rossi,** 1m 42.723s; **4 Biaggi,** 1m 42.756s; **5 Hayden,** 1m 42.847s; **6 Capirossi,** 1m 42.992s; **7 Edwards,** 1m 43.109s; **8 C. Checa,** 1m 43.129s; **9 Barros,** 1m 43.159s; **10 Tamada,** 1m 43.207s; **11 Hopkins,** 1m 43.291s; **12 Nakano,** 1m 43.607s; **13 Roberts,** 1m 43.787s; **14 Hofmann,** 1m 43.864s; **15 Bayliss,** 1m 44.122s; **16 Xaus,** 1m 44.193s; **17 Rolfo,** 1m 44.934s; **18 D. Checa,** 1m 45.310s; **19 Byrne,** 1m 45.636s; **20 Ellison,** 1m 46.750s; **21 Battaini,** 1m 47.599s.

Fastest race laps: **1 Rossi,** 1m 43.195s; **2 Gibernau,** 1m 43.253s; **3 Hayden,** 1m 43.389s; **4 Melandri,** 1m 43.422s; **5 Barros,** 1m 43.498s; **6 Biaggi,** 1m 43.508s; **7 Tamada,** 1m 43.757s; **8 Edwards,** 1m 43.840s; **9 Nakano,** 1m 44.097s; **10 Bayliss,** 1m 44.365s; **11 Hofmann,** 1m 44.439s; **12 Hopkins,** 1m 44.475s; **13 C. Checa,** 1m 44.646s; **14 Roberts,** 1m 44.793s; **15 Capirossi,** 1m 44.889s; **16 Xaus,** 1m 44.962s; **17 Rolfo,** 1m 45.420s; **18 D. Checa,** 1m 45.820s; **19 Byrne,** 1m 46.726s; **20 Ellison,** 1m 48.208s; **21 Battaini,** 1m 48.391s.

World Championship: **1 Rossi,** 145; **2 Melandri,** 87; **3 Biaggi,** 77; **4 Gibernau,** 73; **5 Barros,** 65; **6 Edwards,** 57; **7 Hayden,** 47; **8 Capirossi,** 43; **9 Nakano,** 40; **10 C. Checa,** 33; **11 Bayliss,** 32; **12 Jacque,** 25; **13 Xaus,** 24; **14 Hopkins and Tamada,** 16; **16 Elias,** 15; **17 van den Goorbergh,** 12; **18 Hofmann and Roberts,** 9; **20 Rolfo,** 7; **21 Ellison,** 4; **22 D. Checa,** 3; **23 Ukawa,** 1.

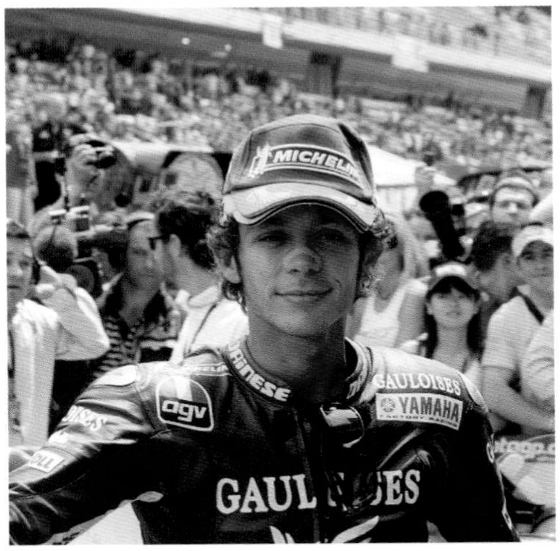

250 cc

23 laps, 67.551 miles/108.721 km

Pos.	Rider (Nat.)	No.	Machine	Laps	Time & speed
1	Daniel Pedrosa (E)	1	Honda	23	41m 29.428s 97.694 mph/ 157.223 km/h
2	Casey Stoner (AUS)	27	Aprilia	23	41m 35.065s
3	Andrea Dovizioso (I)	34	Honda	23	41m 40.025s
4	Hiroshi Aoyama (J)	73	Honda	23	41m 47.066s
5	Simone Corsi (I)	24	Aprilia	23	41m 48.927s
6	Randy de Puniet (F)	7	Aprilia	23	42m 02.663s
7	Yuki Takahashi (J)	55	Honda	23	42m 06.836s
8	Sylvain Guintoli (F)	50	Aprilia	23	42m 06.958s
9	Mirko Giansanti (I)	32	Aprilia	23	42m 12.242s
10	Alex Baldolini (I)	25	Aprilia	23	42m 13.039s
11	Alex Debon (E)	6	Honda	23	42m 13.319s
12	Roberto Locatelli (I)	15	Aprilia	23	42m 15.228s
13	Erwan Nigon (F)	63	Honda	23	42m 27.618s
14	Hugo Marchand (F)	9	Aprilia	23	42m 33.784s
15	Gregory Leblanc (F)	38	Aprilia	23	42m 33.827s
16	Hector Barbera (E)	80	Honda	23	42m 48.557s
17	Martin Cardenas (COL)	36	Aprilia	23	42m 50.337s
18	Frederik Watz (S)	18	Yamaha	23	43m 05.113s
19	Steve Jenkner (D)	17	Aprilia	22	41m 34.096s
20	Gabor Rizmayer (H)	12	Yamaha	22	41m 50.645s
21	Gabriele Ferro (I)	20	Fantic	22	43m 00.107s
	Chaz Davies (GB)	57	Aprilia	20	DNF
	Alex de Angelis (RSM)	5	Aprilia	10	DNF
	Jorge Lorenzo (E)	48	Honda	10	DNF
	Andrea Ballerini (I)	8	Aprilia	6	DNF
	Jakub Smrz (CZ)	96	Honda	5	DNF
	Arnaud Vincent (F)	21	Fantic	2	DNF
	Sebastian Porto (ARG)	19	Aprilia	1	DNF
	Radomil Rous (CZ)	64	Honda		DNS

Fastest lap: **Pedrosa,** 1m 47.373s, **98.479 mph/158.486 km/h.**

Previous record: **Daniel Pedrosa, E (Honda),** 1m 47.302s, **98.544 mph/158.591 km/h (2004).**

Event best maximum speed: **de Angelis,** 170.7 mph/274.7 km/h **(warm-up).**

Qualifying: **1 Pedrosa,** 1m 46.238s; **2 Lorenzo,** 1m 46.617s; **3 Porto,** 1m 46.706s; **4 de Puniet,** 1m 46.825s; **5 Aoyama,** 1m 47.082s; **6 de Angelis,** 1m 47.090s; **7 Barbera,** 1m 47.454s; **8 Stoner,** 1m 47.486s; **9 Dovizioso,** 1m 47.495s; **10 Corsi,** 1m 47.650s; **11 Guintoli,** 1m 48.207s; **12 Takahashi,** 1m 48.217s; **13 Smrz,** 1m 48.661s; **14 Jenkner,** 1m 48.961s; **15 Davies,** 1m 49.012s; **16 Giansanti,** 1m 49.126s; **17 Ballerini,** 1m 49.132s; **18 Debon,** 1m 49.150s; **19 Baldolini,** 1m 49.178s; **20 Nigon,** 1m 49.185s; **21 Marchand,** 1m 49.204s; **22 Locatelli,** 1m 49.277s; **23 Leblanc,** 1m 49.974s; **24 Vincent,** 1m 50.135s; **25 Cardenas,** 1m 50.499s; **26 Rous,** 1m 50.618s; **27 Watz,** 1m 50.995s; **28 Rizmayer,** 1m 51.966s; **29 Ferro,** 1m 53.459s.

Fastest race laps: **1 Pedrosa,** 1m 47.373s; **2 Stoner,** 1m 47.451s; **3 de Puniet,** 1m 47.628s; **4 de Angelis,** 1m 47.632s; **5 Dovizioso,** 1m 47.635s; **6 Lorenzo,** 1m 47.678s; **7 Corsi,** 1m 47.710s; **8 Barbera,** 1m 47.833s; **9 Aoyama,** 1m 47.957s; **10 Giansanti,** 1m 48.711s; **11 Guintoli,** 1m 48.845s; **12 Takahashi,** 1m 48.917s; **13 Baldolini,** 1m 49.037s; **14 Debon,** 1m 49.197s; **15 Ballerini,** 1m 49.275s; **16 Locatelli,** 1m 49.398s; **17 Davies,** 1m 49.607s; **18 Nigon,** 1m 49.664s; **19 Smrz,** 1m 49.701s; **20 Marchand,** 1m 50.015s; **21 Leblanc,** 1m 50.132s; **22 Jenkner,** 1m 50.175s; **23 Cardenas,** 1m 50.686s; **24 Watz,** 1m 51.339s; **25 Vincent,** 1m 51.951s; **26 Porto,** 1m 52.217s; **27 Rizmayer,** 1m 52.384s; **28 Ferro,** 1m 54.889s.

World Championship: **1 Pedrosa,** 123; **2 Stoner,** 96; **3 Dovizioso,** 93; **4 Aoyama,** 58; **5 de Angelis,** 56; **6 Lorenzo,** 54; **7 Porto,** 49; **8 de Puniet,** 46; **9 Barbera,** 44; **10 Corsi,** 38; **11 Takahashi,** 30; **12 Debon,** 29; **13 Guintoli,** 27; **14 Giansanti,** 19; **15 Baldolini, Davies and Locatelli,** 15; **18 Ballerini,** 8; **19 Rous,** 7; **20 Smrz,** 6; **21 Leblanc,** 4; **22 Marchand and Nigon,** 3; **24 Cardenas and Heidolf,** 1.

125 cc

22 laps, 64.614 miles/103.994 km

Pos.	Rider (Nat.)	No.	Machine	Laps	Time & speed
1	Mattia Pasini (I)	75	Aprilia	22	41m 15.125s 93.986 mph/ 151.256 km/h
2	Marco Simoncelli (I)	58	Aprilia	22	41m 24.159s
3	Mika Kallio (SF)	36	KTM	22	41m 27.533s
4	Gabor Talmacsi (H)	14	KTM	22	41m 33.381s
5	Tomoyoshi Koyama (J)	71	Honda	22	41m 33.565s
6	Manuel Poggiali (RSM)	54	Gilera	22	41m 33.669s
7	Thomas Luthi (CH)	12	Honda	22	41m 36.585s
8	Julian Simon (E)	60	KTM	22	41m 36.691s
9	Lorenzo Zanetti (I)	8	Aprilia	22	41m 44.154s
10	Fabrizio Lai (I)	32	Honda	22	41m 44.596s
11	Andrea Iannone (I)	29	Aprilia	22	41m 45.608s
12	Michael Ranseder (A)	76	KTM	22	41m 50.339s
13	Sergio Gadea (E)	33	Aprilia	22	41m 53.764s
14	Alvaro Bautista (E)	19	Honda	22	41m 54.684s
15	Aleix Espargaro (E)	41	Honda	22	41m 59.343s
16	Mike di Meglio (F)	63	Honda	22	41m 59.353s
17	Dario Giuseppetti (D)	25	Aprilia	22	42m 05.376s
18	Federico Sandi (I)	10	Honda	22	42m 06.344s
19	Mateo Tunez (E)	86	Aprilia	22	42m 06.352s
20	Angel Rodriguez (E)	47	Honda	22	42m 10.574s
21	Toshihisa Kuzuhara (J)	9	Honda	22	42m 10.594s
22	Raffaele de Rosa (I)	35	Aprilia	22	42m 10.629s
23	Sandro Cortese (D)	11	Honda	22	42m 16.246s
24	Daniel Saez (E)	49	Aprilia	22	42m 17.058s
25	Raymond Schouten (NL)	16	Honda	22	42m 17.747s
26	Manuel Hernandez (E)	43	Aprilia	22	42m 20.019s
27	Jordi Carchano (E)	28	Aprilia	22	42m 25.797s
28	Gioele Pellino (I)	42	Malaguti	22	42m 30.335s
29	Hugo van den Berg (NL)	78	Aprilia	22	43m 03.006s
	Karel Abraham (CZ)	44	Aprilia	21	DNF
	Imre Toth (H)	45	Aprilia	15	DNF
	Alexis Masbou (F)	7	Honda	11	DNF
	Hector Faubel (E)	55	Aprilia	10	DNF
	Lukas Pesek (CZ)	52	Derbi	4	DNF
	Vincent Braillard (CH)	26	Aprilia	2	DNF
	Stefan Bradl (D)	77	KTM	2	DNF
	Pablo Nieto (E)	22	Derbi	1	DNF
	Enrique Jerez (E)	51	Derbi	1	DNF
	Michele Pirro (I)	15	Malaguti	0	DNF
	Nicolas Terol (E)	18	Derbi	0	DNF
	Joan Olive (E)	6	Aprilia	0	DNF

Fastest lap: **Kallio,** 1m 51.744s, **94.627 mph/152.287 km/h.**

Previous record: **Hector Barbera, E (Aprilia),** 1m 50.903s, **95.344 mph/153.442 km/h (2004).**

Event best maximum speed: **Faubel,** 145.9 mph/234.8 km/h **(race).**

Qualifying: **1 Kallio,** 1m 51.451s; **2 Pasini,** 1m 51.515s; **3 Simoncelli,** 1m 51.562s; **4 Zanetti,** 1m 51.949s; **5 Kuzuhara,** 1m 52.005s; **6 Talmacsi,** 1m 52.052s; **7 Faubel,** 1m 52.056s; **8 Lai,** 1m 52.223s; **9 Poggiali,** 1m 52.285s; **10 Luthi,** 1m 52.407s; **11 Nieto,** 1m 52.579s; **12 Koyama,** 1m 52.586s; **13 Simon,** 1m 52.598s; **14 Pesek,** 1m 52.605s; **15 Gadea,** 1m 52.805s; **16 Bautista,** 1m 52.918s; **17 Iannone,** 1m 52.963s; **18 di Meglio,** 1m 52.985s; **19 Hernandez,** 1m 52.990s; **20 Masbou,** 1m 53.031s; **21 Ranseder,** 1m 53.073s; **22 Giuseppetti,** 1m 53.222s; **23 Tunez,** 1m 53.272s; **24 Espargaro,** 1m 53.319s; **25 de Rosa,** 1m 53.331s; **26 Schouten,** 1m 53.465s; **27 Olive,** 1m 53.511s; **28 Terol,** 1m 53.617s; **29 Carchano,** 1m 53.629s; **30 Pellino,** 1m 53.746s; **31 Cortese,** 1m 53.813s; **32 Rodriguez,** 1m 53.873s; **33 Bradl,** 1m 53.880s; **34 Sandi,** 1m 54.111s; **35 Braillard,** 1m 54.256s; **36 Pirro,** 1m 54.377s; **37 Jerez,** 1m 54.546s; **38 Saez,** 1m 54.779s; **39 van den Berg,** 1m 54.849s; **40 Toth,** 1m 55.022s; **41 Abraham,** 1m 55.647s.

Fastest race laps: **1 Kallio,** 1m 51.744s; **2 Pasini,** 1m 51.793s; **3 Faubel,** 1m 51.835s; **4 Simoncelli,** 1m 51.900s; **5 Talmacsi,** 1m 51.923s; **6 Simon,** 1m 52.048s; **7 Luthi,** 1m 52.230s; **8 Iannone,** 1m 52.279s; **9 Bautista,** 1m 52.314s; **10 Gadea,** 1m 52.323s; **11 Koyama,** 1m 52.345s; **12 di Meglio,** 1m 52.401s; **13 Poggiali,** 1m 52.577s; **14 Lai,** 1m 52.616s; **15 Zanetti,** 1m 52.674s; **16 Espargaro,** 1m 52.690s; **17 Ranseder,** 1m 52.693s; **18 Masbou,** 1m 52.731s; **19 Tunez,** 1m 53.203s; **20 Cortese,** 1m 53.672s; **21 Giuseppetti,** 1m 53.742s; **22 Sandi,** 1m 53.798s; **23 Saez,** 1m 53.809s; **24 Schouten,** 1m 53.828s; **25 Rodriguez,** 1m 53.862s; **26 de Rosa,** 1m 53.892s; **27 Hernandez,** 1m 53.909s; **28 Kuzuhara,** 1m 53.991s; **29 Abraham,** 1m 54.145s; **30 Carchano,** 1m 54.202s; **31 Pellino,** 1m 54.240s; **32 Pesek,** 1m 54.956s; **33 van den Berg,** 1m 55.449s; **34 Toth,** 1m 56.645s; **35 Braillard,** 1m 57.456s; **36 Nieto,** 2m 03.988s; **37 Bradl,** 2m 49.211s.

World Championship: **1 Pasini,** 84; **2 Luthi,** 83; **3 Kallio,** 82; **4 Talmacsi,** 75; **5 Simoncelli,** 72; **6 Lai,** 63; **7 Poggiali,** 51; **8 Simon,** 45; **9 Koyama,** 43; **10 Faubel,** 30; **11 Olive,** 26; **12 Nieto,** 25; **13 di Meglio and Gadea,** 23; **15 Espargaro,** 16; **16 Bautista,** 15; **17 Zanetti,** 14; **18 Hernandez,** 12; **19 Kuzuhara and Masbou,** 9; **21 Pesek and Toth,** 7; **23 Conti and Iannone,** 5; **25 Ranseder,** 4; **26 Carchano, Giuseppetti and Pirro,** 3; **29 Cortese, de Rosa and Terol,** 1.

FIM WORLD CHAMPIONSHIP • ROUND 7

DUTCHTT

ASSEN

More smoke, no mirrors. Rossi fans celebrate another masterful display.
Photograph: Martin Heath

Gibernau leads Melandri, Hayden, Rossi and Capirossi away from the start out onto the north loop... the last time this particular spectacle will be seen.

Photograph: Gold & Goose

ASSEN was an important lesson in history. That it came from a mere honorary and very recent graduate in communication and publicity made it no less telling. The Doctor not only knew and felt the heritage, he added to it significantly. To his perhaps not unmitigated delight, he also had a notable star pupil in the burgeoning Marco Melandri.

The first motorcycle race at Assen was in 1925. Take out the war years, and this was the 75th running, as the only track still on the calendar from the original World Championship of 1949. The mood was more of remembrance than celebration. Far more historic than the numbers was the farewell to what remains of the old track. From next year, the poetry of the north loop will be gone, replaced by a series of long banked right-hand corners turning off from the start-finish straight and sending riders giddy before rejoining a slightly shifted Strubben horseshoe bend, and regaining familiar ground on what will be left of the circuit's trade-mark fast flicks.

Part of the process had already begun, with two corners slowed significantly, making the track marginally shorter but some two mph slower than last year. As Rossi said, in between qualifying on pole and winning the last race on the "old" track: "Already, we have lost some of the taste of Assen." Next year, only traces will remain; the Cathedral will have become a mere church.

The sense of Assen's past reminds us also that these same feelings must have been repeated five times in history... every time the classic track was reduced from the original sprawling 28.4 km of 1925, running for just that year between the villages of Borger and Schoonlo, outside of Assen. Today's "old track" is a short track by comparison. It is itself only 22 years old; Kenny Roberts and Barry Sheene fought their duels on north loop significantly longer than this year's. This is a relentless reduction, which presumably will one day end up with Assen resembling Valencia, twisting and turning round the grandstands and pits, the surrounding open spaces given over to theme parks, or factory outlets, or whatever might eventually transpire.

All the same, the abandonment of the north loop means more than just the loss of a few evocative old names (like Madijk, and Ossebroeken – literally "ox-trousers"). The whole fast and difficult section, nemesis to both Mick Doohan and Alex Criville, among others, was uniquely Assen.

This year's two detail changes to the track basically first used in 1984, widened in 1990, and reprofiled for a larger paddock in 2002, were both controversial, for quite different reasons.

The first was to the fast right-hander and subsequent fast left which terminated the revised old back straight behind the paddock – the famous Veenslang ("peat snake"). Introduced in 2002, the new corners were criticised then as inviting a bad crash – a rider who ran wide off the first corner might come back across the track later on. Just such an accident had tragic consequences in last year's Supersport race, when 20-year-old Italian Alessio Perilli lost his life.

The response was to make both corners much tighter, and the distance between them shorter, making a medium-speed ess-bend... the riders called it a chicane, which it was only in

relation to the high speed of approach. Many had obvious problems judging the braking distance. Run on, and exactly the same thing would happen as before, although at significantly lower speed... as several riders discovered. One of them, Max Biaggi, actually did collide with the unlucky Franco Battaini during just such a manoeuvre, knocking the WMC Blata over, and leaving Franco clinging onto the back of the Honda for a while, before abandoning ship without injury. Mercifully, this was the worst incident. Riders concurred with Rossi's views: "We tried to make it safer, but it is still dangerous. Not so much for a very fast accident like before, but maybe it is not slow enough. Also the gravel should be replaced with hard concrete, so if you go off you can still stay in control."

For Biaggi, this was just one clash in aweekend of them, before the race had even begun. Later that afternoon, in final qualifying, an extraordinary performance saw him stop out on the track to do a practice start some minutes before the session was over, giving Melandri among others a serious fright. The pair met later at the new chicane on the slow-down lap, Max touring, Melandri running faster and overtaking on the inside. Max dived in on him, a collision inevitable; Melandri fended him off with his knee, hooking the factory Honda's clutch lever as he did so, and wrenching the steering. Biaggi all but fell – Melandri continued, shaking his head.

It wasn't over yet. Melandri pulled into parc ferme, being on the front row, to be met with a surprise attacking lunge from an elderly man, who seized him by the throat! It was Max's uncle Valerio.

Top: Another podium revived Edwards's spirits.

Above: Bayliss gives his fans a good laugh.

Left: A kiss for his lucky number from the triumphant Valentino.
Photographs: Gold & Goose

Well, his permanent pass was promptly withdrawn; then both riders were called up before the beak. Race direction judged Melandri innocent; Biaggi was clobbered with a $1,000 fine for the premature test start; and a hefty $5,000 for riding "in an irresponsible manner, causing danger to other riders". His only response was to accuse Melandri of a deliberate attack, adding: "It is a pity that it got uglier. My uncle Valerio is the nicest man in the world."

The more important story of the weekend also involved Biaggi – if passively, in his role as current top factory Repsol Honda rider, and the one least likely to keep his seat next year. It came in HRC's new hospitality unit: a smart suite, purpose-built in the shape of the Honda wing escutcheon, leaving only Yamaha, among the major teams, with the old-style open-sided tent. It was the announcement of a further two years of Repsol sponsorship for the factory team. This meant the end of a major bidding war between Repsol, sponsors of HRC for 11 years, and upstart rivals Telefónica.

There would soon be rumours of a robust earlier attempt by the latter to gazump the former with an offer of 20-million Euros for the whole team, and later still threats from Telefónica that they were considering withdrawing all their very considerable financial backing from motorcycle racing (support that goes right down to grass-roots level) to concentrate on F1, where they were winning the championship with Alonso. The prize was not the HRC contract, but rider Dani Pedrosa. Telefónica had nurtured the 125 and surely soon double 250 champion throughout his glittering career. Now he was top of HRC's shopping list for the factory MotoGP team… and that was out of Telefónica's reach. They were set to lose the man they had groomed to stardom.

History-man Rossi provided a refuge from this high-level turmoil. His sixth win of the year, with the only ever 1:59 lap of the track, meant he was the first ever Yamaha rider to take five races in a row. More unusual was the pressure applied by young pretender Melandri, who had closed on Rossi again at the finish with two fastest laps in a row. He explained he'd taken a good lesson from Rossi in how to be faster through the back section, and had made full use of it. He'd also had a good lesson in how a master treats a threatening young upstart on the last lap.

MOTOGP RACE – 19 laps

"It's a fantastic emotion to do a whole lap on a qualifying tyre at Assen. The bikes are so fast, and also the track." A glowing tribute from Rossi to the last-ever qualifying session on the fine old circuit, after he'd ousted erstwhile pole qualifier Gibernau with the track's first (and undoubtedly last) sub-1:59 lap.

Gibernau had a troubled practice, crew chief Juan Martinez rushed to hospital on the first day with a severe migraine, leaving the rider and his team casting around somewhat. He was back on day two, and Sete was the first of five riders to get below two minutes. Team-mate Melandri was alongside, not four tenths slower on this long lap; Nakano was a best-so-far fourth to head row two from Hayden and Edwards.

The morning dawned as wet and dismal as practice had been baking hot, with Melandri fastest on the wet track. It had dried for the race, but was much cooler, and the rain had washed away the fresh rubber on the racing line. Riding tentatively was one reason why Rossi was submerged in the early rush (only when he realised that everybody was having the same problems, he would say later, did he pick up the rhythm); a slightly slow start was another. Getting off the line would seem to be the only chink in his armour.

Gibernau got the run, but Melandri dived past promptly; Hayden menacing both of them, and Nakano next. Rossi lost another position to Capirossi soon afterwards, and another to Edwards at the new back chicane, the American missing his braking point, scrambling round any old how. Rossi reversed that pass quickly, and also repassed Capirossi into the final chicane, only for the Ducati to power past once again down the front straight. Rossi required another attack at the end of lap two to get ahead finally. Edwards was still well placed; at the back an inspired Hofmann succumbed to Barros on lap two, the German riding his spare bike after warm-up problems, and staying convincingly with the leading pack.

Rossi finally passed Nakano on lap three, Edwards followed one lap later. Ahead of the two Yamahas, Hayden was riding forcefully, until coming off badly at de Strubben horseshoe before the back straight on lap six... pushed wide by an aggressive Gibernau, he was unable to prevent Rossi also slipping underneath. He lost a little ground at once, and next time at the same corner Edwards was also past him.

Rossi loomed, then finally took second off Gibernau at the chicane at the end of lap eight, to breathe down Melandri's neck before a successful pass at the Strubben two laps later. The group was still close, 2.2 seconds covering Rossi, Melandri, Gibernau, Edwards and Hayden.

Rossi upped the pace only slightly, and Melandri responded, almost running into the back of Rossi at de Strubben at one point. But Gibernau seemed to lose heart, and he dropped slowly out of contention. Edwards was delayed for a while, then also forced past, and was soon closing – within a second of Melandri with five laps left. A Yamaha one-two seemed on the cards, until Edwards hit a big front wheel slide into Turn One. "Next lap, same thing. I was really pushing the limit, and I said: there's two-and-a-half laps to go. Let's keep this thing on its wheels."

Melandri was himself almost a second down at this stage, but he was not for giving up, closing up with two consecutive fastest laps to start the last just over half-a-second adrift. Rossi, however, was saving his best for last. He set an even faster lap to secure the final record, and crossed the line 1.58 seconds clear. It had been another magnificent performance, and a fitting farewell to a very special track.

Gibernau had been struggling since half distance, and succumbed to Hayden two laps after losing third to Edwards. Now he fell back as Hayden kept pushing, barely two seconds behind Edwards over the line.

A long way back Barros had seen Hofmann drop back, to eventual retirement with the chain skipping on the sprocket. By lap nine, he had worked his way past both Nakano and then Capirossi to sixth. One lap later, Biaggi was behind him, having worked his way through from 11th on lap one, and the pair of Assen veterans were together to the finish, with Biaggi taking the upper hand, if only narrowly, with six laps to go.

Capirossi lost touch with the remnants of the gang on lap 15, his tyres sliding; Checa had picked up speed, passing Hopkins, then pushing his team-mate, getting ahead in the last laps.

Bayliss was next, getting by Hopkins on the penultimate lap, the Suzuki rider now troubled with a frequent bug-bear... erratic engine management. The Anglo-American lost another place to Xaus on the last lap, the Spaniard's Yamaha battered by stones thrown up by Tamada in the early laps.

Tamada never did get going properly, and was a disappointed 14th, just over a second ahead of David Checa, substituting again for Elias, and also suffering from Tamada's stoning, his arm badly bruised. Roberts was a long way back, though he did hold Byrne's Proton KTM at bay with a final spurt, to retain some dignity. Rolfo and the WCMs trailed in behind.

250 cc RACE – 18 laps

Remarkably, less than two weeks after being fitted with six screws and a plate to his broken left collarbone, Lorenzo claimed a career-first 250 pole at Assen, saying: "This track makes you think so much you can forget the pain." He was narrowly faster than Porto, with Pedrosa and Stoner completing the front row, de Angelis surviving a spectacular crash to head the second.

The same four followed fast starter Lorenzo, joined by Dovizioso, Aoyama, Barbera and de Puniet as they pulled clear. Positions in the middle of the group changed frequently, Dovizioso particularly strong after half-distance, when he pulled up to fourth. But up front it was Lorenzo in control, revelling in leading, with Porto his constant shadow, Stoner holding a close third, for the

Below: Hiroshi Aoyama, getting closer all the time.

Bottom: Porto pulls a hard move on Pedrosa. He was not for being beaten.
Photographs: Gold & Goose

Above: Dr Costa personally applies emergency ice to teenager Jorge Lorenzo after a brave ride to the rostrum with a freshly plated fracture.

Right: Porto, proud to be the last 250 winner at the now defunct classic Assen.

Bottom: Talmacsi took a second win of the year, and moved into joint points lead.

Bottom right: 150 starts for Gibernau didn't bring any special reward.
Photographs: Gold & Goose

first seven laps at least.

Pedrosa was in the thick of it, and seemed cautious, dropping to sixth behind Barbera after six laps. This was as low as he was prepared to go, and over the next two laps he moved steadily back to the head of the group, then took third off Stoner as the Australian started to drop away by a second on the leading pair.

It didn't take Pedrosa long to close that gap, and with seven laps it was a three-man group, locked together, awaiting the final showdown.

By the start of the second-last lap, Pedrosa had passed Porto easily enough, and at the end of it he was lining up Lorenzo into the chicane. But the class rookie was tight on the entry and late on the brakes, forcing both wide, and giving Porto just the chance he needed to pass both of them, and set off for a definitive final 250 lap of the soon-to-be-redundant circuit, setting a lap record barely half a second slower than pole time. "I saved everything to the end, because I knew it would be a tough battle," said the delighted Argentine.

Pedrosa chased all the way; Lorenzo was almost a second adrift at the flag. The 250s had also given Assen a fine farewell.

The next group were still battling to the finish, Barbera finally dropping off the back as de Puniet joined up. Stoner had by now worked his way back to the front, but crucially missed the last lap signal as he tucked in down pit straight. By the end of it, Aoyama and de Angelis were both in front of him, and almost Dovizioso too. De Puniet was next, Barbera a little way back, Corsi a lonely tenth. Locatelli led the next group; Guintoli, Debon, Davies and Takahashi almost abreast for the final points, the luckless Smrz inches behind.

Jenkner crashed out in the early stages; former Assen winner Anthony West, back again, aboard the Wurth Honda this time, to get his eye back in for the future arrival of the KTM, retired to the pits with six laps to go.

125 cc RACE – 17 laps

The KTMs were flying in the smaller class, Kallio taking his fifth pole in seven races, and Talmacsi following him round to slot in just six hundredths slower. The Aprilias of Pasini and Simoncelli completed the front row, Luthi led the second.

Kallio led away for a fierce race, but with a fearsome pack of eight up front, the lead was in dispute over almost every inch of the classic circuit, positions changing corner by corner.

Bautista led next time round over the line, then Luthi for a couple of laps, then Simoncelli and Kallio again for two more each. And this was just in the run up to half distance, by when the tussling octet were still within less than one second. It seemed unlikely that they would all still be there at the finish.

The first to go was erstwhile points leader Kallio, pushed wide and onto the grass and a looping tumble by Luthi with four laps left. The taciturn Finn gesticulated at the departing pack before trudging to the barriers.

The other seven were still all within the same second as they started the last lap. The tall Simoncelli was prominent among them, and riding very aggressively. A bit too much so on the way into the Stekkenwal right-hander, where he was abruptly flicked over the high side. Luthi was right behind, steering perilously between the sliding bike and rider only to run into the gravel, where he managed to keep on board and rejoin, losing some 14 seconds and finishing tenth.

For a second time, Talmacsi was beneficiary of a last-lap tangle, winning by just over half-a-second, and becoming the first Hungarian ever to lead a World Championship (he shared top slot with Pasini).

Faubel was next, with Pasini two tenths down, Bautista almost alongside, then Masbou's top Honda. The first five were covered by less than 1.5 seconds.

This was not all. Less than four seconds down, Simon finally prevailed over a long four-strong battle, from Koyama, Poggiali and Gadea. Then Luthi, with Nieto tenth, ahead of impressive Austrian KTM wild card Michael Ranseder (19), heading a seven-strong gang disputing 12th.

Kuzuhara was an early crash victim; Alex Espargaro next, after a strong early run chasing the leaders.

ASSEN TT RACING CIRCUIT

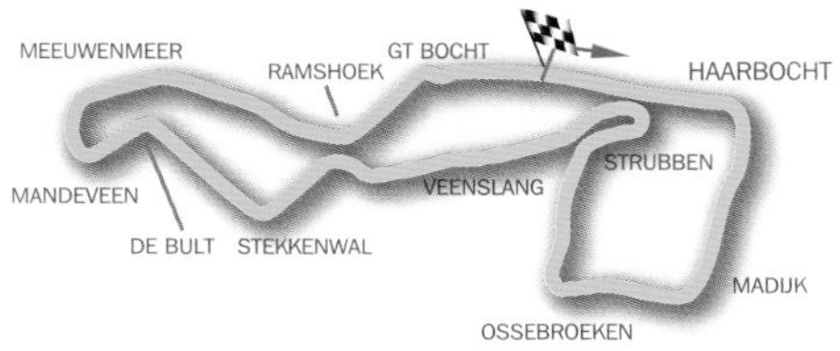
MEEUWENMEER
RAMSHOEK
GT BOCHT
HAARBOCHT
MANDEVEEN
VEENSLANG
STRUBBEN
DE BULT
STEKKENWAL
MADIJK
OSSEBROEKEN

CIRCUIT LENGTH: 3.745 miles/6.027 km

GAULOISES TT ASSEN

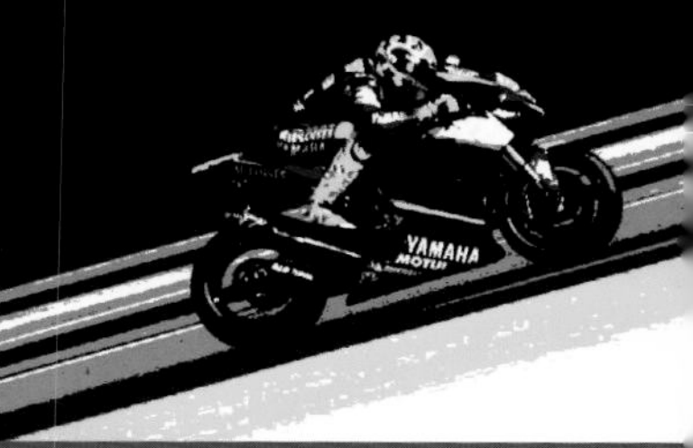

25 JUNE 2005 • FIM WORLD CHAMPIONSHIP ROUND 7

MotoGP

19 laps, 70.801 miles/113.943 km

Pos.	Rider (Nat.)	No.	Machine	Laps	Time & speed
1	Valentino Rossi (I)	46	Yamaha	19	38m 41.808s 109.778 mph/ 176.670 km/h
2	Marco Melandri (I)	33	Honda	19	38m 43.391s
3	Colin Edwards (USA)	5	Yamaha	19	38m 49.451s
4	Nicky Hayden (USA)	69	Honda	19	38m 51.936s
5	Sete Gibernau (E)	15	Honda	19	38m 56.603s
6	Max Biaggi (I)	3	Honda	19	39m 03.383s
7	Alex Barros (BR)	4	Honda	19	39m 04.533s
8	Shinya Nakano (J)	56	Kawasaki	19	39m 08.265s
9	Carlos Checa (E)	7	Ducati	19	39m 12.029s
10	Loris Capirossi (I)	65	Ducati	19	39m 12.273s
11	Troy Bayliss (AUS)	12	Honda	19	39m 25.610s
12	Ruben Xaus (E)	11	Yamaha	19	39m 31.672s
13	John Hopkins (USA)	21	Suzuki	19	39m 32.638s
14	Makoto Tamada (J)	6	Honda	19	39m 35.178s
15	David Checa (E)	94	Yamaha	19	39m 36.773s
16	Kenny Roberts (USA)	10	Suzuki	19	39m 48.747s
17	Shane Byrne (GB)	67	Proton KR	19	39m 48.807s
18	Roberto Rolfo (I)	44	Ducati	19	40m 10.856s
19	James Ellison (GB)	77	Blata	19	40m 25.576s
20	Franco Battaini (I)	27	Blata	18	39m 22.537s
	Alex Hofmann (D)	66	Kawasaki	13	DNF

Fastest lap: Rossi, 2m 00.991s, 110.875 mph/178.436 km/h (record).

Previous record: Valentino Rossi, I (Yamaha), 1m 59.472s, 112.847 mph/181.609 km/h (2004).

Event best maximum speed: Rossi, 190.6 mph/306.7 km/h (free practice no. 2).

Qualifying: 1 Rossi, 1m 58.936s; 2 Gibernau, 1m 59.247s; 3 Melandri, 1m 59.632s; 4 Nakano, 1m 59.760s; 5 Hayden, 1m 59.784s; 6 Edwards, 2m 00.006s; 7 Capirossi, 2m 00.136s; 8 Barros, 2m 00.232s; 9 Biaggi, 2m 00.281s; 10 Hofmann, 2m 00.298s; 11 Tamada, 2m 00.656s; 12 Hopkins, 2m 00.810s; 13 C. Checa, 2m 00.883s; 14 Bayliss, 2m 01.216s; 15 Roberts, 2m 01.836s; 16 Xaus, 2m 01.854s; 17 D. Checa, 2m 02.639s; 18 Rolfo, 2m 02.704s 19 Byrne, 2m 03.442s; 20 Ellison, 2m 03.488s; 21 Battaini, 2m 06.527s.

Fastest race laps: 1 Rossi, 2m 00.991s; 2 Melandri, 2m 01.177s; 3 Edwards, 2m 01.488s; 4 Hayden, 2m 01.702s; 5 Gibernau, 2m 01.864s; 6 Capirossi, 2m 02.052s; 7 Biaggi, 2m 02.152s; 8 Barros, 2m 02.222s; 9 Hopkins, 2m 02.430s; 10 Hofmann, 2m 02.457s; 11 Nakano, 2m 02.526s; 12 C. Checa, 2m 02.678s; 13 Bayliss, 2m 03.255s; 14 Roberts, 2m 03.502s; 15 Xaus, 2m 03.642s; 16 Byrne, 2m 03.896s; 17 D. Checa, 2m 03.997s; 18 Tamada, 2m 04.005s; 19 Rolfo, 2m 05.897s; 20 Ellison, 2m 06.514s; 21 Battaini, 2m 09.650s.

World Championship: 1 Rossi, 170; 2 Melandri, 107; 3 Biaggi, 87; 4 Gibernau, 84; 5 Barros, 74; 6 Edwards, 73; 7 Hayden, 60; 8 Capirossi, 49; 9 Nakano, 48; 10 C. Checa, 40; 11 Bayliss, 37; 12 Xaus, 28; 13 Jacque, 25; 14 Hopkins, 19; 15 Tamada, 18; 16 Elias, 15; 17 van den Goorbergh, 12; 18 Hofmann and Roberts, 9; 20 Rolfo, 7; 21 D. Checa and Ellison, 4; 23 Ukawa, 1.

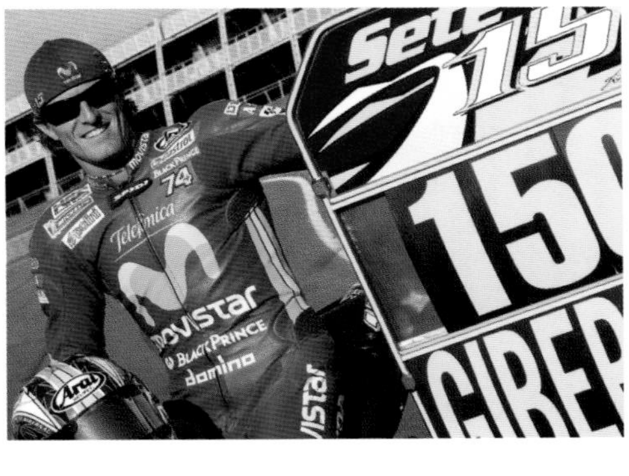

250 cc

18 laps, 67.068 miles/107.496 km

Pos.	Rider (Nat.)	No.	Machine	Laps	Time & speed
1	Sebastian Porto (ARG)	19	Aprilia	18	38m 02.148s 105.807 mph/ 170.280 km/h
2	Daniel Pedrosa (E)	1	Honda	18	38m 02.529s
3	Jorge Lorenzo (E)	48	Honda	18	38m 03.380s
4	Hiroshi Aoyama (J)	73	Honda	18	38m 13.905s
5	Alex de Angelis (RSM)	5	Aprilia	18	38m 14.165s
6	Casey Stoner (AUS)	27	Aprilia	18	38m 14.174s
7	Andrea Dovizioso (I)	34	Honda	18	38m 14.502s
8	Randy de Puniet (F)	7	Aprilia	18	38m 16.083s
9	Hector Barbera (E)	80	Honda	18	38m 16.554s
10	Simone Corsi (I)	24	Aprilia	18	38m 31.442s
11	Roberto Locatelli (I)	15	Aprilia	18	38m 55.832s
12	Sylvain Guintoli (F)	50	Aprilia	18	38m 57.513s
13	Alex Debon (E)	6	Honda	18	38m 57.514s
14	Chaz Davies (GB)	57	Aprilia	18	38m 57.775s
15	Yuki Takahashi (J)	55	Honda	18	38m 58.061s
16	Jakub Smrz (CZ)	96	Honda	18	38m 58.122s
17	Andrea Ballerini (I)	8	Aprilia	18	39m 00.985s
18	Mirko Giansanti (I)	32	Aprilia	18	39m 14.249s
19	Dirk Heidolf (D)	28	Honda	18	39m 14.350s
20	Gregory Leblanc (F)	38	Aprilia	18	39m 27.255s
21	Martin Cardenas (COL)	36	Aprilia	18	39m 27.341s
22	Michele Danese (I)	45	Aprilia	18	39m 34.508s
23	Hans Smees (NL)	66	Aprilia	18	39m 43.338s
24	Arnaud Vincent (F)	21	Fantic	18	38m 56.729s
25	Gabor Rizmayer (H)	12	Yamaha	18	39m 57.796s
	Alex Baldolini (I)	25	Aprilia	12	DNF
	Anthony West (AUS)	14	Honda	12	DNF
	Steve Jenkner (D)	17	Aprilia	3	DNF
	Randy Gevers (NL)	67	Aprilia		DNS
	Jan Roelofs (NL)	68	Yamaha		DNQ
	Alexander Todorov (BUL)	22	Yamaha		DNQ
	Gabriele Ferro (I)	20	Fantic		DNQ
	Mike Velthjzen (NL)	69	Honda		DNQ

Fastest lap: Porto, 2m 05.191s, 107.155 mph/172.450 km/h (record).

Previous record: Daniel Pedrosa, E (Honda), 2m 03.469s, 109.193 mph/175.729 km/h (2004).

Event best maximum speed: de Angelis, 159.0 mph/255.9 km/h (race).

Qualifying: 1 Lorenzo, 2m 04.562s; 2 Porto, 2m 04.738s; 3 Pedrosa, 2m 04.901s; 4 Stoner, 2m 05.251s; 5 de Angelis, 2m 05.456s; 6 Aoyama, 2m 05.702s; 7 Dovizioso, 2m 05.864s; 8 Barbera, 2m 06.255s; 9 de Puniet, 2m 06.263s; 10 Corsi, 2m 06.809s; 11 Smrz, 2m 06.950s; 12 Davies, 2m 07.322s; 13 Takahashi, 2m 07.410s; 14 Jenkner, 2m 07.523s; 15 Giansanti, 2m 07.614s; 16 Baldolini, 2m 07.684s; 17 Guintoli, 2m 07.756s; 18 Heidolf, 2m 07.851s; 19 Ballerini, 2m 07.854s; 20 Locatelli, 2m 07.976s; 21 Debon, 2m 08.412s; 22 Leblanc, 2m 08.952s; 23 West, 2m 09.149s; 24 Vincent, 2m 09.568s; 25 Cardenas, 2m 10.218s; 26 Danese, 2m 10.331s; 27 Gevers, 2m 10.627s; 28 Smees, 2m 10.692s; 29 Rizmayer, 2m 11.204s; 30 Roelofs, 2m 13.529s; 31 Todorov, 2m 14.354s; 32 Ferro, 2m 14.600s; 33 Velthjzen, 2m 15.810s.

Fastest race laps: 1 Porto, 2m 05.191s; 2 Pedrosa, 2m 05.276s; 3 Lorenzo, 2m 05.922s; 4 de Angelis, 2m 06.232s; 5 Stoner, 2m 06.274s; 6 Aoyama, 2m 06.337s; 7 de Puniet, 2m 06.454s; 8 Dovizioso, 2m 06.501s; 9 Barbera, 2m 06.617s; 10 Corsi, 2m 07.296s; 11 Locatelli, 2m 07.974s; 12 Debon, 2m 08.322s; 13 Davies, 2m 08.364s; 14 Takahashi, 2m 08.580s; 15 Smrz, 2m 08.698s; 16 Guintoli, 2m 08.848s; 17 Ballerini, 2m 09.075s; 18 Heidolf, 2m 09.098s; 19 Giansanti, 2m 09.370s; 20 Baldolini, 2m 09.588s; 21 Jenkner, 2m 09.590s; 22 Leblanc, 2m 10.205s; 23 Cardenas, 2m 10.247s; 24 Danese, 2m 10.794s; 25 Smees, 2m 11.053s; 26 West, 2m 11.424s; 27 Vincent, 2m 11.631s; 28 Rizmayer, 2m 11.708s.

World Championship: 1 Pedrosa, 143; 2 Stoner, 106; 3 Dovizioso, 102; 4 Porto, 74; 5 Aoyama, 71; 6 Lorenzo, 70; 7 de Angelis, 67; 8 de Puniet, 54; 9 Barbera, 51; 10 Corsi, 44; 11 Debon, 32; 12 Guintoli and Takahashi, 31; 14 Locatelli, 20; 15 Giansanti, 19; 16 Davies, 17; 17 Baldolini, 15; 18 Ballerini, 8; 19 Rous, 7; 20 Smrz, 6; 21 Leblanc, 4; 22 Marchand and Nigon, 3; 24 Cardenas and Heidolf, 1.

125 cc

17 laps, 63.342 miles/101.949 km

Pos.	Rider (Nat.)	No.	Machine	Laps	Time & speed
1	Gabor Talmacsi (H)	14	KTM	17	38m 09.487s 99.609 mph/ 160.305 km/h
2	Hector Faubel (E)	55	Aprilia	17	38m 10.144s
3	Mattia Pasini (I)	75	Aprilia	17	38m 10.288s
4	Alvaro Bautista (E)	19	Honda	17	38m 10.334s
5	Alexis Masbou (F)	7	Honda	17	38m 10.890s
6	Julian Simon (E)	60	KTM	17	38m 13.459s
7	Tomoyoshi Koyama (J)	71	Honda	17	38m 13.746s
8	Manuel Poggiali (RSM)	54	Gilera	17	38m 13.810s
9	Sergio Gadea (E)	33	Aprilia	17	38m 13.979s
10	Thomas Luthi (CH)	12	Honda	17	38m 23.421s
11	Pablo Nieto (E)	22	Derbi	17	38m 27.749s
12	Michael Ranseder (A)	76	KTM	17	38m 30.180s
13	Joan Olive (E)	6	Aprilia	17	38m 30.578s
14	Mike di Meglio (F)	63	Honda	17	38m 30.683s
15	Lukas Pesek (CZ)	52	Derbi	17	38m 30.791s
16	Nicolas Terol (E)	18	Derbi	17	38m 30.926s
17	Manuel Hernandez (E)	43	Aprilia	17	38m 31.061s
18	Fabrizio Lai (I)	32	Honda	17	38m 31.062s
19	Lorenzo Zanetti (I)	8	Aprilia	17	38m 40.224s
20	Marco Simoncelli (I)	58	Aprilia	17	38m 47.033s
21	Gioele Pellino (I)	42	Malaguti	17	38m 47.264s
22	Angel Rodriguez (E)	47	Honda	17	38m 47.330s
23	Dario Giuseppetti (D)	25	Aprilia	17	38m 50.463s
24	Sandro Cortese (D)	11	Honda	17	38m 50.508s
25	Imre Toth (H)	45	Aprilia	17	38m 59.566s
26	Andrea Iannone (I)	29	Aprilia	17	39m 01.302s
27	Vincent Braillard (CH)	26	Aprilia	17	39m 01.349s
28	Jordi Carchano (E)	28	Aprilia	17	39m 05.483s
29	Gert-Jan Kok (NL)	79	Honda	17	39m 24.648s
30	Joey Litjens (NL)	37	Honda	17	39m 52.722s
31	Hugo van den Berg (NL)	78	Aprilia	17	39m 59.567s
	Raymond Schouten (NL)	16	Honda	14	DNF
	Mika Kallio (SF)	36	KTM	13	DNF
	Mateo Tunez (E)	46	Aprilia	9	DNF
	Raffaele de Rosa (I)	35	Aprilia	6	DNF
	Michele Pirro (I)	15	Malaguti	3	DNF
	Aleix Espargaro (E)	41	Honda	1	DNF
	Federico Sandi (I)	10	Honda	1	DNF
	Toshihisa Kuzuhara (J)	9	Honda	1	DNF
	Karel Abraham (CZ)	44	Aprilia	0	DNF
	Mark van Kreij (NL)	80	Honda		DNQ

Fastest lap: Faubel, 2m 13.536s, 100.459 mph/161.673 km/h (record).

Previous record: Jorge Lorenzo, E (Derbi), 2m 10.123s, 103.609 mph/166.743 km/h (2004).

Event best maximum speed: Toth, 136.5 mph/219.7 km/h (qualifying practice no. 1).

Qualifying: 1 Kallio, 2m 11.855s; 2 Talmacsi, 2m 11.915s; 3 Pasini, 2m 12.300s; 4 Simoncelli, 2m 12.729s; 5 Luthi, 2m 12.911s; 6 Gadea, 2m 13.170s; 7 Poggiali, 2m 13.217s; 8 Masbou, 2m 13.357s; 9 Faubel, 2m 13.370s; 10 Simon, 2m 13.403s; 11 Koyama, 2m 13.403s; 12 Pesek, 2m 13.465s; 13 di Meglio, 2m 13.524s; 14 Bautista, 2m 13.631s; 15 Hernandez, 2m 13.646s; 16 Olive, 1m 13.973s; 17 Ranseder, 2m 13.991s; 18 Lai, 2m 14.272s; 19 de Rosa, 2m 14.363s; 20 Espargaro, 2m 14.389s; 21 Iannone, 2m 14.433s; 22 Terol, 2m 14.463s; 23 Nieto, 2m 14.596s; 24 Cortese, 2m 14.716s; 25 Schouten, 2m 14.975s; 26 Zanetti, 2m 15.150s; 27 Kuzuhara, 2m 15.250s; 28 Rodriguez, 2m 15.370s; 29 Abraham, 2m 15.399s; 30 Toth, 2m 15.457s; 31 Sandi, 2m 15.666s; 32 Pirro, 2m 15.951s; 33 Giuseppetti, 2m 15.965s; 34 Carchano, 2m 16.146s; 35 Braillard, 2m 16.150s; 36 Pellino, 2m 16.321s; 37 Tunez, 2m 16.427s; 38 Litjens, 2m 16.918s; 39 van den Berg, 2m 17.682s; 40 Kok, 2m 18.113s; 41 van Kreij, 2m 22.202s.

Fastest race laps: 1 Faubel, 2m 13.536s; 2 Bautista, 2m 13.561s; 3 Masbou, 2m 13.581s; 4 Simoncelli, 2m 13.582s; 5 Talmacsi, 2m 13.628s; 6 Luthi, 2m 13.636s; 7 Kallio, 2m 13.671s; 8 Pasini, 2m 13.703s; 9 Simon, 2m 13.739s; 10 Koyama, 2m 13.747s; 11 Poggiali, 2m 13.773s; 12 Gadea, 2m 13.903s; 13 Nieto, 2m 14.190s; 14 Ranseder, 2m 14.219s; 15 di Meglio, 2m 14.335s; 16 Pesek, 2m 14.468s; 17 Hernandez, 2m 14.482s; 18 Olive, 2m 14.513s; 19 Pellino, 2m 14.527s; 20 Zanetti, 2m 14.555s; 21 Terol, 2m 14.566s; 22 Lai, 2m 14.668s; 23 de Rosa, 2m 14.756s; 24 Schouten, 2m 14.905s; 25 Rodriguez, 2m 14.955s; 26 Giuseppetti, 2m 15.331s; 27 Cortese, 2m 15.449s; 28 Iannone, 2m 15.537s; 29 Carchano, 2m 15.969s; 30 Toth, 2m 16.005s; 31 Braillard, 2m 16.104s; 32 Kok, 2m 17.376s; 33 Pirro, 2m 18.210s; 34 Tunez, 2m 18.281s; 35 van den Berg, 2m 18.832s; 36 Litjens, 2m 19.179s; 37 Espargaro, 2m 23.539s; 38 Sandi, 2m 25.784s.

World Championship: 1 Pasini and Talmacsi, 100; 3 Luthi, 89; 4 Kallio, 82; 5 Simoncelli, 72; 6 Lai, 63; 7 Poggiali, 59; 8 Simon, 55; 9 Koyama, 52; 10 Faubel, 50; 11 Gadea and Nieto, 30; 13 Olive, 29; 14 Bautista, 28; 15 di Meglio, 25; 16 Masbou, 20; 17 Espargaro, 16; 18 Zanetti, 14; 19 Hernandez, 12; 20 Kuzuhara, 9; 21 Pesek and Ranseder, 8; 23 Toth, 7; 24 Conti and Iannone, 5; 26 Carchano, Giuseppetti and Pirro, 3; 29 Cortese, de Rosa and Terol, 1.

UNITED STATESGP
LAGUNA SECA

FOR all the obvious reasons – greed, money, prestige, and latterly a heaven-sent chance to put F1 racing in the eye after the debacle at Indianapolis a few short weeks before – MotoGP was mad about the return to the USA.

This had been true ever since the last US GP at Laguna in 1994, after a six-year run of dwindling popularity and income. Dorna had been trying hard to restore the States to the calendar ever since. Alternatives had emerged at Elkhart Lake, Homestead near Miami, at the new Barber Raceway in Alabama, and in on-paper plans for several other venues, including Palm Springs. Acting as a Dorna envoy, Mick Doohan himself had even endorsed Homestead. But none of these ever came to anything... driving the ever-more eager Dorna back to Laguna again. It was time to overlook the many shortcomings and forget the previous financial losses. Major concessions would have to be made in all sorts of areas, including track facilities, and even (as it turned out, to the surprise of nobody) in safety.

The enthusiasm from the hosts was hardly less striking. Thanks to $2-million from Yamaha, who had a half-century to celebrate, plus strong event sponsorship from Red Bull, a major spending programme had taken the old Laguna Circuit a significant step forwards towards the 20th Century. Massive earthmoving had shifted though not removed the bank outside Turn One, and made more run-off area towards the next corner. More run-off was claimed up the hill, at the notorious Corkscrew, and at the following Rainey Corner. That the track still lay far behind the standards set by new circuits from Valencia to China, from Istanbul to Losail, was a reflection of how much further back it had been when it started.

The riders? Well, of course the Americans were relishing the prospect: Edwards and Hayden, Roberts and Hopkins all had more or less intimate knowledge of a track with a very distinct and very demanding character. Ex-superbikers Xaus and Bayliss knew it too, but of the remainder only Barros, Biaggi and Checa had raced there before. And there is plenty to get to know. In line with the club-like facilities and organisation, Laguna is short, rather narrow and very busy. Just three out of the 11 corners are anything like flat. The constant changes of elevation are supplemented by a full range of bumps and whoop-de-doos that require intimate knowledge if they are to be exploited, rather than suffered.

Some of the veterans liked it – Barros especially, and Bayliss, set for his best race of the year.

The Laguna virgins were in for a shock, when they saw the wall on the outside of the notorious Turn One (front wheel aviating at close to 165mph just as you're trying to swing left and get the bike planted for some hard braking). And Turn Six, on the climb to the Corkscrew, where the concrete was so close to the track it was "like the entrance to the Autopista in Milan," according to Melandri.

Worries about just how the new-generation MotoGP machines would manage this small, tight track had been growing in the preceding weeks. Melandri was the most outspoken, breaking cover even before practice had begun. Seeing Turn One, he shook his head. "I can't think of anyone making a mistake there – we have walls inside and outside." The pit lane entrance was also a convolution of concrete ... "very dangerous, if you come in quickly on a slick tyre to change in the rain". His criticism was punished by three crashes over a dire weekend that would begin a pause in his strong run as the new young pretender.

Rossi was also a prominent critic, if more diplomatic; though he admitted "every time I go to Turn One or Six, I think... f**k!". Without further detail beyond a need to iron out the bumps by resurfacing, he said: "If they don't change it, I don't think we will be able to race here again. If we compare this track to all others in the championship it is very dangerous. The biggest problem for me is the speeds these bikes do.." And track expert Kenny Roberts Junior echoed this, if inversely. "They seem to have shrunk the track by 15 percent," he said.

Roberts had inspected the track on behalf of the riders (Edwards also shouldered some of the blame, when the nasty talk began), and had previously acknowledged that the Europeans might find it alarming. "American riders come here and think it's great... it's to do with the mind-set." In the normal course of events, he didn't believe there was a big chance of anybody striking a wall "with any significance". But even he had that faraway look as he reeled off a litany of potentially unexpected problems that might have more severe consequences – "a blown engine oiling the back tyre, a tyre exploding, the throttle jamming open". Understandably, since he had himself been victim to each of these problems at least once in the past two seasons.

This all simmered gently, but such was the hoopla that there was never any more than minor fears that riders might refuse to ride. To do so would be to offend Brad Pitt! He was just one of several celebs on the grid. Matt Leblanc of "Friends" was another, with lesser known Hollywood luminaries Adrien Brady and Alan Grier (who distinguished himself by arriving at Yamaha's half-centenary party all togged up in Repsol Honda leathers).

More gratifyingly, if in a different way, there were also a number of ex-racing stars on hand. Wayne Rainey, a leading figure behind the revival of the race within earshot of his house, was a prominent presence. Career rival Kevin Schwantz was

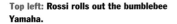

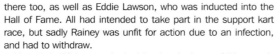

Top left: Rossi rolls out the bumblebee Yamaha.

Centre left: Yamaha's Wataru Hasegawa wishes the company happy 50th birthday.

Top right: Legends at the party– Rossi and Edwards flank Rainey, Roberts behind Rainey, Agostini two to his left, beyond Kel Carruthers.

Bottom row, from left: Nicky, Tommy and Roger Lee Hayden with Michael Jordan; Brad Pitt with Hayden on the grid; more legends – Doohan, Spencer, Rainey , Lawson and Roberts in the Hall of Fame.

Photographs: Gold & Goose

there too, as well as Eddie Lawson, who was inducted into the Hall of Fame. All had intended to take part in the support kart race, but sadly Rainey was unfit for action due to an infection, and had to withdraw.

Yamaha's 50th – overlooked by the denizens of Monterey's famed aquarium – was the reason for their big spend, for the presence of Yamaha world champions and associates from Agostini to Rossi and back, and for an outbreak of Seventies memories, most notably a searing display of yellow – riders' leathers and team livery echoing the historic yellow and broken black of Yamaha Motor USA. One of racing's most iconic images, the bumblebee bikes evoked strong memories of King Kenny Roberts and the way he grabbed the World Championship by the scruff of its neck in the latter part of that decade.

Brad Pitt's personal good-luck grid squeeze to Nicky Hayden may have made all the difference. More likely was a fine piece of opportunism from a MotoGP rider whose machine control is conspicuously dirt-track daring, but who had been taking a little longer than expected to mature. Nicky did not only exploit his track knowledge for his pole position, followed by a very determined flag-to-flag first win. He also protected it, making sure nobody followed him in practice. "Those guys that would never let me follow them anywhere were the ones waiting on me," he said. "I tried to show a few guys some bad lines in a few places. I mean, Sete never let me follow him anywhere." Shakey Byrne had typically humorous response. "I tried to follow the Americans. but they kept clearing off. They've no consideration at all for the slower guys."

The concessions made an uneasy marriage between AMA and MotoGP, and different ways of doing things came up with several anomalies. The sale of paddock passes is against protocol, though not unknown in Europe: here AMA practice was adopted, with 13,000 sold, giving fans a chance to ambush riders as they dashed between the back of the tented pits to the safety of container-offices or motorhomes.

The security and parking attendants had that down-home deputy sheriff-style authoritian approach that visitors found hard to come to terms with. Then some of the flag marshals wan-

dered off, lengthening a delay in the special two-hour free training session scheduled for Friday morning. That eventually got under way 25 minutes late, prompting Rossi's crew chief Burgess to sound off that he couldn't remember a delay like this "for many, many years – even in Brazil or South Africa". Clearly he'd forgotten China, ten weeks before; but his words reflected a widespread hacked-off feeling inside the makeshift paddock.

There were other practical problems... including a failure of local and Dorna TV feed networks to match up. This left the pits without any of the usual array of information – not only lap times, but also section times, speeds, real-time monitoring of riders, and more. This was fixed for Saturday; Friday's solution had PR staff and even Yamaha team manager Davide Brivio lined up in the press room (where the feed did work), reading timing data over to team members by two-way radio. There was little sign that the absence of these people from the pits proper in any way inhibited the progress of the machine development.

In the end, however, they not only got away with it. They did so in gratifying keep-it-Stateside style. The revived US GP was a great success, with an official crowd figure of 57,932, and an all-American results sheet to gladden the patriotic heart. Hayden ran from pole to flag; Edwards defeated Rossi for second. He was the first American winner since Roberts at Motegi in 2000, and this the first American one-two since Schwantz beat Rainey at Jerez in 1993.

So when the winner followed his victory lap with a second one, his father Earl Hayden perched on the seat; then danced a blue-grass/hip-hop jig on the podium, there was never to be heard a discouraging word. Until next year, obviously...

MOTOGP RACE – 32 laps

Experience told at Laguna, and qualifying proved it... not only for pole. That was inspired aggression by Hayden, as well as track intimacy, for a flying lap with everything on the line. But seven of the first eight names on the list were among the elite with prior knowledge. The exception (who else) was Rossi, who

learned fast enough to qualify within three tenths of Hayden, and ahead not only of Barros, but also Superbike veterans Bayliss and Edwards, and local hero Hopkins, who made up the second row. Melandri was down in 11th; Gibernau back in 13th, and said succinctly: "I'm screwed. I could talk for longer, but that says it all." A settings breakthrough in morning warm-up meant his condition for the race was rather different.

Hayden had discussed tactics with his brothers the night before. They were simple enough. Get a flyer, and run away. "I said, dude, I really think I can get away tomorrow if I get the hole shot."

That worked perfectly, with Bayliss taking a runner from his second row start to follow him into Turn One, from Rossi, fast starter Biaggi, Hopkins, Checa and Gibernau, who was ahead of Edwards after charging through from the fifth row.

Top: Strangers in a strange land... far behind the Americans, Tamada, a sickly Capirossi, Rolfo and Hofmann pull the Corkscrew.

Above: Track knowledge helped Bayliss equal his best result. Checa, close behind, is soon to tumble.

Left: Nakano on the grid with crew chief Fiorenzo Fanali. He would gain another top ten.

Photograph: Gold & Goose

133

Above: All yellow: Edwards shows Rossi some Stateside sideways in their battle for second.

Right: Hayden greets the fans who watched him reach maturity.
Photograph: Gold & Goose

Nicky's lead was a second at the end of the first lap, and would stretch to almost three at one point. Later on, Edwards would close up challengingly, but the Honda rider was able to respond. For a first-time winner who had been keeping his supporters waiting, the way he muscled his bike to victory from pole to flag was mighty impressive.

Another front-row starter didn't even finish lap one. Track fan Barros was skittled by Melandri at the final corner – the latter's third tumble of the weekend.

There was plenty of action in the early laps, Rossi up to second by the end of lap one, and then Bayliss losing touch, with a gaggle of growling 990s building up behind him. The fourth lap was hectic – Biaggi attacking Bayliss through the early corners, only for the Honda to fight back with a tighter line over the blind approach to the Corkscrew. Edwards meanwhile was even faster. He came whistling past both of them on the inside. Gibernau was right behind, and in the confusion also slipped through to drop Biaggi from the front to the back of the gang in one bend.

Edwards immediately left this group behind, and started closing on Rossi, more than two seconds ahead, himself a little closer than that to the leader.

The pursuit, as well as Hayden muscling around in the lead, had the movie stars leaning over the railing and the capacity crowd whooping with excitement. Edwards was as much a master of the track as the younger rider, his straight-line approach to the crucial blind and bumpy run into the Corkscrew taking him onto the paint on both sides of the road time and again. It was here that he pounced on Rossi on lap 16, the Italian later admitting he'd been taken by surprise, in spite of watching the gap grow smaller lap by lap.

Could the Texas Tornado catch Hayden? The gap at the end of that lap was 2.67 seconds, a quarter less time next round, then the same reduction again for the next two laps, so that on the 19th Edwards had pinned it back to 1.86. With 12 laps to go, he was on target. But Hayden had it under control, putting in another flyer to re-establish his authority. He was able to maintain it under constant pressure all the way to the flag. The

American fans watched one of their own riders reach maturity at Laguna.

Edwards had to settle for second, and was lapping steadily at the close… to be taken by surprise by Rossi's late charge. With one lap to go, too late to be signalled, he scythed eight tenths off Edwards's advantage. Edwards could hardly believe his eyes when he saw his team-mate right on his back wheel into Turn Two on the last lap.

Rossi might have had the strength to attack, but he also had the vision of celebrating Yamaha's half-century "with both yellow bikes in the gravel", so he backed off to cross the line less than half-a-second behind. It was enough to be the first European, and to have learned a lot about Laguna's quirks from the two Americans ahead of him.

Biaggi had got straight back ahead of Bayliss after the Corkscrew shuffle, and was looming over Gibernau, finally passing with a good run up the inside into Turn Three on the tenth lap. Once again he was to produce a strong race after struggling in qualifying; no less so Gibernau, who kept him honest to the flag, where he was still less than two tenths adrift.

Bayliss maintained control of the next group, with Checa pushing him hard, until he lost the front at the first hairpin and slid to earth. Hopkins and Nakano were there to take up the pursuit. All the time, slow starter Tamada was gaining speed, getting straight past Capirossi, riding as an act of determination, after battling all weekend with severe gastro-enteritis. The Japanese Honda rider then overtook Roberts, dropping backwards from the group, and in the latter part of the race not only closed up on Nakano, but was by the finish past everybody except Bayliss. He was still attacking the Australian as they crossed the line, Hopkins fending off Nakano a short way behind.

Capirossi was next, then Xaus some way back, followed by Hofmann and Elias hard at it. A yawning 23 seconds back came Roberts, apologising to friends and fans for an extraordinarily lacklustre effort. Byrne shaded Ellison in an all-British battle for the last point.

Rolfo ran out of gas on the penultimate lap.

MAZDA RACEWAY LAGUNA SECA

CIRCUIT LENGTH: 2.238 miles/3.610 km

RED BULL
U.S. GRAND PRIX

10 JULY 2005 • FIM WORLD CHAMPIONSHIP ROUND 8

MotoGP

32 laps, 71.776 miles/115.520 km

Pos.	Rider (Nat.)	No.	Machine	Laps	Time & speed
1	Nicky Hayden (USA)	69	Honda	32	45m 15.374s 95.165 mph/ 153.154 km/h
2	Colin Edwards (USA)	5	Yamaha	32	45m 17.315s
3	Valentino Rossi (I)	46	Yamaha	32	45m 17.686s
4	Max Biaggi (I)	3	Honda	32	45m 19.590s
5	Sete Gibernau (E)	15	Honda	32	45m 19.852s
6	Troy Bayliss (AUS)	12	Honda	32	45m 37.755s
7	Makoto Tamada (J)	6	Honda	32	45m 37.867s
8	John Hopkins (USA)	21	Suzuki	32	45m 38.522s
9	Shinya Nakano (J)	56	Kawasaki	32	45m 38.999s
10	Loris Capirossi (I)	65	Ducati	32	45m 41.497s
11	Ruben Xaus (E)	11	Yamaha	32	45m 58.886s
12	Alex Hofmann (D)	66	Kawasaki	32	46m 06.331s
13	Toni Elias (E)	24	Yamaha	32	46m 06.717s
14	Kenny Roberts (USA)	10	Suzuki	32	46m 29.123s
15	Shane Byrne (GB)	67	Proton KR	32	46m 39.630s
16	James Ellison (GB)	77	Blata	32	46m 39.898s
17	Franco Battaini (I)	27	Blata	31	46m 20.215s
	Roberto Rolfo (I)	44	Ducati	30	DNF
	Carlos Checa (E)	7	Ducati	8	DNF
	Marco Melandri (I)	33	Honda	0	DNF
	Alex Barros (BR)	4	Honda	0	DNF

Fastest lap: Edwards, 1m 23.915s, 96.232 mph/154.871 km/h (record).

Previous record: Kevin Schwantz, USA (Suzuki), 1m 25.838s, 92.099 mph/148.219 km/h (1990).

Event best maximum speed: Hayden, 161.1 mph/259.2 km/h (warm-up).

Qualifying: 1 Hayden, 1m 22.670s; 2 Rossi, 1m 23.024s; 3 Barros, 1m 23.312s; 4 Bayliss, 1m 23.358s; 5 Edwards, 1m 23.469s; 6 Hopkins, 1m 23.493s; 7 Biaggi, 1m 23.596s; 8 Checa, 1m 23.597s; 9 Tamada, 1m 23.750s; 10 Nakano, 1m 23.799s; 11 Melandri, 1m 23.905s; 12 Roberts, 1m 24.011s; 13 Gibernau, 1m 24.145s; 14 Capirossi, 1m 24.257s; 15 Hofmann, 1m 24.480s; 16 Xaus, 1m 24.741s; 17 Elias, 1m 25.462s; 18 Rolfo, 1m 25.881s; 19 Byrne, 1m 25.937s; 20 Ellison, 1m 26.800s; 21 Battaini, 1m 28.435s.

Fastest race laps: 1 Edwards, 1m 23.915s; 2 Hayden, 1m 23.984s; 3 Rossi, 1m 24.207s; 4 Biaggi, 1m 24.280s; 5 Gibernau, 1m 24.294s; 6 Tamada, 1m 24.654s; 7 Checa, 1m 24.694s; 8 Capirossi, 1m 24.702s; 9 Nakano, 1m 24.706s; 10 Hopkins, 1m 24.783s; 11 Bayliss, 1m 24.787s; 12 Roberts, 1m 25.187s; 13 Xaus, 1m 25.254s; 14 Elias, 1m 25.371s; 15 Hofmann, 1m 25.437s; 16 Rolfo, 1m 25.951s; 17 Byrne, 1m 26.495s; 18 Ellison, 1m 26.773s; 19 Battaini, 1m 28.638s.

World Championship: 1 Rossi, 186; 2 Melandri, 107; 3 Biaggi, 100; 4 Gibernau, 95; 5 Edwards, 93; 6 Hayden, 85; 7 Barros, 74; 8 Capirossi and Nakano, 55; 10 Bayliss, 47; 11 C. Checa, 40; 12 Xaus, 33; 13 Hopkins and Tamada, 27; 15 Jacque, 25; 16 Elias, 18; 17 Hofmann, 13; 18 van den Goorbergh, 12; 19 Roberts, 11; 20 Rolfo, 7; 21 D. Checa and Ellison, 4; 23 Byrne and Ukawa, 1.

FIM WORLD CHAMPIONSHIP • ROUND 9
BRITISHGP

THERE is a certain sense of inevitability that the British GP will be wet. It made no difference that there'd been such a long hot spell in England, as on mainland Europe, that drought measures were already coming into force. Practice and the preceding Day of Champions had been dry throughout, but the famous English summer obliged most generously on race morning. The heavens opened, and stayed wide open for the rest of the day.

It was easy to say it made for a typical British GP. In fact, though there is seldom a British GP weekend when there isn't at least some rain at some time, the preconception is wrong – in the last 20 years, there have been only three wet races in the top class, 1986 at Silverstone, 2000 and now 2005 at Donington.

And while the discomfort for more than 75,000 fans was considerable, the reward for their endurance was even greater. Rain changes everything, punishing the unwary and paying dividends to the exceptionally skilled. Rossi won – and one almost adds "of course", until remembering that the wet was his

nemesis often enough earlier in his career. This was another towering demonstration of every aspect of his gift for racing. And Kenny Roberts Junior was second – and one almost adds "Who?". It's been that long since the 2000 World Champion had the chance to demonstrate that while he has no appetite for risking his all on a bike not capable of anything more than mid-field finishes, when skill becomes more important than the motorcycle, he still has plenty of that. It was, for Kenny, the end of a long dry season.

The annual charity Day of Champions saw the usual antics and drew the usual crowd, yielding a record £172,000 for the now well-established Riders for Health charity, providing transport for health care in Africa. Charitably also, the crowds overlooked the state of the circuit. The grass on the parkland was fresh-mown, the views over the back section still extensive; but the Spitfire on its Airfix-style plinth down below them was minus one wing, with the tail cockeyed... obviously just about to crash.

Up in the paddock, the down-at-heel feel, coming after the

similarly primitive Laguna Seca, was an uncomfortable reminder to the English-speakers that they host the three GPs with the dowdiest facilities... the prefab Phillip Island being the third. Relief, for Donington, is at hand. In October the bulldozers were due to move in, to flatten the entire paddock area and start again.

Out on the track, a full resurfacing had made a difficult circuit still harder, with grip levels unpredictable, especially when wet. The dual character remained intact – sweeping subtleties down the hill through the Craner Curves and up again via Macleans and Coppice; brawling outbraking and first-gear nerfing moves for the rest of the track. In this way it puts the emphasis on the full range of machine performance. The trouble is, improving the bike for one section of the track makes it worse for the rest, and vice versa. Donington makes engineers think hard.

Of course, the rain changed all that. It hands the power back to the riders. Nowhere was this more clearly illustrated than in the 250 class. KTM's long-awaited 250 had finally arrived. An unorthodox (nowadays) parallel twin, crafted by long-serving two-stroke guru Harald Bartol, who chose the layout to avoid the problems suffered by the preferred V-twins. "When you design an engine, you start with one test cylinder. In my experience with vee engines, if you put two together you never get twice the power of one, because of different cylinder angles, intake and exhaust paths and volumes, etc." The successful partially injected 125 engine had been doubled up, but Bartol had taken a tip from the M1, and added a balance shaft. This allowed him to decouple the crankshaft throws. Having tested conventional (180-degree) timing as well, the preferred engine had the second cylinder delayed by a further 90 degrees, to make a virtual V-twin in the manner of Yamaha's virtual V4.

In practice, a broken con-rod precipitated a crash for rider Anthony West, who qualified 15th. In the rain, the underrated Australian was able to employ the skills that had won Assen in similar conditions in 2003. He finished second.

As it would transpire, the 250 project was being pursued at the cost of the four-stroke MotoGP engine... at least in the sense that at an earlier meeting, KTM had discussed cancelling it in order to release more money for the project with Proton Team KR. They had a revised engine here, aimed to improve mid-range and throttle response of a motor that has reasonable power, but not much user-friendliness with it. More significantly, meetings between the team and the engine supplier ended another step closer to a premature parting of the ways.

Luck was not on the team's side in their attempt to do their part perfectly, with a freak mechanical failure right in front of the pits in practice. A rear suspension link broke, collapsing the back end and sending Byrne onto the grass, where he was able to stop without further misadventure. The overall effect was slightly ridiculous, the failure a first ever, according to team boss Chuck Aksland. The consequences of the same failure on a fast Assen corner, or Turn One at Laguna, did not bear thinking about.

Suzuki's latest round of top-end engine parts this time did offer a tangible improvement, according to both Hopkins and project leader Sahara. "You can feel the difference out of the slow corners here," said the rider. "It's not only smoother coming on the power, but also it feels like it has more grunt." The engineer added: "Of course when you improve torque, you also improve driveability." It was good enough to put Hopkins top qualifier of the Bridgestone runners, heading the similarly shod Capirossi, Nakano and Checa, but down in tenth, because of a conundrum... on this track, the latest soft qualifying tyres didn't work as well as race tyres, which in turn weren't doing that well either. Rain was a blessing for them all... though not all were able to take advantage.

In spite of the grip problems, there was not quite the usual spate of accidents on Craner Curves, though Tamada paved the way in the first practice session with a classic cold-left-tyre slide across the grass. He raced despite a heavy impact to his hip, and also bit his tongue, making it hard for him to speak for the rest of the weekend. Not much change for the reticent Japanese rider, then.

Above: An English summer Sunday afternoon ride. Barros leads, Rossi stalks, Roberts follows.
Photographs: Gold & Goose

Top: Gibernau led, then also sank without trace.

Above: Ducatis in the mist – Checa (7) would leave Capirossi by the end.

Above right: Edwards (5) was close to the front three, until he had one scare too many, and let them go.
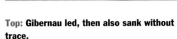
Photographs: Gold & Goose

MOTOGP RACE – 29 laps (shortened)

Half-hearted rain spoiled Friday afternoon; Saturday was dry for a typically exciting climax to qualifying. Rossi claimed pole, almost half a second faster than Melandri, with less than a minute left. Then Gibernau pushed his team-mate to third. Veteran Barros, in his 250th GP start, was off the front by fractions; eight riders within one second of Rossi, first to break below 1:28. "I love riding a MotoGP bike here," he said. Later, he watched his qualifying lap on TV, and was so struck by the symphonic perfection that he decided, if he won, to give a little violin recital over the finish line.

There were some hard miles to be covered first.

The lights failed as they lined up in heavy rain. After an engines-off delay and another warm-up lap, race distance cut by one, they were off.

Gibernau led from Melandri, Barros, Edwards and Bayliss into the first corner; Rossi suffered wheelspin, and was sixth. He picked up two places by the end of that lap; by then Biaggi had fallen, the first of almost half the field. As he remounted, Gibernau led the ball of spray over the line by 2.4 seconds.

People were crashing everywhere – Xaus out on lap two; Melandri on the third, taking Bayliss off and ultimately down too, and Hayden on the same lap. Then the luckless Gibernau, still leading by better than a second as he lined up for the first corner to start his fourth lap. As he touched the brake, he was down. "Usually you get some warning. This time, nothing." It was a common refrain…

Nakano, lying 12th, followed him down a lap later, any chance of a good race on Bridgestones already ruined by the clutch and down-shifting problems that caused him to fall. Biaggi had already fallen for a second time, this one terminal.

It wasn't over yet. On the next lap, Byrne – charging in the wet – also crashed after just touching the brakes – out of an unprecedented sixth place.

Rossi took over from Gibernau, now heading Barros and Roberts. But Hopkins was charging through, starting lap five 2.6 seconds adrift of the leaders, and finishing it in front. He stayed there for two laps, but leading wasn't his plan. He'd hoped that getting out of the spray would clear his misting visor. It didn't help… then the screen misted as well. He'd dropped back to fifth by lap nine, still struggling, when "I opened the gas too soon" at the Old Hairpin. He saved the high-side but careened across the grass, eventually falling at a low enough speed to remount, heading for the pits. His handlebar was bashed straight, and he donned a spare helmet (fitted with a dark smoked visor), and rejoined a lap behind.

Rossi stayed second as Barros took over on lap seven. Then – a real blast from the past – Roberts nosed by to consign the great man to third. Edwards was pressing hard in fourth. Tamada was next, losing ground, Checa and Capirossi closing, the latter after passing Hofmann on lap six.

Highly variable grip meant some shuffling. Roberts took over from Barros on the 11th lap for one lap, Rossi running wide at the chicane as he tried to attack as well, dropping to fourth behind Edwards. Just one of several lucky escapes, this put him almost five seconds behind the leader.

He soon caught up, which gave him an inkling of how he could beat them all. On lap 14, he passed Edwards onto the back straight, and Roberts at the other end of it, and tucked in behind Barros for eight laps. Then he pulled the pin...

At the end of lap 22, he ran inside the Camel Honda at the slow Melbourne Loop, and then gave a display of wet-weather riding to rank with the finest. He took almost two seconds out of Barros on lap 23, 2.5 seconds on the next, 3.3 on the one after that. "It was more like driving a boat than riding a motorcycle," he laughed afterwards.

Roberts, watching from close behind, said later: "When he passed Alex, I thought: 'Okay, let's go'. It took about three corners before I decided: 'Okay, let's race Alex'." He did so with masterly economy, waiting until the last lap before a decisive move up the inside at Macleans. Barros fought back hard, but was beaten by the end.

Edwards had been close until lap 19, when yet another scary slide meant he chose caution and a safe fourth, moving him to third in the championship. At the end, Checa had closed to within three seconds, after setting third-fastest lap in the later stages. Wheelspin at the start, and too much time spent waiting for his tyres to develop a better feeling, spoiled his chances.

Capirossi was outpaced at the finish, though both red bikes were ahead of Tamada. Hofmann was the last rider on the same lap; Elias and Rolfo survived for ninth and tenth, Hopkins was another lap down for 11th, which was still his second-best finish of the year so far. With Ellison and Battaini also both crashing, these were the only finishers.

250 cc RACE – 27 laps

Increasingly importunate, Lorenzo led the first three sessions, only for his rival Pedrosa to claim pole in the final outing by 0.136 seconds. With Dovizioso fourth, third-placed de Angelis rode the only Aprilia among the front-row Hondas.

The rain redrew the map, wet-specialist Aoyama leading away, and immediately drawing clear of de Puniet, Dovizioso, Pedrosa and the rest. Lorenzo was 13th, right in the spray; West had got away well and gained places at every opportunity, finishing the first lap sixth.

Two places behind, de Angelis got briefly ahead of Stoner, then followed him past Pedrosa, to hold a threatening fifth. The defending champion stayed prudently behind, out of trouble. Fast starter Dovizioso had been dropping back from the beginning, and was soon in the clutches of the next group, where Porto and Guintoli got the better of him. Then de Angelis was gone, a lap-nine victim of the treacherous surface.

By lap 11, approaching half distance, Aoyama was almost seven seconds clear. Next time round, he too slid off, under brakes for Redgate.

West had come forging through, dealing easily with the likes of Porto and Pedrosa. Now he scythed past de Puniet to take second, and when Aoyama went, the new KTM was leading its first grand prix.

With half the race to go, the top three were back and forth as though it was the final lap. De Puniet regained his advantage to

Below left: 2000 World Champion Kenny Junior has never lost faith in himself. He had to wait and wait before rain let him prove he hasn't forgotten how.

Below right: Wet specialist Aoyama led almost half the race... until this happened at Redgate. Leblanc (38) and Rous (64) were a lap down.

Bottom: De Puniet (7) recovered from an amazing save to regain the 250 lead from West. Second was still a fine result for the new KTM and the underrated Australian.
Photographs: Gold & Goose

head the trio for three laps, then on lap 17 Stoner was in front over the line. The manoeuvres elsewhere on the track were too numerous to recount. De Puniet seemed strongest, though West got ahead again on lap 22.

What happened next should have finished De Puniet's race, as he narrowly escaped a high-side down through Craner, and took to the grass at very high speed. By some miracle, he lost only half a second before rejoining behind Stoner in third. Nothing daunted, he took the lead again briefly next time round.

It was Stoner who led the end of that lap, however, but he was third next time round, and about to leave the group. His visor fogged, he lost the front into Redgate, regaining control only to run across gravel and grass and almost into the tyre wall. The luckiest man on the track, he rejoined 16 seconds down, still safe in third.

In the end, with the help of some awkwardly placed lapped traffic, de Puniet's bold recovery was rewarded with the win, better than a second clear of a nonetheless jubilant West.

Pedrosa's cautious approach yielded a valuable fourth, free from threat for Porto, also playing it cool. Corsi won out over Dovizioso… the next survivor was Lorenzo, a lonely eighth. He was the last rider on the same lap; behind him Guintoli had

been chasing Porto when he fell, hastily remounting to save ninth place.

The rest of the points-scorers trailed in; 13th-placed Baldolini another to fall and remount; Rous taking the final point from Smrz. All were glad to have finished; plenty didn't. Vincent, Takahashi and Debon were out in a first-lap tangle; as well as de Angelis and Aoyama, Polzer, Barbera, Sekiguchi and Davies also crashed.

125 cc RACE – Nine laps (restart)

Kallio's pole was his sixth of the year, and fourth in succession, by just a tenth from Pasini. Simoncelli made two front-row Aprilias; Luthi's Honda on the far end.

Rain changed everything here as well, with new rules employed after an abortive first race hit a sudden downpour after seven laps, and leader Bautista crashed heavily. Lai and Kallio also fell, the red flags came out, and all were allowed to restart for an abbreviated nine-lap sprint, the first race counting only for starting positions.

The second race was a sodden and slippery crash-fest with 13 fallers, some (including early leader Talmacsi) crashing twice.

Talmacsi took a strong lead from Lai, the field spreading out immediately, but on the second lap he was 25th, after crashing and remounting. He was up seven places when he fell again next time round.

Luthi also left the lead group on the second lap, with a wild ride across the grass at Coppice, regaining the track in ninth. By lap four, there were just three leading the way – di Meglio, Bautista and Simon. Then Bautista went flying again… two terminal race crashes in one day.

Simon took the lead with two laps to go, and was 2.4 seconds clear of di Meglio by the finish… a first rostrum for both teenagers, whose combination of survival and speed was impressive.

Lai prevailed for third from Simoncelli; the experienced Pablo Nieto moved steadily through to fifth, with Luthi and Kallio trailing in behind.

Mattia Pasini was one of four to crash out of the first part of the race, along with Rodriguez, Faubel and Koyama, though he retained a narrow shared points lead with fellow non-scorer Talmacsi.

Promising performances by the five British wild cards were topped by ninth for Dan Linfoot (17, on a Honda). Christian Elkin (24) was 12th; 17-year-old James Westmorland 22nd, Rob Guiver (20) crashing out of seventh on the fourth lap. Luckless Kev Coghlan (17) retired from the aborted first race.

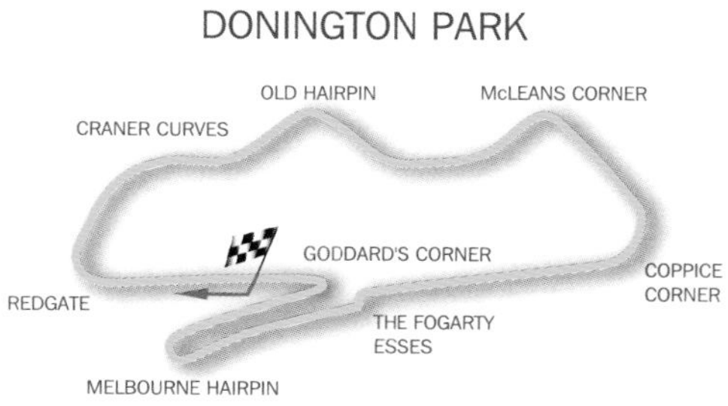
DONINGTON PARK
OLD HAIRPIN
McLEANS CORNER
CRANER CURVES
GODDARD'S CORNER
COPPICE CORNER
REDGATE
THE FOGARTY ESSES
MELBOURNE HAIRPIN

CIRCUIT LENGTH: 2.500 miles/4.023 km

betandwin.com

BRITISH GRAND PRIX

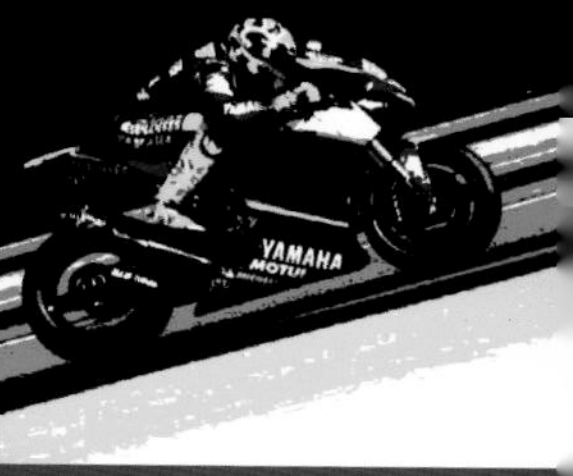

24 JULY 2005 • FIM WORLD CHAMPIONSHIP ROUND 9

MotoGP

29 laps, 72.500 miles/116.667 km

Pos.	Rider (Nat.)	No.	Machine	Laps	Time & speed
1	Valentino Rossi (I)	46	Yamaha	29	52m 58.675s 82.102 mph/ 132.130 km/h
2	Kenny Roberts (USA)	10	Suzuki	29	53m 01.844s
3	Alex Barros (BR)	4	Honda	29	53m 02.681s
4	Colin Edwards (USA)	5	Yamaha	29	53m 08.967s
5	Carlos Checa (E)	7	Ducati	29	53m 11.695s
6	Loris Capirossi (I)	65	Ducati	29	53m 21.996s
7	Makoto Tamada (J)	6	Honda	29	53m 36.508s
8	Alex Hofmann (D)	66	Kawasaki	29	53m 43.292s
9	Toni Elias (E)	24	Yamaha	28	54m 02.294s
10	Roberto Rolfo (I)	44	Ducati	28	54m 35.570s
11	John Hopkins (USA)	21	Suzuki	27	53m 32.212s
	Franco Battaini (I)	27	Blata	25	DNF
	James Ellison (GB)	77	Blata	7	DNF
	Shane Byrne (GB)	67	Proton KR	4	DNF
	Sete Gibernau (E)	15	Honda	3	DNF
	Shinya Nakano (J)	56	Kawasaki	3	DNF
	Max Biaggi (I)	3	Honda	3	DNF
	Marco Melandri (I)	33	Honda	2	DNF
	Troy Bayliss (AUS)	12	Honda	2	DNF
	Nicky Hayden (USA)	69	Honda	2	DNF
	Ruben Xaus (E)	11	Yamaha	1	DNF

Fastest lap: Rossi, 1m 45.377s, 85.399 mph/137.437 km/h.

Previous record: Colin Edwards, USA (Honda), 1m 29.973s, 100.021 mph/160.968 km/h (2004).

Event best maximum speed: Hayden, 172.6 mph/277.8 km/h (qualifying practice).

Qualifying: 1 Rossi, 1m 27.897s; 2 Gibernau, 1m 28.182s; 3 Melandri, 1m 28.295s; 4 Barros, 1m 28.394s; 5 Hayden, 1m 28.415s; 6 Edwards, 1m 28.656s; 7 Bayliss, 1m 28.720s; 8 Biaggi, 1m 28.726s; 9 Tamada, 1m 28.976s; 10 Hopkins, 1m 29.231s; 11 Capirossi, 1m 29.731s; 12 Nakano, 1m 29.742s; 13 Checa, 1m 29.816s; 14 Xaus, 1m 29.890s; 15 Hofmann, 1m 30.151s; 16 Roberts, 1m 30.260s; 17 Elias, 1m 30.342s; 18 Byrne, 1m 31.026s; 19 Rolfo, 1m 31.180s; 20 Ellison, 1m 31.791s; 21 Battaini, 1m 32.684s.

Fastest race laps: 1 Rossi, 1m 45.377s; 2 Barros, 1m 47.362s; 3 Checa, 1m 47.539s; 4 Roberts, 1m 47.630s; 5 Capirossi, 1m 47.693s; 6 Hopkins, 1m 47.697s; 7 Edwards, 1m 47.702s; 8 Tamada, 1m 48.570s; 9 Hofmann, 1m 48.730s; 10 Byrne, 1m 50.673s; 11 Gibernau, 1m 50.698s; 12 Bayliss, 1m 51.307s; 13 Melandri, 1m 51.663s; 14 Biaggi, 1m 52.942s; 15 Elias, 1m 53.114s; 16 Rolfo, 1m 54.030s; 17 Battaini, 1m 55.141s; 18 Nakano, 1m 55.475s; 19 Ellison, 1m 55.561s; 20 Hayden, 2m 00.400s; 21 Xaus, 2m 00.489s.

World Championship: 1 Rossi, 211; 2 Melandri, 107; 3 Edwards, 106; 4 Biaggi, 100; 5 Gibernau, 95; 6 Barros, 90; 7 Hayden, 85; 8 Capirossi, 65; 9 Nakano, 55; 10 C. Checa, 51; 11 Bayliss, 47; 12 Tamada, 36; 13 Xaus, 33; 14 Hopkins, 32; 15 Roberts, 31; 16 Elias and Jacque, 25; 18 Hofmann, 21; 19 Rolfo, 13; 20 van den Goorbergh, 12; 21 D. Checa and Ellison, 4; 23 Byrne and Ukawa, 1.

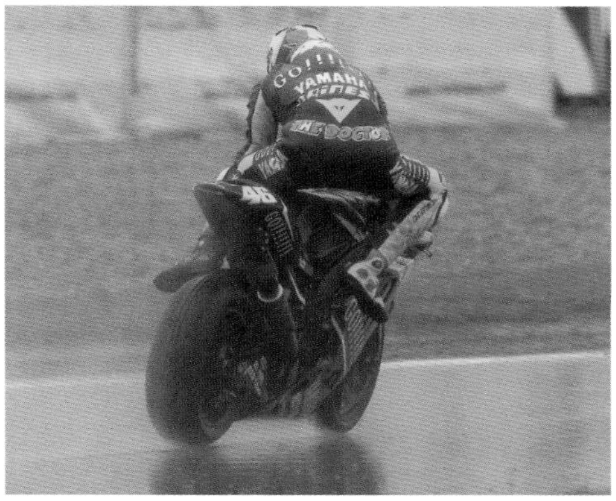

250 cc

27 laps, 67.500 miles/108.621 km

Pos.	Rider (Nat.)	No.	Machine	Laps	Time & speed
1	Randy de Puniet (F)	7	Aprilia	27	49m 11.337s 82.328 mph/ 132.494 km/h
2	Anthony West (AUS)	14	KTM	27	49m 12.573s
3	Casey Stoner (AUS)	27	Aprilia	27	49m 28.077s
4	Daniel Pedrosa (E)	1	Honda	27	49m 59.162s
5	Sebastian Porto (ARG)	19	Aprilia	27	50m 14.786s
6	Simone Corsi (I)	24	Aprilia	27	50m 43.774s
7	Andrea Dovizioso (I)	34	Honda	27	50m 45.897s
8	Jorge Lorenzo (E)	48	Honda	27	50m 57.301s
9	Sylvain Guintoli (F)	50	Aprilia	26	49m 13.761s
10	Andrea Ballerini (I)	8	Aprilia	26	49m 26.863s
11	Mirko Giansanti (I)	32	Aprilia	26	50m 25.686s
12	Roberto Locatelli (I)	15	Aprilia	26	50m 43.000s
13	Alex Baldolini (I)	25	Aprilia	26	51m 02.105s
14	Gregory Leblanc (F)	38	Aprilia	25	49m 12.366s
15	Radomil Rous (CZ)	64	Honda	25	49m 15.134s
16	Jakub Smrz (CZ)	96	Honda	25	49m 16.597s
17	Steve Jenkner (D)	17	Aprilia	25	49m 24.706s
18	Alvaro Molina (E)	41	Aprilia	25	49m 49.803s
19	Gabriele Ferro (I)	20	Fantic	23	50m 13.528s
	Chaz Davies (GB)	57	Aprilia	22	DNF
	Taro Sekiguchi (J)	44	Aprilia	21	DNF
	Hector Barbera (E)	80	Honda	16	DNF
	Hiroshi Aoyama (J)	73	Honda	12	DNF
	Yves Polzer (A)	42	Aprilia	12	DNF
	Alex de Angelis (RSM)	5	Aprilia	8	DNF
	Martin Cardenas (COL)	36	Aprilia	4	DNF
	Dirk Heidolf (D)	28	Honda	2	DNF
	Arnaud Vincent (F)	21	Fantic	0	DNF
	Yuki Takahashi (J)	55	Honda	0	DNF
	Alex Debon (E)	6	Honda	0	DNF
	Andreas Martensson (S)	26	Yamaha		EXC
	Nicklas Cajback (S)	23	Yamaha		DNQ

Fastest lap: West, 1m 47.025s, 84.085 mph/135.321 km/h.

Previous record: Daniel Pedrosa, E (Honda), 1m 33.217s, 96.540 mph/155.366 km/h (2004).

Event best maximum speed: Corsi, 149.2 mph/240.1 km/h (free practice no. 2

Qualifying: 1 Pedrosa, 1m 31.834s; 2 Lorenzo, 1m 31.964s; 3 de Angelis, 1m 32.489s; 4 Dovizioso, 1m 32.597s; 5 Porto, 1m 32.615s; 6 de Puniet, 1m 32.804s; 7 Barbera, 1m 32.812s; 8 Aoyama, 1m 32.826s; 9 Takahashi, 1m 32.984s; 10 Stoner, 1m 32.992s; 11 Locatelli, 1m 33.262s; 12 Guintoli, 1m 33.468s; 13 Debon, 1m 33.488s; 14 Corsi, 1m 33.850s; 15 West, 1m 33.910s; 16 Davies, 1m 33.972s; 17 Smrz, 1m 34.118s; 18 Jenkner, 1m 34.306s; 19 Baldolini, 1m 34.424s; 20 Ballerini, 1m 34.706s; 21 Heidolf, 1m 34.913s; 22 Giansanti, 1m 34.959s; 23 Cardenas, 1m 35.268s; 24 Leblanc, 1m 35.390s; 25 Rous, 1m 35.629s; 26 Sekiguchi, 1m 35.976s; 27 Vincent, 1m 36.421s; 28 Polzer, 1m 36.508s; 29 Molina, 1m 36.561s; 30 Martensson, 1m 37.257s; 31 Ferro, 1m 38.054s; 32 Cajback, 1m 38.673s.

Fastest race laps: 1 West, 1m 47.025s; 2 Stoner, 1m 47.451s; 3 de Puniet, 1m 47.666s; 4 Aoyama, 1m 47.824s; 5 de Angelis, 1m 48.502s; 6 Pedrosa, 1m 49.094s; 7 Porto, 1m 49.439s; 8 Guintoli, 1m 50.350s; 9 Lorenzo, 1m 50.622s; 10 Dovizioso, 1m 50.731s; 11 Corsi, 1m 50.954s; 12 Barbera, 1m 51.321s; 13 Ballerini, 1m 51.613s; 14 Davies, 1m 52.396s; 15 Baldolini, 1m 52.831s; 16 Giansanti, 1m 54.483s; 17 Leblanc, 1m 54.973s; 18 Locatelli, 1m 55.069s; 19 Smrz, 1m 55.336s; 20 Cardenas, 1m 55.483s; 21 Rous, 1m 55.645s; 22 Jenkner, 1m 56.154s; 23 Molina, 1m 56.350s; 24 Sekiguchi, 1m 56.385s; 25 Heidolf, 1m 57.333s; 26 Martensson, 2m 01.475s; 27 Ferro, 2m 04.209s; 28 Polzer, 2m 06.719s.

World Championship: 1 Pedrosa, 156; 2 Stoner, 122; 3 Dovizioso, 111; 4 Porto, 85; 5 de Puniet, 79; 6 Lorenzo, 78; 7 Aoyama, 71; 8 de Angelis, 67; 9 Corsi, 54; 10 Barbera, 51; 11 Guintoli, 38; 12 Debon, 32; 13 Takahashi, 31; 14 Giansanti and Locatelli, 24; 16 West, 20; 17 Baldolini, 18; 18 Davies, 17; 19 Ballerini, 14; 20 Rous, 8; 21 Leblanc and Smrz, 6; 23 Marchand and Nigon, 3; 25 Cardenas and Heidolf, 1.

125 cc

9 laps, 22.500 miles/36.207 km (Race Part 2)*

Pos.	Rider (Nat.)	No.	Machine	Laps	Time & speed
1	Julian Simon (E)	60	KTM	9	17m 35.523s 76.732 mph/ 123.488 km/h
2	Mike di Meglio (F)	63	Honda	9	17m 37.929s
3	Fabrizio Lai (I)	32	Honda	9	17m 44.419s
4	Marco Simoncelli (I)	58	Aprilia	9	17m 44.692s
5	Pablo Nieto (E)	22	Derbi	9	17m 49.360s
6	Thomas Luthi (CH)	12	Honda	9	17m 53.846s
7	Mika Kallio (SF)	36	KTM	9	17m 58.976s
8	Joan Olive (E)	6	Aprilia	9	18m 06.947s
9	Dan Linfoot (GB)	94	Honda	9	18m 09.388s
10	Toshihisa Kuzuhara (J)	9	Honda	9	18m 15.617s
11	Sergio Gadea (E)	33	Aprilia	9	18m 15.868s
12	Christian Elkin (GB)	56	Honda	9	18m 16.284s
13	Jordi Carchano (E)	28	Aprilia	9	18m 18.312s
14	Lorenzo Zanetti (I)	8	Aprilia	9	18m 18.356s
15	Sandro Cortese (D)	11	Honda	9	18m 18.943s
16	Raymond Schouten (NL)	16	Honda	9	18m 19.110s
17	Karel Abraham (CZ)	44	Aprilia	9	18m 20.624s
18	Gioele Pellino (I)	42	Malaguti	9	18m 22.600s
19	Federico Sandi (I)	10	Honda	9	18m 24.424s
20	Raffaele de Rosa (I)	35	Aprilia	9	18m 24.611s
21	Nicolas Terol (E)	18	Derbi	9	18m 30.089s
22	James Westmoreland (GB)	95	Honda	9	18m 35.292s
23	Vincent Braillard (CH)	26	Aprilia	9	18m 36.195s
24	Mateo Tunez (E)	46	Aprilia	9	18m 37.657s
25	Manuel Poggiali (RSM)	54	Gilera	9	19m 01.942s
26	Imre Toth (H)	45	Aprilia	9	19m 03.934s
	Alexis Masbou (F)	7	Honda	8	DNF
	Alvaro Bautista (E)	19	Honda	5	DNF
	Aleix Espargaro (E)	41	Honda	5	DNF
	Gabor Talmacsi (H)	14	KTM	4	DNF
	Rob Guiver (GB)	57	Honda	3	DNF
	Lukas Pesek (CZ)	52	Derbi	1	DNF
	Michele Pirro (I)	15	Malaguti	0	DNF
	Andrea Iannone (I)	29	Aprilia	0	DNF
	Manuel Hernandez (E)	43	Aprilia	0	DNF
	Kev Coghlan (GB)	96	Honda	0	DNF
	Angel Rodriguez	47	Honda		DNS**
	Hector Faubel	55	Aprilia		DNS**
	Tomoyoshi Koyama (J)	71	Honda		DNS**
	Mattia Pasini (I)	75	Aprilia		DNS**
	Dario Giuseppetti (D)	25	Aprilia		DNS

*Race Part 1: 7 laps, result neutralised.
**DNS Race Part 2

Fastest lap: Espargaro, 1m 54.639s, 78.500 mph/126.333 km/h.

Previous record: Alvaro Bautista, E (Aprilia), 1m 38.263s, 91.583 mph/147.388 km/h (2004).

Event best maximum speed: Lai, 131.2 mph/211.2 km/h (free practice no. 2).

Qualifying: 1 Kallio, 1m 37.295s; 2 Pasini, 1m 37.396s; 3 Simoncelli, 1m 37.407s; 4 Luthi, 1m 37.634s; 5 Lai, 1m 37.660s; 6 Simon, 1m 37.701s; 7 Talmacsi, 1m 37.952s; 8 Koyama, 1m 38.034s; 9 di Meglio, 1m 38.060s; 10 Masbou, 1m 38.238s; 11 Poggiali, 1m 38.238s; 12 Bautista, 1m 38.352s; 13 Faubel, 1m 38.372s; 14 Gadea, 1m 38.551s; 15 Olive, 1m 38.745s; 16 Hernandez, 1m 38.820s; 17 Nieto, 1m 38.866s; 18 Terol, 1m 38.978s; 19 Espargaro, 1m 39.040s; 20 Pesek, 1m 39.136s; 21 de Rosa, 1m 39.148s; 22 Iannone, 1m 39.166s; 23 Rodriguez, 1m 39.261s; 24 Tunez, 1m 39.265s; 25 Schouten, 1m 39.417s; 26 Carchano, 1m 39.459s; 27 Zanetti, 1m 39.480s; 28 Cortese, 1m 39.538s; 29 Giuseppetti, 1m 39.579s; 30 Kuzuhara, 1m 39.635s; 31 Sandi, 1m 39.895s; 32 Pirro, 1m 40.110s; 33 Braillard, 1m 40.149s; 34 Toth, 1m 40.293s; 35 Coghlan, 1m 40.301s; 36 Abraham, 1m 40.401s; 37 Westmoreland, 1m 40.742s; 38 Pellino, 1m 40.919s; 39 Linfoot, 1m 40.996s; 40 Guiver, 1m 41.272s; 41 Elkin, 1m 41.699s.

Fastest race laps: 1 Espargaro, 1m 54.639s; 2 Bautista, 1m 55.254s; 3 Simon, 1m 55.262s; 4 Talmacsi, 1m 55.535s; 5 di Meglio, 1m 55.641s; 6 Simoncelli, 1m 56.153s; 7 Nieto, 1m 56.264s; 8 Guiver, 1m 56.298s; 9 Luthi, 1m 56.456s; 10 Lai, 1m 56.655s; 11 Kallio, 1m 58.146s; 12 Kuzuhara, 1m 58.159s; 13 Zanetti, 1m 58.233s; 14 Masbou, 1m 58.236s; 15 Cortese, 1m 58.432s; 16 Linfoot, 1m 58.533s; 17 Olive, 1m 59.025s; 18 Gadea, 1m 59.054s; 19 Carchano, 1m 59.267s; 20 de Rosa, 1m 59.351s; 21 Elkin, 1m 59.624s; 22 Schouten, 1m 59.675s; 23 Poggiali, 1m 59.701s; 24 Pellino, 1m 59.731s; 25 Abraham, 2m 00.091s; 26 Terol, 2m 00.173s; 27 Sandi, 2m 00.375s; 28 Tunez, 2m 00.467s; 29 Westmoreland, 2m 01.082s; 30 Braillard, 2m 01.430s; 31 Toth, 2m 04.847s.

World Championship: 1 Pasini and Talmacsi, 100; 3 Luthi, 99; 4 Kallio, 91; 5 Simoncelli, 85; 6 Simon, 80; 7 Lai, 79; 8 Poggiali, 59; 9 Koyama, 52; 10 Faubel, 50; 11 di Meglio, 45; 12 Nieto, 41; 13 Olive, 37; 14 Gadea, 35; 15 Bautista, 28; 16 Masbou, 20; 17 Espargaro and Zanetti, 16; 19 Kuzuhara, 15; 20 Hernandez, 12; 21 Pesek and Ranseder, 8; 23 Linfoot and Toth, 7; 25 Carchano, 6; 26 Conti and Iannone, 5; 28 Elkin, 4; 29 Giuseppetti and Pirro, 3; 31 Cortese, 2; 32 de Rosa and Terol, 1.

MotoGP restart in the sweltering heat, and Hayden gets the jump for a second time. His clutch never quite recovered from the double punishment.
Photograph: Gold & Goose

FIM WORLD CHAMPIONSHIP • ROUND 10

GERMANGP
SACHSENRING

Right: Rossi slips off in practice. No harm done.

Below: Rossi joined the rostrum of all time with an apology to boyhood hero Hailwood.
Photographs: Gold & Goose

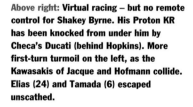

Above right: Virtual racing – but no remote control for Shakey Byrne. His Proton KR has been knocked from under him by Checa's Ducati (behind Hopkins). More first-turn turmoil on the left, as the Kawasakis of Jacque and Hofmann collide. Elias (24) and Tamada (6) escaped unscathed.

Far right: Carlos Checa celebrated his 150th race in the senior class.
Photographs: Gold & Goose

THE Sachsenring, in spite of the compact carnival-style modern venue, is rich in memories and heavy with history. The road to the track, actually part of the old public-roads circuit, passes the immaculately tended memorial to Norton rider Jimmy Guthrie, fatally injured there in 1937. There is the shade of tragic Sixties star Bill Ivy, who died in practice in 1969, on a Jawa. And the lingering presence also of Walter Kaaden, revolutionary pioneer of the racing two-stroke, working at the old MZ factory just south-east of Chemnitz, the former Karlmarxstadt, close to the circuit.

Never far from racing memories is the name of Mike Hailwood, one of the MZ's early riders. The British nine-times World Champion was a hero to the vast crowds at the old East German Grand Prix, a Sachsenring race winner every year from 1961 through to 1967. Rossi's career bears comparison with that of Mike the Bike, but he's never done what Hailwood did, here at the Sachsenring in 1963. Mike won three GPs in one day – 250, 350 and 500cc, all on MV Agustas.

Rossi enjoys his place in history, and was well aware that victory on Sunday at the modern circuit would be the 76th in his career. This put him equal with Hailwood, and still counting, with only Nieto (90 wins) and Agostini (122) ahead of him. "I arrive on the podium of all time. It is a great, great pleasure," he said, after showing a flag on his slow-down lap reading: "Rossi 76, Hailwood 76. I'm Sorry, Mike."

Weather extremes continued in Germany, baking hot as the event got underway, but stricken with violent rain and winds on Friday night that wrought havoc in the packed camp-site, with more than 40 recorded injuries among the canvas devastation. For once again, the crowds had poured in to what has in seven years become an important event.

The second-shortest track of the year (after Laguna) is not dissimilar in character, with even more changes of elevation, and a corner to rival the Corkscrew in roller-coaster effect – the swoop down the short back "straight", approached via a fast blind right, from which the track plunges downhill like a funfair ride. Without safety rails, unfortunately for Checa and Hopkins, both of whom came major croppers down there during practice. The former was straight back on a bike again, unhurt. Hopkins was more badly beaten, and had picked up fractures in his left ankle among other collateral. Full of painkillers and courage, he elected to race anyway... with dire consequences.

This corner is not the compact "car-park" circuit's defining aspect. That is the preceding series of corners, leading from Turn Three, a tight right loop. After that, ringed with grand-stands, the track climbs over the brow of the hill again in the first of a complex series of corners that keep the bike on its left-hand side for almost half the lap. By the time they get to that right onto the roller-coaster, that side of the tyre has cooled right down; by the time they get to the end of the race, the left-hand side has already long since been chewed to a frazzle.

Mixed-compound tyres are nowadays in common usage at many tracks – for this one, harder on the left, harder still in the middle, softer on the right. Getting the balance right is of course crucial; that Michelin continue to lead progress forward in this as in other areas is obvious from continually falling lap times –

this year's lap record more than three tenths faster than last. Bridgestone are following, in fits and starts, and Nakano's impressive sixth marked one of the latter, as he hounded Barros, only five seconds off winner Rossi. For this rider, on the same machine/tyre combination, his best race lap time was fully a second faster than last year, though much of that must be credited to Kawasaki's big-bang motor. (Oddly his qualifying time was actually three tenths slower.)

It was party time at HRC's new unit on race eve... for Nicky Hayden's 24th birthday. Of more satisfaction was his second pole position, at another of those rare left-handed tracks that play to his dirt-track experience and reflexes. "I guess it's like a NASCAR driver joining GPs – on the US ovals, we get used to going left, left, left. One of the things I try to practise is going the other way," he would later tell MOTOCOURSE. Last time he'd been on pole, he'd won the race.

Not among his birthday gifts, a revised chassis, with the swing-arm pivot moved forward. This was only for Max and Sete, though the latter denied he had any such thing. ("He needs to go to church more often," was Hayden's comment.) Biaggi was cagey too, and whatever the benefit, it was not enough to beat Rossi's Yamaha. HRC had by now identified the Yamaha's advantage as being in corner entry. As if to bear them out, long-time race leader Gibernau extended his run of bad luck, with a botched entry to Turn One on the last lap. This handed the race to Rossi on the proverbial plate. "Maybe I thought it was his birthday, instead of Nicky's," Gibernau commented wryly.

All were looking forward to the three-week holiday after this event. Some of the circus would go into the summer break beneath dark clouds. Among them Proton Team KR, still the subject of dire rumours of imminent collapse. This time, with KTM already discussing the issue separately with Dorna, they would turn out to be true.

Alex Barros had a different kind of worry. Shortly before the German race, the courts had found against him in a case brought by Altadis, owners of the Gauloises brand, for skipping out of a two-year contract at the end of 2003 to ride the factory Honda in 2004. Hit with a US $2.9-million damages bill, plus interest and $300,000 costs, he remained tight-lipped, saying that he was turning the matter over to his lawyers.

The story of the weekend concerned Hopkins, who had been slammed down onto the tarmac with devastating force in his Friday fourth-gear high-side on the chute down the hill. As well as getting a face full of rocks scooped into his helmet, chipping a tooth, he had also broken the fifth metatarsal in his left foot, and damaged his right thumb ligament. He wasn't even sure about riding on Saturday, but found he could have a go, running 12 laps in qualifying to place a plucky tenth, one place and a few hundredths slower than team-mate Roberts. "The way I feel, not racing is maybe a smarter option," he said. "But I feel I can get through the race safely, and finish in the points. The team's not pressuring me in any way."

Perhaps somebody should have, but the team suffers from the same racing bug as the rider, and the medical authorities are prepared to defer to the rider in these matters. In

Above: Down again, and this time out. Hopkins's second high-sider stopped the race.

Right: Nakano's strong sixth presaged the forthcoming Bridgestone big step forward.

Photographs: Gold & Goose

retrospect, what happened next was all too predictable, and a clear indication that the system needs serious thought. Early in the race, lying 12th, he suddenly slewed sideways at the second corner, and was flung once more over the high side, luckily taking nobody with him as he slammed down again into the middle of the track. As luckily he sustained no further injury, though he did aggravate those he already had. "It was my fault for going out," he said, revealing that the painkilling injections and strapping had left him with "not too much feeling" in his left foot. On full lean, he had hooked second gear by mistake.

Just why was he allowed out there at all?

MOTOGP RACE – 25 laps (shortened)

Innovative GPS indicators showed real-time bike positioning on the circuit map for TV. If anyone was following Rossi's, it stopped on the second corner, with a rare crash on Friday. Typically, there were no painful consequences. It's not a favourite track, and he was off the front row for the first time since China. With such close times – 14 within one second of pole – it hardly signified.

Hayden's pole was a tenth ahead of Gibernau, triple-faller Barros alongside, then Melandri and Biaggi with Rossi on row two. With the dash into the tight and slow first turn, the positioning could be crucial, and clutch control at a premium.

Hayden won the drag race, and led the first five laps, from Rossi, Barros and Gibernau. Three didn't make the second corner... Byrne first, after braking late, "but not tragically", then clipping Checa as he tried to slow. Independently, wild card Jacque ran into the back of his team-mate Hofmann's Kawasaki, ruining the home rider's chances as both went down. Bayliss was a lap-three faller, tucking the front.

Then Hopkins, lying 12th just behind Roberts, high-sided, and the red flags came out. The restart would be just 25 laps, and five riders short; positions from first race to determine the grid.

Hayden led again from the restart, but soon realised his bike was not what it had been, the clutch giving trouble on down-shifts. Rossi swept past him at the first corner, the first braking point of lap two; Gibernau at the next braking, at the bottom of the downhill straight. One lap later, Barros was on Hayden's back wheel, with Biaggi and Capirossi closing up, Nakano next

after losing one place.

Gibernau played the same downhill move on Rossi next time down the back straight, taking a lead he would hold for every other lap, except the one that mattered.

Until half distance, the pack stayed close and in the same order. Capirossi was running into problems with his tyres, losing sixth to Nakano again on lap eight, and behind the chasing Melandri one lap later. Checa was an early departure, crashing at the bottom of the hill at the end of lap four.

Up front, on lap 13, Hayden made a rare pass on Rossi into the first corner. The champion was only biding his time, however, expecting the real fight to be with Gibernau, and after six more laps he chose the other passing sport for an emphatic overtake to regain second.

At this point, Barros was a short distance back, Biaggi holding station behind him, and Nakano hanging on grimly. He'd been within a second on lap 15, and he was still less than two away.

Gibernau was now in a familiar position, with Rossi breathing down his neck, the latter looking comfortable, and planning his last-lap attack for the bottom of the back straight. He never had to deploy it. Instead, as they ran into the first corner for the last time, Gibernau ran wide, leaving an open invitation. Hayden almost made it past as well, Gibernau cutting in sharply to force him back.

It was a costly lapse in concentration, with an unexpected justification. Sete said he'd been distracted by his team – "a whole bunch of people showing hands to me", as he flashed past pit wall. By the time he looked back at the track, he had missed his braking point.

This settled the first three, crossing the line within nine tenths. Barros and constant companion Biaggi had lost touch slightly over the last seven laps or so, the Brazilian obviously struggling with a lack of grip that meant he finally succumbed with three laps to go.

At the point of the overtake, a heroic ride by Nakano – catching, dropping back, then catching again – had him within a second again, but he was also visibly struggling on every corner, and he had drifted away again at the finish.

There was something of a procession behind… Melandri never in the hunt in the second race, blaming a loss of traction, but clear anyway of Edwards. Then a long gap to Capirossi, fading steadily after a good start. The remaining finishers trailed in: Roberts, Elias, Xaus, Rolfo and Battaini, the WCM rider taking his first point of the season. His team-mate Ellison had crashed out.

250 cc RACE – 29 laps

Aprilias flanked two Hondas on the front row, de Angelis on pole by less than a tenth, Spaniards Pedrosa and Lorenzo alongside, Porto on the far end. Stoner was on row two, West 12th on the KTM, in its second outing.

Precocious rookie Lorenzo muscled his way to the front, Aoyama on his tail from the second row, then de Angelis, Pedrosa, and a brawling pack. There was pushing and shoving galore, then on lap three Aoyama was ahead, Lorenzo third, and Pedrosa right behind.

What happened next was open to interpretation, but the consequences were clear enough. Pedrosa moved ahead, and was swinging in towards the apex of the left at the bottom of the hill just as Lorenzo was barrelling up the inside, travelling faster. He was unable to avoid a collision, and as his front wheel struck Pedrosa's left-hand exhaust, bending it out at a right angle, Lorenzo's bike flipped in the opposite direction and he went flying.

Main photograph: Gibernau, slightly askew, leads Hayden, Rossi, Barros and Biaggi out of the last of the string of left-handers.
Photograph: Gold & Goose

Top: Pedrosa – bent exhaust clearly visible – has just taken the lead from de Angelis, with Dovizioso and Aoyama close behind. There will be no stopping him.

Below: From the left, Kallio, Luthi and Simoncelli dispute the lead of the shortened 125 race.

Opposite: Teak-tough racer Rossi shows his teeth. Being Rossi, he got them from a joke shop.

Photographs: Gold & Goose

Pedrosa dropped behind Porto and Dovizioso as he took stock, and counted his luck at not joining Lorenzo in the gravel. It took him two laps to appreciate that he could still go fast, and to accept that if his pipe was broken, there was nothing he could do about it. He quickly despatched Porto, and set a close watch on the three ahead, with Dovizioso now briefly leading de Angelis. Then the latter moved past to dispute the lead with Aoyama, finally taking over for the tenth and 11th laps. But by now it was Pedrosa in second, and next time he was leading.

Over the next two laps he steadily drew clear, and then the gap started to stretch. Behind him, de Angelis made a concurrent escape. He'd seen the bent pipe, and was hoping the Honda's power might drop off as the race wore on. In vain, and with the gap more than two seconds by two-thirds distance, he slacked off to finish almost eight seconds adrift.

Behind him, Aoyama and Dovizioso had been dropping back gradually, while the Aprilias of Porto and de Puniet closed from behind. The last-named would lose touch, but Porto was always within a second or so of the Hondas, and on lap 24 had closed up and pounced. The three were locked in combat to the finish, but Aoyama stayed in front, and Dovizioso was ahead of the Aprilia again.

Stoner had got away tenth, then moved through to tail Barbera, finally getting ahead for seventh on lap 22. As he drew clear of the class rookie, he was closing fast on the fading de Puniet, taking 2.5 seconds out of him in the last two laps, but still finishing four tenths behind.

Takahashi passed West for ninth with three laps to go, the pair

dropping off Guintoli as they battled to the finish. Debon was narrowly ahead of Heidolf, then Jenkner headed a gang of four over the line with eight tenths, disputing the final points. Cardenas took the last one, Smrz and Giansanti narrowly out of luck.

Locatelli, Baldolini and wild card Franz Aschenbrenner joined Lorenzo on the crash list; Davies retired to the pits.

125 cc RACE – 20 laps (restart)

The first race saw no less than 14 crashes, a spate that started on the first corner, where Pirro, Bautista, Kuzuhara and Terol tangled, the last remounting, only to retire. On the second lap, Faubel also went down, with Iannoni.

Up front, Luthi had dashed away, but was soon under vigorous attack from Lai and Simoncelli, who led lap two. Teammates Talmacsi and pole starter Kallio were close behind, and Masbou's Honda was next. The French teenager was in the front pack for a while more... only to be adjudged as having jumped the start, then excluded for missing the flags calling him in for a ride-through.

By lap five, Luthi was back in front from Simoncelli, Kallio had picked his way to third, with Pasini fourth and pushing hard. Positions were changing almost corner by corner, riders running four or five abreast.

When Kallio took the lead off Simoncelli on lap eight, Pasini followed him through... only to crash out on the ninth.

This shuffled the still-close gang of six survivors – Kallio hanging on up front from Luthi and Talmacsi, with an on-form Pesek, Simoncelli and third KTM rider Simon close behind.

The only constant was Kallio in the lead, with Luthi strong in second, Simoncelli and Talmacsi still threatening, and going to and fro. Then came the 14th and final crash.

The victim was Poggiali, at the back of a five-strong group disputing seventh when he crashed heavily at the top of the downhill straight. He and his Gilera slid all the way down the hill, the bike ending up in the middle of the track, triggering immediate red flags. Results were taken from the previous lap.

This thwarted Luthi, who had been planning a last-lap attack, "and now we have no last lap"; but second gave him the points lead for the break.

It favoured Kallio, who took the win off the Swiss teenager by just over a tenth. Simoncelli was third, narrowly ahead of Talmacsi. Simon and Pesek were just a second adrift.

Lai led the next gang, from Olive, Espargaro, Nieto and Poggiali, classified 11th. Fast wild card Michael Ranseder headed regulars Zanetti and Cortesi for 12th; fellow wild card Stefan Bradl, son of Helmut, was less than a second away from scoring a point.

The crash tally was completed by Gadea, Hommel, Sandi, Schouten, di Meglio and Koyama.

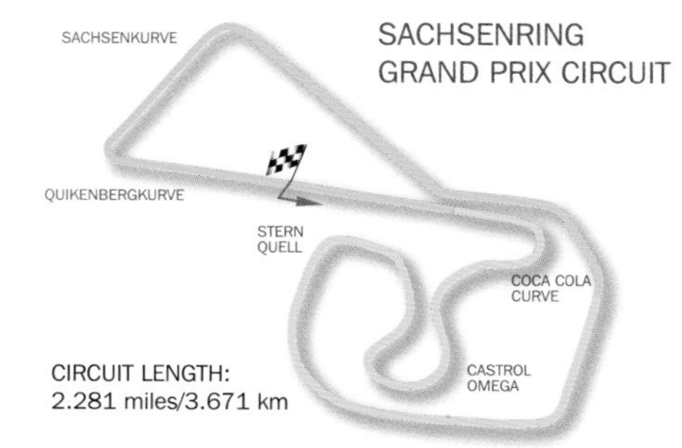
SACHSENKURVE
SACHSENRING
GRAND PRIX CIRCUIT
QUIKENBERGKURVE
STERN
QUELL
COCA COLA
CURVE
CASTROL
OMEGA
CIRCUIT LENGTH:
2.281 miles/3.671 km

ALICE MOTORRAD GRAND PRIX DEUTSCHLAND

31 JULY 2005 • FIM WORLD CHAMPIONSHIP ROUND 10

MotoGP

25 laps, 57.025 miles/91.775 km (Race Part 2)*

Pos.	Rider (Nat.)	No.	Machine	Laps	Time & speed
1	Valentino Rossi (I)	46	Yamaha	25	35m 04.434s 97.553 mph/ 156.997 km/h
2	Sete Gibernau (E)	15	Honda	25	35m 05.119s
3	Nicky Hayden (USA)	69	Honda	25	35m 05.319s
4	Max Biaggi (I)	3	Honda	25	35m 06.799s
5	Alex Barros (BR)	4	Honda	25	35m 07.289s
6	Shinya Nakano (J)	56	Kawasaki	25	35m 08.991s
7	Marco Melandri (I)	33	Honda	25	35m 16.703s
8	Colin Edwards (USA)	5	Yamaha	25	35m 19.283s
9	Loris Capirossi (I)	65	Ducati	25	35m 27.923s
10	Makoto Tamada (J)	6	Honda	25	35m 32.263s
11	Kenny Roberts (USA)	10	Suzuki	25	35m 46.533s
12	Toni Elias (E)	24	Yamaha	25	35m 51.738s
13	Ruben Xaus (E)	11	Yamaha	25	36m 04.609s
14	Roberto Rolfo (I)	44	Ducati	25	36m 12.148s
15	Franco Battaini (I)	27	Blata	24	35m 21.155s
	Carlos Checa (E)	7	Ducati	4	DNF
	Troy Bayliss (AUS)	12	Honda		DNS**
	Olivier Jacque (F)	19	Kawasaki		DNS**
	John Hopkins (USA)	21	Suzuki		DNS**
	Alex Hofmann (D)	66	Kawasaki		DNS**
	Shane Byrne (GB)	67	Proton KR		DNS**
	James Ellison (GB)	77	Blata		DNS**

*Race Part 1: 5 laps, result neutralised.

**DNS Race Part 2.

Fastest lap: Gibernau, 1m 23.705s, 98.104 mph/157.883 km/h (unofficial record set in Race Part 1).

Previous record: Alex Barros, BR (Honda), 1m 24.056s, 97.694 mph/157.223 km/h (2004).

Event best maximum speed: Capirossi, 178.2 mph/286.8 km/h (qualifying practice).

Qualifying: 1 Hayden, 1m 22.785s; 2 Gibernau, 1m 22.889s; 3 Barros, 1m 22.932s; 4 Rossi, 1m 22.973s; 5 Melandri, 1m 23.051s; 6 Biaggi, 1m 23.054s; 7 Edwards, 1m 23.139s; 8 Capirossi, 1m 23.174s; 9 Roberts, 1m 23.212s; 10 Hopkins, 1m 23.296s; 11 Checa, 1m 23.341s; 12 Nakano, 1m 23.382s; 13 Hofmann, 1m 23.405s; 14 Jacque, 1m 23.715s; 15 Tamada, 1m 23.860s; 16 Bayliss, 1m 23.916s; 17 Elias, 1m 24.421s; 18 Xaus, 1m 24.605s; 19 Ellison, 1m 24.988s; 20 Rolfo, 1m 25.011s; 21 Byrne, 1m 25.713s; 22 Battaini, 1m 26.154s.

Fastest race laps (After Race Part 2): 1 Capirossi, 1m 23.708s; 2 Gibernau, 1m 23.745s; 3 Rossi, 1m 23.782s; 4 Barros, 1m 23.799s; 5 Biaggi, 1m 23.805s; 6 Hayden, 1m 23.847s; 7 Nakano, 1m 23.858s; 8 Checa, 1m 23.987s; 9 Melandri, 1m 23.991s; 10 Edwards, 1m 24.242s; 11 Roberts, 1m 24.261s; 12 Tamada, 1m 24.333s; 13 Rolfo, 1m 24.869s; 14 Elias, 1m 25.049s; 15 Xaus, 1m 26.001s; 16 Battaini, 1m 27.079s.

World Championship: 1 Rossi, 236; 2 Melandri, 116; 3 Gibernau, 115; 4 Edwards, 114; 5 Biaggi, 113; 6 Barros and Hayden, 101; 8 Capirossi, 72; 9 Nakano, 65; 10 C. Checa, 51; 11 Bayliss, 47; 12 Tamada, 42; 13 Roberts and Xaus, 36; 15 Hopkins, 32; 16 Elias, 29; 17 Jacque, 25; 18 Hofmann, 21; 19 Rolfo, 15; 20 van den Goorbergh, 12; 21 D. Checa and Ellison, 4; 23 Battaini, Byrne and Ukawa, 1.

250 cc

29 laps, 66.149 miles/106.459 km

Pos.	Rider (Nat.)	No.	Machine	Laps	Time & speed
1	Daniel Pedrosa (E)	1	Honda	29	41m 35.089s 95.444 mph/ 153.602 km/h
2	Alex de Angelis (RSM)	5	Aprilia	29	41m 43.029s
3	Hiroshi Aoyama (J)	73	Honda	29	41m 46.260s
4	Andrea Dovizioso (I)	34	Honda	29	41m 46.435s
5	Sebastian Porto (ARG)	19	Aprilia	29	41m 46.533s
6	Randy de Puniet (F)	7	Aprilia	29	41m 52.625s
7	Casey Stoner (AUS)	27	Aprilia	29	41m 53.038s
8	Hector Barbera (E)	80	Honda	29	41m 57.282s
9	Yuki Takahashi (J)	55	Honda	29	42m 17.377s
10	Anthony West (AUS)	14	KTM	29	42m 17.785s
11	Sylvain Guintoli (F)	50	Aprilia	29	42m 26.372s
12	Alex Debon (E)	6	Honda	29	42m 37.048s
13	Dirk Heidolf (D)	28	Honda	29	42m 38.349s
14	Steve Jenkner (D)	17	Aprilia	29	42m 48.437s
15	Martin Cardenas (COL)	36	Aprilia	29	42m 48.902s
16	Jakub Smrz (CZ)	96	Honda	29	42m 48.965s
17	Mirko Giansanti (I)	32	Aprilia	29	42m 49.240s
18	Taro Sekiguchi (J)	44	Aprilia	29	42m 53.378s
19	Alvaro Molina (E)	41	Aprilia	28	41m 56.887s
20	Radomil Rous (CZ)	64	Honda	28	42m 05.390s
21	Andreas Martensson (S)	26	Yamaha	28	42m 32.853s
22	Nicklas Cajback (S)	23	Yamaha	28	43m 06.208s
23	Thomas Walter (D)	52	Honda	27	41m 36.555s
	Gregory Leblanc (F)	38	Aprilia	20	DNF
	Simone Corsi (I)	24	Aprilia	20	DNF
	Franz Aschenbrenner (D)	16	Honda	19	DNF
	Chaz Davies (GB)	57	Aprilia	8	DNF
	Andrea Ballerini (I)	8	Aprilia	8	DNF
	Alex Baldolini (I)	25	Aprilia	5	DNF
	Jorge Lorenzo (E)	48	Honda	4	DNF
	Roberto Locatelli (I)	15	Aprilia	2	DNF
	Arnaud Vincent (F)	21	Fantic	2	DNF
	Patrick Lakerveld (NL)	53	Honda		DNQ
	Yves Polzer (A)	42	Aprilia		DNQ
	Gabriele Ferro (I)	20	Fantic		DNQ

Fastest lap: Pedrosa, 1m 25.327s, 96.239 mph/154.881 km/h.

Previous record: Sebastian Porto, ARG (Aprilia), 1m 25.118s, 96.476 mph/155.262 km/h (2004).

Event best maximum speed: Corsi, 150.9 mph/242.8 km/h (warm-up).

Qualifying: 1 de Angelis, 1m 24.618s; 2 Pedrosa, 1m 24.714s; 3 Lorenzo, 1m 24.905s; 4 Porto, 1m 25.193s; 5 Aoyama, 1m 25.433s; 6 Takahashi, 1m 25.469s; 7 Stoner, 1m 25.470s; 8 de Puniet, 1m 25.617s; 9 Barbera, 1m 25.643s; 10 Dovizioso, 1m 25.669s; 11 Locatelli, 1m 26.139s; 12 West, 1m 26.278s; 13 Guintoli, 1m 26.303s; 14 Corsi, 1m 26.320s; 15 Davies, 1m 26.360s; 16 Jenkner, 1m 26.449s; 17 Baldolini, 1m 26.507s; 18 Heidolf, 1m 26.512s; 19 Smrz, 1m 26.841s; 20 Giansanti, 1m 26.845s; 21 Debon, 1m 26.983s; 22 Leblanc, 1m 27.678s; 23 Sekiguchi, 1m 27.950s; 24 Ballerini, 1m 27.954s; 25 Rous, 1m 28.105s; 26 Cardenas, 1m 28.522s; 27 Vincent, 1m 28.691s; 28 Molina, 1m 28.979s; 29 Martensson, 1m 29.672s; 30 Aschenbrenner, 1m 29.769s; 31 Cajback, 1m 30.093s; 32 Walter, 1m 30.502s; 33 Lakerveld, 1m 30.630s; 34 Polzer, 1m 30.812s; 35 Ferro, 1m 31.136s.

Fastest race laps: 1 Pedrosa, 1m 25.327s; 2 de Angelis, 1m 25.648s; 3 Aoyama, 1m 25.802s; 4 Barbera, 1m 25.816s; 5 de Puniet, 1m 25.831s; 6 Dovizioso, 1m 25.891s; 7 Porto, 1m 25.979s; 8 Lorenzo, 1m 26.062s; 9 Stoner, 1m 26.149s; 10 Takahashi, 1m 26.501s; 11 Corsi, 1m 26.757s; 12 West, 1m 26.850s; 13 Guintoli, 1m 27.044s; 14 Debon, 1m 27.221s; 15 Heidolf, 1m 27.224s; 16 Locatelli, 1m 27.441s; 17 Davies, 1m 27.514s; 18 Baldolini, 1m 27.527s; 19 Smrz, 1m 27.637s; 20 Cardenas, 1m 27.756s; 21 Sekiguchi, 1m 27.849s; 22 Jenkner, 1m 27.865s; 23 Leblanc, 1m 28.138s; 24 Giansanti, 1m 28.147s; 25 Molina, 1m 28.790s; 26 Ballerini, 1m 28.861s; 27 Rous, 1m 28.963s; 28 Aschenbrenner, 1m 29.896s; 29 Martensson, 1m 30.002s; 30 Cajback, 1m 30.409s; 31 Walter, 1m 31.212s; 32 Vincent, 1m 36.905s.

World Championship: 1 Pedrosa, 181; 2 Stoner, 131; 3 Dovizioso, 124; 4 Porto, 96; 5 de Puniet, 89; 6 Aoyama and de Angelis, 87; 8 Lorenzo, 78; 9 Barbera, 59; 10 Corsi, 54; 11 Guintoli, 43; 12 Takahashi, 38; 13 Debon, 36; 14 West, 26; 15 Giansanti and Locatelli, 24; 17 Baldolini, 18; 18 Davies, 17; 19 Ballerini, 14; 20 Rous, 8; 21 Leblanc and Smrz, 6; 23 Heidolf, 4; 24 Marchand and Nigon, 3; 26 Cardenas and Jenkner, 2.

125 cc

20 laps, 45.620 miles/73.420 km

Pos.	Rider (Nat.)	No.	Machine	Laps	Time & speed
1	Mika Kallio (SF)	36	KTM	20	29m 46.795s 91.916 mph/ 147.925 km/h
2	Thomas Luthi (CH)	12	Honda	20	29m 46.929s
3	Marco Simoncelli (I)	58	Aprilia	20	29m 47.083s
4	Gabor Talmacsi (H)	14	KTM	20	29m 47.276s
5	Julian Simon (E)	60	KTM	20	29m 48.230s
6	Lukas Pesek (CZ)	52	Derbi	20	29m 48.423s
7	Fabrizio Lai (I)	32	Honda	20	30m 01.834s
8	Joan Olive (E)	6	Aprilia	20	30m 02.051s
9	Aleix Espargaro (E)	41	Honda	20	30m 02.100s
10	Pablo Nieto (E)	22	Derbi	20	30m 02.319s
11	Manuel Poggiali (RSM)	54	Gilera	20	30m 02.372s
12	Michael Ranseder (A)	76	KTM	20	30m 07.668s
13	Lorenzo Zanetti (I)	8	Aprilia	20	30m 07.840s
14	Sandro Cortese (D)	11	Honda	20	30m 07.981s
15	Raffaele de Rosa (I)	35	Aprilia	20	30m 12.138s
16	Stefan Bradl (D)	77	KTM	20	30m 13.056s
17	Karel Abraham (CZ)	44	Aprilia	20	30m 13.980s
18	Dario Giuseppetti (D)	25	Aprilia	20	30m 17.933s
19	Mateo Tunez (E)	46	Aprilia	20	30m 19.597s
20	Imre Toth (H)	45	Aprilia	20	30m 20.068s
21	Patrick Unger (D)	13	Aprilia	20	30m 21.213s
22	Vincent Braillard (CH)	26	Aprilia	20	30m 30.867s
23	Manuel Hernandez (E)	43	Aprilia	20	30m 35.162s
24	Manuel Mickan (D)	98	Honda	20	30m 53.540s
25	Hugo van den Berg (NL)	78	Aprilia	20	30m 53.652s
26	Jordi Carchano (E)	28	Aprilia	18	30m 42.641s
	Tomoyoshi Koyama (J)	71	Honda	16	DNF
	Mike di Meglio (F)	63	Honda	16	DNF
	Angel Rodriguez (E)	47	Honda	16	DNF
	Raymond Schouten (NL)	16	Honda	9	DNF
	Mattia Pasini (I)	75	Aprilia	9	DNF
	Sascha Hommel (D)	31	Malaguti	8	DNF
	Federico Sandi (I)	10	Honda	7	DNF
	Sergio Gadea (E)	33	Aprilia	4	DNF
	Andrea Iannone (I)	29	Aprilia	1	DNF
	Hector Faubel (E)	55	Aprilia	1	DNF
	Nicolas Terol (E)	18	Derbi	1	DNF
	Michele Pirro (I)	15	Malaguti	0	DNF
	Alvaro Bautista (E)	19	Honda	0	DNF
	Toshihisa Kuzuhara (J)	9	Honda	0	DNF
	Alexis Masbou (F)	7	Honda		EXC

Fastest lap: Kallio, 1m 28.522s, 92.765 mph/149.291 km/h.

Previous record: Hector Barbera, E (Aprilia), 1m 27.680s, 93.656 mph/150.725 km/h (2004).

Event best maximum speed: di Meglio, 128.4 mph/206.6 km/h (race).

Qualifying: 1 Kallio, 1m 27.965s; 2 Simoncelli, 1m 28.182s; 3 Luthi, 1m 28.240s; 4 Pasini, 1m 28.353s; 5 Simon, 1m 28.375s; 6 Koyama, 1m 28.563s; 7 Pesek, 1m 28.605s; 8 Talmacsi, 1m 28.631s; 9 Faubel, 1m 28.635s; 10 Gadea, 1m 28.735s; 11 Espargaro, 1m 28.736s; 12 Zanetti, 1m 28.917s; 13 Lai, 1m 29.025s; 14 Iannone, 1m 29.116s; 15 Cortese, 1m 29.145s; 16 Kuzuhara, 1m 29.167s; 17 Olive, 1m 29.175s; 18 Nieto, 1m 29.179s; 19 Bautista, 1m 29.182s; 20 di Meglio, 1m 29.254s; 21 Poggiali, 1m 29.329s; 22 Hernandez, 1m 29.465s; 23 Toth, 1m 29.468s; 24 Masbou, 1m 29.480s; 25 de Rosa, 1m 29.535s; 26 Bradl, 1m 29.565s; 27 Randseder, 1m 29.569s; 28 Carchano, 1m 29.906s; 29 Giuseppetti, 1m 30.058s; 30 Abraham, 1m 30.234s; 31 Schouten, 1m 30.298s; 32 Pirro, 1m 30.350s; 33 Rodriguez, 1m 30.389s; 34 Terol, 1m 30.464s; 35 Sandi, 1m 30.508s; 36 Tunez, 1m 30.613s; 37 Unger, 1m 31.076s; 38 Hommel, 1m 31.221s; 39 Braillard, 1m 31.379s; 40 van den Berg, 1m 31.460s; 41 Mickan, 1m 31.924s.

Fastest race laps: 1 Kallio, 1m 28.522s; 2 Talmacsi, 1m 28.575s; 3 Luthi, 1m 28.627s; 4 Pasini, 1m 28.638s; 5 Lai, 1m 28.730s; 6 Gadea, 1m 28.781s; 7 Simoncelli, 1m 28.787s; 8 Pesek, 1m 28.802s; 9 Masbou, 1m 28.822s; 10 Simon, 1m 28.875s; 11 di Meglio, 1m 29.004s; 12 Koyama, 1m 29.034s; 13 Poggiali, 1m 29.088s; 14 Espargaro, 1m 29.124s; 15 Nieto, 1m 29.143s; 16 Zanetti, 1m 29.150s; 17 Ranseder, 1m 29.320s; 18 Olive, 1m 29.383s; 19 de Rosa, 1m 29.491s; 20 Cortese, 1m 29.499s; 21 Bradl, 1m 29.510s; 22 Tunez, 1m 29.598s; 23 Giuseppetti, 1m 29.825s; 24 Toth, 1m 29.888s; 25 Abraham, 1m 29.920s; 26 Unger, 1m 30.086s; 27 Braillard, 1m 30.228s; 28 Hernandez, 1m 30.244s; 29 Carchano, 1m 30.273s; 30 Sandi, 1m 30.304s; 31 Rodriguez, 1m 30.667s; 32 van den Berg, 1m 31.165s; 33 Hommel, 1m 31.226s; 34 Schouten, 1m 31.240s; 35 Mickan, 1m 31.363s; 36 Iannone, 1m 34.232s; 37 Faubel, 1m 34.286s.

World Championship: 1 Luthi, 119; 2 Kallio, 116; 3 Talmacsi, 113; 4 Simoncelli, 101; 5 Pasini, 100; 6 Simon, 91; 7 Lai, 88; 8 Poggiali, 64; 9 Koyama, 52; 10 Faubel, 50; 11 Nieto, 47; 12 di Meglio and Olive, 45; 14 Gadea, 35; 15 Bautista, 28; 16 Espargaro, 23; 17 Masbou, 20; 18 Zanetti, 19; 19 Pesek, 18; 20 Kuzuhara, 15; 21 Hernandez and Ranseder, 12; 23 Linfoot and Toth, 7; 25 Carchano, 6; 26 Conti and Iannone, 5; 28 Cortese and Elkin, 4; 30 Giuseppetti and Pirro, 3; 32 de Rosa, 2; 33 Terol, 1.

CZECHGP
BRNO

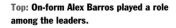

Top: On-form Alex Barros played a role among the leaders.

Above: Mates, but not team-mates: Shakey Byrne sends Jeremy "Belfast" McWilliams out for a gallop.

Above centre: Now you see them, now you don't. KTM engines arrived, were installed, then crated up and taken away again.

Above right: McWilliams beat last year's Proton V5 time, but did not finish.
Photographs: Gold & Goose

THERE is a moment of transition, they say, that is the best of times in motor racing. This apogee occurs just as that particular discipline changes from being a sport to become an industry. The events that marked the reassembly after the summer break suggested that MotoGP may already have gone past that moment of perfect balance.

One sign was the silly season – 2005 style. Usually, this hectic rumour-broking concentrates on which rider will be going where. Now, the scuttlebutt was more about which sponsor would go where. Another symptom of the ascendance of commercialism came from several sets of lawyers, rubbing their hands at all the forthcoming fees, in a pair of burgeoning disputes.

The sponsorship story had two strands, each rather different. The first concerned Rossi, and his recently announced new 2006 deal with Yamaha. Details were confidential, but it was known that he planned to hive off from the Gauloises-backed official factory team, in line with his oft-stated dislike of tobacco sponsorship. He would run in a so-called satellite team, with sponsors of his own choosing (Thought to be Alice, the Italian telecommunications company, and Nastro Azurro beer, his long-time personal and previous Honda team backers... plus a rumour of MacDonalds now offering U.S.$12-million.) Not

surprisingly, Altadis, owners of both Gauloises and current satellite team sponsors Fortuna, were far from delighted at the prospect of sponsoring a much-diminished "factory" team, while the factory star went elsewhere.

At Brno, tight-lipped Yamaha racing boss Lin Jarvis admitted that the future of the Fortuna satellite team (caught in the Gauloises crossfire) was uncertain, and that they were in "cordial" discussions with Altadis about the Rossi situation. Three weeks later in Japan, Altadis were talking tougher, demanding either Rossi, or financial compensation, with the distinct possibility of pulling out.

The second sponsorship tangle was linked, if only by default... because if Altadis were to take their Gauloises and Fortuna sponsorship from Yamaha, then to whom might they give it instead? By coincidence, Honda had a very, very big hole to be filled, for it was now common knowledge that Telefónica MoviStar were about to zip up their money-bags and depart for F1, to put more money behind Alonso, steadily drawing clear for his first World Championship. This was the last act of a long-running opera, triggered by the as yet unconfirmed expectation that they will lose their star pupil and double champion Dani Pedrosa to the factory MotoGP team, and to Repsol in the process.

This would leave Gresini unsponsored, and he was variously rumoured to be in line for Fortuna, or to snitch the Camel backing from Team Pons, Fortuna going there instead. Bad news for Gibernau who, unlike Melandri, had a big-money contract with MoviStar rather than the team.

This shuffling among the heavy hitters somewhat overshadowed (though did not drown out) a different kind of squabble at the other end of the grid. This saw Proton Team KR in the pits, looking rather hapless but eager to please, with two different riders and two different kinds of motorcycle; and over at the Red Bull tent KTM management (and eventually even the proprietor) making a robust defence of the decision that had caused the trouble. During the break the Austrian company had announced they would cease supplying engines to Kenny Roberts's team. Kenny was absent, and had professed himself utterly taken aback by KTM's pull-out. "I've never come across this kind of behaviour in racing before," he said; while at Brno team manager Chuck Aksland showed E-mails and other documents suggesting that while no contract had been signed between the two parties, there had been "a living contract". In the meantime, the team would do its best to fulfil its own commitment, an agreement to race until the end of the year.

KTM CEO (and indirectly majority shareholder) Stefan Pierer forcibly insisted that no contract had been in place, and that KTM's decision, while painful, had been for all the right reasons, mainly an unwillingness to spend any more time or money on a project that had not fulfilled its promise on the track, and would in any case be obsolete in 2007. If the dispute with Proton Team KR came to court, then so be it. "I will trust the court to come to the right decision."

Aksland had heard about the withdrawal from rider Byrne, then via a press release. The team quickly readied one of last year's V5s, and enlisted McWilliams as rider (Byrne being contracted directly to KTM). The Austrian company then offered (again via the rider) to support them for this one more race. Aksland was reluctant, telling them he preferred to stick with the original plan, until the end of the season. On Thursday, KTM technicians arrived unexpectedly with a spare engine, and helped the team prepare two more machines. Then at 5pm, KTM's attorneys faxed the team, saying they had no permission to use these engines. The drama continued until half-an-hour before practice, with both Byrne and McWilliams ready to ride. At that point, with no further response from KTM, Aksland decided to use the old V5.

Inside racing, everyone rallied round Roberts. Dorna's Carmelo Ezpeleta gave his verbal backing, and said that if the team could not complete the season as per contract, Dorna would not penalise them. Michelin chipped in with FOC tyres (they had previously been charging KTM 50,000 Euros per race). McWilliams qualified on the old bike on Michelins, and in morning warm-up was 1.5 seconds faster than Aoki had been on the same bike the year before on Dunlops. "We always thought the tyres were worth 1.5 to two seconds a lap," said Aksland. He retired from the race when a front-wheel sensor failed, throwing the engine management system out of kilter.

Reduced to mere background noise, there were some rider dispositions getting into line, as Hopkins made a massive leap of faith to sign with Suzuki for two more years. His alternative had been Ducati, and he admitted later he felt a bit queasy when one of the much-revived red bikes finished in a strong second place. Gibernau was on the loose, and would from now on increasingly be linked with Ducati; Elias was tipped to take his place at Gresini Honda, unless the Fortuna sponsorship money took him to Pons Honda instead.

To little surprise, Blata's V6 did not appear as promised… a statement issued in the break described how the company's

Below: No V6 in sight, Blata rider Ellison stayed on last year's WCM, and went much faster than it had last year.

Bottom: Nakano enjoyed the new Bridgestones, but the long fast track showed that his Kawasaki, like the Suzukis, still needed more horsepower.
Photographs: Gold & Goose

attention had been very fully occupied defending their copyright against Chinese companies making cut-price copies of Blata minibikes, their staple product.

Honda's very new RC211V was on hand, however – a major redesign of the existing concept, mainly aimed at making the engine shorter to centralise mass still further. The bike was to be tested by Biaggi and Gibernau on the two days after the GP – almost all teams were staying to test. In the end, however, it was mysteriously withdrawn on orders from Japan "for safety reasons", and only released for a short time at the end of the second testing day.

Finally, there was a motorcycle race on Sunday. Another MotoGP, the same winner... in unusual yet essentially familiar circumstances, as Sete Gibernau found yet another way to seize defeat from the jaws of victory. This time, his last-lap failure was entirely down to the bike... and led to a flurry of self-contradiction from HRC, who at first denied that the machine had run out of petrol. In fact, it had – the consequence of an electronic malfunction in a system that constantly measures fuel consumption in real time, and is intended to make mixture and throttle adjustments to ensure there will always be enough to finish any given race. Or, in this case, not.

MOTOGP RACE – 22 laps

Practice had shown a clear improvement in Bridgestone tyres, especially for Ducati, with "the new Capirossi" (as Rossi described him) heading two out of three free practices, fast also on race tyres. Rossi meanwhile had a third crash of the year, colliding with Bayliss on the last corner after the latter slowed suddenly to go into the pits. "The pit entrance is something we have to change," Rossi commented later.

Michelin topped the qualifying, however, Gibernau half a tenth ahead of Hayden and then the Ducati, on the front row for the first time since China. Rossi headed row two from Melandri and Checa. Biaggi, a track specialist with seven wins here, was again complaining about elusive feel problems, and

qualified tenth.

Gibernau led morning warm-up, and into the first corner, under clearing skies. Rossi had made a last-minute change before the race, and was clearly determined not to let Gibernau escape, pushing past brusquely on the right-hander out of the stadium section. Melandri was third after lap one, then Hayden and fast-starter Hopkins... although he had to watch Checa, Capirossi and Barros blow by him before the end of the pit straight.

On lap three, Gibernau took the lead again, and Hayden passed Melandri for a couple of laps of back-and-forth, the Ducati pair Capirossi and Checa close behind. Barros and Edwards made up a close top eight, Hopkins losing ground at the head of the next gang. Right behind him, a steadily advancing Biaggi, up from 11th on lap one.

Now the leading pair gained a little gap from Hayden, Melandri and Capirossi, Checa off the back and about to lose sixth to a charging Barros. Then Rossi ran wide, losing almost a second on lap eight, to give his pursuers a clearer target. In another lap he was back with Gibernau, and starting to lean on him, and the next quartet closer too.

Just after half distance, Rossi attacked with real intent, diving underneath into the last corner to take what would remain the slenderest of leads.

Melandri dropped away from the pursuit group, blaming a lack of traction. On lap 13, Barros was up to third and brought Hayden and Capirossi with him as he closed a small gap on the leaders down to almost half a second on lap 18.

All eyes were on the front, where Gibernau had been shadowing Rossi for five laps. He looked strong and unflustered, and proved it when he passed Rossi firmly at the bottom of the hill on lap 18 to lead for three more laps. Was this Rossi's familiar game, waiting for the end for the final attack – or did Gibernau really have an advantage for once?

There were clues to the answer – one being Rossi's subsequent assertion it had been the hardest race of the year, but no certainty. Because it was now that Gibernau's Honda started to starve of fuel, cutting out momentarily, and playing up going

Above: Rossi fans were as prominent as ever.

Top: Capirossi and the Ducati were resurgent at Brno – a portent of even more to come.
Photographs: Gold & Goose

into turns as the engine braking system cut in and out. "Sometimes I didn't know what gear I was in, because the engine wouldn't rev," he said. He was still ahead into the chicane before starting the last lap, but behind on the way out.

Rossi put his head down. Gibernau was still close at the bottom of the hill. Then he slowed suddenly and moved out wide, to coast to a stop. Rossi's ninth win of the year was ultimately once again unchallenged. He donned a dickey shirt-front on the rostrum and served his champagne to the team – it was Yamaha's 140th win in the premier class, one more than MV Agusta, behind only Honda with 194.

Capirossi was less than two seconds behind, his and the Desmosedici's best result since Australia in 2003. Third was a bit of a surprise...

Biaggi had passed the slowing Checa for eighth just before half distance, and his progress didn't stop. "Once I believed I could move forward, then I could," he would say. Over the next five laps, he passed Edwards and Melandri. Riding with trade-mark consistency, he was rapidly on the next group, passing Hayden with two laps left, and Barros on the last lap. It was his first rostrum since Mugello, but for all his complaints about his top factory machine, his overall consistency meant Max now displaced Melandri in an increasingly close battle for second overall.

With Edwards and Checa spaced out behind, the next battle was for ninth. At mid-distance, Hopkins was holding on grimly, from Roberts and Hofmann, Bayliss and Nakano a little way back. Then came Tamada, passing Elias as he recovered from a slow start.

Now Bayliss started to move forward, passing Hopkins with four laps left. Tamada also picked his way through for tenth, Roberts and Nakano close, and likewise the fading Hopkins, with class rookie Elias ahead of Hofmann at the flag. Ninth to 14th was covered by less than 1.5 seconds.

Wild card Aoki, Rolfo, and the perplexed and increasingly disappointed Xaus trailed in ahead of the WCM-Blata pair.

Above: Lorenzo shows his aggressive style as he heads the tight 250 pack, from Aoyama, de Angelis, Stoner, Dovizioso and Pedrosa.

Opposite bottom: Rossi, regaining strength in the pantomime department, donned a waiter's dickey to serve champagne to Yamaha, whose 140th premier class win had eclipsed MV Agusta.

Photographs: Gold & Goose

250 cc RACE – 20 laps

Qualifying was a bitter dispute between Lorenzo and Pedrosa, the new boy winning out by just three thousandths. Stoner was close, then second rookie Dovizioso, making the front row three Hondas and one Aprilia. The first eight were within a second.

Then the weather took a hand... the track mainly dry but still slippery, and rain spotting as Pedrosa and Lorenzo got away up front. Everybody was somewhat cautious, so Aoyama decided "I would try and go", taking the lead for four laps.

The champion was sixth at the end of lap one, holding his position at the back of a close group, and very mindful about how he had misjudged the rain conditions and lost the race last year. "With the drizzle, I had a flash-back," he said. He watched and waited, as ahead of him the hotheads shuffled to and fro.

De Angelis was second at the end of lap four, but Lorenzo passed him soon afterwards and then took Aoyama at the final chicane to start a long spell in the lead. Aoyama hung on in second until almost half distance.

But Pedrosa had been moving forward, passing Dovizioso and Stoner in one lap, Aoyama the next, and then de Angelis.

With nine laps to go he was in second. Before he could start sizing up Lorenzo, however, de Angelis shouldered past for a couple more laps.

On lap 16, Lorenzo flashed across the line with the fastest lap... instantly eclipsed by Pedrosa, who seized the lead into the next corner. He held it from there to the end, Lorenzo conceding defeat on the final lap to be more than a second behind over the line.

The faster pace spread the pursuit, Stoner finally getting ahead of de Angelis on lap 17, and staying there narrowly to the finish. Close behind, Aoyama repassed Dovizioso on the final lap after an entertaining scrap.

Almost 20 seconds behind, Porto was seventh, his chances spoiled on lap one when he was put off the track by a high-siding Corsi. He rejoined in 13th, and by half-distance had taken seventh off fast starter Guintoli. Further progress was impossible, and he had a lonely ride to the end. It was the Argentine's 150th start.

Team-mate de Puniet had tagged on; at the end Guintoli lost another place to Locatelli. Smrz pipped West's KTM for 12th on the last lap, comfortably clear of the next group.

Like spectacular crasher Corsi, Takahashi and Barbera didn't finish lap one, tangling and falling together; Davies and Ballerini did the same four laps later, the latter remounting. Heidolf and Sekiguchi also crashed out.

125 cc RACE – 19 laps

Luthi put in a flier at the end of qualifying, Pasini nosing into second ahead of Kallio, and Simoncelli pushing Talmacsi to lead the second row. A small army of fans had come across from Hungary to watch him, and he was feeling the pressure.

Light rain was threatening as Luthi led into the first corner. By lap three he had opened up a second gap over Kallio and a big pack. Lai was losing ground within it, Pasini showing strongly, and Simoncelli moving steadily forwards after finishing the first lap barely in the top ten.

Pasini had taken second, but Kallio took over the lead on lap eight, with the Italian rider ahead next time. Behind Luthi by half distance, Simoncelli and Zanetti made a group of five. They were changing places frequently, with Luthi back in front for another four laps. Until Pasini took over on lap 15 ... just as the rain got a bit more serious.

Conditions were tricky, survival the key issue, as Pasini demonstrated at the wettest point, the last corners at the top of the hill, crashing out with two laps to go, just after losing the lead to Luthi.

Luthi said that from then on, the surface increasingly treacherous, "it was just a matter of staying on," and his second win of the year was by better than three seconds from Kallio, who ran the last lap only just fast enough to keep Simoncelli behind.

Gadea came through to take fourth from Zanetti, then Lai narrowly headed team-mate di Meglio and Poggiali. Then came a disappointed Talmacsi, who blamed a reluctance to rev for a poor showing. Simon was close behind; fellow KTM rider, impressive wild card Ranseder crashed out while well up in the top ten, taking Koyama and Masbou with him.

Above: Treacherous conditions in a dramatic 125 race. Pasini had just lost the lead to Luthi when he hit a damp patch and lost the plot. Simoncelli got past unscathed.

Right: Luthi's valuable win was a matter of survival.

Photographs: Gold & Goose

AUTODROM BRNO – CZECH REPUBLIC

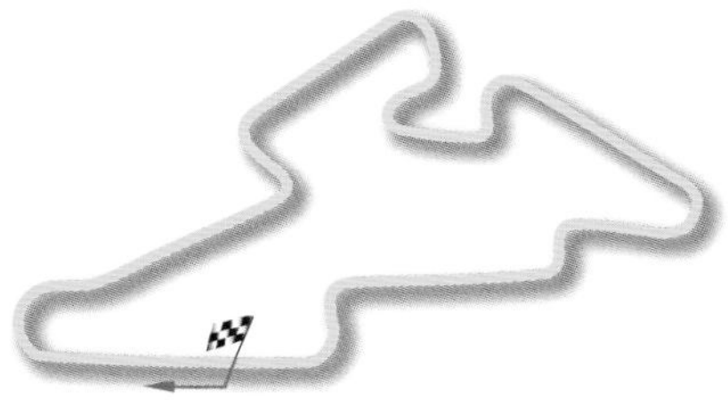

CIRCUIT LENGTH: 3.357 miles/5.403 km

GAULOISES GRAND PRIX CESKE REPUBLIKY

28 AUGUST 2005 • FIM WORLD CHAMPIONSHIP ROUND 11

MotoGP

22 laps, 73.854 miles/118.866 km

Pos.	Rider (Nat.)	No.	Machine	Laps	Time & speed
1	Valentino Rossi (I)	46	Yamaha	22	43m 56.539s 100.850 mph/ 162.302 km/h
2	Loris Capirossi (I)	65	Ducati	22	43m 58.376s
3	Max Biaggi (I)	3	Honda	22	43m 59.983s
4	Alex Barros (BR)	4	Honda	22	44m 00.687s
5	Nicky Hayden (USA)	69	Honda	22	44m 00.902s
6	Marco Melandri (I)	33	Honda	22	44m 07.689s
7	Colin Edwards (USA)	5	Yamaha	22	44m 10.071s
8	Carlos Checa (E)	7	Ducati	22	44m 15.870s
9	Troy Bayliss (AUS)	12	Honda	22	44m 23.664s
10	Makoto Tamada (J)	6	Honda	22	44m 23.787s
11	Kenny Roberts (USA)	10	Suzuki	22	44m 24.223s
12	Shinya Nakano (J)	56	Kawasaki	22	44m 24.342s
13	John Hopkins (USA)	21	Suzuki	22	44m 24.817s
14	Toni Elias (E)	24	Yamaha	22	44m 25.110s
15	Alex Hofmann (D)	66	Kawasaki	22	44m 26.307s
16	Nobuatsu Aoki (J)	9	Suzuki	22	44m 38.317s
17	Roberto Rolfo (I)	44	Ducati	22	44m 54.339s
18	Ruben Xaus (E)	11	Yamaha	22	45m 04.621s
19	James Ellison (GB)	77	Blata	22	45m 38.708s
20	Franco Battaini (I)	27	Blata	22	45m 51.323s
	Sete Gibernau (E)	15	Honda	21	DNF
	Jeremy McWilliams (GB)	99	Proton KR	7	DNF

Fastest lap: Rossi, 1m 58.787s, 101.746 mph/163.745 km/h (record).

Previous record: Alex Barros, BR (Honda), 1m 59.302s, 101.307 mph/163.038 km/h (2004).

Event best maximum speed: Biaggi, 191.4 mph/308.0 km/h (race).

Qualifying: 1 Gibernau, 1m 57.504s; 2 Hayden, 1m 57.551s; 3 Capirossi, 1m 57.685s; 4 Rossi, 1m 57.875s; 5 Melandri, 1m 57.999s; 6 Checa, 1m 58.185s; 7 Barros, 1m 58.223s; 8 Hopkins, 1m 58.277s; 9 Edwards, 1m 58.323s; 10 Biaggi, 1m 58.337s; 11 Nakano, 1m 58.490s; 12 Tamada, 1m 58.610s; 13 Bayliss, 1m 58.662s; 14 Hofmann, 1m 58.793s; 15 Elias, 1m 58.815s; 16 Aoki, 1m 59.495s; 17 Roberts, 1m 59.734s; 18 Ellison, 2m 00.529s; 19 Rolfo, 2m 00.879s; 20 Xaus, 2m 01.535s; 21 Battaini, 2m 02.585s; 22 McWilliams, 2m 04.663s.

Fastest race laps (After Race Part 2): 1 Rossi, 1m 58.787s; 2 Gibernau, 1m 58.819s; 3 Barros, 1m 58.827s; 4 Capirossi, 1m 58.856s; 5 Checa, 1m 58.897s; 6 Edwards, 1m 58.974s; 7 Melandri, 1m 59.044s; 8 Hayden, 1m 59.100s; 9 Biaggi, 1m 59.269s; 10 Roberts, 1m 59.420s; 11 Nakano, 1m 59.529s; 12 Elias, 1m 59.669s; 13 Hopkins, 1m 59.847s; 14 Hofmann, 1m 59.863s; 15 Bayliss, 2m 00.103s; 16 Tamada, 2m 00.103s; 17 Aoki, 2m 00.362s; 18 Rolfo, 2m 01.491s; 19 Xaus, 2m 02.040s; 20 Ellison, 2m 02.377s; 21 McWilliams, 2m 03.332s; 22 Battaini, 2m 03.847s.

World Championship: 1 Rossi, 261; 2 Biaggi, 129; 3 Melandri, 126; 4 Edwards, 123; 5 Gibernau, 115; 6 Barros, 114; 7 Hayden, 112; 8 Capirossi, 92; 9 Nakano, 69; 10 C. Checa, 59; 11 Bayliss, 54; 12 Tamada, 48; 13 Roberts, 41; 14 Xaus, 36; 15 Hopkins, 35; 16 Elias, 31; 17 Jacque, 25; 18 Hofmann, 22; 19 Rolfo, 15; 20 van den Goorbergh, 12; 21 D. Checa and Ellison, 4; 23 Battaini, Byrne and Ukawa, 1.

250 cc

20 laps, 67.140 miles/108.060 km

Pos.	Rider (Nat.)	No.	Machine	Laps	Time & speed
1	Daniel Pedrosa (E)	1	Honda	20	41m 24.944s 97.275 mph/ 156.549 km/h
2	Jorge Lorenzo (E)	48	Honda	20	41m 26.247s
3	Casey Stoner (AUS)	27	Aprilia	20	41m 29.197s
4	Alex de Angelis (RSM)	5	Aprilia	20	41m 30.270s
5	Hiroshi Aoyama (J)	73	Honda	20	41m 33.336s
6	Andrea Dovizioso (I)	34	Honda	20	41m 33.415s
7	Sebastian Porto (ARG)	19	Aprilia	20	41m 50.489s
8	Randy de Puniet (F)	7	Aprilia	20	41m 57.103s
9	Roberto Locatelli (I)	15	Aprilia	20	41m 58.913s
10	Sylvain Guintoli (F)	50	Aprilia	20	42m 00.488s
11	Jakub Smrz (CZ)	96	Honda	20	42m 16.771s
12	Anthony West (AUS)	14	KTM	20	42m 16.993s
13	Alex Debon (E)	6	Honda	20	42m 23.158s
14	Radomil Rous (CZ)	64	Honda	20	42m 23.548s
15	Steve Jenkner (D)	17	Aprilia	20	42m 23.855s
16	Andrea Ballerini (I)	8	Aprilia	20	42m 31.147s
17	Mirko Giansanti (I)	32	Aprilia	20	42m 39.397s
18	Arnaud Vincent (F)	21	Fantic	20	42m 52.697s
19	Martin Cardenas (COL)	36	Aprilia	20	42m 53.466s
20	Alvaro Molina (E)	41	Aprilia	20	43m 13.210s
21	Gregory Leblanc (F)	38	Aprilia	20	43m 14.399s
22	Michal Filla (CZ)	70	Aprilia	19	41m 31.466s
23	Alex Baldolini (I)	25	Aprilia	19	41m 54.951s
24	Nicklas Cajback (S)	23	Yamaha	19	41m 59.054s
	Dirk Heidolf (D)	28	Honda	19	DNF
	Taro Sekiguchi (J)	44	Aprilia	19	DNF
	Chaz Davies (GB)	57	Aprilia	4	DNF
	Simone Corsi (I)	24	Aprilia	0	DNF
	Yuki Takahashi (J)	55	Honda	0	DNF
	Hector Barbera (E)	80	Honda	0	DNF
	Gabriele Ferro (I)	20	Fantic		DNQ
	Alexander Todorov (BUL)	22	Yamaha		DNQ

Fastest lap: Pedrosa, 2m 02.554s, 98.619 mph/158.712 km/h (record).

Previous record: Daniel Pedrosa, E (Honda), 2m 03.332s, 97.996 mph/157.710 km/h (2004).

Event best maximum speed: Corsi, 157.8 mph/254.0 km/h (free practice no. 2).

Qualifying: 1 Lorenzo, 2m 02.261s; 2 Pedrosa, 2m 02.264s; 3 Stoner, 2m 02.468s; 4 Dovizioso, 2m 02.493s; 5 de Puniet, 2m 02.813s; 6 Porto, 2m 02.822s; 7 de Angelis, 2m 02.851s; 8 Aoyama, 2m 03.131s; 9 Takahashi, 2m 03.529s; 10 Guintoli, 2m 03.759s; 11 Locatelli, 2m 03.851s; 12 Barbera, 2m 03.973s; 13 Corsi, 2m 04.302s; 14 Smrz, 2m 04.486s; 15 Davies, 2m 04.674s; 16 Ballerini, 2m 05.224s; 17 Baldolini, 2m 05.360s; 18 Rous, 2m 05.368s; 19 Debon, 2m 05.448s; 20 Heidolf, 2m 05.458s; 21 Giansanti, 2m 05.574s; 22 Jenkner, 2m 05.590s; 23 West, 2m 05.621s; 24 Sekiguchi, 2m 05.774s; 25 Vincent, 2m 06.558s; 26 Leblanc, 2m 07.431s; 27 Cardenas, 2m 08.388s; 28 Filla, 2m 08.816s; 29 Molina, 2m 09.287s; 30 Cajback, 2m 10.123s; 31 Ferro, 2m 11.336s; 32 Todorov, 2m 13.084s.

Fastest race laps: 1 Pedrosa, 2m 02.554s; 2 Lorenzo, 2m 02.814s; 3 de Angelis, 2m 03.164s; 4 Dovizioso, 2m 03.274s; 5 Stoner, 2m 03.282s; 6 Aoyama, 2m 03.554s; 7 Porto, 2m 04.409s; 8 de Puniet, 2m 04.503s; 9 Locatelli, 2m 04.702s; 10 Guintoli, 2m 04.972s; 11 West, 2m 05.525s; 12 Smrz, 2m 05.744s; 13 Rous, 2m 05.831s; 14 Jenkner, 2m 05.991s; 15 Heidolf, 2m 06.017s; 16 Debon, 2m 06.030s; 17 Baldolini, 2m 06.171s; 18 Ballerini, 2m 06.336s; 19 Davies, 2m 06.366s; 20 Giansanti, 2m 06.583s; 21 Cardenas, 2m 07.341s; 22 Sekiguchi, 2m 07.356s; 23 Vincent, 2m 07.363s; 24 Molina, 2m 08.613s; 25 Leblanc, 2m 08.656s; 26 Filla, 2m 09.734s; 27 Cajback, 2m 11.018s.

World Championship: 1 Pedrosa, 206; 2 Stoner, 147; 3 Dovizioso, 134; 4 Porto, 105; 5 de Angelis, 100; 6 Aoyama and Lorenzo, 98; 8 de Puniet, 97; 9 Barbera, 59; 10 Corsi, 54; 11 Guintoli, 49; 12 Debon, 39; 13 Takahashi, 38; 14 Locatelli, 31; 15 West, 30; 16 Giansanti, 24; 17 Baldolini, 18; 18 Davies, 17; 19 Ballerini, 14; 20 Smrz, 11; 21 Rous, 10; 22 Leblanc, 6; 23 Heidolf, 4; 24 Jenkner, Marchand and Nigon, 3; 27 Cardenas, 2.

125 cc

19 laps, 63.783 miles/102.657 km

Pos.	Rider (Nat.)	No.	Machine	Laps	Time & speed
1	Thomas Luthi (CH)	12	Honda	19	41m 32.409s 92.134 mph/ 148.276 km/h
2	Mika Kallio (SF)	36	KTM	19	41m 35.621s
3	Marco Simoncelli (I)	58	Aprilia	19	41m 35.735s
4	Sergio Gadea (E)	33	Aprilia	19	41m 40.163s
5	Lorenzo Zanetti (I)	8	Aprilia	19	41m 46.862s
6	Fabrizio Lai (I)	32	Honda	19	41m 57.565s
7	Mike di Meglio (F)	63	Honda	19	41m 57.656s
8	Manuel Poggiali (RSM)	54	Gilera	19	41m 57.918s
9	Gabor Talmacsi (H)	14	KTM	19	41m 58.182s
10	Julian Simon (E)	60	KTM	19	41m 58.475s
11	Andrea Iannone (I)	29	Aprilia	19	42m 01.386s
12	Alvaro Bautista (E)	19	Honda	19	42m 02.769s
13	Aleix Espargaro (E)	41	Honda	19	42m 02.784s
14	Sandro Cortese (D)	11	Honda	19	42m 03.168s
15	Stefan Bradl (D)	77	KTM	19	42m 06.135s
16	Pablo Nieto (E)	22	Derbi	19	42m 09.289s
17	Raffaele de Rosa (I)	35	Aprilia	19	42m 10.748s
18	Imre Toth (H)	45	Aprilia	19	42m 10.824s
19	Nicolas Terol (E)	18	Derbi	19	42m 13.919s
20	Manuel Hernandez (E)	43	Aprilia	19	42m 17.081s
21	Vincent Braillard (CH)	26	Aprilia	19	42m 19.664s
22	Joan Olive (E)	6	Aprilia	19	42m 35.102s
23	Sascha Hommel (D)	31	Malaguti	19	43m 04.595s
24	Thomas Mayer (D)	99	Aprilia	19	43m 04.777s
25	Julian Miralles (E)	84	Aprilia	19	43m 41.556s
26	David Bonache (E)	48	Honda	19	43m 49.536s
	Mattia Pasini (I)	75	Aprilia	17	DNF
	Hector Faubel (E)	55	Aprilia	17	DNF
	Patrik Vostarek (CZ)	87	Honda	17	DNF
	Jordi Carchano (E)	28	Aprilia	17	DNF
	Lukas Razek (CZ)	97	Honda	17	DNF
	Federico Sandi (I)	10	Honda	13	DNF
	Dario Giuseppetti (D)	25	Aprilia	11	DNF
	Karel Abraham (CZ)	44	Aprilia	10	DNF
	Lukas Pesek (CZ)	52	Derbi	9	DNF
	Tomoyoshi Koyama (J)	71	Honda	5	DNF
	Alexis Masbou (F)	7	Honda	5	DNF
	Michael Ranseder (A)	76	KTM	5	DNF
	Raymond Schouten (NL)	16	Honda	5	DNF
	Michele Pirro (I)	15	Malaguti	5	DNF
	Toshihisa Kuzuhara (J)	9	Honda		DNS

Fastest lap: Gadea, 2m 08.931s, 93.741 mph/150.862 km/h.

Previous record: Lucio Cecchinello, I (Aprilia), 2m 07.836s, 94.544 mph/152.154 km/h (2003).

Event best maximum speed: Gadea, 137.0 mph/220.5 km/h (race).

Qualifying: 1 Luthi, 2m 08.638s; 2 Pasini, 2m 08.670s; 3 Kallio, 2m 08.875s; 4 Simoncelli, 2m 08.953s; 5 Talmacsi, 2m 09.045s; 6 Cortese, 2m 09.205s; 7 Lai, 2m 09.472s; 8 Pesek, 2m 09.533s; 9 Koyama, 2m 09.807s; 10 de Rosa, 2m 09.896s; 11 Masbou, 2m 09.905s; 12 Ranseder, 2m 09.998s; 13 Simon, 2m 10.049s; 14 Poggiali, 2m 10.057s; 15 Zanetti, 2m 10.128s; 16 Faubel, 2m 10.176s; 17 di Meglio, 2m 10.184s; 18 Iannone, 2m 10.227s; 19 Nieto, 2m 10.287s; 20 Gadea, 2m 10.350s; 21 Bautista, 2m 10.499s; 22 Hernandez, 2m 10.587s; 23 Espargaro, 2m 10.787s; 24 Abraham, 2m 11.315s; 25 Toth, 2m 11.339s; 26 Bradl, 2m 11.400s; 27 Schouten, 2m 11.485s; 28 Kuzuhara, 2m 11.723s; 29 Giuseppetti, 2m 11.848s; 30 Pirro, 2m 12.110s; 31 Terol, 2m 12.320s; 32 Olive, 2m 12.328s; 33 Braillard, 2m 12.831s; 34 Vostarek, 2m 12.936s; 35 Sandi, 2m 13.107s; 36 Carchano, 2m 13.433s; 37 Hommel, 2m 13.603s; 38 Mayer, 2m 14.191s; 39 Bonache, 2m 14.771s; 40 Miralles, 2m 15.130s; 41 Razek, 2m 15.603s.

Fastest race laps: 1 Gadea, 2m 08.931s; 2 Kallio, 2m 09.045s; 3 Pasini, 2m 09.207s; 4 Zanetti, 2m 09.267s; 5 Luthi, 2m 09.310s; 6 Simoncelli, 2m 09.337s; 7 Masbou, 2m 09.654s; 8 Koyama, 2m 09.694s; 9 Ranseder, 2m 09.744s; 10 Talmacsi, 2m 09.788s; 11 di Meglio, 2m 09.901s; 12 Faubel, 2m 09.910s; 13 Espargaro, 2m 09.987s; 14 Lai, 2m 10.076s; 15 Simon, 2m 10.151s; 16 Iannone, 2m 10.287s; 17 Bautista, 2m 10.390s; 18 Pesek, 2m 10.514s; 19 Poggiali, 2m 10.632s; 20 Cortese, 2m 10.705s; 21 Hernandez, 2m 10.799s; 22 Vostarek, 2m 10.818s; 23 Nieto, 2m 10.974s; 24 Toth, 2m 11.007s; 25 Braillard, 2m 11.039s; 26 de Rosa, 2m 11.065s; 27 Terol, 2m 11.069s; 28 Bradl, 2m 11.075s; 29 Abraham, 2m 11.148s; 30 Sandi, 2m 11.800s; 31 Giuseppetti, 2m 12.120s; 32 Olive, 2m 12.334s; 33 Carchano, 2m 12.858s; 34 Schouten, 2m 13.020s; 35 Hommel, 2m 13.421s; 36 Pirro, 2m 13.744s; 37 Mayer, 2m 14.053s; 38 Miralles, 2m 15.631s; 39 Bonache, 2m 16.050s; 40 Razek, 2m 16.270s.

World Championship: 1 Luthi, 144; 2 Kallio, 136; 3 Talmacsi, 120; 4 Simoncelli, 117; 5 Pasini, 100; 6 Lai, 98; 7 Simon, 97; 8 Poggiali, 72; 9 di Meglio, 54; 10 Koyama, 52; 11 Faubel, 50; 12 Gadea, 48; 13 Nieto, 47; 14 Olive, 45; 15 Bautista, 32; 16 Zanetti, 30; 17 Espargaro, 26; 18 Masbou, 20; 19 Pesek, 18; 20 Kuzuhara, 15; 21 Hernandez and Ranseder, 12; 23 Iannone, 10; 24 Linfoot and Toth, 7; 26 Carchano and Cortese, 6; 28 Conti, 5; 29 Elkin, 4; 30 Giuseppetti and Pirro, 3; 32 de Rosa, 2; 33 Bradl and Terol, 1.

Left: The invader – in the Japanese industry's homeland Capirossi, Ducati and the Bridgestones were dominant all weekend.

Right: Capirossi enjoys his first win for two years.

Below: At last and at home, last year's winner Tamada claimed a first rostrum for the Konika Minolta team.

Photographs: Gold & Goose

JAPANESEGP
TWIN-RING MOTEGI

Left: A chastened Rossi leads disappointed fan club members back under the tunnel after his collision with the injured Melandri.

Photograph: Gold & Goose

Top: Ukawa, in familiar colours, was the first of a series of replacements for Bayliss.

Above centre: Removing the remains – Luthi's bike, after the 125-class mayhem.

Above: And it's compulsory.

Photographs: Gold & Goose

NO stranger to controversy and the unexpected, Honda's carved-from-solid Twin-Ring Motegi served a several courses of both in 2005, with some cream-of-the-crop ingredients in all classes. At the same time, the quirky and punishing circuit also thwarted Rossi's aim of settling things in Honda's back yard. Not, however, by favouring Honda. They took a beating, from a rather unexpected quarter, from Italy and Ducati, with an extra under-belly slash from countrymen Bridgestone, whose new-generation tyres made the whole upset possible.

This was the first of a trio of back-to-backs, and in many ways the most punishing... jet-lag at its peak, an extremely foreign environment, the championship a foregone conclusion, and the prospect of three weeks of packing cases and suitcases ahead. Ten to one Valentino would wrap it up here. The mathematical variations were many, and in theory any of six riders (Biaggi, Melandri, Edwards, Gibernau, Barros and Hayden) could defeat him. In reality, he needed to keep close to Biaggi and/or Melandri. Not too hard, and a significant group of his Yellow-Shirt brigade had made the long-haul journey, with "Seven Samurai" T-shirts printed up, ready to celebrate his seventh crown. Instead, he would crash right in front of them, where they were preparing a celebration that would never take place.

Ducati's return to glory, their first win since Catalunya in 2003, also with Capirossi, was part of the same pattern that put him second three weekends before at Brno. Partly it was machine balance, achieved after some earlier blind technical alleys; much more it was the tyres. Bridgestone had introduced a new generation at Brno, and now a further upgrade on those tyres for their home track, where they test extensively. Just how well the tyres worked became clear in practice, when Capirossi not only took pole, but reeled off strings of fast laps on race tyres. At this track and the next, the improved side-grip of the tyres would raise the bar, and get all the Michelin runners, including Rossi, on the back foot.

The bellowing Desmosedici was on full song under the scrutiny of the big noises from all the Japanese factories. The echoes from the front-straight grandstands and in the unique pair of underpasses (a deafeningly pleasurable place to stand) rather drowned out the background noise of contract wrangles and who-goes-where rider speculation, much of the latter settled, with Capirossi now also signed to stay put. But there was a rather ominous statement from Altadis, on the brewing Rossi/Yamaha contract situation, the matter now in the hands of their same attorneys who had recently won a $3-million contract suit against Barros. Said communications officer, Dany Hindenoch: "There are only two acceptable conclusions to this matter: that Rossi returns to the Gauloises Yamaha team in 2006 or that Yamaha compensates Altadis." Pending resolution, Gauloises and Fortuna involvement in MotoGP (but not 250) would be frozen, he added.

Rossi himself was answering questions on another topic – an imminent move to F1, following some comments from Ferrari's Ross Brawn that he would be doing a test a month in 2006. Rossi poured cold water on these suggestions – adding: "I don't know what happens next week in my life. For sure in two years, I don't know."

Troy Bayliss was a significant absentee – the former Superbike champion and now struggling new Honda rider capping a highly forgettable season with a motocross training crash that smashed his wrist. Plates and screws had been inserted – rather surprisingly his first such – but the injury would end his season, and ultimately his MotoGP career.

His place was taken by ex-GP man Tohru Ukawa, a one-race break from his HRC test duties on the development version of the V5. Tohru raced a stock machine, and was victim of a rare race breakdown that increased Honda's embarrassment at home, and triggered rumours of fragility at the current rev and horsepower levels of a four-year-old engine design. The new bike, with a more compact engine and longer swing-arm, remained a distant dream for riders Gibernau and Biaggi, who briefly tested it at Brno. The former continued his peculiar combination of good speed and bad luck; the latter salvaged HRC's pride with one of his best races of the year.

The smaller classes were up to all sorts as well. Perhaps the 125 outcome was not so unexpected... a carbon copy of a crash last year that caused the race to be red flagged. Luthi, tussling for the lead with title rival Kallio, high-sided on the exit of the final right-hander onto the pit straight. The entry is blind, and as last year another rider in the following pack, Sergio Gadea, was unable to take avoiding action, running over Luthi's ankles then piling into his Honda with such force that it broke his Aprilia in two. Miraculously, he escaped injury; Luthi with two injured ankles, and a dislocated right shoulder.

With results taken from the previous lap, Luthi was credited with second, Kallio was the winner, Gadea seventh. The unexpected came from KTM's Harald Bartol, who raised a knowingly hopeless protest against Luthi's engine, in order (he explained) to open a debate on another question... whether a rider who triggers a race stoppage is entitled to be included in the results. This could of course decide the title, "and not just in favour of a KTM rider," he said, citing World Speedway as an example where elimination is automatic. The AMA has a similar rule. Race Director Paul Butler agreed to ponder over this, but he and his colleagues had much else on their minds.

It started in a 250 class already topsy-turvy after Pedrosa had not just one uncharacteristic crash in practice, but three – ending up battered and bruised and on the second row of the grid. Lorenzo was soon also in the negative limelight. His downer came in a spirited race, in what Race Direction saw as a rather too spirited last lap move. "Pulling a desperate," Lorenzo dived underneath de Angelis into a tight corner, unable either to stop or make the corner, batting his rival off the track as he crashed. For this, he was judged to have "ridden in an irresponsible manner causing danger to other riders", and was suspended from next week's Malaysian GP. This heavy penalty was explained as a punishment for cumulative infringements.

Explanation was necessary, because it was hard to tell the difference between this and the case of Rossi and Melandri. Especially after Race Direction unanimously overturned a post-race dangerous riding protest against Rossi, from HRC.

Chasing the leaders, Rossi suddenly found himself on Melandri's back wheel. He said later that he'd been surprised by Melandri's slower and tighter line into the bottom corner at the end of the back straight. Or had he just missed his braking point? Either way, he ran right into him at speed. Rossi escaped unhurt; Melandri was unlucky enough to have his right foot

speared by his own footpeg. He was helicoptered off directly to have a savage wound treated with more than 30 stitches.

It was at the same place and not dissimilar to the move that got Makoto Tamada disqualified two years before, after he'd supposedly pushed Gibernau onto the dirt. The same year, a first-corner multiple crash triggered by an over-impetuous Hopkins saw him disqualified from the next race. One year later, Capirossi escaped unpunished after doing much the same thing. Obviously, the hard braking and variety of corner lines of this circuit invite this sort of incident – a fault more with the circuit design, you might think, than the riders.

Now critics saw yet more inconsistency in Race Direction's reaction, when Rossi's crash was regarded as a straightforward racing incident, whereas Lorenzo's was not.

This is a natural consequence, perhaps, of the case-by-case, rider-by-rider approach. But there were critics on the other side as well. Given the complete and apparently whimsical control wielded by Race Direction, why not introduce some commercial nous? A man with the vision of an Ecclestone would have disqualified Rossi from one and maybe two races without even thinking. This would not only postpone premature resolution of the championship. It would also generate a storm of world-wide headlines and controversy. In business terms, a no-brainer.

AAbove: **Deep impact – and dire consequences. Rossi on the left will escape unharmed, but Melandri's right foot is about to be speared by his Honda's projecting footrest.**
Photograph: Gold & Goose

Above: Tamada shares with his home fans the reward after a season of tribulation. Behind, Hopkins (waving) had a career-best fifth.

Right: More than miffed, Nakano stomps away from his beached and blown-up Kawasaki.

Below right: Battaini may have been last, but was just out of the top ten. Finishing at all was beyond many riders.

Photographs: Gold & Goose

MOTOGP RACE – 24 laps

Bridgestone served notice in qualifying, taking the top two grid positions, pole man Capirossi the only rider to beat Tamada's (Bridgestone/Honda) pole of last year. Second-placed Hopkins was almost half-a-second slower, but it was still an impressive performance, at one track where his high corner speed compensated more generously for a lack of top speed. Melandri was top Honda and top Michelin runner, with Tamada, Biaggi and Hayden on a close second row.

And the World Champion elect? Eleventh was Rossi's worst qualification since 2001, and he admitted he was in trouble. Made worse when his team had a rare slip-up in practice. Normally past masters of getting the rider out on a qualifying tyre to cross the line just a few seconds before the chequered flag for an unassailable last flying lap, this time they missed it by some three seconds. The rear spindle had jammed while changing the wheel, costing vital seconds. In any case, the performance of the Bridgestones had put Rossi under unprecedented pressure, and brought new handling and stability issues to light… as generally happens when the pace increases.

For the first time in three years, all riders made it through the first turn. Attrition began soon afterwards, with wild card Matsudo crashing the Moriwaki on the first lap – Ellison had already withdrawn, unable to cope with the hard braking with an elbow injury. On lap three, Alex Hofmann and Roby Rolfo collided, the latter a surprised innocent victim. Hofmann broke a bone in his left ankle, out until the final race.

Melandri took the early lead, chased by Capirossi and Biaggi, Hopkins gradually losing ground, a little on every straight. Rossi had stormed off the line, up to seventh ahead of Hayden on lap one, past Gibernau and Hopkins on the next, then took fourth off Tamada one lap later. Behind him, Checa was also making his way past Gibernau and the Suzuki.

There was a slight gap to the leaders, and it stayed that way for a while, Tamada shadowing Rossi, then Checa, Hopkins and

Gibernau. At this stage, Rossi's position would be good enough for the title. Then they started shuffling up front.

Biaggi's first attack on lap eight actually lost ground, which he quickly regained. On lap ten he took second from Capirossi, and immediately started to hound the long-time leader.

Again his first attempt failed, as he dived inside at the end of the back straight only for Melandri to pass again on the exit. Two laps later, he made it stick, with Capirossi also moving past Melandri through the last underpass... nearly meeting a sticky end as he ran on to oil spilled by Nakano, whose new Kawasaki engine had blown up smokily on the ninth lap. By then Ukawa was long gone, pitting with a mystery mechanical failure after just five laps. Then Gibernau crashed out on the 12th lap, while battling Checa for sixth, leaving just 14 still in the race.

That number was to be cut still further before another lap was done, when Rossi and Melandri went out together, spectacularly. Rossi held his hands up after the crash. He hadn't been trying to overtake, he said. "The problem is Melandri is able, in the last part of the braking, to stop the bike better than me and close the line," he said. Shortly afterwards, Barros – labouring in eighth – also went down, on Nakano's spilled oil.

This left just two scrapping up front, by the end it became clear that while Biaggi was on the limit, his pursuer Capirossi had a little in hand. At the start of lap 19, he forced under Biaggi at the late apex to the first long U-turn, and from then on "tried to push one hundred percent," moving away to win by almost 1.5 seconds.

Biaggi had every reason to be proud of his close second, on tyres he was happy to admit were no match for Capirossi's Bridgestones. Tamada kept pushing on to a lone third, his best of the year.

The attrition left a processional race behind them, with not a single change of position for the last ten laps. Carlos Checa's fourth gave Ducati their best-ever two-rider finish. The Americans were strung out behind – Hopkins soldiering on relentlessly for a career-best fifth; Edwards closed to within 1.3 seconds after fighting front-end problems. Hayden had run off the track

on lap nine while tussling with Barros, doing his front tyre no good and rejoining three places down behind Roberts, getting past the second Suzuki with ten laps to go.

The slowly recovering Elias and the fast-declining Xaus trailed in behind, with Battaini again last, but in a career-best eleventh.

250 cc RACE – 23 laps

Team-mate Aoyama made hay as Pedrosa became a serial crasher, claiming his first pole of the year after the points leader hit the deck painfully three times. Lorenzo was alongside, and then the pole man's younger (by three years) brother Shuhei, a traditionally fast local wild card on a Harc-Prol Honda. His race, however, would end with a crash on lap three.

De Angelis completed the front row, Dovizioso led the second, with Pedrosa further along it, eight tenths down on pole.

Lorenzo took the early lead, with de Angelis shouldering Aoyama to third for a couple of laps. On the fifth, a reshuffle through the right-left saw the Japanese rider in front and Lorenzo third. Aoyama would lead from there to the flag.

At the same time, both Dovizioso and Stoner had got ahead of a cautious Pedrosa, whose usual wait-and-see policy would pay big dividends.

Up front, Aoyama's advantage remained slender, seldom more than half a second. Dovizioso was second from laps seven to nine, but de Angelis was the chief leader of a very close pack. At half distance, the first eight were covered by less than three seconds: Aoyama, de Angelis, Dovizioso, Stoner, Lorenzo, Takahashi, Pedrosa and de Puniet.

Over the next laps they stretched a little, while Pedrosa moved up to fifth. Lorenzo seemed to be losing ground behind him, with a gap of well over 1.5-seconds developing.

Then Aoyama gave it everything, stretching a rapidly growing lead to more than five seconds over the last five laps.

At the same time, Pedrosa was picking off the opposition – Stoner at the right before the entrance to the first tunnel;

Below: Aoyama starts to open up a lead on de Angelis and Dovizioso, with Pedrosa at the back of the group.
Photograph: Gold & Goose

Above: Racing-at-home-syndrome gave 250 regular Takahashi a year's best of fourth.

Above right: The same effect had Aoyama beaming after his only win of the season.

Below: Kallio and Faubel were on the rostrum, but second-placed Luthi was in the medical centre. KTM team boss Harald Bartol (orange shirt on left) was not sure he should be on the results sheet either.

Opposite bottom: Ex-250 racer Naoki Matsudo would not finish the first lap on the Moriwaki.

Photographs: Gold & Goose

Dovizioso in the same place next time round. Now he started to attack de Angelis, getting ahead several times on the penultimate lap.

Lorenzo was also on the charge, up to fourth on lap 21, leaving Stoner trailing slightly. He was lining up for his last-lap lunge, way too fast into the hairpin, with the lucky Pedrosa now ahead of de Angelis, and avoiding most of the carnage… though he did get a nudge on the preceding corner. Both Lorenzo and de Angelis fell, the latter remounting to finish seventh, eight seconds adrift.

Stoner rolled to a safe third, counting himself lucky to get a rostrum on a slowing machine.

A little behind, both Takahashi and de Puniet got ahead of the fading Dovizioso, one each on the final laps. Barbera was alone by the finish, some way behind de Angelis, then Debon prevailed in a three-way battle with Guintoli and Corsi.

The field was depleted by several other crashes. Smrz, Locatelli, Vincent and wild card Ryuji Yokoe crashed on the first lap, followed by West, the younger Aoyama, Chaz Davies and Porto, lying ninth behind his team-mate de Puniet, shortly before half-distance.

125 cc RACE – 15 laps

Talmacsi was on pole, title rivals Kallio and Luthi both on the second row, but it was Pasini who led the first lap of what would remain a very close race until the premature final stages.

Kallio took over for the next three laps, then Luthi for a spell, then Pasini again. These were just positions over the line, however, with places changing at almost every corner, as riders explored different lines and braking tactics.

After eight laps, the top ten were still covered by just a second, Pasini ahead from Talmacsi, Kallio, Luthi and Faubel. Poggiali was prominent in the gang, Simoncelli also – soon to crash out, with the ill-starred Gadea at the back in tenth.

Four more laps went by in similar fashion, nine now in the front gaggle, still within less than two seconds. Now it was Kallio up front, and on lap 13 he started to stretch the pace, only Luthi able to go with him, as they edged away.

By lap 15 they were better than 1.5-seconds clear. Faubel was best of the rest, then Koyama was narrowly ahead of a pack of five, from Pasini, Poggiali, Gadea and Nieto.

The horrific crash happened as they completed lap 16; Gadea unsighted in that big gang. Luthi was left prone, the motorcycles reduced almost to component parts. Amazingly, Gadea was able to run off the track, unhurt.

The result cut Luthi's championship lead to three points. Had he been ruled out of the results as per Harald Bartol's suggestion, he would have been 17 points behind Kallio instead.

It also brought the record of 125 races without a consecutive winner to a round 50.

TWIN RING MOTEGI

CIRCUIT LENGTH: 2.983 miles/4.801 km

GRAND PRIX OF JAPAN

28 AUGUST 2005 • FIM WORLD CHAMPIONSHIP ROUND 12

MotoGP

24 laps, 71.592 miles/115.224 km

Pos.	Rider (Nat.)	No.	Machine	Laps	Time & speed
1	Loris Capirossi (I)	65	Ducati	24	43m 30.499s 98.735 mph/ 158.899 km/h
2	Max Biaggi (I)	3	Honda	24	43m 31.978s
3	Makoto Tamada (J)	6	Honda	24	43m 46.726s
4	Carlos Checa (E)	7	Ducati	24	43m 52.647s
5	John Hopkins (USA)	21	Suzuki	24	44m 03.711s
6	Colin Edwards (USA)	5	Yamaha	24	44m 05.414s
7	Nicky Hayden (USA)	69	Honda	24	44m 16.393s
8	Kenny Roberts (USA)	10	Suzuki	24	44m 26.997s
9	Toni Elias (E)	24	Yamaha	24	44m 42.536s
10	Ruben Xaus (E)	11	Yamaha	24	45m 05.426s
11	Franco Battaini (I)	27	Blata	23	44m 38.510s
	Marco Melandri (I)	33	Honda	12	DNF
	Valentino Rossi (I)	46	Yamaha	12	DNF
	Alex Barros (BR)	4	Honda	12	DNF
	Sete Gibernau (E)	15	Honda	11	DNF
	Shinya Nakano (J)	56	Kawasaki	8	DNF
	Tohru Ukawa (J)	72	Honda	4	DNF
	Roberto Rolfo (I)	44	Ducati	2	DNF
	Alex Hofmann (D)	66	Kawasaki	2	DNF
	Naoki Matsudo (J)	45	Moriwaki	0	DNF
	James Ellison (GB)	77	Blata		DNS

Fastest lap: Capirossi, 1m 47.968s, 99.469 mph/160.080 km/h (record).

Previous record: Makoto Tamada, J (Honda), 1m 48.524s, 98.960 mph/159.260 km/h (2004).

Event best maximum speed: Elias, 192.1 mph/309.2 km/h (free practice no. 1).

Qualifying: 1 Capirossi, 1m 46.363s; 2 Hopkins, 1m 46.861s; 3 Melandri, 1m 46.867s; 4 Tamada, 1m 47.043s; 5 Biaggi, 1m 47.089s; 6 Hayden, 1m 47.166s; 7 Gibernau, 1m 47.168s; 8 Roberts, 1m 47.257s; 9 Checa, 1m 47.323s; 10 Barros, 1m 47.562s; 11 Rossi, 1m 47.563s; 12 Hofmann, 1m 47.594s; 13 Edwards, 1m 47.678s; 14 Nakano, 1m 47.787s; 15 Ukawa, 1m 48.194s; 16 Rolfo, 1m 48.733s; 17 Elias, 1m 48.861s; 18 Matsudo, 1m 49.734s; 19 Xaus, 1m 49.969s; 20 Battaini, 1m 51.902s; 21 Ellison, 1m 51.972s.

Fastest race laps (After Race Part 2): 1 Capirossi, 1m 47.968s; 2 Biaggi, 1m 47.985s; 3 Rossi, 1m 48.014s; 4 Melandri, 1m 48.186s; 5 Tamada, 1m 48.207s; 6 Checa, 1m 48.489s; 7 Hopkins, 1m 48.561s; 8 Gibernau, 1m 48.592s; 9 Barros, 1m 48.731s; 10 Nakano, 1m 48.841s; 11 Hayden, 1m 48.883s; 12 Edwards, 1m 48.945s; 13 Roberts, 1m 48.985s; 14 Ukawa, 1m 49.477s; 15 Rolfo, 1m 50.635s; 16 Elias, 1m 50.748s; 17 Hofmann, 1m 50.864s; 18 Xaus, 1m 51.585s; 19 Battaini, 1m 53.274s.

World Championship: 1 Rossi, 261; 2 Biaggi, 149; 3 Edwards, 133; 4 Melandri, 126; 5 Hayden, 121; 6 Capirossi, 117; 7 Gibernau, 115; 8 Barros, 114; 9 C. Checa, 72; 10 Nakano, 69; 11 Tamada, 64; 12 Bayliss, 54; 13 Roberts, 49; 14 Hopkins, 46; 15 Xaus, 42; 16 Elias, 38; 17 Jacque, 25; 18 Hofmann, 22; 19 Rolfo, 15; 20 van den Goorbergh, 12; 21 Battaini, 6; 22 D. Checa and Ellison, 4; 24 Byrne and Ukawa, 1.

250 cc

23 laps, 68.609 miles/110.423 km

Pos.	Rider (Nat.)	No.	Machine	Laps	Time & speed
1	Hiroshi Aoyama (J)	73	Honda	23	43m 52.454s 93.832 mph/ 151.008 km/h
2	Daniel Pedrosa (E)	1	Honda	23	43m 57.767s
3	Casey Stoner (AUS)	27	Aprilia	23	44m 00.235s
4	Yuki Takahashi (J)	55	Honda	23	44m 02.676s
5	Randy de Puniet (F)	7	Aprilia	23	44m 03.217s
6	Andrea Dovizioso (I)	34	Honda	23	44m 03.508s
7	Alex de Angelis (RSM)	5	Aprilia	23	44m 11.653s
8	Hector Barbera (E)	80	Honda	23	44m 17.119s
9	Alex Debon (E)	6	Honda	23	44m 30.137s
10	Sylvain Guintoli (F)	50	Aprilia	23	44m 30.576s
11	Simone Corsi (I)	24	Aprilia	23	44m 30.648s
12	Steve Jenkner (D)	17	Aprilia	23	44m 46.665s
13	Mirko Giansanti (I)	32	Aprilia	23	44m 48.818s
14	Alex Baldolini (I)	25	Aprilia	23	45m 01.094s
15	Radomil Rous (CZ)	64	Honda	23	45m 01.659s
16	Kouki Takahashi (J)	93	Honda	23	45m 10.436s
17	Martin Cardenas (COL)	36	Aprilia	23	45m 17.550s
18	Dirk Heidolf (D)	28	Honda	23	45m 18.542s
19	Mamoru Akiya (J)	77	Yamaha	23	45m 25.740s
20	Masaki Tokudome (J)	79	Yamaha	23	45m 28.052s
21	Mathieu Gines (F)	56	Aprilia	23	45m 30.006s
	Jorge Lorenzo (E)	48	Honda	22	DNF
	Taro Sekiguchi (J)	44	Aprilia	21	DNF
	Sebastian Porto (ARG)	19	Aprilia	10	DNF
	Andrea Ballerini (I)	8	Aprilia	10	DNF
	Chaz Davies (GB)	57	Aprilia	5	DNF
	Shuhei Aoyama (J)	75	Honda	2	DNF
	Anthony West (AUS)	14	KTM	2	DNF
	Roberto Locatelli (I)	15	Aprilia	0	DNF
	Arnaud Vincent (F)	21	Fantic	0	DNF
	Ryuji Yokoe (J)	78	Yamaha	0	DNF
	Jakub Smrz (CZ)	96	Honda	0	DNF
	Nicklas Cajback (S)	23	Yamaha		DNQ
	Gabriele Ferro (I)	20	Fantic		DNQ
	Alexander Todorov (BUL)	22	Yamaha		DNQ

Fastest lap: Pedrosa, 1m 53.199s, 94.873 mph/152.683 km/h.

Previous record: Shinya Nakano, J (Yamaha), 1m 52.253s, 95.673 mph/153.970 km/h (2000).

Event best maximum speed: Porto, 163.7 mph/263.5 km/h (qualifying practice no. 1).

Qualifying: 1 H. Aoyama, 1m 51.843s; 2 Lorenzo, 1m 51.859s; 3 S. Aoyama, 1m 52.374s; 4 de Angelis, 1m 52.408s; 5 Dovizioso, 1m 52.603s; 6 Y. Takahashi, 1m 52.634s; 7 Pedrosa, 1m 52.662s; 8 de Puniet, 1m 52.890s; 9 Stoner, 1m 52.923s; 10 Porto, 1m 52.966s; 11 Guintoli, 1m 53.768s; 12 Sekiguchi, 1m 53.868s; 13 Barbera, 1m 53.925s; 14 West, 1m 53.970s; 15 Jenkner, 1m 54.060s; 16 Debon, 1m 54.245s; 17 Locatelli, 1m 54.345s; 18 Yokoe, 1m 54.435s; 19 Smrz, 1m 54.458s; 20 Heidolf, 1m 54.512s; 21 Giansanti, 1m 54.539s; 22 Rous, 1m 55.006s; 23 Davies, 1m 55.065s; 24 Corsi, 1m 55.105s; 25 Tokudome, 1m 55.206s; 26 Ballerini, 1m 55.240s; 27 Baldolini, 1m 55.789s; 28 K. Takahashi, 1m 55.815s; 29 Cardenas, 1m 55.986s; 30 Akiya, 1m 56.647s; 31 Vincent, 1m 56.936s; 32 Gines, 1m 56.955s; 33 Cajback, 2m 00.469s; 34 Ferro, 2m 02.055s; 35 Todorov, 2m 03.740s.

Fastest race laps: 1 Pedrosa, 1m 53.199s; 2 H. Aoyama, 1m 53.502s; 3 de Angelis, 1m 53.793s; 4 Dovizioso, 1m 53.820s; 5 Lorenzo, 1m 53.850s; 6 Stoner, 1m 53.896s; 7 de Puniet, 1m 53.932s; 8 Y. Takahashi, 1m 53.988s; 9 Porto, 1m 54.025s; 10 Barbera, 1m 54.300s; 11 Guintoli, 1m 54.940s; 12 Debon, 1m 54.954s; 13 S. Aoyama, 1m 55.050s; 14 Corsi, 1m 55.408s; 15 Jenkner, 1m 55.499s; 16 Heidolf, 1m 55.588s; 17 Giansanti, 1m 55.685s; 18 Sekiguchi, 1m 55.737s; 19 Davies, 1m 55.846s; 20 West, 1m 55.850s; 21 Baldolini, 1m 55.994s; 22 Rous, 1m 56.197s; 23 Cardenas, 1m 56.751s; 24 K. Takahashi, 1m 56.836s; 25 Ballerini, 1m 56.838s; 26 Akiya, 1m 57.289s; 27 Tokudome, 1m 57.365s; 28 Gines, 1m 57.452s.

World Championship: 1 Pedrosa, 226; 2 Stoner, 163; 3 Dovizioso, 144; 4 H. Aoyama, 123; 5 de Angelis, 109; 6 de Puniet, 108; 7 Porto, 105; 8 Lorenzo, 98; 9 Barbera, 67; 10 Corsi, 59; 11 Guintoli, 55; 12 Y. Takahashi, 51; 13 Debon, 46; 14 Locatelli, 31; 15 West, 30; 16 Giansanti, 27; 17 Baldolini, 20; 18 Davies, 17; 19 Ballerini, 14; 20 Rous and Smrz, 11; 22 Jenkner, 7; 23 Leblanc, 6; 24 Heidolf, 4; 25 Marchand and Nigon, 3; 26 Cardenas, 2.

125 cc

15 laps, 44.745 miles/72.015 km

Pos.	Rider (Nat.)	No.	Machine	Laps	Time & speed
1	Mika Kallio (SF)	36	KTM	15	30m 10.854s 88.959 mph/ 143.166 km/h
2	Thomas Luthi (CH)	12	Honda	15	30m 10.965s
3	Hector Faubel (E)	55	Aprilia	15	30m 12.371s
4	Tomoyoshi Koyama (J)	71	Honda	15	30m 13.203s
5	Mattia Pasini (I)	75	Aprilia	15	30m 13.260s
6	Manuel Poggiali (RSM)	54	Gilera	15	30m 13.473s
7	Sergio Gadea (E)	33	Aprilia	15	30m 13.615s
8	Pablo Nieto (E)	22	Derbi	15	30m 13.815s
9	Alvaro Bautista (E)	19	Honda	15	30m 14.574s
10	Fabrizio Lai (I)	32	Honda	15	30m 20.790s
11	Mike di Meglio (F)	63	Honda	15	30m 25.400s
12	Aleix Espargaro (E)	41	Honda	15	30m 25.547s
13	Andrea Iannone (I)	29	Aprilia	15	30m 26.553s
14	Toshihisa Kuzuhara (J)	9	Honda	15	30m 31.687s
15	Enrique Jerez (E)	51	Derbi	15	30m 33.416s
16	Raffaele de Rosa (I)	35	Aprilia	15	30m 34.892s
17	Lorenzo Zanetti (I)	8	Aprilia	15	30m 36.761s
18	Joan Olive (E)	6	Aprilia	15	30m 37.868s
19	Manuel Hernandez (E)	43	Aprilia	15	30m 38.356s
20	Alexis Masbou (F)	7	Honda	15	30m 38.402s
21	Imre Toth (H)	45	Aprilia	15	30m 58.841s
22	Hiroaki Kuzuhara (J)	68	Honda	15	30m 59.191s
23	Federico Sandi (I)	10	Honda	15	30m 59.378s
24	Yuki Hamamoto (J)	64	Honda	15	31m 01.940s
25	Takumi Takahashi (J)	20	Honda	15	31m 04.384s
26	Arata Mori (J)	66	Honda	15	31m 04.464s
27	Vincent Braillard (CH)	26	Aprilia	15	31m 05.506s
28	Karel Abraham (CZ)	44	Aprilia	15	31m 06.308s
29	Kazuki Hanafusa (J)	67	Honda	15	31m 14.418s
30	Jordi Carchano (E)	28	Aprilia	13	30m 18.069s
	Gabor Talmacsi (H)	14	KTM	13	DNF
	Lukas Pesek (CZ)	52	Derbi	13	DNF
	Dario Giuseppetti (D)	25	Aprilia	12	DNF
	Marco Simoncelli (I)	58	Aprilia	9	DNF
	Sascha Hommel (D)	31	Malaguti	9	DNF
	Mateo Tunez (E)	46	Aprilia	7	DNF
	Hiroomi Iwata (J)	65	Honda	6	DNF
	Michele Pirro (I)	15	Malaguti	5	DNF
	Sandro Cortese (D)	11	Honda	3	DNF
	David Bonache (E)	48	Honda	0	DNF
	Julian Simon (E)	60	KTM	0	DNF

Fastest lap: Tunez, 1m 59.018s, 90.234 mph/145.218 km/h.

Previous record: Daniel Pedrosa, E (Honda) 1m 58.354s, 90.741 mph/146.033 km/h (2002).

Event best maximum speed: Tunez, 143.0 mph/230.1 km/h (race).

Qualifying: 1 Talmacsi, 1m 58.653s; 2 Koyama, 1m 58.920s; 3 Pasini, 1m 58.970s; 4 Simoncelli, 1m 59.038s; 5 Kallio, 1m 59.137s; 6 Faubel, 1m 59.143s; 7 Luthi, 1m 59.363s; 8 Poggiali, 1m 59.460s; 9 Bautista, 1m 59.539s; 10 Gadea, 1m 59.596s; 11 Simon, 1m 59.660s; 12 de Meglio, 1m 59.724s; 13 Nieto, 1m 59.874s; 14 Lai, 1m 59.982s; 15 Tunez, 2m 00.106s; 16 Cortese, 2m 00.181s; 17 Jerez, 2m 00.281s; 18 Zanetti, 2m 00.287s; 19 Iannone, 2m 00.288s; 20 T. Kuzuhara, 2m 00.301s; 21 Masbou, 2m 00.436s; 22 de Rosa, 2m 00.453s; 23 Pesek, 2m 00.750s; 24 Espargaro, 2m 00.754s; 25 Toth, 2m 00.756s; 26 Hernandez, 2m 01.015s; 27 Olive, 2m 01.126s; 28 Giuseppetti, 2m 01.788s; 29 Takahashi, 2m 01.974s; 30 Abraham, 2m 02.043s; 31 H. Kuzuhara, 2m 02.080s; 32 Hamamoto, 2m 02.224s; 33 Mori, 2m 02.274s; 34 Sandi, 2m 02.553s; 35 Iwata, 2m 02.664s; 36 Carchano, 2m 02.770s; 37 Pirro, 2m 02.885s; 38 Braillard, 2m 03.341s; 39 Bonache, 2m 03.463s; 40 Hommel, 2m 04.379s; 41 Hanafusa, 2m 04.673s.

Fastest race laps: 1 Tunez, 1m 59.018s; 2 Faubel, 1m 59.510s; 3 Talmacsi, 1m 59.555s; 4 Simoncelli, 1m 59.581s; 5 Luthi, 1m 59.613s; 6 Kallio, 1m 59.660s; 7 Gadea, 1m 59.678s; 8 Bautista, 1m 59.764s; 9 Poggiali, 1m 59.779s; 10 Koyama, 1m 59.785s; 11 Pasini, 1m 59.864s; 12 Nieto, 1m 59.951s; 13 Lai, 2m 00.112s; 14 di Meglio, 2m 00.252s; 15 Espargaro, 2m 00.449s; 16 Iannone, 2m 00.479s; 17 Olive, 2m 00.510s; 18 Masbou, 2m 00.768s; 19 T. Kuzuhara, 2m 00.792s; 20 Jerez, 2m 00.835s; 21 Hernandez, 2m 00.928s; 22 Pesek, 2m 00.942s; 23 de Rosa, 2m 01.020s; 24 Cortese, 2m 01.021s; 25 Zanetti, 2m 01.117s; 26 Toth, 2m 02.226s; 27 Giuseppetti, 2m 02.381s; 28 Takahashi, 2m 02.390s; 29 Mori, 2m 02.548s; 30 Sandi, 2m 02.554s; 31 H. Kuzuhara, 2m 02.608s; 32 Hamamoto, 2m 02.671s; 33 Iwata, 2m 02.703s; 34 Carchano, 2m 02.787s; 35 Pirro, 2m 02.897s; 36 Abraham, 2m 02.900s; 37 Braillard, 2m 03.085s; 38 Hanafusa, 2m 03.381s; 39 Hommel, 2m 03.679s.

World Championship: 1 Luthi, 164; 2 Kallio, 161; 3 Talmacsi, 120; 4 Simoncelli, 117; 5 Pasini, 111; 6 Lai, 104; 7 Simon, 97; 8 Poggiali, 82; 9 Faubel, 66; 10 Koyama, 65; 11 di Meglio, 59; 12 Gadea, 57; 13 Nieto, 55; 14 Olive, 45; 15 Bautista, 39; 16 Espargaro and Zanetti, 30; 18 Masbou, 20; 19 Pesek, 18; 20 T. Kuzuhara, 17; 21 Iannone, 13; 22 Hernandez and Ranseder, 12; 24 Linfoot and Toth, 7; 26 Carchano and Cortese, 6; 28 Conti, 5; 29 Elkin, 4; 30 Giuseppetti and Pirro, 3; 32 de Rosa, 2; 33 Bradl, Jerez and Terol, 1.

MALAYSIANGP
SEPANG

One champion, one winner. Rossi, in Barry Sheene-tribute tee-shirt, congratulates his victorious compatriot Capirossi.
Photograph: Gold & Goose

Above: Snow White and the Seven Championships – this was Rossi's most elaborate show yet.

Right: Jorge Lorenzo was an unwilling pedestrian.

Below right: Flat-screen pit furniture fails to capture Barros's attention.

Centre right: Luckless lizard was a sitting duck for Rossi.

Opposite top: Beaming Shakey Byrne was in at the deep end on Camel's second bike.

Opposite centre: Olivier Jacque got another last-minute call, in place of the injured Hofmann.

Photographs: Gold & Goose

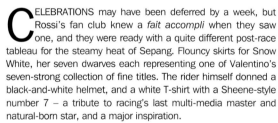

CELEBRATIONS may have been deferred by a week, but Rossi's fan club knew a *fait accompli* when they saw one, and they were ready with a quite different post-race tableau for the steamy heat of Sepang. Flouncy skirts for Snow White, her seven dwarves each representing one of Valentino's seven-strong collection of fine titles. The rider himself donned a black-and-white helmet, and a white T-shirt with a Sheene-style number 7 – a tribute to racing's last multi-media master and natural-born star, and a major inspiration.

If the fact that for once he didn't seal his title with a win took away any of the gloss, he certainly didn't let it show. His vanquisher was an old friend, after all; and Ducatis are as Italian as Valentino himself. That just added to the high.

Rossi would still have been champion if he had finished third... and he very nearly did, as an avenging Carlos Checa closed to within feet over the line. Because whatever advantage the Bridgestone users had found at Motegi was here at Sepang again, with bells on. They had dominated practice and qualifying, with Capirossi reeling off yet more strings of very fast laps on race tyres; and the front two rows of the grid taking in both Suzukis and one Kawasaki, enjoying the same benefit. In Rossi's words: "The Bridgestones are like in another sport."

Michelin race boss Nicolas Goubert was left with little more than his familiar rueful smile, and to promise that things would be different at the upcoming tracks, in Qatar and Phillip Island. Events would prove him at least half-right. Impressive as these Bridgestone lap times were, however, they were not as fast as those set in pre-season tests, and in fact only

Capirossi improved on Rossi's 2004 pole time. Dirt, said some, wear and tear on the surface, said others. The effect was the same for all.

The middle of the three flyaways already had a fair crop of walking wounded, and tales of great personal heroism. Just look at Marco Melandri. On Wednesday he was still in a wheelchair, a drain tube in his gruesome foot wound. On Friday morning, he was on his RC211V, finding ways to get around the problem of not being able to exert full weight on the right footpeg in left-hand corners – an essential element in playing power against traction for a fast exit. James Ellison was also back, braving the pain of his elbow injury at a track more flowing than stop-and-go Motegi. And Luthi was a shining example of true grit. Limping heavily and with a painful shoulder, he qualified on pole and won the race, a week after having been run over. In all cases, this especially, it vindicated the medical authorities who had pronounced them fit to race. Even so, it remained impossible to avoid concern at the prevalence of gung ho over go-slow in the treatment of injuries and injured riders.

On a brighter note – certainly in terms of the yellow leathers and fairing, Shane Byrne at last found himself on a seriously competitive MotoGP bike, an opportunity so far denied the ex-Aprilia, ex-Proton Englishman. His debut on Bayliss's Camel Honda put him right in at the deep end, among riders not only familiar with the machine but also hardened by two-thirds of a season's racing on it. "I didn't wake up nervous," he said on Friday. "Because I didn't go to sleep at all." He'd even slipped his new leathers on during the night, just to have a look. Another stranger on the grid was Olivier Jacque, the Hero of Shanghai back on Hofmann's Kawasaki. On his return to Germany, doctors had discovered no less than eight fractures in his ankle, and he was out for the long haul.

GP folk had taken what R&R they could – some taking rides in an F1 powerboat, Colin Edwards visiting Bangkok in the short break. But he was uneasy about his wife, child and family at home in Texas not far from Houston, currently being evacuated in preparation for Hurricane Rita – not to mention his investment properties in Galveston, threatened with flooding. "It feels kind of weird to be lazing by the pool not knowing what's going on," he said. A week later, all safe and sound, he grinned and said: "We dodged the bullet."

There was light relief of a sort over at Lorenzo's pit, where a sign reading "Back in Qatar" hung over the disqualified rider's empty chair, in shop-keeper style. And some mild excitement to be had from MV Agusta chief executive Claudio Castiglioni, the former Cagiva man promising a future return to GP racing for the famous old marque, recently bought by Proton Cars, hence his presence at Sepang. It remained distant, to come only after a World Superbike campaign, itself still in the planning stage.

And yet another incident with the local wild life... something of a trademark in Malaysia, going back even before the famous incident with a rearing cobra at Johor Bahru in 1998. This time the victim was a large iguana lizard, wandering out onto the start of the pit straight in the closing stages of MotoGP qualifying. The creature was hit first by Rolfo, then Rossi dealt the *coup de grace.* Then arrived Gibernau, at the finish of a lap in which he had set fastest time in all sectors so far, on target to depose Capirossi from a second consecutive pole. He got such a shock when he saw the remains that he dived off into pit-lane instead.

Pedrosa carrying an unrevealed injury, had another crash... this time in the race. It was his first race crash since Jerez at the start of the 2004 season, and had the positive effect of spicing up the title battle. Race winner Casey Stoner may still be 40 points adrift, but a long shot is better than no chance at all.

Ducati's first double rostrum finish, sandwiching a Yamaha, meant the first race without a single Honda on the rostrum for a long time. Sadly, it took place in the absence of Marlboro Ducati team chief Livio Suppo, who flew home on the eve of the meeting because of a family bereavement.

Opposite: *Capirossi ahead of Rossi and Hayden... by the end he was unbeatable.*

Below: *Melandri, out of a wheelchair and onto a motorcycle, rests his injured foot.*

Bottom: *Checa hugs team-mate Loris, after Ducati's first double rostrum.*
Photographs: Gold & Goose

MOTOGP RACE – 21 laps

Again, the Bridgestones were strong, filling the top five with 20 minutes of qualifying to go: Capirossi, Checa, Roberts, Hopkins and Nakano, Rossi down in eighth. By the finish, Gibernau put in a flyer to put Michelin on top, only for Capirossi to go again. Then it was three more Bridgestone users: Hopkins on a second successive front row; Nakano and Roberts heading Hayden's Michelin Honda on the next. Rossi led row three, more than half-a-second slower than he'd been a year ago. Melandri was a remarkable ninth.

It was sultry and overcast for the race, but the ever-threatening showers stayed in abeyance. Capirossi won the drag race from Hayden and Gibernau, but the latter was squeezed into the first tight right by Melandri on the inside, and ran into Hayden, lucky not to fall. This let Melandri and Nakano through, and sent riders behind swerving all over the place. Rossi narrowly escaped involvement, and was past Roberts into sixth before half the lap was done.

Melandri's Honda power meant he could duck under Nakano into the first corner as they started the second lap. Gibernau made the same move on Hayden. Now he had Nakano's green Kawasaki a little way ahead, and he also used his speed to close up on the back straight. His run up the inside, however, was over-ambitious. He ran wide and straight into Nakano, taking them both out of the race. Yet another disaster for Sete...

All the while, Capirossi was inching away. Then Hayden found his way past Melandri to take up the pursuit. The Italian was in no condition to fight back, nor when Rossi eased past also on lap four, to take a closer view on how Hayden was starting to lean on the Ducati. Capirossi was in control, however, easing the pace to save his tyre advantage.

On lap six, Hayden's persistence merely led him to run wide, and Rossi caught right up, the three pulling clear of the gradually fading Melandri. He now had Checa closing – the second Ducati rider a big loser in the first-corner tangle, finishing the first lap eighth. He'd come storming past Roberts on lap three, and in five laps had closed the 1.5 seconds on Melandri, and got past him too. Now the leaders were just 2.5 seconds away, with 13 laps to go, and he was catching them.

Up front, another flawed attack at Turn One put Hayden wide

again, and this time Rossi slipped through into second. But the first three stayed together unchanged for a while, as Checa nibbled away at the gap, using the clear track to the full.

After half-distance, Capirossi had a little wobble. Was he feeling the pressure? Rossi attacked on the very next corner, and took the lead for two laps. The first four were bunching up now.

This was Capirossi's signal. It was time to up the stakes. He easily out-powered Rossi down the pit straight and outbraked him into the first corner as they started lap 14. At the end of it, the first four were still within less than 1.3 seconds, but directly afterwards the leading Ducati started easing away. Soon Capirossi was settled into a string of fast laps at maximum effort, that extended his lead by almost two seconds.

Rossi chased hard, but knew it was hopeless. "I realised he'd been playing with me like a cat with a mouse," he said later. Hayden couldn't keep up, but nor could Checa find a way past him, until the 17th lap, with a do-or-die lunge under braking for the final hairpin. Four laps to go, and a 2.5-second gap to Rossi. Carlos's Ducati-Bridgestone combination was clearly faster, but the race just too short. He pulled almost alongside across the finish line, beaten by just seven hundredths of a second. "I think he has ridden before," the Spaniard joked afterwards.

Hayden, fighting chatter all race long after damaging his front tyre in the first-corner melee, came home a safe fourth. Melandri had been losing ground, but keeping an eye on the group behind. This had been led by Roberts until lap eight, by when Biaggi, Barros and Hopkins were piled up behind, with Edwards in close attendance, all covered by less than three seconds.

Biaggi was the only one who actually managed to pass the former double Sepang winner, having an unusually steadfast race. Barros was close behind at the end, then Hopkins and Edwards a couple of seconds apart. Hopkins's front-row start had been negated in the first turn, when he braked too early, then ran into the muddle of swerving traffic. He finished the first lap 11th, and didn't overtake anybody all race long.

Elias just about still had the off-form Edwards in sight – the rest were widely spaced: Tamada in all sorts of trouble, then Rolfo. V5 rookie Byrne was kept honest by Xaus, whose final attack brought him to within two tenths.

Jacque retired to the pits with 17 laps left; Ellison managed another 13 before following suit.

Above: With Pedrosa out, winner Stoner (centre) saw an inkling of a title chance. De Angelis (left) and Porto were second and third.

Opposite: Two in a row for Loris Capirossi.

Below: Photo-finish for the 125s... but returned injury victim Luthi was still just in front of Kallio.

Photographs: Gold & Goose

250 cc RACE – 20 laps

In Lorenzo's absence, Telefónica's Aoyama took a second successive pole, with team-mate Pedrosa less than a tenth down. The Aprilias of de Angelis and Stoner completed the first row, Porto's led the second.

Pedrosa was at the front as the pack swivelled right to left for the second corner, Dovizioso in around fifth when he slipped and flipped over the high-side in the middle of the corner. Everyone avoided him, though Rous fell a little way behind, probably as a result, but the incident split up the leaders.

Stoner was in front by the end of lap one, and de Angelis also ahead of Pedrosa. The points leader was still close behind as they approached the latter part of lap two, but on the fast rights leading onto the back straight, he slid gracefully off the low side and out of the race. It was his first race crash since early last year. His face, after a scooter ride back to the pits, was a picture of baffled dismay.

Stoner was blissfully clear of all this drama, and used the opportunity to stretch gradually away, all the way to the chequered flag. De Angelis gave chase as best he could, but after just eight laps he was already three seconds adrift. He kept pushing hard until a near crash on lap 14 changed his mind. He eased off, and so too did Stoner, to keep the gap to the finish.

It was a largely processional race, but for some battling in the first half between Aoyama and team-mates Porto and de Puniet. The Japanese rider was up front at first, then de Puniet swept past both of them to hold the position from laps five to 12. He never had an inch, however, and when he ran wide at the start of lap 13 Porto pounced, to hold the rostrum position to the flag... by when his closing gallop had brought him to within a second of de Angelis.

De Puniet was relieved of Aoyama's persistent attacks only in the closing laps. Barbera was a lonely sixth; behind him Takahashi finally triumphed over long-time adversary Locatelli. A long way back came a bitter privateers' battle. Guintoli was the narrow winner from Sekiguchi, with Heidolf close behind, and Davies dropping away in the closing laps, though he did save 12th from Giansanti by half-a-second.

Cardenas had been heading the group, but fell on the last corner in sight of the flag, remounting for 15th behind Jenkner.

Debon had fallen alone on lap one; Ballerini and Corsi also fell. Fellow-tumblers Pedrosa and Dovizioso had been the last two in the class with a perfect scoring record in every race.

125 cc RACE – 19 laps

Luthi's pole was a triumph over pain and awkwardness. Pasini was alongside, then the KTM pair, Kallio and Talmacsi.

A multiple pile-up in the first right-left complex thinned the field and led to an unusually processional race in this class too. The victims were Bautista, Abraham, de Rosa, Braillard and Sandi, Bautista scrambling back on board to rejoin in last.

Luthi was already in the lead and making an early attempt to break away. KTM's rookie Simon was second at the end of lap one, heading Pasini, Kallio and Talmacsi.

Kallio was up to third next time round, and on the fourth lap both he and Talmacsi displaced Simon. At this stage, Luthi was a second clear.

At half distance, the Finnish rider started to close the gap bit by bit, the two of them breaking clear of the brawl, where Simon was still giving good account of himself, up to third again on lap 13.

If Kallio hoped Luthi's injuries would weaken him in the closing stages, it was in vain. The Swiss rider kept a cool head under sustained attack, Kallio's last-corner exit bringing him almost alongside over the line. Luthi won, by just two thousandths.

Over the last four laps Faubel had closed on the pursuit group, and was at the front of it as they started the last one. Pasini regained his rostrum spot over the line; Talmacsi and Simon still close.

Lai narrowly led the next big gang over the line, from Poggiali, Simoncelli, Koyama, di Meglio, Pesek and Nieto. Kuzuhara crashed out on the last lap.

MARLBORO MALAYSIAN MOTOCYCLE GRAND PRIX

25 SEPTEMBER 2005 • FIM WORLD CHAMPIONSHIP ROUND 13

TURN 3
TURN 4
TURN 2
TURN 5
TURN 6
TURN 1
PENANG STRAIGHT
TURN 14
TURN 7
TURN 13
TURN 9
TURN 8
TURN 12
TURN 11

CIRCUIT LENGTH:
3.447 miles/5.548 km

MotoGP

21 laps, 72.387 miles/116.508 km

Pos.	Rider (Nat.)	No.	Machine	Laps	Time & speed
1	Loris Capirossi (I)	65	Ducati	21	43m 27.523s 99.949 mph/ 160.853 km/h
2	Valentino Rossi (I)	46	Yamaha	21	43m 29.522s
3	Carlos Checa (E)	7	Ducati	21	43m 29.592s
4	Nicky Hayden (USA)	69	Honda	21	43m 36.750s
5	Marco Melandri (I)	33	Honda	21	43m 43.409s
6	Max Biaggi (I)	3	Honda	21	43m 44.349s
7	Kenny Roberts (USA)	10	Suzuki	21	43m 44.772s
8	Alex Barros (BR)	4	Honda	21	43m 45.744s
9	John Hopkins (USA)	21	Suzuki	21	43m 47.648s
10	Colin Edwards (USA)	5	Yamaha	21	43m 49.798s
11	Toni Elias (E)	24	Yamaha	21	43m 57.379s
12	Makoto Tamada (J)	6	Honda	21	44m 19.195s
13	Roberto Rolfo (I)	44	Ducati	21	44m 32.888s
14	Shane Byrne (GB)	67	Honda	21	44m 46.629s
15	Ruben Xaus (E)	11	Yamaha	21	44m 46.879s
16	Franco Battaini (I)	27	Blata	21	45m 23.405s
	James Ellison (GB)	77	Blata	17	DNF
	Olivier Jacque (F)	19	Kawasaki	4	DNF
	Shinya Nakano (J)	56	Kawasaki	1	DNF
	Sete Gibernau (E)	15	Honda	1	DNF

Fastest lap: Hayden, 2m 02.993s, 100.903 mph/162.389 km/h (record).

Previous record: Valentino Rossi, I (Yamaha), 2m 03.253s, 100.691 mph/162.047 km/h (2004).

Event best maximum speed: Melandri, 197.2 mph/317.3 km/h (free practice no. 1).

Qualifying:: 1 Capirossi, 2m 01.731s; 2 Gibernau, 2m 01.867s; 3 Hopkins, 2m 02.017s; 4 Nakano, 2m 02.178s; 5 Roberts, 2m 02.215s; 6 Hayden, 2m 02.377s; 7 Rossi, 2m 02.412s; 8 Checa, 2m 02.419s; 9 Melandri, 2m 02.660s; 10 Edwards, 2m 02.805s; 11 Barros, 2m 03.013s; 12 Biaggi, 2m 03.210s; 13 Jacque, 2m 03.364s; 14 Elias, 2m 03.397s; 15 Tamada, 2m 03.974s; 16 Xaus, 2m 04.010s; 17 Rolfo, 2m 05.092s; 18 Byrne, 2m 06.493s; 19 Battaini, 2m 07.492s; 20 Ellison, 2m 08.352s.

Fastest race laps: 1 Hayden, 2m 02.993s; 2 Rossi, 2m 03.328s; Capirossi, 2m 03.435s; 4 Checa, 2m 03.527s; 5 Hopkins, 2m 03.681s; 6 Roberts, 2m 03.686s; 7 Melandri, 2m 03.699s; 8 Biaggi, 2m 03.817s; 9 Barros, 2m 03.854s; 10 Edwards, 2m 04.131s; 11 Elias, 2m 04.471s; 12 Tamada, 2m 05.051s; 13 Jacque, 2m 05.089s; 14 Rolfo, 2m 06.070s; 15 Byrne, 2m 06.743s; 16 Xaus, 2m 07.014s; 17 Ellison, 2m 07.378s; 18 Battaini, 2m 08.652s; 19 Nakano, 2m 09.640s; 20 Gibernau, 2m 10.100s.

World Championship: 1 Rossi, 281; 2 Biaggi, 159; 3 Capirossi, 142; 4 Edwards, 139; 5 Melandri, 137; 6 Hayden, 134; 7 Barros, 122; 8 Gibernau, 115; 9 C. Checa, 88; 10 Nakano, 69; 11 Tamada, 68; 12 Roberts, 58; 13 Bayliss, 54; 14 Hopkins, 53; 15 Elias and Xaus, 43; 17 Jacque, 25; 18 Hofmann, 22; 19 Rolfo, 18; 20 van den Goorbergh, 12; 21 Battaini, 6; 22 D. Checa and Ellison, 4; 24 Byrne, 3; 25 Ukawa, 1.

250 cc

20 laps, 68.940 miles/110.960 km

Pos.	Rider (Nat.)	No.	Machine	Laps	Time & speed
1	Casey Stoner (AUS)	27	Aprilia	20	43m 23.138s 95.350 mph/ 153.451 km/h
2	Alex de Angelis (RSM)	5	Aprilia	20	43m 26.271s
3	Sebastian Porto (ARG)	19	Aprilia	20	43m 27.249s
4	Randy de Puniet (F)	7	Aprilia	20	43m 30.707s
5	Hiroshi Aoyama (J)	73	Honda	20	43m 33.247s
6	Hector Barbera (E)	80	Honda	20	43m 49.261s
7	Yuki Takahashi (J)	55	Honda	20	43m 50.439s
8	Roberto Locatelli (I)	15	Aprilia	20	43m 51.144s
9	Sylvain Guintoli (F)	50	Aprilia	20	44m 22.616s
10	Taro Sekiguchi (J)	44	Aprilia	20	44m 22.717s
11	Dirk Heidolf (D)	28	Honda	20	44m 24.575s
12	Chaz Davies (GB)	57	Aprilia	20	44m 27.142s
13	Mirko Giansanti (I)	32	Aprilia	20	44m 27.941s
14	Steve Jenkner (D)	17	Aprilia	20	44m 35.638s
15	Martin Cardenas (COL)	36	Aprilia	20	44m 44.211s
16	Erwan Nigon (F)	63	Yamaha	20	44m 55.063s
17	Mathieu Gines (F)	56	Aprilia	20	45m 15.113s
18	Nicklas Cajback (S)	23	Yamaha	19	43m 28.930s
19	Jakub Smrz (CZ)	96	Honda	19	44m 05.274s
	Simone Corsi (I)	24	Aprilia	7	DNF
	Alex Baldolini (I)	25	Aprilia	7	DNF
	Anthony West (AUS)	14	KTM	5	DNF
	Daniel Pedrosa (E)	1	Honda	1	DNF
	Andrea Ballerini (I)	8	Aprilia	1	DNF
	Arnaud Vincent (F)	21	Fantic	1	DNF
	Andrea Dovizioso (I)	34	Honda	0	DNF
	Alex Debon (E)	6	Honda	0	DNF
	Radomil Rous (CZ)	64	Honda	0	DNF
	Gabriele Ferro (I)	20	Fantic		DNQ
	Zhu Wang (CHN)	60	Aprilia		DNQ
	Zheng Peng Li (CHN)	61	Aprilia		DNQ

Fastest lap: Stoner, 2m 08.853s, 96.315 mph/155.004 km/h.

Previous record: Daniel Pedrosa, E (Honda), 2m 08.015s, 96.946 mph/156.019 km/h (2004).

Event best maximum speed: de Angelis, 160.7 mph/258.6 km/h (warm-up).

Qualifying: 1 Aoyama, 2m 07.860s; 2 Pedrosa, 2m 07.941s; 3 de Angelis, 2m 08.195s; 4 Stoner, 2m 08.286s; 5 Porto, 2m 08.436s; 6 Dovizioso, 2m 08.523s; 7 de Puniet, 2m 08.762s; 8 Barbera, 2m 09.552s; 9 Guintoli, 2m 09.891s; 10 Corsi, 2m 09.998s; 11 Ballerini, 2m 10.039s; 12 Debon, 2m 10.138s; 13 Smrz, 2m 10.164s; 14 Locatelli, 2m 10.212s; 15 Heidolf, 2m 10.279s; 16 Rous, 2m 10.304s; 17 West, 2m 10.330s; 18 Takahashi, 2m 10.448s; 19 Baldolini, 2m 10.786s; 20 Davies, 2m 10.858s; 21 Giansanti, 2m 10.888s; 22 Jenkner, 2m 11.033s; 23 Sekiguchi, 2m 11.542s; 24 Cardenas, 2m 12.195s; 25 Nigon, 2m 12.369s; 26 Gines, 2m 12.509s; 27 Vincent, 2m 12.537s; 28 Cajback, 2m 15.560s; 29 Ferro, 2m 17.579s; 30 Wang, 2m 17.690s; 31 Li, 2m 17.780s.

Fastest race laps: 1 Stoner, 2m 08.853s; 2 de Angelis, 2m 08.933s; 3 Porto, 2m 09.383s; 4 de Puniet, 2m 09.486s; 5 Aoyama, 2m 09.670s; 6 Barbera, 2m 10.268s; 7 Takahashi, 2m 10.298s; 8 Locatelli, 2m 10.462s; 9 Corsi, 2m 10.904s; 10 Cardenas, 2m 11.346s; 11 Smrz, 2m 11.539s; 12 Sekiguchi, 2m 11.686s; 13 Heidolf, 2m 11.753s; 14 Giansanti, 2m 11.787s; 15 Jenkner, 2m 11.878s; 16 Davies, 2m 11.992s; 17 Guintoli, 2m 12.062s; 18 West, 2m 12.084s; 19 Baldolini, 2m 12.822s; 20 Nigon, 2m 12.879s; 21 Gines, 2m 13.859s; 22 Cajback, 2m 15.892s; 23 Pedrosa, 2m 16.169s; 24 Ballerini, 2m 22.275s.

World Championship: 1 Pedrosa, 226; 2 Stoner, 188; 3 Dovizioso, 144; 4 Aoyama, 134; 5 de Angelis, 129; 6 de Puniet and Porto, 121; 8 Lorenzo, 98; 9 Barbera, 77; 10 Guintoli, 62; 11 Takahashi, 60; 12 Corsi, 59; 13 Debon, 46; 14 Locatelli, 39; 15 Giansanti and West, 30; 17 Davies, 21; 18 Baldolini, 20; 19 Ballerini, 14; 20 Rous and Smrz, 11; 22 Heidolf and Jenkner, 9; 24 Leblanc and Sekiguchi, 6; 26 Cardenas, Marchand and Nigon, 3.

125 cc

19 laps, 65.493 miles/105.412 km

Pos.	Rider (Nat.)	No.	Machine	Laps	Time & speed
1	Thomas Luthi (CH)	12	Honda	19	43m 02.214s 91.317 mph/ 146.960 km/h
2	Mika Kallio (SF)	36	KTM	19	43m 02.216s
3	Mattia Pasini (I)	75	Aprilia	19	43m 11.898s
4	Hector Faubel (E)	55	Aprilia	19	43m 11.923s
5	Gabor Talmacsi (H)	14	KTM	19	43m 12.106s
6	Julian Simon (E)	60	KTM	19	43m 14.150s
7	Fabrizio Lai (I)	32	Honda	19	43m 21.846s
8	Manuel Poggiali (RSM)	54	Gilera	19	43m 21.969s
9	Marco Simoncelli (I)	58	Aprilia	19	43m 22.181s
10	Tomoyoshi Koyama (J)	71	Honda	19	43m 22.285s
11	Mike di Meglio (F)	63	Honda	19	43m 22.372s
12	Lukas Pesek (CZ)	52	Derbi	19	43m 22.641s
13	Pablo Nieto (E)	22	Derbi	19	43m 23.392s
14	Alexis Masbou (F)	7	Honda	19	43m 26.413s
15	Aleix Espargaro (E)	41	Honda	19	43m 26.480s
16	Sergio Gadea (E)	33	Aprilia	19	43m 26.695s
17	Joan Olive (E)	6	Aprilia	19	43m 26.829s
18	Andrea Iannone (I)	29	Aprilia	19	43m 50.252s
19	Enrique Jerez (E)	51	Derbi	19	43m 50.371s
20	Lorenzo Zanetti (I)	8	Aprilia	19	43m 51.307s
21	Sandro Cortese (D)	11	Honda	19	43m 51.421s
22	Imre Toth (H)	45	Aprilia	19	44m 05.208s
23	Dario Giuseppetti (D)	25	Aprilia	19	44m 05.214s
24	Manuel Hernandez (E)	43	Aprilia	19	44m 05.970s
25	Mateo Tunez (E)	46	Aprilia	19	44m 13.802s
26	Alvaro Bautista (E)	19	Honda	19	44m 22.366s
27	David Bonache (E)	48	Honda	19	44m 25.308s
28	Jordi Carchano (E)	28	Aprilia	19	44m 34.947s
29	Wai On Cheung (CHN)	38	Honda	19	44m 49.576s
30	Sascha Hommel (D)	31	Malaguti	19	44m 49.886s
31	Doni Tata Pradita (INA)	72	Yamaha	19	45m 23.068s
	Toshihisa Kuzuhara (J)	9	Honda	17	DNF
	Michele Pirro (I)	15	Malaguti	4	DNF
	Federico Sandi (I)	10	Honda	0	DNF
	Vincent Braillard (CH)	26	Aprilia	0	DNF
	Raffaele de Rosa (I)	35	Aprilia	0	DNF
	Karel Abraham (CZ)	44	Aprilia	0	DNF

Fastest lap: Talmacsi, 2m 14.839s, 92.040 mph/148.123 km/h.

Previous record: Lucio Cecchinello, I (Aprilia), 2m 13.919s, 92.671 mph/149.140 km/h (2002).

Event best maximum speed: Kallio, 136.9 mph/220.3 km/h (free practice no. 2).

Qualifying: 1 Luthi, 2m 14.546s; 2 Pasini, 2m 14.837s; 3 Talmacsi, 2m 14.903s; 4 Kallio, 2m 14.964s; 5 Simoncelli, 2m 15.047s; 6 Pesek, 2m 15.187s; 7 Poggiali, 2m 15.257s; 8 Simon, 2m 15.326s; 9 Faubel, 2m 15.343s; 10 di Meglio, 2m 15.349s; 11 Koyama, 2m 15.594s; 12 Olive, 2m 15.635s; 13 Lai, 2m 15.750s; 14 Espargaro, 2m 15.833s; 15 Masbou, 2m 15.864s; 16 de Rosa, 2m 16.231s; 17 Jerez, 2m 16.277s; 18 Gadea, 2m 16.406s; 19 Zanetti, 2m 16.559s; 20 Bautista, 2m 16.796s; 21 Hernandez, 2m 17.094s; 22 Cortese, 2m 17.611s; 23 Nieto, 2m 17.670s; 24 Iannone, 2m 17.672s; 25 Giuseppetti, 2m 17.799s; 26 Toth, 2m 17.876s; 27 Kuzuhara, 2m 17.997s; 28 Carchano, 2m 18.159s; 29 Bonache, 2m 18.290s; 30 Pirro, 2m 18.623s; 31 Tunez, 2m 18.679s; 32 Braillard, 2m 18.984s; 33 Abraham, 2m 18.996s; 34 Sandi, 2m 19.039s; 35 Hommel, 2m 20.354s; 36 Pradita, 2m 21.017s; 37 Cheung, 2m 21.576s.

Fastest race laps: 1 Talmacsi, 2m 14.839s; 2 Simon, 2m 14.979s; 3 Kallio, 2m 15.003s; 4 Luthi, 2m 15.096s; 5 Faubel, 2m 15.449s; 6 di Meglio, 2m 15.497s; 7 Simoncelli, 2m 15.512s; 8 Nieto, 2m 15.562s; 9 Pasini, 2m 15.658s; 10 Pesek, 2m 15.698s; 11 Lai, 2m 15.711s; 12 Poggiali, 2m 15.863s; 13 Koyama, 2m 15.878s; 14 Gadea, 2m 15.898s; 15 Espargaro, 2m 16.012s; 16 Olive, 2m 16.020s; 17 Masbou, 2m 16.057s; 18 Iannone, 2m 16.397s; 19 Zanetti, 2m 16.540s; 20 Cortese, 2m 16.771s; 21 Jerez, 2m 16.935s; 22 Bautista, 2m 17.576s; 23 Pirro, 2m 17.632s; 24 Hernandez, 2m 17.703s; 25 Kuzuhara, 2m 17.708s; 26 Giuseppetti, 2m 17.954s; 27 Tunez, 2m 17.968s; 28 Toth, 2m 18.053s; 29 Bonache, 2m 18.677s; 30 Carchano, 2m 18.934s; 31 Hommel, 2m 20.406s; 32 Cheung, 2m 20.613s; 33 Pradita, 2m 22.171s.

World Championship: 1 Luthi, 189; 2 Kallio, 181; 3 Talmacsi, 131; 4 Pasini, 127; 5 Simoncelli, 124; 6 Lai, 113; 7 Simon, 107; 8 Poggiali, 90; 9 Faubel, 79; 10 Koyama, 72; 11 di Meglio, 64; 12 Nieto, 58; 13 Gadea, 57; 14 Olive, 45; 15 Bautista, 39; 16 Espargaro, 31; 17 Zanetti, 30; 18 Masbou and Pesek, 22; 20 Kuzuhara, 17; 21 Iannone, 13; 22 Hernandez and Ranseder, 12; 24 Linfoot and Toth, 7; 26 Carchano and Cortese, 6; 28 Conti, 5; 29 Elkin, 4; 30 Giuseppetti and Pirro, 3; 32 de Rosa, 2; 33 Bradl, Jerez and Terol, 1.

FIM WORLD CHAMPIONSHIP • ROUND 14

QATARGP
LOSAIL

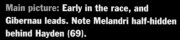

Main picture: Early in the race, and Gibernau leads. Note Melandri half-hidden behind Hayden (69).

Left: Concrete and sand – and a GP in the middle of it.

Centre left: Camel, unbranded.

Below: High winds on the grid almost blew the umbrellas inside out.

Bottom left: Rossi and teamster celebrate his tenth win.

Bottom right: Just follow the signs into the desert… you can't miss it.

Photographs: Gold & Goose

QATAR'S Losail Circuit is unique. It is MotoGP in a bubble, in isolation. Out in the desert, where only the camels are still on their feet at midday, grand prix racing takes place because of itself, and in spite of itself. One might as well be racing in space.

Added to the fatigue of the preceding races on consecutive weekends, this can lead to serious "what-are-we-doing-here" feelings during the restless nights. Philosophical questions of why and wherefore, about the very nature of motorbike racing. How it is at the same time athletic, but also technical. And how it is a team effort, but in the end rests solely on the individual rider.

It took the smallest, and nowadays least relevant, World Championship class to throw this last aspect into sharp (and hilarious) focus.

The question of team orders often arises when world championships are at stake. At this stage only the smaller titles remained to be decided. An unsung epic was under way in 250, where two bruising races had left Pedrosa with a fractured shoulder. He was keeping quiet about it, however. Only those closest to him were aware just how much his march to victory was under threat. The 125 remained fiercely disputed between Luthi on the Honda and Kallio on the KTM.

The smallest class was especially important to the tight-knit all-orange Austrian outfit, led by well-respected veteran two-stroke man Harald Bartol. Among other things was the need to save face after the MotoGP debacle, where they'd stopped supplying engines to Proton Team KR. Concentrating all resources on the 125s meant that the 250 was on the back-burner for the present. To its cost. Since its fine second-place debut in the wet at Donington Park, it had suffered a spate of seizures and bottom end failures because of a big-end problem that nobody had any time to solve. When it seized again in final qualifying at Qatar, and although this time he didn't fall off, it was the last straw for rider Anthony West. Angry words were exchanged in the pit, and KTM promptly withdrew the 250 from this GP, and from the following flyaway rounds as well. Paddock wags were unable to resist commenting that now KTM had stopped supplying engines to themselves as well.

Still, come the race, the 125s saved the day. Title candidate Kallio led lap after lap, team-mate Talmacsi dutifully riding shotgun, though not above pulling alongside every so often on the straight, just so everyone knew he wasn't going his absolute fastest, but was following team orders.

Then he did it once too often. On the last lap. To win the race.

The flabbergasted faces on the KTM pit rail were a picture; likewise Talmacsi's, after taking his helmet off. He hadn't known it was the last lap, he protested. Oh yeah, implied Kallio's blank stare. MOTOCOURSE asked if he had known, would he have done differently? "I don't know. I don't know," replied the Hungarian. The move may or may not cost Kallio the title, but it most certainly cost Talmacsi his job.

Up at the top end of the paddock, there was still second place to be fought for... and for a younger-looking and clearly more carefree Rossi a chance to race without pressure. He could measure up the strength of his rivals for next year, and be (as he put it) "more serene", though that's not the way it looked in a tough fight for his tenth win of the year. His own title might be secure, but there was still the team championship and the manufacturers title. "It is important to Yamaha, and so it is important to me too," he said. Victory avenged his problems here last year – dumped to the back of the grid, then crashing in a mad charge towards the front, and helped defer a triumph eagerly anticipated by Honda, holding their breath for their 600th win. They currently dallied on 598... and for once didn't win a single race all day.

There was, as Michelin's Nicolas Goubert had predicted from pre-season tests, a turnover in tyre fortunes – the hitherto rampant Bridgestones found the track did not provide the clear advantage enjoyed at the previous two, though Capirossi's third pole suggested they were not too far behind. Suzuki in particular were struggling for front grip, according to Hopkins. And the heat was still on, with Goubert acknowledging that they would have to follow Bridgestone's lead in instituting independent test teams with Honda and Yamaha – the direct antithesis of their hopes of cutting back on costs, under discussion just one year ago. "Michelin have realised that having test teams has given Bridgestone a big advantage," he said.

Opposite: Rubber studies: At the top, a Ducati's well-used Bridgestone; below, a Honda's Michelin, more lightly feathered, clearly shows bands of different compounds.

Below: Winner Talmacsi – celebrating. For now.

Bottom: Kallio looks across in baffled amazement as his team-mate steals the race.
Photographs: Gold & Goose

Jacque was back for a second successive replacement ride on the Kawasaki, but the hero of Shanghai became the victim of Qatar, crashing after only six minutes of the first session, on the gravel at a relatively low speed. The ex-250 champion went out again in the same session, but at lunchtime his back and neck started seizing up, and by the next day he was back on an aircraft for Europe, to be checked over for possible spinal injuries. Mercifully, he was cleared, and fit to race again in two weeks.

The rest soldiered on in merciless heat – riding was "like sitting behind 100 hairdryers ", according to Checa; many again resorted to appropriate camel-back drinking systems in the hump on their leathers, while Nakano's Kawasaki acquired an extra heat shield on the right above the exhausts, to stop his foot from getting slow-cooked.

The dusty track gained traction from the start of practice, and had gained a great deal more in the intervening year of sporadic use and steady weathering since the first visit, with pole a full two seconds faster than last year. It was still slippery off line, but not as bad as before... almost like a real race-track. In a few more years, it might even become like a real race, too.

MOTOGP RACE – 22 laps

Capirossi took his third pole in a row, narrowly ousting Gibernau. Rossi was on the far end... remarkably, his first top-three qualifying since the British GP. Times were close, with the second row – Edwards, Melandri and Checa – still within half a second of pole. Elias had showed strongly, second on day one, but on qualifying tyres he was on row three, behind Nakano and Hayden.

Capirossi headed the brawl into the first corner, where paint was exchanged and places shuffled, but nobody fell. He led for the rest of the lap, but was in trouble with rear grip, and powerless to prevent Gibernau piling past into the first corner, and Rossi and Hayden also by the end of lap two. He would continue to slip backwards to sixth on lap eight, when he ran off the track, rejoining 12th.

Gibernau resisted an early challenge from Rossi, but his lead was never as much as a second, as Hayden got in front of Rossi briefly, and Edwards and Melandri closed from behind. Melandri was the flyer, and on lap five was up to third, ahead of Hayden. Edwards was clinging on grimly behind, but before half distance he was dropping away gradually.

Melandri was engaged with Rossi, Hayden seemingly having

trouble hanging on behind. Then came the first indication of how hard Rossi was trying, as he ran wide, letting Melandri pass easily, and almost Hayden as well. The American went with him as he closed up again on Melandri, Gibernau half-a-second odd ahead. On lap ten, the first four were covered by only 1.3 seconds, more than half of that accounted for by Gibernau's lead.

Rossi regained second next time round, and over the next four laps chipped away at Gibernau. The quartet became closer still – until another lunge by Melandri saw him almost collide with Rossi, who ran wide again to let him through. Now the bullish youngster started on his team-mate. With five laps to go, he got in front. Gibernau pushed straight ahead again into the next turn. But it was another ill-judged and flustered move; off line and too fast, he ran off into the gravel at a tangent, once more removing himself from contention. He rejoined behind the fading Edwards.

Melandri led for the next two laps, then Rossi blasted past down the straight with speed to spare. This may have been due to some canny pit work by Burgess – noting the stiff headwind, he geared down by some 20 km/h to let the Yamaha rev out. Hayden was now in familiar mode, not quite able to keep in touch as the other pair slugged it out. On the final lap, Melandri showed how he has developed since his passive second place at Assen, attacking again with some vigour, slipping inside Rossi

with half a lap to go, only to run wide on the exit, puffing dust from the trackside Astroturf as Rossi ran past inside for his tenth win of the year by 1.670 seconds. One of the toughest, and for Melandri a harbinger of a major revival in fortunes.

Edwards and Gibernau accounted for the top five. There was some close racing behind. Rolfo took a blazing start, and it took three laps before Checa, shadowed by Nakano, had slipped by. Nakano harried the Ducati for much of the race, before slipping away, only to close again by the flag.

Biaggi was also ahead of the year-old Ducati by lap four, but one lap later he slowed and pitted, with a bad connection taking the blame for upsetting the complex electronics.

Elias had followed Biaggi past, and now Rolfo fell into the hands of Barros and Roberts. Barros got the best of it, pegged down Elias by half distance, and then passed him too. But only for two laps, the class rookie pulling clear at the finish for his best result so far.

Capirossi passed Roberts with nine laps to go for tenth, Rolfo a now distant 12th, Tamada had struggled to pass him, then promptly crashed out with five laps left. Byrne was having a second Honda ride, taking 13th well clear of the increasingly detuned Xaus. Ellison took the last point ahead of Battaini and Hopkins, who'd pitted for a tyre change after suffering from the start, and running off into the gravel.

Above: Kenny Roberts Jr. strides towards his GSV-R. This would be his last race for Suzuki.

Photograph: Gold & Goose

250 cc RACE – 20 laps

In spite of his concealed injury, Pedrosa qualified on the front row, but it was Lorenzo on pole, on blazing form after his one-race suspension, fastest on both days. De Angelis was second, then Stoner; Porto led row two.

Stoner's title hopes were slender, but still alive, and he rode an emphatic race, seizing a lead of one second on the first lap, and stretching towards five seconds as the race approached half distance. There'd been a spirited pursuit by Lorenzo, with the gap see-sawing back and forth, but Stoner had retained control for what looked like a comfortable win, with 3.4 seconds in hand as he started lap 17. But now his Aprilia started to sing less sweetly, "a spark plug or something playing up", and his pace dropped off. He won by 1.6 seconds, but said: "In another lap or two they'd have caught me."

By now the pursuit had been stretched. From the start, Pedrosa had been quickly displaced by Lorenzo and Dovizioso, with Porto close, but Aoyama soon to lose touch.

The four stayed together until half distance, Dovizioso twice harrying Lorenzo, who was in turn striving to close up on the flying Stoner. After the mid-point, these efforts saw him break free for a dogged and lonely pursuit.

At the same time, Porto took to the lead of the remaining three, locked together – until lap 15, when Pedrosa attacked vigorously, only to run wide shortly afterwards, dropping behind Dovizioso again.

Porto's race did not last much longer, his tyres all used up, and he dropped to the back of the trio and out of touch.

The other two battled for the last rostrum position, Pedrosa

ahead on lap 17, and almost staying there to the finish. On the last lap he fought Dovizioso off once, but could do nothing as the Italian got a better run out of the last corner, and ducked out of his slipstream to steal the spot by half a tenth.

Porto was two seconds adrift, then a great yawning gap to Aoyama, who had Barbera chasing a little way behind. Then Takahashi prevailed for eighth after a long battle with Guintoli.

A big gang disputed the final points, from tenth to 16th covered by only four seconds. Sekiguchi was inches ahead of Debon, Giansanti, Cardenas, Jenkner, Ballerini and Davies, the only one out of the points.

De Angelis was charging with the front men, lying sixth when he became an early crash victim; de Puniet had engine trouble from the start, dropping back to eventual retirement; Locatelli was the only other faller. West did not start, the KTM withdrawn on race eve.

125 cc RACE – 18 laps

Kallio claimed his eighth 125 pole of the season, title rival Thomas Luthi was back on the third row after running into traffic on his final fast lap, waving his fists angrily. Talmacsi was second, then Pasini and front-row first-timer Simon making it three KTMs.

Kallio took the lead from the start, the other two orange bikes following, Simon immediately displaced from third by di Meglio. At the end of the first lap, Luthi was embroiled in an arms-and-elbows gang, eighth, one place behind Pasini. The Italian was able to get straight back to the front, but Luthi couldn't find his way out of the box.

Up front, Kallio and Talmacsi drew steadily away towards their last-lap drama. Talmacsi's rush of blood (he blamed an incorrect lap count on his pit board) gave him the win by 0.017 seconds. "That was not so clever," growled Kallio.

Simon was in the following gang, with Pasini at the head of it from the second lap. Also involved were Poggiali, di Meglio, Simoncelli, Lai, Faubel and Luthi, and the erstwhile points leader wasn't getting anything like the best of it.

Simoncelli was the strongest, up to third on lap five, and immediately pulling off in a lonely and fruitless pursuit of the KTMs, some 2.5 seconds clear.

Behind, Poggiali now led the brawl over the line for a few laps, but it was pretty hectic. Just after half distance Lai lost the grippy line and ran off for a second time, rejoining out of touch. This left six in an all-action free-for-all.

Luthi tried to get to the front of it to escape, but instead collided with Pasini, both losing time as Faubel headed the group for a while. It went all the way. At the finish, fourth to eighth were covered by four tenths, positions decided only on the final sprint, with di Meglio narrowly leading Faubel, Luthi, Poggiali and Simon, Pasini a couple of seconds adrift, and then Lai.

Kallio now led on points again – but by two. Had he won, it would have been by seven. It had been a costly afternoon for him, but vastly amusing for everybody else.

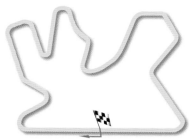

QATAR - LOSAIL GRAND PRIX CIRCUIT

CIRCUIT LENGTH: 3.343 miles/5.380 km

MARLBORO QATAR GRAND PRIX

1 OCTOBER 2005 • FIM WORLD CHAMPIONSHIP ROUND 14

MotoGP

22 laps, 74.546 miles/118.360 km

Pos.	Rider (Nat.)	No.	Machine	Laps	Time & speed
1	Valentino Rossi (I)	46	Yamaha	22	43m 33.759s 101.296 mph/ 163.020 km/h
2	Marco Melandri (I)	33	Honda	22	43m 35.429s
3	Nicky Hayden (USA)	69	Honda	22	43m 39.295s
4	Colin Edwards (USA)	5	Yamaha	22	43m 48.496s
5	Sete Gibernau (E)	15	Honda	22	43m 54.190s
6	Carlos Checa (E)	7	Ducati	22	44m 05.191s
7	Shinya Nakano (J)	56	Kawasaki	22	44m 06.742s
8	Toni Elias (E)	24	Yamaha	22	44m 13.647s
9	Alex Barros (BR)	4	Honda	22	44m 15.551s
10	Loris Capirossi (I)	65	Ducati	22	44m 18.011s
11	Kenny Roberts (USA)	10	Suzuki	22	44m 22.504s
12	Roberto Rolfo (I)	44	Ducati	22	44m 35.750s
13	Shane Byrne (GB)	67	Honda	22	44m 38.564s
14	Ruben Xaus (E)	11	Yamaha	22	44m 47.583s
15	James Ellison (GB)	77	Blata	22	45m 42.401s
16	Franco Battaini (I)	27	Blata	21	43m 59.063s
17	John Hopkins (USA)	21	Suzuki	21	44m 38.818s
	Makoto Tamada (J)	6	Honda	17	DNF
	Max Biaggi (I)	3	Honda	6	DNF

Fastest lap: Hayden, 1m 57.903s, 102.073 mph/164.270 km/h (record).

Previous record: Colin Edwards, USA (Honda), 1m 59.293s, 100.883 mph/162.356 km/h (2004).

Event best maximum speed: Checa, 204.2 mph/328.7 km/h (qualifying practice).

Qualifying:: 1 Capirossi, 1m 56.917s; 2 Gibernau, 1m 56.994s; 3 Rossi, 1m 57.360s; 4 Edwards, 1m 57.447s; 5 Melandri, 1m 57.468s; 6 Checa, 1m 57.481s; 7 Nakano, 1m 57.697s; 8 Hayden, 1m 57.872s; 9 Elias, 1m 57.902s; 10 Tamada, 1m 58.317s; 11 Roberts, 1m 58.329s; 12 Hopkins, 1m 58.527s; 13 Biaggi, 1m 58.622s; 14 Barros, 1m 59.084s; 15 Rolfo, 1m 59.392s; 16 Xaus, 1m 59.482s; 17 Byrne, 2m 00.097s; 18 Ellison, 2m 00.909s; 19 Battaini 2m 01.678s.

Fastest race laps: 1 Hayden, 1m 57.903s; 2 Rossi, 1m 57.910s; 3 Melandri, 1m 57.939s; 4 Gibernau, 1m 58.079s; 5 Edwards, 1m 58.345s; 6 Capirossi, 1m 58.904s; 7 Nakano, 1m 58.939s; 8 Checa, 1m 59.177s; 9 Biaggi, 1m 59.285s; 10 Elias, 1m 59.316s; 11 Barros, 1m 59.434s; 12 Roberts, 1m 59.488s; 13 Hopkins, 1m 59.724s; 14 Tamada, 1m 59.764s; 15 Rolfo, 1m 59.951s; 16 Byrne, 2m 00.526s; 17 Xaus, 2m 01.194s; 18 Ellison, 2m 02.387s; 19 Battaini, 2m 04.663s.

World Championship: 1 Rossi, 306; 2 Biaggi, 159; 3 Melandri, 157; 4 Edwards, 152; 5 Hayden, 150; 6 Capirossi, 148; 7 Barros, 129; 8 Gibernau, 126; 9 C. Checa, 98; 10 Nakano, 78; 11 Tamada, 68; 12 Roberts, 63; 13 Bayliss, 54; 14 Hopkins, 53; 15 Elias, 51; 16 Xaus, 45; 17 Jacque, 25; 18 Hofmann and Rolfo, 22; 20 van den Goorbergh, 12; 21 Battaini and Byrne, 6; 23 Ellison, 5; 24 D. Checa, 4; 25 Ukawa, 1.

---

250 cc

20 laps, 66.860 miles/107.600 km

Pos.	Rider (Nat.)	No.	Machine	Laps	Time & speed
1	Casey Stoner (AUS)	27	Aprilia	20	41m 22.628s 96.951 mph/ 156.028 km/h
2	Jorge Lorenzo (E)	48	Honda	20	41m 24.194s
3	Andrea Dovizioso (I)	34	Honda	20	41m 25.231s
4	Daniel Pedrosa (E)	1	Honda	20	41m 25.287s
5	Sebastian Porto (ARG)	19	Aprilia	20	41m 27.495s
6	Hiroshi Aoyama (J)	73	Honda	20	41m 52.599s
7	Hector Barbera (E)	80	Honda	20	41m 55.336s
8	Yuki Takahashi (J)	55	Honda	20	42m 09.098s
9	Sylvain Guintoli (F)	50	Aprilia	20	42m 09.477s
10	Taro Sekiguchi (J)	44	Aprilia	20	42m 24.310s
11	Alex Debon (E)	6	Honda	20	42m 24.324s
12	Mirko Giansanti (I)	32	Aprilia	20	42m 24.408s
13	Martin Cardenas (COL)	36	Aprilia	20	42m 25.423s
14	Steve Jenkner (D)	17	Aprilia	20	42m 26.580s
15	Andrea Ballerini (I)	8	Aprilia	20	42m 27.545s
16	Chaz Davies (GB)	57	Aprilia	20	42m 28.822s
17	Simone Corsi (I)	24	Aprilia	20	42m 43.632s
18	Dirk Heidolf (D)	28	Honda	20	42m 59.174s
19	Mathieu Gines (F)	56	Aprilia	20	43m 13.673s
20	Alex Baldolini (I)	25	Aprilia	20	43m 24.733s
	Erwan Nigon (F)	63	Yamaha	17	DNF
	Jakub Smrz (CZ)	96	Honda	16	DNF
	Randy de Puniet (F)	7	Aprilia	12	DNF
	Roberto Locatelli (I)	15	Aprilia	6	DNF
	Alex de Angelis (RSM)	5	Aprilia	5	DNF
	Radomil Rous (CZ)	64	Honda	5	DNF
	Arnaud Vincent (F)	21	Fantic	2	DNF
	Gabriele Ferro (I)	20	Fantic		DNQ
	Nicklas Cajback (S)	23	Yamaha		DNQ

Fastest lap: Pedrosa, 2m 03.301s, 97.604 mph/157.079 km/h.

Previous record: Alex de Angelis, RSM (Aprilia), 2m 03.015s, 97.831 mph/157.444 km/h (2004).

Event best maximum speed: de Angelis, 161.7 mph/260.2 km/h (free practice no. 2).

Qualifying: 1 Lorenzo, 2m 02.154s; 2 de Angelis, 2m 02.303s; 3 Stoner, 2m 02.473s; 4 Pedrosa, 2m 02.544s; 5 Porto, 2m 02.704s; 6 Dovizioso, 2m 02.715s; 7 Aoyama, 2m 02.828s; 8 de Puniet, 2m 04.219s; 9 Barbera, 2m 04.282s; 10 Takahashi, 2m 04.327s; 11 Guintoli, 2m 04.419s; 12 Locatelli, 2m 04.485s; 13 Smrz, 2m 04.816s; 14 Ballerini, 2m 04.964s; 15 Giansanti, 2m 04.999s; 16 Jenkner, 2m 05.033s; 17 Debon, 2m 05.039s; 18 Sekiguchi, 2m 05.296s; 19 Corsi, 2m 05.313s; 20 Davies, 2m 05.600s; 21 Cardenas, 2m 05.796s; 22 Heidolf, 2m 06.036s; 23 Nigon, 2m 06.179s; 24 Baldolini, 2m 06.190s; 25 Vincent, 2m 06.669s; 26 Rous, 2m 07.557s; 27 Gines, 2m 07.712s; 28 Ferro, 12.646s; 29 Cajback, 2m 12.962s.

Fastest race laps: 1 Pedrosa, 2m 03.301s; 2 Stoner, 2m 03.350s; 3 Lorenzo, 2m 03.430s; 4 Dovizioso, 2m 03.446s; 5 Porto, 2m 03.511s; 6 de Angelis, 2m 03.614s; 7 Aoyama, 2m 03.795s; 8 de Puniet, 2m 04.309s; 9 Barbera, 2m 04.357s; 10 Guintoli, 2m 05.022s; 11 Locatelli, 2m 05.116s; 12 Takahashi, 2m 05.471s; 13 Giansanti, 2m 05.942s; 14 Davies, 2m 06.003s; 15 Debon, 2m 06.009s; 16 Cardenas, 2m 06.033s; 17 Sekiguchi, 2m 06.096s; 18 Ballerini, 2m 06.269s; 19 Jenkner, 2m 06.390s; 20 Corsi, 2m 06.402s; 21 Heidolf, 2m 06.416s; 22 Baldolini, 2m 06.835s; 23 Smrz, 2m 06.841s; 24 Rous, 2m 07.474s; 25 Gines, 2m 07.960s; 26 Nigon, 2m 08.228s; 27 Vincent, 2m 11.500s.

World Championship: 1 Pedrosa, 239; 2 Stoner, 213; 3 Dovizioso, 160; 4 Aoyama, 144; 5 Porto, 132; 6 de Angelis, 129; 7 de Puniet, 121; 8 Lorenzo, 118; 9 Barbera, 86; 10 Guintoli, 64; 11 Takahashi, 60; 12 Corsi, 59; 13 Debon, 51; 14 Locatelli, 39; 15 Giansanti, 34; 16 West, 30; 17 Davies, 21; 18 Baldolini, 20; 19 Ballerini, 15; 20 Sekiguchi, 12; 21 Jenkner, Rous and Smrz, 11; 24 Heidolf, 9; 25 Cardenas and Leblanc, 6; 27 Marchand and Nigon, 3.

---

125 cc

18 laps, 60.174 miles/96.840 km

Pos.	Rider (Nat.)	No.	Machine	Laps	Time & speed
1	Gabor Talmacsi (H)	14	KTM	18	39m 23.248s 91.664 mph/ 147.519 km/h
2	Mika Kallio (SF)	36	KTM	18	39m 23.265s
3	Marco Simoncelli (I)	58	Aprilia	18	39m 32.819s
4	Mike di Meglio (F)	63	Honda	18	39m 35.063s
5	Hector Faubel (E)	55	Aprilia	18	39m 35.417s
6	Thomas Luthi (CH)	12	Honda	18	39m 35.551s
7	Manuel Poggiali (RSM)	54	Gilera	18	39m 35.565s
8	Julian Simon (E)	60	KTM	18	39m 35.813s
9	Mattia Pasini (I)	75	Aprilia	18	39m 40.819s
10	Fabrizio Lai (I)	32	Honda	18	39m 43.005s
11	Joan Olive (E)	6	Aprilia	18	39m 45.285s
12	Sergio Gadea (E)	33	Aprilia	18	39m 47.453s
13	Raffaele de Rosa (I)	35	Aprilia	18	39m 48.590s
14	Tomoyoshi Koyama (J)	71	Honda	18	39m 51.213s
15	Enrique Jerez (E)	51	Derbi	18	40m 00.489s
16	Lorenzo Zanetti (I)	8	Aprilia	18	40m 06.952s
17	Sandro Cortese (D)	11	Honda	18	40m 08.103s
18	Aleix Espargaro (E)	41	Honda	18	40m 08.118s
19	Andrea Iannone (I)	29	Aprilia	18	40m 08.769s
20	Alexis Masbou (F)	7	Honda	18	40m 12.259s
21	Dario Giuseppetti (D)	25	Aprilia	18	40m 13.272s
22	Alvaro Bautista (E)	19	Honda	18	40m 13.307s
23	Gioele Pellino (I)	42	Malaguti	18	40m 13.547s
24	Mateo Tunez (E)	46	Aprilia	18	40m 20.204s
25	Jordi Carchano (E)	28	Aprilia	18	40m 20.268s
26	Federico Sandi (I)	10	Honda	18	40m 38.175s
27	Toshihisa Kuzuhara (J)	9	Honda	18	40m 52.385s
28	Karel Abraham (CZ)	44	Aprilia	18	40m 52.406s
29	Imre Toth (H)	45	Aprilia	18	41m 03.032s
	Michele Pirro (I)	15	Malaguti	15	DNF
	Angel Rodriguez (E)	47	Aprilia	13	DNF
	Pablo Nieto (E)	22	Derbi	6	DNF
	Lukas Pesek (CZ)	52	Derbi	3	DNF
	Manuel Hernandez (E)	43	Aprilia	3	DNF
	Sascha Hommel (D)	31	Honda	2	DNF
	David Bonache (E)	48	Honda	1	DNF

Fastest lap: Simoncelli, 2m 10.515s, 92.209 mph/148.396 km/h.

Previous record: Jorge Lorenzo, E (Derbi), 2m 09.569s, 92.883 mph/149.480 km/h (2004).

Event best maximum speed: Pesek, 141.4 mph/227.6 km/h (qualifying practice no. 2).

Qualifying: 1 Kallio, 2m 09.455s; 2 Talmacsi, 2m 09.601s; 3 Pasini, 2m 09.653s; 4 Simon, 2m 09.680s; 5 Lai, 2m 09.699s; 6 Poggiali, 2m 09.718s; 7 Simoncelli, 2m 09.850s; 8 Rodriguez, 2m 09.962s; 9 Luthi, 2m 10.010s; 10 di Meglio, 2m 10.024s; 11 Faubel, 2m 10.075s; 12 Bautista, 2m 10.282s; 13 Olive, 2m 10.415s; 14 de Rosa, 2m 10.432s; 15 Masbou, 2m 10.444s; 16 Koyama, 2m 10.489s; 17 Espargaro, 2m 10.728s; 18 Gadea, 2m 11.094s; 19 Nieto, 2m 11.176s; 20 Iannone, 2m 11.411s; 21 Cortese, 2m 11.455s; 22 Zanetti, 2m 11.485s; 23 Pesek, 2m 11.498s; 24 Jerez, 2m 11.618s; 25 Pellino, 2m 11.784s; 26 Hernandez, 2m 12.032s; 27 Giuseppetti, 2m 12.032s; 28 Tunez, 2m 12.313s; 29 Carchano, 2m 12.355s; 30 Pirro, 2m 12.392s; 31 Sandi, 2m 12.588s; 32 Abraham, 2m 13.224s; 33 Bonache, 2m 13.283s; 34 Kuzuhara, 2m 13.491s; 35 Toth, 2m 13.679s; 36 Hommel, 2m 14.299s.

Fastest race laps: 1 Simoncelli, 2m 10.515s; 2 Lai, 2m 10.537s; 3 Talmacsi, 2m 10.569s; 4 Simon, 2m 10.613s; 5 Kallio, 2m 10.629s; 6 Pesek, 2m 10.630s; 7 Pasini, 2m 10.731s; 8 Poggiali, 2m 10.740s; 9 di Meglio, 2m 10.759s; 10 Luthi, 2m 10.765s; 11 Faubel, 2m 10.904s; 12 Olive, 2m 10.950s; 13 Gadea, 2m 11.283s; 14 Masbou, 2m 11.369s; 15 de Rosa, 2m 11.398s; 16 Koyama, 2m 11.588s; 17 Iannone, 2m 11.602s; 18 Jerez, 2m 12.014s; 19 Cortese, 2m 12.137s; 20 Rodriguez, 2m 12.233s; 21 Pellino, 2m 12.322s; 22 Bautista, 2m 12.325s; 23 Zanetti, 2m 12.344s; 24 Espargaro, 2m 12.387s; 25 Giuseppetti, 2m 12.430s; 26 Pirro, 2m 12.866s; 27 Sandi, 2m 13.045s; 28 Nieto, 2m 13.078s; 29 Tunez, 2m 13.140s; 30 Carchano, 2m 13.146s; 31 Kuzuhara, 2m 14.043s; 32 Hernandez, 2m 14.351s; 33 Abraham, 2m 14.541s; 34 Toth, 2m 15.048s; 35 Bonache, 2m 17.368s; 36 Hommel, 2m 44.978s.

World Championship: 1 Kallio, 201; 2 Luthi, 199; 3 Talmacsi, 156; 4 Simoncelli, 140; 5 Pasini, 134; 6 Lai, 119; 7 Simon, 115; 8 Poggiali, 99; 9 Faubel, 90; 10 di Meglio, 77; 11 Koyama, 63; 12 Gadea, 61; 13 Nieto, 58; 14 Olive, 50; 15 Bautisa, 39; 16 Espargaro, 31; 17 Zanetti, 30; 18 Masbou and Pesek, 22; 20 Kuzuhara, 17; 21 Iannone, 13; 22 Hernandez and Ranseder, 12; 24 Linfoot and Toth, 7; 26 Carchano and Cortese, 6; 28 Conti and de Rosa, 5; 30 Elkin, 4; 31 Giuseppetti and Pirro, 3; 33 Jerez, 2; 34 Bradl and Terol, 1.

AUSTRALIANGP
PHILLIP ISLAND

Main picture: A Phillip Island classic: Rossi, Hayden, Melandri and Checa fill the frame, Edwards looms over the brow.

Below left: Checa played the numbers game for a second rostrum in three races.

Below: Stoner's crash, and his own fine win, clinched 250 title number two for the briefly exultant Pedrosa.
Photograph: Gold & Goose

Above: New champion Pedrosa soberly informs a rapt Spanish press corps of the concealed injury that had spoiled recent races.

Photograph: Gold & Goose

SWEEPING circuits with fast corners make for great motorcycle racing. With Assen emasculated, Phillip Island remains a last bastion of this principle. And of its corollary... fast corners make for fast accidents. Fast accidents can hurt.

There were two high-level victims of the circuit's heart-stopping Turn One. The problem with this 150-plus mph right-hand heave, straight after the 200-plus mph downhill straight, lies in what comes before... maybe the most famous feature of a famous circuit. This is the set of left-handers, apexing three times on a crescendo of speed and acceleration, before the run down past the pits. Long enough for the right-hand side of the tyre to cool, and if the compound is not well chosen, to become treacherous.

The first to fall was Roberts on the Suzuki, well into the corner "when it highsided the hell out of me." He thought there might have been some mechanical problem. Then Capirossi did something similar, falling earlier on the corner. Both were on Bridgestone tyres. Were they to blame? If there were further problems, they did not have the same consequences, so the speculation died a natural death.

Roberts suffered fractures to his left wrist, and flew home, where further damage was diagnosed. It would be his last ride

on a Suzuki, after winning his sole title on the marque way back in 2000.

Capirossi fell somewhat faster, and was more severely hurt, with internal bleeding to his left lung requiring drain tubes to be inserted. He was flown back to Italy within days, still festooned with tubes and laid low for some time more. It seemed his season was also done, but Loris is made of stern stuff, and made a courageous return for the last GP.

The question was not so much why they had fallen off (it does, after all, happen from time to time), but what had happened later. Roberts was flying anyway, but Capirossi had been sliding cleanly on the grass and onto the gravel before he started flipping so injuriously. This was an improvement on last year, when a raised lip on the same gravel trap had been responsible for sending Anthony West looping painfully. In the race, Barros would suffer a bruising for the same reason, at another of the new gravel traps.

These had been put in at the request of the riders' safety commission, of which – ironically enough – both Capirossi and Roberts were members, where before there had been open grassland. Questioned later, the third commission member Rossi defended this and other controversial installations. The consequences might have been worse without them, he insisted.

the corners, he said. All the same, he made impressive progress, staying afloat and getting steadily faster by a second every session, to qualify 14th and finish in the points.

This did his immediate career prospects no harm at all, as we would see – and the situation of saddles vacant was becoming fluid. Two old hands not sure of their next season were Checa and Barros; while Yamaha's sponsorship uncertainty with Gauloises simmered on. Checa would have a weekend of numbers to play with. He turned 33 on Saturday night, recorded 333 km/h as the best top speed (actually 333.4, 207.2 mph), and battled with number 33 (Melandri) to come third.

Second overall remained to be decided, and five riders within a spread of just 11 points put seven riders in the frame, as close as anything. Biaggi was the narrow leader, and might yet save his reputation if he were to finish top Honda. Fate had other plans, and his first-lap crash was the prelude to a melt-down that would threaten his whole career.

He and his fellow Honda riders did, however, have the all clear to return to the full 16,500 rpm limit, after two races of being held 500 rpm lower than that, while HRC investigated "lubrication issues" that arose after the Motegi failures.

Suzuki had new and more aerodynamic bodywork, better in crosswinds, said Hopkins, adding: "We still don't have the horsepower to feel the benefit in a straight line." Top speed figures proved the point, the Suzukis slowest of the factory machines, and at 196 mph, more than ten mph down on Checa.

Honda were finally able to put out the banners celebrating 600 GP wins. Luthi's 125 win had been the 599th; Pedrosa took the big one. But nothing could stop Rossi tying up the constructors' title for Yamaha. "Always to race in this track is different, is magic," he said. "I win a lot of times here, a lot of important races for my career. I love this track."

Below left: Capirossi enjoys the sunshine, shortly before his heavy crash.

Below: On a mutual high, rostrum finishers Rossi and Checa share the aftermath of a superlative race.

Bottom: Biaggi crashed before half a lap was done. It was a turning point in a season he had almost salvaged.

Photographs: Gold & Goose

In most respects, after all, the island was in benevolent mood, laying on far better weather than most visitors had ever seen, and the usual good racing. In title terms, the 125 was still open; but Pedrosa convincingly tied up his second consecutive 250 crown. There had been much crowing from Stoner's faction, buoyed up by two recent race wins, but this time it was the Australian who fell out of contention. Directly afterwards, Pedrosa revealed the truth about how he had been carrying shoulder fractures since Motegi. Small, but wound tight, as they say – it was the climax to a second and in many ways much more difficult season of dominance for the diminutive rider, now earmarked for an immediate move to MotoGP, where there are fears that his physique might not be up to the task.

Dani might have been watching another RCV rookie closely – Chris Vermeulen, fresh off a string of Superbike wins, and the next to take over Bayliss's Camel Honda. No problems with physical size or strength for the 23-year-old Australian, who also had home track knowledge. He still found he had much to learn. Firstly the carbon brakes and then the tyres – Michelins against the control Pirellis of SBK. It was hard even to find their limits, let alone start being aggressive with them, and not surprisingly he was losing most of his time going into

MOTOGP RACE – 27 laps

Lap times dropped under 1:30 for the first time, but pole man Hayden was unsure about race pace, and pole might have gone to the more consistent Rossi, if not for being baulked by Xaus on the final sector of a fast lap. Gibernau was alongside, all the Michelin runners worried about grip. Top Bridgestone man was Checa, heading row two from Edwards and Biaggi, but threateningly fast and consistent on race tyres. Elias led row three, his best-yet qualifying position.

Hayden was fastest away, Checa challenging strongly, with Rossi tucked into third. Biaggi fell in the middle of the pack into Honda Hairpin, probably because of the cold right side of the tyre. "One minute I was braking, the next the bike was on its side."

By the end of the lap Rossi was in second, the front three slightly clear of Melandri, Gibernau, and Edwards. It would not last. Rossi drafted up the inside to take the lead from Hayden; one lap later Melandri was through to demote the American one place more, running inside in the long left-hand southern loop.

Hayden was enjoying an improved package after switching his tyre choice, and he shadowed Melandri for less than three laps before firmly getting ahead before the run up to Lukey Heights. Lap six closed with him half-a-second behind Rossi. Melandri was still right up close, but Checa had drifted away by 1.7 seconds, with Gibernau leaning on him. Edwards had

got ahead of the Spaniard for a while, but was now gradually losing touch.

The front three got even closer over the next lap, but Rossi was forcing the pace, and next time round Melandri had lost a second. Not so Hayden. He was still right with the Yamaha, and comfortable. "I tried to go alone two or three times, but Nicky came with me," Rossi said later. He decided to wait and see. There was some seesawing of the gaps over the forthcoming laps, with Hayden hanging on close, Melandri still losing tenths every lap. Gibernau finally passed Checa on lap ten, while behind them Barros got ahead of Edwards one lap later. Checa wasn't done yet, however, and regained fourth from Gibernau on the front straight as they started lap 12.

As they passed half distance, Rossi and Hayden were still glued together, Melandri 1.8 seconds behind, then a similar gap to Checa and Gibernau. The third-placed rider would lose more ground, then suddenly take a full second back again on lap 16, bringing the two Spaniards with him. At the end of lap 18, the top four were covered by less than three quarters of a second, fanning out over the line – Hayden now back in front of Rossi for the past two laps, then Melandri and Checa, with Gibernau a bare second behind. It was shaping up to become a Phillip Island classic.

Rossi started the next movement, diving past into Turn One at the start of lap 19. Melandri was also past Hayden a couple of corners later, and as this pair changed places again the leader made his escape bid. It proved crucial, claiming better than a second's lead after lap 20, and able to run at his own pace.

Hayden did close him down slowly after that, in the process dropping off Melandri. But it was never quite enough, and he crossed the line a second adrift.

Behind them, Melandri had been unable to shake off Checa, and the pair battled over the last lap. Checa took third as they started; Melandri took it back in Honda Corner, the pair clashing on the exit. It came to the run out of the final corners, Melandri spinning up and skittering a little wide. Checa took advantage, and used the Ducati's horsepower to take the rostrum by less than two hundredths.

Gibernau was ten seconds away, then a long gap to Edwards. This had been filled by Barros, travelling alone after passing the American. Then he crashed on lap 23 at the fast Hayshed turn before Lukey Heights, to be flipped end over end by the lip of the gravel trap.

It was tooth and nail for seventh. Nakano, Tamada and Elias had been exchanging places over the closing laps, and carried on all the way to a photo finish, in that order. It was similar for tenth. Vermeulen had passed Hopkins on lap eight, and the MotoGP regular had shadowed him from there to the finish, swerving out of his draft to beat him over the line.

Xaus lost time in the early laps and never recovered, finishing 12th; another 30 seconds behind, Rolfo was the last rider on the same lap. Ellison and Battaini completed the points; Jacque was 16th after twice running on at the hairpin, then pitting to change his rear tyre, another lap down.

250 cc RACE – 25 laps

Stoner was riding high on two wins and a tide of national enthusiasm, and took pole ahead of Lorenzo, de Angelis and Porto. Pedrosa was sixth, almost a second off pole.

The Australian got away first, and set about trying to escape. He had eked out less than three-quarters-of-a-second as he started his third lap, but he wouldn't finish it. Exiting MG hairpin, he spun the rear and flicked over the high side. De Angelis, right behind, also fell victim – clipping the fallen Aprilia, wheelying dramatically, regaining control briefly, only to run off to the inevitable tumble.

This changed the championship picture. If Pedrosa could win, he would be unassailable.

Lorenzo had inherited the lead, but Porto took over next time round, and Pedrosa joined him a lap later. Within a few laps, the pair had left everyone trailing, and they remained inseparable to the end, Pedrosa never as much as two tenths behind over the line, and usually much closer.

The Honda rider took his time to attack, confident not only in his own corner speed but also that his bike was running as strongly as ever. He planned to slipstream him out of the last corner to pass over the line. In fact, he was too close, and was forced to move out of the draft earlier than he wanted. "The bike wasn't quite as fast as I thought, but luckily it was enough to win by a couple of thousandths."

Below left: Chris Vermeulen did well enough in his MotoGP debut on a Honda to earn a factory ride. On a Suzuki.

Below centre: Little giants, with 17 World Championships between them. Angel Nieto (12 plus one) and team owner Jorge "Aspar" Martinez (4) enjoy the sunshine.

Bottom: Deciding moment. Stoner comes to grief as Pedrosa motors safely past.
Photographs: Gold & Goose

Above: New 250-class star Lorenzo leads, but Porto is stalking, and Pedrosa is stalking him. At the flag, the order will be reversed, and Lorenzo out of touch.

Right: Luthi managed an inspired breakaway win to regain the title lead.

Below right: Delighted 125 rookie Tomoyoshi Koyama after a best-ever second.

Bottom: With Luthi away on his mission, the rest were left to battle for second. Pasini heads Simoncelli, Kallio, Faubel and Simon, with Talmacsi off the back.

Opposite: Ruben Xaus, suffering through to the end of the year.
Photographs: Gold & Goose

Any hopes Lorenzo might have had of following were dashed when he was instead mixed up with a persistent Dovizioso, who got in front over the line on lap eight, and several times elsewhere. After that, however, the Spaniard was able to get clear and move away, with no hope of closing on the leaders. He was eight seconds adrift at the end.

The Italian had trouble coming up behind, and by lap 18 Barbera was within striking distance, bringing Aoyama along too. They ran the last seven laps in close formation, Aoyama in front as they started the final lap. By the end of it, both Barbera and Dovizioso were ahead of him.

De Puniet was a distant and lonely seventh – later that evening, it was announced he had signed for next year with the Kawasaki MotoGP team.

Locatelli was equally lonely in eighth; the usual privateer battle somewhat fragmented in his wake. Debon narrowly headed Guintoli across the line, as they had been most of the race. Sekiguchi's Aprilia had been with them, but rattled to a stop on the last lap.

Some way back, Chaz Davies led Heidolf and Smrz in a close trio; Jenkner, Ballerini and Corsi were almost side by side, but the last-named out of the points. Baldolini crashed out.

125 cc RACE – 23 laps

Luthi was on pole, and made short work of the 125cc race. The Swiss title challenger bolted from the green light, taking a lead of almost a full second on the first lap alone, and continued to pull away until almost five seconds clear after half distance. He could afford to slacken his pace and still win by more than half that amount. It was an important turn-about for the title. Luthi had arrived two points behind Kallio. He left 12 points ahead.

"Some people said it would not be possible to break away here, but I said I would try... and that was the reason for victory today," he said later.

The battle for second was more characteristic of the smallest class. It changed hands 11 times in the course of the race; third place even more often than that.

By the end of the race, there were still six riders in the pack, shuffling at every corner. Kallio had managed to get to the head of the group for the start of the last lap, but try as he might he could not get the gap he needed to get away.

They were still trading blows and positions on the run to the flag, with Koyama vaulting from sixth to second, Simoncelli somehow hanging on to third, then Pasini, Kallio and Faubel. Talmacsi and Rodriguez were right behind. It was a matter of tactics and timing – especially of the electronic kind: second to eighth covered by less than three-quarters of a second.

Gadea led the next big gang of six across the line, barely further apart in another classic brawl. All of which made Luthi's escape all the more impressive – and all the more disheartening for Kallio.

PHILLIP ISLAND

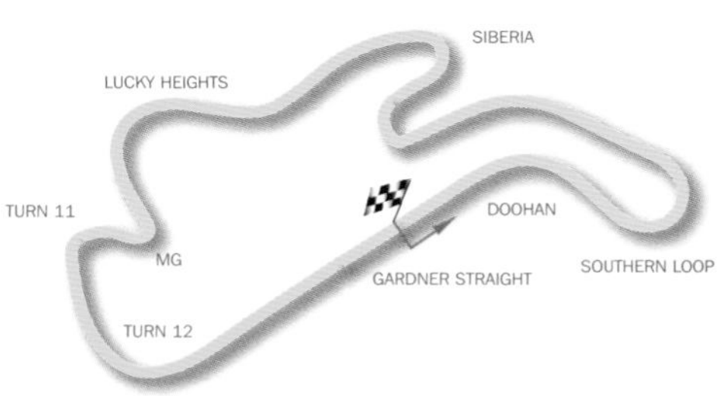

SIBERIA
LUCKY HEIGHTS
TURN 11
DOOHAN
MG
GARDNER STRAIGHT
SOUTHERN LOOP
TURN 12

CIRCUIT LENGTH: 2.764 miles/4.448 km

POLINI AUSTRALIAN GRAND PRIX

16 OCTOBER 2005 • FIM WORLD CHAMPIONSHIP ROUND 15

MotoGP

27 laps, 74.628 miles/120.096 km

Pos.	Rider (Nat.)	No.	Machine	Laps	Time & speed
1	Valentino Rossi (I)	46	Yamaha	27	41m 08.542s 108.828 mph/ 175.142 km/h
2	Nicky Hayden (USA)	69	Honda	27	41m 09.549s
3	Carlos Checa (E)	7	Ducati	27	41m 12.757s
4	Marco Melandri (I)	33	Honda	27	41m 12.774s
5	Sete Gibernau (E)	15	Honda	27	41m 22.630s
6	Colin Edwards (USA)	5	Yamaha	27	41m 41.742s
7	Shinya Nakano (J)	56	Kawasaki	27	41m 53.597s
8	Makoto Tamada (J)	6	Honda	27	41m 53.645s
9	Toni Elias (E)	24	Yamaha	27	41m 53.646s
10	John Hopkins (USA)	21	Suzuki	27	41m 58.802s
11	Chris Vermeulen (AUS)	17	Honda	27	41m 59.239s
12	Ruben Xaus (E)	11	Yamaha	27	42m 16.866s
13	Roberto Rolfo (I)	44	Ducati	27	42m 40.279s
14	James Ellison (GB)	77	Blata	26	41m 43.184s
15	Franco Battaini (I)	27	Blata	26	42m 15.829s
16	Olivier Jacque (F)	19	Kawasaki	25	41m 56.837s
	Alex Barros (BR)	4	Honda	22	DNF
	Max Biaggi (I)	3	Honda	0	DNF

Fastest lap: Melandri, 1m 30.332s, 110.148 mph/177.266 km/h (record).

Previous record: Loris Capirossi, I (Ducati), 1m 31.102s, 109.217 mph/175.767 km/h (2004).

Event best maximum speed: Checa, 207.2 mph/333.4 km/h (free practice no. 3).

Qualifying:: 1 Hayden, 1m 29.337s; 2 Rossi, 1m 29.443s; 3 Gibernau, 1m 29.729s; 4 Checa, 1m 29.775s; 5 Edwards, 1m 29.943s; 6 Biaggi, 1m 30.070s; 7 Elias, 1m 30.094s; 8 Melandri, 1m 30.322s; 9 Tamada, 1m 30.624s; 10 Nakano, 1m 30.628s; 11 Hopkins, 1m 30.667s; 12 Barros, 1m 30.757s; 13 Jacque, 1m 31.079s; 14 Vermeulen, 1m 31.654s; 15 Xaus, 1m 31.728s; 16 Rolfo, 1m 33.495s; 17 Ellison, 1m 33.673s; 18 Battaini, 1m 35.933s.

Fastest race laps: 1 Melandri, 1m 30.332s; 2 Hayden, 1m 30.438s; 3 Rossi, 1m 30.505s; 4 Gibernau, 1m 30.657s; 5 Edwards, 1m 30.827s; 6 Checa, 1m 30.837s; 7 Barros, 1m 31.119s; 8 Elias, 1m 31.618s; 9 Tamada, 1m 31.644s; 10 Nakano, 1m 31.892s; 11 Hopkins, 1m 32.170s; 12 Jacque, 1m 32.282s; 13 Vermeulen, 1m 32.350s; 14 Xaus, 1m 32.895s; 15 Rolfo, 1m 33.841s; 16 Ellison, 1m 34.145s; 17 Battaini, 1m 36.195s.

World Championship: 1 Rossi, 331; 2 Hayden and Melandri, 170; 4 Edwards, 162; 5 Biaggi, 159; 6 Capirossi, 148; 7 Gibernau, 137; 8 Barros, 129; 9 C. Checa, 114; 10 Nakano, 87; 11 Tamada, 76; 12 Roberts, 63; 13 Hopkins, 59; 14 Elias, 58; 15 Bayliss, 54; 16 Xaus, 49; 17 Jacque and Rolfo, 25; 19 Hofmann, 22; 20 van den Goorbergh, 12; 21 Battaini and Ellison, 7; 23 Byrne, 6; 24 Vermeulen, 5; 25 D. Checa, 4; 26 Ukawa, 1.

250 cc

25 laps, 69.100 miles/111.200 km

Pos.	Rider (Nat.)	No.	Machine	Laps	Time & speed
1	Daniel Pedrosa (E)	1	Honda	25	39m 18.195s 105.481 mph/ 169.756 km/h
2	Sebastian Porto (ARG)	19	Aprilia	25	39m 18.222s
3	Jorge Lorenzo (E)	48	Honda	25	39m 26.869s
4	Hector Barbera (E)	80	Honda	25	39m 43.033s
5	Andrea Dovizioso (I)	34	Honda	25	39m 43.063s
6	Hiroshi Aoyama (J)	73	Honda	25	39m 43.067s
7	Randy de Puniet (F)	7	Aprilia	25	39m 55.469s
8	Roberto Locatelli (I)	15	Aprilia	25	40m 05.208s
9	Alex Debon (E)	6	Honda	25	40m 14.797s
10	Sylvain Guintoli (F)	50	Aprilia	25	40m 14.942s
11	Chaz Davies (GB)	57	Aprilia	25	40m 27.321s
12	Dirk Heidolf (D)	28	Honda	25	40m 27.991s
13	Jakub Smrz (CZ)	96	Honda	25	40m 28.025s
14	Steve Jenkner (D)	17	Aprilia	25	40m 32.667s
15	Andrea Ballerini (I)	8	Aprilia	25	40m 32.692s
16	Simone Corsi (I)	24	Aprilia	25	40m 32.966s
17	Martin Cardenas (COL)	36	Aprilia	25	40m 40.275s
18	Mirko Giansanti (I)	32	Aprilia	24	39m 20.688s
19	Arturo Tizon (E)	33	Honda	24	39m 58.000s
20	Mathieu Gines (F)	56	Aprilia	24	40m 40.314s
	Taro Sekiguchi (J)	44	Aprilia	24	DNF
	Alex Baldolini (I)	25	Aprilia	17	DNF
	Arnaud Vincent (F)	21	Fantic	12	DNF
	Yuki Takahashi (J)	55	Honda	10	DNF
	Erwan Nigon (F)	63	Yamaha	6	DNF
	Casey Stoner (AUS)	27	Aprilia	4	DNF
	Alex de Angelis (RSM)	5	Aprilia	3	DNF
	Mick Kelly (AUS)	82	Honda		DNQ
	Nicklas Cajback (S)	23	Yamaha		DNQ
	Mark Rowling (AUS)	81	Yamaha		DNQ
	Gabriele Ferro (I)	20	Fantic		DNQ

Fastest lap: Porto, 1m 33.503s, 106.412 mph/171.254 km/h.

Previous record: Sebastian Porto, ARG (Aprilia), 1m 33.381s, 106.551 mph/171.478 km/h (2004).

Event best maximum speed: Locatelli, 167.7 mph/269.9 km/h (warm-up).

Qualifying: 1 Stoner, 1m 32.756s; 2 Lorenzo, 1m 32.843s; 3 de Angelis, 1m 32.882s; 4 Porto, 1m 33.117s; 5 Barbera, 1m 33.624s; 6 Pedrosa, 1m 33.691s; 7 Dovizioso, 1m 33.733s; 8 Aoyama, 1m 34.134s; 9 de Puniet, 1m 34.341s; 10 Locatelli, 1m 34.715s; 11 Takahashi, 1m 34.739s; 12 Jenkner, 1m 34.998s; 13 Debon, 1m 35.028s; 14 Guintoli, 1m 35.087s; 15 Sekiguchi, 1m 35.104s; 16 Corsi, 1m 35.225s; 17 Davies, 1m 35.710s; 18 Baldolini, 1m 35.761s; 19 Smrz, 1m 35.891s; 20 Ballerini, 1m 36.107s; 21 Heidolf, 1m 36.192s; 22 Giansanti, 1m 36.318s; 23 Cardenas, 1m 36.547s; 24 Tizon, 1m 36.631s; 25 Vincent, 1m 36.756s; 26 Nigon, 1m 37.463s; 27 Gines, 1m 37.611s; 28 Kelly, 1m 39.266s; 29 Cajback, 1m 39.507s; 30 Rowling, 1m 42.395s; 31 Ferro, 1m 59.674s.

Fastest race laps: 1 Porto, 1m 33.503s; 2 Pedrosa, 1m 33.528s; 3 Dovizioso, 1m 33.593s; 4 de Angelis, 1m 33.634s; 5 Stoner, 1m 33.682s; 6 Barbera, 1m 33.840s; 7 Lorenzo, 1m 33.979s; 8 Aoyama, 1m 34.053s; 9 de Puniet, 1m 34.576s; 10 Locatelli, 1m 35.094s; 11 Debon, 1m 35.186s; 12 Takahashi, 1m 35.613s; 13 Sekiguchi, 1m 35.702s; 14 Guintoli, 1m 35.753s; 15 Heidolf, 1m 35.916s; 16 Jenkner, 1m 36.139s; 17 Giansanti, 1m 36.162s; 18 Davies, 1m 36.265s; 19 Corsi, 1m 36.278s; 20 Smrz, 1m 36.342s; 21 Ballerini, 1m 36.357s; 22 Cardenas, 1m 36.479s; 23 Baldolini, 1m 36.627s; 24 Gines, 1m 37.733s; 25 Vincent, 1m 38.002s; 26 Nigon, 1m 38.229s; 27 Tizon, 1m 38.244s.

World Championship: 1 Pedrosa, 264; 2 Stoner, 213; 3 Dovizioso, 171; 4 Aoyama, 154; 5 Porto, 152; 6 Lorenzo, 134; 7 de Puniet, 130; 8 de Angelis, 129; 9 Barbera, 99; 10 Guintoli, 75; 11 Takahashi, 68; 12 Corsi, 59; 13 Debon, 58; 14 Locatelli, 47; 15 Giansanti, 34; 16 West, 30; 17 Davies, 26; 18 Baldolini, 20; 19 Ballerini, 16; 20 Smrz, 14; 21 Heidolf and Jenkner, 13; 23 Sekiguchi, 12; 24 Rous, 11; 25 Cardenas and Leblanc, 6; 27 Marchand and Nigon, 3.

125 cc

23 laps, 63.572 miles/102.304 km

Pos.	Rider (Nat.)	No.	Machine	Laps	Time & speed
1	Thomas Luthi (CH)	12	Honda	23	38m 00.352s 100.356 mph/ 161.507 km/h
2	Tomoyoshi Koyama (J)	71	Honda	23	38m 03.015s
3	Marco Simoncelli (I)	58	Aprilia	23	38m 03.017s
4	Mattia Pasini (I)	75	Aprilia	23	38m 03.025s
5	Mika Kallio (SF)	36	KTM	23	38m 03.212s
6	Hector Faubel (E)	55	Aprilia	23	38m 03.297s7
7	Gabor Talmacsi (H)	14	KTM	23	38m 03.302s
8	Angel Rodriguez (E)	47	Aprilia	23	38m 03.738s
9	Sergio Gadea (E)	33	Aprilia	23	38m 10.898s
10	Alexis Masbou (F)	7	Honda	23	38m 10.903s
11	Raffaele de Rosa (I)	35	Aprilia	23	38m 11.203s
12	Fabrizio Lai (I)	32	Honda	23	38m 11.423s
13	Manuel Poggiali (RSM)	54	Gilera	23	38m 11.485s
14	Mike di Meglio (F)	63	Honda	23	38m 11.981s
15	Joan Olive (E)	6	Aprilia	23	38m 15.400s
16	Alvaro Bautista (E)	19	Honda	23	38m 31.235s
17	Aleix Espargaro (E)	41	Honda	23	38m 31.236s
18	Pablo Nieto (E)	22	Derbi	23	38m 49.410s
19	Sandro Cortese (D)	11	Honda	23	38m 49.483s
20	Lorenzo Zanetti (I)	8	Aprilia	23	38m 49.522s
21	Toshihisa Kuzuhara (J)	9	Honda	23	38m 51.012s
22	Manuel Hernandez (E)	43	Aprilia	23	38m 51.379s
23	Mateo Tunez (E)	46	Aprilia	23	39m 07.669s
24	Gioele Pellino (I)	42	Malaguti	23	39m 10.184s
25	Jordi Carchano (E)	28	Aprilia	23	39m 21.664s
26	Dario Giuseppetti (D)	25	Aprilia	23	39m 28.579s
27	David Bonache (E)	48	Honda	22	38m 06.966s
28	Blake Leigh-Smith (AUS)	69	Honda	21	38m 56.668s
	Federico Sandi (I)	10	Honda	18	DNF
	Tom Hatton (AUS)	81	Honda	16	DNF
	Nicolas Terol (E)	18	Derbi	13	DNF
	Lukas Pesek (CZ)	52	Derbi	8	DNF
	Julian Simon (E)	60	KTM	7	DNF
	Imre Toth (H)	45	Aprilia	6	DNF
	Andrea Iannone (I)	29	Aprilia	3	DNF
	Michele Pirro (I)	15	Malaguti	2	DNF
	Sascha Hommel (D)	31	Honda	0	DNF
	Karel Abraham (CZ)	44	Aprilia		DNS
	Brent Riggoli (AUS)	70	Honda		DNQ
	Rhys Moller (AUS)	83	Honda		DNQ
	Candice Scott (AUS)	82	Honda		DNQ

Fastest lap: Rodriguez, 1m 38.054s, 101.473 mph/163.305 km/h.

Previous record: Daniel Pedrosa, E (Honda), 1m 37.983s, 101.547 mph/163.424 km/h (2002).

Event best maximum speed: Olive, 146.7 mph/236.1 km/h (free practice no. 2).

Qualifying: 1 Luthi, 1m 37.543s; 2 Pasini, 1m 37.704s; 3 Talmacsi, 1m 37.731s; 4 Simoncelli, 1m 37.796s; 5 Kallio, 1m 37.906s; 6 Koyama, 1m 37.930s; 7 di Meglio, 1m 37.983s; 8 Pesek, 1m 38.177s; 9 Lai, 1m 38.182s; 10 Olive, 1m 38.208s; 11 Simon, 1m 38.239s; 12 Rodriguez, 1m 38.449s; 13 Faubel, 1m 38.649s; 14 de Rosa, 1m 38.734s; 15 Poggiali, 1m 38.968s; 16 Cortese, 1m 39.020s; 17 Masbou, 1m 39.107s; 18 Bautista, 1m 39.107s; 19 Espargaro, 1m 39.249s; 20 Terol, 1m 39.368s; 21 Toth, 1m 39.578s; 22 Gadea, 1m 39.610s; 23 Zanetti, 1m 39.656s; 24 Carchano, 1m 39.701s; 25 Nieto, 1m 39.953s; 26 Kuzuhara, 1m 39.963s; 27 Abraham, 1m 40.082s; 28 Hernandez, 1m 40.272s; 29 Pellino, 1m 40.412s; 30 Sandi, 1m 40.418s; 31 Tunez, 1m 40.678s; 32 Pirro, 1m 40.936s; 33 Bonache, 1m 41.172s; 34 Iannone, 1m 41.814s; 35 Giuseppetti, 1m 42.145s; 36 Leigh-Smith, 1m 43.269s; 37 Hommel, 1m 43.285s; 38 Hatton, 1m 43.320s; 39 Riggoli, 1m 45.550s; 40 Moller, 1m 46.071s; 41 Scott, 1m 47.132s.

Fastest race laps: 1 Rodriguez, 1m 38.054s; 2 Faubel, 1m 38.156s; 3 Kallio, 1m 38.285s; 4 Simon, 1m 38.301s; 5 Luthi, 1m 38.302s; 6 Koyama, 1m 38.320s; 7 Simoncelli, 1m 38.323s; 8 de Rosa, 1m 38.372s; 9 Pasini, 1m 38.383s; 10 Masbou, 1m 38.405s; 11 Talmacsi, 1m 38.423s; 12 di Meglio, 1m 38.477s; 13 Lai, 1m 38.515s; 14 Gadea, 1m 38.516s; 15 Pesek, 1m 38.574s; 16 Poggiali, 1m 38.739s; 17 Olive, 1m 38.791s; 18 Espargaro, 1m 38.868s; 19 Bautista, 1m 39.081s; 20 Terol, 1m 39.275s; 21 Zanetti, 1m 39.551s; 22 Hernandez, 1m 39.843s; 23 Cortese, 1m 39.865s; 24 Nieto, 1m 39.881s; 25 Kuzuhara, 1m 40.089s; 26 Sandi, 1m 40.104s; 27 Pellino, 1m 40.434s; 28 Tunez, 1m 40.563s; 29 Carchano, 1m 40.946s; 30 Pirro, 1m 40.988s; 31 Toth, 1m 41.049s; 32 Bonache, 1m 41.789s; 33 Giuseppetti, 1m 41.974s; 34 Iannone, 1m 42.167s; 35 Hatton, 1m 43.356s; 36 Leigh-Smith, 1m 43.390s.

World Championship: 1 Luthi, 224; 2 Kallio, 212; 3 Talmacsi, 165; 4 Simoncelli, 156; 5 Pasini, 147; 6 Lai, 123; 7 Simon, 115; 8 Poggiali, 102; 9 Faubel, 100; 10 Koyama, 93; 11 di Meglio, 79; 12 Gadea, 68; 13 Nieto, 58; 14 Olive, 51; 15 Bautista, 39; 16 Espargaro, 31; 17 Zanetti, 30; 18 Masbou, 28; 19 Pesek, 22; 20 Kuzuhara, 17; 21 Iannone, 13; 22 Hernandez and Ranseder, 12; 24 de Rosa, 10; 25 Rodriguez, 8; 26 Linfoot and Toth, 7; 28 Carchano and Cortese, 6; 30 Conti, 5; 31 Elkin, 4; 32 Giuseppetti and Pirro, 3; 34 Jerez, 2; 35 Bradl and Terol, 1.

TURKISHGP
ISTANBUL

Above: MoviStar team principal Fausto Gresini beams with his latest race winner.

Above centre: Negotiations in the sun – Luis d'Antin hoped to recruit James Ellison for 2006, but Yamaha were also interested.

Top: Shinichi Ito made an inauspicious Ducati debut.

Left: Edwards (5) had his hands full with Elias (24). Gibernau (15) has just regained the track ahead of Checa, and will pass both before the lap is out.

Photographs: Gold & Goose

PADDOCK denizens were very jaded when they arrived in Istanbul, after five races in six weekends, spanning numerous time zones and both hemispheres in the trail from Japan to Malaysia, Qatar, Australia and Turkey. A few had suffered delays in the flight from the Antipodes to the Bosphorus, including Rossi's head man Burgess and Alex Barros, but all the freight had arrived. Only the jet lag was insoluble, with barely three days to accommodate a backwards time displacement of nine hours. It is one thing for the catering staff or the press corps to feel bewildered, dislocated, and inappropriately exhausted at inconvenient times. It is quite another for mechanics to feel the same way. And something else again when it is the riders.

Rossi agreed that it could be a safety issue. "I think 17 races is too many, and five races in six weeks is too much. The jet lag is too difficult. I have spent a lot of time in aeroplanes," said Rossi, who at least had the consolation of first class travel. "We need to think about this for the calendar, and not go back and forth in time zones," he said. (One wag told him he'd better not complain about 17 races, because F1, his rumoured destination, has 19. Rossi laughed, and said: "We try to fix one problem at a time.") By coincidence, or perhaps not, a revised 2006 calendar was announced during the weekend, with Malaysia, Australia and Japan obligingly grouped together on consecutive weekends, with a substantial break at either end.

It followed that this first trip to the gateway to Asia had not been anticipated with much pleasure. A new track, yes... but from the same designer who had inflicted Shanghai onto MotoGP, German Hermann Tilke. Expecting yet more strings of ultra-slow corners and with all but one title already settled, the circus approached this race as just another chore to be completed.

Jaded or not, nothing could have prepared riders and the rest for what they found, as they crested the surrounding hills for the first time to see the new municipal Istanbul Park circuit. Fine paddock buildings and facilities are nothing new, though standards keep rising and here was another leading example... in very stark contrast to its immediate surroundings, let it be said. The joy came from the track itself – diving off into a tricky downhill first corner past the pits before soaring away across the distant hillsides. Some riders criticised the trade-mark "Tilke Twiddles" at the end of the lap – an ultra-tight left-right-left set taken in first gear; but these proved their value in all the races as a mix-and-match counterpoint to the sweeping approach bends.

And what an approach. After a tricky downhill braking section and a second-gear left-right combination, the track climbs in a crescendo of speed to Turn 11, taken flat in fifth at around 160 mph... the fastest corner of the year. This new circuit gave MotoGP riders an opportunity that is unknown at most modern circuits... to open the throttles and let the thing run, on the edge of tyres' and the chassis's abilities, just as hard as they dared. Hayden's "men from the boys" comment on the bend was echoed by many and understood by all.

The next section was the fastest point on the track, with speeds better than 190 mph... directly followed by more hard braking for the first-gear finishing set.

The track was not perfect, however – in spite of its newness, with just one F1 race already, plus a German touring car event, it was already puckering up in the braking zones said Rossi, describing a sort of wave formation with his hands. This was familiar from other tracks shared with F1, notably Catalunya before resurfacing, but not all shared tracks, he said, Sepang (another Tilke circuit) an exception. Grip was not high, with the touring cars blamed for a polishing effect.

With Gauloises now believed sure to go, there were more uncertainties in the paddock than usual, but it was the start of an interesting time for young riders seeking MotoGP opportunities. Vermeulen, back again on the Camel Honda, was one such. In fact, his mind was already made up, it seems, and the announcement at Istanbul that Kenny Roberts Jr. would not be with Suzuki in 2006 cleared the field. On the Friday

after the race it was announced the he had signed a two-year contract with Suzuki. The 23-year-old Australian's reasoning was that he wanted to have a factory bike that could be developed around him, rather than having to take a hand-me-down non-adjustable satellite Honda, though he admitted there was a lot of faith involved in joining a team currently languishing out of contention. Honda had their own plans for him – namely another year in World Superbike to win that title, and only then a step onto the MotoGP ladder. A weekend of frantic doorstepping included a handsome financial offer to do just that, but Vermeulen let it be known that "I'm not in racing for the money," and stuck with his resolve.

Colin Edwards was talking again about having to modify his style, from Superbike point-and-squirt to a smoother 250 manner. He might have picked up some tips in the race from ex-250 MotoGP rookie Elias, who handed him a solid drubbing in the run through the Tilke Twiddles in the race, the pair changing places three times. Edwards was the first MotoGP rider to tumble at the new track – a harmless low-sider that left the engine running with the bike on its side, until he ran to it and hit the kill-switch. This was to have consequences in the afternoon, when the same engine suffered a smoky blow-up, a healthy oil fire brewing up in the belly pan as he stopped. It was a toned-down replay of his fire-ball bail-out at Sachsenring the year before last, when his Aprilia's fuel filler cap came off, and he had to jump off at speed.

Capirossi was recuperating in Italy; his replacement Ito (Ducati's test rider, and former HRC 500 man) had a short afternoon. Failing to see signs calling him in for a jump-start penalty, he was black-flagged after six laps.

Inasmuch as a new track reveals basic readiness to race – having a good base setting, for example, only Gresini's MoviStar team came up smiling from the start. The reward was a fine maiden win for Melandri, a true defeat of Rossi (albeit in post-title mood), and an important score in the battle for second overall with Hayden.

MOTOGP RACE – 22 laps

Melandri dominated free practice, and only lost his first pole to a small slip on his qualifying lap, as well as a timely burst from his team-mate Gibernau. Just over a tenth apart, they were a half-a-second clear of Hayden, who made it the first all-Honda front row since the Sachsenring. Rossi was having trouble with stability, and only caught up right at the end of the session, to head an all-Yamaha second row from Edwards and Elias.

Melandri got the jump into the first turn, from Gibernau, Hayden, Edwards and Elias. Rossi was slow away, and behind Tamada for much of the first lap. He had lost 2.2 costly seconds on the leaders by the time he got by, and was more than a second off Elias.

All in a day's work you might think, had there been a title at stake, and he was soon with the rookie, and straight past him. His problem was that the front three were pulling clear, and he still had to get ahead of Edwards before catching them.

Up front, Melandri was having trouble with a full tank, and though he knew he would get better later in the race, he was worried when Gibernau snatched the lead at the start of the climb to Turn 11 and charged off impressively. He didn't have to worry long... Gibernau led for two laps before leaving his braking too late for an early uphill corner. He was out wide and across the kerb as Melandri, Hayden and by now also Rossi piled past. He regained hard standing almost six seconds adrift, ahead of Checa but behind Edwards, Elias, Barros, though he would pass them all by the end of the lap. In a year of missed chances and rotten luck, this was the third time he'd simply run off the track while leading.

The leaders were still covered by just over a second on lap seven; next time round Rossi pushed past Hayden in the last tight turns. The effort cost some time, and Melandri started lap nine with almost a second in hand.

Normally, Rossi would soon close this up. This time, the gap stayed the same for three laps, and then started to stretch out,

little by little. On lap 16 Melandri's lead was two seconds, and on lap 20 it was three. With just two left, the game was effectively over.

Hayden had stuck with Rossi, close but never threatening, until there were four laps to go. They crossed the line distinctly separated, with Melandri standing on one foot, his other leg cocked up behind him and the bike on its back wheel; Hayden well out of touch.

The angry Gibernau was next. Behind him, Checa – 11th on lap one, and charging – had made short work of Edwards, Elias and Barros, passing all three in one reshuffle in the last corners. Edwards now dropped to the back of the group behind Barros, and the pair swapped places once or twice, but lost ground as Elias stayed close to the Ducati. Three laps later, he found the pace too hot and also ran off briefly, leaving Checa a straightforward run to fifth.

Edwards and Barros flashed past, and also Tamada, but the class rookie was not to be denied. He closed on Tamada, who was himself gaining on the two up front, and despatched the Japanese rider on lap 18.

One lap later he was past the fading Barros as well, and he hounded Edwards from there to the end, with a successful final attack in the last triple-set, finally passing the American round the outside of the final corner for a career-best sixth.

Tamada passed Barros with three laps to go.

Vermeulen finished lap one ninth, and held his place for two more laps after Checa came by, with Nakano, Tamada, Jacque and Hopkins piling up behind. The Japanese pair picked him off, Tamada bound for better things, but the rookie stayed in front of the other two all the way to the flag.

It was a black day for Biaggi. He'd qualified 12th, finished the first lap 15th, behind Itoh and losing touch. He gradually caught the slowing Hopkins, stricken with 'flu, and passed him after half distance, then Jacque also two laps later. That was the end of his progress. There were angry scenes back in the pit, the consequences of which were that Honda decided soon afterwards that Biaggi would never again ride one of their motorcycles.

By the finish, Hopkins had slowed enough to come into range of Xaus, who passed him with two laps to go – an unusual event for the increasingly out-of-place Spaniard.

250 cc RACE – 20 laps

De Angelis and Stoner had a strong battle for pole, with Aoyama following team-mate Pedrosa to push him onto the far end of the front row. Porto again led row two from fast rookies Barbera, Lorenzo and Dovizioso.

Stoner planned to win from the start, and took an immediate lead, which he stretched to almost 1.5 seconds after six laps.

Rivals had started to drop out from the start, de Puniet skittled on the very first corner, team-mate Porto crashing out alone on the second lap.

Scrapping for second, Lorenzo's first-lap advantage did not last, and he was to drop backwards bit by bit as Dovizioso took over. De Angelis and Aoyama stayed with him, Pedrosa tagging on behind on lap four.

Stoner's pace kept the pursuit at full stretch, until Pedrosa made a swoop under braking at the end of the lap six, going from fifth to second in one lap. He was soon outpacing his companions as he nibbled away at the lead of less than 1.5 seconds, a few tenths a lap. On lap 15, with five to go, the blue Honda was on Stoner's tail, and looked set to attack.

Stoner, however, gave him no opportunity, running a string of consistent fast laps, with the final one his fastest of the race (though a little short of Pedrosa's earlier new lap record). Pedrosa started that lap only inches behind, and even pulled almost alongside in the final run through the fast corner. Stoner braked even later than usual for the final bends, and was less than a tenth ahead over the line for his fifth win of the year.

Pedrosa's escape left de Angelis and Aoyama to a fierce battle, Dovizioso fading from the back of it. The fight was resolved with some rough and tumble in the Tilke Twiddles, the pair colliding in the middle right-hander and de Angelis getting the worst of it, so

that he tumbled on the following left.

This left fourth to be disputed by the next trio. Lorenzo had been engaged with Barbera, and now caught and passed Dovizioso with one lap left, Barbera sixth, all three covered by four tenths.

De Angelis scrambled back on board to save seventh, crossing the line less than half a second ahead of Locatelli, who had escaped from a big privateer battle. Guintoli was also clear at the finish, with Davies and Baldolini inches apart as they had been all race long, for tenth and 11th,

Another gang, four-strong, disputed the last points, with Debon taking 12th ahead of Ballerini, Giansanti and Smrz.

Crashes included Sekiguchi, Cardenas, Corsi and Takahashi, as well as Chinese wild card Zhu Wang.

Stoner's win prolonged the battle for the constructors' title, giving Aprilia 323 points to Honda's 324.

Opposite: Melandri on the podium... the picture of Turkish delight.

Below: Lorenzo was still hoping to become the youngest-ever 250 winner.

Bottom: Stoner resisted fearsome pressure for his fifth win in a strong season.
Photographs: Gold & Goose

Above: Tight final turns made a fine 125 brawl. Here eventual winner di Meglio leads Kallio (half-hidden), Luthi (12) and Pasini (75). Talmacsi (14) will also have a turn up front.

Right: Manuel Poggiali, once a winner, now struggling for the top ten.

Below: The 125 rostrum, and Pasini was ready with a special Dunlop fez. Winner di Meglio is flanked by Koyama.

Opposite: Melandri's pit board on the last lap.

Photographs: Gold & Goose

125 cc RACE – 19 laps

Points leader Luthi was in no mood for compromise, claiming pole fully four tenths ahead of Faubel, with Kallio third and Pasini fourth.

The combination of fast sweeping corners, heavy braking and the final twirls made for an epic close race – anyone left behind in the slipstreaming could get another crack at passing everyone again. On the first lap alone, the lead changed hands four times (mainly between Kallio and Luthi), with the braking at the end of the back straight seeing riders coming in four or five abreast. The same thing would happen every lap until the end.

Di Meglio led the next two laps, then Kallio and Luthi took a turn each. By then, the front pack dropped by two, as team-mates Faubel and Gadea crashed into each other in the slow section.

Talmacsi led on lap six, but still in bad odour after his Qatar win, it was only once and he ceded directly to Kallio, with the top five still covered by a mere eight tenths, and Koyama closing up fast to join the gang.

Pasini then took over for five laps, trying but failing to get away.

With four laps left, Luthi was at the back of the group and Kallio once again at the front, and Luthi seemed to be struggling to stay in touch, though he would catch up again hand over fist in the slow last corners. He was just waiting, and as they came in to finish the penultimate lap he was closer, and swooped from fifth to first.

This spurred Kallio to even greater efforts. Too great. He regained the lead on the far left-hander at the top of the hill, but was off-line and too fast. The front wheel slid away, and he was down and out.

In title terms, this meant Luthi needed to finish third to clinch it (fourth would have offered only a potential points tie) – but that wasn't so easy. He came off worst in the final brawl through the slow turns, as Frenchman di Meglio bullied his way to a narrow first win, just inches ahead of Pasini and Koyama, then Talmacsi and Luthi.

There was a similar unseemly brawl for sixth, with Simoncelli leading Lai, Rodriguez and Olivé past the flag. Masbou had been with this group, but crashed out.

ISTANBUL PARK

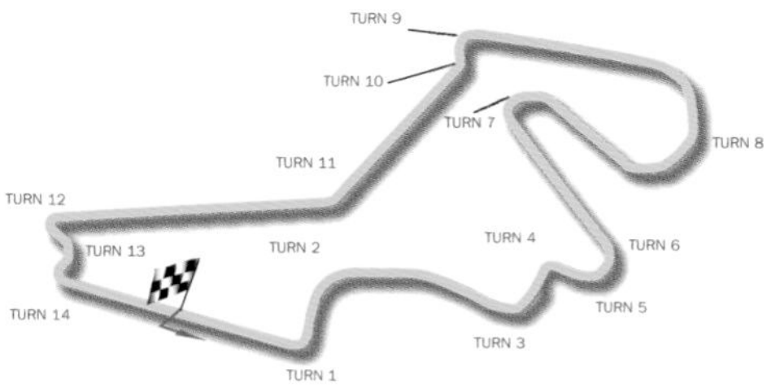
TURN 9
TURN 10
TURN 7
TURN 8
TURN 11
TURN 12
TURN 13
TURN 2
TURN 4
TURN 6
TURN 14
TURN 5
TURN 3
TURN 1

CIRCUIT LENGTH: 3.337 miles/5.340 km

GRAND PRIX OF TURKEY

YAMAHA

23 OCTOBER 2005 • FIM WORLD CHAMPIONSHIP ROUND 16

MotoGP

22 laps, 72.996 miles/117.480 km

Pos.	Rider (Nat.)	No.	Machine	Laps	Time & speed
1	Marco Melandri (I)	33	Honda	22	41m 44.139s 104.944 mph/ 168.891 km/h
2	Valentino Rossi (I)	46	Yamaha	22	41m 45.652s
3	Nicky Hayden (USA)	69	Honda	22	41m 51.012s
4	Sete Gibernau (E)	15	Honda	22	41m 56.559s
5	Carlos Checa (E)	7	Ducati	22	42m 11.102s
6	Toni Elias (E)	24	Yamaha	22	42m 13.244s
7	Colin Edwards (USA)	5	Yamaha	22	42m 13.394s
8	Makoto Tamada (J)	6	Honda	22	42m 17.484s
9	Alex Barros (BR)	4	Honda	22	42m 17.929s
10	Shinya Nakano (J)	56	Kawasaki	22	42m 28.364s
11	Chris Vermeulen (AUS)	17	Honda	22	42m 30.238s
12	Max Biaggi (I)	3	Honda	22	42m 34.323s
13	Olivier Jacque (F)	19	Kawasaki	22	42m 40.905s
14	Ruben Xaus (E)	11	Yamaha	22	42m 45.499s
15	John Hopkins (USA)	21	Suzuki	22	42m 47.530s
16	Roberto Rolfo (I)	44	Ducati	22	43m 01.793s
17	Franco Battaini (I)	27	Blata	21	42m 09.486s
18	James Ellison (GB)	77	Blata	21	42m 47.811s
	Shinichi Ito (J)	23	Ducati		Excluded

Fastest lap: Melandri, 1m 53.111s, 105.606 mph/169.956 km/h (record).

Previous record: none (new circuit).

Event best maximum speed: Checa, 190.6 mph/306.8 km/h (free practice no. 1).

Qualifying: 1 Gibernau, 1m 52.334s; 2 Melandri, 1m 52.463s; 3 Hayden, 1m 52.976s; 4 Rossi, 1m 53.177s; 5 Edwards, 1m 53.219s; 6 Elias, 1m 53.230s; 7 Tamada, 1m 53.667s; 8 Barros, 1m 53.719s; 9 Checa, 1m 53.836s; 10 Nakano, 1m 54.023s; 11 Vermeulen, 1m 54.217s; 12 Biaggi, 1m 54.358s; 13 Jacque, 1m 54.407s; 14 Hopkins, 1m 54.434s; 15 Ito, 1m 54.669s; 16 Xaus, 1m 55.414s; 17 Rolfo, 1m 55.838s; 18 Ellison, 1m 56.576s; 19 Battaini, 1m 58.417s.

Fastest race laps: 1 Melandri, 1m 53.111s; 2 Hayden, 1m 53.270s; 3 Rossi, 1m 53.305s; 4 Gibernau, 1m 53.414s; 5 Checa, 1m 53.507s; 6 Elias, 1m 53.901s; 7 Edwards, 1m 54.327s; 8 Tamada, 1m 54.358s; 9 Barros, 1m 54.376s; 10 Nakano, 1m 54.965s; 11 Vermeulen, 1m 55.136s; 12 Hopkins, 1m 55.235s; 13 Jacque, 1m 55.363s; 14 Biaggi, 1m 55.383s; 15 Ito, 1m 55.478s; 16 Xaus, 1m 55.948s; 17 Rolfo, 1m 56.012s; 18 Ellison, 1m 56.135s; 19 Battaini, 1m 59.639s.

World Championship: 1 Rossi, 351; 2 Melandri, 195; 3 Hayden, 186; 4 Edwards, 171; 5 Biaggi, 163; 6 Gibernau, 150; 7 Capirossi, 148; 8 Barros, 136; 9 C. Checa, 125; 10 Nakano, 93; 11 Tamada, 84; 12 Elias, 68; 13 Roberts, 63; 14 Hopkins, 60; 15 Bayliss, 54; 16 Xaus, 51; 17 Jacque, 28; 18 Rolfo, 25; 19 Hofmann, 22; 20 van den Goorbergh, 12; 21 Vermeulen, 10; 22 Battaini and Ellison, 7; 24 Byrne, 6; 25 D. Checa, 4; 26 Ukawa, 1.

MARCO
P1
0000K

250 cc

20 laps, 66.360 miles/106.800 km

Pos.	Rider (Nat.)	No.	Machine	Laps	Time & speed
1	Casey Stoner	27	Aprilia	20	39m 28.243s 100.878 mph/ 162.348 km/h
2	Daniel Pedrosa (E)	1	Honda	20	39m 28.336s
3	Hiroshi Aoyama (J)	73	Honda	20	39m 39.890s
4	Jorge Lorenzo (E)	48	Honda	20	39m 50.104s
5	Andrea Dovizioso (I)	34	Honda	20	39m 50.183s
6	Hector Barbera (E)	80	Honda	20	39m 50.501s
7	Alex de Angelis (RSM)	5	Aprilia	20	40m 11.998s
8	Roberto Locatelli (I)	15	Aprilia	20	40m 12.348s
9	Sylvain Guintoli (F)	50	Aprilia	20	40m 17.161s
10	Chaz Davies (GB)	57	Aprilia	20	40m 22.619s
11	Alex Baldolini (I)	25	Aprilia	20	40m 22.894s
12	Alex Debon (E)	6	Honda	20	40m 28.034s
13	Andrea Ballerini (I)	8	Aprilia	20	40m 28.325s
14	Mirko Giansanti (I)	32	Aprilia	20	40m 28.468s
15	Jakub Smrz (CZ)	96	Honda	20	40m 28.581s
16	Dirk Heidolf (D)	28	Honda	20	40m 56.327s
17	Mathieu Gines (F)	56	Aprilia	20	41m 02.908s
18	Arturo Tizon (E)	33	Honda	20	41m 13.730s
19	Erwan Nigon (F)	63	Yamaha	19	39m 44.274s
20	Zheng Peng Li (CHN)	61	Aprilia	19	40m 18.354s
21	Nicklas Cajback (S)	23	Yamaha	19	40m 36.811s
	Yuki Takahashi (J)	55	Honda	19	DNF
	Arnaud Vincent (F)	21	Fantic	11	DNF
	Zhu Wang (CHN)	60	Aprilia	11	DNF
	Simone Corsi (I)	24	Aprilia	9	DNF
	Martin Cardenas (COL)	36	Aprilia	4	DNF
	Taro Sekiguchi (J)	44	Aprilia	2	DNF
	Steve Jenkner (D)	17	Aprilia	2	DNF
	Sebastian Porto (ARG)	19	Aprilia	1	DNF
	Randy de Puniet (F)	7	Aprilia	0	DNF
	Gabriele Ferro (I)	20	Fantic		DNQ

Fastest lap: Pedrosa, 1m 57.595s, 101.579 mph/163.476 km/h (record).

Previous record: none (new circuit).

Event best maximum speed: de Angelis, 165.6 mph/266.5 km/h (qualifying practice no. 1).

Qualifying: 1 de Angelis, 1m 56.930s; 2 Stoner, 1m 57.071s; 3 Aoyama, 1m 57.198s; 4 Pedrosa, 1m 57.390s; 5 Porto, 1m 57.408s; 6 Barbera, 1m 57.969s; 7 Lorenzo, 1m 58.093s; 8 Dovizioso, 1m 58.107s; 9 Locatelli, 1m 58.421s; 10 de Puniet, 1m 58.437s; 11 Takahashi, 1m 58.678s; 12 Debon, 1m 59.074s; 13 Guintoli, 1m 59.129s; 14 Jenkner, 1m 59.167s; 15 Corsi, 1m 59.296s; 16 Baldolini, 1m 59.325s; 17 Davies, 1m 59.750s; 18 Cardenas, 1m 59.757s; 19 Smrz, 1m 59.948s; 20 Sekiguchi, 1m 59.951s; 21 Heidolf, 2m 00.007s; 22 Ballerini, 2m 00.147s; 23 Giansanti, 2m 00.180s; 24 Tizon, 2m 00.677s; 25 Gines, 2m 01.217s; 26 Nigon, 2m 02.817s; 27 Vincent, 2m 02.819s; 28 Li, 2m 04.091s; 29 Wang, 2m 04.265s; 30 Cajback, 2m 05.062s; 31 Ferro, 2m 08.940s.

Fastest race laps: 1 Pedrosa, 1m 57.595s; 2 Aoyama, 1m 57.812s; 3 Stoner, 1m 57.934s; 4 de Angelis, 1m 57.935s; 5 Dovizioso, 1m 58.239s; 6 Barbera, 1m 58.751s; 7 Lorenzo, 1m 58.798s; 8 Locatelli, 1m 59.410s; 9 Guintoli, 1m 59.957s; 10 Takahashi, 2m 00.083s; 11 Baldolini, 2m 00.147s; 12 Davies, 2m 00.219s; 13 Corsi, 2m 00.298s; 14 Debon, 2m 00.329s; 15 Ballerini, 2m 00.397s; 16 Smrz, 2m 00.510s; 17 Giansanti, 2m 00.593s; 18 Cardenas, 2m 00.965s; 19 Sekiguchi, 2m 01.334s; 20 Jenkner, 2m 01.513s; 21 Heidolf, 2m 01.598s; 22 Gines, 2m 01.802s; 23 Tizon, 2m 02.382s; 24 Nigon, 2m 03.485s; 25 Vincent, 2m 03.533s; 26 Wang, 2m 04.828s; 27 Porto, 2m 05.199s; 28 Li, 2m 05.460s; 29 Cajback, 2m 06.316s.

World Championship: 1 Pedrosa, 284; 2 Stoner, 238; 3 Dovizioso, 182; 4 Aoyama, 170; 5 Porto, 152; 6 Lorenzo, 147; 7 de Angelis, 138; 8 de Puniet, 130; 9 Barbera, 109; 10 Guintoli, 82; 11 Takahashi, 68; 12 Debon, 62; 13 Corsi, 59; 14 Locatelli, 55; 15 Giansanti, 36; 16 Davies, 32; 17 West, 30; 18 Baldolini, 25; 19 Ballerini, 19; 20 Smrz, 15; 21 Heidolf and Jenkner, 13; 23 Sekiguchi, 12; 24 Rous, 11; 25 Cardenas and Leblanc, 6; 27 Marchand and Nigon, 3.

125 cc

19 laps, 63.042 miles/101.460 km

Pos.	Rider (Nat.)	No.	Machine	Laps	Time & speed
1	Mike di Meglio (F)	63	Honda	19	39m 50.377s 94.947 mph/ 152.802 km/h
2	Mattia Pasini (I)	75	Aprilia	19	39m 50.482s
3	Tomoyoshi Koyama (J)	71	Honda	19	39m 50.533s
4	Gabor Talmacsi (H)	14	KTM	19	39m 50.648s
5	Thomas Luthi (CH)	12	Honda	19	39m 50.794s
6	Marco Simoncelli (I)	58	Aprilia	19	39m 56.129s
7	Fabrizio Lai (I)	32	Honda	19	39m 56.525s
8	Angel Rodriguez (E)	47	Aprilia	19	39m 56.671s
9	Joan Olive (E)	6	Aprilia	19	39m 56.988s
10	Andrea Iannone (I)	29	Aprilia	10	40m 07.496s
11	Manuel Poggiali (RSM)	54	Gilera	19	40m 07.931s
12	Alvaro Bautista (E)	19	Honda	19	40m 11.609s
13	Lukas Pesek (CZ)	52	Derbi	19	40m 11.843s
14	Sandro Cortese (D)	11	Honda	19	40m 32.584s
15	Dario Giuseppetti (D)	25	Aprilia	19	40m 33.175s
16	Nicolas Terol (E)	18	Derbi	19	40m 38.252s
17	Aleix Espargaro (E)	41	Honda	19	40m 38.292s
18	Karel Abraham (CZ)	44	Aprilia	19	40m 38.617s
19	Jordi Carchano (E)	28	Aprilia	19	40m 38.744s
20	Pablo Nieto (E)	22	Derbi	19	40m 39.070s
21	Mateo Tunez (E)	46	Aprilia	19	40m 39.317s
22	Jules Cluzel (F)	89	Malaguti	19	40m 57.551s
23	Gioele Pellino (I)	42	Malaguti	19	40m 57.830s
24	Imre Toth (H)	45	Aprilia	19	41m 03.307s
25	Manuel Hernandez (E)	43	Honda	19	41m 04.119s
26	Sascha Hommel (D)	31	Honda	19	41m 26.653s
	Mika Kallio (SF)	36	KTM	18	DNF
	Alexis Masbou (F)	7	Honda	14	DNF
	Federico Sandi (I)	10	Honda	12	DNF
	Lorenzo Zanetti (I)	8	Aprilia	8	DNF
	David Bonache (E)	48	Honda	5	DNF
	Hector Faubel (E)	55	Aprilia	3	DNF
	Sergio Gadea (E)	33	Aprilia	3	DNF
	Daniel Saez (E)	49	Aprilia	1	DNF
	Raffaele de Rosa (I)	35	Aprilia	0	DNF

Fastest lap: Luthi, 2m 04.428s, 96.000 mph/154.498 km/h (record).

Previous record: none (new circuit).

Event best maximum speed: Koyama, 140.8 mph/226.6 km/h (free practice no. 1).

Qualifying: 1 Luthi, 2m 03.585s; 2 Faubel, 2m 04.064s; 3 Kallio, 2m 04.115s; 4 Pasini, 2m 04.179s; 5 Gadea, 2m 04.833s; 6 di Meglio, 2m 04.888s; 7 Koyama, 2m 05.026s; 8 Talmacsi, 2m 05.107s; 9 Simoncelli, 2m 05.300s; 10 Pesek, 2m 05.368s; 11 Lai, 2m 05.511s; 12 de Rosa, 2m 05.519s; 13 Masbou, 2m 05.643s; 14 Olive, 2m 05.845s; 15 Rodriguez, 2m 05.864s; 16 Bautista, 2m 05.902s; 17 Poggiali, 2m 06.186s; 18 Zanetti, 2m 06.243s; 19 Terol, 2m 06.303s; 20 Nieto, 2m 06.345s; 21 Iannone, 2m 06.455s; 22 Abraham, 2m 06.654s; 23 Espargaro, 2m 06.727s; 24 Carchano, 2m 06.787s; 25 Cortese, 2m 07.007s; 26 Giuseppetti, 2m 07.243s; 27 Toth, 2m 07.293s; 28 Cluzel, 2m 07.861s; 29 Sandi, 2m 07.937s; 30 Hernandez, 2m 08.143s; 31 Saez, 2m 08.290s; 32 Tunez, 2m 08.443s; 33 Pellino, 2m 08.680s; 34 Bonache, 2m 09.432s; 35 Hommel, 2m 09.597s.

Fastest race laps: 1 Luthi, 2m 04.428s; 2 Pasini, 2m 04.495s; 3 Talmacsi, 2m 04.719s; 4 Koyama, 2m 04.846s; 5 Kallio, 2m 04.859s; 6 Rodriguez, 2m 04.946s; 7 Simoncelli, 2m 05.048s; 8 Lai, 2m 05.091s; 9 di Meglio, 2m 05.165s; 10 Masbou, 2m 05.251s; 11 Olive, 2m 05.366s; 12 Bautista, 2m 05.367s; 13 Iannone, 2m 05.500s; 14 Faubel, 2m 05.535s; 15 Poggiali, 2m 05.732s; 16 Pesek, 2m 05.864s; 17 Cortese, 2m 05.909s; 18 Gadea, 2m 06.142s; 19 Espargaro, 2m 06.234s; 20 Terol, 2m 06.764s; 21 Abraham, 2m 06.880s; 22 Tunez, 2m 06.982s; 23 Nieto, 2m 07.031s; 24 Giuseppetti, 2m 07.119s; 25 Carchano, 2m 07.148s; 26 Hernandez, 2m 07.476s; 27 Zanetti, 2m 07.629s; 28 Toth, 2m 07.786s; 29 Cluzel, 2m 08.025s; 30 Sandi, 2m 08.297s; 31 Pellino, 2m 08.500s; 32 Bonache, 2m 08.808s; 33 Hommel, 2m 09.589s.

World Championship: 1 Luthi, 235; 2 Kallio, 212; 3 Talmacsi, 178; 4 Pasini, 167; 5 Simoncelli, 166; 6 Lai, 132; 7 Simon, 115; 8 Koyama, 109; 9 Poggiali, 107; 10 di Meglio, 104; 11 Faubel, 100; 12 Gadea, 68; 13 Nieto and Olive, 58; 15 Bautista, 43; 16 Espargaro, 31; 17 Zanetti, 30; 18 Masbou, 28; 19 Pesek, 25; 20 Iannone, 19; 21 Kuzuhara, 17; 22 Rodriguez, 16; 23 Hernandez and Ranseder, 12; 25 de Rosa, 10; 26 Cortese, 8; 27 Linfoot and Toth, 7; 29 Carchano, 6; 30 Conti, 5; 31 Elkin and Giuseppetti, 4; 33 Pirro, 3; 34 Jerez, 2; 35 Bradl and Terol, 1.

Melandri leads Hayden and the pack into
Turn One. He was still in front at the end.
Photograph: Gold & Goose

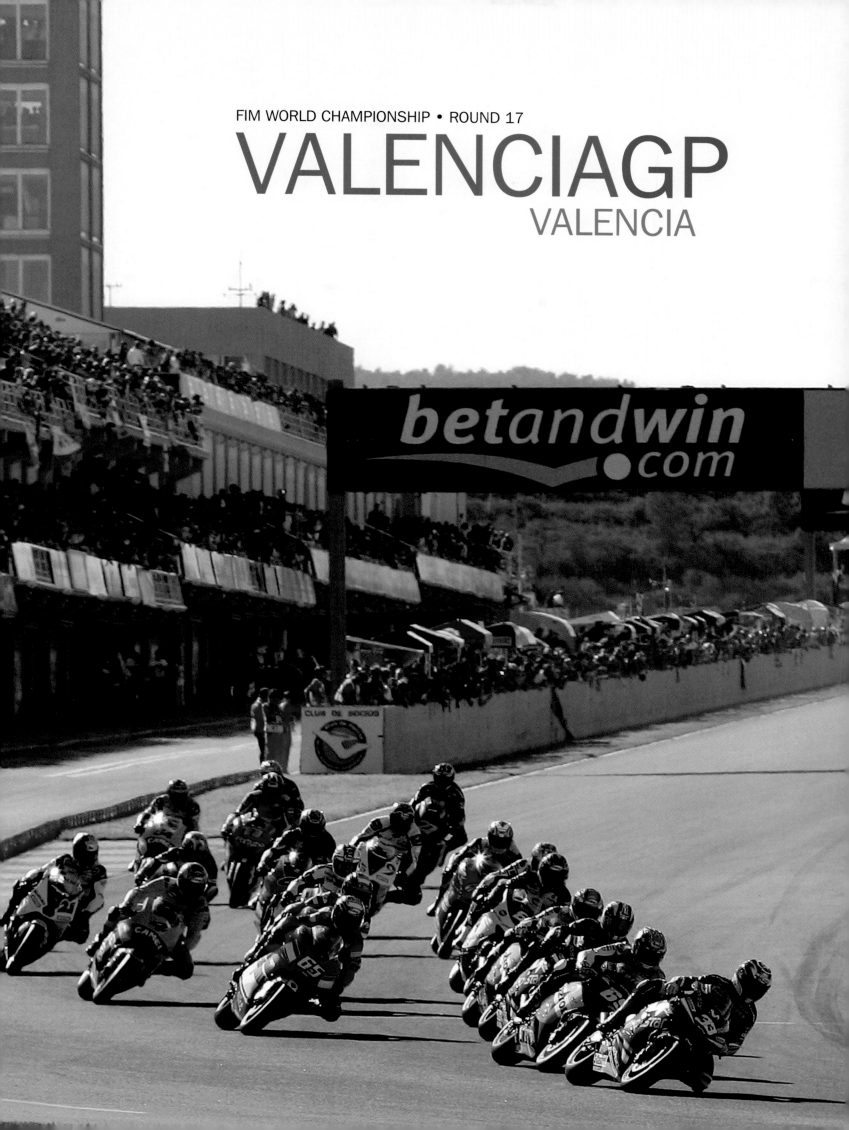

betandwin
.com

Above: **End-of-season paddock, buzzing with rumours, gossip and intrigue.**

Right: **Pubescent paradise as Nicky Hayden meets and greets.**

Centre right: **Thumbs-up from Sete... the BMW for fastest qualifier was his only prize since the start of the year.**
Photographs: Gold & Goose

THERE were still minor titles to be decided – riders' in 125, constructors' in 125 and 250. The 125 decision could hardly have been more tense or ironic. Kallio lost it by five points... exactly the number his team-mate Talmacsi had robbed him of at Qatar.

All the same, Valencia was more about next year than this. And it was a messy business that started long before the first free practice, and lasted well into the Sunday night and beyond.

Much of it centred around Max Biaggi. According to internet rumours, there'd been a blazing row in the pit after the Turkish GP, and Max had been sacked forthwith, and would not even ride at Valencia. Smiling HRC managing director Satoru Horiike denied any rift, but confirmed there would be no factory bike for him next year. But there must have been some substance, for when Camel, sponsors of the Sito Pons satellite team, suggested they'd be pleased to have Max back next year, HRC forbade it. By the end of the evening, a senior spokesman for Camel brand owners JTI, vice president and sponsorship manager Daniel Torras, announced in the press room that talks had broken down with Honda, and that they would seek another alternative within MotoGP. Or failing that,

outside of MotoGP.

This meant a third sponsor threatening to follow Gauloises and Telefónica MoviStar out of MotoGP (a fourth, counting BMW, who confirmed their withdrawal at Valencia). This was a serious battle between manufacturers and sponsors over who is in control of nominating riders."

There was not much consistency in this. Honda imposed no ban when Fortuna (cross-fire casualties in the Gauloises-Yamaha battle) made their sponsorship of the Gresini satellite team conditional on Toni Elias getting the second ride alongside Melandri. This lucky squad changed sponsors quite seamlessly, from blue MoviStar clothing on Sunday to red Fortuna shirts on Monday, for the announcement of the rider change.

Others were caught in the confusion – one being Casey Stoner, who started the weekend with three options: stay with the Carrera 250 team, join an unspecified Yamaha team for a relatively cut price, or sign up with Camel Honda. He took the third... only for it to suddenly go shaky, though the team did test him on the bike in the following weeks. Another wandering erstwhile Camel Honda rider was Shakey Byrne, called in to take over Bayliss's bike for this meeting (Vermeulen's Suzuki

work already in progress for his new Honda-powered Banbury-built hybrid, and work in progress also in trying to find someone to pay for it. Cue also WCM, whose Blata backing remained dependant on increasingly distant-seeming Czech Republic government backing.

There was serious unrest at all levels of MotoGP. What a way to end the season. Never mind – the new one started the very next day, with de Puniet testing his new Kawasaki, Vermeulen the Suzuki, Pedrosa, Stoner and Elias the RCV Honda...

Rossi needed one more win to beat his own record of 11, and equal that of Doohan – achieved in 1997, a year with two fewer races. But, perhaps not surprisingly, in the words of Burgess, "he's gone a bit off the boil", and he made it hard for himself. Again he had trouble in practice. Not even in the top ten with just over ten minutes of qualifying to go, he crashed – a high-speed ton-plus tumble on the way into Turn 11. "I made the change of direction – left to right – very aggressively. My speed was good, but I braked too late, I think. When I touched the brake I lost the front. It was my mistake – nothing technical." He tumbled and slid in relative safety, sitting up afterwards and shaking his head. "I think I swallowed a kilogramme of dust." His bike demonstrated just how much more violent the crash might have been. Shedding white-painted bodywork, it flew right over the barrier and cleared the service road before landing in a ditch. By sheer luck no marshals, photographers or trackside traffic were in the way. He switched to his second, less favoured bike, and tried again – to little avail, and qualified 15th, his worst since his second GP, the 125 round in Sentul, Indonesia, in 1996.

Capirossi was back, riding with a chest pad and shrugging off problems with breathing and discomfort. Another stroke of misfortune came on the way to the race – unwilling to fly any more in his condition, he came by car, following his father driving his elderly motorhome... only to watch it burn to the ground by the road in the south of France.

Yamaha had a second half-centenary celebration... a pale shadow of the lavish US party at the Monterey Aquarium at GP time, canapés in a crowded tent sufficing instead. Agostini was present, however, to see the factory M1s painted in his Yamaha Europe livery, white with a red barred stripe. The riders' leathers and team clothing matched. No Gauloises? No significance, we were assured – the original contract had allowed for two races in corporate livery.

Oh yes, and Gibernau won the BMW M5, for the best qualifying record – an aggregate time (all qualifying sessions plus the Catalunya test) of 30'55.903 was 3.585 seconds better than last year's winner Rossi. He could park it next to the M1 he won at Catalunya... the only prizes of an extraordinary year for the fastest lapper of them all.

Above: MoviStar girl – the sponsors made the most of their last GP.

Top left: "Compared with F1, it's so smooth." Gerhard Berger sampled the two-seater Ducati behind Randy Mamola.

Centre and below left: Before and after. White-suited Rossi paid customary obeisance to his Yamaha... then threw it away so hard it cleared the barriers. The bike's condition shows how lucky he was to escape injury.

Bottom: Long-standing Michelin boss Pierre Dupasquier (standing, holding helmet) retired, and the stars at his farewell party included Rossi (on his left) and Hayden (alongside), Biaggi (on his right), Elias (seated) and Carlos Lavado (blue jacket), then Barros and (standing) Sito Pons. Photographs: Gold & Goose

signing having ruled him out), only to be dumped at the last minute in favour of Ryuichi Kiyonari.

Thus the year ended with Honda's top rider effectively sacked. Somebody had to pay for their lack of success in the quest to beat Rossi. It was Max.

Or had it been Sete? This is what he seemed to suggest, after he found yet another way to lose a race. This time it was a smoky blow up (almost unknown on a Honda) in the early stages. An impassioned briefing after the race hinted at "something fishy" going on at Honda. Sete had qualified on pole and led morning warm-up. Then Japanese technicians, he said, had claimed the engine was leaking oil, and swapped it before the race. The new one vibrated so badly that after two laps he could barely hang on to the bars. Then it expired.

As you may imagine, Sete would only be so free with his criticism of HRC if he expected never to return. Indeed so – Ducati had put a Sunday midnight deadline on their offer to him, but he signed within 15 minutes of the end of the race.

This left Barros and Checa in limbo, likewise Team Pons, and also the Tech 3 satellite Yamaha team, still without a sponsor. Cue Kenny Roberts, back in the paddock with talk of design

MOTOGP RACE – 30 laps

Gibernau claimed a dominant pole, his fifth of the year; Melandri slotting alongside at the end, moving Hayden to third on another all-Honda front row. Checa led the second, Biaggi alongside, making the most of his last Honda factory ride, then Edwards, carrying the white flag for Yamaha.

Melandri led Hayden into the first corner – an order that did not change from there to the finish... though not for want of trying on the American's part, once he'd got over his early misgivings of pushing too hard. "I crashed here the last two years," he recalled. Their battle would go to the last corner.

Hayden was poised to slip through on the inside of the tricky approach... braking while already leaned well over Melandri stayed in even tighter, and then got a little sideways. Hayden swiftly switched to Plan B, to slow up more, square the corner off, take first instead of second, then get him on the way out. He failed by less than a tenth.

It was another steadfast race from the Italian apprentice (rather surprisingly not a candidate for a factory bike next year). "Before the start I thought only to control Nicky for the championship, but when I led into the first corner I decided to take my own rhythm." Into the last one, "I used an extra finger on the lever to brake as hard as possible." In spite of his consequent slide, he was able to retain control.

Gibernau had been a close third for three laps, and on the fourth he was touring to a stop, to drop to his knees at the side of the track, his Honda smoking beside him.

All eyes, of course, were on Rossi, lanky in his white suit. He gained five places before half the first lap was gone, and two more before the end, to finish it eighth. But now he was 2.76 seconds off the lead, and stuck behind Barros for another lap. Ahead of the Brazilian were still both Ducatis to deal with, and then Max.

When Gibernau went, Checa had displaced Biaggi from third, and Rossi was right behind. Capirossi, Barros and Edwards followed on. On lap five Rossi took Biaggi, and Checa one lap later. He was third, and now the gap to the lead was almost five seconds. With 24 laps left, he needed to recoup two tenths a lap. Surely possible.

In fact he got four tenths back next time round, but he couldn't sustain the pace as Melandri responded, and on lap 13 he was more than six seconds adrift.

Again, if there had been a title at stake it might have been different. After lap 20, Rossi did start to take ground back, although erratically, and in the last four laps was closing visibly. But it was too little too late.

Part of the need to push had come from Checa, closing right up again on lap ten, and pushing hard for the next five. Tyre chatter problems were awaiting the last-time Ducati rider, and after lap 16 he lost more time to pose no further challenge.

Behind him, Biaggi, Capirossi and Barros had been battling from the fifth lap. It was tough stuff from Capirossi, who lost touch only in the last couple of laps. Barros had finally got the better of Biaggi the lap before, and held the advantage to the flag.

Edwards dropped away from this group after seven laps. Tamada had an undistinguished ride, finishing more than ten seconds away after a slow start, then waiting behind Hopkins and Elias for five laps while his tyres reached temperature. He had a lonely run to ninth.

Nakano had also got away from this pair, but had hurt his hand in a Friday fall, and when Elias caught him with two laps left, he was unable to resist.

Four seconds away, Kiyonari won out after a long battle with Hopkins; Hofmann – riding with a plate and screws in his ankle – only lost touch at the end. Xaus in 15th was alone and miles behind.

Battaini was the only other runner; Ellison had retired with valve problems with 15 laps to go. One lap later Kurtis Roberts, riding the V5 Proton for one last late return, pitted with gear shifting problems after running in the points. Nobu Aoki, on the second Suzuki, had been ahead of team-mate Hopkins when he stopped out on the track with an electrical problem on lap nine.

Above: **BSB runner up Ryuichi Kiyonari was the latest on the Camel Honda.**

Top: **Melandri led and Hayden chased, from the first to the last.**
Photographs: Gold & Goose

The only crash came in the very first corner, when Nakano and Rolfo collided, the latter tumbling off in the thick of the pack.

Melandri earned second overall with a second consecutive strong win. Surprisingly, HRC had announced two days earlier that his satellite team, now Fortuna sponsored, would not be in line for a factory bike.

We shall have to wait to next year to see about that.

250 cc RACE – 27 laps

New champion Pedrosa led two more Hondas and an Aprilia on the front row, with first-timer Barbera second at home, then de Angelis and Lorenzo. Dovizioso led row two, Stoner two places down, Porto absent – a previous back injury had played up and he withdrew during final qualifying.

It all started promisingly enough, with Barbera snatching the early lead… though Dovizioso put himself out of the picture on only the second corner, running into the back of de Angelis to wobble dangerously into the gravel, rejoining right at the very back.

Pedrosa, Lorenzo and de Angelis tailed the race leader for a couple of laps, with Aoyama and Stoner chasing hard, and de Puniet at the back of the front group. Strongest among them was Stoner, up to fourth on lap five, ahead of de Angelis as well as Aoyama.

Now Lorenzo, riding with typical aggression, took a turn at leading his home GP. Two laps further Barbera ran wide and lost touch with the leading pair, Spain's deadly rivals, young master versus even younger pretender.

Pedrosa patiently shadowed Lorenzo until lap 13, then out-braked him firmly into the first corner. Lorenzo stayed close for a lap or two, but after one more the gap was more than a second and stretching rapidly to comfortably more than three seconds at the end. There was no question about who was in charge.

Left: Disappointed, Rossi failed to equal his record of 12 wins per season.

Below left: Kurtis Roberts returned for one race on the old V5 Proton KR.

Bottom: Dani Pedrosa signed off his 250 career with his eighth win of the season.

Photographs: Gold & Goose

Stoner had passed Barbera on lap eight, still only a couple of seconds adrift of the leading pair. But the gap slowly stretched over the next laps, to a yawning ten seconds at the end. Barbera was fading now, and drifted into the hands of de Angelis, who also got ahead on lap 16. With Aoyama straggling in behind, this accounted for the top six, covered by some 30 seconds.

A battle for seventh was closing at the end, with Takahashi finally prevailing over de Puniet with three laps left. All the while, Dovizioso had been regaining places. His final victim was Locatelli, consigned to tenth two laps from the end.

Debon was clear of the next group, where Smrz narrowly got the better of Cardenas and Guintoli, with Sekiguchi 15th, Davies dropping out of touch for 16th.

Lorenzo's rostrum gave him fifth overall from non-starter Porto; the constructors' title went to Honda by ten points.

As so often this year, especially at the start of it, Pedrosa's sheer class had stretched the pursuit into a processional race. Next year, he will be gone to MotoGP, along with Stoner and de Puniet. The young chargers will have it all to themselves.

125 cc RACE – 24 laps

Serge Gadea claimed not only his first pole but his first front-row start, just three thousandths faster than Pasini, and with title rivals Kallio and Luthi third and fourth, the front row was covered by 0.164 or a second.

Kallio needed to win; if he did so, Luthi needed to finish no worse than 13th. If he was 14th, they would be equal on points and equal on wins, but Kallio would be champion by virtue of four second places to Luthi's three. Of course, if Luthi failed to finish, then Kallio would triumph.

Gadea led for the first four laps. By the time Pasini took over on the fifth, the first pair had a little gap on a to-and-fro pack, currently headed by the KTMs of Kallio and Talmacsi, from Lai, Luthi, and Faubel, with di Meglio and Simon close behind, the Turkish GP winner soon to tumble.

Gadea regained the lead at the start of lap 13, with only the KTMs still close. Faubel was almost three seconds down, then a bigger gap to Luthi, Lai, Koyama and Simon, with Simoncelli gaining speed and closing from behind.

Kallio was up to second three laps later when he survived a big slide in the last corner. This was home hero Gadea's signal to go for a fine first victory, and he had gained a lead of almost 1.5 seconds as they started lap 19. Sadly, his ambitions were too great, and he crashed at the first corner.

Pasini took over, and led until the apex of the final corner. There Kallio pushed inside firmly, and their bikes touched. As the Italian wobbled, Talmacsi also sneaked through for second, leaving Pasini fuming.

Faubel was a lonely fourth, with Simoncelli through to a clear fifth by the end. Behind him there were still three scrapping over every inch, with Koyama just taking sixth from Lai and Simon.

Luthi had left them to it, slowing to finish three seconds adrift, safe in ninth... good enough for a fine and hard-fought championship. Kallio had to be content with a fine race win, and KTM with the constructors' title, 28 points clear of Honda.

As well as di Meglio, Cortesi, Poggiali and nine others crashed out, among them Pesek and Zanetti. The first-named took exception, and gave his assailant a good shaking, earning a US $3,000 fine in the process.

CIRCUITO DE LA COMUNITAT VALENCIANA

CIRCUIT LENGTH: 2.489 miles/4.005 km

G.P. betandwin.com DE LA COMMUNITAT VALENCIA

6 NOVEMBER 2005 • FIM WORLD CHAMPIONSHIP ROUND 17

MotoGP

30 laps, 74.670 miles/120.150 km

Pos.	Rider (Nat.)	No.	Machine	Laps	Time & speed
1	Marco Melandri (I)	33	Honda	30	46m 58.152s 95.370 mph/ 153.483 km/h
2	Nicky Hayden (USA)	69	Honda	30	46m 58.249s
3	Valentino Rossi (I)	46	Yamaha	30	47m 01.111s
4	Carlos Checa (E)	7	Ducati	30	47m 16.870s
5	Alex Barros (BR)	4	Honda	30	47m 18.858s
6	Max Biaggi (I)	3	Honda	30	47m 19.406s
7	Loris Capirossi (I)	65	Ducati	30	47m 21.294s
8	Colin Edwards (USA)	5	Yamaha	30	47m 23.830s
9	Makoto Tamada (J)	6	Honda	30	47m 34.862s
10	Toni Elias (E)	24	Yamaha	30	47m 37.268s
11	Shinya Nakano (J)	56	Kawasaki	30	47m 39.288s
12	Ryuichi Kiyonari (J)	54	Honda	30	47m 43.843s
13	John Hopkins (USA)	21	Suzuki	30	47m 44.659s
14	Alex Hofmann (D)	66	Kawasaki	30	47m 48.008s
15	Ruben Xaus (E)	11	Yamaha	30	48m 17.595s
16	Franco Battaini (I)	27	Blata	29	47m 35.920s
	Kurtis Roberts (USA)	80	Proton KR	16	DNF
	James Ellison (GB)	77	Blata	15	DNF
	Nobuatsu Aoki (J)	9	Suzuki	8	DNF
	Sete Gibernau (E)	15	Honda	3	DNF
	Roberto Rolfo (I)	44	Ducati	0	DNF

Fastest lap: Melandri, 1m 33.043s, 96.288 mph/154.960 km/h (record).

Previous record: Valentino Rossi, I (Honda), 1m 33.317s, 96.005 mph/154.505 km/h (2003).

Event best maximum speed: Capirossi, 197.3 mph/317.5 km/h (free practice no. 1).

Qualifying: 1 Gibernau, 1m 31.874s; 2 Melandri, 1m 32.111s; 3 Hayden, 1m 32.217s; 4 Checa, 1m 32.374s; 5 Biaggi, 1m 32.384s; 6 Edwards, 1m 32.456s; 7 Capirossi, 1m 32.482s; 8 Barros, 1m 32.518s; 9 Nakano, 1m 32.663s; 10 Tamada, 1m 32.682s; 11 Hopkins, 1m 32.785s; 12 Hofmann, 1m 32.966s; 13 Elias, 1m 33.005s; 14 Aoki, 1m 33.393s; 15 Rossi, 1m 33.503s; 16 Kiyonari, 1m 33.846s; 17 Xaus, 1m 34.874s; 18 Rolfo, 1m 34.978s; 19 Ellison, 1m 35.158s; 20 Kurtis Roberts, 1m 35.374s; 21 Battaini, 1m 35.712s.

Fastest race laps: 1 Melandri, 1m 33.043s; 2 Hayden, 1m 33.106s; 3 Rossi, 1m 33.199s; 4 Gibernau, 1m 33.476s; 5 Checa, 1m 33.622s; 6 Capirossi, 1m 33.845s; 7 Edwards, 1m 33.880s; 8 Barros, 1m 33.896s; 9 Tamada, 1m 33.962s; 10 Nakano, 1m 33.981s; 11 Biaggi, 1m 34.008s; 12 Aoki, 1m 34.159s; 13 Kiyonari, 1m 34.272s; 14 Hopkins, 1m 34.391s; 15 Elias, 1m 34.393s; 16 Hofmann, 1m 34.553s; 17 Kurtis Roberts, 1m 35.599s; 18 Xaus, 1m 35.790s; 19 Ellison, 1m 36.030s; 20 Battaini, 1m 36.839s.

Final World Championship Standings: 1 Rossi, 367; 2 Melandri, 220; Hayden, 206; 4 Edwards, 179; 5 Biaggi, 173; 6 Capirossi, 157; 7 Gibernau, 150; 8 Barros, 147; 9 C. Checa, 138; 10 Nakano, 98; 11 Tamada, 91; 12 Elias, 74; 13 Roberts, 63; 14 Hopkins, 63; 15 Bayliss, 54; 16 Xaus, 52; 17 Jacque, 28; 18 Rolfo 25; 19 Hofmann, 24; 20 van den Goorbergh, 12; 21 Vermeulen, 10; 22 Battaini and Ellison, 7; 24 Byrne, 6; 25Kiyonari and D. Checa, 4; 26 Ukawa, 1.

250 cc

27 laps, 67.203 miles/108.135 km

Pos.	Rider (Nat.)	No.	Machine	Laps	Time & speed
1	Daniel Pedrosa (E)	1	Honda	27	43m 33.395s 92.558 mph/ 148.957 km/h
2	Jorge Lorenzo (E)	48	Honda	27	43m 36.843s
3	Casey Stoner (AUS)	27	Aprilia	27	43m 47.767s
4	Alex de Angelis (RSM)	5	Aprilia	27	43m 51.166s
5	Hector Barbera (E)	80	Honda	27	43m 59.628s
6	Hiroshi Aoyama (J)	73	Honda	27	44m 04.639s
7	Yuki Takahashi (J)	55	Honda	27	44m 08.913s
8	Randy de Puniet (F)	7	Aprilia	27	44m 09.883s
9	Andrea Dovizioso (I)	34	Honda	27	44m 16.524s
10	Roberto Locatelli (I)	15	Aprilia	27	44m 17.355s
11	Alex Debon (E)	6	Honda	27	44m 28.889s
12	Jakub Smrz (CZ)	96	Honda	27	44m 30.660s
13	Martin Cardenas (COL)	36	Aprilia	27	44m 31.580s
14	Sylvain Guintoli (F)	50	Aprilia	27	44m 31.940s
15	Taro Sekiguchi (J)	44	Aprilia	27	44m 34.880s
16	Chaz Davies (GB)	57	Aprilia	27	44m 45.507s
17	Steve Jenkner (D)	17	Aprilia	27	44m 56.870s
18	Alex Baldolini (I)	25	Aprilia	27	45m 03.930s
19	Mirko Giansanti (I)	32	Aprilia	27	45m 05.352s
20	Mathieu Gines (F)	56	Aprilia	26	43m 41.745s
21	Zheng Peng Li (CHN)	61	Aprilia	26	44m 45.419s
	Andrea Ballerini (I)	8	Aprilia	26	DNF
	Simone Corsi (I)	24	Aprilia	26	DNF
	Dirk Heidolf (D)	28	Honda	18	DNF
	Erwan Nigon (F)	63	Yamaha	18	DNF
	Zhu Wang (CHN)	60	Aprilia	15	DNF
	Arturo Tizon (E)	33	Honda	9	DNF
	Alvaro Molina (E)	41	Aprilia	6	DNF
	Arnaud Vincent (F)	21	Fantic	6	DNF
	Sebastian Porto (ARG)	19	Aprilia		DNS
	Niklas Cajback (S)	23	Yamaha		DNQ
	Gabriele Ferro (I)	20	Fantic		DNQ

Fastest lap: Pedrosa, 1m 35.792s, 93.524 mph/150.513 km/h (record).

Previous record: Shinya Nakano, J (Yamaha), 1m 36.398s, 92.937 mph/149.567 km/h (2000).

Event best maximum speed: Stoner, 162.3 mph/261.2 km/h (qualifying practice no. 1).

Qualifying: 1 Pedrosa, 1m 35.298s; 2 Barbera, 1m 35.530s; 3 de Angelis, 1m 35.768s; 4 Lorenzo, 1m 35.942s; 5 Dovizioso, 1m 35.995s; 6 Aoyama, 1m 36.038s; 7 Stoner, 1m 36.143s; 8 Takahashi, 1m 36.284s; 9 Porto, 1m 36.522s; 10 de Puniet, 1m 36.537s; 11 Smrz, 1m 36.742s; 12 Heidolf, 1m 36.840s; 13 Debon, 1m 36.870s; 14 Sekiguchi, 1m 36.973s; 15 Baldolini, 1m 37.025s; 16 Locatelli, 1m 37.106s; 17 Guintoli, 1m 37.183s; 18 Jenkner, 1m 37.559s; 19 Cardenas, 1m 37.577s; 20 Davies, 1m 37.639s; 21 Ballerini, 1m 37.746s; 22 Tizon, 1m 38.325s; 23 Gines, 1m 38.530s; 24 Molina, 1m 38.536s; 25 Corsi, 1m 38.544s; 26 Vincent, 1m 38.638s; 27 Giansanti, 1m 39.127s; 28 Nigon, 1m 39.324s; 29 Wang, 1m 40.548s; 30 Li, 1m 41.390s; 31 Cajback, 1m 42.096s; 32 Ferro, 1m 43.778s.

Fastest race laps: 1 Pedrosa, 1m 35.792s; 2 Lorenzo, 1m 36.255s; 3 de Angelis, 1m 36.514s; 4 Stoner, 1m 36.537s; 5 Barbera, 1m 36.721s; 6 de Puniet, 1m 37.038s; 7 Aoyama, 1m 37.066s; 8 Takahashi, 1m 37.080s; 9 Dovizioso, 1m 37.100s; 10 Locatelli, 1m 37.552s; 11 Cardenas, 1m 37.841s; 12 Guintoli, 1m 37.937s; 13 Heidolf, 1m 38.094s; 14 Smrz, 1m 38.129s; 15 Debon, 1m 38.268s; 16 Sekiguchi, 1m 38.421s; 17 Davies, 1m 38.549s; 18 Baldolini, 1m 38.644s; 19 Ballerini, 1m 38.798s; 20 Corsi, 1m 38.968s; 21 Jenkner, 1m 38.975s; 22 Giansanti, 1m 39.247s; 23 Tizon, 1m 39.513s; 24 Gines, 1m 39.574s; 25 Molina, 1m 39.639s; 26 Vincent, 1m 39.681s; 27 Nigon, 1m 39.940s; 28 Li, 1m 41.956s; 22 Wang, 1m 42.123s.

Final World Championship Standings: 1 Pedrosa, 309; 2 Stoner, 254; 3 Dovizioso, 189; 4 Aoyama, 180; 5 Lorenzo, 167; 6 Porto, 152; 7 de Angelis, 151; 8 de Puniet, 138; 9 Barbera, 120; 10 Guintoli, 84; 11 Takahashi, 77; 12 Debon, 67; 13 Locatelli, 61; 14 Corsi, 59; 15 Giansanti, 36; 16 Davies, 32; 16 West, 30; 18 Baldolini, 25; 19 Ballerini, 19; 20 Smrz, 19; 21 Heidolf, Jenkner and Sekiguchi, 13; 24 Rous, 11; 25 Cardenas, 9; 26 Leblanc, 6; 27 Marchand and Nigon, 3.

125 cc

24 laps, 59.736 miles/96.120 km

Pos.	Rider (Nat.)	No.	Machine	Laps	Time & speed
1	Mika Kallio (SF)	36	KTM	24	40m 26.640s 88.606 mph/ 142.597 km/h
2	Gabor Talmacsi (H)	14	KTM	24	40m 26.877s
3	Mattia Pasini (I)	75	Aprilia	24	40m 27.007s
4	Hector Faubel (E)	55	Aprilia	24	40m 39.041s
5	Marco Simoncelli (I)	58	Aprilia	24	40m 43.649s
6	Tomoyoshi Koyama (J)	71	Honda	24	40m 47.275s
7	Fabrizio Lai (I)	32	Honda	24	40m 47.310s
8	Julian Simon (E)	60	KTM	24	40m 47.449s
9	Thomas Luthi (CH)	12	Honda	24	40m 50.157s
10	Pablo Nieto (E)	22	Derbi	24	40m 59.445s
11	Aleix Espargaro (E)	41	Honda	24	41m 02.570s
12	Alvaro Bautista (E)	19	Honda	24	41m 02.655s
13	Raffaele de Rosa (I)	35	Aprilia	24	41m 10.076s
14	Joan Olive (E)	6	Aprilia	24	41m 14.291s
15	Andrea Iannone (I)	29	Aprilia	24	41m 16.027s
16	Nicolas Terol (E)	18	Derbi	24	41m 19.827s
17	Jordi Carchano (E)	28	Aprilia	24	41m 24.616s
18	Enrique Jerez (E)	51	Derbi	24	41m 27.500s
19	Manuel Hernandez (E)	43	Honda	24	41m 27.695s
20	Mateo Tunez (E)	27	Aprilia	24	41m 32.916s
21	Imre Toth (H)	45	Aprilia	24	41m 33.555s
22	Gioele Pellino (I)	42	Malaguti	24	41m 35.119s
23	Vincent Braillard (CH)	26	Aprilia	24	41m 39.929s
24	Esteve Rabat (E)	59	Honda	24	41m 49.322s
25	Julian Miralles (E)	84	Aprilia	24	41m 49.814s
26	Sascha Hommel (D)	31	Honda	24	42m 06.372s
	Alexis Masbou (F)	7	Honda	22	DNF
	Sergio Gadea (E)	33	Aprilia	18	DNF
	Sandro Cortese (D)	11	Honda	17	DNF
	Jules Cluzel (F)	89	Malaguti	17	DNF
	Manuel Poggiali (RSM)	54	Gilera	16	DNF
	Lorenzo Zanetti (I)	8	Aprilia	14	DNF
	Lukas Pesek (CZ)	52	Derbi	14	DNF
	Daniel Saez (E)	49	Aprilia	14	DNF
	Karel Abraham (CZ)	44	Aprilia	10	DNF
	Federico Sandi (I)	10	Honda	6	DNF
	Mike di Meglio (F)	63	Honda	5	DNF
	Dario Giuseppetti (D)	25	Aprilia	0	DNF
	David Bonache (E)	48	Honda	0	DNF

Fastest lap: Gadea, 1m 40.286s, 89.333 mph/143.768 km/h.

Previous record: Steve Jenkner, D (Aprilia), 1m 40.252s, 89.364 mph/143.817 km/h (2002).

Event best maximum speed: Pasini, 139.6 mph/224.7 km/h (warm-up).

Qualifying: 1 Gadea, 1m 39.830s; 2 Pasini, 1m 39.833s; 3 Kallio, 1m 39.899s; 4 Luthi, 1m 39.994s; 5 Lai, 1m 40.101s; 6 Faubel, 1m 40.114s; 7 Cortese, 1m 40.177s; 8 Talmacsi, 1m 40.222s; 9 Koyama, 1m 40.256s; 10 di Meglio, 1m 40.502s; 11 Simoncelli, 1m 40.530s; 12 Simon, 1m 40.643s; 13 Pesek, 1m 40.674s; 14 Espargaro, 1m 40.825s; 15 Poggiali, 1m 41.033s; 16 Iannone, 1m 41.070s; 17 Cluzel, 1m 41.133s; 18 Masbou, 1m 41.351s; 19 Hernandez, 1m 41.521s; 20 Zanetti, 1m 41.534s; 21 de Rosa, 1m 41.557s; 22 Bautista, 1m 41.714s; 23 Carchano, 1m 41.752s; 24 Nieto, 1m 41.855s; 25 Sandi, 1m 41.913s; 26 Terol, 1m 41.982s; 27 Olive, 1m 41.983s; 28 Tunez, 1m 42.095s; 29 Bonache, 1m 42.289s; 30 Giuseppetti, 1m 42.335s; 31 Toth, 1m 42.574s; 32 Saez, 1m 42.587s; 33 Abraham, 1m 42.604s; 34 Pellino, 1m 42.627s; 35 Rabat, 1m 42.788s; 36 Jerez, 1m 42.805s; 37 Miralles, 1m 43.201s; 38 Braillard, 1m 43.215s; 39 Hommel, 1m 44.682s.

Fastest race laps: 1 Gadea, 1m 40.286s; 2 Talmacsi, 1m 40.401s; 3 Kallio, 1m 40.405s; 4 Pasini, 1m 40.439s; 5 Faubel, 1m 40.641s; 6 Lai, 1m 40.743s; 7 di Meglio, 1m 40.759s; 8 Luthi, 1m 40.781s; 9 Koyama, 1m 40.828s; 10 Simon, 1m 40.840s; 11 Simoncelli, 1m 40.893s; 12 Nieto, 1m 40.973s; 13 Masbou, 1m 41.273s; 14 Cluzel, 1m 41.309s; 15 Bautista, 1m 41.339s; 16 Poggiali, 1m 41.415s; 17 Zanetti, 1m 41.454s; 18 Iannone, 1m 41.487s; 19 Pesek, 1m 41.489s; 20 de Rosa, 1m 41.593s; 21 Cortese, 1m 41.613s; 22 Olive, 1m 41.658s; 23 Espargaro, 1m 41.659s; 24 Terol, 1m 42.076s; 25 Carchano, 1m 42.180s; 26 Braillard, 1m 42.424s; 27 Tunez, 1m 42.474s; 28 Saez, 1m 42.484s; 29 Abraham, 1m 42.488s; 30 Toth, 1m 42.543s; 31 Hernandez, 1m 42.564s; 32 Sandi, 1m 42.677s; 33 Jerez, 1m 42.807s; 34 Pellino, 1m 42.878s; 35 Rabat, 1m 43.294s; 36 Miralles, 1m 43.503s; 37 Hommel, 1m 43.869s.

Final World Championship Standings: 1 Luthi, 242; 2 Kallio, 237; 3 Talmacsi, 198; 4 Pasini, 183; 5 Simoncelli, 177; 6 Lai, 141; 7 Simon, 123; 8 Koyama, 119; 9 Faubel, 113; 10 Poggiali, 107; 11 di Meglio, 104; 12 Gadea, 68; 13 Nieto, 64; 14 Olive, 60; 15 Bautista, 47; 16 Espargaro, 36; 17 Zanetti, 30; 18 Masbou, 28; 19 Pesek, 25; 20 Iannone, 20; 21 Kuzuhara, 17; 22 Rodriguez, 16; 23 de Rosa, 13; 24 Hernandez and Ranseder, 12; 26 Cortese, 8; 27 Linfoot and Toth, 7; 29 Carchano, 6; 30 Conti, 5; 31 Elkin and Giuseppetti 4; 33 Pirro, 3; 34 Jerez, 2; 35 Bradl and Terol, 1.

World Championship Points

MOTO GP

Position	Rider	Nationality	Machine	Spain	Portugal	China	France	Italy	Catalunya	Holland	United States	Great Britain	Germany	Czech Republic	Japan	Malaysia	Qatar	Australia	Turkey	Valencia	Points total
1	Valentino Rossi	I	Yamaha	25	20	25	25	25	25	25	16	25	25	25	-	20	25	25	20	16	367
2	Marco Melandri	I	Honda	16	13	16	13	13	16	20	-	-	9	10	-	11	20	13	25	25	220
3	Nicky Hayden	USA	Honda	-	9	7	10	10	11	13	25	-	16	11	9	13	16	20	16	20	206
4	Colin Edwards	USA	Yamaha	7	10	8	16	7	9	16	20	13	8	9	10	6	13	10	9	8	179
5	Max Biaggi	I	Honda	9	16	11	11	20	10	10	13	-	13	16	20	10	-	-	4	10	173
6	Loris Capirossi	I	Ducati	3	7	4	9	16	4	6	6	10	7	20	25	25	6	-	-	9	157
7	Sete Gibernau	E	Honda	20	-	13	20	-	20	11	11	-	20	-	-	-	11	11	13	-	150
8	Alex Barros	BR	Honda	13	25	5	-	9	13	9	-	16	11	13	-	8	7	-	7	11	147
9	Carlos Checa	E	Ducati	6	11	-	-	11	5	7	-	11	-	8	13	16	10	16	11	13	138
10	Shinya Nakano	J	Kawasaki	11	8	-	8	6	7	8	7	-	10	4	-	-	9	9	6	5	98
11	Makoto Tamada	J	Honda	8	-	-	-	8	-	2	9	9	6	6	16	4	-	8	8	7	91
12	Toni Elias	E	Yamaha	4	2	2	7	-	-	-	3	7	4	2	7	5	8	7	10	6	74
13	Kenny Roberts	USA	Suzuki	-	4	-	3	1	1	-	2	20	5	5	8	9	5	-	-	-	63
14	John Hopkins	USA	Suzuki	2	-	9	-	5	-	3	8	5	-	3	11	7	-	6	1	3	63
15	Troy Bayliss	AUS	Honda	10	5	-	6	3	8	5	10	-	-	7	-	-	-	-	-	-	54
16	Ruben Xaus	E	Yamaha	-	6	6	4	2	6	4	5	-	3	-	6	1	2	4	2	1	52
17	Olivier Jacque	F	Kawasaki	-	-	20	5	-	-	-	-	-	-	-	-	-	-	-	3	-	28
18	Roberto Rolfo	I	Ducati	1	3	-	1	-	2	-	-	6	2	-	-	3	4	3	-	-	25
19	Alex Hofmann	D	Kawasaki	5	-	-	-	4	-	-	4	8	-	1	-	-	-	-	-	2	24
20	Jurgen van den Goorbergh	NL	Honda	-	-	10	2	-	-	-	-	-	-	-	-	-	-	-	-	-	12
21	Chris Vermeulen	AUS	Honda	-	-	-	-	-	-	-	-	-	-	-	-	-	-	5	5	-	10
22=	Franco Battaini	I	Blata	-	-	-	-	-	-	-	-	-	1	-	5	-	-	1	-	-	7
22=	James Ellison	GB	Blata	-	1	3	-	-	-	-	-	-	-	-	-	-	1	2	-	-	7
24	Shane Byrne	GB	Proton KR/	-	-	-	-	-	-	-	1	-	-	-	-	2	3	-	-	-	6
25=	Ryuichi Kiyonari	J	Honda	-	-	-	-	-	-	-	-	-	-	-	-	-	-	-	4	-	4
25=	David Checa	E	Yamaha	-	-	-	-	3	1	-	-	-	-	-	-	-	-	-	-	-	4
27	Tohru Ukawa	J	Moriwaki	-	-	1	-	-	-	-	-	-	-	-	-	-	-	-	-	-	1

Position	Rider	Nationality	Machine	Spain	Portugal	China	France	Italy	Catalunya	Holland	Great Britain	Germany	Czech Republic	Japan	Malaysia	Qatar	Australia	Turkey	Valencia	Points total
1	Daniel Pedrosa	E	Honda	25	13	10	25	25	25	20	13	25	25	20	-	13	25	20	25	309
2	Casey Stoner	AUS	Aprilia	-	25	25	13	13	20	10	16	9	16	16	25	25	-	25	16	254
3	Andrea Dovizioso	I	Honda	13	20	20	16	8	16	9	9	13	10	10	-	16	11	11	7	189
4	Hiroshi Aoyama	J	Honda	-	10	16	10	9	13	13	-	16	11	25	11	10	10	16	10	180
5	Jorge Lorenzo	E	Honda	10	6	7	11	20	-	16	8	-	20	-	-	20	16	13	20	167
6	Sebastian Porto	ARG	Aprilia	20	7	11	-	11	-	25	11	11	9	-	16	11	20	-	-	152
7	Alex de Angelis	RSM	Aprilia	16	11	13	-	16	-	11	-	20	13	9	20	-	-	9	13	151
8	Randy de Puniet	F	Aprilia	-	16	-	20	-	10	8	25	10	8	11	13	-	9	-	8	138
9	Hector Barbera	E	Honda	11	5	9	9	10	-	7	-	8	-	8	10	9	13	10	11	120
10	Sylvain Guintoli	F	Aprilia	-	8	4	7	-	8	4	7	5	6	7	7	6	7	6	2	84
11	Yuki Takahashi	J	Honda	-	9	6	6	-	9	1	-	7	-	13	9	8	-	-	9	77
12	Alex Debon	E	Honda	8	3	5	8	-	5	3	-	4	3	7	-	5	7	4	5	67
13	Roberto Locatelli	I	Aprilia	9	-	-	2	-	4	5	4	-	7	-	8	-	8	8	6	61
14	Simone Corsi	I	Aprilia	7	-	8	5	7	11	6	10	-	-	5	-	-	-	-	-	59
15	Mirko Giansanti	I	Aprilia	6	2	-	-	4	7	-	5	-	-	3	3	4	-	2	-	36
16	Chaz Davies	GB	Aprilia	5	-	-	4	6	-	2	-	-	-	4	-	5	6	-	-	32
17	Anthony West	AUS	KTM	-	-	-	-	-	-	-	20	6	4	-	-	-	-	-	-	30
18	Alex Baldolini	I	Aprilia	3	-	3	3	-	6	-	3	-	2	-	-	-	-	5	-	25
19=	Andrea Ballerini	I	Aprilia	2	-	-	1	5	-	-	6	-	-	-	1	1	3	-	-	19
19=	Jakub Smrz	CZ	Honda	-	4	2	-	-	-	-	-	-	5	-	-	-	3	1	4	19
21=	Dirk Heidolf	D	Honda	-	-	-	1	-	-	-	-	3	-	-	5	-	4	-	-	13
21=	Steve Jenkner	D	Aprilia	-	-	-	-	-	-	-	-	2	1	4	2	2	2	-	-	13
21=	Taro Sekiguchi	J	Aprilia	-	-	-	-	-	-	-	-	-	-	-	6	6	-	-	1	13
24	Radomil Rous	CZ	Honda	4	-	-	-	3	-	-	1	-	2	1	-	-	-	-	-	11
25	Martin Cardenas	COL	Aprilia	-	1	-	-	-	-	-	1	-	-	1	3	-	-	-	3	9
26	Gregory Leblanc	F	Aprilia	1	-	-	-	2	1	-	2	-	-	-	-	-	-	-	-	6
27=	Hugo Marchand	F	Aprilia	-	-	-	-	1	2	-	-	-	-	-	-	-	-	-	-	3
27=	Erwan Nigon	F	Honda	-	-	-	-	3	-	-	-	-	-	-	-	-	-	-	-	3

Position	Rider	Nationality	Machine	Spain	Portugal	China	France	Italy	Catalunya	Holland	Great Britain	Germany	Czech Republic	Japan	Malaysia	Qatar	Australia	Turkey	Valencia	Points total
1	Thomas Luthi	CH	Honda	-	16	13	25	20	9	6	10	20	25	20	25	10	25	11	7	242
2	Mika Kallio	SF	KTM	20	25	5	16	-	16	-	9	25	20	25	20	20	11	-	25	237
3	Gabor Talmacsi	H	KTM	11	-	16	10	25	13	25	-	13	7	-	11	25	9	13	20	198
4	Mattia Pasini	I	Aprilia	13	8	25	-	13	25	16	-	-	-	11	16	7	13	20	16	183
5	Marco Simoncelli	I	Aprilia	25	6	10	11	-	20	-	13	16	16	-	7	16	16	10	11	177
6	Fabrizio Lai	I	Honda	16	13	20	-	8	6	-	16	9	10	6	9	6	4	9	9	141
7	Julian Simon	E	KTM	7	7	6	8	9	8	10	25	11	6	-	10	8	-	-	8	123
8	Tomoyoshi Koyama	J	Honda	-	10	11	-	11	11	9	-	-	-	13	6	2	20	16	10	119
9	Hector Faubel	E	Aprilia	9	20	1	-	-	-	20	-	-	-	16	13	11	10	-	13	113
10	Manuel Poggiali	RSM	Gilera	10	11	4	6	10	10	8	-	5	8	10	8	9	3	5	-	107
11	Mike di Meglio	F	Honda	5	5	-	13	-	-	2	20	5	9	5	13	2	25	-	-	104
12	Sergio Gadea	E	Aprilia	-	-	-	20	-	3	7	5	-	13	9	-	4	7	-	-	68
13	Pablo Nieto	E	Derbi	4	4	8	9	-	-	5	11	6	-	8	3	-	-	-	6	64
14	Joan Olive	E	Aprilia	8	-	2	-	16	-	3	8	8	-	-	5	1	7	2	-	60
15	Alvaro Bautista	E	Honda	-	9	-	-	4	2	13	-	4	7	-	-	-	-	4	4	47
16	Aleix Espargaro	E	Honda	2	-	9	4	-	1	-	-	7	3	4	1	-	-	-	5	36
17	Lorenzo Zanetti	I	Aprilia	-	-	-	5	2	7	-	2	3	11	-	-	-	-	-	-	30
18	Alexis Masbou	F	Honda	-	3	-	-	6	-	11	-	-	-	-	2	-	6	-	-	28
19	Lukas Pesek	CZ	Derbi	-	-	7	-	-	-	1	-	10	-	-	4	-	-	3	-	25
20	Andrea Iannone	I	Aprilia	-	-	-	-	5	-	-	-	5	3	-	-	-	6	1	-	20
21	Toshihisa Kuzuhara	J	Honda	-	2	-	-	7	-	-	6	-	-	2	-	-	-	-	-	17
22	Angel Rodriguez	E	Aprilia	-	-	-	-	-	-	-	-	-	-	-	-	8	8	-	-	16
23	Raffaele de Rosa	I	Aprilia	-	-	-	1	-	-	-	1	-	-	-	3	5	-	-	3	13
24=	Manuel Hernandez	E	Honda	6	1	-	2	3	-	-	-	-	-	-	-	-	-	-	-	12
24=	Michael Ranseder	A	KTM	-	-	-	-	-	4	4	-	4	-	-	-	-	-	-	-	12
26	Sandro Cortese	D	Honda	-	-	-	1	-	-	-	1	2	2	-	-	-	2	-	-	8
27=	Dan Linfoot	GB	Honda	-	-	-	-	-	-	-	7	-	-	-	-	-	-	-	-	7
27=	Imre Toth	H	Aprilia	-	-	-	-	7	-	-	-	-	-	-	-	-	-	-	-	7
29	Jordi Carchano	E	Aprilia	3	-	-	-	-	-	-	3	-	-	-	-	-	-	-	-	6
30	Michele Conti	I	Honda	-	-	-	5	-	-	-	-	-	-	-	-	-	-	-	-	5
31=	Christian Elkin	GB	Honda	-	-	-	-	-	-	-	4	-	-	-	-	-	-	-	-	4
31=	Dario Giuseppetti	D	Aprilia	-	-	-	3	-	-	-	-	-	-	-	-	-	-	1	-	4
33	Michele Pirro	I	Malaguti	-	-	3	-	-	-	-	-	-	-	-	-	-	-	-	-	3
34	Enrique Jerez	E	Derbi	-	-	-	-	-	-	-	-	-	-	1	-	1	-	-	-	2
35=	Stefan Bradl	D	KTM	-	-	-	-	-	-	-	-	-	1	-	-	-	-	-	-	1
35=	Nicolas Terol	E	Derbi	1	-	-	-	-	-	-	-	-	-	-	-	-	-	-	-	1

SUZUKI DRINK FROM THE DUCATI CUP

WORLD SUPERBIKE CHAMPIONSHIP • by GORDON RITCHIE

Main picture: **Class of 2005.** Champion Toseland (1) takes centre stage as the riders pose at pre-season tests. Note Corser (11) looming ominously; former 500 GP winners McCoy and Abe on extreme left and right.
Photograph: Gold & Goose

DESPITE all the technical and most of the tyre rules of 2005 already being in place in 2004, politics and the money pit of MotoGP meant that last year only Honda mounted a credible one-man attack on the "Ducati World Championship."

For 2005, one manufacturer from the east took the revised SBK series seriously enough to provide winning-spec machinery from the first ridiculously early race of the year until even after the title was secured at Imola. Suzuki may or may not have broken ranks with their MSMA buddies from Japan, but despite conflicting claims, they certainly gave Corser and Kagayama winning bikes from the off. Just how "factory" were they? We'll never know for sure.

Virtually everyone came back to SBK in 2005 in some form, with Honda, Yamaha, Kawasaki and Suzuki running supported efforts, with big names and proven performers aboard. No factory squads of course, but at season end, few considered "elite" works efforts to be a necessity – despite all the kicking and screaming when they left in a huff after 2003.

It took some time for the racing to become even, but when it did, almost anyone could win. Even Petronas had the podiums dangled tantalisingly close in their field of expectation, at least once.

Only 12 rounds this year, many of them a month apart, made for a sometimes disjointed campaign, especially as we actually started racing in February, at an all new track to SBK. Other territories, like the Czech Republic were returned too, and Oschersleben morphed into Lausitzring for the German round.

After the largely successful Pirelli single-make tyre rules in 2004, the monotyre set-up allowed the racing to get even closer in 2005. Unlike last year, there were very public complaints from many about a lack of consistency from tyre to tyre. These seemed to have been addressed satisfactorily, but returned near the end of the year. This mystery remained unaccounted for, although no one denied Pirelli's huge efforts, and that the circumstances they have to work under limit their freedom for development considerably. The Italian tyre giants could walk tall at season's end anyhow, as they countered the mid season enigma with some new track records, in race and qualifying.

The most impressive aspect of SBK 2005 was, however, the number of participants. Overhead grid shots showed that cheap race bikes, certain knowledge that your tyres are no worse than the guy on pole and the simple impossibility of entering MotoGP, all conspired to put 30 regular bikes on the grids. It was an eclectic mix of young and old riders. SBK perennials and MotoGP leavers, domestic champions and Supersport/Superstock promotees, they all found a welcoming global village. Some of the names who regularly missed Superpole or individual points scores have won multiple GP and/or Superbike races.

Sponsorship may be as hard to get for SBK teams as it's ever been, but the improved feel, scale and self-respect meted out in 2005 all point to even better days ahead. $10 million US for a MotoGP team, or $1.2 million US in World Superbike? Even those of us who can't do rocket science can do arithmetic.

Above: Sponsors Corona brought a sparkle to the series...

Left: ...and won the title. Corser and team-mate Kagayama celebrate appropriately.
Photographs: Gold & Goose

THE WALTZ OF TROY

Above: Battle-hardened, Corser bounced back after a long barren spell.

Above right: The growing Family Corser – Troy and Sam celebrated a further addition during the season.

Right: Out on his own: Corser claimed the first-ever title for a 1000cc four-cylinder machine.

Photographs: Gold & Goose

THE best things come to those who wait. It's a well-worn saying, because in many cases, it's true. For Troy Corser, it needs at least another couple of "waits" added. His second World Championship crown took him nine years to secure, after his impressive start in the premier Superbike category.

Semi-privateer champion in 1996 (then the youngest ever at 24), every subsequent Superbike season bar 1997 has seen him ride for a factory squad. That's if you count his first year off with the Petronas effort as a riding year, as he – you guessed it – waited for his new bike to be ready throughout 2002. But we're getting ahead of ourselves.

He lost 1997 to a disastrous season in MotoGP. Fortune and deliberate policy took him back into Superbikes to stay. He almost took the top prize again in 1998, but a crash in warm-up at the final round in Sugo broke three ribs and split his spleen, breaking his heart in the process. Future team-mate and employer Carl Fogarty took the title.

Crushed by his Ducati team-mate Foggy and his record breaking points haul in 1999 (although Corser himself would deny that even now), Troy has subsequently ridden for Aprilia (2000 and 2001), then until 2004 Petronas. This year, he returned to the winners' fold with team Batta – the Alstare Corona Extra Suzuki team.

Both rider and team were back in from the wilderness, as Alstare skipped SBK in 2004, and Corser counted down what had become a lucrative period of top step inactivity with Petronas. The fact that Corser had scored the odd astonishing result on the machine, in year three of wearing aquamarine clothing, was an indicator that he had lost none of his speed.

His jack-rabbit start to the testing and racing seasons in 2005 proved his hunger had re-appeared in lion's-share proportions, now he could smell the chance of another title.

Often criticised in the past for not being the fittest of riders across a whole season, of being too much of a party animal too often, of simply mislaying the killer instinct inside his boundless confidence when he's on top for a while, Corser just burned his name into the podiums for more than half of the year. Sixteen in a row. It was outstanding stuff by any measure.

In previous years, gripes about tyres, strange vibrations, other things that less analytical riders would just concrete over in their desire to win, have maybe contributed to Corser's downfall. 2005 was different. This year, despite not scoring a single win since Brands Hatch at midseason, he clicked in results when needed, even remounting to score points after his lone serious mistake of the year, falling while leading in Germany. At that point, it has to be said, Vermeulen was looking a lot more convincing than Corser.

Thus Corser's intention in Imola was to leave as race winner and champion. The look on his face, as the weather instead handed him the title without a win, was a study in dissatisfaction. He finally got to celebrate the way he wanted in France, but cruelly, Superpole denied him a further opportunity for a race victory to go with his overall championship.

In the final analysis, he won eight races; six of them in the first seven attempts, and that was largely the story of his second championship season. The first ever 1000cc four-cylinder champion, the first ever for Suzuki, the first ever for Alstare, note it all down, because Corser's achievements have become a gilded SBK milestone for the second time, in a whole new age of Superbike evolution.

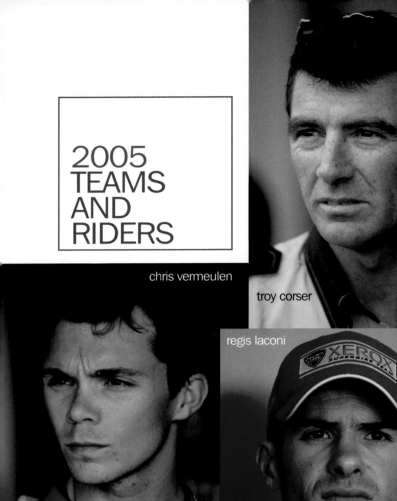
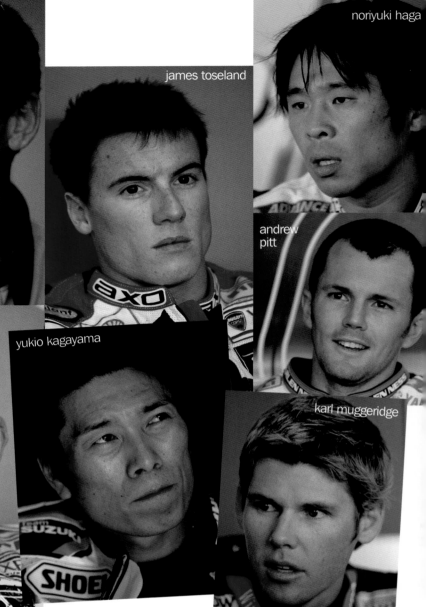

2005 TEAMS AND RIDERS

chris vermeulen

troy corser

regis laconi

yukio kagayama

james toseland

noriyuki haga

andrew pitt

karl muggeridge

Ducati Xerox

In re-signing 2004 world champion James Toseland (24) and runner-up Regis Laconi (30) for their 2005 championship campaign, Ducati made an entirely logical choice of a meritorious riding duo. But despite fewer private riders to service, a deliberate re-introduction of demarcation of the factory equipment levels, and last year's top two in the series, this was a tough year for the previously dominant Bologna factory.

Some obvious internal friction between Toseland and his team (again bestraddled by Davide Tardozzi) was as much to do with misunderstandings as any lack of care. Yet despite the Number One plate Toseland was simply not as highly regarded in the team, personally or professionally, as Laconi.

In turn, Laconi repaid the special attention, proving unquestionably more effective on track – though even the best twin-cylinder riders had their work cut out in 2005.

Ducati SC Caracchi

Madrid-based GP refugee Fonsi Nieto (26) came with a big reputation, but never lived up to it on the track. Stalked by media in Spanish tests and the Valencia race, he was otherwise dogged by some bad luck machinewise. A poor adaptation from 250 two-strokes to Stefano Caracchi's big Dukes combined with an air of laissez-fair saw him labelled lazy.

His team-mate was Ducati's latest Italian hopeful, Lorenzo Lanzi (23) another in his rookie year in SBK. From Superstock to Supersport to Superbike, he looked more assured as the year went on, and claimed his first win by the end of it.

Ducati Pedercini

Veteran team owner-rider Lucio Pedercini (32) had a trio of 999RS twins on his eponymous books. He and his original team-mate Alessandro Velini (26), who had joined him mid-2004, were supplemented by Bertocchi Kawasaki defector Ivan Clementi (30). They toiled away a few places behind their usual spots, and the oft hurt Pedercini himself had his worst year for some time.

DFXtreme Sterilgarda Ducati / Yamaha

Marco Borciani (29) started off riding a Yamaha, just like his loose collection of three DFX team-mates, but his dislike for the R1, and the overstretched nature of the whole effort early season saw him run home to Momma Ducati, his 2004 mount. His results remained, however, equally dire.

Portuguese second year runner Miguel Praia (27) stuck with the R1 Yamaha, running out of the same pit, before being let go before the end of the season.

Klaffi Honda

Having taken the jump up from Supersport, ex-Sidecar racer Klaus Klaffenbock's quick-to-learn team went for the classic mix of youth and experience. At 41 popular veteran Pierfrancesco Chili was the oldest man in the field; at 22 Max Neukirchner was the youngest, last year's World Supersport rookie of the year with the same team, and a Superbike rookie.

Neukirchner proved he really is fast, while Chili really is still fast, if fading somewhat on a sometimes-uncooperative Honda. The machinery was ever-improving, but so were many others.

Winston Ten Kate Honda

After a stunning 2004 season alone in the top Honda team, Chris Vermeulen (23) was joined by his fellow Aussie, fellow WSS champion and fellow early season struggler Karl Muggeridge (31).

In their new blue-and-white fag packet of fibreglass, the Ten Kate crew became all flash and corporate this year, if only on the surface. Gerrit Ten Kate and Co. were still first and foremost very human racers and tuners, albeit with an uncommon desire to win before the Sunday night party.

They didn't do too much winning at first, but were a credible threat to Suzuki after the early season teething problems and rider illness, and stronger still by the end of the year.

At year's end, they lost their top rider Vermeulen to MotoGP, but secured the services of 2004 champion Toseland in his place for 2006.

Renegade Honda Koji

Ben Bostrom (31) came back to play in World Superbike after a return to his AMA haunts. For his trouble, the former championship contender endured a couple of big crashes, the odd bright spark, and a season of much dishevelment and backroom alterations in Mark Griffiths's team.

The joint effort sometimes conspired to make their new Honda Fireblades as unreliable as their 2004 Ducatis, and sometimes as slow as the Petronas. Bostrom was a popular re-entry, if a shadow his former self, no matter how his bike went.

max neukirchner

jose luis cardoso

chris walker

lorenzo lanzi

sebastien gimbert

ben bostrom

norick abe

steve martin

garry mccoy

giovanni bussei

pierfrancesco chili

Alstare Corona Extra Suzuki

Team-Owner Francis Batta's long-time target Troy Corser (33) finally joined the team, got married to long-time companion Sam, had a second child... and had his best season in a decade in World Superbike.

The 1996 champion was hungry from the off, his team-mate Yukio Kagayama (31) even more so, at least until Monza race two. Only Corser had both the long-lasting appetite and the necessary experience of global racing to finish off each weekend with toasted champagne, however. But a wild man on a bike like Kagayama is always welcome in SBK, and the popular ex-BSB star made his mark on the series.

PSG-1 Kawasaki

British veteran Chris Walker (33) moved over from Petronas to the closest thing to a Kawasaki factory team. He may as well have been in a one man Kawasaki outfit, such was the luck and relative lack of velocity of his team-mate Mauro Sanchini (34).

When Sanchini hurt himself, Kawasaki's favourite tester, experienced Spaniard Pere Riba (36), stepped in to make for more respectable two-man PSG-1 showings.

Bertocchi Kawasaki

Early season gripes from Ivan Clementi led to a one-man revolt and a defection to Ducati. This left Giovanni Bussei (32) as the lone green horseman in Kawasaki's conventional colour scheme. He did better than anyone expected, proving that the Kawasaki is not bad, only hard to set-up just so for race day.

Yamaha Motor Italia

How factory were they? In ownership, pretty much – in early season tech specs, not much. But a generally late call to arms for the former Supersport team, sharing premises with the factory MotoGP squad, left a mark that took Noriyuki Haga (30) half a season and more to erase.

The Japanese star had initially watched 2001 Supersport champion Andrew Pitt (29), a class rookie reeling from his MotoGP experiences with Kawasaki, battle up front like a good 'un, at least for a while, in almost every single early season race. The roles were firmly reversed at half season, as the team eventually got man and machine on the same level.

Headed by former racer Mario Meregalli, the team is respected, and was the best Yamaha squad in race trim, despite some early season prowess by other R1 users.

Yamaha Motor France

Crimped locks flailing, long-serving former 500 GP winner Norick Abe (29) came to SBK from MotoGP for 2005, and took to his task in a professional, if seldom challenging, fashion. He did not heap credit on the reputation of MotoGP within this paddock.

Under the tutelage of Yamaha backroom racing legend Martial Garcia, Sebastien Gimbert (27) was unable to replicate early season pace in race situations.

A welcome addition to pit-lane, it was a hard season for all involved in the Yamaha Motor France effort to outdo the resurgent SBK entries.

Yamaha DFXtreme

Jose Luis Cardoso (30) and Lorenzo Alfonsi (24) were a rookie pairing, in a loose four-rider DFX effort, including Borciani and Praia. Ex-250 GP rider Cardoso came with the Spanish Formula Extreme series in his pocket, but scored fewer points than most other riders in races. 2004 Superstock champion Alfonsi was swamped early on, but kept his head down, helped by the experience of Peter Goddard in the pit garage.

Team Italia Lorenzini by Leoni Yamaha

This was one of several ex-Supersport/Superstock teams making the step up to Superbikes. Gianluca Vizziello (25) had lost the 2004 Superstock crown to Alfonsi, but drew level with him in the mediocrity stakes as their rookie SBK seasons unwound.

After scoring end of season points, his overall effort did not seem hampered by the lack of a full-time team-mate.

Foggy Petronas Racing

Hard work with literally no reward for half a season was a hard aquamarine pill to swallow for the pairing of Steve Martin (36) and Garry McCoy (33), each a top-class rider. Jack Valentine (of former V&M fame) formed the management buffer between men and metal, but no amount of rationalisation can help an ineffective design, especially in a year when more than 20 1000cc fours drowned out the two triples' plaintive 900cc yelps.

215

Suzuki GSX-R1000K5

Yamaha R1

Kawasaki ZX-10R

Petronas FP-1

Ducati 999F05

Ducati 999F05

A major winter re-vamp pushed the V-twins into more unknown territory, with significant changes both inside the engines and in ancillary equipment. The finest Öhlins TT25 suspension this side of the MotoGP paddock, lightweight hangers, brackets and bodywork were all to be expected, but in terms of electronics and injection technology, Ducati got even more serious than usual. Alterations even extended to rider aids like low rev range throttle limitation when exiting corners leaning over – with what seemed to be both an active and passive traction control system in the lower gears.

A new alloy fuel tank was called for, as the main Magneti Marelli Marvel 4 EFI brain and wiring loom terminations were centralised behind the steering head. For the beginning of the year, starter motors were retained, to get round the problem restarting a stalled or crashed machine.

Inside the engine, the main changes were to the crankshaft, conrods and pistons, liberating another five horsepower, thanks to an extra 500 revs over the 2004 bike. Ducati now claims 194bhp @ 12,500rpm, from the 104mm x 58.8 mm motor.

All these alterations proved that the factory bike really was a step change over the customer machines. A lack of testing may have muted early season competitiveness while the team achieved full understanding of all the new systems on the works bikes, but when they came good they proved to be a match for even the best Japanese machines.

Honda CBR1000RR

The late go-ahead for both the Winston sponsorship and arrival of pre-production models at Ten Kate did not stop the top Honda being fast from the start, but it did probably stop them being as good in real race situations as they could have been.

Persevering with WP suspension was cited by both riders as no help to set-up and performance, even after the arrival of new 48mm closed-cartridge steel inner forks, replacing last year's all alloy units.

At the rear, they stuck with the standard swing-arm, like most Honda teams, who found no advantage in stiffness worth the change. Stiffer ones gave an automatic loss of tyre feel. Ten Kate did however use their own rear linkages, to improve performance of the suspension unit.

An STM clutch had five more BHP to deal with in 2005, with a great deal of work going into making power more linear than 2004. Titanium rods were used, plus a new ignition and injection system.

Kawasaki ZX-10R

The PSG-1 team took over the mantle of top Kawasaki squad in 2005, combining with the French engine development company, Akira, with great success. The list of engine internals either made by the team itself, or custom made to their spec was impressive and effective. In mid season back-to-back tests with the "factory" race-kit parts in Japan, the PSG-1/Akira kit came out as marginally better.

The chassis was the tricky part for this team, with Walker noting that it was not as predictable as he would have hoped, and every new track meant previous settings were almost invariably required to be revamped.

A Silverstone meeting with top brass from Japan seems to have paved the way with more support for 2006, and certainly more personnel backup at tests and the odd race.

Petronas FP-1

With original technical chief Steve Thomson now a consultant, Jack Valentine took over the on-track reins for the race team, as the Petronas Engine Development Team (originally from Ricardo Engineering) designed new technical specs of the engine mid-season.

The serpentine 3-1-2-3 exhaust system was altered mid-season to feature a horizontally split "clamshell" silencer, the top half of which filled almost the entire seat unit, in an effort to improve both breathing and silencing. An early season new engine spec was soon consigned to the bin, because of poor reliability and a return to the bad old days of frequent engine breakages. This is one of the few of the machine's bugbears which had been brought to acceptable levels, but seemed to justify those who muttered about inherent problems with the reverse-head in-line three-cylinder motor.

The bike had a claimed crank power output of 190bhp @ 13,500rpm and a 14:1 compression ratio. It featured twin injector 55mm throttle bodies, as last year.

Suzuki GSX-R1000K5

When it was wheeled out at first and the Corser and Kagayama road show held an early sway on SBK's collective psyche, the words "factory" and "works" were bandied about like confetti. It seems we were all a little previous, as we could merely have substituted the terms "well-tested" and "properly developed". The Al-stare team's impressive set-up back in Belgium, and the adoption of some new and even higher level engineering personnel into the team, made the early difference for Suzuki.

It seems that they had made their latest GSX-R just as effective as the previous ones. And they had obviously made it ready to win as well, at the start of the season.

Not too different from the previous version, it was, however, better balanced, better across the rev-range and eminently amenable to set-up improvements. The 73.4 x 59.0 mm engine punted out 210 claimed PS, breathing via twin injector ignition, while an Arrow exhaust breathed out the spent gases. Full factory Showa suspension graced the front and rear, with full time Showa service in place at races.

Yamaha R1

They didn't start the season with a Superstock bike, but it was a damn close run thing for the Yamaha Motor Italia boys. Borrowing front mudguards and fork brackets from the MotoGP team in the adjacent workshops in early tests, the first significant engine tuning change came at Assen, but only to one engine at that stage. A cool 4-2-1-2 exhaust provided benefits at Monza, and it was retained for the next races as well.

This was another team to dabble with different rear swing-arms, which also found it hard to beat the one on the showroom bike.

Haga continued to prefer the oil and air springs of old to the more recent Öhlins gas-charged versions, and indeed won with them at Brno. He also preferred widely spaced triple clamps, to help his steering feel.

The Yamaha Motor France team was seen as a development effort for kit parts, with different rear swing-arms on Abe and Gimbert's machines.

Honda CBR1000RR

Round 1
LOSAIL, Qatar
26 February 2005, 3.343-mile/5.380-km circuit

Race 1 18 laps, 60.174 miles/96.840 km

Pl.	Name Nat.(Machine)	No.	Time & gap	Laps
1	Troy Corser, AUS (Suzuki)	11	37m 10.394s	18
			97.124 mph/156.306 km/h	
2	Yukio Kagayama, J (Suzuki)	71	3.065s	18
3	Regis Laconi, F (Ducati)	55	3.496s	18
4	Andrew Pitt, AUS (Yamaha)	88	14.714s	18
5	Noriyuki Haga, J (Yamaha)	41	20.300s	18
6	James Toseland, GB (Ducati)	1	20.562s	18
7	Ivan Silva, E (Yamaha)	22	22.031s	18
8	Chris Vermeulen, AUS (Honda)	77	22.188s	18
9	Karl Muggeridge, AUS (Honda)	31	26.929s	18
10	Norick Abe, J (Yamaha)	3	27.231s	18
11	Giovanni Bussei, I (Kawasaki)	200	38.995s	18
12	Marco Borciani, I (Yamaha)	20	42.208s	18
13	Fonsi Nieto, E (Ducati)	10	43.494s	18
14	Chris Walker, GB (Kawasaki)	9	44.894s	18
15	Steve Martin, AUS (Petronas)	99	49.673s	18
16	Ben Bostrom, USA (Honda)	155	53.884s	18
17	Garry McCoy, AUS (Petronas)	24	1m 01.558s	18
18	Mauro Sanchini, I (Kawasaki)	6	1m 04.028s	18
19	Gianluca Vizziello, I (Yamaha)	45	1m 05.885s	18
20	Miguel Praia, P (Yamaha)	17	1m 27.742s	18

DNF: Sebastien Gimbert, F (Yamaha) 32, 13 laps;
Lorenzo Lanzi, I (Ducati) 57, 13 laps; Max Neukirchner, D
(Honda) 76, 13 laps; Alessio Velini, I (Ducati) 25, 8 laps;
Ivan Clementi, I (Kawasaki) 8, 6 laps; Lucio Pedercini, I
(Ducati) 19, 3 laps; Talal Al Nuami, QAT (Yamaha) 95, 2
laps; Pierfrancesco Chili, I (Honda) 7, 0 laps; José Luis
Cardoso, E (Yamaha) 30, 0 laps.
Fastest lap: Kagayama, 2m 02.135s, 98.536
mph/158.579 km/h (record).

Race 2 18 laps, 60.174 miles/96.840 km

Pl.	Name Nat.(Machine)	No.	Time & gap	Laps
1	Yukio Kagayama, J (Suzuki)	71	37m 00.062s	18
			97.576mph/157.033 km/h	
2	Regis Laconi, F (Ducati)	55	2.454s	18
3	Troy Corser, AUS (Suzuki)	11	5.959s	18
4	Chris Vermeulen, AUS (Honda)	77	7.245s	18
5	Pierfrancesco Chili, I (Honda)	7	8.600s	18
6	James Toseland, GB (Ducati)	1	8.601s	18
7	Norick Abe, J (Yamaha)	3	9.731s	18
8	Max Neukirchner, D (Honda)	76	11.501s	18
9	Andrew Pitt, AUS (Yamaha)	88	11.790s	18
10	Sebastien Gimbert, F (Yamaha)	32	11.808s	18
11	Noriyuki Haga, J (Yamaha)	41	21.364s	18
12	Lorenzo Lanzi, I (Ducati)	57	25.875s	18
13	Fonsi Nieto, E (Ducati)	10	34.084s	18
14	Giovanni Bussei, I (Kawasaki)	200	34.119s	18
15	Mauro Sanchini, I (Kawasaki)	6	47.446s	18
16	Garry McCoy, AUS (Petronas)	24	48.647s	18
17	Gianluca Vizziello, I (Yamaha)	45	1m 03.995s	18
18	Miguel Praia, P (Yamaha)	17	1m 05.222s	18

DNF: Steve Martin, AUS (Petronas) 99, 16 laps; Marco
Borciani, I (Yamaha) 20, 12 laps; Talal Al Nuami, QAT
(Yamaha) 95, 10 laps; Chris Walker, GB (Kawasaki) 9, 9
laps; Karl Muggeridge, AUS (Honda) 31, 9 laps; Ivan
Silva, E (Yamaha) 22, 6 laps; Ivan Clementi, I (Kawasaki)
8, 5 laps; Alessio Velini, I (Ducati) 25, 3 laps; Lucio Ped-
ercini, I (Ducati) 19, 2 laps; Ben Bostrom, USA (Honda)
155, 0 laps; José Luis Cardoso, E (Yamaha) 30, 0 laps.
Fastest lap: Gimbert, 2m 01.852s 98.765
mph/158.947 km/h (record).
Superpole: Laconi, 2m 01.852s, 98.765 mph/158.947
km/h (record).
Previous record: New Circuit.
Championship points: 1 Kagayama, 45; 2 Corser, 41; 3
Laconi, 36; 4 Vermeulen, 21; 5 Pitt and Toseland, 20;
7 Haga, 16; 8 Abe, 15; 9 Chili, 11; 10 Silva, 9; 11
Neukirchner, 8; 12 Bussei and Muggeridge, 7;
14 Gimbert and Nieto, 6.

**Top: Corser and Kagayama, leading race
two, set the pace for the season.**

**Above left: Walker and Muggeridge
collided, and Walker (left) knew whom he
blamed.**

**Above right: Laconi (left) was happy to
split the Suzukis.**

Photographs: Gold & Goose

LOSAIL

The season-opener was an oddity, even given the previous MotoGP experiences at the glitteringly flash and echoingly empty Losail International Circuit.

The fast layout's tarmac had largely been cleaned of sand by a test session enjoyed by the SBK riders old and new in the week leading up to the race. Then it got another rare treat - a cleaning thanks to the rain. Yes, rain in the desert, an inauspicious omen.

The Alstare Corona pair of Troy Corser and Yukio Kagayama, the latter a rookie to the series but well acquainted with a World Superbike spec GSX-R1000, were the main forces through qualifying, and duly scored a win apiece, everyone else looking caught on the hop. It was the first time that Suzuki riders headed both podiums in World Superbike's 18-year history, and it looked like it wouldn't be the last.

To everyone's surprise it was Kagayama who left the Gulf as championship leader, not Corser, even though the latter secured a win and a third place. Corser was well beaten by over five seconds in race two, and even Ducati's perennially combative Regis Laconi, third in race one, outpaced him in the second 18-lapper.

The return of the rains on race day meant two parts for the first race, the result called on aggregate – in favour of Corser. With ten laps completed, the slowly deteriorating wet surface and a subsequent fast off-track excursion from Laconi had brought out the red flags.

Corser kept a canny distance behind Kagayama to finish the second leg second on the road, earning the race win, with Laconi third.

Behind, Andrew Pitt battled front-end set-up problems on the Yamaha for an eventual fourth. He was another SBK newcomer, but team-mate Noriyuki Haga was a seasoned campaigner who stormed to fifth overall. The Yamaha effort was way off form and lacking set-up time, as was shown in the fully dry race two. It was a common problem at this stage, with many teams plainly not ready to race for wins yet.

In the second race an unwise choice of hard rear Pirelli saw Corser stuck in third, Kagayama the winner from an impressive Laconi, but a thrilling fight for fourth place, which featured eight riders at one stage, went to Chris Vermeulen, best Honda finisher on the first day of the new season.

He and new team-mate Karl Muggeridge were the highest-profile riders to suffer all weekend with a nasty flu bug. Vermeulen was almost sickened further at the end by veteran Pierfrancesco Chili in his Klaffi-Honda debut, but middle age contributed to arm pump in the final laps. Max Neukirchner was a revelation, in his first and second SBK races on a full spec Superbike, having tested on a more standard model.

2004 champion James Toseland, recovered from multiple crashes in testing, one a flat-out highsider in fifth – to take two sixths. Considering his practice woes, before taking Superpole with an adrenaline-fuelled lap, these could be considered impressive.

Norick Abe was an assured class debutant, and wild card Ivan Silva Albertola (La Glisse Yamaha) put in an outstanding shift in race one, taking seventh. He crashed out of race two.

Muggeridge and Chris Walker clashed and crashed in the second, with Walker firmly blaming Muggeridge for a miserable no-score.

Petronas? Pointless, and plainly worried.

Right: Fast rookie Neukirchner temporarily leads Corser.

Photographs: Gold & Goose

PHILLIP ISLAND

It was Australia, so we can forgive the fact that several things ended up upside down. Like the look of the qualifying order, in many respects. Having left the Petronas team after three near fruitless years, and having stamped his authority on the winter's proceedings with a ruthless Suzuki boot, Troy Corser actually found himself behind a Petronas at one of the fastest tracks on the calendar. After Superpole qualifying at least.

The front row, post Superpole, was not headed by Corser, but by his team-mate Kagayama. It even had rookie Neukirchner in third place, not to mention Steve Martin, in second. Only then came Corser, but he would have his revenge on them all.

The start of the PI weekend had been balmy, the mercury well up... countered by a stiff breeze hustling down the main straight, and dampened only by Pierfrancesco Chili breaking his collarbone in qualifying. In this year of the all-conquering fours, the heady tailwind, towards the sea for a change, allowed Ducati man Laconi to belt out a 197.6 mph/318 km/h symphony from his 999F05's exhausts. This was claimed as the fastest ever top speed in SBK by the organisers. Not bad for a supposedly outgunned piece of Pantah-plus technology, and no longer with Michelin levels of traction exiting the preceding long lefts.

The upside-down theme continued with the threatening rains arriving on race morning. Muggeridge and Kagayama crashed in a wet warm-up.

A dry first race was depleted by crashes, with only 16 finishers. Worse to come in the second, with only 14 finishers, and a point going begging.

Corser won the first in a howling gale of up to 40 knots, with Qatar King Kagayama second and Vermeulen third, but only after an abrasive race with precocious German rookie Neukirchner. Paint and rubber were exchanged, but Vermeulen was the sleeker and one season older fox, with better knowledge of his local lair.

As the winds died down the rain reappeared, stopping race two after 12 laps, making for an aggregated event and ten laps left to run in the wet.

It was a slithering crash-fest, especially at the Hayshed corner, as Walker, Pitt and Haga all fell there, and Laconi lost out on a second spot after the highside save of the year, only to be claimed by the wet grass at the top of Lukey Heights. Restarting for his second seventh place of the day, he had merely to punch the starter button, after a wise retention of the road-bike system on bikes which can't be bump started.

Despite the promise of qualifying, none of the Petronas machines finished, in what was an unscripted end to their riders' home town fairytale.

It was arguably even more of a disaster for Toseland, who finished his day with a 14th and a crash, in one race almost a minute behind Corser. He had tangled with Muggeridge, falling to earth gracelessly. The least effective championship defence in history seemed to be failing on all fronts.

Chris Walker had another firm showing for a while, even leading the race in the wet section, until his Kawasaki slipped from under him at the infamous Hayshed exit.

One rider who would keep his feet, and earn a surprise top five, was the thus far lacklustre Nieto. His team-mate, Lorenzo Lanzi, was disqualified when his Ducati failed weight checks.

Race 1 22 laps, 60.764 miles/97.790 km

Pl.	Name Nat.(Machine)	No.	Time & gap	Laps
1	Troy Corser, AUS (Suzuki)	11	35m 15.199s	22
			103.418 mph/166.435 km/h	
2	Yukio Kagayama, J (Suzuki)	71	8.279s	22
3	Chris Vermeulen, AUS (Honda)	77	12.551s	22
4	Max Neukirchner, D (Honda)	76	12.761s	22
5	Andrew Pitt, AUS (Yamaha)	88	13.204s	22
6	Norick Abe, J (Yamaha)	3	15.116s	22
7	Regis Laconi, F (Ducati)	55	17.195s	22
8	Karl Muggeridge, AUS (Honda)	31	33.821s	22
9	Chris Walker, GB (Kawasaki)	9	34.010s	22
10	Giovanni Bussei, I (Kawasaki)	200	42.594s	22
11	Sebastien Gimbert, F (Yamaha)	32	42.851s	22
12	Mauro Sanchini, I (Kawasaki)	6	44.556s	22
13	Ivan Clementi, I (Kawasaki)	8	44.804s	22
14	James Toseland, GB (Ducati)	1	1m 01.011s	22
15	Andrew Stroud, NZ (Suzuki)	93	1m 32.156s	22
16	Miguel Praia, P (Yamaha)	17	1 lap	21

DNF: Ben Bostrom, USA (Honda) 155, 21 laps; Steve Martin, AUS (Petronas) 99, 14 laps; Marco Borciani, I (Yamaha) 20, 13 laps; Noriyuki Haga, J (Yamaha) 41, 11 laps; Lorenzo Alfonsi, I (Yamaha) 12, 10 laps; Alessio Corradi, I (Ducati) 27, 8 laps; Gianluca Vizziello, I (Yamaha) 45, 5 laps; Garry McCoy, AUS (Petronas) 24, 4 laps; Lucio Pedercini, I (Ducati) 19, 4 laps; Fonsi Nieto, E (Ducati) 10, 3 laps; José Luis Cardoso, E (Yamaha) 30, 0 laps.

DSQ: Lorenzo Lanzi, I (Ducati) 57, 22 laps.

Fastest lap: Corser, 1m 34.917s, 104.75 mph/168.589 km/h.

Race 2 22 laps, 60.764 miles/97.790 km

Pl.	Name Nat.(Machine)	No.	Time & gap	Laps
1	Troy Corser, AUS (Suzuki)	11	37m 34.183s	22
			97.042 mph/156.174 km/h	
2	Yukio Kagayama, J (Suzuki)	71	5.822s	22
3	Max Neukirchner, D (Honda)	76	10.897s	22
4	Chris Vermeulen, AUS (Honda)	77	18.757s	22
5	Fonsi Nieto, E (Ducati)	10	53.089s	22
6	Alessio Corradi, I (Ducati)	27	54.127s	22
7	Regis Laconi, F (Ducati)	55	58.076s	22
8	Norick Abe, J (Yamaha)	3	1m 03.328s	22
9	Giovanni Bussei, I (Kawasaki)	200	1m 04.355s	22
10	Mauro Sanchini, I (Kawasaki)	6	1m 08.754s	22
11	Ben Bostrom, USA (Honda)	155	1m 14.447s	22
12	Andrew Stroud, NZ (Suzuki)	93	1m 16.710s	22
13	Lorenzo Lanzi, I (Ducati)	57	1m 20.004s	22
14	Miguel Praia, P (Yamaha)	17	2m 44.473s	22

DNF: Lorenzo Alfonsi, I (Yamaha) 12, 16 laps; Chris Walker, GB (Kawasaki) 9, 15 laps; Steve Martin, AUS (Petronas) 99, 14 laps; Noriyuki Haga, J (Yamaha) 41, 13 laps; Andrew Pitt, AUS (Yamaha) 88, 12 laps; Garry McCoy, AUS (Petronas) 24, 12 laps; Marco Borciani, I (Yamaha) 20, 11 laps; Sebastien Gimbert, F (Yamaha) 32, 9 laps; José Luis Cardoso, E (Yamaha) 30, 7 laps; James Toseland, GB (Ducati) 1, 5 laps; Karl Muggeridge, AUS (Honda) 31, 5 laps; Ivan Clementi, I (Kawasaki) 8, 1 lap; ; Gianluca Vizziello, I (Yamaha) 45, 1 lap; Lucio Pedercini, I (Ducati) 19, 1 lap.

Fastest lap: Corser, 1m 34.979s, 104.688 mph/168.479 km/h.

Superpole: Kagayama, 1m 33.241s, 106.640 mph/171.620 km/h.km/h.

Lap record: Troy Corser, AUS (Ducati), 1m 33.019s, 106.894 mph/172.029 km/h (1999).

Championship points: 1 Corser, 91; ; 2 Kagayama, 85; 3 Laconi, 54; 4 Vermeulen, 50; 5 Neukirchner, 37; 6 Abe, 33; 7 Pitt, 31; 8 Toseland, 22; 9 Bussei, 20; 10 Nieto, 17; 11 Haga, 16; 12 Muggeridge, 15; 13 Chili, Gimbert and Sanchini, 11.

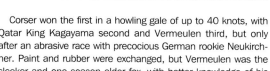

Above left: Pitt came back bearing the scars of battle.

Left: Abe focused on the task – two finishes, little distinction.

Far left: Corser celebrates a home-race double.

Photographs: Gold & Goose

Round 3
VALENCIA, Spain
24 April 2005, 2.489-mile/4.005-km circuit

Race 1 23 laps, 57.247 miles/92.115 km

Pl.	Name Nat.(Machine)	No.	Time & gap	Laps
1	Troy Corser, AUS (Suzuki)	11	37m 31.052s	23
			91.537 mph/147.315 km/h	
2	Chris Vermeulen, AUS (Honda)	77	9.116s	23
3	Yukio Kagayama, J (Suzuki)	71	12.788s	23
4	Chris Walker, GB (Kawasaki)	9	16.867s	23
5	Noriyuki Haga, J (Yamaha)	41	17.882s	23
6	Sebastien Gimbert, F (Yamaha)	32	26.495s	23
7	Pierfrancesco Chili, I (Honda)	7	28.784s	23
8	James Toseland, GB (Ducati)	1	36.604s	23
9	Sergio Fuertes, E (Suzuki)	16	39.524s	23
10	David Checa, E (Yamaha)	94	39.775s	23
11	Ivan Clementi, I (Kawasaki)	8	40.047s	23
12	Ben Bostrom, USA (Honda)	155	42.941s	23
13	Giovanni Bussei, I (Kawasaki)	200	47.505s	23
14	Lorenzo Alfonsi, I (Yamaha)	12	47.585s	23
15	Ivan Silva, E (Yamaha)	22	48.993s	23
16	Gianluca Vizziello, I (Yamaha)	45	49.064s	23
17	Fonsi Nieto, E (Ducati)	10	53.338s	23
18	Marco Borciani, I (Yamaha)	20	54.572s	23
19	Michel Nickmans, B (Yamaha)	21	1 lap	22

DNF: Norick Abe, J (Yamaha) 3, 21 laps; Karl Muggeridge, AUS (Honda) 31, 19 laps; Mauro Sanchini, I (Kawasaki) 6, 16 laps; Garry McCoy, AUS (Petronas) 24, 14 laps; Miguel Praia, P (Yamaha) 17, 10 laps; Steve Martin, AUS (Petronas) 99, 9 laps; Alessio Velini, I (Ducati) 25, 7 laps; Andrew Pitt, AUS (Yamaha) 88, 5 laps; Lucio Pedercini, I (Ducati) 19, 5 laps; José Luis Cardoso, E (Yamaha) 30, 3 laps; Lorenzo Lanzi, I (Ducati) 57, 0 laps; Max Neukirchner, D (Honda) 76, 0 laps.
Fastest lap: Corser, 1m 36.721s, 92.627 mph/149.068 km/h.

Race 2 23 laps, 57.247 miles/92.115 km

Pl.	Name Nat.(Machine)	No.	Time & gap	Laps
1	Troy Corser, AUS (Suzuki)	11	37m 52.057s	23
			90.691mph/145.953 km/h	
2	Chris Vermeulen, AUS (Honda)	77	5.361s	23
3	Chris Walker, GB (Kawasaki)	9	7.184s	23
4	Noriyuki Haga, J (Yamaha)	41	10.600s	23
5	Norick Abe, J (Yamaha)	3	11.903s	23
6	Ben Bostrom, USA (Honda)	155	19.200s	23
7	Yukio Kagayama, J (Suzuki)	71	19.345s	23
8	Andrew Pitt, AUS (Yamaha)	88	23.246s	23
9	David Checa, E (Yamaha)	94	24.787s	23
10	Pierfrancesco Chili, I (Honda)	7	25.299s	23
11	Sebastien Gimbert, F (Yamaha)	32	25.495s	23
12	Max Neukirchner, D (Honda)	76	27.833s	23
13	Ivan Clementi, I (Kawasaki)	8	31.339s	23
14	Gianluca Vizziello, I (Yamaha)	45	33.013s	23
15	Lorenzo Alfonsi, I (Yamaha)	12	34.024s	23
16	Sergio Fuertes, E (Suzuki)	16	39.889s	23
17	Steve Martin, AUS (Petronas)	99	41.728s	23
18	Mauro Sanchini, I (Kawasaki)	6	50.192s	23
19	James Toseland, GB (Ducati)	1	1 lap	22

DNF: : Karl Muggeridge, AUS (Honda) 31, 15 laps; Fonsi Nieto, E (Ducati) 10, 15 laps; Marco Borciani, I (Yamaha) 20, 12 laps; José Luis Cardoso, E (Yamaha) 30, 10 laps; Miguel Praia, P (Yamaha) 17, 10 laps; Ivan Silva, E (Yamaha) 22, 10 laps; Michel Nickmans, B (Yamaha) 21, 8 laps; Giovanni Bussei, I (Kawasaki) 200, 5 laps; Lucio Pedercini, I (Ducati) 19, 4 laps; Garry McCoy, AUS (Petronas) 24, 3 laps; Alessio Velini, I (Ducati) 25, 3 laps;
Fastest lap: Corser, 1m 37.756s 91.646 mph/147.490 km/h.
Superpole: Corser, 1m 35.676s, 93.638 mph/150.696 km/h.
Lap record: Neil Hodgson, GB (Ducati), 1m 35.007s, 94.297 mph/151.757 km/h (2003).
Championship points: 1 Corser, 141; 2 Kagayama, 110; 3 Vermeulen, 90; 4 Laconi 54; 5 Abe, 44; 6 Neukirchner, 41; 7 Haga, 40; 8 Pitt, 39; 9 Walker, 38; 10 Toseland, 30; 11 Chili and Gimbert, 26; 13 Bussei, 23; 14 Bostrom, 19; 15 Nieto, 17.

Top: Corser leads the pack into the first corner.

Above left: Vermeulen (77) had a torrid time shaking off Walker's Kawasaki.

Above right: Podium trio – Walker, double-winner Corser and Vermeulen.

Photographs: Gold & Goose

VALENCIA

Corser's steamroller eased open its inlet valve a little more at Valencia, and got two more big shiny decorations to hang over the footplate. This weekend Corser even managed to hex out his own team-mate Kagayama, who had been largely matching him until this point.

Trends were emerging, and once more the four-cylinder riders ruled the roost, now at a track the direct opposite of either Qatar or Phillip Island. Valencia in general was a full-on disaster for the Italian marque, with a weekend best of eighth in race one and 19th in race two. No Ducati of any kind finished race two in the points, and only three Ducatis managed to cross the line all weekend. Unprecedented, and given the near mono-formula status of the year before, it showed just how transient the dip in Superbike's overall fortunes had been.

Negating the fast starting Pitt in one race, Corser placed a provisional order for his end of season ermine robe with two largely unchallenged victories. He won by nine seconds in the opener and five in race two. It was too easy, at least for the watching spectators to get excited about.

The former Kings of Superbike, Ducati, were up to their necks in Clinica Mobile admittance forms and general misfortune. Laconi tangled with another rider and fell hard in qualifying, his dazed expression and unsure gait enough to show right away that the doctors were right to stop him racing.

For the other Ducati lead rider, Toseland, anything would have been better than nothing this weekend. And that's just about what he got. He battled through in manful fashion in race one for eighth, but tyre woes, poor team-work and another

frosty shoulder from a heartless lady luck made him the only Ducati finisher in race two, dead last and pointless in 19th, having been lapped after a tyre change mid-race.

This left Honda as the least ineffective of Suzuki's challengers this week, as Vermeulen worked hard for two seconds. In the opener the surprisingly competitive Norick Abe fell while trying to wrestle second from Vermeulen, gifting third to Kagayama.

Just behind Chris Walker, on a Kawasaki with a willing beast of an engine but with an untamed and unpredictable chassis, was showing that logic sometimes plays little part in racing. The ZX-10 chose the slow and exacting Valencia to challenge for podiums – fourth in race one, and a fully deserved third in race two. It was now a three-horse Japanese machine showcase, with only Yamaha now looking for its first podium of 2005.

Haga was still in the sharp end of competition but complaining bitterly of a lack of feel; Pitt was still coming to terms with the real-world race limitations of the available rubber and the team's lack of development time and budget. Abe, in the Yamaha Motor France team took fifth in race two, his team-mate Gimbert sixth in race one.

Ben Bostrom finally showed himself in race two; sixth out of nowhere creating at least a blip on an otherwise static Renegade Honda radar. The nearby Manises airport traffic control may have had a noontime radar blip just after the start of race one, as Neukirchner suffered the fastest, highest and longest highside of this or any other season. His spinning machine took out Ducati privateer Lorenzo Lanzi, breaking the Italian's collarbone and punting Muggeridge off line and off track for a time. An injured right hand would dampen Neukirchner's outstanding early season competitiveness for a while. But it could have been worse – he could have been riding a Ducati...

Right: Another win kept up Corser's momentum.

Below: Toseland, heading Pitt, regained some self-respect.

Below centre: Fast circuits equal close racing: Laconi pulls the train.

Photographs: Gold & Goose

MONZA

No double for Corser this particular weekend, even though it looked very possible, despite the squeaking close finish to the opening race. He had made his usual break at the earliest opportunity; his 1.2 second lead eventually nibbled off by Laconi and Kagayama. With the advent of Toseland on another red shifter near the end of the 18 laps, the top four were covered by only 1.757 seconds. Fast tracks make for close racing they say, and yet again Monza's chicane-riddled speed bowl offered handlebar-to-handlebar combat, between mechanised cavalry of very different designs.

After their Valencia drubbing and other early season comedy-hour catastrophes – which had stopped being funny for even the most hardened Desmo-bashers in the paddock – Ducati got back their motivation mojo at Monza. Home ground shouldn't have helped that much, as the theoretically more powerful four-cylinder machines should have had a high-speed advantage at this circuit where speed is sometimes all. Yet the Ducatis lost little of anything anywhere, proving that they can't be written off in the class they believe is their own property.

Only a bamboo curtain of defensive riding by Kagayama on the last section stopped Toseland's resurrection from earning him silver for second. Along with self-respect he got to take home some particularly shiny nuggets of bronze for third.

Ten Kate Honda invariably bring some high velocity ammunition to this racetrack. Vermeulen did not use the special Monza-engines team boss/tuner Gerrit so relishes working on over the winter, and they paid the price in race one, when his motor ground to a steaming halt. Using the Monza motor in race two, he won … from Laconi, by just under half a second.

Corser, complaining of braking imperfections at this supreme test of any braking system, had to fight hard for third, just ahead of Muggeridge, who showed he has lost little speed since his step up a division, but that he was still riding it like a Supersport machine on normal circuits.

Monza, however, is far from normal.

At one stage of race two there were eight riders in the leading group (usually headed by Laconi), before it splintered into two pairs, Vermeulen and Laconi, plus Corser and Muggeridge.

Toseland scored a fifth in race two, double-digit points again, with the perennially pushing Pitt seventh, one down on his race one sixth. His team-mate Haga was down among the also rans in ninth and 11th, much to the discomfort of the locally based Yamaha Motor Italia team.

Former Monza race winners were not exactly thick on the ground this year, but in Chili, Honda had one other pre-race potential winner, but not the seemingly unstoppable Neukirchner. Yet Chili was still not making enough sweet music with his multi-valve CBR to be a force, and Neukirchner was missing from his post, after an operation on his right hand injury from Valencia. Chili's bike leaked fluid on the line, causing a delay to the start of race two.

The illogicality of Kawasaki's season continued, as Walker took only a pair of eighth-place finishes on the PSG-1 ZX, at a fast circuit that should have suited it above all.

Round 4
MONZA, Italy
8 May 2005, 3.600-mile/5.793-km circuit

Race 1 18 laps, 64.800 miles/104.274 km

Pl.	Name Nat.(Machine)	No.	Time & gap	Laps
1	Troy Corser, AUS (Suzuki)	11	32m 40.906s	18
			118.952 mph/191.435 km/h	
2	Yukio Kagayama, J (Suzuki)	71	0.985s	18
3	James Toseland, GB (Ducati)	1	1.040s	18
4	Regis Laconi, F (Ducati)	55	1.757s	18
5	Andrew Pitt, AUS (Yamaha)	88	8.609s	18
6	Karl Muggeridge, AUS (Honda)	31	12.435s	18
7	Pierfrancesco Chili, I (Honda)	7	12.628s	18
8	Chris Walker, GB (Kawasaki)	9	16.656s	18
9	Gianluca Nannelli, I (Ducati)	69	20.481s	18
10	Norick Abe, J (Yamaha)	3	21.119s	18
11	Noriyuki Haga, J (Yamaha)	41	23.169s	18
12	Marco Borciani, I (Ducati)	20	39.874s	18
13	Giovanni Bussei, I (Kawasaki)	22	40.080s	18
14	Mauro Sanchini, I (Kawasaki)	6	41.484s	18
15	Ivan Clementi, I (Kawasaki)	8	41.955s	18
16	Fonsi Nieto, E (Ducati)	10	44.944s	18
17	Sebastien Gimbert, F (Yamaha)	32	45.063s	18
18	Ben Bostrom, USA (Honda)	155	47.162s	18
19	José Luis Cardoso, E (Yamaha)	30	47.225s	18
20	Luca Conforti, I (Ducati)	92	54.378s	18
21	Gianluca Vizziello, I (Yamaha)	45	1m 05.562s	18
22	Alessio Velini, I (Ducati)	25	1m 15.797s	18
23	Miguel Praia, P (Yamaha)	17	1m 16.849s	18
24	Paolo Blora, I (Yamaha)	113	1m 20.243s	18
25	Michel Nickmans, B (Yamaha)	21	1 lap	17

DNF: Garry McCoy, AUS (Petronas) 24, 17 laps; Steve Martin, AUS (Petronas) 99, 14 laps; Andrea Mazzali, I (MV Agusta) 26, 4 laps; Chris Vermeulen, AUS (Honda) 77, 1 lap; Lorenzo Alfonsi, I (Yamaha) 12, 0 laps; Luca Pedersoli, I (Ducati) 97, 0 laps.

Fastest lap: Kagayama, 1m 48.082s, 119.895 mph/192.953 km/h.

Race 2 17 laps, 61.200 miles/98.481 km

Pl.	Name Nat.(Machine)	No.	Time & gap	Laps
1	Chris Vermeulen, AUS (Honda)	77	30m 49.758s	17
			119.095 mph/191.664 km/h	
2	Regis Laconi, F (Ducati)	55	0.582s	17
3	Troy Corser, AUS (Suzuki)	11	2.458s	17
4	Karl Muggeridge, AUS (Honda)	31	3.379s	17
5	James Toseland, GB (Ducati)	1	9.901s	17
6	Andrew Pitt, AUS (Yamaha)	88	10.076s	17
7	Pierfrancesco Chili, I (Honda)	7	11.116s	17
8	Chris Walker, GB (Kawasaki)	9	11.587s	17
9	Noriyuki Haga, J (Yamaha)	41	26.936s	17
10	Gianluca Nannelli, I (Ducati)	69	33.459s	17
11	Giovanni Bussei, I (Kawasaki)	200	35.184s	17
12	Norick Abe, J (Yamaha)	3	35.612s	17
13	Mauro Sanchini, I (Kawasaki)	6	36.817s	17
14	Luca Conforti, I (Ducati)	92	45.473s	17
15	Ivan Clementi, I (Kawasaki)	8	47.350s	17
16	Lorenzo Alfonsi, I (Yamaha)	12	47.685s	17
17	Alessio Velini, I (Ducati)	25	1m 12.244s	17
18	Ben Bostrom, USA (Honda)	155	1m 23.146s	17
19	Paolo Blora, I (Yamaha)	113	1m 28.432s	17
20	Andrea Mazzali, I (MV Agusta)	26	1m 28.468s	17
21	Garry McCoy, AUS (Petronas)	24	1 lap	16

DNF: Marco Borciani, I (Ducati) 20, 16 laps; Yukio Kagayama, J (Suzuki) 71, 10 laps; Michel Nickmans, B (Yamaha) 21, 9 laps; Sebastien Gimbert, F (Yamaha) 32, 6 laps; Steve Martin, AUS (Petronas) 99, 4 laps; Fonsi Nieto, E (Ducati) 10, 3 laps; Luca Pedersoli, I (Ducati) 97, 2 laps; Gianluca Vizziello, I (Yamaha) 45, 0 laps; José Luis Cardoso, E (Yamaha) 30, 0 laps; Miguel Praia, P (Yamaha) 17, 0 laps.

Fastest lap: Vermeulen, 1m 48.233s, 119.728 mph/192.684 km/h.

Superpole: Kagayama, 1m 47.439s, 120.613 mph/194.108 km/h.

Lap record: Troy Bayliss, AUS (Ducati), 1m 47.434s, 120.619 mph/194.117 km/h (2002).

Championship points: 1 Corser, 182; 2 Kagayama, 130; 3 Vermeulen, 115; 4 Laconi, 87; 5 Pitt, 60; 6 Toseland, 57; 7 Abe and Walker, 54; 9 Haga, 52; 10 Chili, 44; 11 Neukirchner, 41; 12 Muggeridge, 38; 13 Bussei, 31; 14 Gimbert, 26; 15 Bostrom, 19.

Left: Chili threw boots, leathers and kisses to his avid home fans.

Photograph: Gold & Goose

Round 5
SILVERSTONE, Great Britain
29 May 2005, 2.213-mile/3.561-km circuit

Race 1 28 laps, 61.964 miles/99.708 km

Pl.	Name Nat.(Machine)	No.	Time & gap	Laps
1	Regis Laconi, F (Ducati)	55	40m 58.899s	28
			90.707 mph/145.979 km/h	
2	Troy Corser, AUS (Suzuki)	11	0.096s	28
3	James Toseland, GB (Ducati)	1	1.136s	28
4	Chris Vermeulen, AUS (Honda)	77	11.285s	28
5	Pierfrancesco Chili, I (Honda)	7	14.649s	28
6	Chris Walker, GB (Kawasaki)	9	16.461s	28
7	Max Neukirchner, D (Honda)	76	40.465s	28
8	Giovanni Bussei, I (Kawasaki)	200	43.265s	28
9	José Luis Cardoso, E (Yamaha)	30	46.411s	28
10	Karl Muggeridge, AUS (Honda)	31	49.211s	28
11	Yukio Kagayama, J (Suzuki)	71	51.706s	28
12	Mauro Sanchini, I (Kawasaki)	6	56.374s	28
13	Andrew Pitt, AUS (Yamaha)	88	1m 11.602s	28
14	Alessio Velini, I (Ducati)	25	1m 25.186s	28
15	Miguel Praia, P (Yamaha)	17	1m 25.974s	28
16	Michel Nickmans, B (Yamaha)	21	1m 26.774s	28

DNF: Steve Martin, AUS (Petronas) 99, 27 laps; Noriyuki Haga, J (Yamaha) 41, 25 laps; Norick Abe, J (Yamaha) 3, 22 laps; Massimo Roccoli, I (Yamaha) 52, 11 laps; Garry McCoy, AUS (Petronas) 24, 8 laps; Lorenzo Lanzi, I (Ducati) 57, 1 lap; Lorenzo Lanzi, I (Ducati) 57, 1 lap; Lorenzo Alfonsi, I (Yamaha) 12, 0 laps; Fonsi Nieto, E (Ducati) 10, 0 laps; Sebastien Gimbert, F (Yamaha) 32, 0 laps; Ivan Clementi, I (Ducati) 8, 0 laps.

Fastest lap: Laconi, 1m 27.130s, 91.424 mph/147.132 km/h (record).

Race 2 28 laps, 61.964 miles/99.708 km

Pl.	Name Nat.(Machine)	No.	Time & gap	Laps
1	James Toseland, GB (Ducati)	1	40m 55.190s	28
			90.844 mph/146.200 km/h	
2	Troy Corser, AUS (Suzuki)	11	0.473s	28
3	Noriyuki Haga, J (Yamaha)	41	3.187s	28
4	Chris Vermeulen, AUS (Honda)	77	6.691s	28
5	Pierfrancesco Chili, I (Honda)	7	16.923s	28
6	Chris Walker, GB (Kawasaki)	9	17.057s	28
7	Yukio Kagayama, J (Suzuki)	71	28.248s	28
8	Norick Abe, J (Yamaha)	3	31.760s	28
9	Andrew Pitt, AUS (Yamaha)	88	32.084s	28
10	Karl Muggeridge, AUS (Honda)	31	36.492s	28
11	Lorenzo Lanzi, I (Ducati)	57	39.470s	28
12	Ivan Clementi, I (Ducati)	8	40.182s	28
13	Garry McCoy, AUS (Petronas)	24	41.325s	28
14	Ben Bostrom, USA (Honda)	155	46.096s	28
15	Massimo Roccoli, I (Yamaha)	52	56.251s	28
16	Giovanni Bussei, I (Kawasaki)	200	56.733s	28
17	Mauro Sanchini, I (Kawasaki)	6	58.902s	28
18	Max Neukirchner, D (Honda)	76	1m 04.667s	28
19	Alessio Velini, I (Ducati)	25	1m 13.561s	28
20	Steve Martin, AUS (Petronas)	99	1m 17.669s	28
21	Michel Nickmans, B (Yamaha)	26	1m 25.339s	28

DNF: Fonsi Nieto, E (Ducati) 10, 20 laps; ; Miguel Praia, P (Yamaha) 17, 12 laps; Regis Laconi, F (Ducati) 55, 1 lap; José Luis Cardoso, E (Yamaha) 30, 1 lap.

Fastest lap: Corser, 1m 27.166s, 91.386 mph/147.071 km/h.

Superpole: Kagayama, 1m 26.679s, 91.899 mph/147.897 km/h.

Previous circuit record: Gregorio Lavilla, E (Suzuki), 1m 53.629s, 99.140 mph/159.551 km/h (2003).

Championship points: 1 Corser, 222; 2 Kagayama, 144; 3 Vermeulen, 141; 4 Laconi, 112; 5 Toseland 98; 6 Walker, 74; 7 Pitt, 70; 8 Haga, 68; 9 Chili, 66; 10 Abe, 62; 11 Muggeridge and Neukirchner, 50; ; 13 Bussei, 39; 14 Gimbert, 26; 15 Bostrom, 21.

Top: Toseland's revival continued, with his only win of the year, from Corser and Haga (41).

Above left: Midfield action – Muggeridge heads Abe and Cardoso.

Above right: First-race winner Laconi crashed on lap one of the second. Cardoso (30) was also out, but Neukirchner (76) got going again.

Photographs: Gold & Goose

SILVERSTONE

Quite why Silverstone proved to be just about the happiest Ducati hunting ground of the year is a mystery, as there is nothing in its make up that seems particularly Ducati-friendly. Or unfriendly. The most ludicrously slow, bumpy and ill-considered chicane known to man, surrounded mostly by big fast corners, mile-wide straights and rippled sections – the big Silverstone circuit has it all. But no bike should have any particular advantage because of this.

Not that it mattered, as we didn't get to use the big Silverstone anyway. Late news had dawned that we would be running on the shorter "International" circuit layout as used - with typical British logic – for national racing. It was a bolt from the red, white and blue.

Most heard about the change from the 2003/4 full track layout a week or so beforehand, but many of the riders turned up still expecting full rations even on Thursday. The official SBK website still had the wrong track details showing right up to race eve. It was not SBK's shiniest moment, not least because riders like Pitt hated the layout and pined for the bigger, older version.

The racing proved to be entertaining enough, whatever the track layout; the local crowd got to see something unique and, in many ways, totally unexpected. Toseland almost won a race in the opener and then went on and scored his first 2005 victory in the second outing.

That his team-mate won the other was proof enough that you could accuse the Ducati effort of many things, but in with the negatives there were an increasing number of rapid upswings.

Yamaha, after a reversal of fortune when Haga's fuel pump dropped him from a possible podium in race one, achieved their first top three status of 2005.

In the opener Laconi took the win, from Corser and Toseland.

Corser, the long-time race leader in race two, saw Toseland pass on lap 18, and with Laconi out after a crash on his second lap, it transpired to be Corser easing away from a fading Haga for second. Nonetheless, Haga earned Yamaha's best finish so far, after he simply found "feel" from his suspension, rather than any greater power or electronic trickery from his machine.

In the big picture, Corser increased his championship lead over Kagayama, the Superpole winner having fallen in race one, recovering for 11th; then fought it out for seventh in the second. At a track where this BSB veteran could have been expected to have an advantage, it was poor luck and poor stuff.

Chili's difficult season continued, with the Italian battling leg cramps to take a pair of fifths, each time from Walker.

Pitt's Yamaha carried on Silverstone's traditional engine cut-out controversy, first flagged up by Troy Bayliss in years gone by after a fall in warm up. As his machine patently continued to turn over while lying prostrate, Pitt had to take a ride-through penalty in race one. Controversy continued, as Kagayama's machine seemed not to cut out either, when he fell from the leading pack in race one, and yet he was not penalised. Vermeulen capitalised on Kagayama's bad luck, scoring a brace of fourths.

Garry McCoy had originally been given a ride-through penalty for having too many holes cut into the surface of his Petronas's bodywork to counteract the high winds in qualifying, but as the new rule had not been properly ratified, this was withdrawn. He scored his first points of the year, and sighed with relief at such a meagre feat.

MISANO

You need four sides to make a rectangle and just as many to make a square. A quadrilateral has four sides as well, though each of them can be of a different length. Excuse the cod geometry but race one and race two at Misano were symmetrical along the four leading edges, with Laconi taking the wins, Vermeulen the seconds, Corser the thirds and Toseland two fourths.

Ducati's recent regime of testing – tyres for Pirelli to work out their own mid-season wobble, and riders to get their race performances up – certainly paid dividends, with strong results in each race, even though each was very different.

The first race was halted five laps in after a backmarker crashed, and an aggregate result called. The second heat was trimmed a lap after the start lights began to misbehave, sending a few riders off at the wrong moment.

With track temperatures into the fifties on race day, tyres were always going to be an issue. Corser opted for the new and bigger-section 200 Pirelli. He found it a little off in race conditions, hence his inability to challenge Laconi or Vermeulen with any surety of footing.

Both second place man Vermeulen and Corser got closer to Laconi in race two, but for the French faction in SBK it was a double glory day for the first time of the year.

Behind the repeat top four finishers, there were 30 race starters, and despite two races of sheer attrition (14 non-finishers in race one, 15 in race two) there were still 20 and 18 race finishers respectively.

Lanzi continued his growth hormone intake, earning his best result to date, only four seconds behind Toseland's factory Duke in race one. He had made up ground in the last third of the race, setting the fastest laps of all in that period, just as the tyres got chewy.

In sixth Haga slid into the double-digit scores again, beating Chili and Walker. He was to take another sixth, indicating far from ideal grip from the tyre and bike combination. Behind the top eight, Nieto had his best ride since Australia, only ninth but looking like a racer again. Steve Martin, battering away every weekend on his Petronas scored 11th in race one, a brilliant ride in the hot conditions. He was to ace it with eighth in race two, another small miracle for the largely Pommie Petronas personnel.

Behind the leading four of race two, Chili took a fifth place, with Haga and Muggeridge in his wake.

What of Kagayama? A brief fist fight between him and this year's crash-prone Spaniard Jose Luis Cardoso after a qualifying session saw him fined. He crashed with nine laps to go in race one, finished a depressed 12th in race two after injuring his hand and having to race his number two bike. His constant Suzuka 8-Hour testing commitments were taking a toll, it appeared, as his slide from grace gathered the momentum his race pace had lost.

Neukirchner's dramatic rookie SBK season carried on its mid point flattening out, as he collided with team-mate Chili just as the first race was stopped. In heat two of the opener he suffered brake problems, crashing once more. In race two he toiled against a cracked exhaust and another mysterious lack of traction (a common complaint from all the riders recently) before retiring.

Round 6
MISANO, Italy
26 June 2005, 2.523-mile/4.060-km circuit

Race 1 24 laps, 60.552 miles/97.440 km (aggregate)

Pl.	Name Nat.(Machine)	No.	Time & gap	Laps
1	Regis Laconi, F (Ducati)	55	39m 07.157s	24
			92.865 mph/149.451 km/h	
2	Chris Vermeulen, AUS (Honda)	77	4.439s	24
3	Troy Corser, AUS (Suzuki)	11	8.043s	24
4	James Toseland, GB (Ducati)	1	10.198s	24
5	Lorenzo Lanzi, I (Ducati)	57	14.105s	24
6	Noriyuki Haga, J (Yamaha)	41	16.841s	24
7	Pierfrancesco Chili, I (Honda)	7	18.000s	24
8	Chris Walker, GB (Kawasaki)	9	20.110s	24
9	Fonsi Nieto, E (Ducati)	10	21.468s	24
10	Karl Muggeridge, AUS (Honda)	31	22.590s	24
11	Steve Martin, AUS (Petronas)	99	24.800s	24
12	Mauro Sanchini, I (Kawasaki)	6	26.201s	24
13	José Luis Cardoso, E (Yamaha)	30	27.795s	24
14	Ben Bostrom, USA (Honda)	155	31.185s	24
15	Ivan Clementi, I (Ducati)	8	34.975s	24
16	Lorenzo Alfonsi, I (Yamaha)	12	37.297s	24
17	Gianluca Vizziello, I (Yamaha)	45	53.084s	24
18	Miguel Praia, P (Yamaha)	17	1m 25.485s	24
19	Giuseppe Zannini, I (Yamaha)	73	2m 12.092s	24
20	Adam Badziak, POL (Suzuki)	74	1 lap	23

DNF: Garry McCoy, AUS (Petronas) 24, 20 laps; Alessio Velini, I (Ducati) 25, 18 laps; Yukio Kagayama, J (Suzuki) 71, 15 laps; Lucio Pedercini, I (Ducati) 19, 15 laps; Luca Conforti, I (Ducati) 92, 12 laps; Marco Borciani, I (Ducati) 20, 10 laps; Max Neukirchner, D (Honda) 76, 6 laps; Giovanni Bussei, I (Kawasaki) 200, 6 laps; Norick Abe, J (Yamaha) 3, 6 laps; Norino Brignola, I (Ducati) 75, 4 laps; Paolo Blora, I (Ducati) 113, 4 laps; Michel Nickmans, B (Yamaha) 21, 3 laps; Andrew Pitt, AUS (Yamaha) 88, 2 laps; Michele Gallina, I (MV Agusta) 72, 2 laps.

Fastest lap: Vermeulen, 1m 36.666s, 93.952 mph/151.201 km/h.

Race 2 25 laps, 63.075 miles/101.500 km

Pl.	Name Nat.(Machine)	No.	Time & gap	Laps
1	Regis Laconi, F (Ducati)	55	40m 46.260s	25
			92.815 mph/149.371 km/h	
2	Chris Vermeulen, AUS (Honda)	77	1.491s	25
3	Troy Corser, AUS (Suzuki)	11	3.143s	25
4	James Toseland, GB (Ducati)	1	14.562s	25
5	Pierfrancesco Chili, I (Honda)	7	16.291s	25
6	Noriyuki Haga, J (Yamaha)	41	18.600s	25
7	Karl Muggeridge, AUS (Honda)	31	24.065s	25
8	Steve Martin, AUS (Petronas)	99	24.503s	25
9	Lorenzo Lanzi, I (Ducati)	57	25.865s	25
10	Giovanni Bussei, I (Kawasaki)	200	28.458s	25
11	Chris Walker, GB (Kawasaki)	9	28.522s	25
12	Yukio Kagayama, J (Suzuki)	71	31.223s	25
13	Mauro Sanchini, I (Kawasaki)	6	33.345s	25
14	Lorenzo Alfonsi, I (Yamaha)	12	35.792s	25
15	Norick Abe, J (Yamaha)	3	39.660s	25
16	Miguel Praia, P (Yamaha)	17	1m 25.453s	25
17	Giuseppe Zannini, I (Yamaha)	73	1m 37.770s	25
18	Adam Badziak, POL (Suzuki)	74	1 lap	25

DNF: Warwick Nowland, AUS (Suzuki) 12, 19 laps; Sergio Fuertes, E (Suzuki) 16, 19 laps; Miguel Praia, P (Ducati) 50, 18 laps; Gianluca Nannelli, I (Ducati) 69, 6 laps; Pierfrancesco Chili, I (Ducati) 7, 5 laps; David Garcia, E (Ducati) 48, 3 laps; Alessio Velini, I (Yamaha) 25, 1 lap.

Fastest lap: Laconi, 1m 36.806s, 93.816 mph/150.982 km/h.

Superpole: Corser, 1m 35.330s, 95.269 mph/153.320 km/h.

Lap record: John Kocinski, USA (Ducati), 1m 34.296s, 96.313 mph/155.001 km/h (1996).

Championship points: 1 Corser, 254; 2 Vermeulen, 181; 3 Laconi, 162; 4 Kagayama, 148; 5 Toseland, 124; 6 Haga, 88; 7 Walker, 87; 8 Chili, 86; 9 Pitt, 70; 10 Muggeridge, 65; 11 Abe, 63; 12 Neukirchner, 50; 13 Bussei, 45; 14 Lanzi, 30; 15 Sanchini, 27.

Above left: Ben Bostrom with guardian angel – gentlemen prefer them blonde.

Above right: Crouching tiger, hidden Haga.

Left: Unbeatable Laconi took the double in the heat.

Photographs: Gold & Goose

Round 7
BRNO, Czech Republic
17 July 2005, 3.357-mile/5.403-km circuit

Race 1 20 laps, 67.140 miles/108.060 km

Pl.	Name Nat.(Machine)	No.	Time & gap	Laps
1	Troy Corser, AUS (Suzuki)	11	41m 42.829s	20
			96.580 mph/155.431 km/h	
2	James Toseland, GB (Ducati)	1	6.592s	20
3	Regis Laconi, F (Ducati)	55	7.477s	20
4	Chris Walker, GB (Kawasaki)	9	9.060s	20
5	Pierfrancesco Chili, I (Honda)	7	9.183s	20
6	Lorenzo Lanzi, I (Ducati)	57	10.778s	20
7	Noriyuki Haga, J (Yamaha)	41	13.760s	20
8	Chris Vermeulen, AUS (Honda)	77	15.069s	20
9	Norick Abe, J (Yamaha)	3	16.320s	20
10	Andrew Pitt, AUS (Yamaha)	88	19.676s	20
11	Yukio Kagayama, J (Suzuki)	71	21.822s	20
12	Fonsi Nieto, E (Ducati)	10	24.782s	20
13	Karl Muggeridge, AUS (Honda)	31	25.830s	20
14	Max Neukirchner, D (Honda)	76	27.486s	20
15	David Checa, E (Yamaha)	94	31.003s	20
16	José Luis Cardoso, E (Yamaha)	30	32.625s	20
17	Steve Martin, AUS (Petronas)	99	47.653s	20
18	Marco Borciani, I (Ducati)	20	50.494s	20
19	Sebastien Gimbert, F (Yamaha)	32	50.526s	20
20	Ben Bostrom, USA (Honda)	15	56.070s	20
21	Gianluca Vizziello, I (Yamaha)	45	57.136s	20
22	Lorenzo Alfonsi, I (Yamaha)	12	57.196s	20
23	Miguel Praia, P (Yamaha)	17	1m 24.067s	20
24	Michel Nickmans, B (Yamaha)	21	1m 40.187s	20
25	Adam Badziak, POL (Suzuki)	74	1m 43.866s	20
26	Jiri Drazdak, SVK (Yamaha)	79	1m 52.574s	20
27	Milos Cihak, CZ (Suzuki)	81	2m 01.857s	20
28	Jiri Trcka, CZ (Ducati)	59	1 lap	19

DNF: Alessio Velini, I (Ducati) 25, 16 laps; Ivan Clementi, I (Ducati) 8, 5 laps; Marek Svoboda, SVK (Yamaha) 80, 5 laps; Garry McCoy, AUS (Petronas) 24, 4 laps; Mauro Sanchini, I (Kawasaki) 6, 4 laps; Giovanni Bussei, I (Kawasaki) 200, 4 laps; Jiri Mrkyvka, CZ (Ducati) 23, 2 laps.

Fastest lap: Corser, 2m 03.812s, 97.617 mph/157.099 km/h (record).

Race 2 20 laps, 67.140 miles/108.060 km

Pl.	Name Nat.(Machine)	No.	Time & gap	Laps
1	Noriyuki Haga, J (Yamaha)	41	41m 43.525s	20
			96.553 mph/155.387 km/h	
2	Troy Corser, AUS (Suzuki)	11	3.233s	20
3	Chris Vermeulen, AUS (Honda)	77	11.012s	20
4	Norick Abe, J (Yamaha)	3	12.268s	20
5	Pierfrancesco Chili, I (Honda)	7	12.361s	20
6	Lorenzo Lanzi, I (Ducati)	57	13.511s	20
7	Regis Laconi, F (Ducati)	55	14.141s	20
8	James Toseland, GB (Ducati)	1	16.439s	20
9	Karl Muggeridge, AUS (Honda)	31	16.820s	20
10	Chris Walker, GB (Kawasaki)	9	19.737s	20
11	Yukio Kagayama, J (Suzuki)	71	24.777s	20
12	Fonsi Nieto, E (Ducati)	10	25.244s	20
13	Ivan Clementi, I (Ducati)	8	26.700s	20
14	David Checa, E (Yamaha)	94	28.119s	20
15	Giovanni Bussei, I (Kawasaki)	200	42.082s	20
16	Steve Martin, AUS (Petronas)	99	43.952s	20
17	Sebastien Gimbert, F (Yamaha)	32	48.776s	20
18	Ben Bostrom, USA (Honda)	155	54.908s	20
19	Alessio Velini, I (Ducati)	25	56.372s	20
20	Lorenzo Alfonsi, I (Yamaha)	12	56.694s	20
21	Miguel Praia, P (Yamaha)	17	1m 23.029s	20
22	Michel Nickmans, B (Yamaha)	21	2m 04.091s	20
23	Milos Cihak, CZ (Yamaha)	81	1 lap	19
24	Jiri Trcka, CZ (Ducati)	59	1 lap	19

DNF: Andrew Pitt, AUS (Yamaha) 88, 18 laps; Adam Badziak, POL (Suzuki) 74, 12 laps; Max Neukirchner, D (Honda) 76, 12 laps; Jiri Mrkyvka, CZ (Ducati) 23, 10 laps; José Luis Cardoso, E (Yamaha) 30, 5 laps; Marco Borciani, I (Ducati) 20, 4 laps; Gianluca Vizziello, I (Yamaha) 45, 2 laps; Jiri Drazdak, SVK (Yamaha) 79, 0 laps;

DNS: Marek Svoboda, SVK (Yamaha) 80.

Fastest lap: Haga, 2m 03.747s, 97.668 mph/157.182 km/h (record).

Superpole: Corser, 2m 02.694s, 98.507 mph/158.531km/h

Previous record: Troy Corser, AUS (Ducati), 2m 04.019s, 97.454 mph/156.837 km/h (1996).

Championship points: 1 Corser, 299; 2 Vermeulen, 205; 3 Laconi, 187; 4 Kagayama, 158; 5 Toseland, 152; 6 Haga, 122; 7 Chili, 108; 8 Walker, 106; 9 Abe, 83; 10 Pitt, 76; 11 Muggeridge, 75; 12 Neukirchner, 52; 13 Lanzi, 50; 14 Bussei, 46; 15 Nieto, 32.

Above left: Vermeulen shows his pre-race nerves on the grid.

Above right: Abe, on familiar ground, claimed his best result of the year with fourth in race two.

Photographs: Gold & Goose

BRNO

A return to an old SBK venue marked a return to top form for the most enigmatic and unpredictable talents in World Superbike, Noriyuki Haga. Having frustrated his team, Yamaha and himself with some bursts of speed, then abrupt deflations of mood and pace, Haga made amends in typically flamboyant fashion. His best so far a lone third place, he wrote a new script in the second race at Brno – a thriller of breathtaking ambition and greed, all conducted at lightning pace. Seventh in the opener, he tore even Corser apart in race two, winning by three seconds as he skipped and slid his R1 around one of the best tracks the world has to offer. Not bad for a man who had qualified 18th – out of Superpole indeed – and who had collided with Vermeulen in the early laps, bending his brake lever in the process.

Possibly the most important, if not the most memorable, aspect of a busy race weekend was nothing whatever to do with Haga. It was the resurgence of Corser.

Winless since Monza in early May, some were pointing to the end of the big push, and predicting the onset of a mid-season fade that has taken the shine off many a Corser championship challenge. Not a bit of that this weekend, as he took a full 25 points in race one, after dominating the latter stages of practice and Superpole, then bumped in a close second in race two. It even looked like a yellow and purple parade was on the cards again for most of race two, but for the astonishing advances made by Haga.

According to the statisticians on site, no-one had ever won an SBK race after starting outside the top 16, but few watching would ever forget his new lap record pace and spine-tingling overtakes. It was, that most overused of racing expressions, an historic victory.

A shocking start for Toseland in race one did not stop him battling through for second, finishing his 20 laps ahead of team-mate Laconi, but over six seconds from Corser.

Walker's Kawasaki was singing a sweet refrain around the Brno hillsides, taking him to fourth in race one, just a second and a half from another podium finish. Just behind privateers Chili and Lanzi, compatriots at very different wavelengths of the spectrum of experience, came the race-one Haga, in turn just ahead of an unhappy Vermeulen in eighth.

Oil on the track made for an early complete re-start of race two, and in one of the most changeable afternoons in SBK history many of the leading riders in race one were tearing up their podium press conference speeches.

Corser's second, one ahead of a resurgent Vermeulen, punished his championship rivals badly. Out of the top ten in race one, Abe was only 12 seconds from a win in race two, all the Yamahas obviously a potent force at Brno.

Chili and Lanzi repeated their fifth and sixths from the opener, but behind the two lead Ducatis suffered unexpectedly once more, with Laconi seventh and Toseland eighth. Even Walker, so close to a podium in race one, slipped to tenth.

Slowly failing by degrees, Kagayama left Brno with only a pair of 11th places, and a hangdog expression.

An impressive 24 people finished race two, despite the eight non-finishers and one non-starter, but that was nothing. In race one, a whopping 28 riders crossed the line, all but one on the same lap as the winner.

Down in Petronas country, it was another dry weekend in the points table, with Martin 17th in each race, and McCoy initially a crasher then an injured non-starter in race two.

Left: Haga, heading Corser, regained winning form at last in Brno.

Right: Chris Walker, twice top Briton, leads an off-form Toseland.

Below left: Corser, Haga and Vermeulen share the race-two rostrum.

Below right: Petronas on parade – Steve Martin (99) and Garry McCoy were scratching for scraps.

Photographs: Gold & Goose

BRANDS HATCH

The biggest SBK race on the calendar may not have the same allure as during the Foggy years, but after the hardcore all-weekend crowd had been boosted nicely by the one-day warriors, Brands on Sunday was still a crowded air-horn festival. A sort of mini-FA Cup final, just no longer between Man U and Arsenal.

For SBK nuts it's still unmissable, and the action up front sent them reeling to the exit roads on adrenaline overload.

Kent constabulary might have laid assault charges against the leaders in some stages of each race, especially the last lap of the second, when race-one winner Corser and race-two leading light Haga tangled out the back of the circuit. Corser ran wide, off track, then back on to finish second.

It was Corser's pride that drove him on, as his most realistic championship challenger, Vermeulen, had finished only fourth in race one, then third in race two. Corser clearly wanted to win the double or nothing, after taking an advantage of only 0.186 over Haga in race one. The Aussie had started from pole (his third in a row), and he and Haga took turns to pass and lead over the line no fewer than seven times in the first race, and four in the second.

Haga made set-up changes between races, and went some six seconds faster in the second leg, showing why teams are prepared to put up with some excess baggage charges and inconsistency to gain his signature each year.

Laconi, back in the big mix again for Ducati, was a close third in race one, and would be a remote fifth in race two, slower

second time out. His team-mate, James Toseland, was once more off song at Brands, especially when his machine quit in race one with an "electrical problem". Recovering to finish a struggling and slowing seventh in race two, Toseland was riding hard, but still suffering in Ducati's most difficult season for years. The fitment of a Pirelli's 200mm rear tyre in race two was the reason given, but a steely expression and curt replies may have indicated another cause.

In 2004 it was factory Ducatis versus Ducati privateers, with a saffron coating of Ten Kate Honda at most races. This time it was fours to the floor, and the two-cylinder future was looking bleak again, after some recent rallies in their fortunes.

Just to cap it for Ducati, the second 25-lap race delivered an eventual lonely third for Honda man Vermeulen.

Walker stepped up as top local again in fourth. Easily the best Kawasaki rider of the season, he'd been clattered on the entrance to Paddock Hill Bend at the start of consecutive races at Brands, and but for this, may have clung onto the leaders more closely. Pitt just lost fifth to Laconi in the second race.

A lousy rookie SBK season for Muggeridge continued with a crash in race two, after a strong sixth in race one, in which he got the better of his fellow SBK rookie Pitt.

In race two Walker made it four makes in four places – the sort of result the current technical rules and tyre regulations were brought in to facilitate. Better late than never, after 2004's Ducati dominance.

Suzuki's second early season force, Kagayama, had now completed his Suzuka 8-Hour testing duties and, if not quite liberated from continual jet-lag and Dunlop grip-envy hangovers, he had at least started on his road to recovery, with two ninths.

Round 8
BRANDS HATCH, Great Britain
7 August 2005, 2.608-mile/4.197-km circuit

Race 1 25 laps, 65.200 miles/104.925 km

Pl.	Name Nat.(Machine)	No.	Time & gap	Laps
1	Troy Corser, AUS (Suzuki)	11	36m 45.074s	25
			106.441 mph/171.300 km/h	
2	Noriyuki Haga, J (Yamaha)	41	0.186s	25
3	Regis Laconi, F (Ducati)	55	1.976s	25
4	Chris Vermeulen, AUS (Honda)	77	4.590s	25
5	Chris Walker, GB (Kawasaki)	9	5.746s	25
6	Karl Muggeridge, AUS (Honda)	31	8.428s	25
7	Andrew Pitt, AUS (Yamaha)	88	8.598s	25
8	Lorenzo Lanzi, I (Ducati)	57	15.628s	25
9	Yukio Kagayama, J (Suzuki)	71	15.671s	25
10	Max Neukirchner, D (Honda)	76	28.250s	25
11	Norick Abe, J (Yamaha)	3	32.470s	25
12	Ben Bostrom, USA (Honda)	155	32.500s	25
13	Dennis Hobbs, GB (Yamaha)	98	32.683s	25
14	Pere Riba, E (Kawasaki)	96	32.885s	25
15	Steve Martin, AUS (Petronas)	99	35.171s	25
16	Sebastien Gimbet, F (Yamaha)	32	35.272s	25
17	Gianluca Vizziello, I (Yamaha)	45	46.876s	25
18	Lorenzo Alfonsi, I (Yamaha)	12	48.628s	25
19	Ivan Clementi, I (Ducati)	8	50.123s	25
20	José Luis Cardoso, E (Yamaha)	30	1 lap	24

DNF: Giovanni Bussei, I (Kawasaki) 200, 22 laps; Fonsi Nieto, E (Ducati) 10, 15 laps; Pierfrancesco Chili, I (Honda) 7, 13 laps; Miguel Praia, P (Yamaha) 17, 10 laps; James Toseland, GB (Ducati) 1, 9 laps; Michel Nickmans, B (Yamaha) 21, 9 laps; Alessio Velini, I (Ducati) 25, 7 laps; Garry McCoy, AUS (Petronas) 24, 6 laps; Marco Borciani, I (Ducati) 20, 4 laps.

Fastest lap: Haga, 1m 27.489s, 107.310 mph/172.698 km/h.

Race 2 25 laps, 65.200 miles/104.925 km

Pl.	Name Nat.(Machine)	No.	Time & gap	Laps
1	Noriyuki Haga, J (Yamaha)	41	36m 39.815s	25
			106.696 mph/171.710 km/h	
2	Troy Corser, AUS (Suzuki)	11	2.686s	25
3	Chris Vermeulen, AUS (Honda)	77	8.062s	25
4	Chris Walker, GB (Kawasaki)	9	12.053s	25
5	Regis Laconi, F (Ducati)	55	13.044s	25
6	Andrew Pitt, AUS (Yamaha)	88	13.184s	25
7	James Toseland, GB (Ducati)	1	14.215s	25
8	Lorenzo Lanzi, I (Ducati)	57	21.026s	25
9	Yukio Kagayama, J (Suzuki)	71	21.175s	25
10	Ben Bostrom, USA (Honda)	155	21.257s	25
11	Max Neukirchner, D (Honda)	76	29.315s	25
12	Pere Riba, E (Kawasaki)	96	30.591s	25
13	Pierfrancesco Chili, I (Honda)	7	34.619s	25
14	Sebastien Gimbet, F (Yamaha)	32	39.732s	25
15	Dennis Hobbs, GB (Yamaha)	98	39.879s	25
16	Lorenzo Alfonsi, I (Yamaha)	12	49.646s	25
17	Gianluca Vizziello, I (Yamaha)	45	49.663s	25
18	Garry McCoy, AUS (Petronas)	24	1m 14.032s	25

DNF: Steve Martin, AUS (Petronas) 99, 18 laps; Norick Abe, J (Yamaha) 3, 18 laps; Ivan Clementi, I (Ducati) 8, 16 laps; Fonsi Nieto, E (Ducati) 10, 11 laps; Alessio Velini, I (Ducati) 25, 11 laps; Giovanni Bussei, I (Kawasaki) 200, 10 laps; José Luis Cardoso, E (Yamaha) 30, 10 laps; Marco Borciani, I (Ducati) 20, 8 laps; Michel Nickmans, B (Yamaha) 21, 7 laps; Miguel Praia, P (Yamaha) 17, 4 laps; Karl Muggeridge, AUS (Honda) 31, 1 lap.

Fastest lap: Haga, 1m 27.272s, 107.577 mph/173.128 km/h.

Superpole: Corser, 1m 26.672s, 108.321 mph/174.326 km/h.

Lap record: Shane Byrne, GB (Ducati), 1m 26.755s, 108.217 mph/174.159 km/h (2003).

Championship points: 1 Corser, 344; 2 Vermeulen, 234; 3 Laconi, 214; 4 Kagayama, 172; 5 Haga, 167; 6 Toseland, 161; 7 Walker, 130; 8 Chili, 111; 9 Pitt, 95; 10 Abe, 88; 11 Muggeridge, 85; 12 Lanzi, 66; 13 Neukirchner, 63; 14 Bussei, 46; 15 Bostrom, 33.

Left: How close do you want it? Corser and Haga changed places over and over again.

Photograph: Gold & Goose

Round 9
ASSEN, Holland
4 September 2005, 3.726-mile/5.997-km circuit

Race 1 16 laps, 59.616 miles/95.952 km

Pl.	Name Nat.(Machine)	No.	Time & gap	Laps
1	Chris Vermeulen, AUS (Honda)	77	33m 36.029s	16
			106.466 mph/171.340 km/h	
2	James Toseland, GB (Ducati)	1	3.396s	16
3	Noriyuki Haga, J (Yamaha)	41	4.876s	16
4	Troy Corser, AUS (Suzuki)	11	6.815s	16
5	Andrew Pitt, AUS (Yamaha)	88	10.075s	16
6	Yukio Kagayama, J (Suzuki)	71	12.526s	16
7	Lorenzo Lanzi, I (Ducati)	57	12.661s	16
8	Max Neukirchner, D (Honda)	76	20.595s	16
9	Karl Muggeridge, AUS (Honda)	31	20.872s	16
10	Pierfrancesco Chili, I (Honda)	7	27.691s	16
11	Ivan Clementi, I (Ducati)	8	36.444s	16
12	Sebastien Gimbert, F (Yamaha)	32	36.844s	16
13	Garry McCoy, AUS (Petronas)	24	37.012s	16
14	Steve Martin, AUS (Petronas)	99	39.262s	16
15	Giovanni Bussei, I (Kawasaki)	200	39.339s	16
16	Gianluca Vizziello, I (Yamaha)	45	40.702s	16
17	José Luis Cardoso, E (Yamaha)	30	48.399s	16
18	Ben Bostrom, USA (Honda)	155	49.359s	16
19	Mauro Sanchini, I (Kawasaki)	6	56.678s	16
20	Jurgen vd Goorbergh, NL (Suzuki)	33	1m 03.440s	16
21	Miguel Praia, P (Yamaha)	17	1m 27.412s	16
22	Robert Menzen, NL (Suzuki)	85	1m 35.286s	16
23	Paul Mooijman, NL (Yamaha)	83	1m 41.900s	16

DNF: Norick Abe, J (Yamaha) 3, 13 laps; Alessio Velini, I (Ducati) 25, 11 laps; Bob Withag, NL (Yamaha) 82, 11 laps; Michel Nickmans, B (Yamaha) 21, 9 laps; Marco Borciani, I (Ducati) 20, 8 laps; Jiri Mrkyvka, CZ (Ducati) 23, 5 laps; Lucio Pedercini, I (Ducati) 19, 4 laps; Lorenzo Alfonsi, I (Yamaha) 12, 2 laps; Chris Walker, GB (Kawasaki) 9, 0 laps.

Fastest lap: Vermeulen, 2m 04.685s, 107.590 mph/173.150 km/h (record).

Race 2 16 laps, 59.616 miles/95.952 km

Pl.	Name Nat.(Machine)	No.	Time & gap	Laps
1	Chris Vermeulen, AUS (Honda)	77	33m 34.053s	16
			106.570 mph/171.508 km/h	
2	Noriyuki Haga, J (Yamaha)	41	0.085s	16
3	James Toseland, GB (Ducati)	1	3.318s	16
4	Troy Corser, AUS (Suzuki)	11	5.938s	16
5	Andrew Pitt, AUS (Yamaha)	88	6.394s	16
6	Lorenzo Lanzi, I (Ducati)	57	16.480s	16
7	Max Neukirchner, D (Honda)	76	17.255s	16
8	Karl Muggeridge, AUS (Honda)	31	22.338s	16
9	Norick Abe, J (Yamaha)	3	30.801s	16
10	Ben Bostrom, USA (Honda)	155	34.071s	16
11	Yukio Kagayama, J (Suzuki)	71	36.480s	16
12	Garry McCoy, AUS (Petronas)	24	36.658s	16
13	Sebastien Gimbert, F (Yamaha)	32	37.165s	16
14	Pierfrancesco Chili, I (Honda)	7	37.888s	16
15	Giovanni Bussei, I (Kawasaki)	200	38.414s	16
16	Steve Martin, AUS (Petronas)	99	40.110s	16
17	Jurgen vd Goorbergh, NL (Suzuki)	33	42.910s	16
18	Alessio Velini, I (Ducati)	25	1m 16.543s	16
19	Miguel Praia, P (Yamaha)	17	1m 16.863s	16
20	Michel Nickmans, B (Yamaha)	21	1m 36.225s	16
21	Robert Menzen, NL (Suzuki)	85	1m 41.029s	16
22	Paul Mooijman, NL (Yamaha)	83	2m 04.053s	16

DNF: Ivan Clementi, I (Ducati) 8, 11 laps; Jiri Mrkyvka, CZ (Ducati) 23, 10 laps; Gianluca Vizziello, I (Yamaha) 45, 8 laps; Mauro Sanchini, I (Kawasaki) 6, 6 laps; Lorenzo Alfonsi, I (Yamaha) 12, 6 laps; José Luis Cardoso, E (Yamaha) 30, 6 laps; Lucio Pedercini, I (Ducati) 19, 6 laps.

Fastest lap: Haga, 2m 04.799s, 107.492 mph/172.992 km/h.

Superpole: Vermeulen, 2m 04.179s, 108.028 mph/173.855 km/h.

Lap record: Colin Edwards, USA (Honda), 2m 02.395s, 110.152 mph/177.272 km/h (2002).

Championship points: 1 Corser, 370; 2 Vermeulen, 284; 3 Laconi, 214; 4 Haga, 203; 5 Toseland, 197; 6 Kagayama, 187; 7 Walker, 130; 8 Chili, 119; 9 Pitt, 117; 10 Muggeridge, 100; 11 Abe, 95; 12 Lanzi, 85; 13 Neukirchner, 80; 14 Bussei, 48; 15 Bostrom, 39.

Right: Toseland and Haga dispute second while chasing Vermeulen in race one.

Below centre left: Van den Goorbergh tumbles in practice, setting the scene for a dismal wild-card weekend.

Bottom left: Laconi and his crew in conference before his crash.

Above left: Vermeulen was simply unstoppable, twice.

Photographs: Gold & Goose

ASSEN

Another weekend of high speed high jinks proved that the remodelled Assen was still a track on which only the best artists can put in for the annual turners' prize, the many high speed changes of direction and cambered corners revealing any rider's true talent.

What was not in short supply from any of this year's would-be winners was aggression. In the opening 16-lap dance with the laws of physics around the Circuit van Drenthe's special Möbius loop, a meeting of minds between Haga, Corser and Vermeulen was resolved first by a chase of Vermeulen by a re-vitalised Toseland and now effervescent Haga; and then a comfortable double win for the Aussie rider in the second, from Haga and Toseland.

The action in race one was for second; a loftily paced and enthralling game of close contact elbow wrestling and brinksmanship. Toseland was to prove the most adept, winning the final count by 1.5 seconds.

Corser was the early force, but as he dropped back it seemed like we were in for a bit of 2005 history. It was chronicled in two unwelcome doses of new reality for the runaway championship leader, who was to finish one place from a podium on two occasions, his first and second no podium finishes of the year.

In the second race, also held in warm and dry conditions (very un-Assen like weather was a welcome feature over race weekend) the opening laps were a three-way war between eventual winner Vermeulen plus Haga and Toseland, all taking turns to lead, on multiple occasions.

Ducatis have always gone well at Assen – it's a place where any good bike can shine – but the factory team was reduced to one, as Laconi crashed in qualifying and injured his right elbow tendons. He gruesomely ground one of them into the tarmac as his highsiding bike landed on his arm at speed and quickly erased the protection of his leathers. Minus skin, flesh and tendon control he was unable to push against the bars at all, and for the second time in 2005 Laconi had to sit out races after a practice crash.

In Ten Kate's home country, Vermeulen had taken Superpole. Given his 2004 winning prowess and continual ability to qualify well, it was a peculiarity that it was his first ever Superpole win in two years of trying. Just to over-egg the Ten Kate pudding Vermeulen also took the new Superbike lap record at the new track layout, with a 2'04.685. It will live forever, as this is the last year for the North Loop section.

Rookie Pitt showed the green shoots of continued recovery, with two fifth places; only ten and six seconds down on the winners of each race.

As one Honda rider rose to ascendancy a Ducati rider born in the same year was marking himself out for special notice again. Lanzi impressed again with a seventh and sixth, on a customer Duke. He was the obvious replacement for Laconi at the next round, and would duly become a Xerox man for a time.

A wild-card ride for Jurgen van den Goorbergh, on one of the Crescent BSB team's spare bikes, went from bad to worse. A 20-something shocker in qualifying and two non-scoring rides to 20th and 17th at his home circuit were as nothing compared to his collision with Walker in the early part of race one. He slammed into Walker, hitting his right elbow. The Englishman suffered a double break, and was out for not just Assen, but Lausitz as well.

LAUSITZRING

Until Lausitz, the championship had been a foregone conclusion for Corser. Some 110 points ahead at one stage, his first non-podium finishes only came at Assen. But at Lausitz he was to have even worse luck, in race two at least.

As one megastar prepared to meet his first real nemesis of the year, another budding head boy was suddenly out of short trousers and lifted off the coat hooks of Ducati's middle school. As expected, Lorenzo Lanzi was given Laconi's bikes. This left his SC Caracchi team bereft, for they had also sacked Spanish disappointment Fonsi Nieto.

In the four hours of practice and qualifying, Lanzi was an instant hit, finishing no lower than fourth in any single session. He went on to win Superpole in spectacular fashion, teeing himself up for a perfect start to his factory career, and a more than lukewarm favourite for many at the start of race one.

Then he had a moment of nervous insanity and ran off down the slip road at turn one, onto the banked Indy car section. He ploughed back into the midfield maelstrom and finished eighth.

That man Vermeulen, desperate to put pressure on Corser, won the race, with Haga behind and Corser third. It lasted only 20 laps, with Vermeulen and Co calling a halt when the first threatening spots of rain hit their visors. This relieved Vermeulen of a fight to the bitter end with Haga, only 0.269 seconds adrift at the red flag, but he knew that gaining nine points on Corser

every race would not be enough. It was his third win in a row.

Corser's thirst to regain glory led him to push too hard in the lead of the second lap of race two. He lost the front on turn one; all his fault, he said. He remounted to finish 13th, for three points.

Ironically, the weekend's eventual accidental hero rescued Corser from losing even more points to Vermeulen. Lanzi's race two was simply outstanding, and even Vermeulen could not live with him on the final frantic lap. After his botched first race, Lanzi looked like a seasoned race winner from lap one to lap 24.

Haga was third in the second outing, his Nipponese battle with Kagayama a taste of things to come later in the year. But the headlines were all Lanzi's, the first true winning product of SBK's Superstock-Supersport-Superbike ladder. A super-sub indeed.

Toseland took fourth in race one, fighting for his career in the class. But 11th in race two was not in the script, as relations between rider and team cooled still more.

Kagayama's return continued apace, as he took a fifth and then a fourth. Pitt, still looking for a podium finish, scored two sixes in a year that was becoming something of a summer-long draw in his own personal Ashes series. Chatter stopped his progress. A fading tyre prevented Muggeridge from capitalizing on a good start and aggressive first few laps, with fifth in race two.

At home in Germany, a slowly rebuilding Max Neukirchner had a reasonable weekend, finishing with two sevenths, a number he got stuck on frequently in 2005.

Top left: Vermeulen heads Haga – there were still this close when the race was stopped.

Top right: Race two winner Lorenzo Lanzi made a blazing works-team debut.

Above left: Max Neukirchner gets set for two sevenths.

Above right: Corser crashes! He remounted after his first mistake of the year.

Right: Ducati crew celebrate Lanzi's fine maiden win.

Photographs: Gold & Goose

Round 10
LAUSITZ, GERMANY
11 September 2005, 2.650-mile/4.265-km circuit

Race 1 20 laps, 53.000 miles/85.300 km

Pl.	Name Nat.(Machine)	No.	Time & gap	Laps
1	Chris Vermeulen, AUS (Honda)	77	33m 36.341s	20
			94.632 mph/152.296 km/h	
2	Noriyuki Haga, J (Yamaha)	41	0.269s	20
3	Troy Corser, AUS (Suzuki)	11	2.299s	20
4	James Toseland, GB (Ducati)	1	7.058s	20
5	Yukio Kagayama, J (Suzuki)	71	12.708s	20
6	Andrew Pitt, AUS (Yamaha)	88	14.053s	20
7	Max Neukirchner, D (Honda)	76	16.616s	20
8	Lorenzo Lanzi, I (Ducati)	57	19.023s	20
9	Norick Abe, J (Yamaha)	3	24.651s	20
10	Ben Bostrom, USA (Honda)	155	34.354s	20
11	Garry McCoy, AUS (Petronas)	24	44.385s	20
12	Giovanni Bussei, I (Kawasaki)	200	45.020s	20
13	José Luis Cardoso, E (Yamaha)	30	51.811s	20
14	Norino Brignola, I (Ducati)	75	51.943s	20
15	Stefano Cruciani, I (Kawasaki)	68	1m 04.111s	20
16	Miguel Praia, P (Yamaha)	17	1m 18.520s	20
17	Michel Nickmans, B (Yamaha)	21	1m 37.408s	20
18	Steve Martin, AUS (Petronas)	99	2 laps	18

DNF: Michael Schulten, D (Honda) 15, 19 laps; Gianluca Vizziello, I (Yamaha) 45, 15 laps; Sebastien Gimbert, F (Yamaha) 32, 13 laps; Pierfrancesco Chili, I (Honda) 7, 7 laps; Alessio Velini, I (Ducati) 25, 5 laps; Ivan Clementi, I (Ducati) 8, 4 laps; ; Lucio Pedercini, I (Ducati) 19, 3 laps; Karl Muggeridge, AUS (Honda) 31, 2 laps; Jiri Mrkyvka, CZ (Ducati) 23, 0 laps; Ralf Waldmann, D (Honda), 14, 0 laps.
NC: Marco Borciani, I (Ducati) 20, 12 laps.
Fastest lap: Haga, 1m 39.828s, 95.570 mph/153.805km/h.

Race 2 24 laps, 63.600 miles /102.360 km

Pl.	Name Nat.(Machine)	No.	Time & gap	Laps
1	Lorenzo Lanzi, I (Ducati)	57	40m 20.947s	24
			94.580 mph/152.212 km/h	
2	Chris Vermeulen, AUS (Honda)	77	0.840s	24
3	Noriyuki Haga, J (Yamaha)	41	4.598s	24
4	Yukio Kagayama, J (Suzuki)	71	5.291s	24
5	Karl Muggeridge, AUS (Honda)	31	16.236s	24
6	Andrew Pitt, AUS (Yamaha)	88	18.362s	24
7	Max Neukirchner, D (Honda)	76	26.360s	24
8	Norick Abe, J (Yamaha)	3	26.453s	24
9	Steve Martin, AUS (Petronas)	99	27.076s	24
10	Pierfrancesco Chili, I (Honda)	7	37.303s	24
11	James Toseland, GB (Ducati)	1	40.997s	24
12	Giovanni Bussei, I (Kawasaki)	200	44.309s	24
13	Troy Corser, AUS (Suzuki)	11	44.485s	24
14	Sebastien Gimbert, F (Yamaha)	32	48.459s	24
15	Ben Bostrom, USA (Honda)	155	53.264s	24
16	Norino Brignola, I (Ducati)	75	1m 04.546s	24
17	Alessio Velini, I (Ducati)	25	1m 24.524s	24
18	Miguel Praia, P (Yamaha)	17	1m 24.896s	24

DNF: Garry McCoy, AUS (Petronas) 24, 23 laps; Michel Nickmans, B (Yamaha) 21, 21 laps; Marco Borciani, I (Ducati) 20, 16 laps; José Luis Cardoso, E (Yamaha) 30, 10 laps; Ivan Clementi, I (Ducati) 8, 10 laps; Jiri Mrkyvka, CZ (Ducati) 23, 6 laps; Lucio Pedercini, I (Ducati) 19, 6 laps; Stefano Cruciani, I (Kawasaki) 68, 5 laps; Gianluca Vizziello, I (Yamaha) 45, 3 laps; Michael Schulten, D (Honda) 15, 2 laps.
Fastest lap: Haga, 1m 39.790s, 95.606 mph/153.863 km/h.

Superpole: Lanzi, 1m 39.019s, 96.350 mph/155.061 km/h.
Lap record: Ruben Xaus, E (Ducati), 1m 39.679s, 95.712 mph/154.034 km/h (2002).

Championship points: 1 Corser, 389; 2 Vermeulen, 329; 3 Haga, 239; 4 Toseland, 215; 5 Laconi, 214; 6 Kagayama, 211; 7 Pitt, 137; 8 Walker, 130; 9 Chili, 125; 10 Lanzi, 118; 11 Muggeridge, 111; 12 Abe, 110; 13 Neukirchner, 98; 14 Bussei, 56; 15 Bostrom, 46.

Round 11
IMOLA, Italy
2 October 2005, 3.065-mile/4.933-km circuit

Race 1 21 laps, 64.365 miles/103.593 km

Pl.	Name Nat.(Machine)	No.	Time & gap	Laps
1	Chris Vermeulen, AUS (Honda)	77	39m 35.789s 97.539 mph/156.973 km/h	21
2	Troy Corser, AUS (Suzuki)	11	0.297s	21
3	Noriyuki Haga, J (Yamaha)	41	8.313s	21
4	James Toseland, GB (Ducati)	1	15.339s	21
5	Steve Martin, AUS (Petronas)	99	49.638s	21
6	Chris Walker, GB (Kawasaki)	9	50.072s	21
7	Max Neukirchner, D (Honda)	76	52.175s	21
8	Sebastien Gimbert, F (Yamaha)	32	52.381s	21
9	Regis Laconi, F (Ducati)	55	57.834s	21
10	Gianluca Vizziello, I (Yamaha)	45	1m 05.727s	21
11	Giovanni Bussei, I (Kawasaki)	200	1m 08.332s	21
12	Mauro Sanchini, I (Kawasaki)	6	1m 10.289s	21
13	Ben Bostrom, USA (Honda)	155	1m 10.786s	21
14	Marco Borciani, I (Ducati)	20	1m 27.905s	21
15	Yukio Kagayama, J (Suzuki)	71	1m 33.440s	21
16	Andrew Pitt, AUS (Yamaha)	88	1m 37.849s	21
17	Maurizio Prattichizzo, I (Kawasaki)	36	1 lap	20

DNF: Fonsi Nieto, E (Kawasaki) 10, 18 laps; Luca Pini, I (Honda) 35, 10 laps; Jiri Mrkvyka, CZ (Ducati) 23, 9 laps; Michel Nickmans, B (Yamaha) 21, 9 laps; Andrea Mazzali, I (MV Agusta) 26, 6 laps; Norick Abe, J (Yamaha) 3, 5 laps; Lorenzo Lanzi, I (Ducati) 57, 5 laps; Giuseppe Zannini, I (Ducati) 73, 4 laps; Ivan Clementi, I (Ducati) 8, 3 laps; Lucio Pedercini, I (Ducati) 19, 3 laps; Alessio Velini, I (Ducati) 25, 2 laps; ; Karl Muggeridge, AUS (Honda) 31, 2 laps; Alex Gramigni, I (Yamaha) 39, 2 laps; Pierfrancesco Chili, I (Honda) 7, 2 laps; Ivan Silva, E (Yamaha) 21, 1 lap; Mauro Lucchiari, I (Yamaha) 37, 1 lap.

Fastest lap: Corser, 1m 50.632s, 99.743 mph/160.521 km/h.

Superpole: Vermeulen, 1m 48.075s, 102.103 mph/164.319 km/h.

Lap Record: Troy Bayliss, AUS (Ducati), 1m 48.389s, 101.807 mph/163.843 km/h (2002).

Championship points: 1 Corser, 409; 2 Vermeulen 354; 3 Haga, 255; 4 Toseland, 228; 5 Laconi, 221; 6 Kagayama, 212; 7 Walker, 140; 8 Pitt, 137; 9 Chili, 125; 10 Lanzi, 118; 11 Muggeridge, 111; 12 Abe, 110; 13 Neukirchner, 107; 14 Bussei, 61; 15 Bostrom, 49.

Race 2 Cancelled due to torrential rain and flooded track.

This page, clockwise from top: Corser celebrates his title win; determined Vermeulen holds off Corser for victory; Haga awaits a decision on race two.

Opposite page, top right: A vicious tangle of bikes and bodies: Bussei in mid-air, Steve Martin in the midst of it, Pitt (right) about to go flying and Muggeridge (31) also involved.

Opposite page: bottom left: Tyres for the melting pot – used rubber at Magny Cours.

Opposite page, bottom right: Behind every good rider, there is a good woman.

Photographs: Gold & Goose

IMOLA

As Johnny Rotten so famously said, as he signed off the Sex Pistols' (almost) last ever gig, in San Francisco: "Ever get the feeling you've been cheated?" So thought the impressively large crowd – drenched, long-suffering and intoxicated by vitriol – after being presented with only one Superbike race at the wonderful, if ultimately flawed, Imola circuit.

The crowds had come to see Lanzi (now back in SC Caracchi colours, but with factory engines and personnel at his disposal) win for Ducati on its local circuit. Even the rains on race morning did not quell their desmo-worshipping enthusiasm. He had their hopes high after qualifying well and taking fifth in Superpole, but they had not come just to see him crash in race one.

Epic rains between race one and the race-that-never-was simply overwhelmed the whoops and dips of the scarred old Imola track. Trackside drains were functioning, but could simply not shift enough water to stop deep pools appearing at several places; elsewhere rivulets an inch deep ran across the track.

The top riders dictated the stoppage from the start line. After a long wait, a delegation of Corser, Vermeulen and Laconi was sent out in the pace car for one last look, as everyone prayed for a let up before it was too late. Race Direction were left to make the final decision, and race two was duly cancelled. The locals made their feelings plain.

In reality, the jeering masses had to blame global warming or some-such. Cancellation was the only prudent course of action, however unpalatable.

On a grander scale, it meant that Troy Gordon Corser took his second World Superbike crown there and then, after Vermeulen was robbed of the chance of taking a second win of the day, and maybe sweeping the title fight all the way to the final round at Magny-Cours.

Vermeulen had taken a new best Imola lap in practice, with a 1'48.075; he and Corser played out a classic race one. The Honda rider made a risky choice of an intermediate front on tarmac drying from pre-race rain. It shouldn't really have been up to the job of keeping him in front of a determined Corser, but even after Troy's mid-race leading stint, it was. Even Pirelli

were surprised.

A margin of victory of 0.297 told the first part of the podium story, an 8.313 gap back to the chasing Haga an equally lucid tale of the chasms in relative performance.

A remarkable top six was somewhat determined by the wet start and dry finish, but with Toseland fourth, Martin fifth and the still-injured Walker a heroic sixth, we had Honda, Suzuki, Yamaha, Ducati, Petronas and Kawasaki machines in a running flush of all participating makes. You could see the grins on the FGSport bosses' faces from behind the darkened glass of their offices. Their monotyre and technical regulation hard line from 2003 was once again perfectly vindicated.

The smiles lasted only as long as the unequal battle of man against a vengeful mama nature allowed, and in losing race two altogether, no-one left Imola feeling much like a winner – even if Corser was finally, and deservedly, crowned champ.

Proof that nothing is ever predictable in SBK comes in the shape of Sebastien Gimbert (Yamaha Motor France) who went from the bottom of the scoreboard to a powerful eighth. The previously ascendant Kagayama fell and remounted, scoring only a single point for 15th. Laconi, hurting, physically weak but mentally determined to rescue his top five finish, was ninth, with rookie Gianluca Vizziello a season-best tenth. There were 17 finishers, and a monstrous 16 who failed to make all 21 laps.

Round 12
MAGNY COURS, France
9 October 2005, 2.741-mile/4.411-km circuit

Race 1 23 laps, 63.043 miles/101.453 km

Pl.	Name Nat.(Machine)	No.	Time & gap	Laps
1	Chris Vermeulen, AUS (Honda)	77	39m 03.405s	23
			96.844 mph/155.855 km/h	
2	Yukio Kagayama, J (Suzuki)	71	8.200s	23
3	James Toseland, GB (Ducati)	1	13.336s	23
4	Karl Muggeridge, AUS (Honda)	31	13.887s	23
5	Troy Corser, AUS (Suzuki)	11	14.299s	23
6	Andrew Pitt, AUS (Yamaha)	88	15.270s	23
7	Chris Walker, GB (Kawasaki)	9	16.136s	23
8	Max Neukirchner, D (Honda)	76	16.616s	23
9	Lorenzo Lanzi, I (Ducati)	57	18.201s	23
10	Norick Abe, J (Yamaha)	3	31.000s	23
11	David Checa, E (Yamaha)	94	34.310s	23
12	Ben Bostrom, USA (Honda)	155	34.493s	23
13	Giovanni Bussei, I (Kawasaki)	200	38.601s	23
14	Fonsi Nieto, E (Kawasaki)	10	38.914s	23
15	Sebastien Gimbert, F (Yamaha)	32	40.508s	23
16	Mauro Sanchini, I (Kawasaki)	6	50.824s	23
17	Ivan Clementi, I (Ducati)	8	56.953s	23
18	Vincent Philippe, F (Suzuki)	62	58.385s	23
19	Michel Nickmans, B (Yamaha)	21	1 lap	22

DNF: Andy Notman, GB (Petronas) 38, 13 laps; Pierfrancesco Chili, I (Honda) 7, 10 laps; Steve Martin, AUS (Petronas) 99, 10 laps; Julien Da Costa, F (Yamaha) 40, 10 laps; Laurent Brian, F (Kawasaki) 60, 9 laps; Alessio Velini, I (Ducati) 25, 8 laps; Noriyuki Haga, J (Yamaha) 41, 2 laps; Giuseppe Zannini, I (Ducati) 73, 1 lap; Gianluca Vizziello, I (Yamaha) 45, 1 lap.

DNS: Regis Laconi, F (Ducati) 55.

Fastest lap: Vermeulen, 1m 40.985s, 97.709 mph/157.247 km/h (record).

Race 2 23 laps, 63.043 miles/101.453 km

Pl.	Name Nat.(Machine)	No.	Time & gap	Laps
1	Lorenzo Lanzi, I (Ducati)	57	39m 01.858s	23
			96.908 mph/155.958 km/h	
2	Yukio Kagayama, J (Suzuki)	71	6.662s	23
3	Noriyuki Haga, J (Yamaha)	41	10.722s	23
4	Troy Corser, AUS (Suzuki)	11	13.457s	23
5	Chris Walker, GB (Kawasaki)	7	16.651s	23
6	James Toseland, GB (Ducati)	1	17.005s	23
7	Andrew Pitt, AUS (Yamaha)	88	20.863s	23
8	Max Neukirchner, D (Honda)	76	22.280s	23
9	Norick Abe, J (Yamaha)	3	22.713s	23
10	Pierfrancesco Chili, I (Honda)	7	31.108s	23
11	Ben Bostrom, USA (Honda)	155	32.271s	23
12	David Checa, E (Yamaha)	94	38.195s	23
13	Fonsi Nieto, E (Kawasaki)	10	45.314s	23
14	Julien Da Costa, F (Yamaha)	40	46.922s	23
15	Gianluca Vizziello, I (Yamaha)	45	50.604s	23
16	Vincent Philippe, F (Suzuki)	62	50.803s	23
17	Mauro Sanchini, I (Kawasaki)	6	51.434s	23
18	Alessio Velini, I (Ducati)	25	1m 23.608s	23
19	Michel Nickmans, B (Yamaha)	21	1 lap	22
20	Laurent Brian, F (Kawasaki)	60	1 lap	22
21	Giuseppe Zannini, I (Ducati)	73	1 lap	22

DNF: Chris Vermeulen, AUS (Honda) 77, 18 laps; Sebastien Gimbert, F (Yamaha) 32, 12 laps; Ivan Clementi, I (Ducati) 8, 6 laps; Marco Borciani, I (Ducati) 20, 4 laps; Andy Notman, GB (Petronas) 38, 4 laps;

DNS: Steve Martin, AUS (Petronas) 99; Karl Muggeridge, AUS (Honda) 31; Giovanni Bussei, I (Kawasaki) 200.

Fastest lap: Lanzi, 1m 40.601s, 98.082 mph/157.847 km/h (record).

Superpole: Vermeulen, 1m 39.836s, 98.833 mph/159.057 km/h.

Previous record: Neil Hodgson, GB (Ducati), 1m 41.219s, 97.483 mph/156.884 km/h (2003).

Championship points: 1 Corser, 433; **2 Vermeulen,** 379; **3 Haga,** 271; **4 Toseland,** 254; **5 Kagayama,** 252; **6 Laconi,** 221; **7 Walker,** 160; **8 Pitt,** 156; **9 Lanzi,** 150; **10 Chili,** 131; **11 Muggeridge,** 124; **12 Neukirchner,** 123; **13 Abe,** 123; **14 Bussei,** 64; **15 Bostrom,** 58.

MAGNY-COURS

Even if Thursday was wet at times and Friday morning misty, the remarkably sunny weather which bathed Magny-Cours's magnificent facilities and so-so track layout for most of the weekend was a welcome splash of invigorating tonic to counter Imola's drowned sorrows. Even though the championship was now decided (it was at around mid-season, if we're honest), everyone bar Corser and Vermeulen had a position to fight for. And as the racing showed, even the top two had something to prove after Imola's unsatisfactory outcome.

As is often the case, the difference in track temperature between noon and the planned 15.30 start of race two played a part for many riders.

Having scored a double only once this year, Vermeulen was well placed to sign off the season in style, after scorching to an absolute track record in Superpole . His win in race one was a superb display of flag-to-flag racing, beating Hodgson's old Michelin race lap record just for fun. Yo-yo Yukio Kagayama was second, eight seconds down, Toseland third and Muggeridge a close fourth. But where was our new World Champion?

It was a short long story. On the pace pre-Superpole, someone on his team had messed up the tyre pressures, and his rear was 50 percent over-inflated. His Superpole time put him last from the 16 hopefuls. But it was impressive to watch the new champ slither smokily around Magny-Cours, shaking his head while exiting corners sideways, his rear Pirelli unable to do for him what it had done for four of his peers in the contest – break the old track best time. He overcame his fourth row starts in both legs with fifth in race one, and an even more impressive fourth in race two.

Pitt, Walker, Neukirchner and Lanzi finished off the top nine in the opener, with Abe taking a top ten finish in race one in his

team's native land.

A truly terrible weekend for the Foggy Petronas team, which had lost Garry McCoy to a coccyx fracture at Imola, continued with stand-in rider Andy Notman, a frequent practice crasher and double non-finisher.

It just got worse in race two, for different reasons.

The start of the second 23-lap race provided a reminder that racing is not ever to be taken lightly, last day of term or not. Muggeridge and Pitt tangled as they got off the start line, and with Muggeridge unseated, he and Pitt careened into the following Bussei and Martin. Wildcard rider, Julien Da Costa was pushed off track, hitting Bussei as he lay motionless. Bussei suffered severe concussion, and neck and shoulder injuries, Martin received a kidney injury (discovered a couple of days later), and Muggeridge had a lucky escape with "only" internal and external scalp stitches inserted to a head injury, after his footpeg dug into and under the rim of his crash helmet.

Pitt lost skin from his hands, but made it back to the start with the mother of all headaches; as did da Costa.

The long delay until the re-start summed up some endlessly messy Sundays of the season, but it was encouraging that two of the younger stars in the series, Vermeulen and Lanzi, battled for the win. Lanzi won unopposed, eventually, as Vermeulen's rear sprocket, new before the race, wore out – possibly due to stone damage, and he was out, leaving Lanzi six seconds clear for his second win of his rookie SBK season.

Just behind, Haga (punted off by team-mate Pitt in race one) had a fabulously entertaining fight with Kagayama, until the Suzuki rider eased away to second, on better-preserved tyres.

Walker and Toseland contested fourth, the Kawasaki rider taking it.

A harsh end to a long but often frantic and staccato season, which had started way back in February.

229

Position	Rider	Nationality	Machine	Losail/1	Losail/2	Phillip Island/1	Phillip Island/2	Valencia/1	Valencia/2	Monza/1	Monza/2	Silverstone/1	Silverstone/2	Misano/1	Misano/2	Brno/1	Brno/2	Brands Hatch/1	Brands Hatch/2	Assen/1	Assen/2	Lausitz/1	Lausitz/2	Imola/1	Imola/2	Magny-Cours/1	Magny-Cours/2	Points total
1	Troy Corser	AUS	Suzuki	25	16	25	25	25	25	25	16	20	20	16	16	25	20	25	20	13	13	16	3	20	-	11	13	433
3	Chris Vermeulen	AUS	Honda	8	13	16	13	20	20	-	25	13	13	20	20	8	16	13	16	25	25	25	20	25	-	25	-	379
3	Noriyuki Haga	J	Yamaha	11	5	-	-	11	13	5	7	-	16	10	10	9	25	20	25	16	20	20	16	16	-	-	16	271
4	James Toseland	GB	Ducati	10	10	2	-	8	-	16	11	16	25	13	13	20	8	-	9	20	16	13	5	13	-	16	10	254
5	Yukio Kagayama	J	Suzuki	20	25	20	20	16	9	20	-	5	9	-	4	5	5	7	7	10	5	11	13	1	-	20	20	252
5	Regis Laconi	F	Ducati	16	20	9	9	-	-	13	20	25	-	25	25	16	9	16	11	-	-	-	-	7	-	-	-	221
7	Chris Walker	GB	Kawasaki	2	-	7	-	13	16	8	8	10	10	8	5	13	6	11	13	-	-	-	-	10	-	9	11	160
8	Andrew Pitt	AUS	Yamaha	13	7	11	-	-	8	11	10	3	7	-	-	6	-	9	10	11	11	10	10	-	-	10	9	156
9	Lorenzo Lanzi	I	Ducati	-	4	-	3	-	-	-	-	5	11	7	10	10	8	8	9	10	8	25	-	-	-	7	25	150
10	Pierfrancesco Chili	I	Honda	-	11	-	-	9	6	9	9	11	11	9	11	11	11	-	3	6	2	-	6	-	-	-	6	131
11	Karl Muggeridge	AUS	Honda	7	-	8	-	-	-	10	13	6	6	6	9	3	7	10	-	7	8	-	11	-	13	-	-	124
12	Max Neukirchner	D	Honda	-	8	13	16	-	4	-	-	9	-	-	-	2	-	6	5	8	9	9	9	9	-	8	8	123
13	Norick Abe	J	Yamaha	6	9	10	8	-	11	6	4	-	8	-	1	7	13	5	-	-	7	7	8	-	-	6	7	123
14	Giovanni Bussei	I	Kawasaki	5	2	6	7	3	-	3	5	8	-	-	6	-	1	-	-	1	1	4	4	5	-	3	-	64
15	Ben Bostrom	USA	Honda	-	-	-	5	4	10	-	-	-	2	2	-	-	-	4	6	-	6	6	1	3	-	4	5	58
16	Sebastien Gimbert	F	Yamaha	-	6	5	-	10	5	-	-	-	-	-	-	-	-	-	2	4	3	-	2	8	-	1	-	46
17	Fonsi Nieto	E	Ducati	3	3	-	11	-	-	-	-	-	7	-	4	4	-	-	-	-	-	-	-	-	-	2	3	37
18	Steve Martin	AUS	Petronas	1	-	-	-	-	-	-	-	-	-	5	8	-	-	1	-	2	-	-	7	11	-	-	-	35
19	Mauro Sanchini	I	Kawasaki	-	1	4	6	-	-	2	3	-	4	3	-	-	-	-	-	-	-	-	-	4	-	-	-	31
20	Ivan Clementi	I	Kawasaki	-	-	3	-	5	3	1	1	-	4	1	-	-	3	-	-	5	-	-	-	-	-	-	-	26
21	David Checa	E	Yamaha	-	-	-	-	6	7	-	-	-	-	-	-	1	2	-	-	-	-	-	-	-	-	5	4	25
22	Garry McCoy	AUS	Petronas	-	-	-	-	-	-	-	-	3	-	-	-	-	-	-	-	3	4	5	-	-	-	-	-	15
23=	José Luis Cardoso	E	Yamaha	-	-	-	-	-	-	7	-	3	-	-	-	-	-	-	-	-	-	3	-	-	-	-	-	13
23=	Gianluca Nanelli	I	Ducati	-	-	-	-	-	-	7	6	-	-	-	-	-	-	-	-	-	-	-	-	-	-	-	-	13
25=	Marco Borciani	I	Yamaha	4	-	-	-	-	-	4	-	-	-	-	-	-	-	-	-	-	-	2	-	-	-	-	-	10
25=	Alessio Corradi	I	Ducati	-	-	-	10	-	-	-	-	-	-	-	-	-	-	-	-	-	-	-	-	-	-	-	-	10
25=	Ivan Silva	E	Yamaha	9	-	-	-	1	-	-	-	-	-	-	-	-	-	-	-	-	-	-	-	-	-	-	-	10
28	Gianluca Vizziello	I	Yamaha	-	-	-	-	-	2	-	-	-	-	-	-	-	-	-	-	-	-	-	-	6	-	-	1	9
29	Sergio Fuertes	E	Suzuki	-	-	-	-	-	7	-	-	-	-	-	-	-	-	-	-	-	-	-	-	-	-	-	-	7
30	Pere Riba	E	Kawasaki	-	-	-	-	-	-	-	-	-	-	-	-	2	-	4	-	-	-	-	-	-	-	-	-	6
31=	Lorenzo Alfonsi	I	Yamaha	-	-	-	-	2	1	-	-	-	-	-	-	2	-	-	-	-	-	-	-	-	-	-	-	5
31=	Andrew Stroud	NZ	Suzuki	-	-	1	4	-	-	-	-	-	-	-	-	-	-	-	-	-	-	-	-	-	-	-	-	5
33	Dennis Hobbs	GB	Yamaha	-	-	-	-	-	-	-	-	-	-	-	-	-	-	-	-	3	1	-	-	-	-	-	-	4
34	Miguel Praia	P	Yamaha	-	-	-	2	-	-	-	1	-	-	-	-	-	-	-	-	-	-	-	-	-	-	-	-	3
35=	Norino Brignola	I	Ducati	-	-	-	-	-	-	-	-	-	-	-	-	-	-	-	-	-	-	-	-	-	2	-	-	2
35=	Luca Conforti	I	Ducati	-	-	-	-	-	-	2	-	-	-	-	-	-	-	-	-	-	-	-	-	-	-	-	-	2
35=	Julien Da Costa	F	Yamaha	-	-	-	-	-	-	-	-	-	-	-	-	-	-	-	-	-	-	-	-	-	-	-	2	2
35=	Alessio Velini	I	Ducati	-	-	-	-	-	-	-	2	-	-	-	-	-	-	-	-	-	-	-	-	-	-	-	-	2
39=	Stefano Cruciani	I	Kawasaki	-	-	-	-	-	-	-	-	-	-	-	-	-	-	-	-	-	-	-	-	1	-	-	-	1
39=	Massimo Roccoli	I	Yamaha	-	-	-	-	-	-	-	1	-	-	-	-	-	-	-	-	-	-	-	-	-	-	-	-	1

SPLIT PERSONALITIES

By GORDON RITCHIE

Top: Champion Charpentier tied the Supersport title up early.

Above: Fujiwara leads Nannelli, Charpentier and Curtain at Monza.

Above right: 1999 champion Chambon was twice on the rostrum.

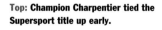

Photographs: Gold & Goose

IF we cover over the last third of the 2005 Supersport championship table, look at the final points score and the distribution of rewards over the first few rounds, it was a Honda walkover. More than that, it was a Ten Kate kicking for the rest, in a season where the strength in depth had soaked away to Superbike, leaving a few grains of golden wheat – and a hell of a load of mouldy old chaff.

In a year that Ten Kate and Honda scored their fourth Championship in a row, their duo won everything all the time. With credible factory Kawasaki, Suzuki and Ducati efforts noticeable on the entry list only by their absence, it was a hollow victory, in a sparse season.

Well, it commenced that way, but after the Clinica Mobile was almost forced to fit revolving doors facing the Ten Kate garage, it didn't end that way. Not when you uncover the final third of the table.

Everyone suspected that trimming down the possible winner's list to two or three (maybe four), was inevitable after some riding talent moved to SBK, and some top teams pushed upwards to boot. Yamaha Motor Italia, most of Alstare Suzuki, the bulk of the Klaffi Honda outfit, and even Ducati's single bike

749 factory crew were the highest profile defectors.

In the Winston Ten Kate Team, armed with new and more race-ready CBR600RRs, Sebastien Charpentier and Katsuaki Fujiwara were the favourites, with Charpentier burning the biggest holes in the time sheets in winter testing. For Yamaha Motor Germany, Kevin Curtain and ex-Ten Kate rider Broc Parkes were experienced R6 runner and utter R6 novice respectively. Honda's "second" entry, from the Team Italia Megabike squad, always looked like being poor relations, despite fielding 2002 champion Fabien Foret and forceful up-and-comer, Michel Fabrizio.

Alstare Suzuki had only Spanish kid Javi Fores on their outdated and outclassed GSX-R600. Ducati had two possible surprises, one being Jurgen van den Goorberg (Ducati Selmat) and the other a rapid hard case, Gianluca Nannelli (SC Caracchi Ducati).

Early season, the Ten Kate Hondas of Sebastien and "Kats" frustrated the rest, as they shared wins like alcoholics share the latest communal bottle. By necessity, but grudgingly all the same.

To everyone's amazement, Kats won the opening race in

Qatar, recovering from a dreadful start to overhaul Charpentier, with Fabrizio a distant third.

Ten Kate's French connection returned the compliment with interest at Phillip Island, as Curtain took second, Foret third and Fujiwara "only" fourth.

In Valencia, back on the Euro-tour, Charpentier punched another win into the time clock, with Kats second and Curtain a brave but performance-limited third, finding the top Ten Kate machines too tough to smash.

Unable to get used to the 749R twin, van den Goorbergh got out of Selmat Ducati's own private Dodge City as soon as he could after Valencia, despite scoring fifth at Phillip Island.

Monza was a return to prominence for Fujiwara, with his team-mate second and – the shape of things to come – Nannelli's Ducati third.

The top rider at Silverstone was Charpentier, on a track at which 1999 Champion Stephane Chambon (GIL Honda CBR600RR) scored the first of two fourth places in his first non-Alstare Suzuki season for aeons. In this year's "European" British round a new name also appeared on the podium. Or rather, an old name, with a glorious history – Foret. The 'other' Frenchman was third, behind the epitome of the Aussie battler, Curtain, and his close-but-no-cigar Yamaha. Unable to get the bike to steer properly, grip at the front properly and stop chattering on the Pirellis, Curtain was nonetheless a minor miracle worker again.

In flaming June on the Adriatic coast, that man Foret scored second at Misano, with Fujiwara third. Oh yeah, Charpentier won.

A lot changed before Brno. Fujiwara had fallen in one of his many tests for the Suzuka 8-Hour, smacking his back and burning his neck – missing the return of the SBK circus to the Czech republic. His place was taken, for one race only, by young Brit Craig Jones. He went sixth, and impressed his temporary team.

Charpentier, almost inevitably, took the win after Curtain crashed. This year's Great One simply catapulted himself clear of the immediate opposition in the fight for the championship itself. Fabrizio, a double no-scorer in Silverstone and Misano, bounced back with second, his countryman Nannelli riding his baby Duke to the second third place of his racing year.

Back in Britain for the second time, Charpentier took his fourth straight win, from Fabrizio and a recovering Curtain, in third. It was to be Charpentier's last race win of 2005, an amazing prophecy at this stage, as he was only ten points from perfect at this point.

Charpentier dropped another five in Assen, but couldn't have cared less. He had won the championship with three races left to run, in his team's home country.

Foret made a Megabike breakthrough win in Holland, stealing a jewel from the new King's crown. A thoroughly good weekend for the Megabike crew put Fabrizio third. Curtain was fourth, and looked like he was maybe going to have to settle for a season-ending third overall, behind a blue-and-white Winston Honda banner of supremacy. Fujiwara had spoiled his day by finishing sixth.

On the team's home track, at Lausitz in Germany, Curtain

and Parkes found a sudden change in fortunes, based on their combined chassis set-up suddenly chiming in, rather than chattering them out of contention.

Curtain, lauded by all the neutrals, won from Parkes, with Foret third. But where had Charpentier gone? Into the kitty litter, while chasing the disappearing Yamahas, while Fujiwara was fourth.

After Charpentier had won overall, the Ten Kate duo came apart at the seams, though Fujiwara could not be blamed for a backmarker moving across his path in his first practice lap at Imola. He broke a finger and hurt his arm in the subsequent crash, at a closing speed of 60 mph, putting him out. Charpentier could not explain why, after taking his tenth pole within seven laps of qualifying – a time unbeaten all weekend – he had then fallen, injuring his shoulder. That ended his 2005 championship participation.

This left the race open. A two-parter, stopped for rain, went to the Nannelli's Ducati, with Curtain second and Alessio Corradi (van den Goorbergh's generally-effective replacement) third. Deep joy for the Ducatisti.

The last race, with Fujiwara but sans Charpentier (a double nightmare for the French race promoters, as Laconi was out of Superbike as well) saw the sixth different race winner of the year, as Parkes took his first class victory ahead of Curtain. Fabrizio was a good third, but Foret's fourth could not quite displace Fujiwara from a final third overall.

A year that started with little expectation of either dramatic merit or variety show brassiness ultimately became a game of pass the grenade. For a series which had taken a knock in status, with Superbikes absorbing a big burst of energy and talent, this was very good news. Unless your name was Katsuaki Fujiwara, or even the unlikeliest of triple no-score merchants, Sebastien Charpentier.

Two other series followed SBK and WSS around Europe. The Superstock 1000 FIM Cup was the old European Superstock re-branded upwardly, and featuring a higher age limit for participation. There was now also European 600 Superstock, for riders from school leaving age to 20.

The 1000cc favourite Kenan Sofuoglu (Yamaha Motor Germany) lost his chance of a title win that seemed certain at one stage, after a couple of falls and a last race/last corner block pass by his team-mate, and new Superstock champion, Didier Van Keymeulen. Despite a horrific last race crash and broken collarbone, when hit by a competitor's crashing bike, EMS Suzuki rider Craig Coxhell took third overall.

In the all-new 600cc division, Claudio Corti (Trasimeno Yamaha) only had to score a single point in the denouement at Magny-Cours to beat Yoann Tibero (Megabike Junior Team Honda). Corti cruised to the finish line to win yet another new class designed to provide a ladder for new talent, for SBK as a whole.

Above: Supersport runner up Kevin Curtain – personification of the Aussie battler.

Left: Former champion Fabien Foret claimed a win at Assen.

Below: Sebastien Charpentier won and won for Ten Kate.

Bottom: Australian Broc Parkes took the final round.
Photographs: Gold & Goose

THE END OF AN ERA

ANYONE expecting 2005 to be another season of "Webster enters, Webster wins" would have been more than slightly astonished. Watching Steve Webster and Paul Woodhead win the first two races would have reinforced those expectations. It was never going to be that straightforward.

The same applied to the plan for a 16-race championship, over eight circuits. Four of those venues– Brands Hatch, Schleiz in Germany, Rijeka and St Petersburg – were to run three full-points championship races over a single weekend. The programme was inventive… a frantic "Match" race of three to five laps; a ten-to-15-lap "Sprint"; and a traditional full length 20-to-30-lap "Gold" race.

Then the Russian round was cancelled mid-August, because track safety modifications had not been carried out. The three lost rounds were replaced with a two-round season-end special at the Sachsenring, and one additional race at Rijeka. These circumstances threw up an unprecedented (and chaotic) four-race, 100-point weekend that sealed the series for the likeable Kent brothers Tim and Tristan Reeves.

A further quirk was the introduction of "success ballast". Race winners would have 10kg attached to their outfit after each win, up to a 30kg maximum. Reeves had amassed this maximum weight penalty at Rijeka, qualified with it, and was about to race with it when safety concerns prompted the FIM to change their minds abruptly, applying an arbitrary time penalty instead.

This hasty decision so enraged Reeves's only challenger, Jorg Steinhausen, that he walked away from the championship, declining to take any further part.

The Reeves brothers ended up comfortable and worthy winners with 334 points, 123 more than Manninen. After all the shenanigans, there was at least no doubt about the fairness of the final outcome. Tim Reeves is one of the few drivers to have emerged in recent years who might have made a good account of himself in the golden era two decades ago, with the Big Four of Biland, Streuer, Michel and Webster.

Once again, we have to accept that as a professional sport, international sidecar racing is still on the precipice, but hope persists. At the time of writing, confident plans for another full championship in 2006 were well under way.

Round 1, Brands Hatch, Great Britain
7 & 8 May 2005

Webster and Woodhead won the opening five-lap Match Race by just over half a second from local hero Reeves after a fierce battle, claiming a new lap record. World Championship returnee Jorg Steinhausen (who raced in Germany in 2004) took third.

The 14-lap Sprint race saw more fireworks, until Webster grabbed the advantage and made it stick by 2.3 seconds. Both machines returned to pit lane battle-scarred, Webster's nose cone stoved in against Reeves's fairing. The riders shook hands, accepting it as part of the battle. Steinhausen was again third.

Webster had shaved a further tenth off his lap record. Who present could have thought it would prove to be the ten-times World Champion's last win?

The 30-lap Gold race remained. Reeves took the early lead, but by half distance, Webster had motored away to a six-second advantage. Then his engine started to misfire. His retirement after 16 laps gifted the race to Reeves, who had to ease his own machine home after the dashboard came loose in the cockpit. "I had to hold it in. If it had come away, that would have cut the ignition," said Reeves.

Round 2, Hungaroring, Hungary
28 & 29 May 2005

In searing heat, Webster took over from Reeves on lap nine of 19. Then, at the start of lap 14, the leader slowed suddenly along the main straight and he retired at the second corner.

Passenger Woodhead tried to climb from the outfit, but immediately collapsed. Prompt attention and an hour on a saline drip restored him, but it underlined the immense physical demands upon the passenger by this unique motor sport.

Was there ever a more understated job title? The passenger's carbon fibre platform is immediately behind the radiator, fielding a staggering amount of heat. Compounded by the tight Kevlar racing suit and exhaust fumes, 13 laps in the sweltering conditions had done for the man universally seen as the fittest passenger in the paddock.

Reeves was able to cruise home with a comfortable 16-second lead over Mike Roscher and Adolf Hanni, who recorded their best ever result. Martin and Tonnie van Gils were third.

Round 3, Nürburgring, Germany
18 & 19 June 2005

The story of the weekend was that defending champion Steve Webster conceded the 2005 title, forced to withdraw after qualifying on pole for the 31st consecutive race. Webster revealed that continuing health problems were affecting his ability to concentrate.

"I just didn't feel totally in control," he said, hoping to be back "firing on all cylinders" in September for Assen, his favourite circuit.

The race was left for Reeves and Steinhausen, and on the final lap, Steinhausen controversially hit his rival at Turn One, sending him spinning. Despite an heroic recovery from Reeves, Steinhausen took the win, with passenger Hopkinson ripping off the damaged sidecar wheel arch as they crossed the line.

Furious, Reeves refused to attend the rostrum ceremony – incurring a 1,000 fine. The FIM Jury, who determined that the coming together was merely a racing incident, then rejected his official protest. He had the consolation of a healthy championship lead, 110 points to Steinhausen's 86.

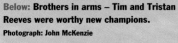

Below: Brothers in arms – Tim and Tristan Reeves were worthy new champions.
Photograph: John McKenzie

Round 4, Schleiz, Germany
9 & 10 July 2005

This was the second three-race meeting, and Reeves missed the three-lap Match Race after an earthing fault silenced his machine minutes before the start. In desperation he borrowed Billy Galross's Sourcecom outfit but was forced off the grid, temper flaring. Steinhausen's win was relatively simple.

In the 11-lap Sprint race, Reeves won a thriller from Steinhausen by a tenth. It was left to the 22-lap Gold race to provide a spectacular and painful finale.

Reeves took the lead early on, but slowed, inviting a reluctant Steinhausen to set the pace. Then with six laps to go, the Team Roberts duo retook the lead, steadily building a safe 6.5-second cushion.

With two laps remaining, Reeves ran low on fuel, and Steinhausen was within two seconds as they began the final lap. Approaching the last right-hander he dived for an imaginary gap. This dropped his wheels off the track, and the Q8-Suzuki outfit slid and then flipped. Steinhausen was airlifted to hospital with neck pains, and passenger Trev Hopkinson sustained a suspected broken wrist and ribs, Reeves had regained 25 points, quite unaware of the melee behind him.

Round 5, Salzburgring, Austria
6 & 7 August 2005

The growing Anglo-German grudge match would continue at the fearsome Salzburgring.

Reeves hit the front on the first lap of the single race, pole qualifier Steinhausen tucked in close behind, and the two outfits jockeyed and swapped positions. Steinhausen had suffered from a blown water hose from the seventh lap; but backmarkers prevented Reeves from taking full advantage.

Onto the final lap, the two outfits were still nose to tail, Reeves hanging on by just 0.7 seconds. For once no paint was exchanged – perhaps in deference to the unforgiving nature of the spectacular Alpine circuit. Laidlaw and Farrance made up the rostrum.

Round 6, Rijeka, Croatia
20 & 21 August 2005

Three-round Rijeka added a fourth after the St Petersburg cancellation, with an extra ten-lap Sprint on Saturday afternoon.

Reeves took his first pole, carrying the full 30kg ballast. He was then surprised as he was putting his helmet on for the first race by the FIM Jury. They had decided that 30kg of ballast was a safety issue. He was to remove 10kg immediately, and accept a ten-second time penalty instead. When he remonstrated, he was told if he did not comply, he was out of the race.

He lined up for the start. Nerves stretched to the limit, his machine crept forward. Steinhausen went with him, and as both dropped their revs the lights went green, and they were swamped, third qualifiers Pekka Paivarinta and Peter Wall leading. Reeves was gaining ground when he was called in for a "drive-through" penalty for jumping the start. He rejoined tenth, and although he fought back to fifth on the track, the time penalty pushed him down to eighth, some 22 seconds down on winner Paivarinta. Steinhausen's had an identical penalty, but recovered to take second.

It was nevertheless a popular and historic win for Paivarinta – Finland's first since 1972.

It was now confirmed that Reeves's time penalty (in lieu of weight) would be apportioned pro-rata across the three races remaining: five seconds for the Match race, ten seconds for the Sprint, and 15 for the Gold.

The Steinhausen team had become increasingly irritated by these ad hoc rule changes, and now believed Reeves had argued down his time penalty. This was the last straw, and he packed up and left at once, his campaign over.

In the three-lap Match race, Reeves crossed the line first, but his time penalty put him last, with Paivarinta first. In the second race, Reeves's challenge was to make up the ten seconds over

Above: Farewell to a legend: ten times World Champion, Steve Webster (with Paul Woodhead) retired after yet one last fastest lap.
Photograph: John McKenzie

ten laps. Once more Reeves crossed the line first, this time some 6.5 seconds clear of Paivarinta. He was classified second.

The complex turn of events now presented Reeves with an early championship chance. He was told just before his sighting lap that a win in the 20-lap race would secure the title. The penalty meant he had to do it by more than 15 seconds.

A fluffed start left him in the pack at the first corner, but by lap two they had disposed of Roscher, Knight, Hanks and Manninen, and were after race leader Paivarinta. By lap six Reeves was clear and racing against the clock to build as big a gap as possible.

"With one lap to go, my pit board said plus 14.1, but it started to rain, and I just thought: 'Don't back off.' Everyone else did," said Reeves, a worthy champion.

Series returnees Tom Hanks and Phil Biggs took second place on the second Team Hanni outfit, with the consistent Manninen third.

Round 7, Assen, Holland
3 & 4 September 2005

Assen's big news was the return of Webster and Woodhead. He had decided it would be his final race, but hopes of finishing a magnificent career on a high note were quashed. Woodhead was thrown out under heavy braking for the first right-hander during Friday's timed session, and sustained heavy bruising to his arms and a possible wrist fracture.

They did manage a couple of fast laps subsequently to qualify an uncharacteristic fourth, but after two laps Webbo was forced to pull into the pits for the final time, when Woody could no longer grip safely.

In his two last laps, Webster set a new lap record. He quit racing as the fastest man on the track. He parked the outfit, grabbed a beer and sat down to watch the race with a smile.

His successors Tim and Tristan Reeves stormed to another victory in the two-part race disrupted by a red-flagged crash. Second, a career best, were Andy Laidlaw and Patrick Farrance, with Hanks and Biggs back on the rostrum with third.

Round 8, Sachsenring, Germany
10 & 11 September 2005

Sachsenring's late replacement race had a large and welcoming crowd, overcoming any end-of-term feeling.

Reeves won the ten-lap Sprint race by over ten seconds from Manninen; and then he won the 22-lap Gold race from the same rival, taking his season tally to nine. Spurred by the appreciative spectators, he also set a new lap record, a fitting season finale for the new champion.

Still notable by his absence was Steinhausen. In fact, he was there, but he only entered the German Championship races run on the same day... and then broke a drive chain.

ISLE OF MAN TT RACES
ALL CHANGE ON THE ISLAND

By MAC McDIARMID

Above: John McGuinness won both Superbike and Senior for Yamaha, and the Joey Dunlop Trophy for himself.
Photograph: Dave Collister/www.photocycles.com

THE year 2005 marked the end of the anachronistic old TT programme in favour of classes more in keeping with what was going on in the rest of the racing world. Out went the Formula One race, a hangover from the FIM's concessions to maintain the TT's World Championship profile almost 30 years before, in favour of a Superbike race. Both the 125 and 250cc classes departed, with the Supersport machines now having two races (an expensive notion, it would transpire), whilst the TT Production classes were replaced by a single race for Super-stock machines. The Senior TT, the week's final and once most prestigious event, would now be open to all three solo classes. Effectively, the TT was now a four-stroke-only event.

PRACTICE

Whilst being welcomed in many quarters, notably the motorcy-cle industry, there was plenty of dissent at the demise of "proper" racing classes. The Manx gods, judging by the weather which greeted the first practice session, took the latter view. The revamped programme got underway in the teeth of a howl-ing Force 8 gale. Although conditions were otherwise perfect, in the interests of safety the session was untimed.

Later in the week, Wednesday's and Thursday's sessions were rained off, Friday's began late due to more uncertain weather, and Saturday's short session was again untimed, this time due to partially wet roads which saw the Superbike race postponed to Sunday. Although the situation never became crit-

ical enough for emergency practice periods to be used, most teams found themselves seriously pressed for adequate track time – in marked contrast to the 2004 TT.

The gale conditions de-tuned all the solo hotshots. "That's the worst I've ever known it", exclaimed Richard Britton, now an official Honda rider on Ten Kate-tuned machines. The Enniskillen man, who would be tragically killed racing at County Kerry's Ballybunnion meeting in mid-September, was third-fastest in the Superbike class with his fastest-ever Mountain Course lap.

"It's hell out there" parodied Britton's team-mate, Ian Lougher. Winner of the NW200 Superstock race, he wore a preoccupied air throughout practice, brightened only by his Fireblade's second place in the Superstock class. Yet the Welshman, by far the most experienced TT campaigner in the paddock, has a Joey Dunlop-like habit of keeping his powder dry.

Meanwhile Bruce Anstey, second-favourite to John McGuin-ness for major honours, was more concerned with the virus which would mar most of TT fortnight. Looking haggard and drained, he failed to make the Superbike leaderboard. His TAS Suzuki team-mate, Adrian Archibald, was second on the Super-bike but a lowly sixth in both other classes.

McGuinness himself was coming off a frustrating season in British Superbikes which hadn't improved at the rain-lashed NW200. Now without his mentor/manager, Jim Moodie, the Morecambe rider knew he'd be lucky to have a fortnight as smooth as he'd enjoyed in 2004. Whilst never quite scaling the record-shattering heights of the previous year, the Yamaha man would set the pace throughout practice on both Superbike and Superstock machines, topping the leaderboard in both. Veteran team-mate Jason Griffiths simply kept his head down in his first outing of the year, placing fifth on both the Superbike and Su-perstock R1s.

Ryan Farquhar, who'd scored his debut TT win in '04, was now riding for Nick Morgan's MSS Discovery Kawasaki squad. Despite a practice week troubled by set-up problems, particu-larly with the big ZX-10, the sometimes volatile Irishman seemed to wear a new mantle of calm confidence. As one of the few Kawasaki campaigners, he spent most of practice week posting the marque's fastest-ever TT laps, culminating at 124.23mph, to emerge an impressive fourth in the Superbike division, and topping the Supersports class on the ZX-6R.

Of the young pretenders, Martin Finnegan's practice week was the most impressive, fourth in the Supersports class. Hav-ing spent much of the week rebuilding the Superstock Honda smashed to pieces during the NW200 meeting, his team were left to rebuild it again when a missing oil-way bolt caused it to trash itself during Friday practice.

If the spoils were shared in the solo classes, one man tow-ered over the field in the sidecar division – even into the teeth of the gale. Dave Molyneux, with fellow Manxman Dan Sayle in the chair of the Dave Hagon-tuned DMR Honda, startled every-one with his fastest-ever standing start lap, 112.44mph – just eight seconds outside the record the pair set last year.

From there the week went downhill as his engine was plagued by generator, fuelling and ignition problems, preventing him completing a single practice lap. But during Friday's final practice session, when in danger of failing to qualify for an event he had won ten times, Moly startled everyone. His lap at 115.916mph was not only the first sub-20-minute sidecar lap, it carved an astonishing 28 seconds off the old record. Even the top solo stars were incredulous at such a time, which would have placed him 14th in the similarly powered 600cc Super-sport solo class, in the same session.

"I knew it was going to be a quick 'un", said the Manxman afterwards, "under 20 minutes, but nothing that quick." Dan Sayle, Moly's passenger, added that the lap was "pretty smooth…no moments. Conditions were good, but I think we can go quicker still." The rest – 35 seconds in arrears – had been warned.

SIDECAR RACE A

With the Superbike race postponed, the chairs opened race week's proceedings. Molyneux made his usual lightning start to lead by 48 seconds after one lap of the weather-delayed race, and we all settled down to await the predictable outcome. Then at Barregarrow, 12 miles into the second lap, his Honda CBR600 engine lost power due to an ignition amplifier fault, handing the lead to fellow Manxmen Nick Crowe and Darren Hope, whose DMR outfit Molyneux himself built.

Crowe's Slick Bass-tuned Honda was overhauled by Castle-ford's Steve Norbury and Andy Smith by the end of lap two, but when their Yamaha-powered outfit began to suffer fuel starva-tion from the 11th Milestone on the final lap, they were power-less to prevent the local duo from eating into their lead to win the 113 mile race by just 2.3 seconds.

"We were never going to be on Moly's pace" admitted a gracious Crowe after his debut TT win. "In fact we've been struggling all week, doing lots of engine swaps." Crowe spoke of "massive slides" due to the tricky part-wet conditions and "nearly tripping over a few times" in the final rush over the Mountain to overhaul Norbury. Nonetheless his race average time, 109.85mph, was slightly up on his pace when finishing second to Molyneux in the same race last year.

The race was marred by the death of Les Harah, from Brough, Yorkshire, after crashing at the exit from Parliament Square. A policeman attending the incident narrowly missed being struck by another sidecar, an occurrence which would cause the police to reconsider their involvement in future meetings.

SUPERBIKE

John McGuinness scored an emphatic win in the first-ever Su-perbike TT, postponed by wet weather to Sunday. His strategy, as in the previous year, was to dominate the opposition from the start on his AIM Racing Yamaha R1.

The Morecambe rider was visibly quickest away as he screamed the R1 off the line. By Glen Helen, 10 miles into lap one, he led by 2.6 seconds from Richard Britton's Honda, and saw the signal "+3" eight miles later at Ballaugh. "Hell," I thought, "someone's on my case. So I just kept pressing."

By the end of lap one, McGuinness led Britton by 8.1 sec-onds with TAS Suzuki's Adrian Archibald a further five seconds adrift. Archibald overhauled Britton on lap three, but the Yamaha man extended his lead to win his seventh TT by over 36 seconds at the end of the 226 mile race. When Britton re-tired on lap four, Eire's Martin Finnegan assumed third place on the Vitrans Honda, holding the position to the flag for his first rostrum finish.

"It's the first time I've won a six lap TT", explained McGuinness. "I got into a real good rhythm after the first lap, where before I'd been really tense, gripping the bike for grim death. Once the lead was around 30 seconds, I rode to my signals. When Adrian closed slightly I had a real good crack over the Mountain and pulled further ahead again. I didn't rev the engine over 12,000 on the last lap – compared to 13,500 when I had to go for it."

"The bike was working well," he continued. "Apart from a huge slide coming out of Tower Bends – feet off the pegs job – I didn't have any big moments. There was a bit of dampness around Ramsey Hairpin, otherwise conditions were good. But the track seems to be dirtier and bumpier than last year, so the record didn't go." His fastest lap, his second, was seven seconds outside his record from last year. But fittingly, the R1's victory came on the 40th anniversary of Yamaha's first TT win, in the year in which the factory celebrated its 50th birthday.

Second-place man Archibald acknowledged that his Suzuki "didn't feel that quick for the first couple of laps, but I really got my head down after the pit stop when I knew I had to shake Richard off. I knew from my signals that John's lead was to-ing and fro-ing only a bit, so I settled for second before the final lap." Behind Finnegan came Lougher, the rapidly emerging Ray Porter and Guy Martin, the newcomer sensation of the 2004 TT.

SUPERSTOCK

The world's most gruelling road test – 113 miles around the TT course – put Suzuki's new GSX-R1000 at the top of the pile, followed by Honda, Kawasaki and Yamaha. Yet it was TAS Suzuki who suffered the greatest disappointment.

In ideal conditions, Adrian Archibald led throughout the three lap race only to run out of fuel at the Bungalow on the final lap. TAS Suzuki team boss Hector Neill instantly ac-cepted the blame, adding that he expected to be lynched by

Above: First sidecar race winners Nick Crowe and Darren Hope.
Photograph: Dave Collister/www.photocycles.com

Below: Supersport winner Ian Lougher flirts with his shadow.
Photograph: Dave Collister/www.photocycles.com

Bottom: Bruce Anstey (Suzuki) inherited victory in the Superstock race, world's toughest road test.
Photograph: Dave Purves

the crestfallen Archibald.

Archibald's misfortune handed victory to team-mate Bruce Anstey – winner of last year's equivalent event, the 1000cc Production TT – ahead of Ian Lougher's Fireblade, Ryan Farquhar's Kawasaki ZX-10 and Jason Griffiths's R1 Yamaha. Farquhar's ride, on a machine many considered too nervous for the TT course, was a particularly fine performance.

Practice leader John McGuinness pulled out after two lurid slides early on lap one. The first, at the same Crosby Corner which had claimed his close friend David Jefferies two years before, completely de-tuned the Superbike winner. "I lost the front", he explained with a quiver "I was just a passenger, foot down at 180mph. It just brought it all back."

Such is the potential of these slightly modified production machines that even on treaded tyres Archibald's fastest lap, 126.641mph, was a mere two seconds slower than McGuinness had recorded in winning the Superbike TT. Just two clicks on the rear suspension was all it took to turn the GSX-R1000 into a winner.

SUPERSPORT JUNIOR RACE A
After a characteristically unspectacular practice week and a disappointing showing in the Superbike race, Ian Lougher overcame a case of Douglas Belly – "a dodgy lasagne" – to put it all together and win the opening Supersport TT for Honda after an explosive duel with Ryan Farquhar's MSS Discovery ZX-6R. After two laps a mere 0.6 seconds separated the pair, but when the Irishman pulled out with an overheating engine, Lougher rode to his signals and controlled the race to the finish, clocking up his

seventh TT win.

"I had the shits, basically, in the morning", explained Lougher about his day's work, "which is why I was off the pace early on in the Superstock race. In fact I almost threw up going into Ramsey, but felt a lot better after that."

Second was McGuinness, unable to summon his customary blistering opening lap after his Superstock dramas. Jason Griffiths brought the second Yamaha R6 into third, ahead of Anstey's Suzuki, with Guy Martin fifth despite a 10 second "stop box" penalty.

The luck of the Irish deserted them. As well as Farquhar's retirement, Richard Britton's clutch went when he was lying in fourth, whilst Martin Finnegan's steering damper blew a seal, covering him in oil. The TAS Suzuki GSX-R600s were off the pace throughout – a far cry from Tom Sykes's British Supersports machine. Top placed Irishman was Ray Porter, winner of the NW200 Supersports race, in sixth.

SUPERSPORT JUNIOR RACE B
It quickly emerged that expecting a 15,000-rpm Supersports engine to manage two 150 mile races in the space of three days is pushing optimism two far. Although in short circuit conditions the 600s are usually good for 1,000km (620miles), Wednesday's failure rate clearly showed that all the 600s are marginal for practice and two races – say 500 miles at racing speeds.

Ryan Farquhar ended his own streak of breakdowns to emerge from the war of attrition and claim the only Irish win of the week. "To be the only Irish winner is very special", he said, putting him in mind of the days he used to listen to his hero Joey Dunlop's exploits on the radio, crackling over the Irish Sea.

Even though many of his top adversaries fell by the wayside, the MSS Discovery rider fully deserved his win, the first by a Kawasaki in one of the major classes since the days of Mick Grant and the two-stroke triples. After one lap he held a four second lead over Ian Lougher, winner of the first Supersports race, with Jason Griffiths a further nine seconds down in third.

"I knew I was going to be pushed hard by John and Ian, so really went for it from Union Mills on the first lap. I got my first signal on the Mountain, "P1 +14". Then, on the second lap, into Ramsey, I saw "Lougher out, +17". By the pit stop this had extended to "+37". Jason closed the gap but I rode to my signals and had it under control."

Practice leader McGuinness retired when his Yamaha R6 ate a valve on lap one, having led narrowly at Glen Helen, ten miles into the first lap. With Farquhar only 0.7 seconds astern, and Lougher a further 1.0 seconds adrift, it looked like becoming an exhilarating race, but the unreliability of highly-stressed street-based 600s pitted against the Mountain Course put paid to that. As well as McGuinness, retirements included Archibald (clutch slip, leaking hose), Anstey (steering damper), Lougher (valve problems) and Britton (thrown con rod). Even the podium men had their dramas. Third-placed Ray Porter ran out of fuel at Signpost but managed to splutter home for his first rostrum finish.

SIDECAR RACE B
After being sidelined by ignition problems in the first Sidecar race, Dave Molyneux and Dan Sayle put the racing world back on its axis with a record-shattering, start-to-finish victory in the second. The race produced the first official sub-20 minute sidecar lap, and the first sub-one-hour overall race time. It was Moly's 11th win, a record for the sidecar class.

The Manx duo smashed the lap record from a standing start with a lap at 114.683mph to give them a 33 second lead over fellow Manxmen Nick Crowe and Darren Hope, winners of the earlier race. The second lap was quicker still, 116.044mph, almost 30 seconds faster than Molyneux's old lap record.

Yet even these speeds almost failed to guarantee victory. At Governor's Bridge on the last lap, just half a mile from the finish, the rear wheel-bearing of the DMR Honda collapsed.

"There was a clunk and the bike started squirming", explained Sayle. "It just felt like the rear tyre had blown off the rim. Moly looked at me. I had a look down and just yelled to keep going."

Despite clunking over the line at barely 30mph, at the finish

Above: Gathering no moss... but Adrian Archibald ran out of fuel to lose certain Superstock victory
Photograph: Dave Collister/www.photocycles.com

Left: Ryan Farquhar's second-race Supersport win made him the only Irish winner of the year.
Photograph: Dave Purves

Far left: Dave Molyneux and Dan Sayle jump for joy during their record-breaking second sidecar win.
Photograph: Dave Collister/www.photocycles.com

Moly described the historic race as "the easiest we've done. It didn't feel all that quick." Yet the DMR's chassis certainly felt the pace. "Stuff's been breaking and cracking that we've never had problems with before", explained Sayle. "Maybe we've found the limit for this sort of technology over the Mountain Course. Maybe the next step will need something very different."

SENIOR

In near-perfect conditions, John McGuinness confirmed his standing as the TT's top exponent with a typically dominant win in the final race of the week. It was his eighth TT victory and his first Senior TT win, also giving him the lucrative Joey Dunlop trophy for the best combined performance in the Superbike and Senior races.

"Pretty straightforward, actually", beamed McGuinness after the race. "I went fast from the off. It took me a while to get Monday's slides out of my system, but I was on it today. The R1 isn't the fastest thing, but it's reliable, a good package. You can work it hard. It's fantastic over the Mountain, and the Dunlops gave so much grip." McGuinness R1 was running a new generation of synthetic belted KR106/108 tyres, similar to those which debuted in MotoGP in 2004 which, like the ubiquitous Pirellis, reduce tyre growth and increase stability.

In a race in which slow pit stops robbed both Richard Britton and Martin Finnegan of potential rostrum positions, McGuinness had "two fantastic pit stops", but by then had already set the fastest lap of the race, a new Senior record at 127.326mph, on his opening lap.

Adrian Archibald, winner of the Dunlop trophy for the past three years, picked up the pace after a typically steady start and was holding McGuinness until he suffered a puncture and stopped at Ramsey on the second lap. A wretched day for TAS Suzuki was compounded when Bruce Anstey, one of the pre-event favourites but out of sorts for much of the week, retired in the pits with a bike that "just didn't feel right".

With Archibald out and Britton slowed in the pits, Ian Lougher slotted into second place after two weeks struggling with the handling of his DMRR Honda Fireblade. "The handling wasn't too bad with a new tyre – laps one, three and five. We took a bit of a gamble dropping the front end before the race, but it was definitely better."

Ryan Farquhar, whose ZX-10 Kawasaki lay third in the early stages, dropped out when his ZX-10 ran a big end on lap two. This left the way open for a nail-biting battle for third between Martin Finnegan and his former mechanic, Guy Martin. The lead oscillated between the two at practically every timing point, until Martin emerged ahead by less than two seconds. Both men recorded career-best TT laps during the final circuit. Finnegan's 127.014mph was the third fastest ever and the quickest by any Irishman, whilst Martin posted 126.481mph in only his second TT. Fifth was Richard Britton, with Japan's Jun Maeda rounding off an impressive week with his first leaderboard finish.

Motorcycle journalist Gus Scott, riding in his first TT, was killed when he collided with a marshal crossing the road at Kirk Michael. The marshal was also killed. It was another tragedy that will do little for the race's reputation.

MUCH MORE MLADIN

By PAUL CARRUTHERS

YOU could almost hear the collective groan in the AMA paddock when it was announced in July, at the Mid-Ohio Sports Car Course, that Mat Mladin had signed a new three-year contract with Suzuki to contest the AMA Superbike Championship. After all, based on Mladin's dominance of late, it means the others don't have much of a chance until 2009.

With a record six championships already on his résumé, few would argue the likelihood of that becoming nine by the time the Australian hangs up his boots and concentrates full time on being a parent and businessman. If you're a rival with hopes of winning an AMA Superbike title, Mladin's name on the bottom of another Suzuki contract spells nothing but doom.

Unless you're a bright young racer like Roger Lee Hayden. The youngest of the Hayden brothers signed a contract at the end of the 2005 season that will see him in the Superbike class for the first time in 2006, riding a ZX-10R against Mladin and the rest of the Superbike men. Hayden, you see, views it differently. With Mladin in the series, Roger Lee realizes there's a permanent benchmark against which to compare your racing skills. And, more importantly, a rival who is known around the world for just how good he is. In other words, beat Mladin and you may end up going somewhere. World Superbike racing... MotoGP, perhaps. Hey, it worked for big brother Nicky – the last to take an AMA title from Mladin.

But enough of the future.

In 2005, Mladin again made the AMA Superbike Championship his own. He controlled virtually every race from beginning to end. Only a mechanical glitch and a crash, which was no fault of his own, stopped him from running away and hiding in the series. In the end, he had to take it to the finale to earn his sixth title, but there was never any doubting the inevitable. Everyone was racing for second place, and you got the feeling they knew it.

It wasn't so much that Mladin got stronger (really, how much better can he possibly get), but that his competition got weaker. On paper, this series looked set to be a doozy. But the paper and the racetrack are two different entities.

The year started as always at Daytona, though this one was different from past Daytonas. For starters, the track was modified in an effort to make it safer. Which it was, though to what extent? Truly different was the fact that the Superbikes were no longer in the headline Daytona 200. Coerced somewhat by the Speedway and the notion that 1000cc Superbikes were just too fast for the racetrack, the AMA opted to run Formula Xtreme bikes (highly modified 600s) in the 200. Just like that, the Superbike race became a support class.

Still, it was the season starter and everyone was there with the fresh hopes that a new season brings.

Mladin had an even better GSX-R1000 to work with, and his Yoshimura Suzuki team now included not only Aaron Yates but speedy rookie Ben Spies, the young Texan ready to make a full run at Superbike racing. The Yosh team was strong, especially so on the Mladin side where he was armed with his ultra-experienced, near all-Aussie crew.

Last year, the Honda CBR1000RR proved to be a highly capable Superbike in the hands of Jake Zemke and Miguel Duhamel. In fact, both had challenged Mladin to the very end for the title. And both had won races.

But they wanted more out of the motorcycle and they somehow came up with the notion that they could get it themselves if given the freedom to do so. You know, cut that pesky HRC thing out of the picture and bring it all in house. It was the perfect case of "be careful what you wish for". For most of the season, they were horribly uncompetitive, and it got to the point where you didn't even give much thought to them getting any better. In fact, they didn't win a race. A season without a Honda Superbike victory... how can that be? But there was improvement and Duhamel ended the series fifth overall. It will be interesting to see where it goes in 2006.

Former World Superbike Champion Neil Hodgson was a welcome visitor to the AMA paddock, the Brit who calls the Isle of Man home coming across the Pond to race for the factory Ducati Austin team. He came full of hope, and left somewhat disappointed. But he did win a race, and learned aplenty. He'll

be back in 2006 and should be a threat, though he knows what a formidable opponent Mr. Mladin can be. Win or lose, he was a popular figure in the series: Likeable, witty and truly professional. Hell, even Mladin seemed to like him.

Hodgson was teamed with Eric Bostrom, the Californian returning to the team for another season and happy to be reunited with Dunlop after a less-than-satisfying year on Michelins. Bostrom would have an up-and-down '05. He'd look fantastic in winning some races, but then fail miserably and be off the pace in others. He was consistent in only one thing – his inconsistency. But his wins were enough to put him third overall.

The third Japanese manufacturer in the series was Kawasaki, though they came only with a satellite team, run by Attack Racing, with rider Josh Hayes running at the back of the factory men and sometimes in front of the Ducatis and Hondas.

The Kawasaki effort was superior compared to Yamaha's, who again failed to come to the party. At season's end, Kawasaki announced they would return with a full factory effort with Roger Lee and Tommy Hayden, but Yamaha was still out, content to run in the support classes.

Opposite page: Australian Mat Mladin remained the dominant force, with a record sixth AMA Superbike title.

Below: Mladin has no intention of hanging up his helmet, having signed for another three years.
Photographs: Gold & Goose

There were a few quality privateer teams, most notably the Michael Jordan Motorsports squad of Steve Rapp and Jason Pridmore. Pridmore had his usual bad luck and suffered injury, but Rapp had some good results and ended up well in the top ten in the final point standings. But it was Mat Mladin Motorsports (yes, that Mat Mladin) who fared the best with steady Australian Marty Craggill always in the top ten, seventh and top privateer in the final standings.

But at the very top in 2005 it was back to Mladin vs. the rest and it all started at Daytona, with the class now reduced to secondary status.

Mladin put it to 'em in the race, beating Hodgson by almost three and a half seconds to again establish himself as the man to beat. Hodgson, meanwhile, had fared well in his AMA debut, though he could already tell there was work to do to match Mladin. Third place went to Spies over his Yoshimura team-mate Yates. Then came the two Hondas – Zemke then Duhamel – with their troubles starting to show, but with things not nearly as bad as they'd get.

Running around Daytona in a support role didn't suit Mladin, the Aussie feeling like the class had been slapped in the face. And it was difficult to find someone who disagreed with him.

"The fact that Xtreme is the main race here at Daytona, I think, is pathetic," Mladin stated after winning. "The fact that the Superbike guys had a 15-minute" (actually 25-minute, but you get his point) "race and is almost a support race for this weekend, I think, is crazy. Our qualifying times were five seconds a lap quicker than theirs. If they are going to call that the main class, then it's a slow main class."

The Daytona 200, now with Formula Xtreme bikes, was won by Duhamel over his team-mate Zemke – the only two factory bikes in the field. It was Duhamel's fifth Daytona 200 victory, matching Scott Russell's record. But you didn't get the feeling that Duhamel was overly pleased with Daytona's way of thinking on the Superbike dilemma, though he's never one to publicly demean a circuit with which his name will be linked forever.

Either way, not all looked back at Daytona with fond memories, and the entire paddock was pleased to head to Barber Motorsports Park for the first of many Superbike double-headers. And if the competition was worried after Daytona, they were even more so after Barber. Mladin went out and won both races at the picturesque circuit outside of Birmingham in the southern state of Alabama, and he did so in dominant fashion, running away in both races.

In fact of the 71 race laps thus far run in the series, Mladin had led 69 of them. The competition was in trouble. And the worst part: they knew it.

Second was split up over the two days, with Yates getting it on Saturday and Hodgson on Sunday. Spies turned in a pair of thirds over the course of the weekend, showing that he was very close to being someone to worry about.

Beyond the three Suzukis and Hodgson, the rest were in a world of hurt. It was disaster with a capital D for Honda. Duhamel turned in his normal gritty performance to finish fifth and fourth over the two days, but after that things went downhill quickly. Zemke didn't finish either race, the man many predicted to be Mladin's toughest foe was hardly that. His CBR1000RR had picked up a "gremlin", and it stayed for the weekend. In fact, it stayed for most of the year. After three races, Zemke had 26 points to Mladin's 113. Hasta la vista, title hopes.

Mladin's season featured two hiccups. The first came at California Speedway on the outskirts of Los Angeles. And it was of the mechanical variety. The clutch, they said.

With Mladin out of Saturday's race, young Texan Spies rolled to the first AMA Superbike win of his promising career, the Suzuki rider taking the spot when Hodgson blundered on the final lap. The next day, Spies finished second to Mladin and things went all topsy-turvy, the youngster leading the championship by three points when all was said and done in Southern California.

Hodgson also took advantage of Mladin's woes, though not as much as he could have. On the final lap, it looked like he was going to win his first AMA event when he overshot Turn

Three, a fever and illness having an effect on him – though he's not the sort to make excuses.

On Sunday, Hodgson was even sicker and he went from infield hospital bed to the racetrack and back to the hospital bed – with a fifth-place finish stuck in between. Too ill even to practice on Sunday, Hodgson showed his toughness, surprising all those who knew his condition. Especially the track medical crew. Now he was just six points behind Mladin and nine behind Spies, but Hodgson's been around this block before and he knows a tough customer when he sees one. And he knew Mladin was still in the catbird seat.

Normality returned to the series when it headed north to Infineon Raceway near San Francisco. Two races, two wins for Mladin. And two dominating wins at that. "I sort of can't hang with him, and I'll crash trying, and then I'll be even more annoyed with myself. Seeing him pull away is very frustrating. At the moment, there's not a lot I can do. So I'm just going to keep pushing as hard as I can," said the realist Hodgson, after second and fifth place finishes over the two races.

Yates was second best at Infineon, the Georgian ending up behind Mladin in both races, though not close enough to leave with much confidence. Hodgson was third on day one with Spies earning the final podium spot a day later.

Top: Neil Hodgson – high-class rookie.
Photograph: Gold & Goose

Above: Fast-rising Ben Spies ran Yoshimura Suzuki team-mate Mladin close on points during the year.
Photograph: Andrew Wheeler

Left: Aaron Yates was a third strong Suzuki team member.

Opposite page: Ducati teamsters Neil Hodgson (top) and Eric Bostrom. Photographs: Gold & Goose

Above: Josh Hayes claimed a Kawasaki rostrum at Road America.

Below left: Tommy Hayden, oldest of the three racing brothers, clinched the 600cc Supersport crown for Kawasaki.
Photographs: Andrew Wheeler

Below right: Honda team-mates Jake Zemke (98) and Miguel Duhamel had more luck in the Xtreme series than Superbikes, splitting race wins. Duhamel took the crown.
Photograph: Tom Hnatiw/Flick Of The Wrist Photography

The factory Hondas were 25th and sixth (Duhamel) and 20th and fourth (Zemke), the pair continuing to struggle.

All Eric Bostrom generally needs to cure whatever ails him is a trip to the Rocky Mountains in Colorado. The winner of five AMA Superbike Nationals at Pikes Peak Raceway, Bostrom arrived frustrated, lacking any real results in the series thus far, and completely outgunned by rookie team-mate Hodgson.

That all changed at Pikes, with Bostrom getting his sixth win at the little bull-ring racetrack, beating Yates by 0.255 of a second after the Suzuki rider erred on the penultimate lap. Third place went to Spies.

And Mladin... well, his Pikes problems continued at the only track in the series on which he's yet to win. For the fourth year in a row, he had to pit for a new rear tyre. Still, he finished fourth, and left with a 15-point lead. For him that was almost as good as victory.

Bostrom's win was balanced within the factory Ducati team by Hodgson's 31st-place finish, the Brit's 999 F04 blowing a hose off and forcing an extended pit stop.

Hodgson's luck turned around a few weeks later when the series headed to Wisconsin for the Road America double-header. In conditions even Hodgson called the worst he'd ever raced in, Saturday's National was hit by a deluge. So much so that the AMA called it complete after halfway, giving Hodgson his first AMA Superbike victory. Mladin ended up second, his pit stop for tyres proving to be very timely, as when the AMA stopped the race and went back a lap, the Suzuki rider was still on track and running second.

Attack Kawasaki's Josh Hayes had his best-ever Superbike finish, riding the privateer ZX10R to third in the atrocious conditions.

Sunday dawned sunny and clear and it was all Mladin, the Aussie winning for the seventh time of the season. Zemke stayed close initially, but Mladin gradually pulled away, and Spies ended up taking the runner-up spot with a last-lap pass on Zemke. Still, Zemke's third was a bright spot in an otherwise forgettable season, the two Hondas finally getting some new engine parts that moved them a bit closer to the Suzukis.

Hodgson was in a pack fighting for third in the dry race, but he ran off in Turn Five and ended up 19th. "I'm really pissed off as you can imagine," Hodgson said. "I only had a quarter of a lap to go."

The Superbikes were relegated to support level again in 2005, but this time it was at Laguna Seca and it was a different sort of support level. MotoGP was in town for the first time since

1993, and the place was going absolutely crazy because of it.

Racing in front of more people than they would all year, the Superbikers did what they'd done all year. They unsuccessfully chased Mladin during practice and qualifying and looked set to do the same in the race. But someone forgot to tell Bostrom that he wasn't supposed to win here.

And that's exactly what he did, beating Mladin in a straight fight in what was the most surprising race outcome of the season. Really. Nobody saw it coming. And Bostrom proved in winning the big race that he's not just a one-track wonder (Pikes Peak), and in fact it was his third at Laguna. It all came down to a pre-race gamble by rider and crew in an effort to rid the Ducati of the chatter problem he'd had all weekend. Wholesale changes were made, and they worked – much to Bostrom's relief. "On the warm-up lap, I knew that things were right and we'd basically improved the bike in every way," Bostrom said.

He put his head down straight away and was never headed, beating Mladin, Yates and Spies. Hodgson was the most notable non-finisher, taken out on the opening lap in a scary incident on the entrance to the Corkscrew. Hayes collected Hodgson from behind, sending them both to the dirt and out of the race. Hodgson was irate, and rightfully so, but he even handled that with class.

Mladin dropped the bomb on everyone at Mid-Ohio. He wasn't going MotoGP racing, wasn't going World Superbike racing, and most definitely wasn't going home to retire to Australia. Instead he signed a three-year contract with Suzuki to do AMA Superbikes, so they could instead look forward to three more years of knowing that to win this thing they'll have to beat him.

A day after letting everyone know, Mladin gave them all a dose of what they have to not look forward to. On Saturday, he beat Spies by 12 seconds for the 40th win of his AMA Super-bike career, and Suzuki's 75th.

A day later, we found out just as quickly why they continue to hold races and not just hand out championships in the pre-season. On Sunday, while biding his time behind Bostrom and his team-mate Yates in the early going, Mladin helplessly watched as Yates crashed in front of him. Taking evasive action, Mladin went off track, lost control and also fell. He remounted to finish last, earning a single point.

Bostrom went on to a well-deserved victory, again proving that if there are just a few men capable of winning AMA Super-

Above: Duhamel leads the Formula Xtreme
pack at Sears Point.
Photograph: Tom Hnatiw/Flick Of The Wrist Photography

bike races, he's one of them. And we shouldn't forget it.

As for Mladin, all the work of recouping the points lost from the California Speedway debacle had been undone. The lead of 37 points just 24 hours earlier was suddenly reduced to just nine. Game on. Again. He led Spies by 397-388, with four races to go in what was now a two-man race for the title.

Mladin's two-race performance at Virginia International Race-way may have been the best of his AMA career. On Saturday, he came from behind three times in a race that kept being stopped by red flags, and he did so with an undisclosed bike problem in the back of his mind for the duration. But he did the business anyway.

On Sunday, it was vintage Mladin. He got a decent start, sliced and diced his way to the front in five laps and was gone. By the end he was a Virginia country mile in front of Yates and well on to a sixth AMA Superbike crown, a title that would be in his back pocket a week later in Atlanta.

For the fourth and fifth times this year, Suzuki swept the podium, the order behind Mladin switched each time. On Satur-day it was Spies, Yates. On Sunday the other way round. Either way, it further proved the team's dominance.

On Saturday at Road Atlanta, Mladin won his 11th race of the season, stretching his career mark to 43 wins. On Sunday, he cel-ebrated an unprecedented sixth championship after cruising to fourth, leaving a first win of the year to team-mate Yates, with Spies second and Hodgson third. But as it started, it was all about Mladin – the most prolific AMA Superbike champion of all time.

And just think – he's got three more years to add to the legacy.

Although at times the class is the laughing stock of the series, mainly down to only the factory Honda team contesting it, no one could argue that the Formula Xtreme class had the best finish to its season. With Duhamel and team-mate Zemke exchanging wins all season long, it came down to the very last race. The winner would be champion. In a battle reminiscent of the whole preceding season, the pair fought it out at the front. Until Zemke crashed on the final lap, handing overall victory to Duhamel. It was the French Canadian's eighth AMA Pro title.

Although Roger Lee Hayden was quickly becoming the star of AMA road racing by season's end, it was older brother Tommy who earned the coveted 600cc Supersport crown. Roger Lee won four races to Tommy's three, but Tommy was there from the start and was in the battle at the front each and every race. Although he finished his season with a badly broken hand (from a crash at Laguna Seca), he also ended it with the title, after gutsy performances riding hurt at the very end of the championship.

Roger Lee also came on strong at the end of the Superstock Series, but that title ultimately went to Suzuki man Yates, the Georgian winning five times. That was plenty to defeat Yamaha's top gun Jason DiSalvo, the New Yorker winning once along the way. Third in the series went to Michael Jordan Motorsports' Steve Rapp, the Californian earning himself a return ride on the team's Suzukis next year.

Although most thought a class would be dropped at the end of the season, the AMA has opted to retain the status quo for 2007. Superbikes will return, along with Xtreme, Superstock and Supersport.

WORLD CLASS, FOREIGN WINNER

By GARY PINCHIN, Motorcycle News

NO Hollywood script writer could have penned a more perfect plot for the 2005 British Superbike Championship. The underdog (Gegorio Lavilla), riding a bike everyone said was past its best (Ducati 999), took on the biggest factory team ever seen in BSB (HRC's HM Plant Honda team). And clinched the title in the final race of the year.

For a sub-plot, the season was punctuated by thrilling races, spectacular smashes, all underpinned by political infighting, rider sackings and stories of amazing determination in the face of adversity. What more could any BSB race fan ask for?

After a year on the sidelines Darrell Healey's GSE Racing returned to the series they dominated in 1999 (with Troy Bayliss) and 2000 (Neil Hodgson) before switching to WSB (from 2001 to 2003), paving the way for both Hodgson and James Toseland to title glory with the factory team.

For 2005 GSE, with backing from Wrigley's Airwaves chewing gum, opted to run ex-factory F04 Ducatis – even though the 999 was derided throughout the 2003 season by Sean Emmett as being obsolete.

Even though Paul Bird's MonsterMob Ducati team had won the title the previous two years with 998s (with Steve Hislop in 2002 and Shane Byrne in 2003), nothing they tried seemed to make Emmett happier about the way the new bike worked.

For their homecoming, GSE's team boss Colin Wright signed Leon Haslam and James Haydon. Haslam had Ducati experience from 2004 in WSB with Mark Griffiths's Renegade team, and had even won a BSB race at Brands on Pirellis in tricky wet conditions. But he still wasn't considered ready to be a title contender, despite his wide experience on different types of machinery at world level.

Haydon had shrugged off his "crasher" tag in 2004, having joined Virgin Yamaha mid-term to replace injured Steve Plater. He put together an impressive season with a far-from-sorted R1 and ran so many races without falling that he joked how the bodywork on his bike was worn out with stone damage and needed replacing!

No chance of that continuing on the Ducati. Haydon crashed twice in the very first pre-season test at Almeria because, according to sources within the team, he was spooked by the sheer speed of his new team-mate and tried to beat his lap time before getting himself up to speed on the V-twin. Then on the eve of the first race, he crashed again testing at Albacete, the force of the highside breaking his thumb, little finger and knuckle joint.

With Haydon out, Wright drafted in Gregorio Lavilla, who was sitting at home in Spain with no ride, having missed out on berths at Rizla Suzuki (in favour of 2004 golden boy Scott Smart) and Stobart Honda (in favour of MotoGP refugee Jeremy McWilliams).

Lavilla turned up at the first Brands Hatch race with no pre-season testing of any kind and no seat time with the 999 F04. He had WSB experience on the Brands GP circuit, but the BSB opener was on the short track. It didn't stop him pulling off the pass of the weekend, stuffing the 999 underneath Hawk Kawasaki's Glen Richards at Clearways to finish second in race one. He was third in race two.

Lavilla also knew which way to go at second-round venue Thruxton, having subbed for the injured Yukio Kagayama on the Rizla Suzuki there in 2004. On the Ducati Lavilla again finished third and second, but not without some controversy since Haydon turned up at the meeting, telling anyone who would listen he was race fit and ready to ride and would definitely be back in action on the Ducati at round three, at Mallory. He even had a certificate to prove his fitness from the circuit medical staff but as far as Colin Wright was concerned, Haydon had still not been passed fit by their own specialist and, until he was, there was no chance of him riding their bike.

Airwaves Ducati were in a very difficult position. HM Plant Honda's Ryuichi Kiyonari was unbeaten in all four races on the full factory machine, and had amassed 100 points but Lavilla was second in the championship with 72, and the only rider in the four races so far to pressure Kiyonari or Honda team-mate Michael Rutter. Missing four races meant Haydon was effectively out of the title chase. By Mallory, GSE Racing had paid him off and signed Lavilla for the remainder of the year. Wright said: "No one ever won the title after scoring nothing in the first four rounds. To have dropped Greg would have handed the title to Honda there and then. We were not prepared to do that. We had obligations to sponsors. What made it tough was that I really wanted to work with James."

Even though Lavilla got the job, the consensus was that his world-class finesse wouldn't help him once he got to the more contentious circuits. Like Mallory, Mondello, Croft, Knockhill, or even Oulton Park: a mix of tight little twisters where you must be prepared to bounce off the landscape once in a while, and undulating courses with blind apexes, where you need massive experience to know where to throw it in or, more importantly, where to make a killer pass.

Above: Growing experience – Leon Haslam made a strong team-mate to Lavilla.
Photograph: Clive Challinor Motor Sport Photgraphy

Opposite top: Gregorio Lavilla went from unemployed to BSB champion within nine months.

Opposite: Methodical and masterful – Lavilla at work.
Photographs: Martin Heath

Below: Bennett's showed off their title sponsorship to good effect.
Photograph: Clive Challinor Motor Sport Photgraphy

Lavilla was up to the task on all counts. Meeting followed meeting with a familiar format. Lavilla would be off the pace Friday, learning his way around, trying all manner of different lines to see where he could and couldn't pass. Saturday he'd move closer to the pace, chucking in qualifiers only once he was happy with race distance rubber. Sunday, regardless of grid slot he'd grind out results. He proved time and again he was the only rider in the series capable of coming from the back. His overtaking moves were clean and effortless.

The much-derided 999 seemed to turn on a sixpence and hold whatever line Lavilla wanted to run. The way he stuffed the Ducati inside Kiyonari at Croft highlighted not just how agile the bike was, but how much the Spaniard wanted to win. Okay, the Honda blew him away on acceleration down the next straight, but Lavilla's pressure eventually told as Kiyo made an error in tricky conditions and the calculating Gregorio won again.

GSE pinpointed that the 999's inability to hold a line was down to too much grip – accentuated by the sticky new Dunlops. Wright said: "We realised what was causing the front end issue when we put soft (qualifying) tyres in. There was no way Greg could go any quicker. You can't steer when the front's not on the ground. Leon didn't have such an issue because he had a different style and was slower than Greg mid-corner." Wright claimed it was something Emmett overlooked in 2004, but the new 200-section N-tec Dunlops highlighted the grip issue. With the old 205s it was possible to steer the bike by spinning the rear – even when the front wheel was in the air. But the new 200s gave so much grip the riders couldn't spin them at will.

The team didn't use the new rubber until round three, once they had got used to how the 999 responded to changes. The big change came at Mondello in May, when Lavilla asked the team for a softer engine map, to take some of the harshness out of the power delivery. They also lowered the bike and extended the wheelbase to the maximum, to help curtail the bike's propensity for wheelies. These effectively became the base chassis settings for the remainder of the year – although they were soon back to running the engine at full power for virtually every track bar Cadwell.

Wright added: "It took a lot more effort to ride the bike. And once Greg got it down into a corner, it wanted to stay down, so instead of running wide he was turning too tight. It became a lot more physical for him to ride." The season became a testament to Lavilla's ability as a racer and a tactician – and GSE Racing's skills in turning the underdog bike into a winner.

It wasn't just Lavilla though. The team also helped Leon Haslam hone his very obvious natural talent. Being part of a world class team, meant he started the season looking more confident than ever before, and as the year progressed he matured into one of the most competitive racers in the championship. He won three races and by the last two rounds was more than capable of beating anyone in the series, including his team-mate!

Round three at Mallory was a pivotal moment. Kiyonari was running his usual blistering pace in the first race but got into Edwina's chicane a bit too hot, had the back end slew around on him, and speared off the track, clipping the tyre wall with his Shoei as he slid along the grass. Otherwise unhurt, Kiyonari suffered concussion and subsequent scans the following week showed some bruising to his brain. That ruled him out of round four at Oulton a week later.

But there was no crisis at Honda, since team-mate Rutter was bang on the pace. He won both Mallory races, took the first Oulton scrap and was runner-up to Haslam in the second, to build a healthy 56-point lead over Lavilla.

Kiyo bounced back with a first-race win at Mondello; Lavilla countered by winning race two. In the next two rounds the same three riders filled the rostrum positions but Kiyo looked to be back in control, winning three out of four. Rutter, thanks to his consistent run of four runner-up finishes, still controlled the series, with 275 points, but Kiyo was now second on 232 and Lavilla third with 216.

Snetterton was the turning point in the series, though on paper, Silverstone six weeks later might appear to have had the

greater effect.

Rutter highsided at the tight Russell's chicane during Saturday morning qualifying. He didn't tell anyone except those closest to him in the team but he had broken his right collarbone and displaced his left. Luckily the right fracture wasn't displaced so though he was in some discomfort, it wasn't the real agony he knew only too well from previous similar injuries, where the bones spread and cause real problems.

Rutter finished a hard man's fifth and third in the two races. With 27 points, he actually out-scored his championship rivals, each of whom won a race but failed to score in the other. Kiyonari took the first, then crashed out in race two. Lavilla lost the front at Sears in race one, then won race two.

Rutter was still suffering from his shoulder injuries at Silverstone – and he was far from happy with his latest Michelins. In race one, he looked set for the podium when he lost the front end at the stupidly tight final chicane, though he managed to remount for 15th and one point. But he lacked confidence in the front tyre in race two, and could only finish fourth.

Kiyo also suffered a front-end crash in the chicane earlier in the race. He too remounted to finish eighth, then won race two from first-race victor Lavilla. His charge was now on. Rutter still led the points 316 to Kiyo's 290, but Lavilla was closer now on 286.

Rutter's season fell apart after that. He scored just 14 points and crashed twice in the next four races and was suddenly an also ran. It was down to Kiyonari to salvage Honda's honour. He was off-form at Cadwell, Honda Racing's back yard, but GSE failed to capitalise fully on the situation. Lavilla looked set to win the first race but Haslam, seemingly desperate to win at all costs, managed to take his team-mate grass-tracking and hand victory to Virgin Yamaha's Tommy Hill. Luckily neither of them crashed and Lavilla finished second with Haslam third but there were some harsh words back in the pits.

Ironically there were still no team orders in race two, as Haslam took his second win of the year with Lavilla second and Kiyonari a distant third. For the first time all year Lavilla led the series with 326 points – just two ahead of Rutter while Kiyonari trailed in third on 317.

Kiyo won both Oulton races, but Lavilla kept up the pressure with two seconds, so it was now a one-point game, with Kiyo just holding the upper hand.

For the penultimate round at Donington, Dunlop upped their game – at a track everyone expected to suit Kiyonari and the Michelins, as in 2004 when the Japanese rider scored a memorable end-of-season double. How wrong they were.

Rutter's confidence by now was in tatters. A seized back brake in the first Oulton race and a crash in the second didn't help matters. A bad tyre in race one at Donington just piled on the agony.

Kiyonari didn't live up to the pre-Donington hype either – making several small mistakes to make Lavilla's job easier. Dunlop's massive offensive, drawing in staff from MotoGP and AMA Superbike, ensured Airwaves Ducati got every scrap of technical support they required. It worked to perfection with Lavilla winning both races – in front of Ducati Corse boss Paolo Ciabatti, who had jetted in specially to savour BSB for the first time.

Haslam was right in the mix too, making good starts to act as a buffer between hole-shot man Lavilla and the rest of the pack in the first few laps. He finished third behind Kiyonari in race one but helped the team's title cause no end by beating the HRC rider back to third in race two. Lavilla would go to the final Brands round with a 13-point lead over Kiyonari.

In the two-week gap to the final Brands race Honda Racing made some curious decisions. Team boss Neil Tuxworth told Michael Rutter his services would no longer be required for 2006. The team also built a third factory bike from spares for Karl Harris – ostensibly as a thank-you for his services in the past three years with Honda. But the reality was more likely that they hoped Harris might act as a spoiler against the Ducatis to help Kiyonari – especially with Rutter suffering such an appalling lack of confidence in his tyres.

It was a strange task, since Harris had run WP suspension all year and now had to use factory Showa kit. That didn't please

Above: Michael Rutter holds his injured shoulder.

Top left: John Reynolds (chatting with Niall Mackenzie) was injured before the season began in earnest, and struggled manfully thereafter.
Photographs: Clive Challinor Motor Sport Photgraphy

WP. Harris continued to run Dunlop rubber though – the British firm were being asked to supply tyres to a team who were trying to beat the Dunlop-shod Ducati team to the title.

And if Kiyonari didn't already have enormous pressure on his shoulders, HRC top brass including HRC managing director Satoru Horiike jetted in for the final round.

What they witnessed was a humiliating defeat as the Airwaves Ducati duo dominated. Lavilla won the first race with Haslam second. And with the title virtually sewn up, Haslam was let off the leash to do his own thing and even Lavilla's lap-record breaking pace wasn't enough to stop his team-mate taking his third win of the year. Kiyonari couldn't even get on the podium, and suffered the ignominy of being beaten back to fourth in the final race of the year by Steve Plater on a Hydrex Honda, working better than usual thanks to special help from WP technicians and some trick Dunlop rubber. The result was just what Plater needed, after a disappointing year that started with an uncompetitive Sendo Kawasaki and almost ended prematurely when the mobile phone company went into liquidation.

In the final reckoning Kiyonari won 12 races, five more than Lavilla, but BSB was proclaiming a Spanish champion for the first time in its history. Kiyonari just didn't have the consistency to make the most of his impressive win record.

Lavilla said: "It's been an amazing year, especially the way I arrived with no testing and no experience of BSB. But the team worked perfect for me. Everyone said the 999 was no good but we worked on the bike, learned the tracks and the combination was perfect.

"I went into every race thinking anything is possible. I feel happy to have proved something to those who forgot how competitive I am." Although it took until the second race of round four for his first win, Lavilla looked strong everywhere. Everyone kept waiting for a mistake. He didn't make any. Lavilla and GSE Racing simply ground the Honda effort into submission as first Rutter and then Kiyonari crumbled under the pressure.

The final tally gave Lavilla 461 points from Kiyonari's 429. Rutter scored just 51 points in the final eight races (Lavilla scored 175!), but still clung to third in the final standings on 371 with Haslam fourth on 350.

Top: Ryuichi Kiyonari won the most races, but lacked consistency.
Photograph: Clive Challinor Motor Sport Photgraphy

Above: Glen Richards pushed beyond the limits time and again on the Kawasaki.
Photograph: Martin Heath

Above left: James Haydon was paid off by Team GSE, but ended the year on the Rizla Suzuki.
Photograph: Clive Challinor Motor Sport Photgraphy

Hawk Kawasaki pair Glen Richards and Dean Thomas were fifth and sixth respectively in the championship – pretty much where team boss Stuart Hicken had predicted his low budget outfit would finish on the ZX10s.

Richards often ran up front early in the race, but being down on power he simply couldn't live with the faster Hondas and Ducatis over a full race distance. His best weekend came at Mallory with two second places. Thomas, in his first year with the team, took a while to adapt from a Ducati to the four-cylinder Japanese bike, but seemed to gain strength in the latter half of the year, with a string of top six finishes.

Karl Harris finished seventh overall on the www.honda-racing.co.uk entry. In his first season back in the top flight after back-to-back Supersport titles for HM Plant Honda in 2003 and 2004. Harris started the season solidly enough among the top six but suffered a mid-term loss of form. He pulled himself together by the end of the year to earn that factory bike for Donington, though a first race crash left him nursing a broken foot. But at least he had some good news – an HM Plant Honda Superbike ride replacing Rutter in 2006.

Gary Mason was the top scorer of the three Stobart Honda riders. The Paul Bird-owned team took longer than expected to make the FireBlade competitive, but they did follow a path less travelled than other rival privateer Honda teams. Where most opted to run WP suspension and Motec engine management, and glean data from Honda Racing-run teams (Harris plus Jonathan Rea on the Red Bull Rookie Blade), the Stobbies went for Ohlins suspension and Magneti Marelli, figuring independent development meant the chance to get the jump on their rivals.

When they did finally get the bikes up to speed, it was BSB rookie Michael Laverty who put the bike on the podium: with third place at Knockhill and then again at Snetterton where he finished second to Lavilla and ahead of HRC's Rutter.

It seemed only a matter of time before the stylish 24-year-old Ulsterman would clinch an elusive race win, but at Silverstone he was involved in a nasty accident, and was still not fully recovered in the final Brands round. He had crashed, unhurt, at Copse when fluids leaking from his own bike got onto the rear tyre. Just as he was picking himself up, Harris crashed on the same fluids and his bike slid across the high-friction run-off at high speed (great for cars but not so good for bikes) centre-

punching the unsuspecting Laverty. Incredibly he suffered no broken bones but did suffer some massive muscle and ligament damage that took an age to mend.

Nevertheless, Laverty was a real star of the series, and should be one of the pacemakers in 2006 on the now well-sorted Stobart Honda. His far more experienced team-mate Jeremy McWilliams never got a chance to shine. The former MotoGP man crashed at Brands, suffering nerve damage to his right shoulder that rendered his bicep and some of his shoulder muscles useless. He tried to continue, but finally gave up after Mondello in May, and didn't return until the final round – even though he had ridden a MotoGP bike in the meantime.

Injuries also meant Rizla Suzuki became a shadow of the title-winning team of 2005. John Reynolds never got a chance to defend his Number One plate. On the morning of the very first pre-season test of the year at Valencia he crashed and badly broke his right leg. That meant new signing Scott Smart shouldered the brunt of development riding, not an ideal situation since he was coming off a year of racing the ZX10 – a very different animal to the new K5 Suzuki.

Lavilla had been drafted in for the next pre-season test, but Reynolds was back in the saddle for the Brands first round, even though he was still on crutches. It was a typically gutsy performance from JR, but the reality was that one crash would have risked everything with the injured leg. He scored two ninth places at Brands but struggled over the Thruxton bumps and decided not to race at Mallory.

By then, though, Lavilla had been snapped up by a shrewd Colin Wright, so Rizla turned to out-of-work James Haydon from fourth-round Oulton until Mondello.

Meanwhile Smart was struggling to get to grips with the Suzuki – and the team. The feelings were mutual, and when relationships became sufficiently strained he was finally sacked after Croft. Reynolds was back in the saddle by then and Haydon, after doing Croft on a Virgin Yamaha subbing for injured Sean Emmett, was signed for the remainder of the season by Rizla.

Even with Smart gone (he subsequently boosted the Vivaldi Kawasaki ranks to three from Knockhill on, alongside youngsters Ben Wilson and Tristan Palmer), Rizla Suzuki didn't really sort the K5 until the final round at Brands, with a radical set-up

Above: Tommy Hill claimed a win at Cadwell for Virgin Yamaha.
Photograph: Clive Challinor Motor Sport Photography

Top: BSB rookie Michael Laverty leads the pack – he would score Stobart Honda's first podium.
Photograph: Martin Heath

to the Ohlins gas forks which Reynolds initially tried in the previous Donington round.

With the team owner away running the Suzuki's MotoGP effort, the BSB team had lost direction, so Reynolds's old crew chief Dave "Oz" Marton was brought back in late June for a coherent development programme.

In the final round Haydon scored his best result of the year with third, holding off Kiyonari, in race one, though he crashed out of race two.

Despite both physical and machine weakness, Reynolds ground out four podium finishes, but then suffered multiple injuries after crashing at the start of Friday practice for the final Brands round. He sustained two broken vertebrae, a broken collarbone, four broken ribs and a punctured lung. On the Sunday night, from his hospital bed, he announced his retirement from racing. Ironically, the previous Wednesday he had agreed terms to remain with the Rizla Suzuki team for one more season.

Reynolds (42) said: "As soon as I hit the barrier I knew that was it – it was one more warning I could not ignore."

Injury also plagued Sean Emmett. After his disappointing year with MonsterMob Ducati, Emmett hoped to turn around his fortunes with Virgin Yamaha's big-bang R1. Pre-season testing had shown the bike capable of running lap record pace, but it all went wrong in the first round when Emmett was highsided and suffered an injured elbow. He continued to race, scoring three fifths and a fourth in the opening four rounds, but clearly not able to ride at his best. Unfortunately it wasn't until after Mondello in June that he discovered his elbow was actually broken, and he'd need an operation to pin a shard of bone back in place.

Even when he returned to racing late in the year he struggled to get on the pace and was put in the shade by his much less-experienced team-mate, 20-year-old Tommy Hill. The youngster had taken until halfway through the season to understand how to get the best from the big-bang engine – that its strength was high corner speed, in the same way the old GP500 two-stroke twins used to be able to run fast lap times against the point and squirt GP500 fours.

Hill was the only rider outside the top four in the championship to score a win. It came at Cadwell after the Ducati duo messed each other up. Hill was waiting for the mistake, and claimed a memorable victory. But the problem with the big-bang was a lack of development tyres to suit it. The newer 200-section Dunlops were built to suit modern point-and-squirt screamers, so with that in mind, the team are going back to a conventional firing order engine for 2006 – for Hill and R6 Cup champion Billy McConnell, a talented 19-year-old Aussie.

James Buckingham won the Privateer Cup with an outstanding season on his GSX-R1000. Buckingham even managed to out-qualify the Rizla Suzuki team at Croft, and was impressive in a one-off non-championship Castle Combe outing, guesting on the factory bike. He also rode for injured Reynolds at the final Brands rounds but, at the time of MOTOCOURSE going to press - despite showing a lot of talent, the 22-year-old still hadn't secured the top class ride he so richly deserved for 2006.

If this year's series was the best BSB season yet, 2006 promises to be even better. Lavilla and Haslam have re-signed with GSE Racing and will get factory F06 Ducatis to take on HRC duo Kiyonari and Harris. Rutter will bounce back on a Stobart Honda – with the added incentive of wanting to prove a point with a privateer FireBlade against the factory teams.

Rizla Suzuki have to bounce back after a year in the doldrums and start winning again. Haydon was already signed, but it still wasn't clear who would be his new team-mate. Whoever it is will have his work cut out. BSB simply is so competitive these days.

Support Classes

Leon Camier added the British Supersport title to the 125 title he won in 2001. But it was an impressive one-off Suzuka Eight Hour ride on a Moriwaki Honda FireBlade that got everyone talking about the 19-year-old from Kent. He was offered a ride with basketball legend Michael Jordan's Jumpman 23 Suzuki

team in the States but opted instead to stick with Honda, signing for Gary Ekerold's team in order to defend his Supersport title, but with the promise of a factory Honda BSB ride in 2007.

British Supersport was rich with raw young talent in 2005. Craig Jones finished runner-up in the series and got himself a deal with Carl Fogarty's Petronas team in WSB. Cal Crutchlow was third overall, probably showing the best form in the end of season races - enough to unsettle Ekerold Honda team-mate Jones. Crutchlow stays with the team in 2006 alongside new-signing Camier.

Tom Sykes was a strong contender early in the year on the TAS Suzuki but smashed his hand badly at Snetterton and wasn't fully race fit when he returned for the final few races of the year.

Twenty-four-year-old Christian Elkin won the British 125 title for the second year in succession and announced plans to race in British Supersport in 2006 – though at the time of writing he still had no confirmed ride.

Going into the final round any one of three riders could have won the title but Elkin's rivals, James Westmorland and Rob Guiver both suffered machine failure in the early stages of the Brands race.

The 125 series was marred by the death of Red Bull Rookie Chris Jones after a start-line accident Cadwell Park. The 14-year-old from Bromsgrove was airlifted to hospital but succumbed to his injuries the following day. Jones had scored five podium finishes in his nine rounds.

Lee Jackson won the National Superstock title after his main threat Adrian Coates crashed out of the final Brands round, and former R6 Cup contender Peter Ward won the Superstock Cup title, scoring seven wins in the series.

Below: **Sean Emmet.**
Photograph: Clive Challinor Motor Sport Photgraphy

Above: **Above: Karl Harris's all-action style at Donington Park.**
Photograph: Clive Challinor Motor Sport Photgraphy

Left: **British Supersport champion and impressive talent Leon Camier celebrates his title at Brands.**
Photograph: Martin Heath

MAJOR RESULTS

OTHER CHAMPIONSHIP RACING SERIES WORLDWIDE

Compiled by KAY EDGE

AMA Chevrolet Superbike Championship

Presented by Parts Unlimited

DAYTONA INTERNATIONAL SPEEDWAY – Daytona Beach, Florida, 9-12 March, 44.25 miles

1. Mat Mladin (Suzuki GSX-R1000); **2** Neil Hodgson (Ducati 999); **3** Ben Spies (Suzuki GSX-R1000); **4** Aaron Yates (Suzuki GSX-R1000); **5** Jake Zemke (Honda CBR1000RR); **6** Miguel Duhamel (Honda CBR1000RR); **7** Jason Pridmore (Suzuki GSX-R1000); **8** Geoff May (Suzuki GSX-R1000); **9** Kurtis Roberts (Honda CBR1000RR); **10** Steve Rapp (Suzuki GSX-R1000).

BARBER MOTORSPORTS PARK – Birmingham, Alabama, 22-23 April, 64.4 miles/103.040 km

Race 1

1 Mat Mladin (Suzuki GSX-R1000); **2** Aaron Yates (Suzuki GSX-R1000); **3** Ben Spies (Suzuki GSX-R1000); **4** Neil Hodgson (Ducati 999); **5** Miguel Duhamel (Honda CBR1000RR); **6** Jason Pridmore (Suzuki GSX-R1000); **7** Steve Rapp (Suzuki GSX-R1000); **8** Eric Bostrom (Ducati 999); **9** Vincent Haskovec (Suzuki GSX-R1000); **10** Marty Craggill (Suzuki GSX-R1000).

Race 2

1 Mat Mladin (Suzuki GSX-R1000); **2** Neil Hodgson (Ducati 999); **3** Ben Spies (Suzuki GSX-R1000); **4** Miguel Duhamel (Honda CBR1000RR); **5** Eric Bostrom (Ducati 999); **6** Josh Hayes (Kawasaki ZX-10RR); **7** Vincent Haskovec (Suzuki GSX-R1000); **8** Aaron Yates (Suzuki GSX-R1000); **9** Marty Craggill (Suzuki GSX-R1000); **10** John Haner (Suzuki GSX-R1000).

CALIFORNIA SPEEDWAY – Fontana, California, 29 April-1 May, 66.080 miles/106.345 km

1 Ben Spies (Suzuki GSX-R1000); **2** Aaron Yates (Suzuki GSX-R1000); **3** Neil Hodgson (Ducati 999); **4** Miguel Duhamel (Honda CBR1000RR); **5** Eric Bostrom (Ducati 999); **6** Jake Zemke (Honda CBR1000RR); **7** Josh Hayes (Kawasaki ZX-10RR); **8** Steve Rapp (Suzuki GSX-R1000); **9** Marty Craggill (Suzuki GSX-R1000); **10** Vincent Haskovec (Suzuki GSX-R1000).

Race 2

1 Mat Mladin (Suzuki GSX-R1000); **2** Ben Spies (Suzuki GSX-R1000); **3** Aaron Yates (Suzuki GSX-R1000); **4** Eric Bostrom (Ducati 999); **5** Neil Hodgson (Ducati 999); **6** Jake Zemke (Honda CBR1000RR); **7** Steve Rapp (Suzuki GSX-R1000); **8** Marty Craggill (Suzuki GSX-R1000); **9** Clint McBain (Suzuki GSX-R1000); **10** Larry Pegram (Honda CBR1000RR).

INFINEON RACEWAY – Sonoma, California, 13-15 May, 60.320 miles/97.060 km

Race 1

1 Mat Mladin (Suzuki GSX-R1000) **2** Aaron Yates (Suzuki GSX-R1000); **3** Neil Hodgson (Ducati 999); **4** Ben Spies (Suzuki GSX-R1000); **5** Josh Hayes (Kawasaki ZX-10RR); **6** Steve Rapp (Suzuki GSX-R1000); **7** Jacob Holden (Suzuki GSX-R1000); **8** Larry Pegram (Honda CBR1000RR); **9** Marty Craggill (Suzuki GSX-R1000); **10** Eric Bostrom (Ducati 999).

Race 2

1 Mat Mladin (Suzuki GSX-R1000) **2** Aaron Yates (Suzuki GSX-R1000); **3** Aaron Yates (Suzuki GSX-R1000); **4** Jake Zemke (Honda CBR1000RR); **5** Neil Hodgson (Ducati 999); **6** Miguel Duhamel (Honda CBR1000RR); **7** Eric Bostrom (Ducati 999); **8** Josh Hayes (Kawasaki ZX-10RR); **9** Marty Craggill (Suzuki GSX-R1000); **10.** Larry Pegram (Honda CBR1000RR).

PIKES PEAK INTERNATIONAL RACEWAY – Fountain, Colorado, 22 May, 56.2 miles/84.160 km

1 Eric Bostrom (Ducati 999); **2** Aaron Yates (Suzuki GSX-R1000); **3** Ben Spies (Suzuki GSX-R1000); **4** Mat Mladin (Suzuki GSX-R1000); **5** Josh Hayes (Kawasaki ZX-10RR); **6** Steve Rapp (Suzuki GSX-R1000); **7** Mark Ledesma (Honda CBR1000RR); **8** John Haner (Suzuki GSX-R1000); **9** Miguel Duhamel (Honda CBR1000RR); **10** Brent George (Suzuki GSX-R1000).

ROAD AMERICA – Elkhart Lake, Wisconsin, 4-5 June, 64 miles/102.998 km

Race 1

1 Neil Hodgson (Ducati 999); **2** Mat Mladin (Suzuki GSX-R1000); **3** Josh Hayes (Kawasaki ZX-10RR); **4** Ben Spies (Suzuki GSX-R1000); **5** Marty Craggill (Suzuki GSX-R1000); **6** Jake Zemke (Honda CBR1000RR); **7** Miguel Duhamel (Honda CBR1000RR); **8** Larry Pegram (Honda CBR1000RR); **9** John Haner (Suzuki GSX-R1000); **10** Akira Tamitsuji (Suzuki GSX-R1000).

Race 2

1 Mat Mladin (Suzuki GSX-R1000); **2** Ben Spies (Suzuki GSX-R1000); **3** Jake Zemke (Honda CBR1000RR); **4** Eric Bostrom (Ducati 999); **5** Aaron Yates (Suzuki GSX-R1000); **6** Josh Hayes (Kawasaki ZX-10RR); **7** Kurtis Roberts (Honda CBR1000RR); **8** Steve Rapp (Suzuki GSX-R1000); **9** Lee Acree (Suzuki GSX-R1000); **10.** Clint McBain (Suzuki GSX-R1000).

MAZDA RACEWAY LAGUNA SECA – Monterey, California, 9 July, 61.600 miles/98.560km

1 Eric Bostrom (Ducati 999); **2** Mat Mladin (Suzuki GSX-R1000); **3** Aaron Yates (Suzuki GSX-R1000); **4** Ben Spies (Suzuki GSX-R1000); **5** Jake Zemke (Honda CBR1000RR); **6** Miguel Duhamel (Honda CBR1000RR); **7** Kurtis Roberts (Honda CBR1000RR); **8** Steve Rapp (Suzuki GSX-R1000); **9** Jacob Holden (Suzuki GSX-R1000); **10** Jason Pridmore (Suzuki GSX-R1000).

MID-OHIO SPORTS CAR COURSE – Lexington, Ohio, 22-24 July, 62.4 miles/99.840 km

Race 1

Mat Mladin (Suzuki GSX-R1000); **2** Ben Spies (Suzuki GSX-R1000); **3** Eric Bostrom (Ducati 999); **4** Miguel Duhamel (Honda CBR1000RR); **5** Neil Hodgson (Ducati 999); **6** Josh Hayes (Kawasaki ZX-10RR); **7** Kurtis Roberts (Honda CBR1000RR); **8** Jason Pridmore (Suzuki GSX-R1000); **9** Jacob Holden (Suzuki GSX-R1000); **10** Marty Craggill (Suzuki GSX-R1000)

Race 2

1 Eric Bostrom (Ducati 999); **2** Miguel Duhamel (Honda CBR1000RR); **3** Ben Spies (Suzuki GSX-R1000); **4** Neil Hodgson (Ducati 999); **5** Kurtis Roberts (Honda CBR1000RR); **6** Steve Rapp (Suzuki GSX-R1000); **7** Jason Pridmore (Suzuki GSX-R1000); **8** Jacob Holden (Suzuki GSX-R1000); **9** Aaron Yates (Suzuki GSX-R1000); **10** Larry Pegram (Honda CBR1000RR).

VIRGINIA INTERNATIONAL RACEWAY, Alton, Virginia, 26-28 August, 62.300 miles/99.680km

1 Mat Mladin (Suzuki GSX-R1000); **2** Ben Spies (Suzuki GSX-R1000); **3.** Aaron Yates (Suzuki GSX-R1000); **4.** Jake Zemke (Honda CBR1000RR); **5.** Miguel Duhamel (Honda CBR1000RR); **6.** Eric Bostrom (Ducati 999); **7** Josh Hayes (Kawasaki ZX-10RR); **8.** Marty Craggill (Suzuki GSX-R1000); **9** Jeremy Toye (Honda CBR1000RR); **10** Lee Acree (Suzuki GSX-R1000).

Race 2

1 Mat Mladin (Suzuki GSX-R1000)

2 Aaron Yates (Suzuki GSX-R1000); **3** Ben Spies (Suzuki GSX-R1000); **4** Miguel Duhamel (Honda CBR1000RR); **5.** Neil Hodgson (Ducati 999); **6.** Josh Hayes (Kawasaki ZX-10RR); **7.** Eric Bostrom (Honda CBR1000RR); **8.** Jason Pridmore (Suzuki GSX-R1000); **9** Steve Rapp (Suzuki GSX-R1000); **10.** Cory Denton West (Suzuki GSX-R1000).

Race 2

1 Mat Mladin (Suzuki GSX-R1000)

2 Aaron Yates (Suzuki GSX-R1000); **3** Ben Spies (Suzuki GSX-R1000); **4** Miguel Duhamel (Honda CBR1000RR); **5** Neil Hodgson (Ducati 999); **6.** Josh Hayes (Kawasaki ZX-10RR); **7** Eric Bostrom (Ducati); **8** Jason Pridmore (Suzuki GSX-R1000); **9** Steve Rapp (Suzuki GSX-R1000); **10.** Cory Denton West (Suzuki GSX-R1000).

ROAD ATLANTA – Braselton, Georgia, 2-4 September, 63.5 miles/101.389km

Race 1

1 Mat Mladin (Suzuki GSX-R1000); **2** Ben Spies (Suzuki GSX-R1000); **3** Miguel Duhamel (Honda CBR1000RR); **4** Neil Hodgson (Ducati 999); **5** Eric Bostrom (Ducati 999); **6** Josh Hayes (Kawasaki ZX-10RR); **7** Jason Pridmore (Suzuki GSX-R1000); **8** Kurtis Roberts (Honda CBR1000RR); **9** Marty Craggill (Suzuki GSX-R1000); **10** Lee Acree (Suzuki GSX-R1000).

Race 2

1 Aaron Yates (Suzuki GSX-R1000); **2** Ben Spies (Suzuki GSX-R1000); **3** Neil Hodgson (Ducati 999); **4** Mat Mladin (Suzuki GSX-R1000); **5** Jake Zemke (Honda CBR1000RR); **6** Josh Hayes (Kawasaki ZX-10RR); **7** Jason Pridmore (Suzuki GSX-R1000); **8** Eric Bostrom (Ducati 999); **9** Miguel Duhamel (Honda CBR1000RR); **10** Steve Rapp (Suzuki GSX-R1000).

Final Championship Points

1.	Mat Mladin	536
2	Ben Spies	514
3	Eric Bostrom	431
4	Aaron Yates	414
5	Miguel Duhamel	392
6	Neil Hodgson	384

7 Marty Craggill, 331; 8 Steve Rapp, 305; 9 Josh Hayes, 302; 10. Lee Acree, 301.

Endurance World Championship

ASSEN 500, Assen Circuit, Holland, 12 April 2004.

Endurance World Championship, round 1. 129 laps of the 2.412-mile/3.881-km circuit, 311.148 miles/500.649 km

1 Suzuki Castrol Team, F: Vincent Philippe/Olivier Four/Matthieu Lagrive (Suzuki GSXR), 3h 01m 29.671s, 102.843 mph/165.509 km/h. **2** Yamaha GMT 94, F: Sebastien Gimbert/William Costes/David Checa (Yamaha YZF), 129 laps; **3** Yamaha Endurance Moto 38, F: Gwen Giabbani/FrÈdÈric Jond/Stephane Duterne (Yamaha YZF), 126; **4** WRT Honda Austria, A: Erwin Wilding/Karl Truchsess (Honda CBR 1000), 124; **5** Bridgestone Bikers, D: Tim Rˆthig/Ralf Schwickerath (Suzuki GSXR), 123; **6** Suzuki Jet Team, CH: Claude Alain Jaggi/Eric Monot/Sylvain Waldmeier (Suzuki GSXR), 122; **7** Diablo 666 Bolliger, GB: James Hutchins/Nick Pilborough/Mike Edwards (Kawasaki ZX10R), 122; **8** Ducati Team Spring, I: Lorenzo Mauri/Matteo Colombo/Bellezza (Ducati 999R), 122; **9** Suzuki Team Innodrom, D: Sandor Bitter/Lars Albrecht/Niggi Schmassmann (Suzuki GSXR), 122; **10** Suzuki No Limits Team, I: Roberto Ruozi/Andrea Giachino/Moreno Codeluppi (Suzuki GSXR), 121; **11** Burger King Lust Team, D: Gerd Peter Meyer/Stefan Meyer/Mattias Bormann (Suzuki), 121; **12** Yamaha Endurance Belgie, B: Danny Scheers/Koen Reymenants (Yamaha YZF), 120; **13** Benelli X-One, I: Andrea Perselli/Paolo Tessari/Maurizio Barghiacchi (Benelli Tornado), 119; **14** Pajic-Kawasaki, NL: Mile Pajic/Visscher (Kawasaki ZX10R), 118; **15** Kawasaki Endurance, D: Sebric/Hahn (Kawasaki ZX10), 118.

Fastest lap: Gimbert/Costes/Checa, 1m 21.925s, 105.969 mph/170.541 km/h.

Championship points: 1 Suzuki Castrol Team, 25; **2** Yamaha GMT 94, 20; **3** Yamaha Endurance Moto 38, 16; **4** WRT Honda Austria, 13; **5** Bridgestone Bikers, 11; **6** Suzuki Jet Team, 10.

8 HORAS NOCTURNAS DE ALBACETE, Albacete, Spain, 21 May 2004.

Endurance World Championship, round 2. 299 laps of the 2.199-mile/3.539-km circuit, 657.501 miles/1058.161 km

1 Suzuki-Castrol Team, F: Vincent Philippe/Keiichi Kitagawa/Olivier Four (Suzuki GSXR), 8h 00m 08.820s, 82.158 mph/132.220 km/h. **2** Folch Endurance 23, E: Daniel Ribalta/Salvador Cabana/Kenny Noyes (Yamaha R1), 296 laps; **3** Yamaha Austria Racing Team, A: Igor Jerman/Thomas Hinterreiter/Gwen Giabanni (Yamaha YZFR), 294; **4** Bolliger Team Switzerland, CH: Marcel Kellenberger/David Morillon/Patric Muff (Kawasaki ZX10R), 293; **5** Yamaha Phase One Endurance, GB: Warwick Nowland/Andy Notman/Damian Cudlin (Yamaha YZFR), 288; **6** Sapeurs Pompiers 18, F: Stéphane Molinier/Guillaume Pialoux/Guillaume Grelaud (Suzuki), 287; **7** Shell Endurance Academy, GB: Marko Rothlaan/Ben Wylie/Calvin Hogan (Yamaha YZFR), 287; **8** Diablo 666 Bolliger, GB: James Hutchins/Steve Mizera/Kevin Falcke (Kawasaki ZX10R), 287; **9** No Limits & RT Racing Team, I: Roberto Ruozi/Giancarlo de Matteis/Andrea Giachino (Suzuki GSXR), 284; **10** Fabi Corse, I: Eric Monot/Marc Dos Santos/Anthony Dos Santos (Suzuki GSXR), 282; **11** Bridgestone Bikers Profi, D: Tim Röthig/Stefan Strauch/Franck Heidger (Suzuki GSXR), 281; **12** Ducati Spring Team, I: Matteo Colombo/Lorenzo Mauri/Maurizio Gennari (Ducati 999), 281; **13** Team Power Bike, F: David Barrot/Patrick Vieira/Michael Lalevee (Yamaha R1), 280; **14** MVA Burger King-Lust, D: Gerd Peter Meyer/Stefan Meyer/Toni Heiler (MV Agusta), 279; **15** Projecteam Honda, D: Philipp Ludwig/Hubertus Junker/Roger Maher (Honda CBR), 272.

Fastest lap: Philippe/Kitagawa/Four, 1m 33.660s, 84.524 mph/136.028 km/h.

Championship points: 1 Suzuki-Castrol Team, 55; **2** Bolliger Team Switzerland, 36; **3** Yamaha Austria Racing Team, 30; **4** Diablo 666 Bolliger and Yamaha Phase One Endurance, 26; **6** Folch Endurance 23, 24.

SUZUKA EIGHT HOURS, Suzuka International Circuit, Japan, 31 July 2005.

Endurance World Championship, round 3. 204 laps of the 3.617-mile/5.821-km circuit, 737.868 miles/1187.484 km

1 Seven Stars Honda 7, J: Ryuichi Kiyonari/Tohru Ukawa (Honda CBR1000), 8h 01m 22.351s, 91.969 mph/148.010 km/h. **2** Seven Stars Honda 11, J: Chris Vermeulen/Katsuaki Fujiwara (Honda CBR1000), 201 laps; **3** Suzuki-Castrol Team, F: Vincent Philippe/Keiichi Kitagawa/Matthieu Lagrive (Suzuki GSXR), 196; **4** Yamaha Austria Racing Team, A: Gwen Giabanni/Igor Jerman/Horst Saiger (Yamaha YZFR), 194; **5** Yoshimura Suzuki Jomo Srixon, J: Yukio Kagayama/Atsushi Watanabe (Suzuki GSXR), 193; **6** Int Power Factory Roadway, J: Shuichi Shimizu/Hiroaki Matoba (Suzuki GSXR), 190; **7** Yamaha Phase One Endurance, GB: Warwick Nowland/Damian Cudlin/Paul Young (Yamaha YZFR), 189; **8** Akai Sanrinsha Racing Club, J: Takestsuna Morii/Hideki Matsui (Honda CBR1000), 187; **9** Shell Endurance Academy, GB: Marko Rothlaan/Ben Wylie/Calvin Hogan (Yamaha YZFR), 185; **10** DRT Banana Hands, J: Tadatoshi Okazaki/Daisuke Sato (Yamaha YZFR), 184; **11** Team Twenty One, J: Yoshiyuki Torii/Takenori Kawasuji (Suzuki GSXR), 180; **12** No Limits & RT Racing Team, I: Roberto Ruozi/Andrea Giachino/Moreno Codeluppi (Suzuki GSXR), 179; **13** Aprilia Motociclismo Test Team, I: Federico Aliverti/Daniele Vechini/Samuela de Nardi (Aprilia RSV1000), 177; **14** Team Surf Suzuki, J: Yoshinobu Yamamoto/Hisayoshi Masuda (Suzuki GSXR), 176; **15** HMF Verity, J: Yoshifumi Takamiya/Yoshinobu Takahashi (Suzuki GSXR), 174.

Fastest lap: Kagayama/Watanabe, 2m 09.849s, 100.277 mph/161.380 km/h.

Championship points: 1 Suzuki-Castrol Team, 74; **2** Yamaha Austria Racing Team, 46; **3** Yamaha Phase One Endurance, 37; **4** Bolliger Team Switzerland, 36; **5** Seven Stars Honda 7, 30; **6** Shell Endurance Academy, 28.

24 STUNDEN VON OSCHERSLEBEN, Oschersleben Circuit, Germany, 13-14 August 2005.

Endurance World Championship, round 4. 855 laps of the 2.279-mile/3.667-km circuit, 1948.545 miles/3135.285 km

1 Suzuki-Castrol Team, F: Vincent Philippe/Keiichi Kitagawa/Matthieu Lagrive (Suzuki GSXR), 24h 00m 42.339s, 81.134 mph/130.573 km/h. **2** Bolliger Team Switzerland, CH: Marcel Kellenberger/David Morillon/Roman Stamm (Kawasaki ZX10R), 832 laps; **3** Diablo 666 Bolliger, GB: James Hutchins/Steve Mizera/Russell Baker (Kawasaki ZX10R), 825; **4**

No Limits & RT Racing Team, I: Andrea Giachino/Roberto Ruozi/Eric Monot (Suzuki GSXR), 812; **5** Bridgestone Bikers Profi, D: Tim Röthig/Stefan Strauch/Toni Heiler (Suzuki GSXR), 811; **6** Suzuki Austria Team 76, A: Gerhard Klein/Malec Marjan/Sandor Bitter (Suzuki GSXR), 805; **7** Aprilia Motociclismo Test Team, I: Fabrizio Pellizzon/Daniele Veghini/Federico Aliverti (Aprilia RSV1000), 794; **8** Team Fagersjo-el.se 2, S: Eric Hulth/Jim Agombar/Niklas Carlberg (Suzuki GSXR), 794; **9** Shell Endurance Academy, GB: Marko Rothlaan/Ben Wylie/Calvin Hogan (Yamaha YZFR), 786; **10** Maco Moto Racing Team, SLO: Jiri Drazdak/Marek Svoboda/Martin Kuzma (Yamaha YZFR), 785; **11** Eurosport Benelux, NL: Eddy Peeters/Fabian Le Grelle/Marc Dos Santos (Suzuki GSXR), 782; **12** Projecteam Honda, D: Hubertus Junker/Roger Maher/Frank Spenner (Honda CBR1000), 761; **13** Innodrom Racing, D: Agoston Rosivall/Matthias Bormann/Niggi Schmassmann (Suzuki GSXR), 759; **14** Cro-Moto 1 Valvoline, CRO: Davor Barukcic/Alen Vrdoljak/Drazen Kemenovic (Kawasaki ZX10R), 755; **15** Polizei NRW, D: Wolfgang Stamm/Eric van Loock/Dirk Druve (Suzuki GSXR).

Fastest lap: Lagrive, 1m 30.676s, 90.463 mph/145.586 km/h.

Championship points: **1** Suzuki-Castrol Team, 109; **2** Bolliger Team Switzerland, 64; **3** Diablo 666 Bolliger, 48; **4** Yamaha Austria Racing Team, 46; **5** Shell Endurance Academy, 38; **6** Yamaha Phase One Endurance, 37

200 MIGLIA DI VALLELUNGA, Vallelunga Circuit, Italy, 25 September 2005.

Endurance World Championship, round 5. 79 laps of the 2.554-mile/4.110-km circuit, 201.766 miles/324.690 km

1 Suzuki-Castrol Team, F: Keiichi Kitagawa/Matthieu Lagrive (Suzuki GSXR), 2h 17m 11.868s, 88.231 mph/141.994 km/h.

2 Yamaha Phase One Endurance, GB: Warwick Nowland/Damian Cudlin (Yamaha YZFR), 79 laps; **3** Yamaha Austria Racing Team, A: Igor Jerman/Thomas Hinterreiter (Yamaha YZFR), 78; **4** Bolliger Team Switzerland, CH: Marcel Kellenberger/David Morillon (Kawasaki ZX10R), 78; **5** Ducati Spring Team, I: Matteo Colombo/Lorenzo Mauri/Maurizio Gennari (Ducati 999), 77; **6** Team Fagersjo-el.se, S: Andy Notman/Lars Carlbark (Suzuki GSXR), 77; **7** Shell Endurance Academy, GB: Calvin Hogan/Ben Wylie/Marko Rothlaan (Yamaha YZFR), 77; **8** Team X-One, I: Paolo Tessari/Riccardo Ricci/Federico Clementini (Yamaha YZFR), 77; **9** No Limits & RT Racing Team, I: Roberto Ruozi/Andrea Giachino/Moreno Codeluppi (Suzuki GSXR), 76; **10** Team RMT 21, D: Thomas Fluckiger/Thomas Roth/Marc Wildisen (Kawasaki ZX10R), 76; **11** Aprilia Motociclismo Test Team, I: Daniele Veghini/Federico Aliverti (Aprilia RSV1000), 76; **12** Fabi Corsi, I: Marc Dos Santos/Lorenzo Cangini (Suzuki GSXR), 76; **13** Team Fagersjo-el.se 2, S: Tobias Andersson/Niklas Carlberg (Suzuki GSXR), 76; **14** Team Fagersjo-el.se 3, S: Por Johanson/Jan Grevan (Suzuki GSXR), 75; **15** Maco Moto Racing Team, SLO: Martin Kuzma/Marek Svoboda (Yamaha YZFR), 75.

Fastest lap: Kitagawa/Lagrive, 1m 41.619s, 90.473 mph/145.602 km/h.

Final World Championship points

1	Suzuki-Castrol Team, F	134
2	Bolliger Team Switzerland, CH	77
3	Yamaha Austria Racing Team, A	62
4	Yamaha Phase One Endurance, GB	57
5	Diablo 666 Bolliger, GB	48
6	Shell Endurance Academy, G	47

7 No Limits & RT Racing Team, I, 43; **8** Seven Stars Honda 7, J, 30; **9=**Folch Endurance 23, E and Seven Stars Honda 11, J, 24; **11** Aprilia Motociclismo Test Team, I, 22; **12** Bridgestone Bikers Profi, D, 21; **13** Team Fagersjo-el.se, S, 20; **14=**Ducati Spring Team, I, and Team X-One, I, 16.

Isle of Man Tourist Trophy Races

ISLE OF MAN TOURIST TROPHY COURSE, 4-10 June 2005. 37.73-mile/60.72-km course.

Duke Superbike TT (6 laps, 226.38 miles/364.32 km)

1 John McGuinness (1000 Yamaha R10), 1h 49m 25.74s, 124.124 mph/199.758 km/h. **2** Adrian Archibald (1000 Suzuki GSXR), 1h 50m 02.04s; **3** Martin Finnegan (1000 Honda CBR), 1h 51m 18.16s; **4** Ian Lougher (1000 Honda CBR), 1h 51m 42.70s; **5** Raymond Porter (1000 Yamaha R1), 1h 52m 09.16s; **6** Guy Martin (1000 Suzuki), 1h 52m 22.87s; **7** Jason Griffiths (1000 Yamaha), 1h 52m 26.88s; **8** Chris Heath (998 Honda CBR), 1h 53m 05.38s; **9** Jun Maeda (1000 Honda CBR), 1h 53m 55.19s.

Fastest lap: McGuinness, 17m 50.53s, 126.879 mph/204.192 km/h.

Supersport Junior TT: Race A (4 laps, 150.92 miles/242.88 km)

1 Ian Lougher (600 Honda CBR), 1h 14m 52.84s, 120.928 mph/194.615 km/h. **2** John McGuinness (600 Yamaha R6), 1h 15m 15.46s; **3** Jason Griffiths (600 Yamaha R6), 1h 15m 50.07s; **4**Bruce Anstey (600 Suzuki GSXR), 1h 15m 56.10s; **5** Guy Martin (600 Honda CBR), 1h 16m 25.36s; **6** Raymond Porter (600 Yamaha R6), 1h 16m 29.25s; **7** Darran Lindsay (600 Honda CBR), 1h 16m 35.18s; **8** Adrian Archibald (600 Suzuki GSXR), 1h 17m 00.04s; **9** Jun Maeda (600 Honda CBR), 1h 17m 06.03s; **10** Nigel Beattie (600 Yamaha R6), 1h 17m 13.69s; **11** Ian Hutchinson (600 Honda CBR), 1h 17m 22.35s; **12** Davy Morgan (600 Yamaha R6), 1h 17m 39.77s; **13** Gary Carswell (600 Yamaha R6), 1h 18m 03.74s; **14** Chris Palmer (600 Honda), 1h 18m 19.61s; **15** Dean Silvester (600 Yamaha R6), 1h 18m 35.48s.

Fastest lap: Ryan Farquhar (600 Kawasaki ZX6R), 18m 27.54s, 122.639 mph/197.368 km/h.

IOM Steam Packet Supersport Junior TT: Race B (4 laps, 150.92 miles/242.88 km)

1 Ryan Farquhar (600 Kawasaki ZX6R), 1h 15m 01.42s, 120.697 mph/194.243 km/h. **2** Jason Griffiths (600 Yamaha R6), 1h 15m 15.72s; **3** Raymond Porter (600 Yamaha R6), 1h 15m 30.53s; **4** Guy Martin (600 Honda CBR), 1h 15m 55.99s; **5** Martin Finnegan (600 Honda CBR), 1h 16m 01.00s; **6** Jun Maeda (600 Honda CBR), 1h 16m 26.66s; **7** Ian Hutchinson (600 Honda CBR), 1h 16m 28.89s; **8** Nigel Beattie (600 Yamaha R6), 1h 16m 48.28s; **9** Gary Carswell (600 Yamaha R6), 1h 17m 07.78s; **10** Chris Palmer (600 Honda), 1h 17m 10.52s; **11** Cameron Donald (600 Honda CBR), 1h 17m 26.39s; **12** Davy Morgan (600 Yamaha R6), 1h 17m 33.35s; **13** Dean Silvester (600 Yamaha R6), 1h 18m 11.94s; **14** Kevin Mawdsley (600 Honda CBR), 1h 18m 23.89s; **15** Paul Owen (600 Honda CBR), 1h 18m 35.44s; **16** Keith Stewart (600 Yamaha R6), 1h 18m 45.43s.

Fastest lap: Griffiths, 18m 28.44s, 122.540 mph/197.209 km/h.

Scottish Life International Superstock TT (3 laps, 113.19 miles/182.16 km)

1 Bruce Anstey (1000 Suzuki GSXR), 54m 39.74s, 124.242 mph/199.948 km/h. **2** Ian Lougher (1000 Honda CBR), 55m 15.73s; **3** Ryan Farquhar (1000 Kawasaki), 55m 16.82s; **4** Jason Griffiths (1000 Yamaha), 55m 34.28s; **5** Guy Martin (1000 Suzuki GSXR), 55m 34.53s; **6** Paul Hunt (1000 Suzuki GSXR), 55m 37.39s; **7** Martin Finnegan (1000 Honda CBR), 55m 40.22s; **8** Richard Britton (998 Honda), 55m 57.54s; **9** Ian Hutchinson (1000 Honda), 56m 33.00s; **10** Chris Heath (1000 Yamaha YZF), 56m 35.93s; **11** Gary Carswell (1000 Yamaha R1), 56m 43.30s; **12** Rob Frost (1000 Suzuki GSXR), 57m 17.44s.

Fastest lap: Adrian Archibald (1000 Suzuki GSXR), 17m 52.54s, 126.641 mph/203.809 km/h (record).

Strand Shopping Centre Senior TT (6 laps, 226.38 miles/364.32 km)

1 John McGuinness (1000 Yamaha R1), 1h 49m 15.16s, 124.324 mph/200.080 km/h. **2** Ian Lougher (1000 Honda CBR), 1h 49m 49.84s; **3** Guy Martin (1000 Suzuki), 1h 50m 08.19s; **4** Martin Finnegan (1000 Honda CBR), 1h 50m 09.50s; **5** Richard Britton (998 Honda), 1h 50m 21.24s; **6** Jun Maeda (1000 Honda CBR), 1h 51m 07.10s; **7** Jason Griffiths (1000 Yamaha), 1h 51m 23.12s; **8** Ian Hutchinson (1000 Honda), 1h 52m 55.19s; **9** Nigel Beattie (1000 Yamaha), 1h 53m 20.24s; **10** Chris Palmer (1000 Yamaha R1), 1h 53m 49.29s; **11** Rob Frost (1000 Suzuki GSXR), 1h 54m 03.50s; **12** Dean Silvester (750 Suzuki), 1h 54m 29.67s; **13** Thomas Montano (1000 MV Agusta), 1h 54m 41.40s.

Fastest lap: McGuinness, 17m 46.77s, 127.326 mph/204.911 km/h (record).

Sidecar TT: Race A (3 laps, 113.19 miles/182.16 km)

1 Nick Crowe/Darren Hope (600 DMR Honda), 1h 01m 49.30s, 109.85 mph/176.786 km/h. **2** Steve Norbury/Andy Smith (600 Shelbourne), 1h 01m 51.60s; **3** John Holden/Jamie Winn (600 Honda), 1h 03m 06.50s; **4** Philip Dongworth/Stuart Castles (600 Ireson), 1h 04m 18.60s; **5** Simon Neary/Stuart Bond (600 Baker Yamaha), 1h 04m 23.20s; **6** Tony Baker/Mark Hegerty (600 Baker Yamaha), 1h 04m 40.30s; **7** Ben Dixon/Mark Lambert (600 Honda), 1h 04m 44.60s.

Fastest lap: Dave Molyneux/Daniel Sayle (600 DMR Honda), 20m 12.80s, 111.990 mph/180.230 km/h.

Hilton Hotel & Casino Sidecar TT: Race B (3 laps, 113.19 miles/182.16 km)

1 Dave Molyneux/Daniel Sayle (600 DMR Honda), 59m 06.39s, 114.901 mph/184.915 km/h. **2** Nick Crowe/Darren Hope (600 DMR Honda), 1h 00m 28.37s; **3** Steve Norbury/Andy Smith (600 Shelbourne), 1h 01m 40.06s.

Fastest lap: Molyneux/Sayle, 19m 30.49s, 116.044 mph/186.755 km/h (record).

British Championships

BRANDS HATCH INDY CIRCUIT, 28 March 2005. 1.226-mile/1.973-km circuit.

Bennetts British Superbike Championship, rounds 1 and 2 (2 x 30 laps, 36.780 miles/59.190 km)

Race 1

1 Ryuichi Kiyonari (Honda), 23m 17.575s, 94.80 mph/152.56 km/h.

2 Gregorio Lavilla (Ducati); **3** Glen Richards (Kawasaki); **4** Michael Rutter (Honda); **5** Sean Emmett (Yamaha); **6** Karl Harris (Honda); **7** Jeremy McWilliams (Honda); **8** Dean Thomas (Kawasaki); **9** John Reynolds (Suzuki); **10** Tommy Hill (Yamaha); **11** Ben Wilson (Kawasaki); **12** Danny Beaumont (Honda); **13** Jonathan Rea (Honda); **14** Tristan Palmer (Kawasaki); **15** Michael Laverty (Honda).

Fastest lap: Kiyonari, 45.954s, 96.06 mph/154.59 km/h (record).

Race 2

1 Ryuichi Kiyonari (Honda), 23m 16.796s, 94.85 mph/152.65 km/h.

2 Michael Rutter (Honda); **3** Gregorio Lavilla (Ducati); **4** Leon Haslam (Ducati); **5** Sean Emmett (Yamaha); **6** Karl Harris (Honda); **7** Glen Richards (Kawasaki); **8** Scott Smart (Suzuki); **9** John Reynolds (Suzuki); **10** Gary Mason (Honda); **11** Dean Thomas (Kawasaki); **12** Tommy Hill (Yamaha); **13** Ben Wilson (Kawasaki); **14** John McGuinness (Yamaha); **15** Michael Laverty (Honda).

Fastest lap: Lavilla, 46.093s, 95.77 mph/154.12 km/h.

Championship points: **1** Kiyonari, 50; **2** Lavilla, 36; **3** Rutter, 33; **4** Richards, 25; **5** Emmett, 22; **6** Harris, 20.

Metabo British Supersport Championship, round 1 (28 laps, 34.328 miles/55.244 km)

1 Jay Vincent (Honda), 22m 22.207s, 92.13 mph/148.27 km/h.

2 Stuart Easton (Ducati); **3** Craig Jones (Honda); **4** Leon Camier (Honda); **5** Pere Riba (Kawasaki); **6** Eugene Laverty (Honda); **7** Tom Tunstall (Honda); **8** Kieran Murphy (Honda); **9** Luke Quigley (Honda); **10** Jamie Robinson (Honda); **11** Paul Young (Honda); **12** Steven Neate (Honda); **13** Steve Allan (Kawasaki); **14** Andy Weymouth (Yamaha); **15** Lee Dickinson (Honda).

Fastest lap: Vincent, 47.242s, 93.44 mph/150.37 km/h (record).

Championship points: **1** Vincent, 25; **2** Easton, 20; **3** Jones, 16; **4** Camier, 13; **5** Riba, 11; **6** Laverty, 10.

British 125GP Championship, round 1 (21 laps, 25.746 miles/41.433 km)

1 Kev Coghlan (Honda), 18m 46.747s, 82.33 mph/132.50 km/h.

2 Rob Guiver (Honda); **3** Brian Clark (Honda); **4** Christian Elkin (Honda); **5** Bradley Smith (Honda); **6** James Webb (Honda); **7** Dan Linfoot (Honda); **8** Joel Morris (Honda); **9** Alex Lowes (Honda); **10** Alex Gault (Malaguti); **11** Kris Weston (Honda); **12** Ashley Beech (Honda); **13** B. J. Toal (Honda); **14** Matthew Kuhne (Honda); **15** Benji Dawson (Honda).

Fastest lap: Coghlan, 49.437s, 89.29 mph/143.70 km/h.

Championship points: **1** Coghlan, 25; **2** Guiver, 20; **3** Clark, 16; **4** Elkin, 13; **5** Smith, 11; **6** Webb, 10.

THRUXTON CIRCUIT, 10 April 2005. 2.356-mile/3.792-km circuit.

Bennetts British Superbike Championship, rounds 3 and 4 (2 x 22 laps, 51.832 miles/83.424 km)

Race 1

1 Ryuichi Kiyonari (Honda), 28m 05.231s, 110.72 mph/178.19 km/h.

2 Michael Rutter (Honda); **3** Gregorio Lavilla (Ducati); **4** Leon Haslam (Ducati); **5** Sean Emmett (Yamaha); **6** Karl Harris (Honda); **7** Scott Smart (Suzuki); **8** Dean Thomas (Kawasaki); **9** Glen Richards (Kawasaki); **10** Tommy Hill (Yamaha); **11**James Buckingham (Suzuki); **12** Gary Mason (Honda); **13**Steve Plater (Kawasaki); **14** John Reynolds (Suzuki); **15** Michael Laverty (Honda).

Fastest lap: Lavilla, 1m 15.699s, 112.04 mph/180.31 km/h (record).

Race 2

1 Ryuichi Kiyonari (Honda), 28m 45.734s, 108.12 mph/174.00 km/h.

2 Gregorio Lavilla (Ducati); **3** Michael Rutter (Honda); **4** Sean Emmett (Yamaha); **5** Glen Richards (Kawasaki); **6** Dean Thomas (Kawasaki); **7** Leon Haslam (Ducati); **8** Karl Harris (Honda); **9** Jeremy McWilliams (Honda); **10** Steve Plater (Kawasaki); **11** Kieran Clarke (Honda); **12** Jonathan Rea (Honda); **13** Gary Mason (Honda); **14** Steve Brogan (Honda); **15** Ben Wilson (Kawasaki).

Fastest lap: Lavilla, 1m 15.577s, 112.22 mph/180.60 km/h (record).

Championship points: **1** Kiyonari, 100; **2** Lavilla, 72; **3** Rutter, 69; **4** Emmett, 46; **5** Richards, 43; **6** Harris, 38.

Metabo British Supersport Championship, round 2 (16 laps, 37.696 miles/60.672 km)

1 Leon Camier (Honda), 20m 55.339s, 108.10 mph/173.97 km/h.

2 Stuart Easton (Ducati); **3** Jay Vincent (Honda); **4** Craig Jones (Honda); **5** Kieran Murphy (Honda); **6** Jamie Robinson (Honda); **7** Cal Crutchlow (Honda); **8** Pere Riba (Kawasaki); **9** Tom Sykes (Suzuki); **10** Simon Andrews (Suzuki); **11** Paul Young (Honda); **12** Steve Allan (Kawasaki); **13** Sam Owens (Honda); **14** Steven Neate (Honda); **15** Luke Quigley (Honda).

Fastest lap: Camier, 1m 17.580s, 109.32 mph/175.94 km/h (record).

Championship points: **1** Vincent, 41; **2** Easton, 40; **3** Camier, 38; **4** Jones, 29; **5** Murphy and Riba, 19.

British 125GP Championship, round 2 (14 laps, 32.984 miles/53.088 km)

1 Christian Elkin (Honda), 19m 18.388s, 102.50 mph/164.96 km/h.

2 Kev Coghlan (Honda); **3** Michael Wilcox (Honda); **4** Brian Clark (Honda); **5** Ashley Beech (Honda); **6** Alex Lowes (Honda); **7** Joel Morris (Honda); **8** Rob Guiver (Honda); **9** James Webb (Honda); **10** John Pearson (Honda); **11** Kris Weston (Honda); **12** James Ford (Honda); **13** Matthew Kuhne (Honda); **14** Tom Grant (Honda); **15** Paul Robinson (Honda).

Fastest lap: Coghlan, 1m 21.700s, 103.81 mph/167.07 km/h.

Championship points: **1** Coghlan, 45; **2** Elkin, 38; **3** Clark, 29; **4** Guiver, 28; **5** Lowes, Morris and Webb, 17.

MALLORY PARK CIRCUIT, 24 April 2005. 1.390-mile/2.237-km circuit.

Bennetts British Superbike Championship, rounds 5 and 6

Race 1 (25 laps, 34.750 miles/55.925 km

1 Michael Rutter (Honda), 21m 48.024s, 95.64 mph/153.92 km/h.

2 Glen Richards (Kawasaki); **3** Leon Haslam (Ducati); **4** Sean Emmett (Yamaha); **5** Scott Smart (Suzuki); **6** Dean Thomas (Kawasaki); **7** Michael Laverty (Honda); **8** Gary Mason (Honda); **9** Danny Beaumont (Honda); **10** Steve Brogan (Honda); **11** John McGuinness (Yamaha); **12** Dennis Hobbs (Yamaha); **13** Tristan Palmer (Kawasaki); **14** Jonathan Rea (Honda); **15** James Buckingham (Suzuki).

Fastest lap: Rutter, 51.590s, 96.99 mph/156.09 km/h (record).

Race 2 (12 laps, 16.680 miles/26.844 km)

1 Michael Rutter (Honda), 10m 27.220s, 95.73 mph/154.06 km/h.

2 Glen Richards (Kawasaki); **3** Gregorio Lavilla (Ducati); **4** Dean Thomas (Kawasaki); **5** Leon Haslam (Ducati); **6** Karl Harris (Honda); **7** Gary Mason (Honda); **8** Scott Smart (Suzuki); **9** Michael Laverty (Honda); **10** Sean Emmett (Yamaha); **11** Ben Wilson (Kawasaki); **12** John McGuinness (Yamaha); **13** Tristan Palmer (Kawasaki); **14** Jonathan Rea (Honda); **15** Kieran Clarke (Honda).

Fastest lap: Lavilla, 51.513s, 97.14 mph/156.33 km/h (record).

Championship points: 1 Rutter, 119; **2** Kiyonari, 100; **3** Lavilla, 88; **4** Richards, 83; **5** Emmett, 65; **6** Haslam, 62.

Metabo British Supersport Championship, round 3 (23 laps, 31.970 miles/51.451 km)

1 Leon Camier (Honda), 20m 30.490s, 93.53 mph/150.52 km/h.

2 Tom Sykes (Suzuki); **3** Craig Jones (Honda); **4** Cal Crutchlow (Honda); **5** Jamie Robinson (Honda); **6** Jay Vincent (Honda); **7** Stuart Easton (Ducati); **8** Pere Riba (Kawasaki); **9** Paul Young (Honda); **10** Eugene Laverty (Honda); **11** Luke Quigley (Honda); **12** Simon Andrews (Suzuki); **13** Gary Johnson (Kawasaki); **14** Sam Owens (Honda); **15** Lee Dickinson (Honda).

Fastest lap: Sykes, 52.808s, 94.75 mph/152.49 km/h.

Championship points: 1 Camier, 63; **2** Vincent, 51; **3** Easton, 49; **4** Jones, 45; **5** Riba, Robinson and Sykes, 27.

British 125GP Championship, round 3 (22 laps, 30.580 miles/49.214 km)

1 Christian Elkin (Honda), 20m 49.820s, 88.08 mph/141.75 km/h.

2 Dan Linfoot (Honda); **3** Rob Guiver (Honda); **4** Ashley Beech (Honda); **5** James Webb (Honda); **6** James Westmoreland (Honda); **7** John Pearson (Honda); **8** Michael Wilcox (Honda); **9** Tom Grant (Honda); **10** Matthew Kuhne (Honda); **11** Sam Lowes (Honda); **12** Joel Noon (Honda); **13** Davy Haire (Honda); **14** James Ford (Honda); **15** Daniel Harrison (Honda).

Fastest lap: Bradley Smith (Honda), 54.395s, 91.99 mph/148.04 km/h (record).

Championship points: 1 Elkin, 63; **2** Coghlan, 45; **3** Guiver, 44; **4** Clark and Linfoot, 29; **6** Beech and Webb, 28.

OULTON PARK INTERNATIONAL, 2 May 2005. 2.692-mile/4.332-km circuit.

Bennetts British Superbike Championship, rounds 7 and 8 (2 x 18 laps, 48.456 miles/77.976 km)

Race 1

1 Michael Rutter (Honda), 29m 43.001s, 97.83 mph/157.44 km/h.

2 Gregorio Lavilla (Ducati); **3** Karl Harris (Honda); **4** Leon Haslam (Ducati); **5** Glen Richards (Kawasaki); **6** Dean Thomas (Kawasaki); **7** Gary Mason (Honda); **8** James Haydon (Suzuki); **9** Scott Smart (Suzuki); **10** Kieran Clarke (Honda); **11** Steve Plater (Kawasaki); **12** Jonathan Rea (Honda); **13** Michael Laverty (Honda); **14** John Laverty (Honda); **15** Ben Wilson (Kawasaki).

Fastest lap: Rutter, 1m 37.967s, 98.92 mph/159.20 km/h.

Race 2

1 Leon Haslam (Ducati), 32m 41.250s, 88.94 mph/143.14 km/h.

2 Michael Rutter (Honda); **3** Karl Harris (Honda); **4** James Haydon (Suzuki); **5** Julien Da Costa (Kawasaki); **6** Glen Richards (Kawasaki); **7** Steve Plater (Kawasaki); **8** Kieran Clarke (Honda); **9** Jonathan Rea (Honda); **10** Michael Laverty (Honda); **11** Sean Emmett (Yamaha); **12** Jon Kirkham (Kawasaki); **13** Tristan Palmer (Kawasaki); **14** Ben Wilson (Kawasaki); **15** Dean Thomas (Kawasaki).

Fastest lap: Thomas, 1m 45.906s, 91.50 mph/147.26 km/h.

Championship points: 1 Rutter, 164; **2** Lavilla, 108; **3** Richards, 104; **4** Haslam and Kiyonari, 100; **6** Harris, 80.

Metabo British Supersport Championship, round 4 (16 laps, 43.072 miles/69.312 km)

1 Tom Sykes (Suzuki), 29m 46.937s, 86.77 mph/139.64 km/h.

2 Cal Crutchlow (Honda); **3** Paul Young (Honda); **4** Craig Jones (Honda); **5** Kieran Murphy (Honda); **6** Luke Quigley (Honda); **7** Paul Shoesmith (Yamaha); **8** Paul Seward (Kawasaki); **9** Lee Longden (Honda); **10** Steven Neate (Honda); **11** Craig Sproston (Honda); **12** Eugene Laverty (Honda); **13** Neil MacQueen (Honda); **14** Lee Dickinson (Honda); **15** Darren Cooper (Yamaha).

Fastest lap: Jamie Robinson (Honda), 1m 47.526s, 90.12 mph/145.04 km/h.

Championship points: 1 Camier, 63; **2** Jones, 58; **3** Sykes, 52; **4** Vincent, 51; **5** Easton, 49; **6** Crutchlow, 42.

British 125GP Championship, round 4 (14 laps, 37.688 miles/60.648 km)

1 Christian Elkin (Honda), 27m 02.292s, 83.63 mph/134.59 km/h.

2 Dan Linfoot (Honda); **3** Chris Jones (Honda); **4** Ashley Beech (Honda); **5** Rob Guiver (Honda); **6** Tom Grant (Honda); **7** Aaron Walker (Aprilia); **8** Brian Clark (Honda); **9** James Westmoreland (Honda); **10** Tom Hayward (Honda); **11** Sam Lowes (Honda); **12** Toby Markham (Honda); **13** James Ford (Honda); **14** Ashley Martin (Honda); **15** Jon Vincent (Honda).

Fastest lap: Elkin, 1m 52.574s, 86.08 mph/138.54 km/h.

Championship points: 1 Elkin, 88; **2** Guiver, 55; **3** Linfoot, 49; **4** Coghlan, 45; **5** Beech, 41; **6** Clark, 37.

MONDELLO PARK, 15 May 2005. 2.176-mile/3.502-km circuit.

Bennetts British Superbike Championship, rounds 9 and 10 (2 x 18 laps, 39.168 miles/63.036 km)

Race 1

1 Ryuichi Kiyonari (Honda), 30m 22.490s, 77.39 mph/124.55 km/h.

2 Michael Rutter (Honda); **3** Gregorio Lavilla (Ducati); **4** Karl Harris (Honda); **5** Scott Smart (Suzuki); **6** Michael Laverty (Honda); **7** Sean Emmett (Yamaha); **8** Gary Mason (Honda); **9** Jeremy McWilliams (Honda); **10** James Haydon (Suzuki); **11** Kieran Clarke (Honda); **12** Jon Kirkham (Kawasaki); **13** Ben Wilson (Kawasaki); **14** Steve Plater (Kawasaki); **15** Dean Thomas (Kawasaki).

Fastest lap: Glen Richards (Kawasaki), 1m 40.582s, 77.90 mph/125.37 km/h (record).

Race 2

1 Gregorio Lavilla (Ducati), 30m 21.071s, 77.45 mph/124.64 km/h.

2 Leon Haslam (Ducati); **3** Ryuichi Kiyonari (Honda); **4** Michael Laverty (Honda); **5** Michael Rutter (Honda); **6** Glen Richards (Kawasaki); **7** Karl Harris (Honda); **8** Scott Smart (Suzuki); **9** Gary Mason (Honda); **10** Jeremy McWilliams (Honda); **11** Steve Plater (Kawasaki); **12** Jon Kirkham (Kawasaki); **13** Dean Thomas (Kawasaki); **14** Tommy Hill (Yamaha); **15** Ben Wilson (Kawasaki).

Fastest lap: Lavilla, 1m 40.076s, 78.29 mph/126.00 km/h (record).

Championship points: 1 Rutter, 195; **2** Lavilla, 149; **3** Kiyonari, 141; **4** Haslam, 120; **5** Richards, 114; **6** Harris, 102.

Metabo British Supersport Championship, round 5 (16 laps, 34.816 miles/56.032 km)

1 Tom Sykes (Suzuki), 27m 27.820s, 76.08 mph/122.44 km/h.

2 Craig Jones (Honda); **3** Pere Riba (Kawasaki); **4** Cal Crutchlow (Honda); **5** Stuart Easton (Ducati); **6** Eugene Laverty (Honda); **7** Jamie Robinson (Honda); **8** Sam Owens (Honda); **9** Kieran Murphy (Honda); **10** Matt Llewellyn (Honda); **11** Steven Neate (Honda); **12** Andy Weymouth (Yamaha); **13** Gary Johnson (Kawasaki); **14** Craig Sproston (Honda); **15** Alan O Connor (Yamaha).

Fastest lap: Riba, 1m 42.042s, 76.79 mph/123.58 km/h (record).

Championship points: 1 Jones, 78; **2** Sykes, 77; **3** Camier, 63; **4** Easton, 60; **5** Crutchlow, 55; **6** Vincent, 51.

British 125GP Championship, round 5 (12 laps, 26.112 miles/42.024 km)

1 Rob Guiver (Honda), 21m 29.205s, 72.93 mph/117.37 km/h.

2 Dan Linfoot (Honda); **3** James Westmoreland (Honda); **4** Christian Elkin (Honda); **5** Bradley Smith (Honda); **6** Kris Weston (Honda); **7** Brian Clark (Honda); **8** Ashley Beech (Honda); **9** Chris Jones (Honda); **10** James Webb (Honda); **11** Joel Morris (Honda); **12** Michael Wilcox (Honda); **13** John Pearson (Honda); **14** Ashley Martin (Honda); **15** James Ford (Honda).

Fastest lap: Linfoot, 1m 46.148s, 73.81 mph/118.80 km/h (record).

Championship points: 1 Elkin, 101; **2** Guiver, 80; **3** Linfoot, 69; **4** Beech, 49; **5** Clark, 46; **6** Coghlan, 45.

CROFT CIRCUIT, 5 June 2005. 2.127-mile/3.423-km circuit.

Bennetts British Superbike Championship, rounds 11 and 12 (2 x 22 laps, 46.794 miles/75.306 km)

Race 1 (22 laps, 46.794 miles/75.306 km)

1 Ryuichi Kiyonari (Honda), 29m 58.160s, 93.68 mph/150.76 km/h.

2 Michael Rutter (Honda); **3** Gregorio Lavilla (Ducati); **4** Michael Laverty (Honda); **5** Glen Richards (Kawasaki); **6** Leon Haslam (Ducati); **7** Jonathan Rea (Honda); **8** James Haydon (Yamaha); **9** Gary Mason (Honda); **10** Dean Thomas (Kawasaki); **11** Steve Plater (Kawasaki); **12** Ben Wilson (Kawasaki); **13** Scott Smart (Suzuki); **14** Marty Nutt (Honda); **15** Steve Brogan (Honda).

Fastest lap: Kiyonari, 1m 20.931s, 94.61 mph/152.26 km/h (record).

Race 2 (14 laps, 29.778 miles/47.922 km)

1 Gregorio Lavilla (Ducati), 20m 10.015s, 88.59 mph/142.57 km/h.

2 Michael Rutter (Honda); **3** Ryuichi Kiyonari (Honda); **4** Glen Richards (Kawasaki); **5** Gary Mason (Honda); **6** Dean Thomas (Kawasaki); **7** Steve Plater (Kawasaki); **8** Kieran Clarke (Honda); **9** Steve Brogan (Honda); **10** John Laverty (Honda); **11** Chris Martin (Suzuki); **12** John Reynolds (Suzuki); **13** Scott Smart (Suzuki); **14** James Buckingham (Suzuki); **15** Tristan Palmer (Kawasaki).

Fastest lap: Lavilla, 1m 21.489s; 93.96 mph/151.22 km/h.

Championship points: 1 Rutter, 235; **2** Lavilla, 190; **3** Kiyonari, 182; **4** Richards, 138; **5** Haslam, 130; **6** Harris, 102.

Metabo British Supersport Championship, round 6 (20 laps, 42.540 miles/68.460 km)

1 Stuart Easton (Ducati), 28m 03.883s, 90.94 mph/146.35 km/h.

2 Leon Camier (Honda); **3** Craig Jones (Honda); **4** Tom Sykes (Suzuki); **5** Pere Riba (Kawasaki); **6** Jamie Robinson (Honda); **7** Rob Frost (Honda); **8** Sam Owens (Honda); **9** Tom Tunstall (Honda); **10** Kieran Murphy (Honda); **11** Craig Sproston (Honda); **12** Lee Dickinson (Honda); **13** Gary Johnson (Kawasaki); **14** Andy Weymouth (Yamaha); **15** Lee Longden (Honda).

Fastest lap: Camier, 1m 22.974s, 92.28 mph/148.51 km/h (record).

Championship points: 1 Jones, 94; **2** Sykes, 90; **3** Easton, 85; **4** Camier, 83; **5** Crutchlow, 55; **6** Riba, 54.

British 125GP Championship, round 6 (16 laps, 34.032 miles/54.768 km)

1 Chris Jones (Honda), 23m 47.574s, 85.82 mph/138.11 km/h.

2 Dan Linfoot (Honda); **3** Kris Weston (Honda); **4** James Westmoreland (Honda); **5** Rob Guiver (Honda); **6** Michael Wilcox (Honda); **7** Tom Hayward (Honda); **8** James Ford (Honda); **9** Christian Elkin (Honda); **10** Sam Lowes (Honda); **11** John Pearson (Honda); **12** William Dunlop (Honda); **13** B. J. Toal (Honda); **14** Joel Noon (Honda); **15** Alex Gault (Malaguti).

Fastest lap: Ashley Beech (Honda), 1m 27.356s, 87.65 mph/141.06 km/h (record).

Championship points: 1 Elkin, 108; **2** Guiver, 91; **3** Linfoot, 89; **4** Beech, 49; **5** Jones, 48; **6** Clark and Westmoreland, 46.

KNOCKHILL CIRCUIT, 26 June 2005. 1.299-mile/2.091-km circuit.

Bennetts British Superbike Championship, rounds 13 and 14 (2 x 30 laps, 38.970 miles/62.730 km)

Race 1

1 Ryuichi Kiyonari (Honda), 25m 04.260s, 93.23 mph/150.04 km/h.

2 Michael Rutter (Honda); **3** Michael Laverty (Honda); **4** Glen Richards (Kawasaki); **5** Leon Haslam (Ducati); **6** Gregorio Lavilla (Ducati); **7** John Reynolds (Suzuki); **8** Karl Harris (Honda); **9** Gary Mason (Honda); **10** Dean Thomas (Kawasaki); **11** James Buckingham (Suzuki); **12** Scott Smart (Kawasaki); **13** Tristan Palmer (Kawasaki); **14** Ben Wilson (Kawasaki); **15** Tommy Hill (Yamaha).

Fastest lap: Kiyonari, 49.787s, 93.89 mph/151.11 km/h (record).

Race 2

1 Ryuichi Kiyonari (Honda), 25m 06.287s, 93.10 mph/149.83 km/h.

2 Michael Rutter (Honda); **3** Gregorio Lavilla (Ducati); **4** Michael Laverty (Honda); **5** Leon Haslam (Ducati); **6** John Reynolds (Suzuki); **7** Glen Richards (Kawasaki); **8** James Haydon (Suzuki); **9** Jonathan Rea (Honda); **10** Dean Thomas (Kawasaki); **11** Karl Harris (Honda); **12** Tommy Hill (Yamaha); **13** Gary Mason (Honda); **14** Kieran Clarke (Honda); **15** Tristan Palmer (Kawasaki).

Fastest lap: Rutter, 49.651s, 94.15 mph/151.53 km/h (record).

Championship points: 1 Rutter, 275; **2** Kiyonari, 232; **3** Lavilla, 216; **4** Richards, 160; **5** Haslam, 152; **6** Harris, 115.

Metabo British Supersport Championship, round 7 (17 laps, 22.083 miles/35.547 km)

1 Leon Camier (Honda), 14m 42.469s, 90.05 mph/144.92 km/h.

2 Stuart Easton (Ducati); **3** Craig Jones (Honda); **4** Jamie Robinson (Honda); **5** Eugene Laverty (Honda); **6** Pere Riba (Kawasaki); **7** Rob Frost (Honda); **8** Cal Crutchlow (Honda); **9** Simon Andrews (Suzuki); **10** Tom Tunstall (Honda); **11** Kieran Murphy (Honda); **12** Steven Neate (Honda); **13** Torquil Paterson (Honda); **14** Bob Grant (Honda); **15** Andy Weymouth (Yamaha).

Fastest lap: Easton, 51.516s, 90.74 mph/146.04 km/h (record).

Championship points: 1 Jones, 110; **2** Camier, 108; **3** Easton, 105; **4** Sykes, 90; **5** Crutchlow and Riba, 63.

British 125GP Championship, round 7 (24 laps, 31.176 miles/50.184 km)

1 Kev Coghlan (Honda), 22m 00.076s, 84.99 mph/136.78 km/h.

2 James Westmoreland (Honda); **3** Chris Jones (Honda); **4** Bradley Smith (Honda); **5** Ashley Beech (Honda); **6** Brian Clark (Honda); **7** William Dunlop (Honda); **8** Daniel Cooper (Honda); **9** Rob Guiver (Honda); **10** Kris Weston (Honda); **11** Tom Hayward (Honda); **12** Sam Lowes (Honda); **13** Joel Noon (Honda); **14** Nathan Pallett (Honda); **15** Ashley Martin (Honda).

Fastest lap: Coghlan, 54.313s, 86.07 mph/138.52 km/h (record).

Championship points: 1 Elkin, 108; **2** Guiver, 98; **3** Linfoot, 89; **4** Coghlan, 70; **5** Westmoreland, 66; **6** Jones, 64.

SNETTERTON CIRCUIT, 10 July 2005. 1.952-mile/3.141-km circuit.

Bennetts British Superbike Championship, rounds 15 and 16 (2 x 25 laps, 48.800 miles/78.525 km)

Race 1

1 Ryuichi Kiyonari (Honda), 27m 34.719s, 106.16 mph/170.85 km/h.

2 Leon Haslam (Ducati); **3** John Reynolds (Suzuki); **4** James Haydon (Suzuki); **5** Michael Rutter (Honda); **6** Karl Harris (Honda); **7** Steve Plater (Honda); **8** Gary Mason (Honda); **9** Ben Wilson (Kawasaki); **10** Tommy Hill (Yamaha); **11** Dean

Thomas (Kawasaki); **12** Richard Wren (Yamaha); **13** Tristan Palmer (Kawasaki); **14** Scott Smart (Kawasaki); **15** Dennis Hobbs (Yamaha).
Fastest lap: Kiyonari, 1m 05.685s, 106.98 mph/172.17 km/h (record).

Race 2
1 Gregorio Lavilla (Ducati), 27m 39.538s, 105.86 mph/170.37 km/h.
2 Michael Laverty (Honda); **3** Michael Rutter (Honda); **4** John Reynolds (Suzuki); **5** Steve Plater (Honda); **6** Ben Wilson (Kawasaki); **7** Tommy Hill (Yamaha); **8** Gary Mason (Honda); **9** Dean Thomas (Kawasaki); **10** Chris Burns (Yamaha); **11** Danny Beaumont (Honda); **12** Richard Wren (Yamaha); **13** Lee Jackson (Kawasaki); **14** Scott Smart (Kawasaki); **15** Steve Brogan (Honda).
Fastest lap: Laverty, 1m 05.713s, 106.93 mph/172.09 km/h.
Championship points: **1** Rutter, 302; **2** Kiyonari, 257; **3** Lavilla, 241; **4** Haslam, 172; **5** Richards, 160; **6** Harris, 125.

Metabo British Supersport Championship, round 8 (19 laps, 37.088 miles/59.679 km)
1 Leon Camier, 21m 59.766s, 101.16 mph/162.80 km/h.
2 Pere Riba (Kawasaki); **3** Cal Crutchlow (Honda); **4** Jamie Robinson (Honda); **5** Rob Frost (Honda); **6** Tom Tunstall (Honda); **7** Sam Owens (Honda); **8** Matt Llewellyn (Honda); **9** Eugene Laverty (Honda); **10** Martin Jessopp (Ducati); **11** Steven Neate (Honda); **12** Paul Young (Honda); **13** Craig Sproston (Honda); **14** Kieran Murphy (Honda); **15** Anthony Cooper (Suzuki).
Fastest lap: Stuart Easton (Ducati), 1m 08.588s, 102.45 mph/164.88 km/h (record).
Championship points: **1** Camier, 133; **2** Jones, 110; **3** Easton, 105; **4** Sykes, 90; **5** Riba, 83; **6** Crutchlow, 79.

British 125GP Championship, round 8 (18 laps, 35.136 miles/56.538 km)
1 Chris Jones (Honda), 22m 28.057s, 93.83 mph/151.00 km/h.
2 Rob Guiver (Honda); **3** James Westmoreland (Honda); **4** Christian Elkin (Honda); **5** Brian Clark (Honda); **6** Michael Wilcox (Honda); **7** John Pearson (Honda); **8** William Dunlop (Honda); **9** James Ford (Honda); **10** Nathan Pallett (Honda); **11** Sam Lowes (Honda); **12** Joel Noon (Honda); **13** Tom Hayward (Honda); **14** Alex Barkshire (Honda); **15** Alex Gault (Malaguti).
Fastest lap: Jones, 1m 13.794s, 95.22 mph/153.25 km/h.
Championship points: **1** Elkin, 121; **2** Guiver, 118; **3** Jones and Linfoot, 89; **5** Westmoreland, 82; **6** Coghlan, 70.

SILVERSTONE INTERNATIONAL CIRCUIT, 21 August 2005. 2.213-mile/3.561-km circuit.
Bennetts British Superbike Championship, rounds 17 and 18
Race 1 (19 laps, 42.047 miles/67.659 km)
1 Gregorio Lavilla (Ducati), 27m 50.122s, 90.47 mph/145.60 km/h.
2 Leon Haslam (Ducati); **3** John Reynolds (Suzuki); **4** Karl Harris (Honda); **5** Glen Richards (Kawasaki); **6** Dean Thomas (Kawasaki); **7** Gary Mason (Honda); **8** Ryuichi Kiyonari (Honda); **9** Tommy Hill (Yamaha); **10** James Haydon (Suzuki); **11** Steve Plater (Honda); **12** Jonathan Rea (Honda); **13** Dennis Hobbs (Yamaha); **14** Tristan Palmer (Kawasaki); **15** Michael Rutter (Honda).
Fastest lap: Kiyonari, 1m 26.870s, 91.70 mph/147.59 km/h (record).

Race 2 (16 laps, 35.408 miles/56.976 km)
1 Ryuichi Kiyonari (Honda), 23m 15.938s, 91.12 mph/146.64 km/h.
2 Gregorio Lavilla (Ducati); **3** Leon Haslam (Ducati); **4** Michael Rutter (Honda); **5** Glen Richards (Kawasaki); **6** Dean Thomas (Kawasaki); **7** Gary Mason (Honda); **8** James Haydon (Suzuki); **9** Karl Harris (Honda); **10** Tommy Hill (Yamaha); **11** Jonathan Rea (Honda); **12** James Buckingham (Suzuki); **13** Dennis Hobbs (Yamaha); **14** Tristan Palmer (Kawasaki); **15** Kieran Clarke (Honda).
Fastest lap: Lavilla, 1m 26.681s, 91.90 mph/147.91 km/h (record).
Championship points: **1** Rutter, 316; **2** Kiyonari, 290; **3** Lavilla, 286; **4** Haslam, 208; **5** Richards, 182; **6** Harris, 145.

Metabo British Supersport Championship, round 9 (12 laps, 26.556 miles/42.732 km)
1 Pere Riba (Kawasaki), 18m 06.455s, 87.74 mph/141.20 km/h.
2 Craig Jones (Honda); **3** Cal Crutchlow (Honda); **4** Leon Camier (Honda); **5** Jamie Robinson (Honda); **6** Stuart Easton (Ducati); **7** Julien Da Costa (Suzuki); **8** Simon Andrews (Suzuki); **9** Rob Frost (Honda); **10** Jay Vincent (Honda); **11** Steven Neate (Honda); **12** Tom Tunstall (Honda); **13** Martin Jessopp (Ducati); **14** Andy Weymouth (Yamaha); **15** Gary Johnson (Kawasaki).
Fastest lap: Riba, 1m 29.515s, 89.00 mph/143.23 km/h.
Championship points: **1** Camier, 146; **2** Jones, 130; **3** Easton, 115; **4** Riba, 108; **5** Crutchlow, 95; **6** Sykes, 90.

British 125GP Championship, round 1 (12 laps, 26.556 miles/42.732 km)
1 James Westmoreland (Honda), 18m 54.020s, 84.06 mph/135.28 km/h.
2 Chris Jones (Honda); **3** Kev Coghlan (Honda); **4** Bradley Smith (Honda); **5** Brian Clark (Honda); **6** Rob Guiver (Honda); **7** Christian Elkin (Honda); **8** Dan Linfoot (Honda); **9** Ashley Beech (Honda); **10** Michael Wilcox (Honda); **11** Tom Hayward (Honda); **12** Sam Lowes (Honda); **13** James Ford (Honda); **14** Nathan Pallett (Honda); **15** Alex Gault (Malaguti).
Fastest lap: Westmoreland, 1m 32.917s, 85.74 mph/137.98 km/h (record).
Championship points: **1** Elkin, 130; **2** Guiver, 128; **3** Jones, 109; **4** Westmoreland, 107; **5**Linfoot, 97; **6** Coghlan, 86.

CADWELL PARK CIRCUIT, 29 August 2005. 2.180-mile/3.508-km circuit.
Bennetts British Superbike Championship, rounds 19 and 20 (2 x 18 laps, 39.240 miles/63.144 km)
Race 1
1 Tommy Hill (Yamaha), 27m 41.871s, 85.00 mph/136.79 km/h.
2 Gregorio Lavilla (Ducati); **3** Glen Richards (Kawasaki); **4** Karl Harris (Honda); **5** Ryuichi Kiyonari (Honda); **6** Leon Haslam (Ducati); **7** James Haydon (Suzuki); **8** Michael Rutter (Honda); **9** Dean Thomas (Kawasaki); **10** James Buckingham (Suzuki); **11** Gary Mason (Honda); **12** John Reynolds (Suzuki); **13** Sean Emmett (Yamaha); **14** Ben Wilson (Kawasaki); **15** Danny Beaumont (Honda).
Fastest lap: Kiyonari, 1m 28.409s, 88.76 mph/142.86 km/h (record).

Race 2
1 Leon Haslam (Ducati), 26m 41.146s, 88.22 mph/141.98 km/h.
2 Gregorio Lavilla (Ducati); **3** Ryuichi Kiyonari (Honda); **4** Tommy Hill (Yamaha); **5** Karl Harris (Honda); **6** James Haydon (Suzuki); **7** Dean Thomas (Kawasaki); **8** John Reynolds (Suzuki); **9** Steve Plater (Honda); **10** Gary Mason (Honda); **11** James Buckingham (Suzuki); **12** Tristan Palmer (Kawasaki); **13** Kieran Clarke (Honda); **14** Chris Martin (Suzuki); **15** Glen Richards (Kawasaki).
Fastest lap: Lavilla, 1m 28.098s, 89.08 mph/143.36 km/h (record).
Championship points: **1** Lavilla, 326; **2** Rutter, 324; **3** Kiyonari, 317; **4** Haslam, 243; **5** Richards, 199; **6** Harris, 169.

Metabo British Supersport Championship, round 10 (12 laps, 26.160 miles/42.096 km)
1 Cal Crutchlow (Honda), 18m 22.791s, 85.39 mph/137.42 km/h.
2 Simon Andrews (Suzuki); **3** Leon Camier (Honda); **4** Craig Jones (Honda); **5** Pere Riba (Kawasaki); **6** Eugene Laverty (Honda); **7** Rob Frost (Honda); **8** Jay Vincent (Honda); **9** Julien Da Costa (Suzuki); **10** Steven Neate (Honda); **11** Tom Tunstall (Honda); **12** Matt Llewellyn (Honda); **13** Martin Jessopp (Ducati); **14** Gary Johnson (Kawasaki); **15** Kieran Murphy (Honda).
Fastest lap: Crutchlow, 1m 30.784s, 86.44 mph/139.12 km/h (record).
Championship points: **1** Camier, 162; **2** Jones, 143; **3** Crutchlow, 120; **4** Riba, 119; **5** Easton, 115; **6** Sykes, 90.

British 125GP Championship, round 10 (12 laps, 26.160 miles/42.096 km)
1 James Westmoreland (Honda), 18m 54.972s, 82.97 mph/133.53 km/h.
2 Rob Guiver (Honda); **3** Alex Lowes (Honda); **4** Christian Elkin (Honda); **5** Daniel Cooper (Honda); **6** Dan Linfoot (Honda); **7** Aaron Walker (Aprilia); **8** Michael Wilcox (Honda); **9** Kris Weston (Honda); **10** Joel Noon (Honda); **11** James Ford (Honda); **12** Tom Hayward (Honda); **13** Dean Hipwell (Honda); **14** Ashley Martin (Honda); **15** Alex Barkshire (Honda).
Fastest lap: Westmoreland, 1m 32.945s, 84.43 mph/135.88 km/h (record).
Championship points: **1** Guiver, 148; **2** Elkin, 143; **3** Westmoreland, 132; **4** Jones, 109; **5** Linfoot, 107; **6** Coghlan, 86.

OULTON PARK INTERNATIONAL, 11 September 2005. 2.769-mile/4.456-km circuit.
Bennetts British Superbike Championship, rounds 21 and 22 (2 x 18 laps, 49.842 miles/80.208 km)

Race 1
1 Ryuichi Kiyonari (Honda), 29m 15.364s, 99.37 mph/159.92 km/h.
2 Gregorio Lavilla (Ducati); **3** John Reynolds (Suzuki); **4** Leon Haslam (Ducati); **5** Glen Richards (Kawasaki); **6** James Haydon (Suzuki); **7** Tommy Hill (Yamaha); **8** Karl Harris (Honda); **9** Gary Mason (Honda); **10** Michael Rutter (Honda); **11** Dean Thomas (Kawasaki); **12** James Buckingham (Suzuki); **13** Sean Emmett (Yamaha); **14** Ben Wilson (Kawasaki); **15** Tristan Palmer (Kawasaki).
Fastest lap: Lavilla, 1m 36.314s, 100.62 mph/161.93 km/h (record).

Race 2
1 Ryuichi Kiyonari (Honda), 29m 14.768s, 99.41 mph/159.98 km/h.
2 Gregorio Lavilla (Ducati); **3** John Reynolds (Suzuki); **4** Leon Haslam (Ducati); **5** Karl Harris (Honda); **6** Tommy Hill (Yamaha); **7** Dean Thomas (Kawasaki); **8** Glen Richards (Kawasaki); **9** Gary Mason (Honda); **10** Steve Plater (Honda); **11** Sean Emmett (Yamaha); **12** James Buckingham (Suzuki); **13** Richard Wren (Yamaha); **14** Steve Brogan (Honda); **15** John McGuinness (Honda).
Fastest lap: Reynolds, 1m 36.698s, 100.22 mph/161.29 km/h.
Championship points: **1** Kiyonari, 367; **2** Lavilla, 366; **3** Rutter, 330; **4** Haslam, 269; **5** Richards, 218; **6** Harris, 188.

Metabo British Supersport Championship, round 11 (16 laps, 44.304 miles/71.296 km)
1 Cal Crutchlow (Honda), 26m 47.948s, 96.43 mph/155.19 km/h.
2 Leon Camier (Honda); **3** Tom Sykes (Suzuki); **4** Craig Jones (Honda); **5** Pere Riba (Kawasaki); **6** Stuart Easton (Ducati); **7** Jamie Robinson (Honda); **8** Matt Llewellyn (Honda); **9** Simon Andrews (Suzuki); **10** Jay Vincent (Honda); **11** Martin Jessopp (Ducati); **12** Rob Frost (Honda); **13** Steven Neate (Honda); **14** Tom Tunstall (Honda); **15** Pete Spalding (Honda).
Fastest lap: Crutchlow, 1m 39.357s, 97.53 mph/156.97 km/h (record).
Championship points: **1** Camier, 182; **2** Jones, 156; **3** Crutchlow, 145; **4** Riba, 130; **5** Easton, 125; **6** Sykes, 106.

British 125GP Championship, round 11 (14 laps, 38.766 miles/62.384 km)
1 Bradley Smith (Honda), 25m 07.556s, 89.99 mph/144.82 km/h.
2 Rob Guiver (Honda); **3** James Westmoreland (Honda); **4** Kev Coghlan (Honda); **5** Dan Linfoot (Honda); **6** Ashley Beech (Honda); **7** Christian Elkin (Honda); **8** Aaron Walker (Aprilia); **9** Daniel Cooper (Honda); **10** John Pearson (Honda); **11** James Ford (Honda); **12** Kris Weston (Honda); **13** Nathan Pallett (Honda); **14** Tom Hayward (Honda); **15** Joel Noon (Honda).
Fastest lap: Westmoreland, 1m 45.819s, 91.58 mph/147.38 km/h (record).
Championship points: **1** Guiver, 168; **2** Elkin, 152; **3** Westmoreland, 148; **4** Linfoot, 118; **5** Jones, 109; **6** Coghlan, 99.

DONINGTON PARK GRAND PRIX CIRCUIT, 25 September 2005. 2.500-mile/4.023-km circuit.
Bennetts British Superbike Championship, rounds 23 and 24 (2 x 20 laps, 50.000 miles/80.460 km)

Race 1
1 Gregorio Lavilla (Ducati), 30m 49.746s, 97.25 mph/156.51 km/h.
2 Ryuichi Kiyonari (Honda); **3** Leon Haslam (Ducati); **4** Glen Richards (Kawasaki); **5** John Reynolds (Suzuki); **6** Michael Rutter (Honda); **7** Scott Smart (Kawasaki); **8** Tommy Hill (Yamaha); **9** Dean Thomas (Kawasaki); **10** Gary Mason (Honda); **11** Steve Plater (Honda); **12** Ben Wilson (Kawasaki); **13** Sean Emmett (Yamaha); **14** Julien Da Costa (Kawasaki); **15** James Buckingham (Suzuki).
Fastest lap: Lavilla, 1m 31.718s, 98.12 mph/157.91 km/h (record).

Race 2
1 Gregorio Lavilla (Ducati), 31m 26.230s, 95.36 mph/153.47 km/h.
2 Leon Haslam (Ducati); **3** Ryuichi Kiyonari (Honda); **4** Michael Rutter (Honda); **5** James Haydon (Suzuki); **6** Dean Thomas (Kawasaki); **7** Gary Mason (Honda); **8** Scott Smart (Kawasaki); **9** Karl Harris (Honda); **10** Michael Laverty (Honda); **11** Jonathan Rea (Honda); **12** Dean Ellison (Honda); **13** Ben Wilson (Kawasaki); **14** Marty Nutt (Honda); **15** Luke Quigley (Yamaha).
Fastest lap: Lavilla, 1m 32.463s, 97.33 mph/156.64 km/h.
Championship points: **1** Lavilla, 416; **2** Kiyonari, 403; **3** Rutter, 353; **4** Haslam, 305; **5** Richards, 231; **6** Harris, 195.

Metabo British Supersport Championship, round 12 (18 laps, 45.000 miles/72.414 km)
1 Pere Riba (Kawasaki), 32m 44.740s, 82.39 mph/132.59 km/h.
2 Jay Vincent (Honda); **3** Eugene Laverty (Honda); **4** Craig Jones (Honda); **5** Stuart Easton (Ducati); **6** Jamie Robinson (Honda); **7** Leon Camier (Honda); **8** Simon Andrews (Suzuki); **9** Matt Llewellyn (Honda); **10** Lee Dickinson (Honda); **11** Gary Johnson (Kawasaki); **12** Craig Sproston (Honda); **13** Steven Neate (Honda); **14** Kieran Murphy (Honda); **15** Tom Tunstall (Honda).
Fastest lap: Jones, 1m 46.159s, 84.77 mph/136.43 km/h.
Championship points: **1** Camier, 191; **2** Jones, 169; **3** Riba, 155; **4** Crutchlow, 145; **5** Easton, 136; **6** Sykes, 106.

British 125GP Championship, round 12 (15 laps, 37.500 miles/60.345 km)
1 James Westmoreland (Honda), 25m 48.752s, 87.09 mph/140.16 km/h.
2 Christian Elkin (Honda); **3** Ashley Beech (Honda); **4** Michael Wilcox (Honda); **5** Matthieu Lussiana (Honda); **6** Kris Weston (Honda); **7** Brian Clark (Honda); **8** Clement Dunikowski (Honda); **9** Tom Hayward (Honda); **10** Dean Hipwell (Honda); **11** James Ford (Honda); **12** William Dunlop (Honda); **13** Nathan Pallett (Honda); **14** Kyle Kentish (Honda); **15** Ben Tye (Honda).
Fastest lap: Westmoreland, 1m 41.848s, 88.36 mph/142.21 km/h.
Championship points: **1** Westmoreland, 173; **2** Elkin, 172; **3** Guiver, 168; **4** Linfoot, 118; **5** Jones, 109; **6** Coghlan, 99.

BRAND HATCH GRAND PRIX CIRCUIT, 9 October 2005. 2.608-mile/4.197-km circuit.
Bennetts British Superbike Championship, rounds 25 and 26 (2 x 20 laps, 52.160 miles/83.940 km)

Race 1
1 Gregorio Lavilla (Ducati), 29m 07.520s, 107.50 mph/173.00 km/h.
2 Leon Haslam (Ducati); **3** James Haydon (Suzuki); **4** Ryuichi Kiyonari (Honda); **5** Dean Thomas (Kawasaki); **6** Michael Rutter (Honda); **7** Gary Mason (Honda); **8** Steve Plater (Honda); **9** Jeremy McWilliams (Honda); **10** Jonathan Rea (Honda); **11** Michael Laverty (Honda); **12** Scott Smart (Kawasaki); **13** Ben Wilson (Kawasaki); **14** Kieran Clarke (Honda); **15** David Johnson (Kawasaki).
Fastest lap: Haslam, 1m 26.631s, 108.38 mph/174.42 km/h (record).

Race 2
1 Leon Haslam (Ducati), 28m 58.591s, 108.05 mph/173.89 km/h.
2 Gregorio Lavilla (Ducati); **3** Steve Plater (Honda); **4** Ryuichi Kiyonari (Honda); **5** Dean Thomas (Kawasaki); **6** Glen Richards (Kawasaki); **7** Gary Mason (Honda); **8** Michael Rutter (Honda); **9** Tommy Hill (Yamaha); **10** Jonathan Rea (Honda); **11** Michael Laverty (Honda); **12** Ben Wilson (Kawasaki); **13** Danny Beaumont (Honda); **14** James Buckingham (Suzuki); **15** Sean Emmett (Yamaha).
Fastest lap: Lavilla, 1m 25.728s, 109.52 mph/176.26 km/h (record).

Metabo British Supersport Championship, round 13 (16 laps, 41.728 miles/67.152 km)

1 Stuart Easton (Ducati), 23m 49.879s, 105.11 mph/169.16 km/h.

2 Craig Jones (Honda); **3** Cal Crutchlow (Honda); **4** Tom Sykes (Suzuki); **5** Leon Camier (Honda); **6** Eugene Laverty (Honda); **7** Jamie Robinson (Honda); **8** Rob Frost (Honda); **9** Simon Andrews (Suzuki); **10** Tom Tunstall (Honda); **11** Steven Neate (Honda); **12** Martin Jessopp (Ducati); **13** Gary Johnson (Kawasaki); **14** Joe Dickinson (Honda); **15** Craig Sproston (Honda).

Fastest lap: Pere Riba (Kawasaki), 1m 28.688s, 105.87 mph/170.38 km/h (record).

British 125GP Championship, round 13 (15 laps, 39.120 miles/62.955 km)

1 Christian Elkin (Honda), 23m 59.561s, 97.88 mph/157.52 km/h.

2 Sam Lowes (Honda); **3** Dan Linfoot (Honda); **4** Aaron Walker (Aprilia); **5** Joel Noon (Honda); **6** James Ford (Honda); **7** Kris Weston (Honda); **8** Nathan Pallett (Honda); **9** John Pearson (Honda); **10** Nikki Coates (Honda); **11** Ben Tye (Honda); **12** Alex Barkshire (Honda); **13** Michael Smith (Honda); **14** Anthony Rogers (Honda); **15** Paul Dobbs (Honda).

Fastest lap: Elkin, 1m 34.600s, 99.25 mph/159.73 km/h (record).

Final British Superbike Championship points

1	Gregorio Lavilla	461
2	Ryuichi Kiyonari	429
3	Michael Rutter	371
4	Leon Haslam	350
5	Glen Richards	241
6	Dean Thomas,	198

7 Karl Harris, 195; **8** Gary Mason, 174; **9** John Reynolds, 139; **10** Michael Laverty, 129; **11** James Haydon, 126; **12** Tommy Hill, 123; **13** Steve Plater, 111; **14** Scott Smart, 97; **15** Sean Emmett, 94.

Final British Supersport Championship points

1	Leon Camier	202
2	Craig Jones	189
3	Stuart Easton	161
4	Cal Crutchlow	161
5	Pere Riba	155
6	Tom Sykes	119

7 Jamie Robinson, 112; **8** Jay Vincent, 91; **9** Eugene Laverty, 84; **10** Simon Andrews, 67; **11** Rob Frost, 57; **12** Kieran Murphy, 53; **13** Tom Tunstall, 50; **14** Steven Neate, 48; **15** Paul Young, 37.

Final British 125GP Championship points

1	Christian Elkin	197
2	James Westmoreland	173
3	Rob Guiver	168
4	Dan Linfoot	134
5	Chris Jones	109
6	Kev Coghlan	99

; **7** Ashley Beech, 93; **8** Brian Clark, 87; **9** Michael Wilcox, 75; **10** Bradley Smith, 73; **11** Kris Weston, 72; **12** James Ford, 53; **13** Sam Lowes, 49; **14** John Pearson, 45; **15** Tom Hayward, 41.

Supersport World Championship

LOSAIL, Qatar, 26 February 2005. 3.343-mile/5.380-km circuit.

Supersport World Championsip, round 1 (18 laps, 60.174 miles/96.840 km)

1 Katsuaki Fujiwara, J (Honda), 37m 54.414s, 95.244 mph/153.281 km/h.

2 Sébastien Charpentier, F (Honda); **3** Michel Fabrizio, I (Honda); **4** Kevin Curtain, AUS (Yamaha); **5** Fabien Foret, F (Honda); **6** Broc Parkes, AUS (Yamaha); **7** Stéphane Chambon, F (Honda); **8** Javi Fores, E (Suzuki); **9** Gianluca Nannelli, I (Ducati); **10** Tatu Lauslehto, SF (Honda); **11** Andrea Berta, I (Ducati); **12** Tomas Miksovsky, CZ (Honda); **13** Pawel Szkopek, POL (Honda); **14** Matteo Baiocco, I (Kawasaki).

Fastest lap: Charpentier, 2m 04.686s, 96.520 mph/155.334 km/h (record).

Championship points: **1** Fujiwara, 25; **2** Charpentier, 20; **3** Fabrizio, 16; **4** Curtain, 13; **5** Foret, 11; **6** Parkes, 10.

PHILLIP ISLAND, Australia, 3 April 2005. 2.762-mile/4.445-km circuit.

Supersport World Championship, round 2 (21 laps, 58.002 miles/93.345 km)

1 Sébastien Charpentier, F (Honda), 34m 28.920s, 100.926 mph/162.424 km/h.

2 Kevin Curtain, AUS (Yamaha); **3** Fabien Foret, F (Honda); **4** Katsuaki Fujiwara, J (Honda); **5** Jurgen van den Goorbergh, NL (Ducati); **6** Johan Stigefelt, S (Honda); **7** Broc Parkes, AUS (Yamaha); **8** Stéphane Chambon, F (Honda); **9** Tatu Lauslehto, SF (Honda); **10** Christophe Cogan, F (Suzuki); **11** Javi Fores, E (Suzuki); **12** David Garcia, E (Kawasaki); **13** Tomas Miksovsky, CZ (Honda); **14** Pawel Szkopek, POL (Honda).

Fastest lap: Charpentier, 1m 37.438s, 102.047 mph/164.228 km/h.

Championship points: **1** Charpentier, 45; **2** Fujiwara, 38; **3** Curtain, 33; **4** Foret, 27; **5** Parkes, 19; **6** Chambon, 17.

VALENCIA, Spain, 24 April 2005. 2.489-mile/4.005-km circuit.

Supersport World Championship, round 3 (23 laps, 57.247 miles/92.115 km)

1 Sébastien Charpentier, F (Honda), 38m 27.276s, 89.307 mph/143.725 km/h.

2 Katsuaki Fujiwara, J (Honda); **3** Kevin Curtain, AUS (Yamaha); **4** Michel Fabrizio, I (Honda); **5** Fabien Foret, F (Honda); **6** Broc Parkes, AUS (Yamaha); **7** Barry Veneman, NL (Suzuki); **8** Gianluca Nannelli, I (Ducati); **9** Stéphane Chambon, F (Honda); **10** Johan Stigefelt, S (Honda); **11** Javi Fores, E (Suzuki); **12** Werner Daemen, B (Honda); **13** Sébastien Le Grelle, B (Honda); **14** Arturo Tizon, E (Yamaha); **15** Tatu Lauslehto, SF (Honda).

Fastest lap: Charpentier, 1m 38.976s, 90.516 mph/145.672 km/h.

Championship points: **1** Charpentier, 70; **2** Fujiwara, 58; **3** Curtain, 49; **4** Foret, 38; **5** Fabrizio and Parkes, 29.

MONZA, Italy, 8 May 2005. 3.600-mile/5.793-km circuit.

Supersport World Championship, round 4 (16 laps, 57.600 miles/92.688 km)

1 Katsuaki Fujiwara, J (Honda), 30m 15.930s, 114.177 mph/183.750 km/h.

2 Sébastien Charpentier, F (Honda); **3** Gianluca Nannelli, I (Ducati); **4** Michel Fabrizio, I (Honda); **5** Kevin Curtain, AUS (Yamaha); **6** Tatu Lauslehto, SF (Honda); **7** Broc Parkes, AUS (Yamaha); **8** Stéphane Chambon, F (Honda); **9** Ivan Goi, I (Yamaha); **10** Sébastien Le Grelle, B (Honda); **11** Javi Fores, E (Suzuki); **12** Barry Veneman, NL (Suzuki); **13** Johan Stigefelt, S (Honda); **14** Tomas Miksovsky, CZ (Honda); **15** Matteo Baiocco, I (Kawasaki).

Fastest lap: Charpentier, 1m 52.726s, 114.956 mph/185.004 km/h.

Championship points: **1** Charpentier, 90; **2** Fujiwara, 83; **3** Curtain, 60; **4** Fabrizio, 42; **5** Foret and Parkes, 38.

SILVERSTONE, Great Britain, 29 May 2005. 2.213-mile/3.561-km circuit.

Supersport World Championship, round 5 (28 laps, 61.964 miles/99.708 km)

1 Sébastien Charpentier, F (Honda), 41m 53.540s, 88.736 mph/142.806 km/h.

2 Kevin Curtain, AUS (Yamaha); **3** Fabien Foret, F (Honda); **4** Stéphane Chambon, F (Honda); **5** Broc Parkes, AUS (Yamaha); **6** Barry Veneman, NL (Suzuki); **7** Gianluca Nannelli, I (Ducati); **8** Alessio Corradi, I (Ducati); **9** Katsuaki Fujiwara, J (Honda); **10** Tatu Lauslehto, SF (Honda); **11** Sébastien Le Grelle, B (Honda); **12** Javi Fores, E (Suzuki); **13** Julien Da Costa, F (Kawasaki); **14** Tom Tunstall, GB (Honda); **15** Jarno Janssen, NL (Suzuki).

Fastest lap: Charpentier, 1m 29.027s, 89.476 mph/143.997 km/h (record).

Championship points: **1** Charpentier, 115; **2** Fujiwara, 90; **3** Curtain, 80; **4** Foret, 54; **5** Parkes, 49; **6** Chambon, 45.

MISANO, Italy, 26 June 2005. 2.523-mile/4.060-km circuit.

Supersport World Championship, round 6 (23 laps, 58.029 miles/93.380 km)

1 Sébastien Charpentier, F (Honda), 38m 14.344s, 91.043 mph/146.520 km/h.

2 Fabien Foret, F (Honda); **3** Katsuaki Fujiwara, J (Honda); **4** Kevin Curtain, AUS (Yamaha); **5** Broc Parkes, AUS (Yamaha); **6** Simone Sanna, I (Honda); **7** Javi Fores, E (Suzuki); **8** Alessandro Antonello, I (Kawasaki); **9** Cristiano Migliorati, I (Kawasaki); **10** Tatu Lauslehto, SF (Honda); **11** Robbin Harms, DK (Honda); **12** Barry Veneman, NL (Suzuki); **13** Johan Stigefelt, S (Honda); **14** Camillo Mariottini, I (Honda); **15** Stéphane Chambon, F (Honda).

Fastest lap: Charpentier, 1m 38.821s, 91.903 mph/147.904 km/h.

Championship points: **1** Charpentier, 140; **2** Fujiwara, 106; **3** Curtain, 93; **4** Foret, 74; **5** Parkes, 60; **6** Chambon, 46.

BRNO, Czech Republic, 17 July 2005. 3.357-mile/5.403-km circuit.

Supersport World Championship, round 7 (18 laps, 60.426 miles/97.254 km)

1 Sébastien Charpentier, F (Honda), 38m 44.765s, 93.580 mph/150.602 km/h.

2 Michel Fabrizio, I (Honda); **3** Gianluca Nannelli, I (Ducati); **4** Robbin Harms, DK (Honda); **5** Javi Fores, E (Suzuki); **6** Craig Jones, GB (Honda); **7** Stéphane Chambon, F (Honda); **8** Alessio Corradi, I (Ducati); **9** Werner Daemen, B (Honda); **10** Barry Veneman, NL (Suzuki); **11** Johan Stigefelt, S (Honda); **12** Tatu Lauslehto, SF (Honda); **13** Cristiano Migliorati, I (Kawasaki); **14** Matthieu Lagrive, F (Suzuki); **15** Sébastien Le Grelle, B (Honda).

Fastest lap: Charpentier, 2m 07.316s, 94.931 mph/152.776 km/h (record).

Championship points: **1** Charpentier, 165; **2** Fujiwara, 106; **3** Curtain, 93; **4** Foret, 74; **5**Fabrizio, 62; **6** Parkes, 60.

BRANDS HATCH, Great Britain, 7 August 2005. 2.608-mile/4.197-km circuit.

Supersport World Championship, round 8 (23 laps, 59.984 miles/96.531 km)

1 Sébastien Charpentier, F (Honda), 34m 33.153s, 104.157 mph/167.625 km/h.

2 Michel Fabrizio, I (Honda); **3** Kevin Curtain, AUS (Yamaha); **4** Stéphane Chambon, F (Honda); **5** Fabien Foret, F (Honda); **6** Katsuaki Fujiwara, J (Honda); **7** Alessio Corradi, I (Ducati); **8** Craig Jones, GB (Honda); **9** Matthieu Lagrive, F (Suzuki); **10** Cal Crutchlow, GB (Honda); **11** Javi Fores, E (Suzuki); **12** Tom Tunstall, GB (Honda); **13** Robbin Harms, DK (Honda); **14** Tatu Lausleto, SF (Honda); **15** Johan Stigefelt, S (Honda).

Fastest lap: Charpentier, 1m 29.380s, 105.040 mph/169.045 km/h.

Championship points: **1** Charpentier, 190; **2** Fujiwara, 116; **3** Curtain, 109; **4** Foret, 85; **5** Fabrizio, 82; **6** Chambon, 68.

ASSEN, Holland, 4 September 2005. 3.726-mile/5.997-km circuit.

Supersport World Championship, round 9 (16 laps, 59.616 miles/99.952 km)

1 Fabien Foret, F (Honda), 34m 37.800s, 103.301 mph/166.247 km/h.

2 Sébastien Charpentier, F (Honda); **3** Michel Fabrizio, I (Honda); **4** Kevin Curtain, AUS (Yamaha); **5** Katsuaki Fujiwara, J (Honda); **6** Robbin Harms, DK (Honda); **7** Broc Parkes, AUS (Yamaha); **8** Stéphane Chambon, F (Honda); **9** Tatu Lauslehto, SF (Honda); **10** Javi Fores, E (Suzuki); **11** Matthieu Lagrive, F (Suzuki); **12** Johan Stigefelt, S (Honda); **13** Arie Vos, NL (Honda); **14** Jarno Janssen, NL (Suzuki); **15** Vesa Kallio, SF (Yamaha).

Fastest lap: Fujiwara, 2m 08.865s, 104.100 mph/167.533 km/h (record).

Championship points: **1** Charpentier, 210; **2** Fujiwara, 127; **3** Curtain, 122; **4** Foret, 110; **5** Fabrizio, 98; **6** Chambon, 76.

LAUSITZ, Germany, 11 September 2005. 2.650-mile/4.265-km circuit.

Supersport World Championship, round 10 (23 laps, 60.950 miles/98.095 km)

1 Kevin Curtain, AUS (Yamaha), 39m 39.394s, 92.222 mph/148.417 km/h.

2 Broc Parkes, AUS (Yamaha); **3** Fabien Foret, F (Honda); **4** Katsuaki Fujiwara, J (Honda); **5** Michel Fabrizio, I (Honda); **6** Stéphane Chambon, F (Honda); **7** Alessio Corradi, I (Ducati); **8** Johan Stigefelt, S (Honda); **9** Tatu Lauslehto, SF (Honda); **10** Werner Daemen, B (Honda); **11** Arne Tode, D (Honda); **12** Kai Borre Andersen, NOR (Kawasaki); **13** Robbin Harms, DK (Honda); **14** Javi Fores, E (Suzuki); **15** Jarno Janssen, NL (Suzuki).

Fastest lap: Curtain, 1m 42.438s, 93.135 mph/149.886 km/h (record).

Championship points: **1** Charpentier, 210; **2** Curtain, 147; **3** Fujiwara, 140; **4** Foret, 126; **5** Fabrizio, 109; **6** Parkes, 89.

IMOLA, Italy, 2 October 2005. 3.065-mile/4.933-km circuit.

Supersport World Championship, round 11 (21 laps, 64.365 miles/103.593 km)

1 Gianluca Nannelli, I (Ducati), 42m 55.695s, 89.968 mph/144.790 km/h.

2 Kevin Curtain, AUS (Yamaha); **3** Alessio Corradi, I (Ducati); **4** Michel Fabrizio, I (Honda); **5** Broc Parkes, AUS (Yamaha); **6** Alessandro Antonello, I (Kawasaki); **7** Arie Vos, NL (Honda); **8** Johan Stigefelt, S (Honda); **9** Camillo Mariottini, I (Honda); **10** Matthieu Lagrive, F (Suzuki); **11** Fabien Foret, F (Honda); **12** Julien Enjolras, F (Yamaha); **13** Tomas Miksovsky, CZ (Honda); **14** Sami Penna, SF (Honda); **15** Niccolo Canepa, I (Kawasaki).

Fastest lap: Fabrizio, 1m 52.646s, 97.960 mph/157.651 km/h (record).

Championship points: **1** Charpentier, 210; **2** Curtain, 167; **3** Fujiwara, 140; **4** Foret, 131; **5** Fabrizio, 122; **6** Parkes, 100.

MAGNY COURS, France, 9 October 2005. 2.741-mile/4.411-km circuit.

Supersport World Championship, round 12 (23 laps, 63.043 miles/101.453 km)

1 Broc Parkes, AUS (Yamaha), 40m 12.350s, 94.076 mph/151.400 km/h.

2 Kevin Curtain, AUS (Yamaha); **3** Michel Fabrizio, I (Honda); **4** Fabien Foret, F (Honda); **5** Javi Fores, E (Suzuki); **6** Johan Stigefelt, S (Honda); **7** Katsuaki Fujiwara, J (Honda); **8** Stéphane Chambon, F (Honda); **9** Gianluca Nannelli, I (Ducati); **10** Matthieu Lagrive, F (Suzuki); **11** Arie Vos, NL (Honda); **12** Tatu Lauslehto, SF (Honda); **13** Ivan Goi, I (Yamaha); **14** Jarno Janssen, NL (Suzuki); **15** Sami Penna, SF (Honda).

Fastest lap: Fabrizio, 1m 44.071s, 94.811 mph/152.584 km/h (record).

Final World Championship points

1	Sébastien Charpentier, F	210
2	Kevin Curtain, AUS	187
3	Katsuaki Fujiwara, J	149
4	Fabien Foret, F	144
5	Michel Fabrizio, I	138
6	Broc Parkes, AUS	125

7 Stéphane Chambon, F, 94; **8** Gianluca Nannelli, I, 88; **9** Javi Fores, E, 71; **10** Tatu Lauslehto, SF, 60; **11** Johan Stigefelt, S, 58; **12** Alessio Corradi, I, 50; **13** Robbin Harms, DK, 34; **14** Barry Veneman, NL, 33; **15** Matthieu Lagrive, F, 26.